J V Whiting.
20, East Wonford Hill,

CW01666765

SAINTS AND THEIR SYMBOLS

SAINTS
AND THEIR SYMBOLS

RECOGNIZING SAINTS IN ART AND IN POPULAR IMAGES

BY FERNANDO AND GIOIA LANZI

Drawings by
Ermanno Leso

Translated by
Matthew J. O'Connell

LITURGICAL PRESS
Collegeville, Minnesota

www.litpress.org

This book was originally published in Italian under the title *Come riconoscere i santi e i patroni nell'arte e nelle immagini popolari.*

Printed in Italy.

1 2 3 4 5 6 7 8

Library of Congress Cataloging in Publication Data

Lanzi, Fernando.
[Come riconoscere i santi. English]
Saints and their symbols : recognizing saints in art and in popular images / by Fernando and Gioia Lanzi ; drawings by Ermanno Leso ; trasnslated by Matthew J. O'Connell.
p. cm.
Includes bibliographical references and index.
ISBN 0-8146-2970-9 (alk. paper)
1. Christian saints. I. Lanzi, Gioia. II. Title.

BX4655.3.L3613 2004
282'.092'2—dc22

2004005806

Contents

INTRODUCTION
The Nature and Characteristics of the Images of the Saints
Page 9

HISTORICAL SURVEY OR HISTORICAL ATLAS OF THE SAINTS

Introduction

The Nature and Characteristics of the Images of the Saints

1. Why This Book?

Our churches, as well as our museums and art collections, and not least the streets of our cities and the countryside, are filled with two- and three-dimensional images. Today, as in the past, not everyone understands these images.

The images in question are illustrations that tell the story of Christian salvation, which began at the creation; they depict the divine and human persons who played, and play, a part in the first and former covenant as well as in the second, new, and definitive covenant between humanity and its creator.

But while people today see these images, not all of them are able now to recognize the characteristic features of the actors in that history. Some, of course, are well known and clear to all: Our Lady, Jesus, and the eternal Father are still recognizable, one reason being that their names appear clearly in the titles and captions of works representing them. But the other actors are not only no longer known to all; there is no longer a tradition enabling people to distinguish one from another; whether they belong to the first or the second covenant, their names, even in titles and captions, convey only a general sense, as, for example a "Madonna with Child and some saints." Our intention here is to deal with some individuals of the new covenant, starting with those who surrounded Jesus during his earthly life and then, ideally, to survey the centuries down to our own time. We shall be dealing, therefore, with the images of the saints, and we shall try to explain why so many of them appear in the various depictions of Jesus and the Virgin. What is the significance of this phenomenon, in time and history, for us, and what does it say about us?

An explanation of the images of the saints requires some reflection on two subjects: holiness and images. We shall start with the former.

2. Holiness

God alone is holy, and from him alone can holiness come as a gift whereby we share in his life. To the extent that human beings participate in that life and become pure reflections of his glory, as Christ did, they too are holy. This fact holds for and is acknowledged by all, but we do not know, in all cases, the degree and manner in which they are "saints." In fact, only a relative few have been universally acknowledged to be saints and have for this reason been proposed to all living human beings as models to be imitated. From its very beginning the Church has kept lists of its saints in order that they might be more easily remembered and might serve as examples for all and that their intercession might be invoked, since they are the very special friends both of Christ and of humanity.

An episode in the Gospel of Luke explains what sanctity means in practice:

On Golgotha there is a dialogue that has its roots in Genesis. On the one hand, there is a criminal who challenges Jesus and tries to pass judgment on God: "Are you not the Messiah?

Save yourself and us!" (Luke 23:39). On the other hand, there is Dismas, who has entered history because of his emblematic goodness and is known as the "Good Thief"; he rebuked his companion: "Do you not fear God, since you are under the same sentence of condemnation?" and he asked: "Jesus, remember me when you come into your kingdom." He thus became an image of Christian holiness, being one who acknowledges Christ and his kingdom and surrenders himself wholly to him. For this reason, a man who was obviously a sinner entered paradise immediately.

Holiness has been a mark of Christianity throughout its history. "This invention of God that becomes a reality among human beings"[1] consists in a complete adherence to the will of God, in imitation of Christ and under the guidance of the Holy Spirit. For this reason, it can be said that holiness consists "not in the fact that a human being gives everything, but in the fact that the Lord takes everything."[2] People have always turned to the saints as to friends of Christ, in order to secure help. This help is not simply an act of condescension, for in answer to prayer the saints intervene by broadening the horizon of the devotee, revealing the "meaning" of the latter's personal lot, and showing this to be connected with the history of salvation, that is, with the manifestation of glory. The successful outcome of intercession, namely, the favor, even a material one (the petition for this is obviously a sign of faith), leads to a secondary end: the important thing for the devotees is that they find themselves directed toward God, able now to grasp the meaning of the events of their lives; they experience a revival of faith, hope, and especially charity as the "bond of perfection." In other words, it is important that the very being of the devotees be directed toward holiness.

3. "Sacred" and "Saint"

"Sacred" and "saint(ly)" (holy) are closely related words, inasmuch as they have the same Indo-European root: *sak*[3] "sacred" is used in opposition to "profane" or secular, and signifies that which is completely other than all existing beings and possesses, in the maximum and utterly self-sufficient degree, the attribute of existence. In religion the term is reserved for that which possesses this attribute in the supreme degree, that which *truly is, without any dependence on anything outside itself.*[4]

In order to determine the meaning of the "sacred" as clearly as possible, it is appropriate to take as a starting point the word "saint(ly)." The Latin *sanctus* is the past participle of the Latin verb *sancire,* which means precisely to make something *sak,* that is, to bestow reality and validity on something, or to acknowledge the real existence of something. The verb is a typically juridical one and, in addition to signifying a confirmation, establishment, ratification, or affirmation, it also means *to bestow validity on an institution, to make real, to acknowledge the reality of a state of things*. It follows that the root *sak*—and the words deriving from it in the Indo-European languages—refers to the foundation of what is real.

Sancire means to recognize and render something *sacred:* the *saints* are therefore persons, things, and even places that belong to *being* or are intended to belong to it and are seen to be opposed to whatever is alien to being.

Whatever is holy (sanctus) and those who are holy (saints) become by that very fact *distinct and separated* from everything else; they realize fully their own nature. Holy men and women, therefore, *exist* in the fullest way and by that fact realize the supreme potentialities characteristic of humanity; each of them does so in the most personal manner possible. Since, then, the most distinctive trait of human beings is their capacity for *consciously relating them-*

selves to their creator,[5] those who do it with the greatest deliberation, by opening themselves to the ultimate consequences of this relationship and making it the center of their lives, realize their humanity in the fullest way. To be a saint is to be a *truly human being.*

It is not given to human beings to decide what is not holy; we cannot say this even of the wicked thief or Judas. In contrast, it is possible to recognize some of the external signs that something is holy. A "truly human being" is one who accepts the ultimate consequences of belonging to Christ, one who makes Christ the center of his or her life, and this in concrete daily activities amid the flow of time. The suggestive popular expression "to die in the *odor of sanctity,*" which refers to those saints whose bodies have been preserved incorrupt and sweet-smelling, bears witness to the fact that for some saints there are sensible signs that render their condition directly accessible, so much so that they have been regarded as holy ever since people knew and encountered them.

It is this recognizableness, this visibility, that marks the holy people who are later on "proclaimed" as such, because it is this recognition by all or at least by some that sets in motion the complex process of canonization. Bystanders realize from the very lives of such people a human *truth* that is unmistakable and demands to be publicly declared and made fruitful so that we may enjoy their intercession.

In the Church there are individuals who are given the title of "saint"; they are venerated and are remembered on certain days. Christians, individually and as communities, turn to them as intermediaries and intercessors in order to obtain from the Creator what they desire for themselves. The Church also calls these individuals "servants of God"[6] and from the beginning has taken it upon itself to keep a list of them,[7] expressly in order "to foster the sanctification of the people of God," that is, to help all Christians acquire the qualities of the saints.[8]

We need to ask who these individuals are and in what their holiness consists. Then, in the light of the very numerous, varied, and sometimes seemingly contradictory characteristics of all these persons, we naturally ask what is their distinctive trait that also unites them?

Let us take the Romans as a paradigm of what happened in the religions of humanity. For the Romans, the term "holy" described everything having to do with the divinity and with worship, but it also described high dignitaries and especially the emperor, since all of these were made "sacred and inviolable" by their "authority."[9]

For Christians things were comparable yet different. The "belonging to being" that marks sanctity is described by the Church as "participation in the divine life," which was the original state of humanity at its creation.[10]

The *saint,* then, is a human being who has regained the original human condition: a being who is turned to the Father by the Son and makes fully real the nature of his or her humanity, which is to be an obedient and grateful creature.

In their encounter with Christ present in the Church, the saints found in him the model of humanity in its fullness. To live a life of following and imitating this model became the task set them, the activity by which they contributed to the building of the kingdom. In so acting, they also became models for others.

Christ explicitly summed up as follows the mandate given to him: to bear witness to the Truth. But since the Truth is he who said of himself, "I am the truth," to bear witness to the Truth means simply to acknowledge that Christ is the Son of God who came to save humanity and thus reconcile heaven and earth, and to bring everything back to the Father.

For this reason, in the language of Christians of the very early period, the term "saints," used in the plural signified all the faithful,[11] who are justified by the sole fact of following

Jesus and John.
Drawing of a wood sculpture, ca. 1320, from the Nardreth orphanage in Sigmaringen (Baden-Württemberg), preserved today in the Foundation for the Prussian Cultural Heritage (Berlin). This is a faithful representation of the passage in the Gospel of John that tells how, when Jesus said that one of the Twelve would betray him, John, at Peter's urging, addressed Jesus: "So while reclining next to Jesus, he [John] asked him, 'Lord, who is it?'" (13:25). But the sculpture goes further and suggests, by its placing of John's hand in that of Jesus and by the smiling head that rests on the shoulder of the Master, an utter, trustful abandonment, a surrender of himself, and a placing of his own will in that of Another, which is one of the distinctive traits of Christian holiness.

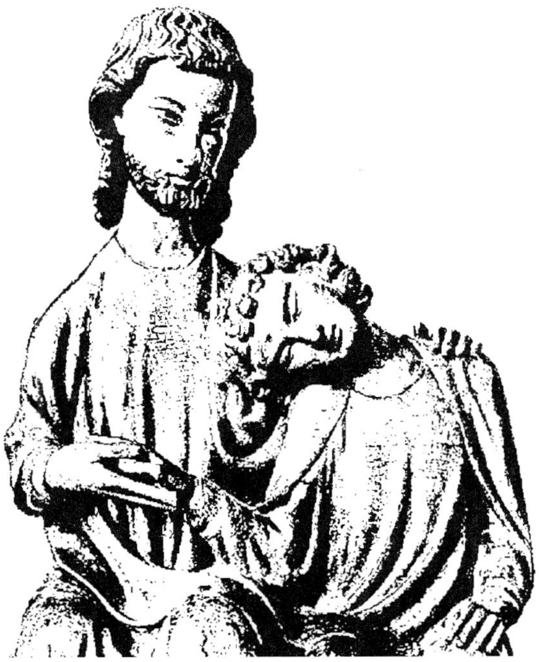

Christ and entering the Church,[12] which is not only *holy* but *sanctifying*[13]: it is in the Christian community that *holiness* "happens."

4. The First Saints: The Martyrs

The "faithful witness" to the truth, of whom the Apocalypse speaks (1:13), is Christ himself; he can therefore be called the first martyr.[14] Martyrdom is likened to a combat in which the witnesses die rather than deviate from their testimony.

"Those who in their turn imitate Christ in bearing witness to the truth are martyrs, that is, they are themselves witnesses; every martyr makes the Savior present again in his act of redemptive self-sacrifice."[15] Among all those who follow Christ, some immediately stand out because they follow him in the most complete way,[16] and they are therefore set before us as models and objects of veneration. They have, in fact, been acknowledged to have contributed in bringing salvation to humanity, each according to his or her own special vocation. This applied first to the Virgin and to St. John the Baptist as precursor. After them came the apostles and the great throng of those who were not ashamed of Christ and would not pay honor to idols even in order to save their lives. They were remembered not so much in order to commemorate them as in order to take them as exemplars.[17]

The first story of persecution that we have is found in a letter about the martyrs of Lyons in 177; the letter is recorded by Eusebius of Caesarea in his *History of the Church*.[18] The letter was not yet a work intended as a commemoration, but simply conveyed news to the Christians of Asia.[19]

For the most part no *Acts* were as yet compiled. The martyr was a person, the anniversary of whose earthly death and "birthday" *(dies natalis)* or entrance into true life and the glory of heaven[20] was commemorated in a special way not only by his or her family but by the entire community, which the bishop called together for a celebration of the Eucharist.[21] In time, a sermon with a eulogy was added, followed by the public reading (once such documents existed) of the *Life* or the *Passion,* that is, the story of the sufferings the martyr had to endure.

The first organized "commemoration" in the full and proper sense took place in North Africa; we know of it from the *Passion of Perpetua, Felicity, and Their Companions,* who were martyred at Carthage in 203, under Emperor Septimius Severus.[22]

Also from the third century are the *Acts* of St. Fructuosus, bishop of Tarragona, who was slain under Valerian in 257/58. These *Acts* attest to the cult of the martyrs throughout Spain. In Rome, too, the third century marks the commemoration of the martyrs in an organized form, in imitation of what had begun to take place in Africa.

In the last decades of the fourth century the veneration of the saints became a fundamental part of Christian piety and spread throughout Christendom.[23]

Perseverance in the confession of the faith to the point of shedding one's blood was the mark of the martyrs; systematic persecutions, and especially that of Diocletian in 304/5 C.E., greatly increased their numbers.

Local churches immediately recognized and proclaimed the holiness of their martyrs and commemorated them at their tombs; the Eucharist was celebrated, and the community prayed to the Lord for the saint and through the saint, who was regarded as an intercessor with God, as can be seen from the Roman graffiti in the *Memoria Apostolorum* (ca. 260).

A list giving the day and place of the burial of the martyrs' bodies is provided by the *Depositio martyrum* (Burial of the Martyrs). This document is found in the *Filocalian*

St. Stephen.
Votive painting in the Catacombs of Domitilla (Rome), 7th cent. The writing identifies the figure as Stephen the Protomartyr and shows him, not in the "story" of his suffering, as was to become customary, but in the posture of an orant, who both asks and offers praise. The picture concretizes the essential relationship between creature and Creator, redeemed and Redeemer.

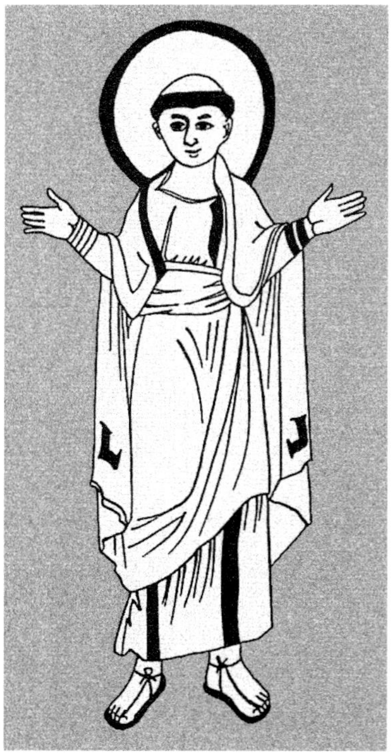

Chronograph, a work named after its compiler, Furius Dionysius Filocalus. The *Chronograph* also contains, among other things, a calendar and a description of Rome.

5. Intercessors and Patrons

The subject of intercession takes us to the heart of the relationship between human beings and God, that is, to prayer. Prayer is the most limpid and simple action of creatures when they turn to their creator and acknowledge that they have received and continually receive every good thing from him. Within the broad context of this acknowledgment every prayer is based also on the awareness of the fall of humanity in their first parent, Adam. From this Fall, the Redeemer has raised up the entire human family, but he has not resolved the human problem of choosing between good and evil. This choice is a struggle that remains difficult and calls for help, although the final victory of the good is a certainty.[24] For this reason, every kind of prayer—praise, petition, self-surrender—becomes an active, programmatic attitude in which a participation in the divine life is both desired and activated, as Pope John Paul II has said so clearly: "Prayer is not only our work to which we devote ourselves and in which we place ourselves before God and his infinite majesty and goodness. Prayer is also a dialogue of two powers. We come before him, our God and Father, before the Most Holy Trinity, before our redeemer, before the Holy Spirit. But he immediately enters into dialogue with us with the intention of giving us the energy that makes our life divine."[25]

Arnold von Harff Invokes St. Catherine of Alexandria. Wood engraving, 1496–1499. German knight Arnold von Harff invokes St. Catherine of Alexandria during a visit to the monastery on Mt. Sinai that was named after the martyr. Incidents during their lives and after their deaths create indissoluble bonds between the saints and the places where they lived and where they are especially remembered.

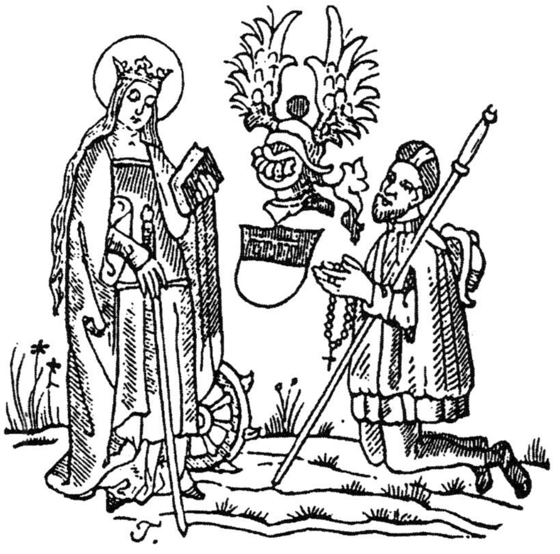

If everybody prays, all the more do those who are already close to God. "The witnesses who have preceded us into the kingdom, especially those whom the Church recognizes as saints, share in the living tradition of prayer by the example of their lives, the transmission of their writings, and their prayer today. They contemplate God, praise him and constantly care for those whom they have left on earth. When they entered into the joy of their Master, they were 'put in charge of many things.' Their intercession is their most exalted service to God's plan. We can and should ask them to intercede for us and for the whole world."[26]

In the *Passion* of Perpetua, cited above, we already find reference to intercession and cures. In fact, in the visions she has before her death, Perpetua sees her sick brother and says: "I understood that from then on I was worthy of praying for him and that I ought to do so"; in a subsequent vision she sees her brother cured. The complete imitation of Christ even to the shedding of blood qualifies and, judging by Perpetua's words, even obliges the martyr to make intercession, that is, to pray for the brethren.

Intercession, then, can be regarded as an integral part of the following of Christ: he himself first intercedes with the Father and, at the moment of his final obedience, prays for sinners: "Father, forgive them." In the Church, prayer is unequivocally addressed to the Father, and the first to give an example of this is Jesus Christ himself. He, first, and then Mary his Mother show themselves to be intercessors.[27]

The martyrs thus imitate Christ even in their intercession, and those who are still on earth can rightfully appeal to them. And because in glory human affections reach their true dimensions, the saints who have reached the Father do not forget those they have loved on earth, their relatives and followers: they remember them before God and present to him their prayers and needs.

We should note here that the family of any saint broadens out. They intercede, indeed, for the members of their families, but their true family is the family born of the Spirit, made up of those who do the Father's will, their brothers and sisters in the faith.[28] They now have a different genealogy, one that does not cancel their natural genealogy but elevates[29] and broadens it. In this setting, new and privileged relationships between human beings and the saints arise, and the ways in which this process takes place are extremely varied and seem to share in the inexhaustible imagination of God. This new relationship in the family of God leads to the idea of "patronage."

"Patron" is a word from the juridical terminology of classical Latin and means a lawyer for the defense. A patron, therefore, is not a simple protector to whom one occasionally turns, but rather the individual by whom one expects to be defended at the particular and universal judgments of God.

To identify one's patrons, whether of an individual or of a category of persons, means, first and foremost, to establish with them a fiduciary relationship that has publicly known characteristics and is not arbitrary but is based on something patron and client "have in common," something that precedes the choice of patron and is understood as part of a providential plan and as a binding directive.

The first bond arises simply from the name[30] given at baptism.[31] There are other bonds as well, based, for example, on the work a person does and on the tools he uses, on his state in life, on illnesses, on the trials he must face and on the situations in which he lives, on a similarity of events in the life of patron and client, on the tasks the client must carry out, and so on.[32] Even simple coincidences of time and place play a role.[33] It can be said that there is no human situation that has not been sanctified by witness to the faith, thus proving that nothing created is incapable of salvation. Every human activity and condition has always found specific intercessors, patrons who offer themselves as protectors to whom one may turn and as models to those who find themselves in the same circumstances as those of the patrons. The saints thus seem to specialize, so to speak, in relation to the incidents, the things, and the persons of their lives and of their early veneration, as well as to the narratives contained in the various versions of their stories, and, further, to the events in which those seeking their intercession find themselves.

Given the very concrete character of Christianity,[34] however, it is necessary, if a patronage or patronal relationship is to be established, that there be a point of contact, which is then shown in the iconography of the saints. The fact remains, however, that in the establishment of a patronage the principal element is the history of the saint; in the case of the martyrs, then, the point of contact is the moment of martyrdom itself and the instruments used in it.

St. Lucy, in whose suffering there is a strong emphasis on sight and the eyes, is invoked on behalf of the petitioner's sight, and she is the patron of oculists. St. Apollonia, whose teeth were battered, is the patron of dentists and is invoked against toothache. St. Stephen, who was stoned, is the patron of stonecutters. St. Matthew the evangelist, who collected taxes, is the patron of accountants. St. Benedict, founder of monasteries, became for that reason the patron of engineers, who build things. St. Agatha, whose breasts were cut off, is today invoked against breast tumors, an illness which in her time was not known as such; she has always been the protector of nursing mothers.

To patrons thus identified Christians entrust themselves if they are devout, and the patrons become models for their behavior. When no specific and real incidents are found in the lives of the patrons, the paradigm is simply their witness to the faith. Devotion to them is closely connected with imitation of them: "Devotion means, on the part of the believer, accepting a saint as patron; but a fruitful devotion is one in which the petition for patronage takes shape in a real conformity to the model. A saint protects those who have developed a real likeness to his or her spiritual character. To have a patron must mean the development of an habitual similarity to that saint."[35]

In the patronal relationship, a kind of dialogue begins, in history, between the protected and their protectors. Influenced by their patrons, their spirituality, and their example as transmitted in verbal and figural stories, the protected show themselves in history as strengthened by a companionship that overcomes every obstacle.

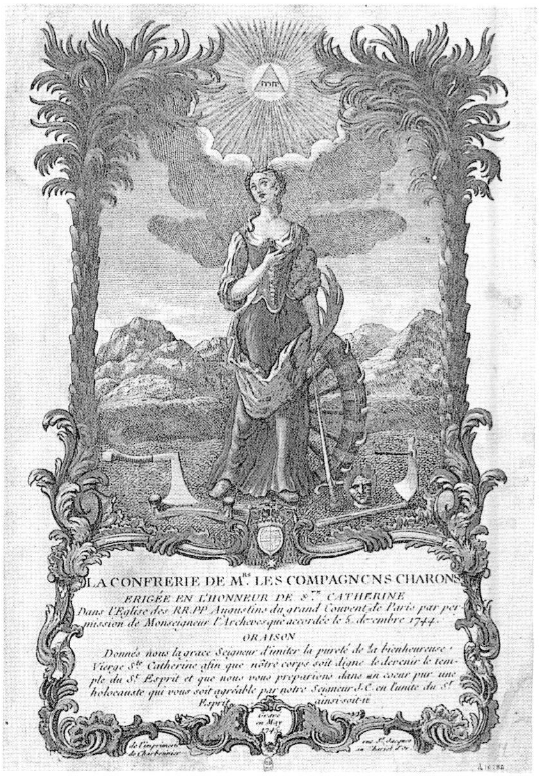

St. Catherine of Alexandria.
A print published in May 1745, by the Charbonnier Printery on the rue Saint-Jacques, Paris, or a sheet intended for the Company of the Carradorians (Charons in 17th-cent. French and Charrons in the modern spelling) of which St. Catherine was patroness. She was linked to this confraternity of craftsmen by the wheel, which they used in their work, while for her it was an instrument of martyrdom. Other attributes of the saint are also present, such as the sword and the palm. In accordance with a habitual practice the saint is standing upright as though to unite earth and heaven, while from the clouds, which foretell a theophany, the trinitarian triangle, with Yahweh written on it in Hebrew letters, radiates power and grace on the martyr. Her gaze, raised to heaven, and her hand, laid on her heart, express the intensity of Catherine's sentiments and her constant directedness to God.

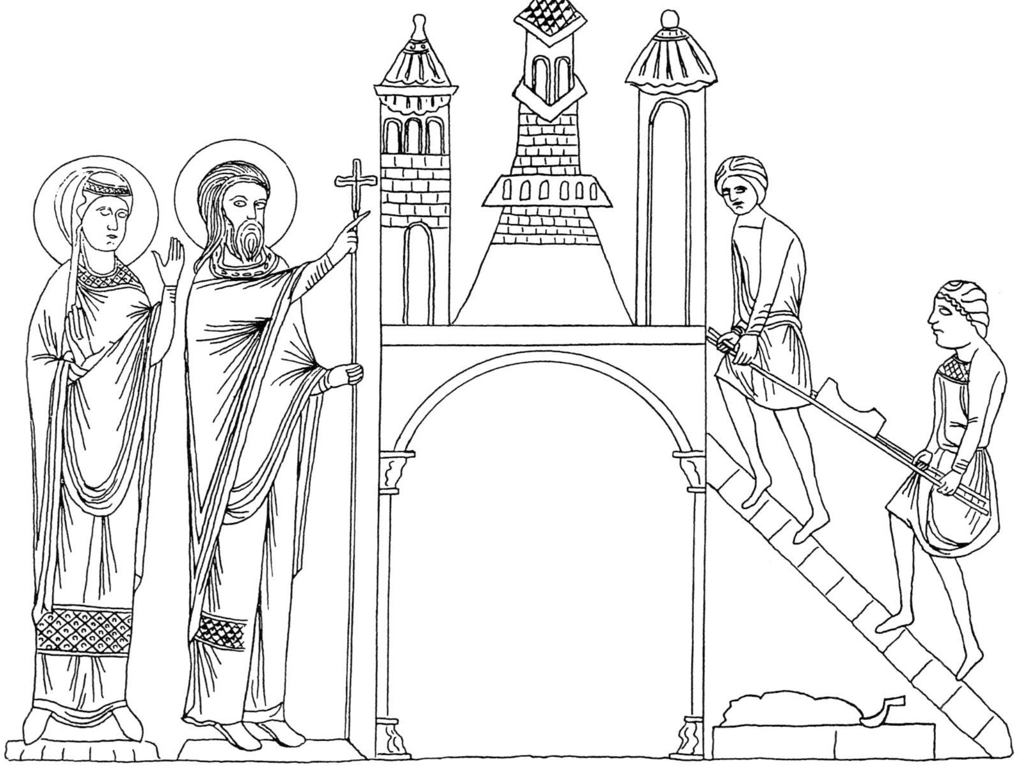

SS. Calminus and Namadia Found a Monastery. This drawing of the Reliquary of Mozac (Puy-de-Dome, end of the 12th, beginning of the 13th cent.) pictures the founding of a monastery under the supervision of the holy spouses Calminus of Mozac and Namadia. Calminus was Duke of Aquitaine and governor of Alvernia in the 7th cent.; together with his wife Namadia, he founded three monasteries: Le Monastier in Velay, Tuule in Limoisin, and Mozac in Alvernia. The two saints were naturally the patrons of the monasteries they founded. The building of a place of worship and prayer was a symbolic equivalent of the building of the heavenly city and an anticipation of heaven here on earth.

6. Patrons of Places and Peoples

Among the various ways of establishing the bond between the saints and human beings still in the world, physical nearness is surely an important one.

Christianity moves on from the general holiness of places to the holiness of men and women to whom God has revealed that the fullness of their humanity consists in the following of Christ and the practice of the evangelical counsels in accordance with their various states and conditions. From these human beings, who lived historically in particular places, the places themselves receive a holiness because they have been the scene of a hierophany in the true and proper sense, a hierophany that used as its medium of manifestation not the splendor of nature nor the fear roused by a grove or a harsh landscape, but persons of flesh and blood, namely, the followers of Jesus Christ, who call upon him.

From the presence in these individuals of the divine life, made evident by their virtues, places themselves receive a new meaning, a new holiness, that is as concrete as relics, miracles, and deeds are. As a result, a geography of the sacred is born, made up of places that enjoy a special patronage because there the saints were born, lived, and died; their relics have been deposited there and are venerated there. The ways of determining the parts of this geography are likewise varied. For saintly bishops it is natural that they should become patrons in a special way of the cities where they carried on their pastoral ministry. For all the saints the places of their birth, their activities, their burial, their relics, the stories about them, and, finally, the places where they are venerated are subjects of special attention.

The new freedom created by Constantine after 313 C.E. fostered the rise of churches that were built near the burial places of the martyrs, sometimes right over their tombs.

The practice of building churches near the tombs of the martyrs and also burying people *ad sanctos,* near the holy bodies, became widespread due to the desire of being affected by the *virtus,* that is, the miraculous power of the saint manifested in its fullness where the body or relics of the saints were. The *virtus* was desirable because it produced *salus,* salvation: health for the living and eternal life for the deceased; it was also powerful against the evil spirits that were always at work.

That was the period when there was a great desire for relics, and the spread of the latter contributed to the unity of the Church.[36] Tertullian wrote that *sanguis martyrum semen christianorum* ("the blood of the martyrs is the seed of Christians").[37] As the universal Church was born of the blood of Christ, the first martyr,[38] so each local church endeavored to be built on the fruitful blood of the martyrs; it sought to possess their relics[39] and regarded these as its foundation. Every church wanted to have its own saints, while, on the other hand, there were and are saints who are venerated throughout the entire Church.

Present in foundation after foundation, relics came to be everywhere in Christendom; as a result, there arose this new geography of the sacred that transcended pre-Christian cults and at times reinterpreted these and took over their deepest longings. This geography had as its point of reference not only the Holy Land but also the major sanctuaries, where apostles and saints were buried.

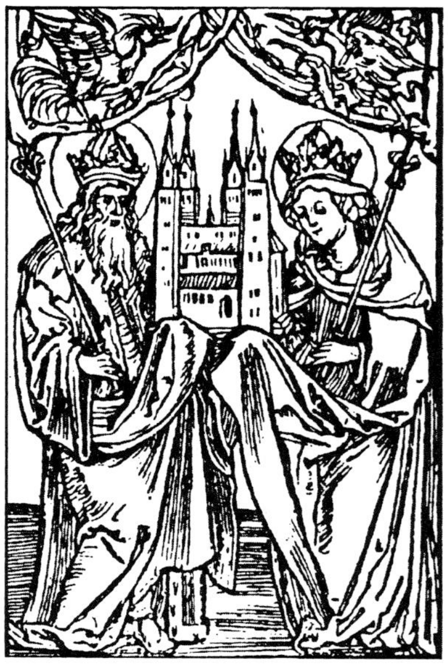

The place in which the relics of a saint rest is chosen by the latter as his or her own protectorate. The saint loves the place in which his or her relics are preserved,[40] and the inhabitants of the place invoke him or her as their patron, as a privileged intercessor among the many whom they cultivate.

Since, then, the saints are held up for the edification or building up of the Church, that is, of its holiness, they are also models of Christian life. Their virtues become exemplars for their clients, who in a sense are defined by this model and can be said to borrow from the patron some traits of character and some types of behavior. It is thus that by reference to their own special saints even the cultural identity of a people is formed and expressed; it can be said that in the relationship between patron and clients the choice is reciprocal. If the saint has chosen a particular place as his regular residence, as, for example, Anthony chose Padua, the devotion of the Paduans to him is, as it were, a response to his choice; this is confirmed by the fact that the Paduans regard Anthony as the ideal model for their lives, as the older brother whom they wish to resemble. In some instances, the bond is such that the inhabitants take the name of the saint; thus the Milanese are also known as "Ambrosians" after the patron of the city.

The bond with the saint is not always experienced with that degree of awareness. The reason is perhaps that for quite some time now the veneration of the saints has slipped into second place in the Church itself. On the other hand, in Italy for example, the feast day of the saint is everywhere a civil holiday as well, thus showing the historical and civil importance of the connection with the patron.

It is not only trades and cities that have their patron saints and refer back to them. Nations, too, have their protectors. In these instances the civil importance and the power of the patron to set an example are obvious and can escape only an eye habituated to think of persons as divided into various types of activity.

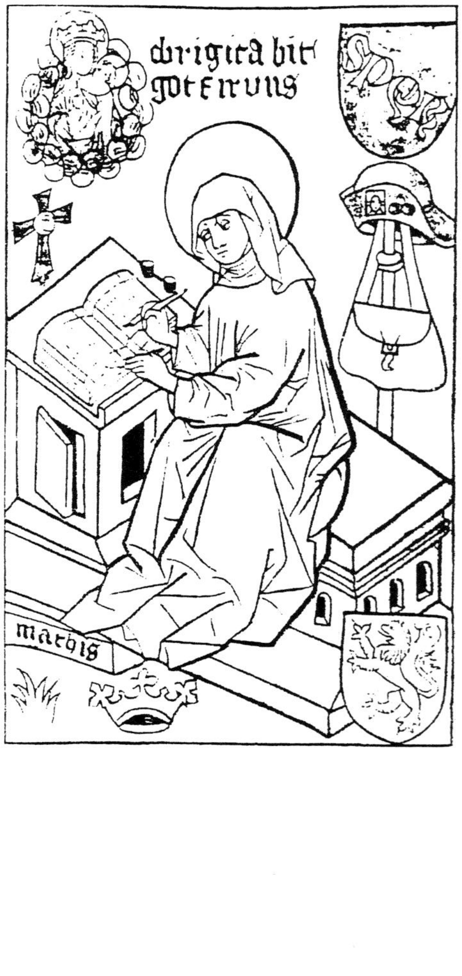

Ludmila Grygiel confirms this observation: "In the early period of European history, it was the saints themselves who established new social, political, and cultural structures. . . . The political sphere is not the place of the Church as an institution, but Christians cannot remain completely indifferent to everything that belongs to Caesar. Many European saints show us how it is possible to serve God and to serve the people in political activity."[41]

Let me give just a few examples by way of confirmation: Leopold III, Margrave of Austria, was a husband, a father, and a wise and far-sighted ruler; Ferdinand of Castile unified Castile and Andalusia and led the *reconquista* of Spain from Arab domination; Louis IX, king of France, thought of his rule as a service to God; and Nicholas of Flue, a Swiss hermit, gave some advice to the delegates of the cantons who gathered at Stans in 1481, and thereby influenced Swiss political life.

In the present volume, because of the strong bond between the saints and the countries and nations they protect, we have given precedence to the patrons of nations over other saints better known and represented by images. It seems to us important to recall, for example, the patrons of the nations of Europe, because in their persons honor is now given to those shared cultural roots that are capable of being the basis of enterprises in the economic and political spheres.

The special bond with places and their residents has its roots in history. This bond has not always been officially underscored by a pontifical decree, but when it has, the fact is important, inasmuch as the Church of the place is thereby more strongly exhorted to look to the patron as a model of life.

It must also be said that rarely does a city or a nation have but one patron; to the principal patron are added others who are usually connected with particular historical events. They are therefore usually decided on over time; they have their roots in the city's or nation's traditions and can be said to provide the framework for these. As we said earlier, traditions are often complemented by a deliberate choice, a solemn proclamation that confirms a very ancient devotion and cult. In other instances, as, for example, the choice of St. Clare as patron of the communications media because of a particular incident in her life, the patronage is only recently established. A list containing all patronages does not exist. It can be composed from tradition, while for some there has been an identifiable moment when an official proclamation was made.

SS. Henry II, Emperor, and His Wife Conegunda.
Wood engraving from a drawing by Albrecht Dürer in his *Salus animae* (1503, Nuremberg).
Emperor Henry II (973–1024), last emperor from the House of Saxony, was canonized in 1146; he was brother of Giselle, at that time wife of St. Stephen, king of Hungary. Henry became duke of Bavaria in 995 and king of Germany in 1002. He was crowned emperor, along with his wife Cunegunda as empress, in 1014 in St. Peter's, Rome, by Pope Benedict VIII. He concerned himself solicitously with the Church, promoted a monastic reform, and founded the Diocese of Bamberg. He obtained a miraculous cure at Montecassino. Here, with his wife Cunegunda, he holds a model of the cathedral of Bamberg, where their remains rest.

7. Why Images?

Given all this, the question still arises: Why images? The general reason for them is their power to engage the viewer; this is all the more useful to those who, like Christians, feel an urgent need to proclaim and convince. Images impact the interior life by acting on the imagination and feelings; through successive processes of identification and assimilation, they set forth a plan of life and tend to become archetypes.[42] An image, thus introduced, is suited to stir devotion, and devotion is in its turn the way to sanctification. For this reason, iconography renders an important service to the same goal for the sake of which the Church has, since its beginnings, proposed saints to all the faithful[43] as models to make their own in order to imitate Christ, as particular expressions, in different individuals, of the one perfect obedience to the Father that Christ rendered.

For this reason Christians did not reject images but soon began to make use of them in those places, namely, burial places, where, in the presence of death and of the final, mysterious passage, they realized more fully the need of being confirmed in the idea of possibly sharing in the divine life and of being fortified through teaching and example.

The first Christians lived in the Jewish world that had inherited the law in the book of Exodus: "You shall not make for yourself an idol, whether in the form of anything that is in heaven above, or that is on the earth beneath, or that is in the water under the earth. You shall not bow down to them or worship them" (20:4-5). But the Jewish world in its turn, before and especially after the Diaspora of 70 C.E.,[44] was immersed in that wider universe reflected in a language, namely, Hellenistic *koinê*. In this language, contributions made by the different peoples who were united by the *Pax Romana* of Augustus were intermingled and caught up in a continual process of exchanges. Generally speaking, it was undoubtedly a world rich in images, a world in which images played a prominent cultural and social role. In such a world the first Christians created images for themselves, not, of course, to turn them into idols but to have aids for memory. For this purpose they used the pre-Christian iconographic heritage of symbols. Of special interest here is research aimed at finding out what Christians took from this patrimony, how they gave new meaning to what they took, what they added, and how they did so.[45]

St. Bridget of Sweden.
Etching (15th cent.) in the Metropolitan Library of Prague. The image summarizes the life of St. Bridget, patroness of Sweden. It connects her life with two events: her pilgrimage to Rome, indicated by the shield that surmounts her pilgrim's broad-brimmed hat, and her visions, of which she writes in her *Revelations*. We also see the crown, the title of marchioness, and the shield of the House of Sweden. The bit of writing says: "Bridget prays to God for us."

In regard, too, to the language of iconography, what can be said of the pre-Christian religions holds true here: that in them a great *praeparatio evangelica* was being made. For this reason, the iconographical language of pre-Christian art prepared the way for that of Christian art and was in turn explained by the latter.[46]

The first Christian images belong to the funerary art[47] on sarcophagi and in paintings in the catacombs. Here we find images (signs, that is, general ideas expressed in very simple language that became meaningful *in a specific context*). These images-signs can be divided into two categories: those representing sacraments and those representing divine interventions. The former say, in a general way, that it is membership in the Church that saves the deceased person; the latter express wishes and are a *commendatio animae* in which God is asked: "as you saved others, save also this dead person."

The repertory of images was gradually built up; along with images of the deceased in scenes of paradisal fellowship, the figures of the martyrs began to appear.

When Constantine decreed freedom of worship, Christian art drew even more freely on the patrimony of Roman art, and descriptive pictures began to appear which were also used for the representation of dogmas. Thus large paintings were made that depicted the majesty of Christ, who is accompanied by the apostles, especially Peter and Paul, in scenes of the *traditio legis* (the delivery of the law) and the *traditio clavum* (the delivery of the keys to heaven).

Of special importance is the fact that the first "portraits" of the saints appeared; their features began to take a fixed form in images. At the same time, reflection on the value and liceity of these images began. Gregory of Nyssa compared an artist's painting to a "book that speaks plainly" and said that paintings made pleasing the tombs that would otherwise be avoided. The images of the martyr's feats, with the description of his torments and the representation of Christ presiding over the whole matter, invited those who saw it "to draw close to the reliquary, in the persuasion that to touch it was to be sanctified and receive a blessing."[48] The image was useful, therefore, because it was an invitation to gaze on the holy martyr and, implicitly, to imitate him. Holy Pope Gregory the Great saw in images "the Scriptures of the illiterate," a means therefore of knowing "the things of the faith and thereby a means of teaching religion and its mysteries."

But Gregory first made a distinction: "It is one thing to adore a painting, another to learn from a painting of a historical scene what ought to be adored."[49] The time was 600, and Pope Gregory was responding to Serenus, bishop of Marseilles, who had had sacred images removed from the churches. This anticipated a controversy over the use of images and the worship of them to which the use might lead, a controversy which, later on, would lead to an out-and-out iconoclasm, especially in the East.

8. The Controversy over Images

Earlier, in the first decades of the fourth century, when Eusebius of Caesarea was asked by the Empress Constantia for an image of Christ, he showed very little regard for the human figure of Christ. He asked her what kind of image she wanted: if an image of his divinity, there could be none; of his humanity, this was unworthy of being represented. In support of his view, he appealed to the passage of Exodus cited above and directed his correspondent to the Scriptures alone as the sole true image of Christ.[50] Almost as if in reply to Eusebius, Theodore the Studite in the sixth century maintained the liceity of images, which he regarded as the equivalents of the Scriptures. He cited an item of information later repeated in a famous eighteenth-century work on iconography, *The Interpretation of Painting* by Dionyius of Phurna.[51] The information was that St. Luke received a divine inspiration; others desirous of learning the art of painting ought to pray thus to Jesus: "You who by the action of your Holy Spirit inspired your divine apostle and evangelist Luke to paint the appearance of your flawless Mother, who carried you as an infant in her arms and who says: 'May the grace of him who was born of me be with them due to my action.'"[52] It was also said that the Virgin herself was satisfied with the icons of St. Luke: "She thanked and blessed the holy apostle and evangelist Luke for his artistic painting, saying: 'The grace of him who was born of me be with them through my intercession.'"[53]

It was this episode that gave rise to the most widespread image of the evangelist, showing him as he paints the Mother of God with her Son in her arms.

In the year 730 C.E. Byzantine Emperor Leo III Isauricus mandated the destruction of all icons for the purpose of rooting out what he regarded as idolatry.[54] The controversy, which was striking and bloody, brought forth St. John Damascene as the "theoretician" who defended icons and made these a result of the Incarnation. For if Christ became flesh and if in

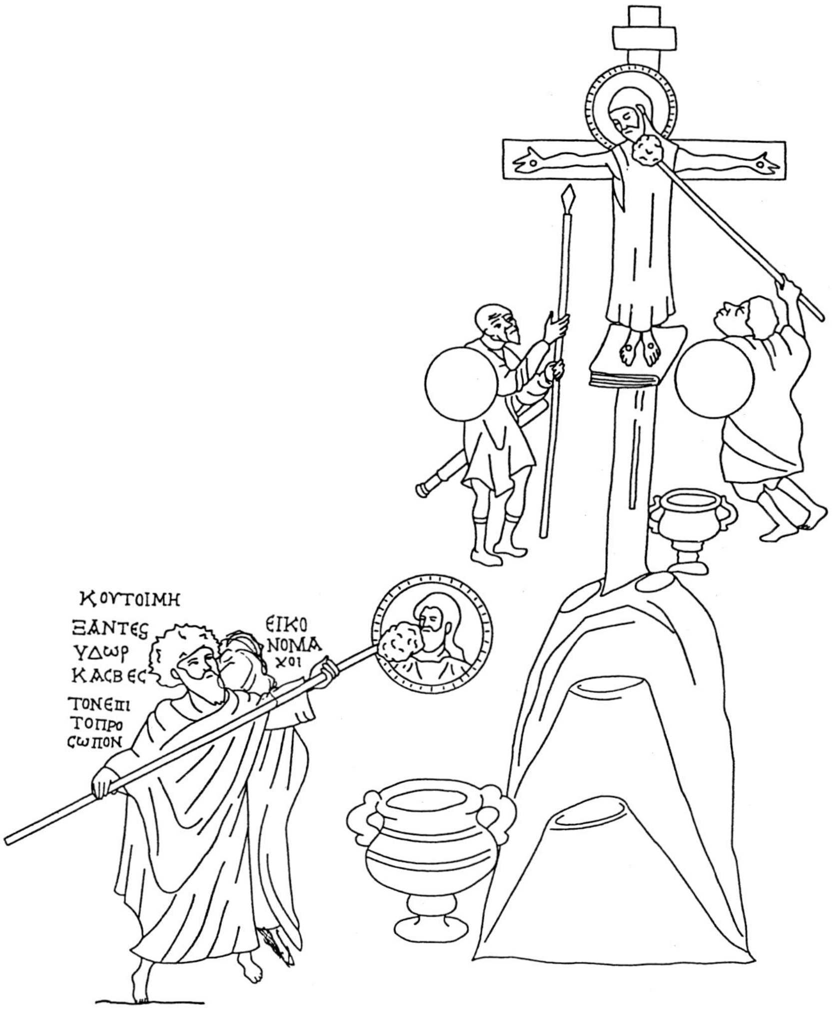

Crucifixion and the Controversy over Images. Drawing after the miniature on fol. 67 of the Chloudow codex = cod. 129, Historical Museum of Moscow. The codex is a Greek Psalter from the end of the 9th cent. The illustration is evidently aimed at the iconoclasts. The iconoclasts, that is, those who fought against images, are shown trying to erase the face of Christ, and their action is likened to that of the soldiers who mocked Christ by giving him a sponge soaked in vinegar and gall, which he refused.

his person the human and divine natures are inseparable, then he can be represented; indeed, to deny this would amount to denying the Incarnation. The controversy was settled by the Second Council of Nicaea in 787, which cleared away all doubts and clearly asserted the liceity of images. It said that "the honour paid to an image traverses it, reaching the model; and he who venerates the image, venerates the person represented in that image."[55] Later on, canon 3 of the Fourth Council of Constantinople (869–870) clearly linked Scripture and art: "As speech teaches and portrays through syllables, so too does painting by means of colours."[56] Thus an icon is "written" just as a book is written, and it is not by chance that painters of icons are called "iconographers," that is, "writers of images."

The point at issue in the controversy over images does not seem to have been simply whether images were to be honored or who was being honored, the image or the model. The question was rather how to depict the person of Christ without either confusing or separating his two natures, the human and the divine. But this question had to do not only with the possibility of a Christian art but also with the very Incarnation itself. Images were in fact being rejected as false, useless, and misleading. This (it was said) was true whether one said that the icons showed the divinity, since it is not possible to represent the divinity, or whether one claimed that they represented the humanity apart from the divinity, since the humanity alone is not worth representing.

Thus it was from the Incarnation as a mystery that the iconoclasts were separating themselves, and from the great dignity of the flesh with which the Son of God clothed himself for the salvation of humanity. Pope Hadrian I (867–872) took up the idea of a divine economy involving the flesh when he wrote: "In the presence of the visible face, our mind will be transported, as by a spiritual attraction, toward the invisible majesty of the divinity as we contemplate the image representing the flesh which the Son of God condescended to make his own for our salvation."[57] The fathers of Constantinople IV, which was convoked by Emperor Constantine I and his mother Irene, accepted Pope Hadrian's teaching on images and even warmly recommended the production of "revered and holy images, whether painted or made of mosaic or of other suitable material": images of Jesus Christ or of Mary his mother, of the angels and "of any of the saintly holy men." The fathers went on to say: "The more frequently they [those represented] are seen in representational art, the more are those who see them drawn to remember and long for those who serve as models."[58]

Once the objection to the liceity of images of the divine persons and of those belonging to the new family of Christ had been surmounted, images filled the churches and the homes of Christians, where they served as exemplars and gave support in the practice of the faith and in devotion. In the eighth and subsequent centuries images of the saints flourished; these had already been used at their tombs and on their relics,[59] but now they were also detached from these places and became autonomous as depictions of intercessors and protectors, making their "models" present in other places as well.

It must be noted that later on the East and the West began to go their separate ways. The East developed a theory of images St. John Damascene formulated and the Second Council of Nicaea clarified in 787. According to the theory, there is in an icon a divinely effected presence of the model to be venerated, a presence due in particular to "fidelity" to the prototype, that is, to the one represented in the icon.[60] This fidelity had to be acknowledged by the Church before the icon was blessed; after that it could be exhibited and venerated.[61]

Finally, it was agreed that the internal law governing the writing of an icon was this: "the icon has its value independently of both the artist and the spectator; it does not stir emotion but gives rise to the coming of the transcendent to whose presence it attests. The artist hides himself and makes himself the intermediary of the tradition which speaks in the icon; the work thus becomes a manifestation of God."[62]

The West, too, accepted the teaching of Nicaea II,[63] but in the matter of images the position taken at the court of Charlemagne was adopted and became common throughout the Middle Ages. An image, which can make present the features of a person and report events, remains nonetheless simply a material object and cannot be an object of worship; its value consists in its ability to teach.[64] Nevertheless, the ideal of a fidelity to models, combined with an implicit iconographical standard, was cultivated in the West as well and is easily verifiable.

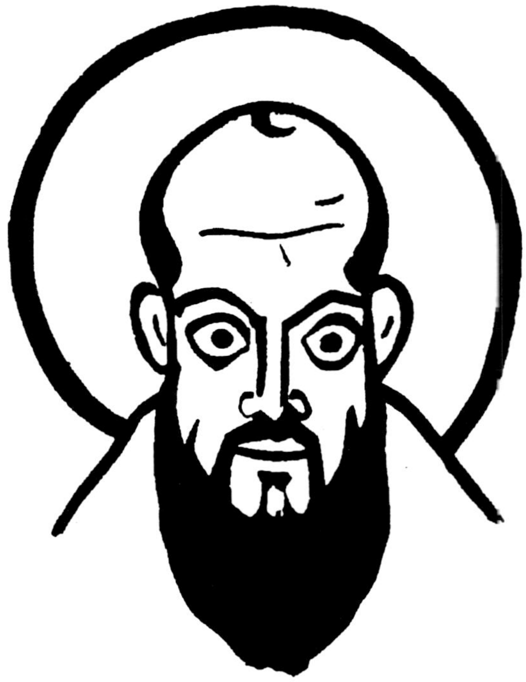

9. How the Saints Are to Be Represented

Representations of the saints, their lives, and their deeds are a constant in Christian art and constitute a fundamental element of it. In fact, if the Christian repertory of images had remained limited to events of the Old and New Testaments, we would have only a limited series of events and personages to be represented, even though these are and could be represented in many manners and styles. But that is not the case, and Christian art has faithfully obeyed the teaching of the Council of 787, which urged the acceptance of tradition.[65] Tradition, however, is not a closed series of facts but is open to infinity, since Christ continues to be present in the Church, that is, in Christians, so that holding up saints as models is simply another way of holding up Christ as a model. The result is an almost unlimited multiplicity of iconographical suggestions, of canons, symbols, and signs that are interwoven and refer to one another in the course of their bimillenial history. The lives of the saints, when crystallized as it were in the images of them that have come down to us, are an invitation to imitate and follow them. It is certainly not an accident that during the rite of canonization an image of the saint is displayed, just as it is not an accident that care is taken of the places and relics of the saints.

St. Paul.
The head of St. Paul from the frescoes in the apse of the Red Monastery, second half of the 5th cent. From the very beginning, representations of St. Paul show the intention of presenting a portrait; in fact, down the centuries the characteristics of his face remained the same.

In the course of time, images have become quite varied. Initially, figures were barely sketched out; later came images that instead tended to be portraits. Think, for example, of the wooden panel in the monastery on Mt. Sinai, on which the Virgin appears enthroned with the child in her arms, while at the sides, in addition to two angels, are SS. Theodore and Demetrius. Here we have two portraits, and this image of Demetrius can readily be compared with the image of him in the church dedicated to him at Thessalonica, where he is seen as interceding for two devotees.

The tendency to portraiture, which we can verify for other persons as well, for example, Peter and Paul, whose features are always very much the same, serves also to make clearly identifiable the saint being represented; the latter is not an abstract model but a real person to whom one can turn with devotion. Devotion, moreover, is not reducible to a simple official request of a believer for the patronage of a saint. The saint in fact protects those who have acquired a real likeness to his spiritual self; the request for protection implies supplying the saint with a concrete reason for intervening, and this concrete motive is the petitioner's real conformity to the model of life given by the saint. The theme of patronage thus includes the idea of a habitual likeness to the patron in the form of an imitation of his virtues.

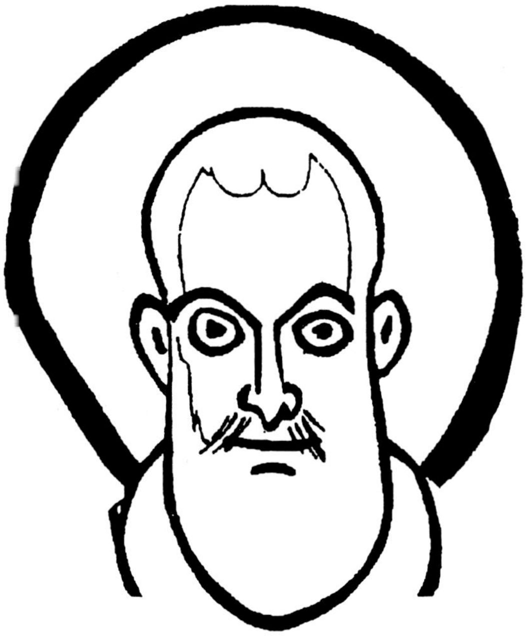

St. Mark.
The head of St. Mark from the frescoes in the apse of the Red Monastery. In this case, however, it is not possible to say that his features were preserved through time, although here there is evidently the intention of presenting a portrait.

10. From Portrait to Attributes

For the achievement of this likeness, the model must be exact, clear, and identifiable if a process of identification and imitation is to be activated. Believers must recognize not only that the saint was a human being like themselves, but also that they share the condition of the saint, experience the same difficulties, and are able to turn these into advantages. A woman must be able to say: "If Rita, who was an unhappy wife, a worried mother, and a widow could become a saint, so too I, who am now widowed and worried about my children, can become a saint."

In some representations of groups of saints (the best known example is the sixth-century procession of virgins and martyrs in Sant'Apollinare Nuovo in Ravenna), the artist does not look so much for the special features of each; rather he emphasizes the choral character of an event and an action.[66] But attentive observers, who do not stop at the fixity of the gaze and the lack of any gesture, will be able to identify particular traits that show Agatha and Agnes, both present, to be two different persons; the names, written underneath, help in this identification.

Generally speaking, then, to a simple likeness of the saint other elements are added, namely, the "attributes," which are capable of suggesting to the viewer the entire activity of the saint; as a result, a single image can call to mind an entire history and the virtues embodied in that history and offered for imitation.

We can point out two ways of representing the saints: one is narrative, the other emblematic.

To the first category belong the representations that relate in images the lives of the saints from birth to earthly death and their presence now in the glory of God; they do this with a more or less extensive abundance of scenes and incidents. In this context it is to be remarked that the life of the saints does not end with their death. It continues not only in heavenly glory but also in the devotion paid to them, in prayer for their intercession, and in events in the lives of their devotees and followers, which end by becoming part of the saint's story. It is a history that originates in the followers and inspires those who ask for their intercession and profit by their intervention. As a result, instances of the protection and intercession by the saint now in glory become part of the iconographical repertory of the facts of his life. Let one example stand for all: St. James, who is represented as a warrior who intervenes in defense of the Spaniards in a ninth-century battle.

In the second category are to be included those representations in which a single image sums up the virtues practiced by the saint,[67] the trials suffered, the condition or state, and, in short, the entire life of the saint, who is shown alone or with others as they accompany, for example, the Virgin enthroned with her Child.

We shall not dwell here on the distinction between the kinds of images: the large fresco, the valuable fabrics, the painting by a craftsman, the ex-voto, the print or holy picture. In all of these, the iconographical and iconological problem remains the same.

In the emblematic category, then, the icons of the saint show him in an attitude or posture typical of or peculiar to him; they link him explicitly to whatever of importance he did in his life or is brought out in his cult. To this end, the image places in his hand or at his feet or in the hands of angels nearby the attributes that contribute to, among other things, the identification of the saint, especially when the subject is a saint whose physical features cannot but be unknown to us.

11. The Attributes

The attribute is fundamental, especially in the case of patronage, because by means of it the faithful recognize themselves and/or the special role of the saint; they know him or her to be a human being like themselves because he shares their condition. They perceive that the holiness set as a goal for him is offered to them as well.

Thus the inhabitants of Santhià (a contraction of Sant'Agata) in the Piedmont and those of Catania in Sicily recognize the beautiful young woman who holds up a plate with her breasts on it as an offering to heaven, to be their common patroness even though, for example, a wooden statue of her may be found in an Austrian church. The people of San Marino recognize their St. Marinus in the quite callow youth, but also in the fine old man with a flowing beard: it is enough that he carries in his hand, as an offering to heaven, their beloved "three *penne*."[68] From the bottles and scalpels in the image, physicians recognize Cosmas and Damian, the saintly doctors who asked no payment for their work and who became martyrs.

The attribute, then, also makes it possible to identify saints for whom it is difficult to find any accurate details of their appearance when age and condition make them similar to other saints. Thus in the dense ranks of holy bishops, all in bishops' robes and miter, staff and book (a clear reference to the gospel and to their teaching in the line of apostolic succession), it would be impossible to single out St. Ambrose, St. Nicholas, St. Augustine, St. Lazarus, and St. Blaise, for example, if they were not accompanied, the first by a beehive and a scourge, the second by three bags of money that look like three balls and by three children, the third by a flaming heart with three arrows, the fourth by a small coffin, and the fifth by a carder's comb.

Each of these attributes refers to an important episode in the saint's life and one also easy to sum up in a sign. It is said of St. Ambrose that when he was an infant a swarm of bees entered his mouth and emerged again, as though foretelling his eloquence, while the scourge alludes to an appearance in which he drove enemies from his Milan in a battle. The three balls held by Nicholas recall the secret alms, consisting of three bags of gold, which he gave to three girls who, because of their poverty, were on their way to becoming prostitutes; while the three children recall those whom a wicked innkeeper killed and pickled in brine, but whom the saint restored to life. The heart recalls Augustine's own words "my heart is restless" and his thinking about the Trinity. The small coffin recalls Lazarus' death and raising to life. The carder's comb recalls Blaise's martyrdom. Examples could be multiplied. Usually the saints have one or more attributes that can be described as the principal ones, because these refer to the saints' fundamental qualities or activities and, in the case of martyrs, to their martyrdom. They have further attributes I prefer to describe as "other" and not as "secondary"; these refer to different and less fundamental incidents, which are therefore less often represented but are not, for that reason, of less importance.

The ways of deciding on the attributes are very diverse and at times seem to follow the logic of the language of symbols and dreams. In the case of martyrs, the most common at-

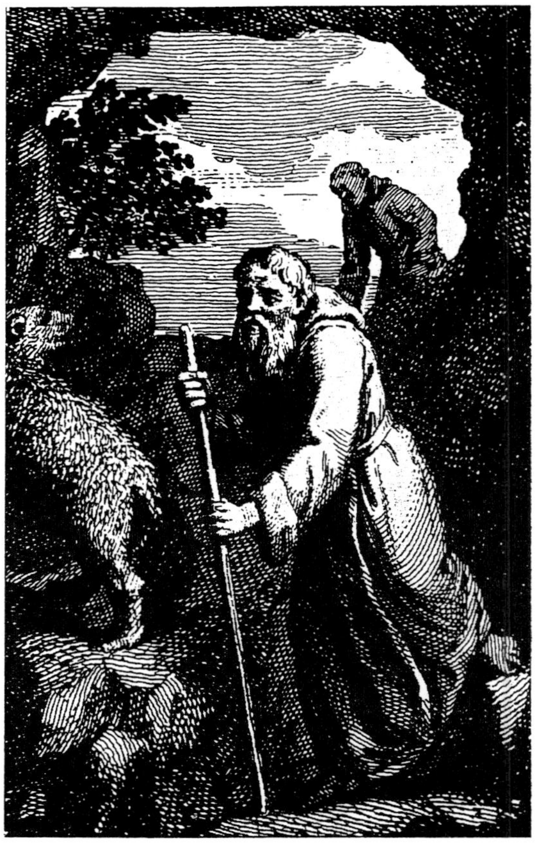

St. Columbanus.
An etching from *The Lives of the Western Fathers of the Desert,* by Burgoing of Villefore (Paris, 1708). St. Columbanus of Bobbio lived in a cave which a bear vacated for him; a bear intervenes in his life on several occasions. The bear is therefore his principal attribute. The docility of the wild animals who submitted to the saints is an obvious symbol of the mastery of instinct and the dominion over natural forces that is proper to Christ.

tributes, as I shall say in greater detail further on, are the instruments of their martyrdom, such as the grill of St. Lawrence, or the tortured parts of the body, such as the breasts of St. Agatha. But if a somewhat more extensive hagiographical narrative is available, a sentence of which lends itself to evocative metaphorical interpretations, then other signs come into play, leading in their turn to new and more imaginative stories and begetting omnipresent attributes. This is the case with the eyes of St. Lucy, which were not torn from her; rather there is a reference to them by the martyr herself in the narrative of her sufferings.

The richer, then, the passion (the narrative of sufferings),[69] the more numerous the attributes that can be derived from it. One example applies to all: the case of St. Barbara whose executioner, her very own father, was burned up by a stroke of lightning. Because lightning is accompanied by thunder, the saint became the protectress of those who use weapons and cannons; as a result, among her attributes the barrel of a cannon can be seen. Or there is the case of St. Anthony Abbot, who probably had nothing to do with pigs, and yet, by complex ways that will be explained in the notice on him, a piglet became a principal attribute of this saint.

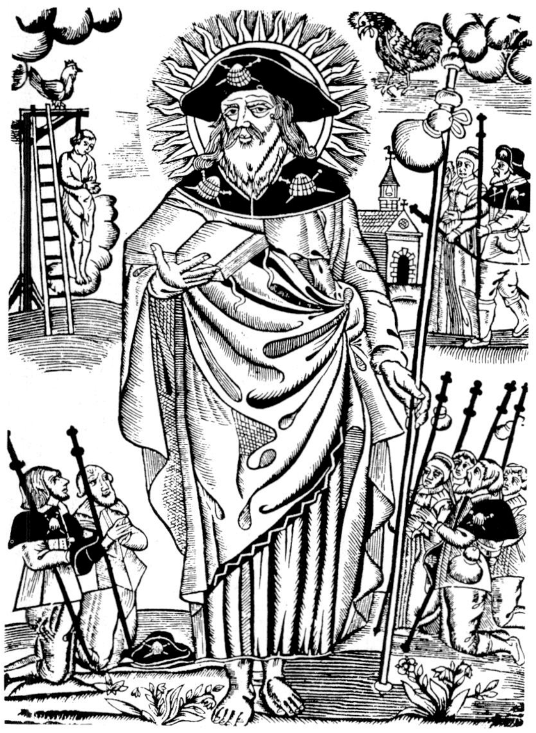

St. James the Apostle.
A popular French print. St. James, patron of pilgrims, is shown as one of them and with the emblems of the pilgrimage to his tomb at Santiago de Campostela. In his hand he carries the Gospel, because he was the evangelizer of Spain. He is surrounded by pilgrims, and in the upper left-hand corner the miracle of the hanged man is memorialized: a young pilgrim was unjustly accused of theft and was hanged, but his parents, who had been given assurances by St. James, turned to the authorities: the resuscitation of an already roasted chicken convinced the authorities to have their son's body taken down from the gibbet, and he was found to be alive. The aureole, or nimbus, does not always take the same form; here it is like a radiant sun, in order to emphasize the saint's power and his likeness to Christ.

12. Signs for All the Saints

There are, then, some standard figures that need to be mentioned. Martyrs, to begin with, are all young and handsome; think, for example, of the already mentioned virgins in Sant'Apollinare Nuovo in Ravenna. It is clear that their uniform beauty is a sign of a spiritual quality rather than a physical and that it translates into material form their virginity and virtue. In this case, as in many others, it may be said that the artist has "idealized" his subject; however, it would be better to say that he gives a realistic representation of the interior face, without losing himself in superficial details, because he sees and represents the truth, and this is more important to him.

The deeper reason for this *beauty,* which seems to be an attribute of all the saints, is traceable to the very nature of holiness. For holiness, as we have seen, is the fullness of humanity after the model of Christ.

In him, who is "the image of the invisible God,"[70] "the light of the face of God shines in all its beauty."[71] Having become like him by their complete following, the martyrs and other saints are "beautiful" independently of any physical feature. For "beauty is the splendor of truth,"[72] which in them, as in Christ whom they imitate, necessarily shines out.

The recurrence of external features that are pleasing in the highest degree according to the canons of esthetics is simply a way of representing this beauty in a visual form; in other words, the beauty here does not reside in any purely outward quality but arises out of a deep interior truthfulness.

Splendor is the radiance of a light. Beauty, heightened by the aureole, is a "formal" attribute of the saints, inasmuch as it expresses the "form" of their life, which is the imitation of Christ.

Physical beauty becomes a deposit and communication of all desirable qualities summed up in it.

In the iconography of the saints, in addition to beauty, other characteristics have also appeared frequently: an upright posture in all cases; the veil of virgins for consecrated virgins; crowns; and, further, the instruments of martyrdom, which are a means of bringing out the special mode of holiness in each martyr. The martyrs always carry the palm of victory and the signs and instruments of the torments they underwent; these become distinctive traits.

The *upright posture* shows a person ready to act, to perform a task; it becomes especially meaningful when we find it in the martyrs.

In iconography, then, this posture is seen when the figure of the saint or martyr is presented in an emblematic and not a narrative manner. It is always accompanied by the saint's attributes and allusions to the particular situation.

St. Francis of Paola.
By Francisco de Goya, 1770, in Vienna.
Eyes raised to heaven are a constant in symbolic images of the saints; they represent the human condition, which must make constant reference to the divine, from which men and women derive inspiration and strength.

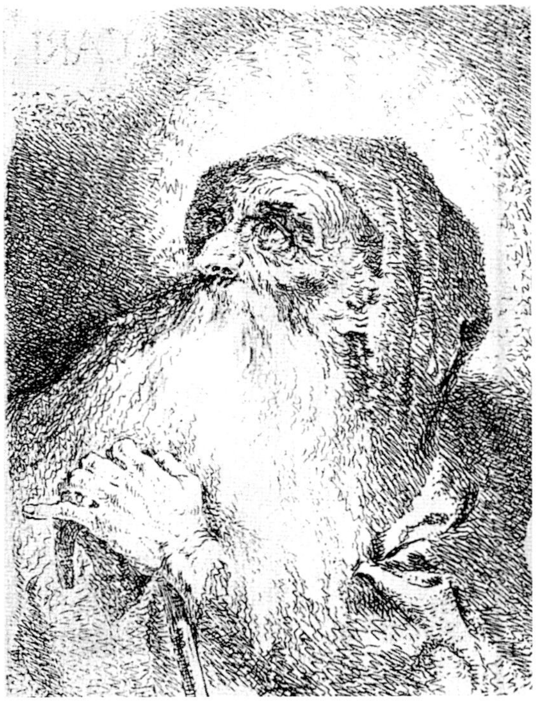

The *eyes raised to heaven* seen in so many images seem to embody St. Paul's exhortation: *Seek the things that are above.* They are an allusion to the close bond between the saints and heaven, a bond that reaches out to include those who pray to the saints.

Clouds and rays of light often envelop the saints. "God is light and in him there is no darkness," St. John writes;[73] he also compares light to the beginning of things, as though to establish and reveal the order in creation.[74] Light is one of the most obvious symbols of the divinity, connected as it is with the blessing that is the sun and with life[75] and therefore with the heavens, which are the first and original hierophany of the sacred.[76]

Light from on high descends upon the saints, signifying both their election and the power that sustains them.

The light often comes from clouds that open up and allow it to pass through, frequently together with angels. The clouds, also connected with heaven, were especially beneficial in the hot regions in which the iconographical repertory of the great religions was formed. In both literary and figural representations, clouds and light almost always accompany the manifestation and appearance of the divinity; they conceal and at the same time reveal, while also alluding to the fact that the direct vision of God would be terrifying.

In iconography clouds seem, as it were, to support the divine persons, either surrounding their feet or providing a seat for them; from the clouds emerge rays of light and angels, both of which are signs of the divine presence. For example, in representations of St. Agatha of Catania light illumines the darkness of her cell and accompanies the visit of St. Peter, who heals her.

The *veil* is seen in the images of virgins, as well as, in a differently developed form, in images of the holy foundresses of convents. The veil suggests the concept of the *velatio virginis* (the "veiling of virgins"). We find it, in fact, as a characteristic of consecrated virgins as well as of martyred women. With its very delicate and sometimes transparent material it is a symbol of separation from the world and of modesty and virtue. The veil of a married woman in the Roman world was thought of as repelling the demons of lust. The vestal virgins, regarded as chaste spouses of the divinities, wore a veil, which served as a sign that they belonged to a god. The veil then became the sign of consecrated virginity; from the representational point of view, the fillets and lengthy ribbons on the head seem to have the same meaning, even if the artists were not always fully aware of this.

Carried in the hand, the *cross* or *crucifix* appears as an attribute of various saints, such as St. Francis, St. Rita of Cascia, and St. Vincent Ferrer, in whom it is connected with particular incidents or qualities. In general, it refers to the saints' full imitation of Christ; it is a source of light, which is not infrequently represented, and it strengthens.

The *Book of the Gospels* is typical of the apostles, whose mandate was to proclaim it, and of their successors, the bishops. But other saints, too, may carry it; in these cases it is an allusion to their meditation on it and to their collaboration in spreading it.

The color *red* recurs in images of the martyrs as being the color of fire and blood. Even when it is the color of authority, as in Roman commanders and emperors, it still refers to the shedding of blood, because a leader must be more ready than others for sacrifice. This is why cardinals, the princes of the Church, wear red robes, for these robes express their readiness for martyrdom. This is also why red is the color of the martyrs and why red vestments are worn on their feast days.

St. John the Evangelist.
Engraving by Agostino Veneziano.
The eagle, which is this saint's principal attribute, supports him amid the clouds (which symbolize a hierophany) as he is intent on his inspired writing. Divine inspiration is emphasized by the blaze of light that radiates around him and from him.

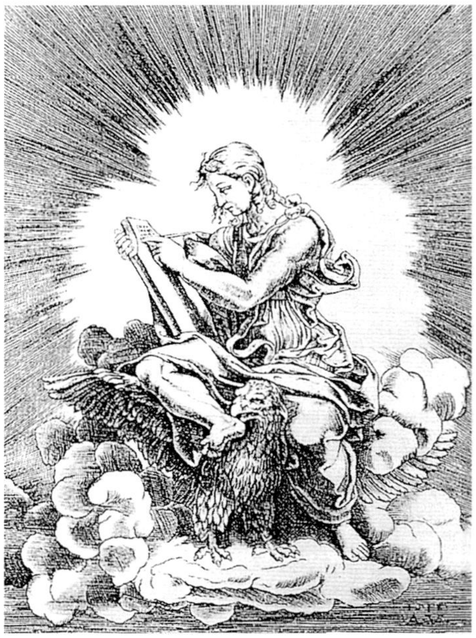

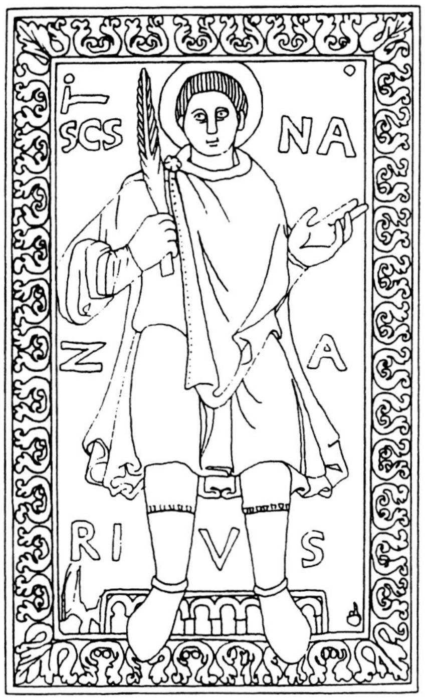

St. Nazarius.
Drawing of an Ottonian ivory of the 10th cent., representing the saint in a way that imitates models of the 5th cent. (Triers, Kestner Museum). The palm branch is an attribute common to all the martyrs, so much so that when other more specific attributes are shown, the palm may not be present.

Images of the martyrs very often show them with two attributes common to all of them: the *palm* and the *crown* of leaves and flowers or of some precious metal. The palm is presented in several ways: it is offered, along with the crown, by angels, or it is carried in the hand, or it is simply there at the side.

These two attributes originate in the Greco-Roman and Jewish-Oriental worlds. But they are signs not so much of sufferings as of victory over the forces of evil: "Those crowned possess palms."[77] A historical study of the use of crowns and palms also shows them to be closely connected.

When Jesus went up to Jerusalem for the Passover, he was greeted by a crowd waving palm branches, a gesture proper to the Hebrew tradition.[78]

The date palm is a special tree in the eyes of Orientals. Everything about it is useful. Its duration and height far surpass human measure, so much so that in Mesopotamia it was regarded as a sacred tree, for it evokes the ideas of immortality, rebirth, victory, and asceticism, and is a metaphor for what is elevated and sublime,[79] a metaphor of victory.

In Egypt palm branches were a symbol of unending life and were carried in funeral processions.[80] The palm tree combined the symbolism of victory with that of resurrection. Thus, while conquerors were greeted with palm branches, the Apocalypse shows the martyrs, those victors[81] over death and in the struggle with the demons, carrying palm branches. Martyrdom was often likened to a struggle not against wild beasts, which, however, they did often have to face, but over the devil himself, who tempted them in every way to deny the faith. The palms, then, automatically likened the martyr to Christ, who was prophetically greeted with palms at his entrance into Jerusalem before his passion.

Coronation of SS. Elzearius and Delphina.
Small portable devotional altar of the 15th cent.; an etching of the original is in the collection of Abbot Couissinier. Franciscan Museum, Rome. Coronation signifies the full accomplishment of a person's task and the achievement of his or her destiny. The emphasis is on the support given by Francis to the two spouses; the whole evidently had in mind other spouses desirous of the saint's protection.

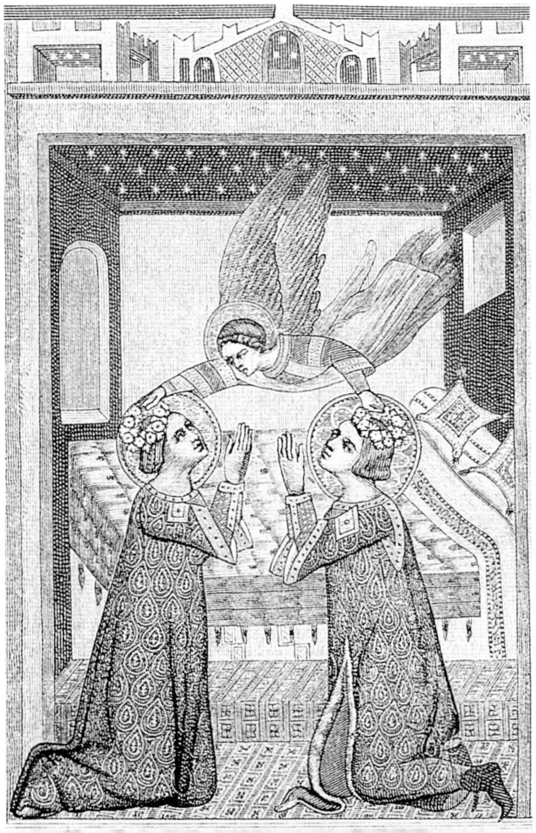

Crowns or *garlands*[82] are signs that convey meaning both by their location and by the material of which they are made. When placed on the head, they share in the transcendent meaning of the head itself, which is the part of the body closest to heaven, and of the person standing upright, ready to carry out a task. Being round, they call to mind the idea of perfection and of participation in the divine nature, symbolized by the circle. In addition, the circle, having neither beginning nor end, is also a symbol of eternal life. Even in the Bible, crown and garland stand for fame, honor, joy, royalty, fullness of life, and eternal life.

The *garland,* which is a round festoon made of leaves or flowers, was an adornment worn during sacrifices and banquets. Its symbolism is also connected with that of plants whose branches are interwoven. Garlands, branches, and flowers suggest the transmission of life and vitality.[83]

In the Greco-Roman world, the laurel was par excellence the tree that supplied garlands. Being evergreen, it suggested the idea of eternal life. The crown of laurel, which was bestowed on victors in battle, was meant to purify them from the shedding of blood. Later on, the idea of victory and, consequently, of honor was associated with the crown; it was also given to the winner in athletic competitions. Bridegrooms wore garlands on their heads; John Chrysostom interprets the garland in this context as a sign of victory, because the bride entered the nuptial chamber as an unconquered virgin.

In the Hebrew world the crown was a sign of victory: the book of Wisdom describes the virtuous person as "crowned in triumph, victor in the contest for prizes that are undefiled" (4:2). On the Feast of Tents[84] the crowns had an eschatological significance and pointed to eternal life. This symbolism passed over into the Christian world, where the crown signified the glory of the elect and the incorruptible life they had won.

The patrimony of the Jewish world and that of the classical world are tightly interwoven in the words of St. Paul as he explains the meaning of the crown for Christians: "Athletes exercise self-control in all things; they do it to receive an imperishable wreath, but we an imperishable one."[85]

When the crown is made of metal, its value and that of the gems that adorn it recall the fullness of power and sovereignty.[86] Such are the crowns of the elders who sit on seats around the throne of the Lamb and wear white robes.[87]

Martyrs wear the crown on their heads or else receive it from angels[88] or even from the divine persons themselves.[89] At times Christ himself gives the crown and by this gesture confirms the meaning of the crown as a sign and acknowledgment of participation in the divine life and of the complete execution of the task assigned to the martyr.

But it is not only in connection with the martyrs that crowns appear in Christian iconography. In fact, crowns would soon become the symbols of sovereigns. As a result, in the majority of cases what is depicted is crowns laid down, the saints thereby attesting that the only real sovereignty belongs to Christ.

The *aureole* or *nimbus* (literally, "little cloud") is a shining disk that surrounds the heads of the divine persons and the saints. It is of Eastern origin and represents the sun, the royal crown; it appeared previously in images of the Olympian gods. The images of kings showed the nimbus as a symbol of earthly sovereignty, while the circular form was a reference to the completeness of their dominion; it appears also in images of the Roman emperors. From the fourth century on, it appears around the head of Christ in the frescoes in the catacombs of St. Callistus, and from then on marks holiness generally. It represents symbolically the outpouring of the divine life that radiates from things holy as light radiates from the sun.

The next things to appear as specific attributes in the representations of the martyrs were the *instruments and signs of martyrdom,* which became emblems of glory. Just as the cross, an instrument of torture and shame to the Romans, was transformed by Christ into a throne and was the reason why he will sit at the right hand of the Father at the Judgment, so these instruments, now precious and dear, are inseparable from the martyrs, who turn them into distinctive signs of themselves, a kind of prolongation of their very name (that is, "martyr"). Here again the iconography of the martyrs is analogous with that of Christ, who displays his wounds and carries the cross as a banner.[90]

For this reason,[91] when Christ is shown in his glory, he is often depicted in the act of displaying the wounds on account of which he is a judge at the General Judgment.[92] Similarly, the martyrs display the wounds from the tortures inflicted on them and carry the instruments of torment in their hands as though these were scepters.

A brief remark on two ways of representing the martyrs: martyrs who carry the instruments and martyrs to whom these are offered by angels. When the instruments of martyrdom are being offered, the emphasis is on the idea that martyrdom is a privilege, a divine investiture. When the martyr carries them in his hands, the emphasis is on the voluntary character of martyrdom. Similarly, in many representations of the crucifixion, Christ is shown in the act as it were of mounting the cross, underscoring the idea of the passion as a voluntary submission to suffering.

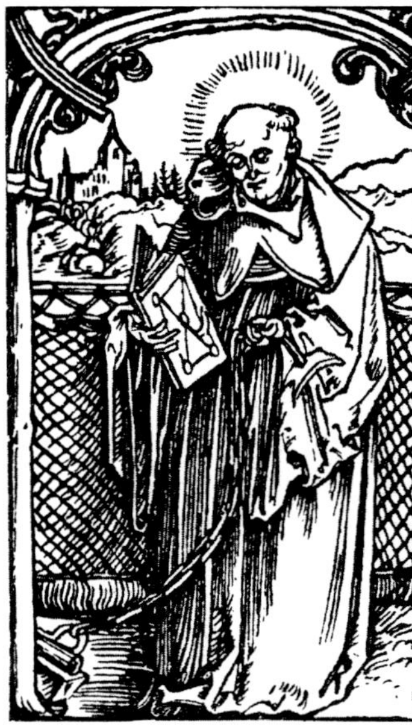

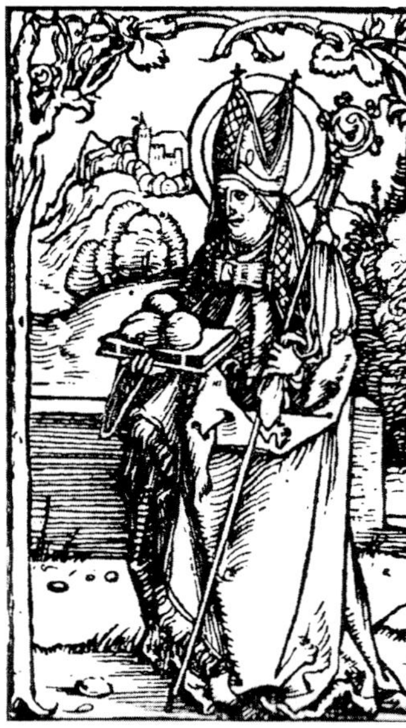

St. Leonard and St. Nicholas of Bari.
Woodcuts from *Salus animae* (Nuremberg, 1503). As in the image of St. James (a few pages back), we see here the different forms the aureole can take. That of St. Leonard (upper image) consists of rays around his head. St. Leonard of Nibliacum (= Limoges) was a hermit who lived between the 5th and the 10th cent. and became very popular in the 11th; we have little information about his life. He was a monk in the retinue of St. Remigius and, like him, acquired the ability to liberate prisoners; he liberated a large number of them, so that a chain became his attribute. St. Nicholas of Bari (lower image) is identified by his episcopal garb and by the three purses on top of the Book of Gospels; his aureole here takes the form of a double circle.

13. Bishops

Bishops are the successors to the apostles, and the garb that characterizes their images is highly symbolic. The vestments to be mentioned are almost all present in the images of all bishops. Conspicuous are the *white tunic* or *coat,* recalling the white garment Herod caused to be put on Jesus; it is a sign of chastity, of the purity of soul bestowed by grace. The tunic is tied on with the *cincture,* a cord representing the cord with which Jesus was bound and the whip with which he was scourged. It binds the one who wears it to the service of Christ. It is a sign of priestly chastity and spiritual vigilance.

The *stole* represents the yoke of Jesus and is therefore a sign both of priestly authority and of priestly dignity. The *chasuble* or *planeta* is the royal robe proper to the celebrant; it is worn

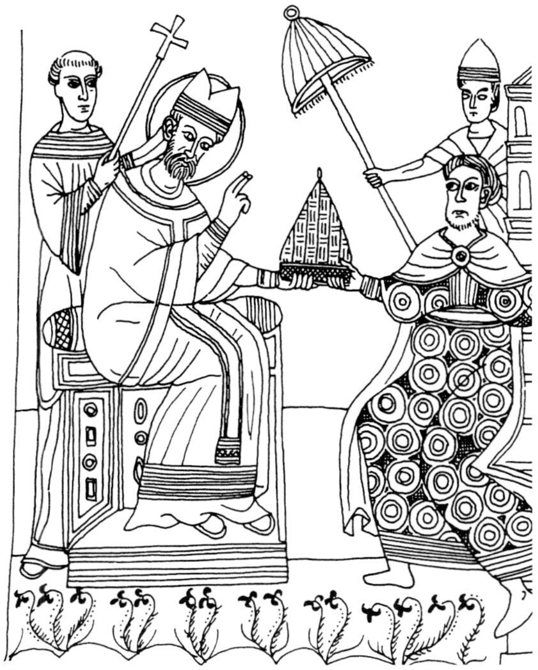

Constantine Gives the Tiara to Pope Sylvester.
Drawing of a fresco in the oratory of St. Sylvester in Rome (13th cent.).
The pope is represented as a bishop: he wears a chasuble with its sign of the cross and a miter, the two points of which symbolize the Old and New Testaments and also, according to Durandus, love of God and of neighbor. The two bands that run down his back, the fanons, allude to the literal and mystical interpretations of Scripture. The fringes, red at times, which adorn the fanons, represent the readiness of the bishop to give his life for his faith and, since they run over the shoulders, they say that the bishops must bear the weight of what they teach, that is, put it into practice. The white color of the miter signifies purity and, placed on his head, refers to watchfulness over the senses. The miter symbolizes the crown of thorns; according to the typical-dogmatic sense it signifies the Church of Christ which surrounds the bishop's head as an adornment, and the exaltation of the humanity of Christ in its hypostatic union with the person of the Son of God.

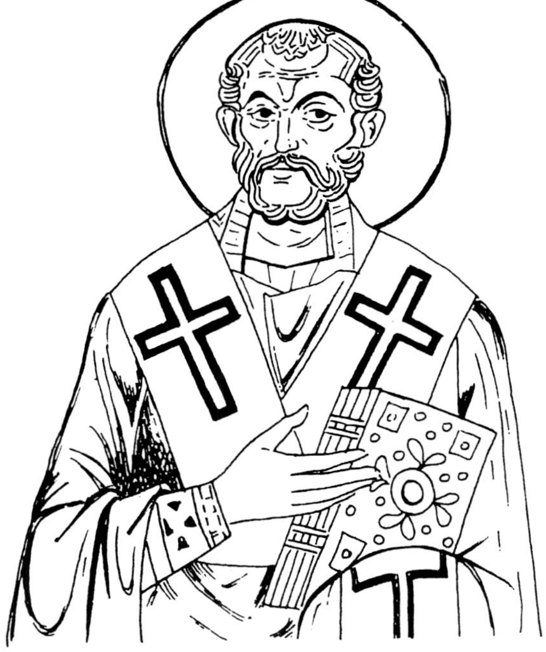

A Holy Bishop
This representation of a bishop comes from the church of Daphni in Greece; the drawing is of an 11th-cent. mosaic. In accordance with Eastern practice there is no miter, while the emphasis is on the stole with its large crosses. As in Western images of bishops, the Gospel is the principal attribute of bishops, because their special task is its proclamation.

over the tunic. This vestment is a reminder of the seamless garment of Jesus as well as of the purple garment that the "King of the Jews" was forced to wear. The cross on the back is the cross carried even to Calvary; the stripe on the front represents the pillar of the scourging; because the chasuble covers the other vestments it signifies the protection given by charity.

The *chair* (cathedra) of the bishop signifies his authority; it is the place of one who teaches and also of one who blesses. In a *blessing* the three extended fingers recall the Most Holy Trinity and the two fingers folded together recall the Second Person, Jesus Christ. The bishop carries the *pastoral staff,* the curve of which represents the curly hair of a ram; the staff recalls the staff of the shepherd kings of the Semitic world, who were prepared to give their lives for the flock. This is perhaps the most meaningful emblem of bishops and is always present along with the *Book of the Gospels;* the two express the bishop's role as leader and teacher.

A *white stripe covered with black crosses,* fastened with white and black pins, is the mark par excellence of archbishops; it is reserved to the pope and archbishops. This is the *pallium* (Latin *pallium* = outer garment, cloak), which was the garb of Greek philosophers and was worn by Christ and the apostles. It is a symbol of the pastoral office and of a readiness for sacrifice. It is woven of the wool of two white lambs that are blessed on the feast of St. Agnes, who is herself a symbol of meekness and sacrifice. Archbishops had to ask the pope for the pallium and go in person, not through a delegate, to receive it, if they were to be able to take possession of their see. It is worn on the shoulders as an admonition to the wearer to prove himself a good shepherd in the exercise of his authority. The *miter* (a Greek word meaning a fillet for the head, a turban) recalls the head gear of the Levites; its two pointed ends represent the Old and New Testaments.

The *gloves* a bishop often wears are a symbol of honor and purity of heart, while on his hand the *ring* (which by its circular form symbolizes completeness and eternity) is a sign of eternal union and marriage to the Church. The *pluviale,* a large decorated cloak, often embroidered with meaningful images, derives its name from the Latin *pluvialis,* "rainy"; it originated in a cloak with a hood to ward off rain. It is a processional robe, underscoring the bishop's role as leader of his people.

14. Protectors and Founders

In many images the patron saints of a city in a manner dictated by an iconographical typology that has a special meaning: the saint carries the city in his arms or on his or her lap. This is an imagery that goes far back and follows, perhaps, the iconographical model of the emperor who holds a globe, which symbolizes the entire world over which he has dominion. One of the earliest uses of this typology in Christian art is to be seen in the mosaic in the apse of the basilica of SS. Cosmas and Damian. It also appears in the mosaic on the arch in the basilica of St. Lawrence. Here Popes Felix IV and Pelagius, surrounded by SS. Peter and Paul and holy martyrs, present to the glorified Christ a model of the basilica they decreed and founded. This is an image of paradisal glory; it expresses the historical fact of glorified holiness, while it also offers to God the churches that have been built and, at the same time, foretells their destiny.

Similarly at Constantinople in Hagia Sophia: in the mosaic on the southwest interior arch, Justinian and Constantine the Great offer, respectively, the church of Hagia Sophia and the city of New Constantinople. There is a similar image in the cathedral of Monreale: here, in mosaics from the end of the twelfth century, William II presents the cathedral to the Virgin.

These images have in common that models of buildings and cities are presented by the persons who decreed their erection or founded them or, in the case of New Constantinople, refounded. The connection between building and offerer or city and offerer is that the offerer has full possession based on his founding action. By reason of his protective activity the saint is as it were the new founder of the city and is no longer separable from it. So close is the connection that the city often becomes his attribute, just as the model of a church or a monastery becomes a distinctive attribute of its founder; the founder becomes the first member and citizen, as though this were his native place.

The connection between the saints and these places is also expressed by the composition of the scene: the saints, standing or kneeling before the divine Persons, present cities or places that are in the background or at their feet, and they show this by the gesture of open and outstretched hands (the gesture is one both of showing and of prayer).

These images of cities and places that are protected by the saints and depicted as clasped in their arms have also a deeper meaning. For this meaning we turn, in addition to the images described above, to the literary image of Jerusalem the Holy as described in the book of Revelation: "And I saw the holy city, the new Jerusalem, coming down out of heaven from God, prepared as a bride adorned for her husband. And I heard a loud voice from the throne saying, 'See, the home of God is among mortals. He will dwell with them as their God; they will be his people, and God himself will be with them'" (Rev 21:2-3). These are all emblematic cities that can be wholly grasped in a single glance; they are cities reduced in size, but they are exemplars, paradigms, summaries of everything that can happen in them in space and time. They are atemporal, metahistorical, and prophetic images; they say that the saint is the one who knows and sustains the city of which he is the patron and, ideally, the founder; he knows it because he has established it; he unveils its interior and better face and presents it, as such, to God.

Not infrequently the founders of orders, monasteries, and congregations carry in their hands a *book* in which one can see their motto written down. The book itself signifies the rule they set for their followers.

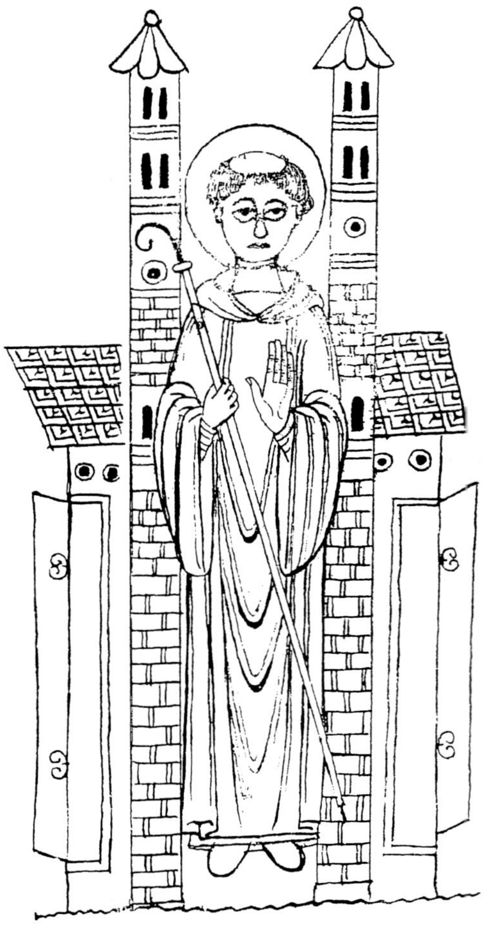

St. Othmar and the Abbey of St. Gall.
As depicted in the Passional of Stuttgart, which came from Zwiefalten, ca. 1150; now in the Württ. Bibl., Stuttgart, fol. 58, f. 118v.
St. Othmar († 759) was abbot of the abbey of St. Gall, of which he is regarded as the second founder. He is represented with his pastoral staff, because the abbot is the shepherd of the monks, and he wears the episcopal insignia.

15. Our citizenship is in heaven *(Phil 2:20)*

There is a special iconographical model that shows a series of saints around the Virgin and the Son, at various moments in the life of Jesus, from his birth to his crucifixion, or at the feet of the Most Holy Trinity, or gathered around a crucifix, and so on.

These are often grandiose images that share the characteristic of being completely non-historical. In fact, none of the persons represented could ever have been in the represented situation while they were on earth. In this kind of image, found especially on polyptychs, the saints appear each with their principal attribute, their typical garments, their characteristic appearance.

These images are often summarized in their captions as "Madonna and Saints," as though those viewing them are not and ought not be interested in who these saints are.

This type of image is one which, since there are no authoritative traditions regarding them, I like to describe as *conversatio coelestis,* "a conversation in heaven." What the images represent is the happy intimacy of the saints with the divine persons; transported as they are into the atemporality of eternity, the saints are witnesses contemporary with us at every moment.

In these images, too, the entire Church is represented emblematically, for it is present in them through its saints, behind whom can be glimpsed all those whom these saints protect. This is true whether the images be spacious representations of paradise in which myriads of angels and saints are arrayed around the Most Holy Trinity and the Virgin, or, instead, show only a few persons around the Christ Child. The philosophy in both kinds of images is the same; they show humanity sharing in glory.

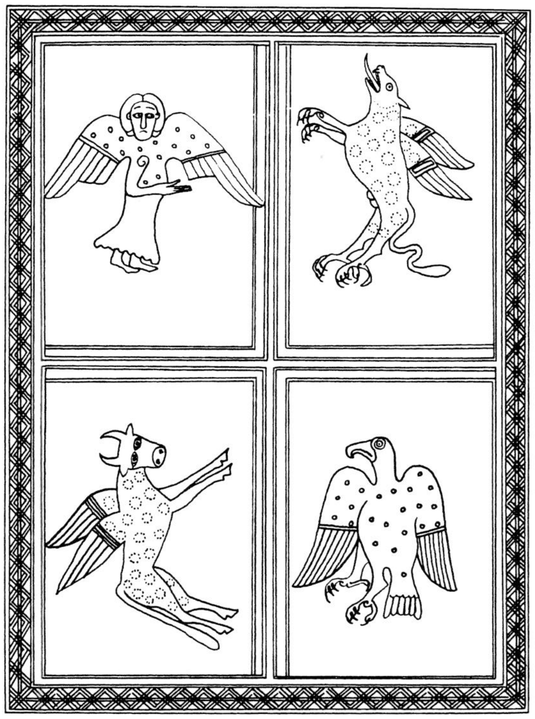

The Four Evangelists.
Book of Litchfield, beginning of 8th cent., Cathedral of Litchfield.
The saints are often grouped according to their special callings and the characteristics of their actions. Among the earliest groups are the evangelists, who could even be represented solely by their symbols, which are taken from the incipits of their respective writings. The image here is of the Tetramorph (literally: fourfold form) and is taken from St. John who, in his Apocalypse, describes four living creatures around the throne of God; these have the appearance, the first of a lion, the second of an ox, the third of a man, and the fourth of an eagle (Rev 4:7-9). Irenaeus of Lyons stresses the correspondence between Christ's plan of salvation and the Gospel, both of them taking four forms. The lion symbolizes energy, primacy, kingliness; the calf, or bull, signifies sacrifice; the human face refers to the self-manifestation of the Son of God as a human being; the eagle flies up to the Spirit who descends as a gift upon the Church. In addition, the four animals are a reminder that Jesus is a man by his birth, a bull in his sacrificial death, a lion in his resurrection (lions were thought to sleep with their eyes open), and an eagle in his ascent to heaven (it was thought that eagles could fix their gaze on the sun). In the moral sense, the human figure is a reminder that a Christian must first of all be a human being, that is, a rational creature; the lion exhorts the Christian to be courageous and fear nothing in this world; the bull exhorts him to sacrifice himself and not be bound by the pleasures of the present world; the eagle urges him to turn his eyes to heaven and to mount up there like Christ in his ascension.

16. Groups of Saints

By reason of their distinctive traits and, above all, by reason of the kind of protection they offer, the saints have been grouped together according to homogeneous types.

Thus there is the group of the twelve apostles, which is certainly the best known and most commonly found in images. Some of the saints appear in the quartet of evangelists: Matthew, Mark, Luke, and John, who are quite often depicted on ambos and pulpits with their symbols, which evidently allude to the Gospel each one proclaimed. We find them also on the facades of cathedrals in the symbolic form of the Tetramorph, that is, a lion, an ox, an eagle, and a human face, the four symbols of the evangelists arranged around Christ. The beginning of each Gospel can be connected with one of these symbols. Mark begins with the preaching of St. John the Baptist, who was "the voice of one shouting in the wilderness" like a lion. Luke begins with the sacrifice offered by Zechariah, who as a Jewish priest sacrificed calves. John, in his Gospel, has his eyes fixed as it were on the light of God, and it was thought that only an eagle could stare at the sun. Matthew begins with the human genealogy of Jesus, and his sign is the human face. But the symbolism is even richer: on the facades of cathedrals the Tetramorph is also an image of the Church that carries the Gospel to the ends of the earth. The Tetramorph goes back to the book of Revelation (4:7-8) and to Ezekiel (1:4ff.).

The group of four evangelists is often matched with the group of the four doctors of the Western Church: Gregory the Great, Augustine, Ambrose, and Jerome. In the Eastern Church, the group of four doctors is made up of Athanasius, Basil, Gregory of Nazianzus, and John Chrysostom.

Another group is that of the holy Helpers or Intercessors. This is a group of fourteen saints who in the Middle Ages were specially invoked in some situations: Acacius against migraine and against the torments of the final agony; Barbara against lightning and a sudden, unprovided death; Blaise against diseases of the throat; Catherine of Alexandria for the protection of philosophers and theologians; Cyriacus against demonic possession and at the moment of death; Christopher against accidents while traveling; Dionysius, a martyr, against demonic possession and headaches; Egidius (or Giles) against epilepsy and madness; Erasmus against lightning and intestinal diseases; Eustachius against the fire of hell; George against diseases of the skin; Margaret against the pains of childbirth; Pantaleon against tuberculosis; Vitus against snakebite and lethargy. The group is not everywhere completely the same: Umberto can replace Eustachies; Roch (Rocco) may replace Pantaleon; Leonard and Nicholas may replace Erasmus and Dionysius. Almost all of them will be found among the saints in this volume.

Finally, there is the group of Four Virgins: Barbara, Catherine, Margaret, and Dorothea.

17. From the Altars to the Streets

The images of the saints become a powerful vehicle for spreading the special virtues of each when they pass from the altars of the churches to prints and holy cards. These sacred images, reduced in size and not infrequently accompanied by prayers and short biographical notes, fostered a greater familiarity with the saints represented and over the course of time have been especially important in the spread of their models of life. Because they helped personal meditation and contemplation, they promoted an internalization of these models.

Moreover, the images of the saints have always been companions on the way for every kind of traveler. Whether painted on walls, reproduced in print, or simply hung on trees, whether located in the shelter of wooden or even marble houses or houses of other material, placed at the top of pillars or in niches in the walls of houses,[93] in both city and countryside,[94] these sacred images attest to the spread of popular devotion not only to the Virgin and her Son but also to many saints such as Anthony of Padua, Anthony the Hermit, and John Nepomuk. The Council of Trent urged seemliness in the making and use of them.[95] Prints were soon replaced by ceramic tablets, which were almost indestructible. Private and individual devotion took on a choral and public dimension along the streets and in the squares.

The images on posters, holy cards, and public sacred images display an exemplary conciseness, because they had their origin in the necessity of giving expression to the entire life and the entire spirituality of a saint, and even of the traditions about him, and of doing so with a few strokes of the pen. The holy cards have been accused in various quarters of being excessively schematic, of promoting a mechanical and repetitive devotion, of being superficial, and indeed it is very difficult to find them in churches. My view, on the other hand, is that their gradual disappearance was an impoverishment and fostered a loss of memory. However beautiful the altar piece or the fresco or the mosaic that one gazes on, the memory of it is not enough to cause the beneficent effects to carry over into domestic and personal meditation. The little holy card, however, though perhaps lacking in graphic and esthetic touches, was able to keep the memory of mosaic or fresco alive and give rise to reflection. It was like a good summary of a book which one will not read but whose essential content is made known through the summary. Yet this is enough to stir devotion and a desire to be like the model, and this is the ultimate purpose of every sacred image.

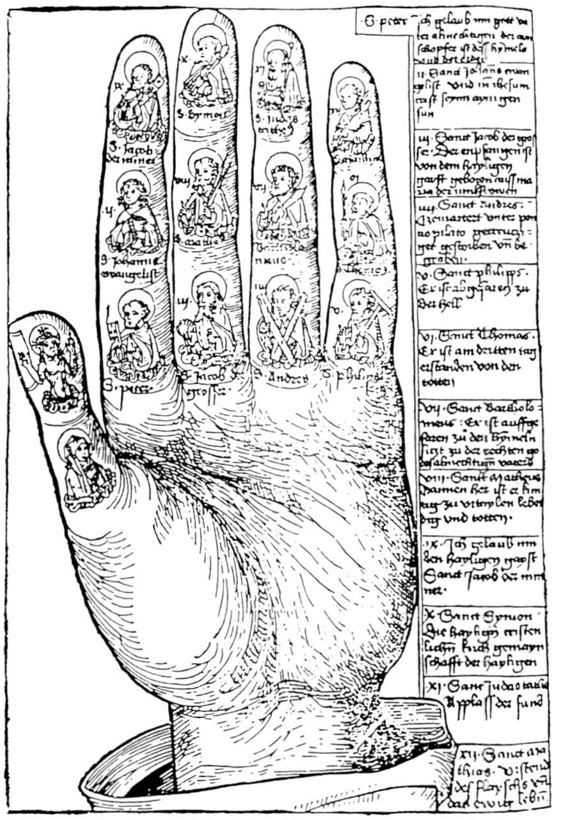

The Creed of the Apostles.
Woodcut by Stephen Fridolin, Nuremberg, 1491. The apostles are represented as the fingers of a hand, showing the unity of their activity and their preaching as the foundation of the Church. On the thumb, the finger without which the hand cannot grip and operate, Jesus and Mary can be seen. On the index finger are James, John, and Peter, the three closest to Jesus and present at his Transfiguration and in the Garden of Olives.

18. Today's Images

Today, however, we face a further problem: the iconography of the saints has been reduced in an immense degree, and it is not easy to find attributes for newly canonized persons. Indeed, it has seemed that if a good photograph of the saint is available, there is no need of calling upon artists to represent them and run the risk of failing to get a likeness.

But very rarely do photographs have the emblematic conciseness of a portrait, which is the genre that seems[96] closest to the photograph.

A photograph seizes a moment, not "*the* moment" of a person's life, that is, the instant in which the whole soul is reaching out to its destiny. The obvious reason for this is that this reaching out is the fruit of a life, of a disposition, of a spiritual attitude that finds expression in countless gestures and moments, in none of which it is contained in its entirety. A photograph of a person is always a "falsehood"[97] in comparison to what the individual really is, because it singles out a particular moment and, although this moment is not emblematic of the whole life of the person, offers this snapshot as being exemplary and paradigmatic.

Photographs of the saints do not satisfy in the least the need that gives rise to images of the saints, and so they are misleading. The rich life of St. Frances Xavier Cabrini, for example, is not represented by a snapshot that is taken almost without her knowledge and that gives posterity the austere and mute image of a religious woman.

This problem will be resolved only if we get artists to play a role once again in the formation of images and if these artists are guided by a religious community that has given its heart to the saint, calls upon her, and seeks conformity with her.

NOTES

[1] G. Biffi, "Preface," in L. Gherardi, *Il sole sugli argini* (Bologna, 1989) ix.
[2] A. von Speyr, *Mistica oggettiva* (Milan, 1975).
[3] J. Ries, *Il sacro* (Milan, 1982) 151ff.
[4] Speaking to Moses on Mount Horeb, God describes himself as "I am who I am" (Exod 3:14), that is, as He who *truly is* and has in himself the source of his own existence, in contrast not only to the gods, who do not exist, but to everything created, which depends on him for its existence.

The Latin words *sanctus* and *sancitus* were used of places that were well circumscribed and separated from everything around them because they were so distinguished for their beauty, their majesty, or other significant and impressive qualities, that people saw manifested in them the power of being, the power of what we today call the divine. These places, in other words, were recognized as being utterly *different,* utterly *other,* from human beings and from all creatures, which are by their nature perishable and ephemeral. In the history of religions, there were, first, holy places in which the divine, the sacred, manifested itself (see M. Delahoutre, "Il sacro e la sua espessione estetica: spazio sacro, arte sacra, monumenti sacri," in *Le origini e il problema dell' homo religiosus* [Milan, 1989] 119ff.). Next came things and human beings that were holy because they were linked in various ways to these holy places: since the *sacred* can draw other things into its sphere and manifest itself in them, persons and things thereby become *holy*. It is evident that holiness is a quality which neither things nor human beings give to themselves, and that it is a gift. This principle, which becomes evident through an analysis of the origins of the idea of holiness, was given a thoughtful formulation by Adrienne von Speyr: "Holiness consists not in the fact that a human being gives everything, but in the fact that God takes everything" *(Mistica oggettiva).*

[5] See L. Giussani, *Il senso religioso* (Milan, 1986) 39: "The human person is that level of nature at which nature becomes conscious of itself; it is the level of reality at which reality begins to become self-consciousness, that is, begins to become reason."
[6] *Code of Canon Law,* Can. 1187: "Veneration through public cult is permitted only to those servants of God who are listed in the catalog of the saints or of the blessed by the authority of the Church" (page 429).
[7] A brief sketch of the history of the ways of "canonizing" is appropriate here.

First, the Christian people began spontaneously to venerate martyrs and confessors, bishops and ascetics, for they saw in these individuals a living and tangible testimony to the new life that had begun in Christ. Between the sixth and eighth centuries there was "episcopal canonization"; this, too, was based on popular veneration and on miracles, but it was the bishops who caused the saint's life and the story of his or her miracles to be written. Above all, it was the bishop who ordered the "elevation" of the body to a more honorable tomb or its "translation" to an altar which took its name from the saint. On such an occasion, the church itself was often enlarged and dedicated to the saint.

Then episcopal canonization began to be replaced by papal canonization, which included the insertion of the saint's name in the *Martyrology* and the creation of a rite for celebrating his or her feast annually. The first example of this is found in 1041, and the saint was Simon of Trier. Of great importance, because the claim was made that canonization was the pope's work, were the pontificates of St. Leo IX (1002–1054; Pope from 1042) and of Alexander III (Pope from 1159 to 1181). Innocent IV (1191–1254; Pope from 1243) set down the procedure and reserved canonization to the pope, who made of it a solemn liturgical action. At the canonization of St. Francis in 1228 the ritual form was already set, and Gregory IX wanted a regulated process to be followed for St. Francis and St. Dominic.

In 1588 Sixtus V established the Sacred Congregation of Rites, which handled the procedure; the latter was subsequently regulated by decrees of the Inquisition (1635) that sought to rein in the proliferation of unauthorized cults. In 1634, in the apostolic letter *Coelestis Hierusalem cives,* Urban VIII (1568–1644; Pope from 1623) distinguished between beatification and canonization, introduced the concept of heroic virtues, and set down the form to be followed in the process. Innocent XI (1615–1700; Pope from 1691) set down the preliminary process carried out by the local bishop, and Benedict XIV, an expert on the subject, further clarified the idea of heroic virtue, stressing the point that the practice had to be consistent and radical. Pius X (1835–1914; Pope from 1903) and Pius XI (1857–1939; Pope from 1922) further defined the procedure. Pius XI also established the historical section of the Congregation of Rites, which since 1988 has been called the Congregation for the Causes of Saints.

Until 1983, the process, called "ordinary" in its first part and "apostolic" in its second, could begin only fifty years after the death of the candidate. It led first to beatification, the proclamation of which involved, and involves, solemn ceremonies, which ever since 1662, by the will of Pope Alexander VII, are held in St. Peter's in Rome. Beatification allowed the veneration of the blessed only in his local church or his religious congregation or order.

Beatification was followed by canonization after a process that certified two more miracles. Canonization included, and still includes, the solemn enrollment in the list of saints, with a ceremony that always takes place at St. Peter's in Rome. This ceremony with its various parts is a true affirmation and triumph of the universal Church, which is aided by the Spirit and is called together by invocations addressed to the several parts of the Church: militant, suffering, and triumphant.

The processes of beatification and canonization could be, and perhaps still can be, very lengthy and exhausting. Indeed, the fact that the entire process reaches a conclusion could almost be considered as itself a miracle proving that by God's will the person in question is to be venerated and taken as a model.

The current procedure, introduced in 1988, provides for an easier, quicker, and more collegial process. The part of the process in which the heroic virtue of the candidate is discussed can begin immediately after the person's death; the miracles required are now one for beatification (not required for martyrs) and a further one for canonization. There is a law, introduced in 1940, that in order to start a process a *nihil obstat* (there is no obstacle) is needed; this attests that there is nothing in the Vatican archives that forbids going ahead with the cause.

[8] *Code of Canon Law,* Can. 1186: "To foster the sanctification of the people of God the Church recommends to the particular and filial veneration of the Christian faithful the Blessed Mary ever Virgin, the Mother of God, whom Christ established as the Mother of the human race; it also promotes true and authentic devotion to the other saints by whose example the Christian faithful are edified and through whose intercession they are sustained."
[9] This underscored the divine origin of civil authority. Also called *sancti* in epitaphs were virtuous persons. This calls attention to a second aspect, that of morality, so that a virtuous behavior, that is, behavior in accordance with the will (note well: not the example!) of the divinity, was a sign of a proper attitude toward the sacred.
[10] I am using recent points of reference, in which what in the beginning was practiced and asserted in action has reached full consciousness and exact formulation.
[11] We must wait for the fifth century for the term to describe the person whose name it precedes.
[12] As we still read in the *Catechism of the Catholic Church,* which in no. 823 cites Ecumenical Council Vatican II: "The Church . . . is held, as a matter of faith, to be unfailingly holy. . . . The Church . . . is 'the holy People of God,' and her members are called 'saints.'"
[13] This is emphasized in the *Catechism,* no. 824: "United with Christ, the Church is sanctified by him; through him and with him she becomes *sanctifying*" (emphases added).
[14] The Greek word *martys* (genitive: *martyros;* plural: *martyres)* means "witness"; from it is derived the verb *martyreô,* which means "I bear witness, I assert, I attest." The word is of special interest to us here because it comes from a Sanskrit root *smarati,* which means "to remember" and therefore calls our attention also to the Latin word *memor* ("remembering, mindful of"). In other words the martyr is a person who "remembers" that which is the foundation of his life, and who bears witness to it.
[15] The words are those of Cardinal Giacomo Biffi, on November 4, 1994, when remembering SS. Vitalis and Agricola, the protomartyrs of Bologna.
[16] We see here something unique and special to Christianity. Christianity is offered to and set before everyone, but the response and acceptance take place on a journey; they become more definitive and complete with time.
[17] Until the third century, the Western Church did not have particular commemorations of saints or the deceased, and Christians honored their dead as everyone else did: on the anniversary the family of the deceased person came together at the tomb and had a meal there, part of which was offered to the deceased.
[18] Eusebius of Caesarea, *History of the Church* 5, 1, 3–63 (trans. G. A. Williamson; Baltimore: Penguin, 1965).
[19] This was a letter sent by the communities of Lyons and nearby Vienne to the brethren in some Oriental Churches. It attests to the persecution of 177; in the text there is abundant reference to the theme of Christ who lives in the martyrs; he not only "helps" them but also "suffers" in them.
[20] Apart from the nativity of Jesus, the only earthly birthdays the Church celebrates are those of the Virgin and Saint John the Baptist: of the Virgin because she was conceived without original sin, and of St. John because in his mother's womb, that is, before his earthly birth, he recognized the Savior when the Virgin visited his mother, St. Elizabeth.

21 The eucharistic liturgy was thus added to the ancient practice of meals at the grave; only from the end of the fourth century on did the bishops combat that practice.

22 Two Latin texts and one Greek text contain the narrative of the martyrdom of Perpetua and Felicity and their companions in the faith. The first Latin text and the Greek (this last possibly composed by Tertullian) are titled *Acts of the Martyrdom . . .*; the second Latin text, which is a slightly later abridgment, is titled *Minor Acts . . . .* The texts show clearly that they were read at celebrations. Thus: "It is useful to read, at celebrations of the Church, the most virtuous life of the blessed martyrs . . . , no less than the ancient narratives" (*Atti del martirio delle sante Perpetua e Felicità, in Atti dei Martiri* [Milan, 1985] 207). Again: "Drawing faithfully on these memoirs, brothers, which are read in the church for the edification of all, the acts of these very famous and most blessed martyrs. . . . When you read them, pray to our merciful God, that through their prayers and those of all the saints he may take pity on us and deign to make us sharers in their lives, to the praise and glory of his Name, which is forever and ever blessed. Amen" (*Atti minori delle sante Perpetua e Felicità*, ibid., 214).

23 Along with the martyrs, "confessors" were also venerated; the name was given to those who, though not slain, did endure suffering or exile for the faith.

24 Among the signs of theological and spiritual soundness was precisely this awareness. See G. Biffi, *La bella, la bestia e il cavaliere* (Milan, 1984) 39: "The keen sense of the difference between good and evil, the consciousness that an irreducible conflict is even now going on between good and evil, and the conviction that in this conflict—which is a present reality and will be until the coming of the Lord—each of us is called upon to struggle in the ways and according to the possibilities given to us."

25 John Paul II, Address to a meeting with married couples, in *L'Osservatore Romano,* October 30–31, 1989, 7.

26 *Catechism of the Catholic Church* (1994), no. 2683.

27 Passages to this effect are very numerous in the New Testament. Examples may be seen in John 15–17, in which we read, among other things: "If you ask the Father anything in my name, he will give it to you" (16:23) and: "I ask not only on behalf of these, but also on behalf of those who will believe in me through their word" (17:20). The Virgin's intercession occurred at the beginning of the public life of Jesus, at the marriage in Cana: "When the wine gave out, the mother of Jesus said to him, 'They have no wine.' And Jesus said to her, 'Woman, what concern is that to you and to me? My hour has not yet come.' His mother said to the servants, 'Do whatever he tells you'" (John 2:3-4).

28 Jesus was the first to give a different interpretation of "family": "Pointing to his disciples, he said: 'Here are my mother and my brothers! For whoever does the will of my Father in heaven is my brother and sister and mother'" (Matt 12:49-50).

29 All good things come from God. Their natural goodness is a kind of prophecy and sample of the goodness of God; this natural goodness is fully "activated" when it is seen in its connection with the Creator.

30 *Catechism,* no. 2158: "God calls each one by name. Everyone's name is sacred. The name is the icon of the person." This passage sums up clearly the great value all peoples assign to the names given to individuals, names identified with the destiny of these persons.

31 *Catechism,* no. 1256: "In baptism, the Lord's name sanctifies man, and the Christian receives his name in the Church. This can be the name of a saint, that is, of a disciple who has lived a life of exemplary fidelity to the Lord. The patron saint provides a model of charity; we are assured of his intercession."

32 Nothing is neglected in the tradition of the Catholic Church. New occupations are given their protectors. In fact, in St. Rita of Coscia, we even have a saint to be invoked in *impossible cases;* she is therefore called "the advocate in desperate cases," "the saint of things impossible."

33 A prime example here is the case of St. Agatha as patron of the Republic of San Marino, as can be seen from the entry on her in the historical survey. It was not only the historically ascertainable facts about the lives of the saints that proved to be the source of legends. When historically ascertainable texts were not to be had, people were satisfied with fanciful stories and narratives in which the intention of astonishing readers was primary and obvious. All this did not, however, prevent the gathering of connections and the formalizing of these in the form of patronage.

34 Biffi, *La bella, la bestia e il cavaliere,* 36: "We are not a 'people of the book'; strictly speaking, we are not even a 'people of the word'; we are a 'people of the event.'" In all their outward manifestations the Christian people show a need of concreteness that descends into details and that is connected with the origin of this people in the very heart of the Incarnation.

35 A. Vecchi, *Il culto delle immagini nelle stampe populari* (Florence, 1968) 7.

36 On the other hand, the continual process of taking relics and carrying them elsewhere meant the despoliation of the cemeteries.

37 Tertullian, *Defense of Christians (Apologeticum)* 50, 13.

38 The iconography of the saints clearly illustrates this concept when it shows the blood and water gushing from the wound in the side of Jesus. See C. Rusconi, *Fulget Crucis Mysterium* (Rimini, 1991) 93: "The blood and water come gushing forcefully from the wound: they are elements in the delivery in which the new humankind and the Church are born." The entire concept and illustration remind us of the parable of the seed: "Unless a grain of wheat falls into the earth and dies, it remains just a single grain; but if it dies, it bears much fruit" (John 12:24). See the painting of the crucifixion by Fra Angelico, which is a part of the altar piece in San Marco, Florence.

39 The desire to possess and preserve the relics gave rise, not infrequently, to thefts and abductions. We may mention the theft of the relics of St. Nicholas from the city of Myra, where he had been bishop, by sailors from Bari. The relics were solemnly received in Bari on May 9, 1087, and today Nicholas is the principal patron of Bari and other cities.

40 Thus viewed, the intercession of St. Agatha on behalf of Catania in the famous incident of Frederick II is testimony of a love that is almost jealous and angry.

41 L. Grigyel, "L'Europa dei Santi," in *La Liturgia della Chiesa*.

42 R. Guardini, "L'immagine sacra e il Dio invisibile," *Rivista di estetica,* no. 1 (1961): "An image reaches down much more deeply to the roots of the interior life, which is not a matter merely of doctrine. An image acts on the imagination and the feelings. It tends to become an archetype and then, being assimilated and transformed, enters the life of the observer."

43 See Vecchi, *Il culto delle immagini,* 1ff.: "To offer a holy image is therefore to body forth an ideal of the life of piety, and to seek to conform thoughts and actions to this ideal. . . . Every image of a saint represents the triumph of a virtue which can be offered for imitation by a category of persons or as an example of a state of life or a profession."

44 Seventy was the year in which Titus conquered Jerusalem, with the resultant destruction of the Temple and the scattering of the Jews throughout the Roman Empire.

45 Of particular interest is the study of the nature and form of what A. Grabar has called the "graphic vector" of the changed meaning of the image, that is, the element which, being introduced into an earlier image, gives it a new meaning; see A. Grabar, *Le vie della creazione nell'iconografia cristiana* (Milan, 1983). In Christian iconography we see a continuous sedimentation at work; nothing in what expresses the relation to the sacred is ever abandoned or completely put aside, and we can say that the Christian iconographic vocabulary is the result of this sedimentation.

46 See J. Ries, "Cristianesimo, religioni e culture," a lecture given at Bologna in 1986, and J. M. Laboa, *Momenti cruciali nella storia della Chiesa* (Milan, 1996) 57ff.

47 A fact brought out clearly by A. Grabar in the work cited earlier, in note 45.

48 Gregory of Nyssa, *Oratio laudatoria sancti ac magni martyris Theodori* (PG 46:737-39).

49 Gregory the Great, *Letter to Bishop Serenus,* in MGH, *Gregorii I Papae Registrum epistularum* II, 1, lib. IX, 208, p. 195; Italian trans. in C. Costantini, "La legislazione ecclesiastica sull'arte," *Fede e arte* 5 (1957) 360. See also Grabar, 221ff.

50 H. Hennephof (ed.), "Lettera di Eusebio all'imperatrice Costanza," in *Textus byzantinos ad iconomachiam pertinentes* (Leiden, 1969) 42–45.

51 The reference is to the famous handbook of the monks of Mt. Athos, which was discovered in 1845 and translated into Italian for the first time at Naples in 1971 (edited by Giovanni Donato Grasso, with an introduction by Sergio Bettini). The text, composed in the eighteenth century, attests to traditions that had become well established in previous eras.

52 Dionysius of Phurna, *Ermeneutica della pittura* (Naples, 1971) 7.

53 Ibid., 10.

54 D. Menozzi correctly remarks that we have no documents directly from the iconoclasts, because these were destroyed by the iconodules. It is therefore not easy completely to explain their arguments that the emperor officially interpreted. See D. Menozzi, *La Chiesa e le immagini* (Milan, 1995).

55 N. P. Tanner (ed.), *Decrees of the Ecumenical Councils* (2 vols.; London: Sheed & Ward, and Washington, D.C.: Georgetown University Press, 1990) 1:136.

56 Ibid., 168.

57 *Letter of Hadrian I to the Generals* (Mansi 12:1061C-D).

58 *Decrees of the Ecumenical Councils* 1:136.

59 See H. Belting, *Il culto delle immagini* (Urbino, 2001) 110ff.

60 M. Donadeo, *Le Icone* (Brescia, 1980) 19.

61 The result was a proliferation of handbooks describing in minute detail how the divine Persons, the saints, and the incidents in their lives were to be represented; a good example of these manuals is the above-mentioned *Ermeneutica della pittura* of Dionysius of Phurna.

62 P. Evdokimov, *La teologia della belleza* (Rome, 1971) 21ff.

63 At the time of the council's twelfth-hundred anniversary, its teaching was repeated by Pope John Paul II in his apostolic letter *Duodecimum saeculum* of December 4, 1987.

64 This point has been underscored by A. Grabar, *Le vie della creazione* (note 45, above) 222: "This diversity of views in regard to religious art has, generally speaking, not been brought out by historians. In this they have been mistaken since the area of the arts, whether looked at from the viewpoint of artistic creation in itself or from the viewpoint of the role of works of art in religious devotion, is a great revealer of the real content of the faith in the consciousness of various ethnic, political, and social groups."

65 After having asserted that the tradition of the Catholic Church is to be followed in all matters, Nicaea II sets down four anathemas. The fourth reads: "If anyone rejects any written or unwritten tradition of the church, let him be anathema" (*Decrees of the Ecumenical Councils* 1:138).

66 The action in this case is the movement of a solemn procession-pilgrimage toward the divine Persons.

67 Vecchi, *Il culto delle immagini,* 7: "Every image of a saint represents the triumph of a virtue that can be offered for imitation by a category of persons or as an exemplar of a state of life or a profession."

[68] The reference is to the three peaks on which the Republic of San Marino stands. *Penne* (*penna* = feather; quill) stands here for *cime* ("peaks"), *penna* having been at one time a customary word for "mountain, rock, point." In this meaning the word fell into disuse in the rest of Italy and was no longer understood, generally speaking, even by the "men of the *penne*" (as the people of San Marino were called), that is, "men of the peaks."

[69] When there had been a martyrdom, the local church gathered at the place of the execution or the burial of the witness to Christ. Every year the church met to celebrate the anniversary of the death and to listen, during the liturgy of the word, to the account of the testimony rendered; in his sermon the celebrating bishop might bring out that testimony more fully. It was in this setting that the *acta martyrum* came into being, and in many passages our ancient sources speak of the *acta martyrum* being read along with the sacred books in the course of the liturgical prayer. Both conciliar documents (such as, for example, those from the Council of Hippo in 393) and the writings of individual authors (such as Augustine in Africa, Caesarius of Arles in Gaul, Braulio in Spain) attest to the existence of this practice. See B. de Gaiffier, "La lecture des passions des martyrs à Rome avant le IXe siècle," *Analecta Bollandiana* 87 (1969) 134ff.

As for the earliest period, it can be noted that the writings of Perpetua and Satyrus, published at the beginning of the third century, were compiled for the purpose of reading them aloud, doubtless at a meeting of a liturgical kind. From the fourth century on we find a special phenomenon: narratives of dubious authenticity kept on multiplying, and when popular piety did not find a narrative written close to the time of the events, it created legends. In any case, these extreme instances attest to tendencies that were there from the beginning: once a martyr had borne witness at the cost of his or her life, the Church to which the martyr belonged wanted that witness to become permanent by being written down for the edification of future generations. That same Church also had no objection against the martyr's glory being reflected on it.

Another term for writings on martyrdom was *passiones,* which was in use from the beginning of Christian Latinity with the meaning "passions of the martyrs." It is found, for example, in a canon of the Council of Hippo in 393 (see C. Munier, Concilia Africae a. 345–a. 525 [CCL 149; Turnholt, 1975] 21 and 43); the canon decrees that alongside the canonical Scriptures the *passiones martyrum* are also to be read in church. It is obvious that this term, on the one hand, emphasizes the idea of suffering, and, on the other, brings out the narrative element: a *passio* is thus a narrative of struggle and suffering, culminating in death.

The distinction between *acta martyrum* and *passiones martyrum* is, strictly speaking, only one of viewpoint. The *acta* can be distinguished from the *passiones* by taking the former to be the trial and the latter to be a description of the trial. There is a difference of form, with the result that the *acta* are closer to drama, the *passiones* to narrative. The *acta* are simply a copy, derived from officials or taken down by a Christian eyewitness, of the official record of the several phases of the debate in court, the sentence, and the execution of the condemnation, all this in the version of the chancery. The *passiones* are later compositions, characterized by a fuller compositional structure, made up of set pieces, and aimed at moral edification. These documents are the source of hagiography.

[70] Paul, Colossians 1:15.

[71] John Paul II, encyclical *Veritatis splendor,* no. 2.

[72] St. Thomas Aquinas, *Commentary on the First Book of Sentences of Peter Lombard,* distinction 3, question 2, article 3, explanation of the text.

[73] 1 John 1:5.

[74] Genesis 1:3.

[75] Evident here is the exceptional concreteness of symbols, which are often thought of, wrongly, as abstract. No bibliography is needed for the fact that the light of the sun is at the physical origin of life on earth.

[76] M. Eliade, *Patterns in Comparative Religion,* trans. R. Sheed (New York: Sheed & Ward, 1958; Meridian Books, 1963) 38: "There is no need to look into the teachings of myth to see that the sky itself directly reveals a transcendence, a power and a holiness. Merely contemplating the vault of heaven produces a religious experience in the primitive mind."

[77] Antiphon in the third Nocturn of the Liturgy of the Martyrs in the Breviary of Pius X.

[78] See J. Daniélou, *I simboli cristiani primitivi* (Rome, 1990) 11–33. The feast of Tents or Huts was originally a seasonal celebration (for the grape harvest) in which "Hebrew thought had concretized its memory of an event of its history" so that it might remember "the sojourn of the people in tents *(schnai)* in the wilderness during the time of the exodus." After living for seven days in huts made of branches *(schnai),* the people processed around the altar, holding in their hand a bundle of willow, myrtle, and palm branches, as well as the fruit of the lemon tree. "To the Jews, the feast of Tents, in which each individual ate and drank with his or her family in their own hut adorned with varied branches, seemed to be a prefiguration of the material joys of the messianic kingdom." It is therefore not surprising that Jesus should be greeted in this way at this moment.

[79] Psalm 92:12: "The righteous flourish like the palm tree."

[80] It is not certain just when the symbolism of death and eternal life first mingled with the iconography of Christ. Let one case stand for all: the myrrh offered to the infant Christ, which is a sign both of embalming, therefore of death, and of incorruption, therefore of resurrection.

[81] Recall here that martyrdom was likened to a combat; in addition, the theme of struggle was also applied to Christ in the sequence of the Easter Vigil, *Victimae paschali:* "Death and life fought a marvelous duel; the Lord of life who was dead lives and reigns" *(Mors et vita duello conflixere mirando: Dux vitae mortuus, regnat vivus).*

[82] *Corona* (crown) derives from the Greek *korônê* (a round object); garland is derived from the Germanic *wieren,* "to surround."

[83] All the religions humanity has practiced find in plant life the symbols of a life that renews itself; the reason for this is the fact that after apparent death plant life continually renews itself. The symbolism appears whenever rituals use branches, trees, or flowers.

[84] Daniélou cites the Jewish book of *Jubilees* XVI, 30: It is ordained forever concerning Israel so that they should observe it [the feast of booths] and that they should dwell in tents and that they should place crowns on their heads and so that they should take branches of leaves and willow from the stream" (J. H. Charlesworh, ed., *The Old Testament Pseudepigrapha* 2 [New York, 1985] 89). He comments: "The reference is evidently to crowns of leaves" (*I simboli cristiani primitivi,* 25).

[85] 1 Corinthians 9:25. See also Isaiah 28:5: "On that day the Lord of hosts will be a garland of glory, and a diadem of beauty, to the remnant of his people"; 1 Peter 5:4: "And when the chief shepherd appears, you will win the crown of glory that never fades away"; Revelation 2:10: "Be faithful unto death, and I will give you the crown of life"; James 1:12: "Such a one [who endures temptation] has stood the test and will receive the crown of life."

[86] For this reason, the crown, being the insignia of royalty, is a treasure to the entire people and not only to the sovereign, and is connected with the idea of the people's identity.

[87] Acts 4:4: "Around the throne are twenty-four thrones, and seated on the thrones are twenty-four elders, dressed in white robes, with golden crowns on their heads. . . . Whenever the living creatures give glory . . . the twenty-four elders fall before the one who is seated on the throne and worship the one who lives forever and ever."

[88] The angel, who is a messenger, announces both a task and a destiny. In iconography the pointer to the task is the presentation of his sign. Examples: the archangel Gabriel, who presents himself to the Virgin Mary while holding a lily that signifies both election and purity; on holy cards, the angels who hold out to the infant Jesus the crown of thorns and the cross that are the instruments of his suffering. Or we may think of the angel in Gethsemane: "Then an angel from heaven appeared to him and gave him strength"; this angel is always shown in the act of handing the cup to Jesus.

[89] On the vault of the apse in the basilica of St. Vitalis in Ravenna, Christ himself extends the crown to the saint.

[90] Images of Christ showing his wounds are rare before the thirteenth century.

[91] Philippians 2:8-10: "[Jesus Christ] humbled himself and became obedient to the point of death—even death on a cross. *Therefore* God also highly exalted him and gave him the name that is above every name, so that at the name of Jesus every knee should bend." The signs of the Passion are signs of obedience and therefore also of glory.

[92] Among many examples I mention only the mosaic showing the general judgment in the Basilica of Torcello (thirteenth century) and the sculpture of the Glory Portico of Santiago de Compostela (end of twelfth century).

[93] Such manufactured objects became widespread throughout all of Europe, but the name given to them changed from place to place. The manner of representation has given them the name I prefer for these objects: I call them "majesties" (Italian: *maestà*), because the persons are shown frontally, according to an iconographic model early Christian art took over from the imperial court, a model dominated visually by the emperor seated on his throne *in maiestate,* that is, with the signs that display his greatness. Other names for these objects: "little pillar," from the shape of the support; "little house," from Latin *aedicula* = little sanctuary, small temple, referring to the shape of the construction that accommodates the image; "little madonna" and "little virgin," with reference to the image most frequently found; "little cell," from the Latin *cella,* which was the name of the part of a temple in which the image of a god stood in a niche; "shrine" (Latin *sacellum,* a small consecrated enclosure; "tabernacle"; "hermitage," because such shrines arose in isolated places; and "oratory," because it was a place at which to pray. In Germany these shrines are known as *Bildstöcke* ("supports with an image"), a name harking back to an arboreal typology (perhaps the most ancient of all), or *Waldandacht* ("devotion in the forest"), which alludes rather to the influence they exert on the spirit of the wayfarer, who is invited to meditate. I could go on citing names.

[94] The phenomenon has wrongly been thought to be a rural one; in fact, recent counts of these objects in the cities has shown how numerous are sacred images unconnected with places of worship.

[95] Council of Trent, Session 25, in *Decrees of the Ecumenical Councils* 2:774–76.

[96] It only seems close, because a portrait, if it be a true portrait, ought by its nature to capture the spirit of the subject and the interior depths of the subject's life; the success of the work is anything but accidental, even when it has the appearance of a mere calligraphic imitation.

[97] Except in cases in which the camera is used to capture a particular, well thought-out pose or scene; but then the photographer is as much an artist as a painter is. But this is not the essence of photography nor its most common approach.

St. Peter and St. Januarius.
5th cent., from the catacombs of St. Januarius, Naples. St. Januarius, guided by St. Peter, holds the crown of martyrdom that brought completion to his earthly life. The theme of the martyr who guides other saints and leads them to heaven is often found in early iconography.

Coronation of Mary.
By Fra Angelico (Louvre Museum, Paris). The coronation of the Virgin by Fra Giovanni of Fiesole, known as Fra Angelico (1387–1455), effectively represents Paradise in which the different saints, their individual characters expressed by their attributes, form a single harmonious expression of praise and glorification.

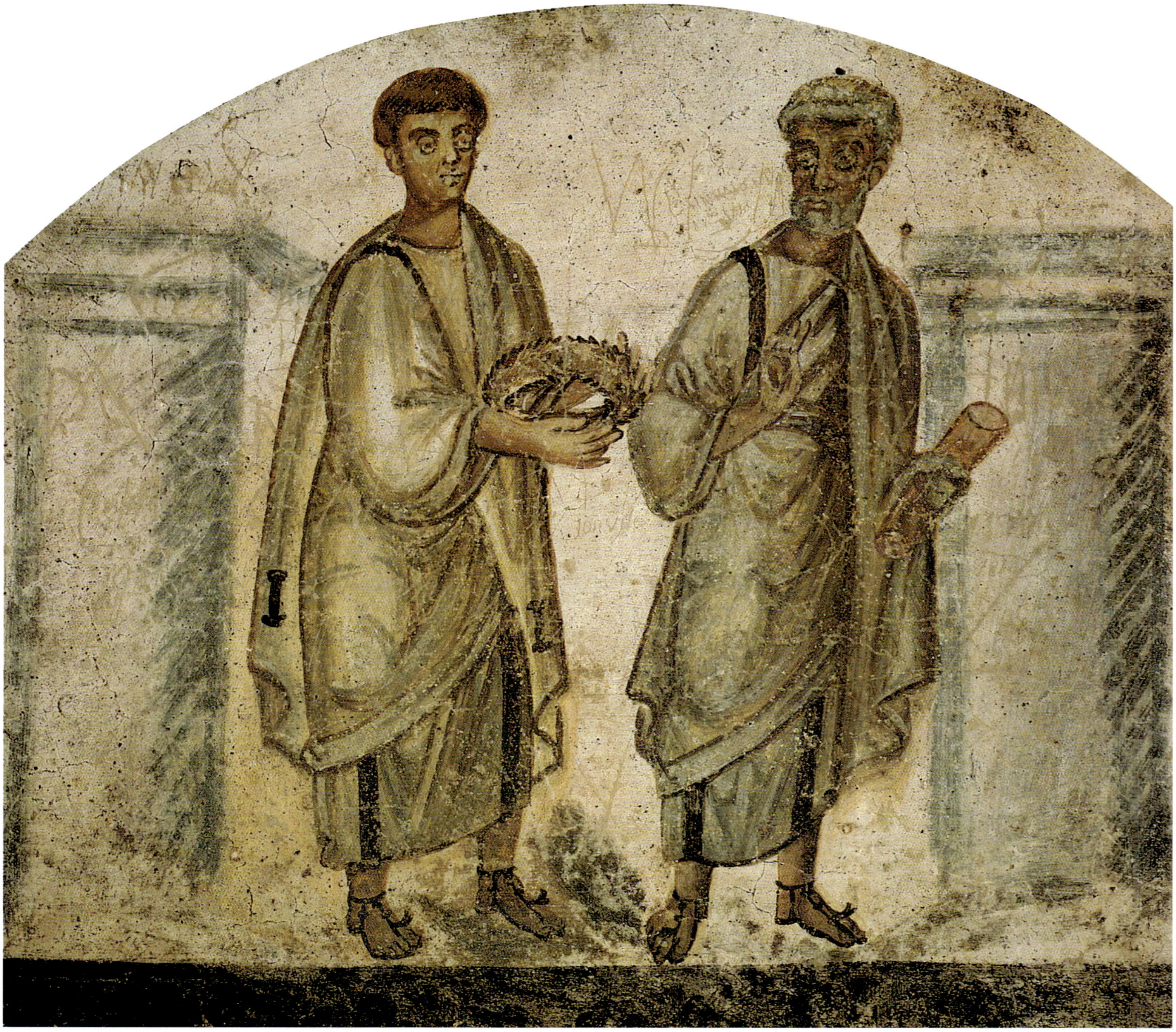

Historical Survey

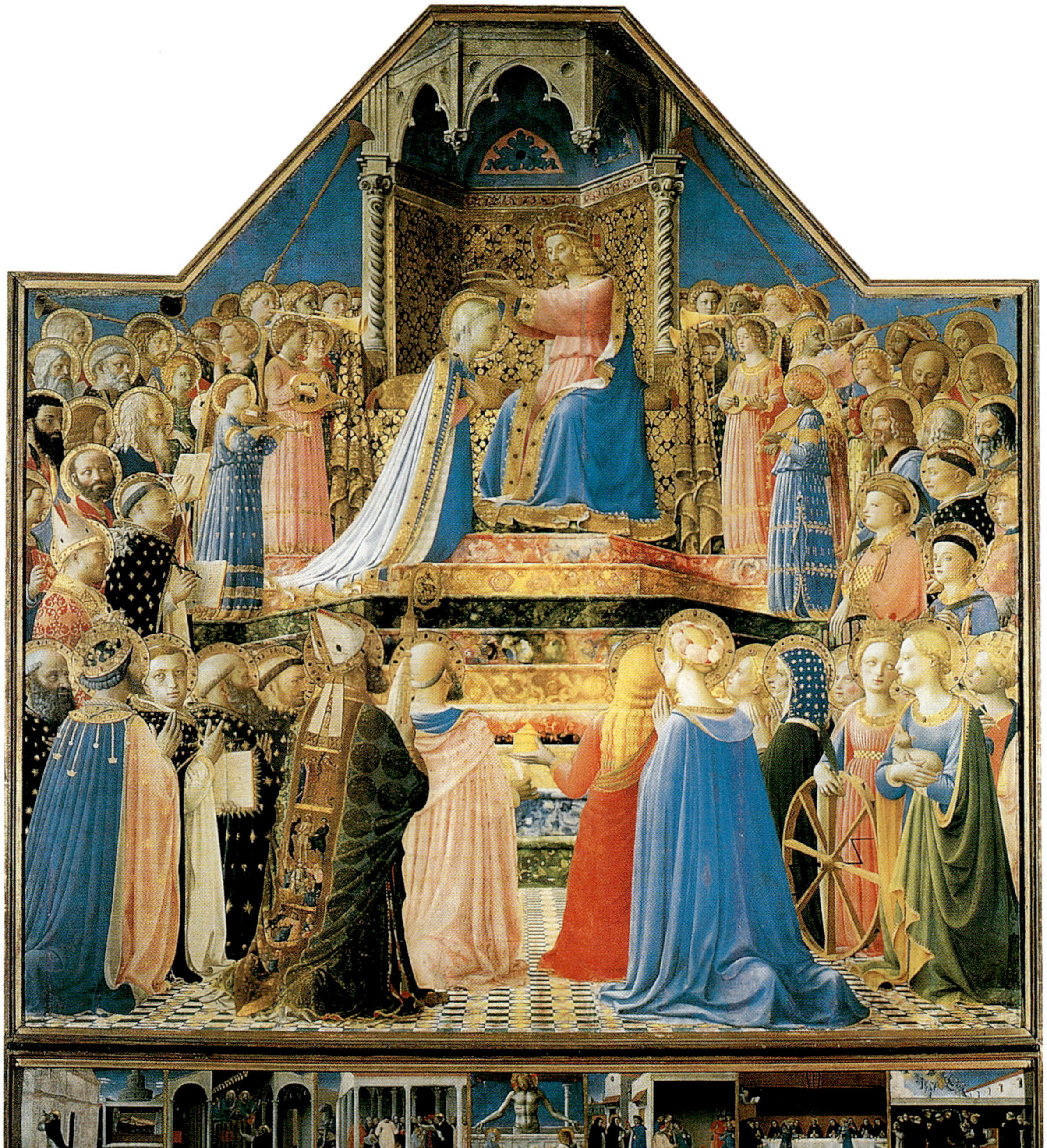

Editorial Note:

In choosing the saints for this list I have taken into consideration not only the extent to which their cult is practiced but also their patronages and, in particular, their patronages of countries and nations. The latter usually have a historical explanation, that is, the saints are patrons of the land in which they were born or in which they lived and worked. The popular choice of a patron has sometimes been confirmed by official proclamations that ratify a tradition; if there has been no popular choice, the proclamation creates one and directs it. No wonder, then, that there are saints little known outside their own country, in which, however, they are greatly venerated.

For each saint I have given the dates of birth and death, the names and even the diminutives (so far as I could determine them) used for them in the various languages. The Latin name, which heads the list, is that used in the *Roman Martyrology;* it is followed by the name in Greek, Italian, French, English, German, Dutch, Polish, Russian, Hungarian, and Rumanian. The first name under each of these headings is the one best attested in that language; the others are the best-known regional variants and indicate the broad spread of the cult.

For each saint I have indicated whether he or she is commemorated in the universal calendar with a solemnity, a feast, or a memorial. When this information is lacking, it means that I have not found the saint in the universal calendar. The reason for this is that while the universal Church remembers the saint on a certain day (usually the *dies natalis* or birthday, that is, the day on which the saint died to earthly life and was born into the life of heaven), the choice of the kind of celebration has been left to the local church. The dates I have taken from the *Roman Martyrology;* these sometimes differ from the dates given in the *Bibliotheca Sanctorum* or in other texts and traditions. When the historical reasons for these changes are of special importance, I have mentioned them. In some cases, further dates are given which refer, for example, to the translation or transferal of their bodies.

The short description given of the life of each saint takes into account what is said in the *Roman Martyrology,* which sets down in summary fashion the main aspects of the holiness, spirituality, and work of the individual.

In each case, a summary life of the saint is given, as is a listing of the saint's patronages of places, categories and activities, animals, and things. I then mention the things for or against which he or she is invoked; these are, of course, linked to the saint's patronages. For example, a saint who is patron of women in labor protects them and is invoked for a safe birth and against the pains of childbirth.

I have given, in boldface type, the saint's attributes as well as those incidents and entities in the story of the life that are present in the iconography as attributes, as becomes immediately evident when I come to the attributes.

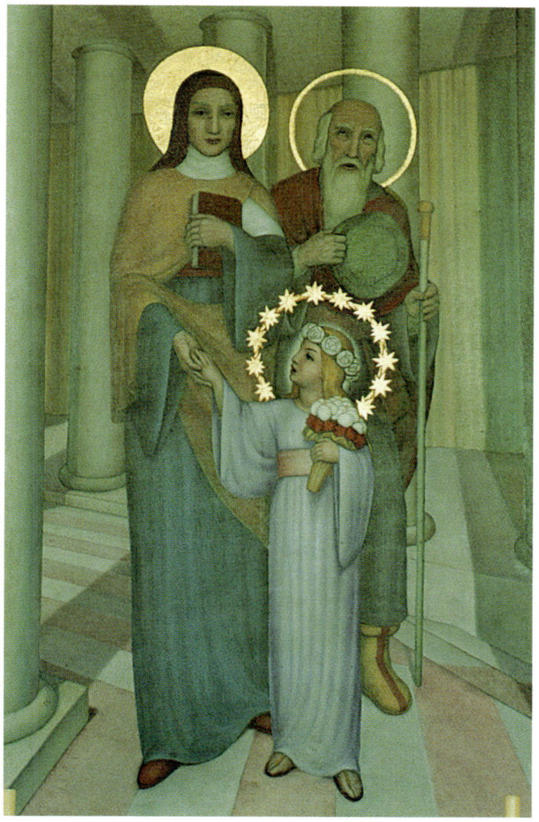

SS. Anna and Joachim with the Child Mary. Fresco in the shrine of Maria Lussari, in Pontebba, Italy, beginning of the 20th cent. Joachim's staff is a reminder that he took refuge in the wilderness among the shepherds. Anna's monastic garb is a reference to her advanced age.

Anna and Joachim, Parents of the Blessed Virgin Mary

Memorial: July 26

Lat.: Anna; It.: Anna, Anita, Nanna; Fr.: Anne, Annette; Sp.: Ana, Anita; Eng.: Anna, Anne, Nan, Nancy; Ger.: Anna, Anita.
Lat.: Ioachim; It.: Gioacchino, Giovacchino, Joachino; Sp.: Joaquin; Ger.: Joachim, Achim.

According to ancient Christian tradition, the names of Mary's parents were preserved for us by the Jews in various apocryphal writings. The name "Anna" was also that of the mother, herself long barren, of Samuel the priest (1 Sam 2:19) and was derived from the Hebrew "Hannah" which means "grace." Anna was the daughter of Mathan, a priest of Bethlehem, and had two sisters, Maria and Sobe, who married two Bethlehemites and became the mothers respectively of Mary Salome and Elizabeth. The *Protevangelium of James* (second century) speaks of Anna in chapters 1–7; the *Gospel of Pseudo-Matthew* in chapters 1–5; and the *Book of the Nativity of Mary* in chapters 1–6.

From these texts we learn that Anna married Joachim, who was perhaps a Galilean, and remained childless for a long time. Joachim, whose name means "preparation of the Lord," was presenting his offering in the Temple when he was accused of being unworthy to do so because he had no children; in his humiliation he withdrew into the wilderness in order to pray. After forty days and forty nights an angel appeared to him and told him that Anna had conceived. Joachim then offered a sacrifice of ten lambs and returned to his home. Anna was in turn instructed by an angel and went to meet her husband at the gate of the city; this moment is known as "The Meeting at the Golden Gate" of Jerusalem and became famous in Eastern iconography; the gate would have been called "golden" because it was gilded, but we have no historical evidence on the subject.

After Mary had been born and had been presented in the Temple at the age of three, we hear nothing more of Joachim. Later apocryphal texts, however, speak of Anna as living to the age of eighty. A late tradition tells of two further marriages of Anna, first to Clopas, brother of Joachim, and then to Salome. According to this tradition, Anna gave birth to Mary, daughter of Clopas, who became the wife of Alphaeus and mother of Simon, Jude Thaddeus, James the lesser, and Joseph the Just; the last-named was presented to the apostles, along with Matthias, as a replacement for Judas Iscariot; Matthias was chosen. After the death of Clopus, Anna married Salome and by him had Mary, daughter of Salome, who married Zebedee and by him had James the Greater and John the Evangelist.

The mother of Jesus, together with her two sisters, was said to constitute the group known as the "Three Marys." It is to be observed that all these cousins of Jesus were also his disciples or apostles. This attractive legend was publicized by the *Golden Legend* and then rejected by the Council of Trent, but it did not therefore die out, especially in the German-speaking countries. In fact, there is an iconographical typology of the "Holy Relatives," which represents all these personages together as in a family portrait. In it, the children, the cousins of Jesus, are already identifiable because they play with the things that

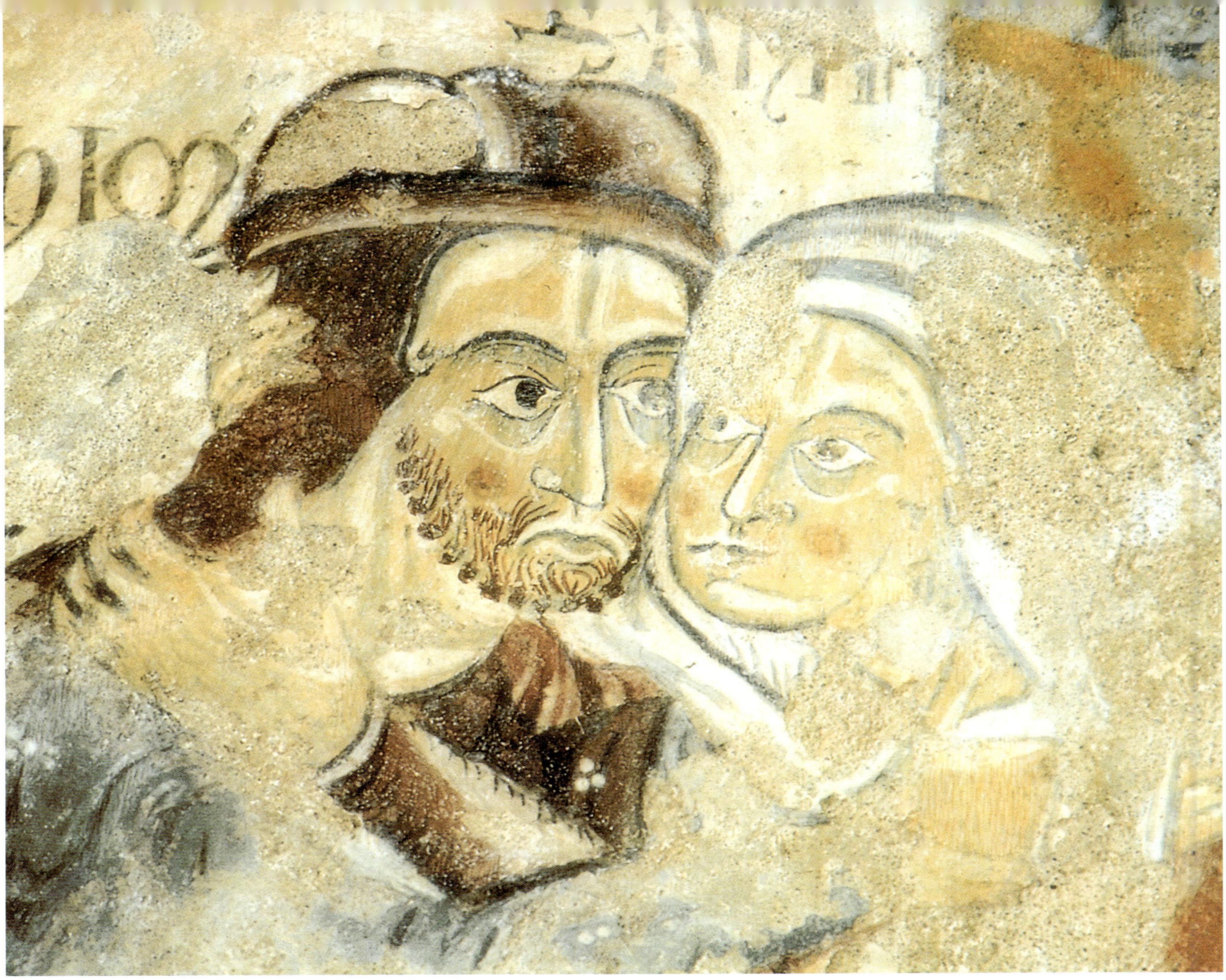

will later on become the instruments of their martyrdom and also, therefore, their iconographical attributes. James, for example, who will become the knight Matamoros, "Slayer of Moors," plays with a horse, Simon with a saw, and Jude Thaddeus with a stick.

The cult of Anna and Joachim spread first in the East and then in the West (partly due to the many relics brought back by the Crusaders) and was connected with the Marian feasts. It was linked in particular to the theme of the Immaculate Conception, which was defended by the Franciscans in the thirteenth century, then ratified by Sixtus IV in 1483, and defined as a dogma in 1854. After spreading throughout Europe, the veneration of Anna was brought to Canada by emigrating Bretons, who were most devoted to her and repeated this saying: "Dead or alive, every Breton must go once to St. Anna."

Today Anna and Joachim are remembered together on July 26.

▷▷ The origin of the many patronages of Anna is connected with Mary. Because Anna carried the hope of the world in her womb, her cloak is green; for this reason she is invoked in Brittany in connection with the hay harvest. As mother-in-law of Joseph the carpenter but chiefly because she was the living "tabernacle" of Mary conceived without sin, she is the patroness of those who work with wood (tabernacles used to made primarily of wood). She therefore protects joiners, carpenters, cabinet makers, and wood turners. Because she guarded Mary like a jewel in a casket, she protects goldsmiths and also coopers. She is the patroness of miners, because they dig up treasures hidden in the depths of the earth, and because the Virgin was Anna's treasure. She taught Mary to clean house and therefore she protects broommakers; to weave, and she protects weavers; to sew, and she protects tailors

Anna and Joachim Kiss When They Meet at the Golden Gate.
Fresco, 13th cent., in the church of Notre Dame, Pozauges-le-Vieux, France.

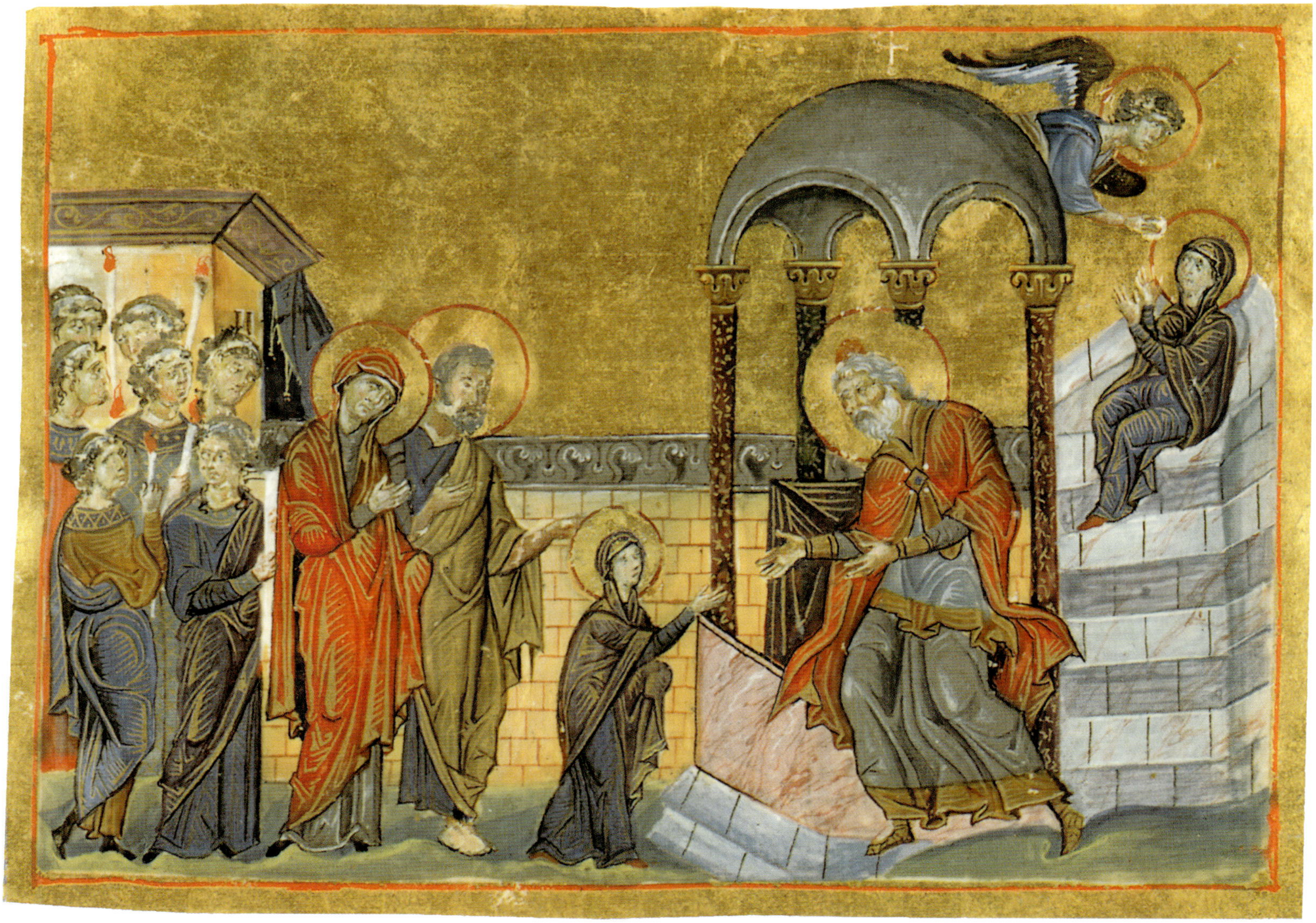

Presentation of the Virgin in the Temple. Miniature, end of 10th, beginning of 11th cent., in the Menology of Basil II (Vat. gr. 1613 f. 198) in the Vatican Apostolic Library.

and those who make cloth, trade in it, and sew it for the home, or make linens and lace. One legend has it that she made knitted gloves; she is therefore patroness of glove makers. Her protection of junk dealers can also be linked to her management of the home. As mother of Mary, *Stella maris,* Anne is patroness of sailors. She is also patroness of Christian mothers of families and of widows.

She is also invoked against conjugal barrenness, on behalf of pregnancies and therefore against the pains of childbirth and as protector against difficult births. Having been the excellent mother of the Virgin, she is asked for help in raising children properly. Since Jesus spared her the fears connected with the final agony, she is invoked for a good death. Tuesday is consecrated to her, because it is thought that she was born and died on that day.

▷▷ In images the couple may be shown together or separately. Joachim has an attribute that is all his own: the **two doves** prescribed as an offering in the Temple. More commonly, however, he is shown with Anna at the meeting at the golden gate, in which it can be said that **each is the attribute of the other**. When shown separately, Anna is most often seen in the act of **teaching Sacred Scripture to little Mary.**

The iconography of Anna has been more developed than that of Joachim; it always shows her as the grandmother par excellence. We see her with the **child Mary**, who is in fact Anna's principal attribute. We also see her with Mary who is holding the infant Jesus in her arms. There are two iconographical types expressing this relationship: one is more intimate, with Anna caressing Jesus; the other is more hieratic with the figures shown frontally as though the one were the royal throne of the other.

Joseph, Husband of the Blessed Virgin Mary

Solemnity: March 19

Lat.: Josephus, faber lignarius, sponsus Mariae, nutritor Domini; It.: Giuseppe; Fr.: Joseph; Sp.: José, Juepe, Pepe, Pepito; Eng.: Joseph, Joe; Ger.: Joseph; Dutch: Josef; Russ.: Osip; Arab.: Yusuf.

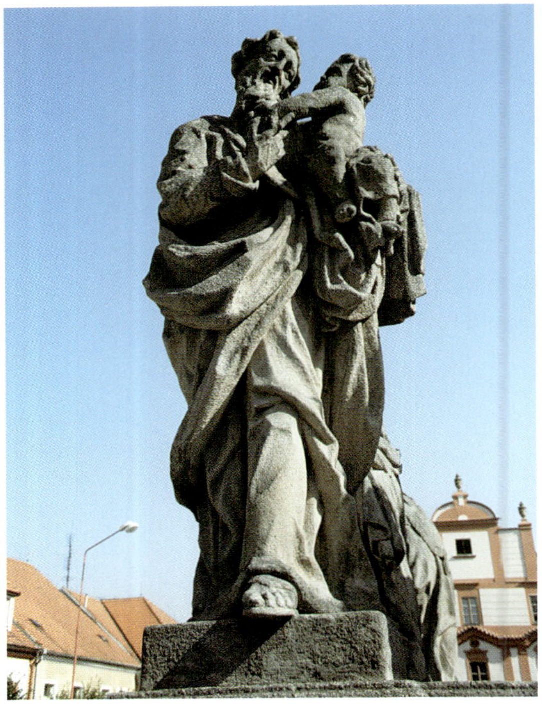

St. Joseph with the Child Jesus.
Statue, 1754–1757, on a bridge over the Otava River in Pisek, Czech Republic.

This righteous man of the House of David served as father to the Son of God, Jesus Christ, who decided to be called the son of Joseph and was submissive to him as a son to his father. The Church honors him especially as a patron, since God himself appointed him protector of his family. Pius IX established his perpetual veneration on January 30, 1859, and later, in the decree *Quemadmodum Deus* of December 8, 1870, proclaimed him patron of the Universal Church. The spread of his cult is attested by the spread of the name, which is the most common male name in Italy and perhaps in the world.

He was espoused to Mary, when the young girl was found to be pregnant; he did not wish, however, to send her away publicly and expose her to the weighty condemnations common at the time. He also knew how to listen, and he listened to the angel who came and told him: "Do not be afraid to take Mary as your wife, for the child conceived in her is from the Holy Spirit" (Matt 1:20). He listened to the angel when the latter urged him to flee quickly into Egypt, and listened again when he was told to return (Matt 2:13-14, 21). We know little else about him, and almost all of it is from the apocrypha, especially the *Protevangelium of James* (datable to the fifth/sixth century). Here, after being chosen as husband of Mary by a dove that came to rest on his staff, Joseph objects, saying: "I already have sons and am old, but she is a girl" (*Protevangelium* 9, 2). This tradition probably goes back to Epiphanius (*Contra Haer.* 73, 10).

Joseph is always referred to as a "carpenter"; Matthew (13:55) uses the Greek work *tektôn,* i.e., builder; today we might call him a contractor or carpenter. Since he was appointed the guardian of Jesus, his entire iconography focuses on this role. We see him sleeping when the angel first comes to him; then he looks for lodging as he guards Mary, who rides a donkey, and is guided by an angel; in the images of the manger, we see him in various attitudes: prayer, watchfulness, solicitude, wonder, concern. In icons and in many Western images representing the manger he appears seated and absorbed, according to the tradition that doubts were raised in him by the devil, who appeared to him in the guise of the shepherd Thyrsus; Thyrsus was the name of the staff of Dionysus, which was used by satyrs and bacchants. These were said to have provoked Joseph by saying, in order to make him doubt the divine maternity of his wife: "As this staff cannot produce leaves, so an old man like you cannot beget and, on the other hand, a virgin cannot give birth."

After the childhood and adolescence of Jesus, often seen in images of the Holy Family and are summarily described in the Gospel of Luke with the words: "He was obedient to them" (2:51), the Gospels provides no further information about Joseph. People have nonetheless imagined his death, at which he is strengthened by Our Lady and by Jesus, with the result that Joseph is invoked more than any other saint for the blessing of a good death. There is an ejaculation: "Jesus, Joseph, and Mary, I give you my heart and soul; Jesus, Joseph, and Mary, be with me in my last moments; Jesus, Joseph, and Mary, may my soul go forth in peace with you."

In the encyclical John Paul II devoted to Joseph (*Redemptoris custos* 8) he writes: "St. Joseph was called by God to serve directly the person and mission of Jesus through the exercise of his paternal role. It was precisely in this way that in the fullness of time he co-operated in the great mystery of the redemption and was truly a minister of salvation."

St. Bernardino of Siena (1380–1444) described St. Joseph thus: "Joseph, the most cheerful old man who ever lived, guardian of the great treasure that was the glorious Virgin Mary, and, how much more! his sweet little son, Jesus!"

▷▷ The cult of Joseph has spread throughout the world. Since 1624 he has been patron of Canada, where a great shrine of his is to be found in Montreal. His altars are almost always marked by the words "Go to Joseph!" In the Bible the expression is used of Joseph, son of Jacob, who had been sold into Egypt and later became the savior of Egypt and of his own family. But the words apply to St. Joseph as well: whoever turns to him is not disappointed.

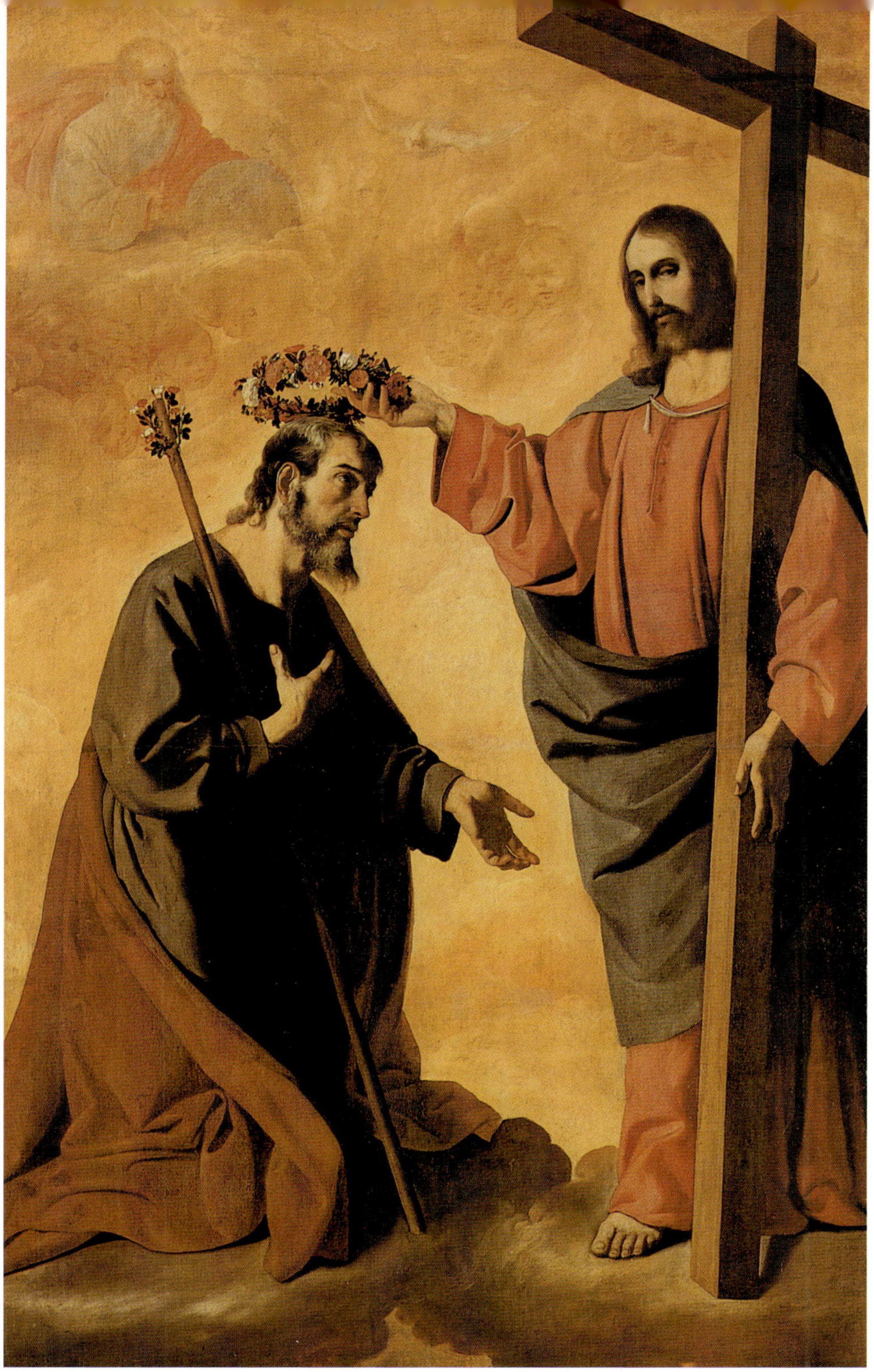

Jesus Crowns St. Joseph.
By Francisco de Zurbaran, 1598–1664, in the Provincial Museum of Seville.
Obvious here is the attribute of the flowering staff. The crowning of Joseph by his putative son is an unusual image, showing the acknowledgment of his collaboration in the work of redemption.

Since 1956 Joseph is remembered on May 1 as a craftsman; on this festival of workers, Christian workers take as their example and protector the man who by his toil supplied the needs of Mary and Jesus and made the Son of God acquainted with human labor.

In many places his feast in March is celebrated not only with bonfires and special fried sweets ("St. Joseph's sweets") but also with works of charity, since for the sake of his family Joseph often fell back on the charity of his neighbors. One example will suffice: the Italian practice of inviting some poor people to dinner, three of them representing Joseph, Mary, and Jesus, who are served by the head of the house; there is a similar custom in the Philippines.

Joseph is patron of a great many societies, confraternities, congregations, and pawnbrokers *(Monti di Pietà)*. He was proclaimed patron of Canada on January 18, 1963, by John XXIII. His role as patron of Bohemia goes back to 1665 and was renewed by Pius X on May 14, 1914, and by Pius XI on December 11, 1935. He was proclaimed patron of

Austria in 1675, of the missions in China by Innocent XI on August 17, 1678, of Belgium and Peru by Pius XII on March 19, 1957.

▷▷ Joseph is the patron of fathers of families but also, because his marriage was exceptional, of celibates as well, being a model of chastity; he is patron, too, although it might seem almost disrespectful, of husbands who have been betrayed. He is, furthermore, the patron of the working class and workers generally and of all who work with wood in any way: joiners, carvers, builders of boxes and coffers, carpenters, and cartwrights. He is patron of the homeless because he himself had to search for lodging; of travelers because of his flight into Egypt, as well as of barrel makers, because he is sometimes shown slaking his thirst from a small cask during his journey; of bridge builders because they do carpenters' work in bridging rivers.

He is invoked, not only for a good death and against the fear of death, but also by all who are homeless or poorly sheltered, and against exile. He is invoked for the preservation of chastity and therefore against subservience to instinct; for this reason people used to wear the "St. Joseph's cordon." In Scotland he is invoked for rain or sun depending on need.

▷▷ As guardian of Jesus, the **Child Jesus** himself becomes his attribute. The staff, which he always has, and his appearance are derived from apocryphal writings, which describe him as elderly. The Gospels make no reference to his age, and over the course of time there has been a gradual tendency to represent him as less elderly.

His principal attribute is the **flowering staff**, more specifically almond blossoms. This kind of sign goes back to the Old Testament, where Aaron is singled out as a priest alongside Moses by the fact that his staff had flowers and the fruit of the almond tree (see Num 18); the flowering implied a divine "choice." The apocrypha describe the wonders that pointed to Joseph as a husband for Mary. The versions differ but they have in common that the priests invited all who might be suitors to bring their staffs to the Temple; the flowering would indicate the one predestined (thus the *Protevangelium of James,* the *Gospel of Pseudo-Matthew,* the *Armenian Infancy Gospel,* the *Book of the Nativity of Mary,* and the *History of Joseph the Carpenter*). The wonder that pointed to Joseph as the predestined husband was, according to the *Gospel of Pseudo-Matthew* (8, 3), a dove that emerged from his staff, but according to the *Protevangelium of James* (9, 1) a dove that came to rest on it.

The almond (Greek: *amigdalê* is proper to Joseph, not only because its hard shell and inner sweetness symbolize the inclusion of a precious content within an impenetrable shell that conceals it, but also because the Hebrew word *shaked,* that is, "almond," is assonant with *shakad,* "watch over," and Joseph watched over Mary and Jesus. The flowering of the staff may also allude to the episode, described in the apocrypha, in which the devil said mockingly to Joseph that if Mary's motherhood was divine, then his dry staff could flower—and the staff did flower. The staff also suggests a scepter, a word that in Greek means "staff," and which in turn elicits the idea of power and strength and royalty (Joseph belonged to the royal house of David), and of the control of natural forces and the powers commanded by the magical wand of magicians; the staff is thus a sign of authority and strength. The staff is the emblem of shepherd kings and of warrior kings who defended their flock by force and is the ancestor of the pastoral staff of bishops, which even in its form recalls the flowering staff of Aaron.

The iconography also includes the **lily**, which signifies purity and virginity and, in keeping with the reference to the lilies of the field (Matt 6:28), also signifies complete trust in God. The **dove**, which is connected with marriage, is decidedly rare; one of the few images of Joseph with the dove sitting on his flowering staff, is in the Baroncelli Chapel in the church of the Holy Cross in Florence. **Two doves** appear as offerings at the presentation of Jesus in the Temple. Secondary attributes are the tools used in a carpenter's work: **saw**, **axe**, **plane**, and **square**.

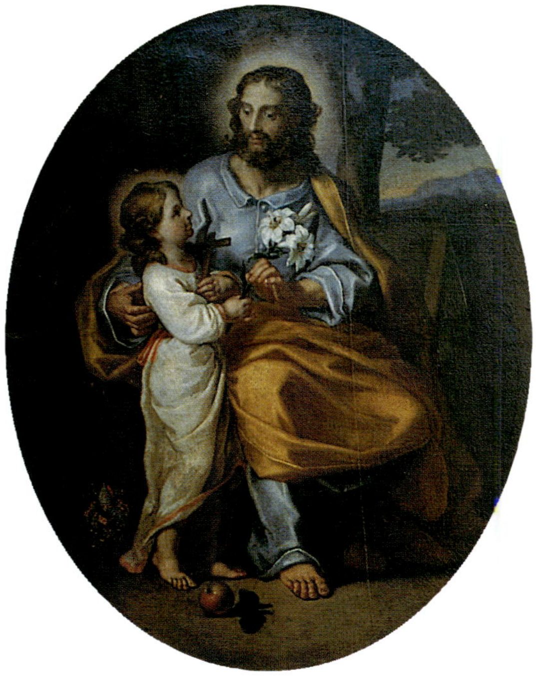

St. Joseph and the Child Jesus.
Abbey church of Viktring, Austria.

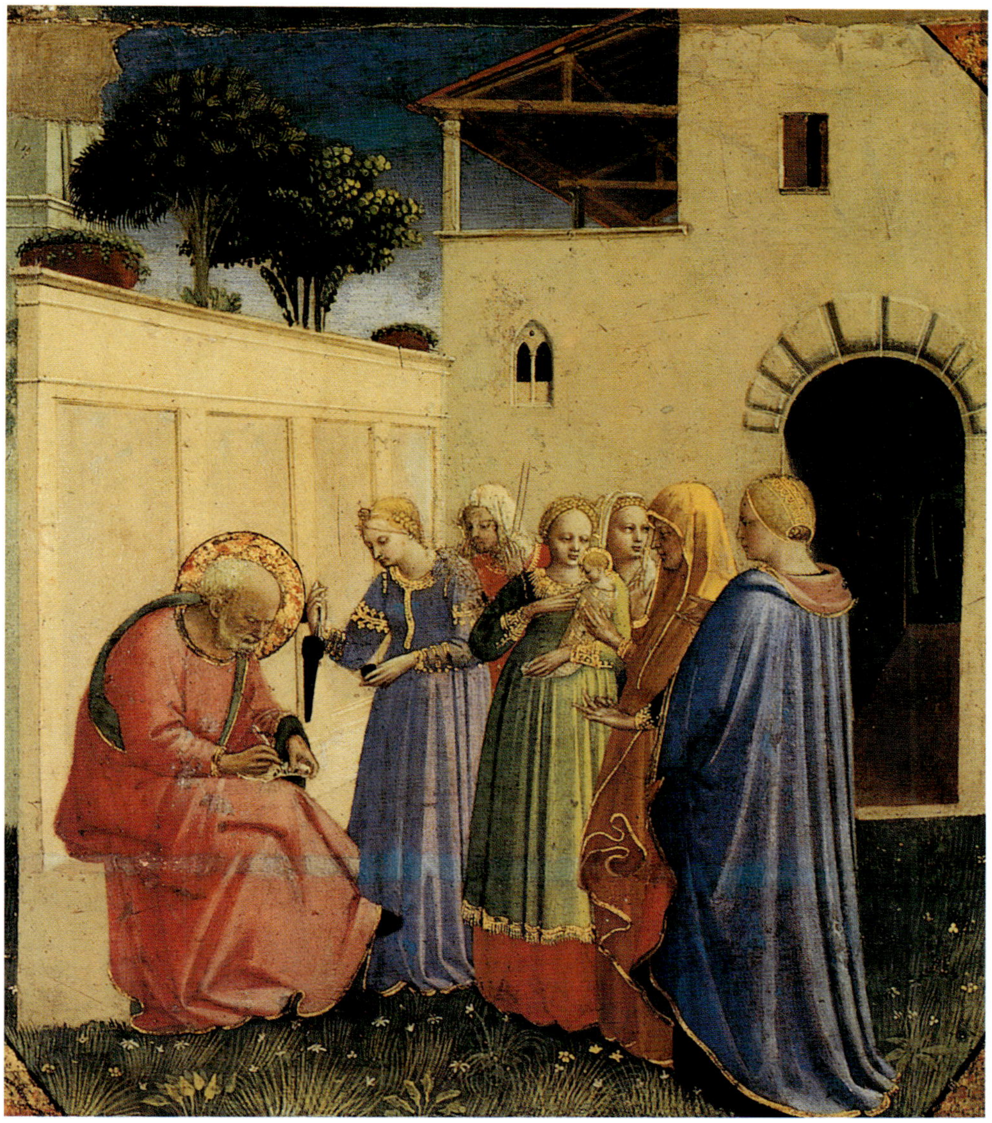

Bestowal of the Name of John the Baptist.
Fra Angelico, 15th cent., Museum of St. Mark, Florence.

The Visitation.
Fresco, 14th cent., castle of Zvikov, Slovakia. "Visitation" is the name given to the visit of Mary to her pregnant cousin Elizabeth. What cannot be shown is John's leaping for joy in the womb of his mother. It is, however, described in the writing, which identifies the scene through the words of Mary and Elizabeth.

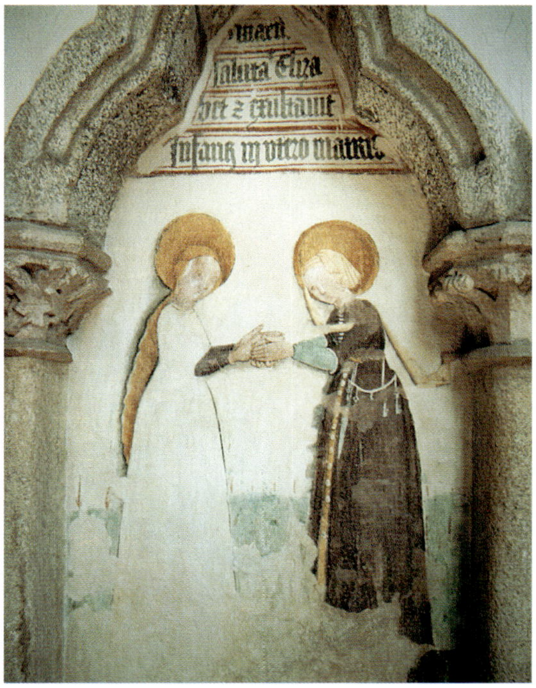

Elizabeth and Zechariah, High Priests, Parents of John the Baptist

Commemoration: September 23
Lat.: Elisabeth, mater Joannis Baptistae; It. var.: Isabeta, Bettina; Fr.: Élisabeth de Jérusalem, Alice, Elysabel, Helisabel, Isabelle, Isabeau, Ysabeau; Sp.: Isabel; Ger.: Elisabeth, Elsbeth, Elsa, Ilsa, Lisbeth; Hung.: Erszébet; Pol.: Elzbieta.
Lat.: Zacharias; Fr.: Zacharie; Ger.: Zacharias.

Remembered as the parents of John the Baptist, Elizabeth and Zechariah respectively have left us words constantly repeated in the "Hail Mary" and the canticle *Benedictus*. Elizabeth greeted her young cousin Mary thus: "Blessed are you among women and blessed is the fruit of your womb." Zechariah, for his part, took his son John in his arms and sang a song of thanksgiving: "Blessed be the Lord God of Israel, for he has looked favorably on his people and redeemed them!"

The name Elizabeth means, in Hebrew, "God has sworn" or "God is perfection." She was a cousin of Anna and married the priest Zechariah. The Gospel of Luke speaks of them as "righteous before God" (Luke 1:6); it tells of how the Archangel Gabriel appeared to Zechariah and made known to him the birth and destiny of a son who was to be called John; because Zechariah doubted and hesitated, he was stricken dumb. Elizabeth then conceived in her advanced age and hid herself for five months; during this period occurred the meeting with Mary, who had received from the same archangel the news of Elizabeth's extraordinary pregnancy, and was immediately inspired to visit her.

▷▷ The scene of the meeting known as the **"Visitation"** may be said to constitute the principal attribute of Elizabeth, but we do find her in various other representations such as the birth of the Baptist or in compositions depicting "the Holy Kinship," of which we spoke above.

Elizabeth, too, owes everything to her son: from the son who leapt in her womb when he recognized in Mary the Mother of the Savior. Although we hear nothing more of her after the birth of John, she remains very vivid in our memories. Shown as she usually is at the birth of her son, she is the patroness of both barren and childbearing women, while Zechariah is invoked against hemorrhages, especially of the nose, because in the apocryphal tradition his blood indelibly stains the steps of the Temple.

Scripture likewise says no more about Zechariah, but the *Protevangelium of James* (13–14) identifies him with Zechariah son of Barachiah who was "slain between the sanctuary and the altar," and of whom Matthew (23:35) speaks. It therefore makes him a martyr under Herod, who was infuriated that little John escaped the slaughter of the innocents.

▷▷ Above all, however, his memory remains alive due to the canticle *Benedictus,* which he chanted when, by writing "John is his name," he confirmed Elizabeth's choice of a name for the child and so expressed his acceptance of the divine plan. The phrase **"John is his name"** can be said to be his attribute, together with the secondary attribute of a **censer**; he is often shown robed as a high priest.

John the Baptist

Solemnity of his birth: June 24; memorial of his beheading: August 29

Lat.: Joannes Baptista; Heb.: Iehohanon; Gr.: Ioannes Prodromos (the precursor); Fr.: Jean Baptiste, and var.: Jehan, Jouan, Juan; Sp.: Juan Bautista, El Precursor; Ger.: Johannes der Täufer, der Vorläufer; Dutch: Jan de Doper, de Voorloper; Pol.: Jan; Russ.: Ioann Krestitel, Predtetcha.

John, known as the Precursor, is the only saint whose earthly birth is celebrated, because, even before entering the world, he was filled with the Holy Spirit and leaped in his mother's womb as he recognized the Savior; thus his very birth was a prophecy of Christ. His life and his death were a witness to the truth and were rendered so resplendent by grace that Jesus himself said of him: "Among those born of women no one has arisen greater than John the Baptist; yet the least in the kingdom of heaven is greater than he" (Matt 11:11). The *Golden Legend* lists his nine special privileges: his birth was announced by the same angel who gave the message to Mary; he leaped in his mother's womb at his meeting with Jesus; the first person to take him in her arms at his birth was Mary; he restored his father's ability to speak; he instituted baptism; he announced the mission of Jesus; he baptized Jesus; Jesus praised him; he made known the imminent coming of Jesus to those in Limbo.

The name John means "Yahweh is propitious." The essential facts about him are found in the Gospels (Matt 3, 4, 9, 11, 14, 17, 21; Mark 1, 3, 4, 6, 9, 11; Luke 1, 3, 7, 9, 20; John 1, 3, 4) and in the apocrypha (in the *Protevangelium of James* and the *Book of John*). His life and the images of him are all connected with Jesus, whose cousin he was; he was older than Jesus by six months and as a child in the extended family would have played with him. Many images in Western iconography, which like to tell of everyday life, show him intently playing with Jesus, who is sitting on Mary's knee and who is almost as big as he. Even in these scenes he wears a garment made of camel's hair and carries the sign that is his principal attribute, namely, **a cross with a banner bearing the words "Ecce Agnus Dei."**

But the time for play was long past "when the word of God came to John" (Luke 3:2) and John's life changed. It is likely that, as in the case of Jesus, John had until then been a youngster like so many others. He now began to live in the wilderness, living an austere life,

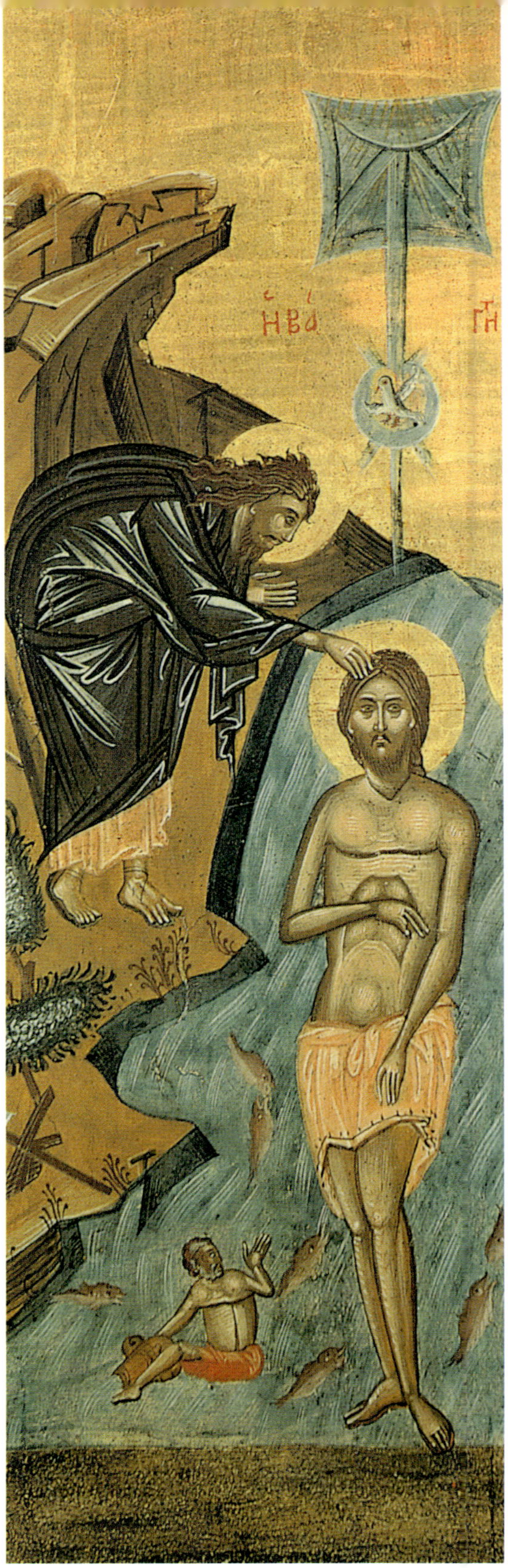

The Baptism of Jesus.
18th-cent. icon belonging to the Venerable Archconfraternity of the Purification, Livorno.
The baptism of Jesus is also known as the Epiphany, because on this occasion there was an explicit manifestation of the divinity of Jesus, on whom the Holy Spirit descended and whom the Father acknowledged as his Son. The scene also includes John the Baptist and sums up his role and his destiny.

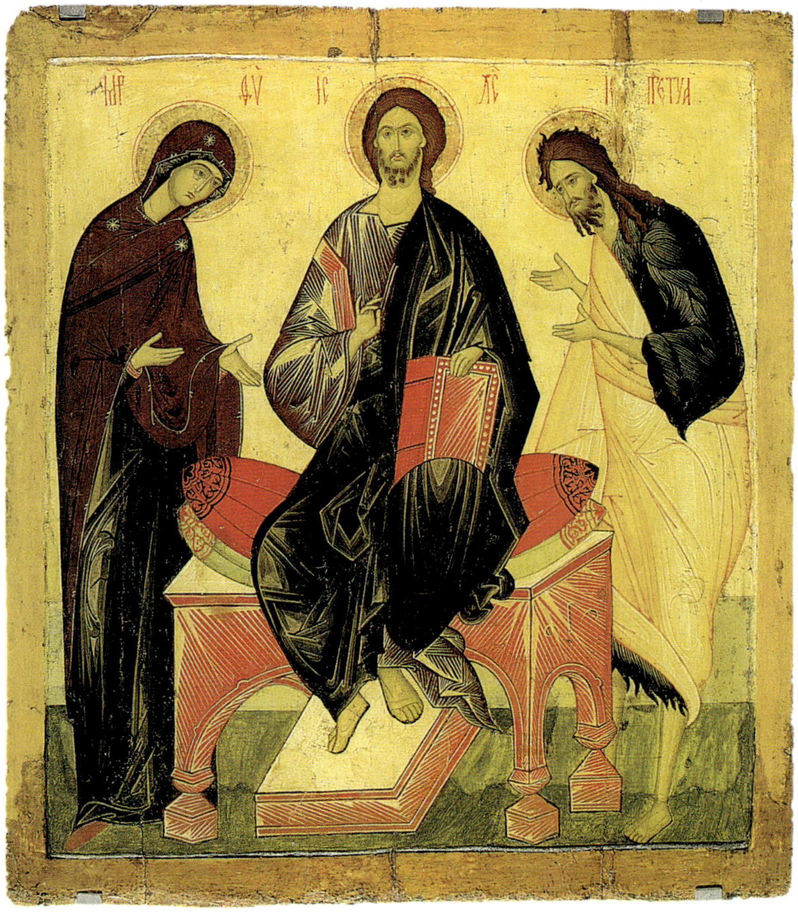

Deêsis ("Petition").
Icon of the 15th cent. in the Tret'jakov Gallery, Moscow. Here, as in other images, John's garment of camel's skin is combined with the red mantle of martyrdom.

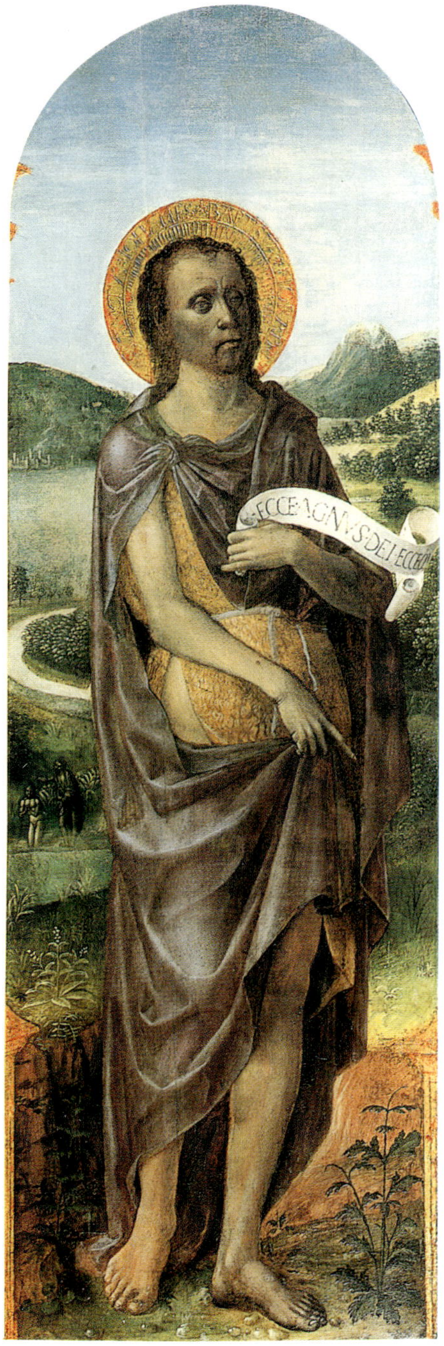

St. John the Baptist.
Tempera on wood, by Vincenzo Foppa, in the Pinacoteca Tosio Martinengo, Brescia.

wearing a garment of camel's hair, and feeding on locusts. He brought the explicit judgment of God to men and women, urged them to convert, and baptized them. The word "baptism," which means "immersion," refers to the repentance and cleansing of which this immersion in water is the image; baptism is as it were a return to the waters of the maternal womb in order to experience a new birth and a deep interior purification.

Essential episodes in the life of John are the moments in which he meets Jesus, baptizes him, bears witness to him, and prophesies: *He must increase, but I must decrease* (John 3:30); and, finally, when he continues to attest to the truth before Herod and condemns the latter for his marriage to Herodias, his brother's wife; this led to his imprisonment in a fortress beyond the Jordan, where he was finally beheaded as a gift to Salome, daughter of Herodias, for her dance during a banquet. Herod had promised her whatever she desired; instructed by her mother, she asked for the head of the Baptist; Herod agreed and had John immediately beheaded in prison.

His cult, which is worldwide, is marked in June by the rituals typical of solstice festivals: the lighting of fires and dancing around and over them. These rituals celebrate not only the saint but also the passage from the old covenant to the new, from the time of promise to the fullness of time, from the promises of fruit and life in the spring to the fulfillment at the harvest in summer. The vigil of his feast was therefore celebrated with bonfires and dances, and people stayed out in the fields in order to bathe in the dew, which was a clear reminder of baptism and constituted an excellent omen.

▷▷ John is the patron of tailors (because he made his own garments of camel's hair in the wilderness) and of furriers. Because he wore a leather belt, he is protector of beltmakers and tanners. Because one of his attributes is a lamb, he protects wool carders. Because of the banquet of Herod in which he participated in so unusual a way, he is the patron of hotel keepers and innkeepers. Because he was imprisoned, he is the patron of prisoners and of those condemned to death. Because he was "put into a cage," he became the patron of bird breeders. He was beheaded with a sharp sword and is therefore the patron of those who make knives and scissors, as well as of swordmakers. By reason of his hairy appearance, he is the patron of chimney sweeps.

His patronage of singers and musicians is due to the fact that when Guido of Arezzo (999–ca. 1050) gave names to the musical notes, he used the initial syllables of a hymn in honor of John: *"UT queant laxis/REsonare fibris/MIra gestorum/FAmuli tuorum/SOlve polluti/LAbii reatum,/Sancte Ioannes"* (the note SI is taken from the first letters of the words "Sancte Ioannes"). The lines mean: "In order that the devout may be able to sing your wonderful deeds with all their strength, remove the guilt that pollutes their lips, O St. John." (UT was replaced by DO in seventeenth-century Italy.)

He is the patron of foundlings because he protects the doors of baptisteries, where newborns were abandoned. He is patron of the Order of Malta as well as of various Confraternities of Mercy, whose task is to be present with those condemned to death; John's head on a platter is often their emblem.

He protects lambs and carrier pigeons, the reason being the descent of the Holy Spirit on Jesus at his baptism; the water there motivates John's protection of springs.

▷▷ Because of his beheading, he is invoked against headaches, epilepsy, diseases of the throat and neck, suffocation, and condemnation to death.

▷▷ Iconography focuses on three moments in John's life: as a child and at the baptism of Jesus in Western art, and as an intercessor in the *Deêsis* scenes of Oriental art. *Deêsis* means "petition, entreaty," and such scenes show Christ at the center with Mary interceding at his right hand and John the Baptist at his left.

The scene most associated with him is the **baptism of Jesus**, one of three moments in the epiphany or manifestation of Jesus, the other two being the adoration of the Magi and the first miracle at Cana. John always wears a **garment of camel's hair**, like Elijah, who was described as *A hairy man, with a leather belt around his waist* (2 Kgs 1:8). In addition to a garment of camel's skin he wears a **red cloak**, red being the color of martyrdom; he holds a **banner in the form of a cross** with the words *"Ecce Agnus Dei"* on it, which he himself had spoken (John 1:29). Not infrequently, he has in his hand a **shell** from which he pours water on the head of Jesus.

His face is usually quite emaciated due to his austere life in the wilderness; at the foot of the cross he is recognizable by his **garment of camel's hair**.

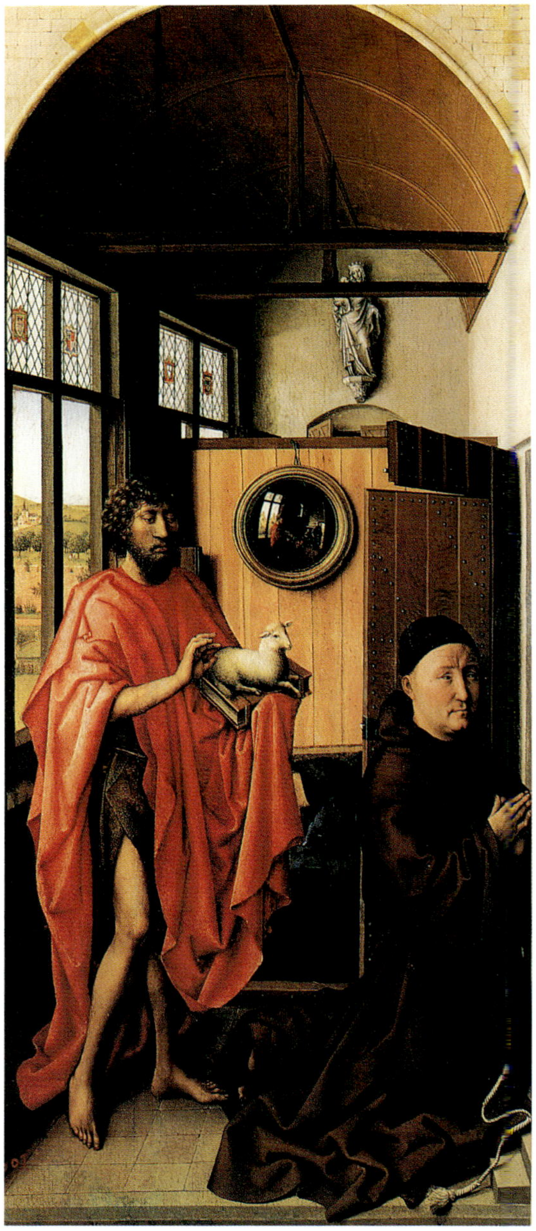

St. John the Baptist Presents Heinrich von Werl.
Detail from a painting by Robert Campin, 15th cent., Prado Museum, Madrid.

Lazarus and Mary of Bethany

Commemoration: July 29
Lat.: Lazarus Massiliensis; Fr.: Lazare, Ladre, Lazaron, Lazer; Sp.: Lazaro; Ger.: Lazarus von Bethanien.

Lazarus is remembered in the Church today along with his sisters Martha and Mary. He is remembered in particular as one at whose death Jesus wept and whom Jesus then raised from death. Mary is remembered as sitting at the feet of Jesus and listening to his words. According to the *Golden Legend* Lazarus belonged to a royal family: he was son of Sirus and Eucharia and brother to Martha and Mary Magdalene. This very wealthy family owned the fortress of Magdala near Lake Gennesaret, Bethany near Jerusalem, and a sizable part of the latter city. In the division of the family possessions by lot, Mary obtained Magdala from which she derived her name; Lazarus and Martha received Jerusalem and Bethany respectively.

This Lazarus, who is often confused with Lazarus the beggar in the parable of the rich glutton in Luke, was a friend of Jesus; after being raised from the dead, he became a living witness to the power of Jesus, an awkward witness for those who hated him and who there-

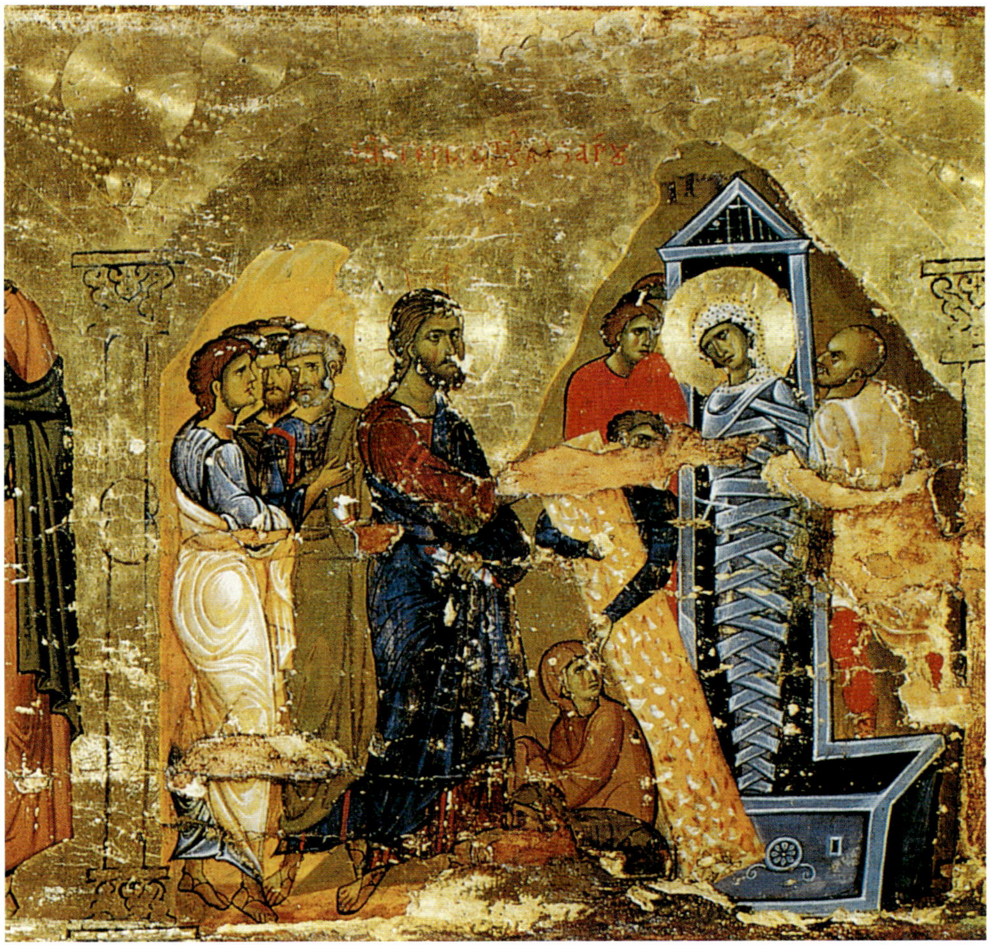

Jesus Raises Lazarus.
12th cent., Monastery of St. Catherine, Sinai. Detail of painting of "The Theophany, Transfiguration, Deêsis, and Resurrection."
The scene of the resuscitation identifies Lazarus.

St. Lazarus and the Dog.
Small devotional image, 20th cent., Cuba.
The image shows the confusion between Lazarus the beggar, who was regarded as a saint, and the brother of Martha and Mary. The cult of Lazarus the poor man is very widespread and strong in Cuba and the Caribbean, where it is easy to find many who regard themselves as like him.

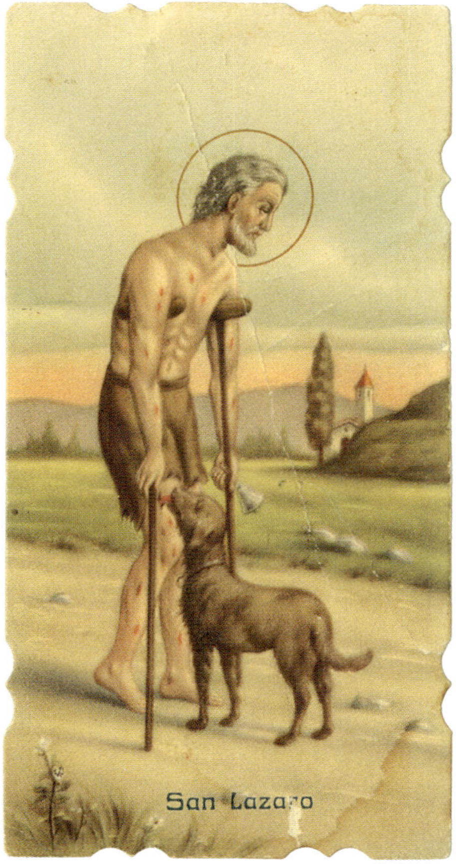

fore tried to have him killed. After the miracle, Jesus returned to Bethany six days before the Passover in order to attend the supper at which Mary perfumed the feet of Jesus with a pound of precious ointment, thus evoking the disapproval of Judas Iscariot.

After this supper nothing more is said of Lazarus in the Gospels; one tradition has him a martyr in Cyprus, where the remains of Mary Magdalene, who died in Ephesus, were later joined to his. Another tradition, the one reported in the *Golden Legend,* says that Lazarus and his sisters went to France, disembarking in Provence; Lazarus became bishop of Marseilles, whence the addition of "Massiliensis" to his name. Here he suffered martyrdom; his relics were transferred to Autun in the twelfth century, to prevent them being possibly stolen by Saracen pirates. The confusion with Lazarus the beggar was at the source not only of an iconography that shows him as poor, in rags, and covered with sores, but of his becoming the patron of hospitals and lazarettos (hospitals for contagious diseases, which take their name from him). The confusion also explains the extensive occurrence of his name in the names of places associated with the presence of hospitals (this because of his sores, which were identified with those of plagues or leprosy) and with places where the sick and pilgrims were welcomed; these were usually on the eastern side of cities and gave their name to numerous outlying hamlets. The cult of Lazarus is widespread in Latin America as well.

▷▷ The raising of Lazarus has made him the protector of sextons, but his cult and his patronage are also marked by the confusion with Lazarus the beggar and his sores: he is protector of lepers, lazarettos, hospitals generally, and bakers, who considered themselves especially exposed to plague by reason of their work.

▷▷ The iconography of Lazarus shows him especially at two fundamental points of his life: when he came forth from the tomb still in **burial wrappings** and in **episcopal robes**. When he is shown as a bishop, his principal attribute is a **coffin**.

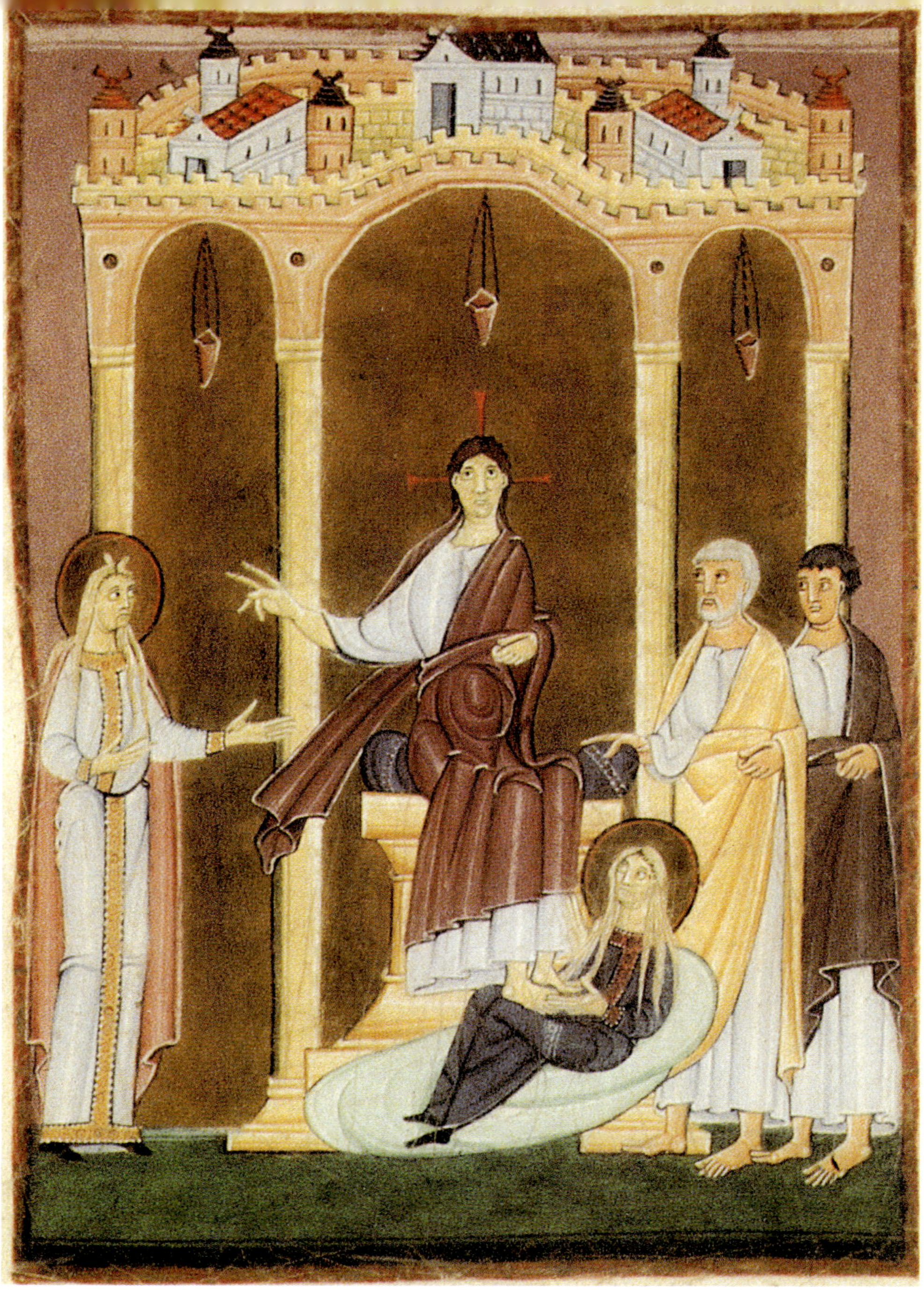

Martha of Bethany

Memorial: July 29
Lat.: Martha, hospes Christi; It.: Marta, Albergatrice di Cristo; Ger.: Martha.

This sister of Lazarus and Mary Magdalene was, like them, a friend of Jesus and his hostess on several occasions. It was she who worked to give Jesus a hospitable welcome when he came (Luke 10:38-42); it was she who went out to meet him after the death of Lazarus, and she who said she believed that Jesus is "the Messiah, the Son of God, the one coming into the world" (John 11:27). The Fathers regarded her as a model of the active mystical life. We know nothing more about her.

Tradition has it that she went to Provence with her brother and sister, and there led many to the faith by her eloquence and powers of persuasion. The *Golden Legend* tells that the banks of the Rhone river between Avignon and Arles were plagued by a fierce dragon; the population called for Martha's help. She found the dragon intent on devouring a man; she showed it the cross and sprinkled it; in this way she subdued it and tied it with her belt, so that the people were able to kill it. The name of the region is derived from "Tarasca," the dragon's name. Here Martha remained and worked miracles such as the raising of a drowned man, in memory of the raising of her brother. She practiced fasting and prayer,

Jesus in the House of Martha and Mary.
Evangeliary of Henry II, ca. 1000, in the Bayerische Staatsbibliothek, Munich.
The figures of Martha and Mary, who traditionally have been seen as symbols respectively of the active life and the contemplative life in the Church (which is symbolized by the buildings and arches of the framework), are here united and represented together. Mary is the footstool on which Christ—the Church—rests his feet, while he also extends his hand in blessing toward Martha with the key on her belt.

founded a monastery, and, finally, knowing the date of her own death a year in advance, prepared for it with great care. Christ himself put to flight the evil spirits who tried to upset the saint, and he received her into heaven as she had received him into her house.

▷▷ Martha is the patroness of Provence. Having herself given hospitality to Jesus, she is the patroness of the heads of households and of all whose work is connected with hospitality, such as innkeepers and restaurateurs, as well as laundresses and domestic servants. She cooked for Jesus and is therefore the patroness of cooks; she carries a spoon as an attribute.

▷▷ She is represented with a **bunch of keys at her belt**; this constitutes her principal attribute, others being a **spoon**, **broom**, **aspergil**, and **a dragon chained to her belt**.

Mary Magdalene

Memorial: July 22

Lat.: Magdalena; Fr. var.: Magdaleine, Magdeleine, Madelon; Sp.: Magdalena; Ger.: Magdalena, Magda.

Mary Magdalene is the penitent par excellence. Pope Gregory the Great identified as a single person three women of whom the Scriptures speak. One was the sister of Lazarus, that is, the woman who, after the raising of Lazarus, entered the dining room at Bethany and anointed the feet of Jesus (John 12:1-8; Matt 26:6-12; Mark 14:3-9), thereby evoking the indignation of Judas Iscariot. A second was the penitent sinner, "from whom seven demons had gone out" (Luke 8:2; Mark 16:9) and who, after being converted, followed Jesus even to staying at the foot of the cross with the Virgin (Matt 27:55-56; Mark 15:40-41; Luke 23:49; John 19:25); with other women she went to the tomb and found it empty; she was then the first of the disciples to see and recognize him (John 20:1-28). The third woman was the nameless sinner who entered the dining room of Simon the leper, anointed the feet of Jesus (Luke 7:36-50), and dried them with her hair.

Historians today are inclined to see here three distinct women.

Noli me tangere ("Do not hold on to me"). Cretan icon, 16th cent., in the Museum of Icons, Dubrovnik, Croatia. The meeting of Mary Magdalene and Jesus at dawn on Easter is identified as such by the words of Jesus to the saint. This is the episode most associated with the saint.

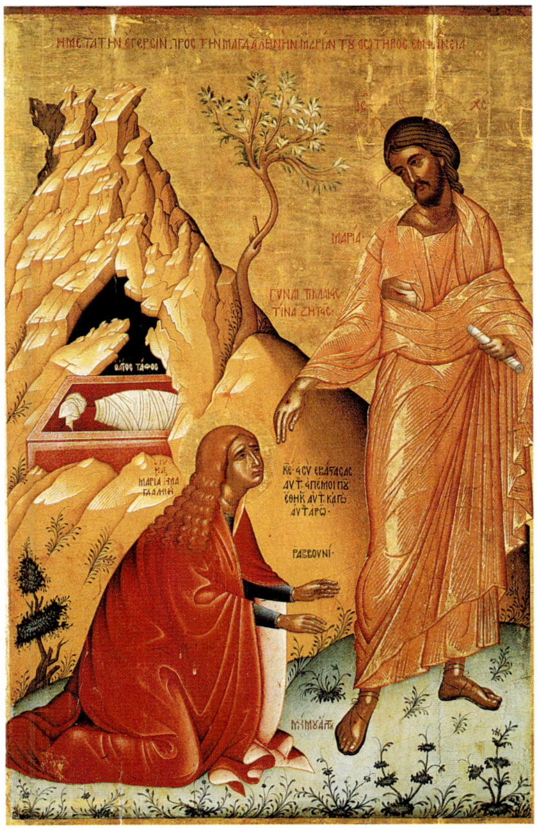

Whether or not she was the sister of Lazarus and Martha, this Mary Magdalene was venerated along with them. Her presence at the foot of the cross linked her with the Blood of Christ, which she supposedly collected and preserved in a cup that in the Arthurian cycle was identified with the Holy Grail. The Church also remembers her as one who was freed from seven demons, followed Jesus to Calvary, and at dawn on Easter was the first to see the Savior and to announce his resurrection to the disciples. A very wealthy woman and one absorbed by pleasures before her conversion, she then followed and served Jesus. She went with the other women to the tomb and then ran to tell the apostles of the empty tomb and the vision. Then, outside the tomb, Jesus appeared to her in the guise of a gardener; when she recognized him and extended her hand to him, he spoke to her the well-known words: **"Do not hold on to me"** (John 20:16).

The Gospels have nothing more to say of Mary Magdalene. Her hagiography, however, records various traditions, but the active center of her cult was France. After the Resurrection, Peter entrusted Mary Magdalene to Blessed Maximinus; persecutors of Christians put her, along with Maximinus, Lazarus, Martha, and many others, on a boat without a pilot, in order that all of them might perish. But, steered by Providence the boat reached Marseilles, where all of them found refuge in the portico of a temple. It was there that in an effort to turn the people from idolatry, Mary began her apostolic mission; she also converted the ruler of the region, and Lazarus became bishop of Marseilles. Then the group went to Aix-en-Provence, where Maximinus was consecrated a bishop. After this, Mary Magdalene withdrew to an isolated place where she lived for thirty years without clothing or food. When she felt death to be near, she sent word to Bishop Maximinus, who brought the Eucharist to her. The saint wept because of her consolations and she fell asleep in the Lord.

Her body was stolen from Aix-en-Provence and taken to Vézelay, the center from which her cult mainly spread from the twelfth century on and where the great basilica dedicated to her now stands. This has become a goal of pilgrimage and the starting point of the pilgrimage to Santiago de Compostela.

Another tradition has it that when she reached Provence, Mary Magdalene immediately withdrew to a cave prepared for her by angels on a mountain in the Sainte-Baume, where she lived as a penitential hermit.

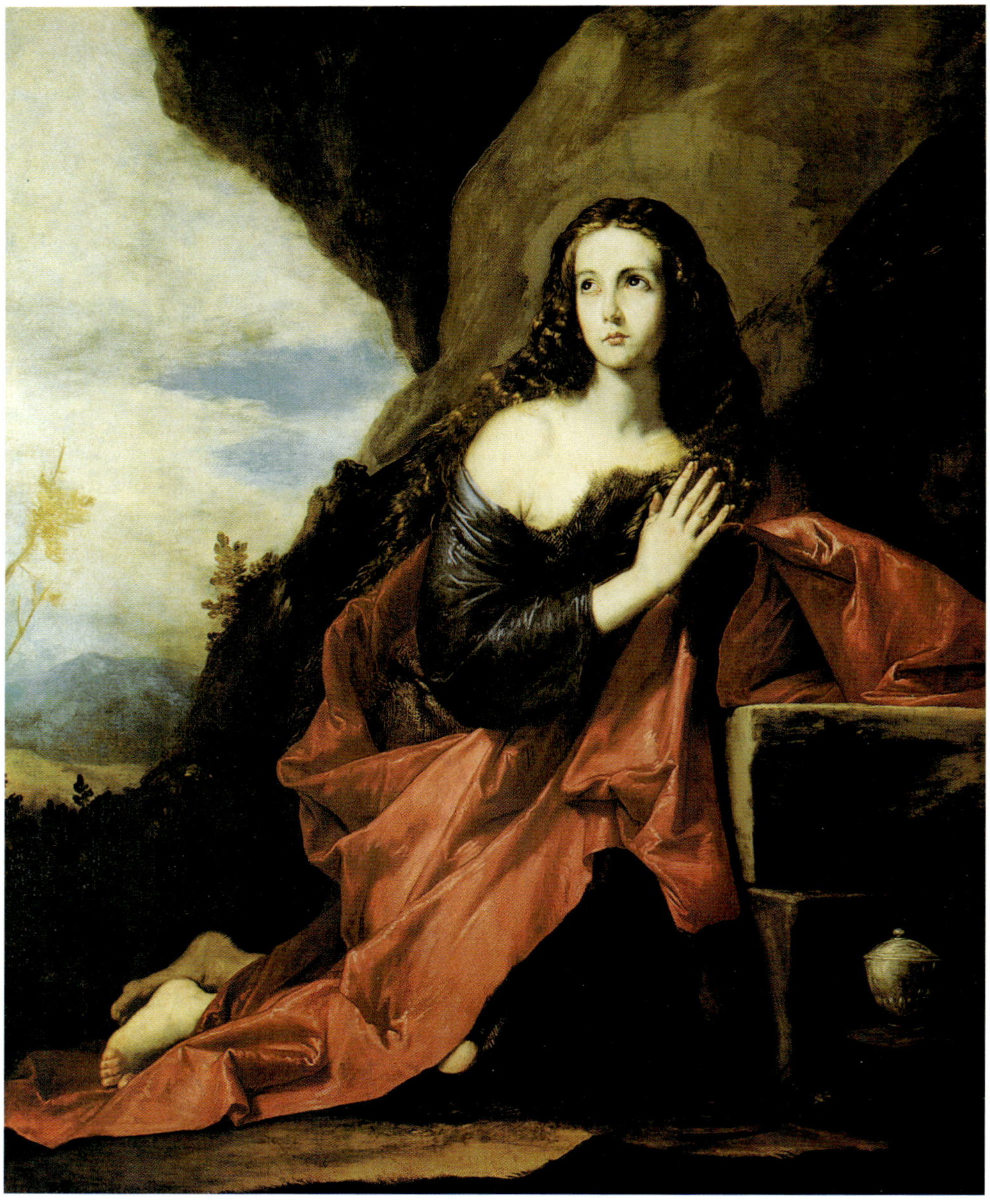

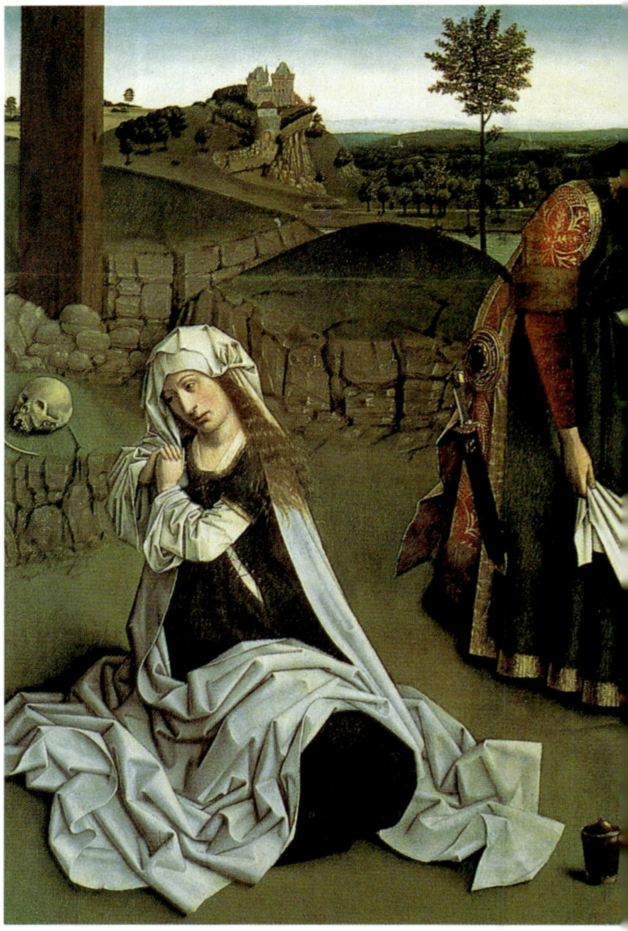

▷▷ Because of the ointment she used, Magdalene became the patroness of perfumers and glove makers (in the Middle Ages gloves were perfumed and were also a sign of coquetry). Because the vessel she used suggested a pitcher or even a perfume bottle, she is patroness of water-sellers and pharmacists. Because she dried the feet of Jesus with her hair, she is patroness of hairdressers of women, sellers of combs, and even of podiatrists. She is patroness of gardeners because Jesus appeared to her in that guise. In France, by a play on the sound of words: Madeleine/*amas de laine* (Magdalene/pile of wool), she became the patroness of carders.

Because she was freed from demons and sin, she is the patroness of prisoners; the latter, once freed, used to give her their chains as an ex-voto offering. Those who desire healing from persistent fevers should rest their heads on the stone she used as a pillow in her hermitage, now in the abbey of St. Victor in Marseilles.

Most important of all, she is the patroness of repentant sinners.

Magdalene as Penitent.
José de Ribeira, 17th cent., Prado Museum, Madrid.
In the iconography of Mary Magdalene the dazzling beauty of her bare shoulders contrasts sharply with the setting and mortified life of a hermit.

Mary Magdalene, Detail of a Pietà.
Petrus Christus, Musées Royaux des Beaux-Arts de Belgique, in Brussels.
The skull is a symbol of penance.

▷▷ The iconography shows us various moments in the life of Mary Magdalene. We see her before her conversion and at her conversion itself, where she is clad in rich robes but deeply moved. We see her with her **hair loosed** in order to dry the feet of Jesus. We see her at the foot of the cross, supporting the Virgin, or among the mourners, weeping for sorrow. We find her with the devout women, the "myrrh-bearers," bringing spices to the tomb, and in the act of stretching out her hands to Jesus, who is often clad as a gardener, because that is how he appeared to her on Easter morning. Finally, we find her as a penitent, emaciated but still beautiful, her fine **hair spilling down over her bare shoulders**, or, more rarely, at her final communion.

Frequently in these episodes of her life, and always when she is seen alone, her principal attribute is a **vessel of ointment** in the form of a covered goblet or wooden cup, which alludes both to the perfumed ointment or nard she poured out on the feet of Jesus in order to anoint his body for the tomb, and to his blood she collected at the foot of the cross and preserved. Another attribute is the episode of the **"Do not hold on to me."**

Longinus of Caesarea, Centurion

Commemoration: October 16

Lat.: Longinus, Languinus, Longius; Fr.: Longin, Longis; Ger.: Longinus; Russ.: Login sotnik (the centurion).

The Gospels speak of soldiers, probably from the Roman garrison, standing beneath the cross of Jesus. John (19:34) tells us that when they came to hasten the death of the crucified men by breaking their legs, they saw that Jesus was dead; then "one of the soldiers pierced his side with a **spear**, and at once blood and water came out": this was strange since corpses do not bleed. Mark (15:39) mentions the centurion who stood facing him: when he "saw that in this way he breathed his last, he said, 'Truly this man was God's Son.'" Matthew, too (27:54) mentions this centurion and the soldiers of the guard who, when frightened by the earthquake and the death of Jesus, said: "Truly this man was God's Son!"

Tradition identifies the soldier with the **spear** and the centurion under a single name derived from the word for "spear": Longinus. The latter might appear to be simply the personification of a particular moment: the moment in which the Church was born, springing from the providentially pierced side of Christ and represented by the gush of water (representing the human nature of Christ) and of blood (representing the divine nature).

The same Longinus then supposedly collected the blood and water in the cup of the Holy Grail, which, together with the **spear**, constituted an outstanding and fascinating relic. This legend appropriated the cup, but another tradition, though a late one, said that Longinus carried the cup to Mantua, where the relic of the Blood of Jesus is venerated in the basilica of St. Andrew; for this reason Longinus is the patron of Mantua. The spear is now to be found in the Treasury of Vienna.

Against the idea that Longinus is simply the personification of an idea stands St. Gregory of Nyssa, who speaks of him in one of his letters (Letter 17, 15) and leads us to believe that as early as the fourth century Longinus was regarded as the evangelizer of Cappadocia and first bishop of the region.

Although the Eastern and Western traditions disagree on some details, they agree that Longinus abandoned military life, received instruction in the faith, and then led a holy life at Caesarea in Cappadocia; he converted others and finally died a martyr by beheading.

In the Greek tradition we find the theme of sight: according to the *Golden Legend,* Longinus had weak sight but was cured when he accidentally touched his eyes with his hands that were wet from a drop of Christ's Blood that had run down his spear. The governor who had him beheaded because he would not sacrifice to the idols himself went mad and became blind; he was cured only when the martyr, now in glory, interceded for him. Longinus' head was taken to Jerusalem and then thrown away; it was found by a blind widow who regained her sight.

▷▷ Longinus is patron of the city of Mantua and protector of horsemen and horse trainers.

▷▷ In iconography Longinus is garbed in **military dress**; in the oldest representations of the crucifixion he is always there in those containing a lot of figures. In these images blood and water can clearly be seen gushing from the pierced side of Christ, these representing the humanity and the divinity; the blood and water are often seen being collected by angels. The principal and indeed sole attribute of Longinus is a **spear**.

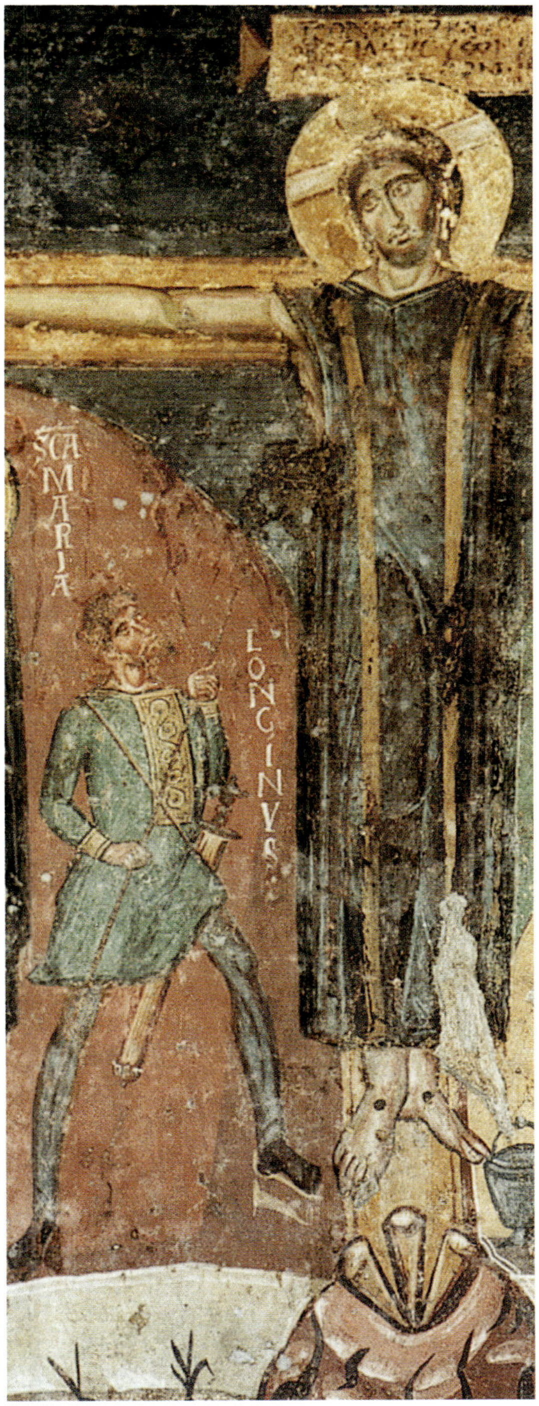

Longinus Pierces Jesus.
Detail from a Crucifixion. Fresco of the 6th–7th cent., Chapel of Theodotus in the church of Santa Maria Antiqua, Rome.

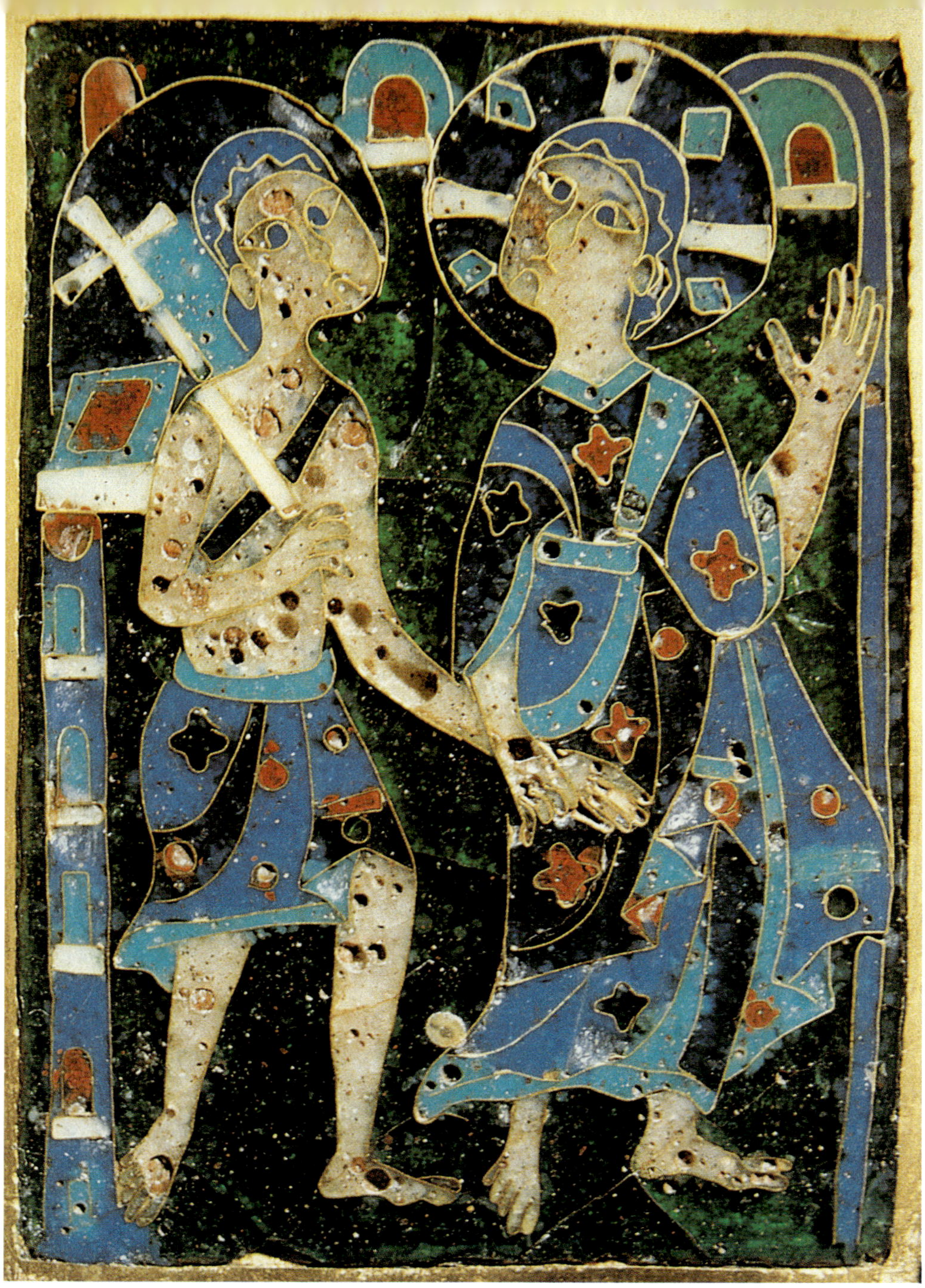

Dismas, the Good Thief

Commemoration: March 25

Lat.: Sanctus Latro, Bonus Latro; Fr.: Dismas, Dysma, Dysmas, Demas; Sp.: Dimas, El Buen Ladrón; Ger.: Der büssende, bussfertige, reumütige, gute Schächer; Dutch: De Goede Moordenar; Russ.: Blagorazoumni Razboïnik.

Dismas is venerated because on the cross he acknowledged the divinity of Christ, who therefore told him: "Today you will be with me in Paradise" (Luke 23:43). His justification is due to his recognition of his guilt, his repentance, and, above all, his acknowledgment that Jesus is the Savior, these being the necessary and sufficient conditions for salvation.

This man, who was immediately received into Paradise, is given the name Dismas in the apocryphal writings. According to these, he was an Egyptian by origin, had killed his father, and first met Jesus when he attacked the Holy Family on their flight into Egypt but, moved by Mary's beauty, ended up protecting them.

▷▷ He is the patron of those condemned to death, of sinners and repentant thieves, of antiquarians and dealers in paintings. He is invoked against condemnation to death.

▷▷ Dismas is always present in representations of the crucifixion; we also find him among the "repentant sinners," that is, King David, Peter, and Mary Magdalene.

When he is shown alone, his attributes are his **chains** (he had been imprisoned as a criminal), the **club** with which his legs were broken, and the **cross**.

The Good Thief Is Led by Christ into Paradise.
On the silver cover of the Evangeliary of Ariberto, ca. 1025, in the Cathedral Museum, Milan.
This precious object was later turned into a *"Pax"* and called "The Pax of Ariberto." The scene seems to be a faithful representation of the exhortation to take up one's cross and follow Christ, which Dismas is doing.
A "peace *(Pax),*" which is short for "Instrument of peace," was a metal plate, with a handle, that often had a sacred image on the plate. Beginning in the 12th cent. this was presented at the "kiss of peace" of the faithful. It was clearly a token of, and at the same time a request for, reconciliation with God.

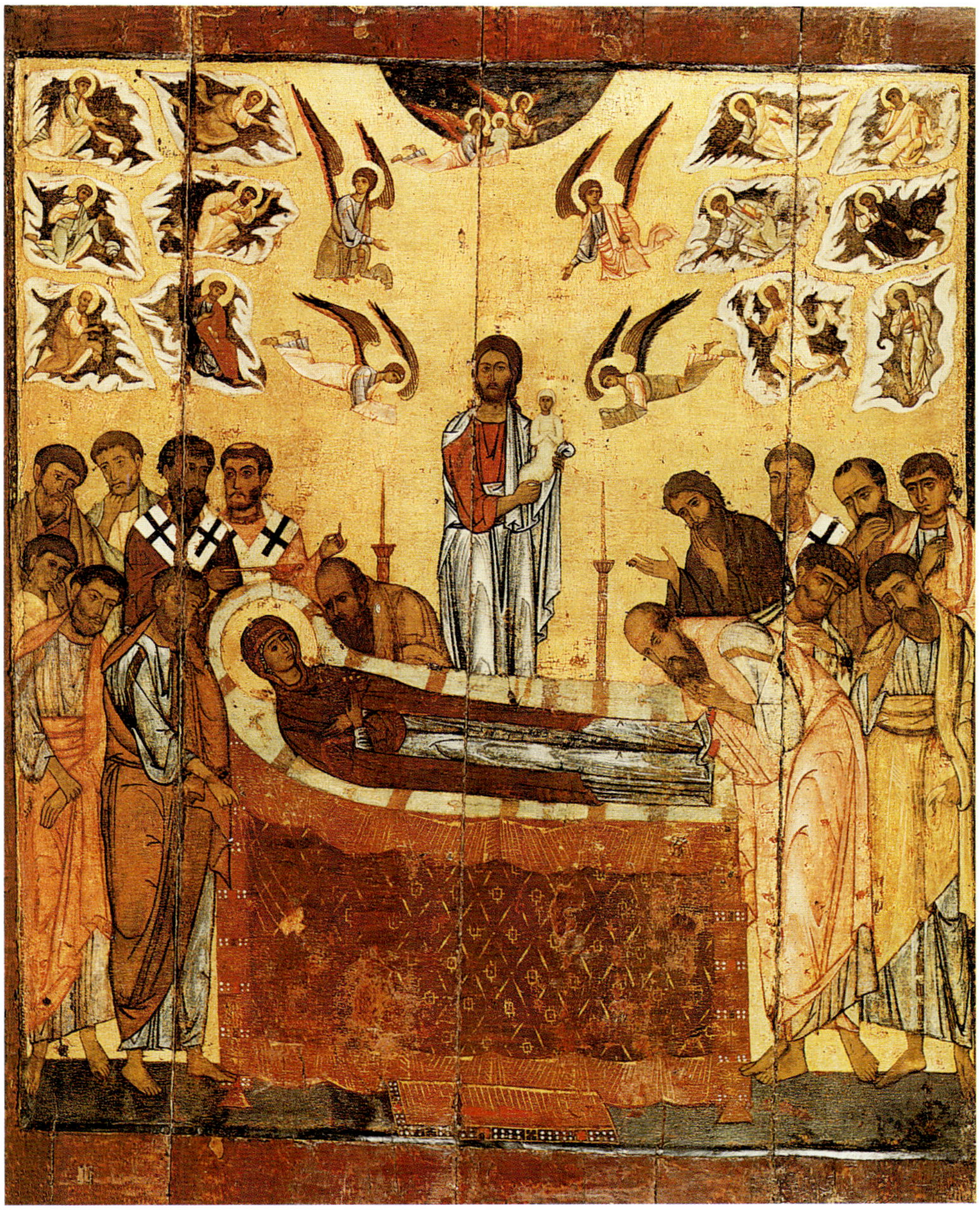

The Apostles

The word means, in Greek, "persons sent," and describes them in terms of the apostolic mission entrusted to them; the bishops of the Church with their role as teachers and as guardians of the word, of the rite of consecration, and of orthodoxy are their successors. The various ecclesial communities have always tried, by means of diverse and even complicated intermediate links, to trace their origin back to one of the apostles. The reason for this is that the connection with the apostles was an explicit proof that this community was the community founded by Christ; in this way, too, the communities bore witness to their union with the Apostolic See par excellence, namely, Rome. A good example of this point is the representation of Pentecost in the church of St. Francis, Ravenna: here all the apostles wear the dress and insignia of bishops.

The first to follow Christ were two disciples of the Baptist, Andrew and John son of Zebedee; they did so after John the Baptist had said of Jesus: "Look, here is the Lamb of God!" (John 1:36). Jesus then said to them: "Come and see," words signifying both Jesus as teacher and Christian experience. Andrew then brought his brother Simon to Jesus; Jesus changed Simon's name and destiny: "You are to be called Cephas (which is translated Peter, that is, 'rock')" (John 1:42). The connection with Jesus is clear, for in one of the psalms he

Dormition of the Virgin.
13th-cent. icon in the Tret'jakov Gallery, Moscow. The scene of the Dormition is one of those that show all the apostles gathered together. Also present at this moment, and representing apostolic succession, are three Oriental bishops, identifiable by their stoles with large black crosses on a white background. In this icon, moreover, the apostles appear twice: once as historical personages (with bare feet) gathered around the Virgin and again as atemporal figures in the eternal glory of heaven where they are ready to receive Mary's soul (shown as a little white figure) that has been accepted by Jesus and will be carried to heaven by angels.

himself was prophetically called a cornerstone, as is the connection with the invitation of Jesus to Peter to build his own house on a rock, that is, his own life in the Church.

Jesus next met Philip, who, like Peter, was from Bethsaida on Lake Gennesaret, and said to him: "Follow me." Philip in turn met Nathanael (also known as Bartholomew) and brought him to Jesus (John 1:43, 51). After John had been imprisoned, Jesus definitively called this group of men to follow him, men of varied background, different ages, and some of them familiar with the shores of the Sea of Galilee. He called John the Evangelist and his brother James, sons both of Zebedee (Mark 1:14-20). We may think that Philip and Bartholomew were of the group, since they had already been called. Later on Jesus met Levi, called Matthew, as he sat at his customs post (Mark 2:13-14). He then chose the Twelve "to be with him, and to be sent out to proclaim the message, and to have authority to cast out demons" (Mark 3:14). Within this common call we may distinguish the group formed by Peter, James, and John; next came Andrew, Philip, Bartholomew, and Matthew (in this list of the Twelve the order of their original call is pretty well respected); Thomas, James son of Alphaeus, Jude Thaddeus or "brother of James," Simon the Canaanite, called the Zealot, and Judas Iscariot (Matt 10:2-4; Luke 6:12-16; Mark 3:13-19).

There is another way of listing the apostles in which a phrase of the creed known precisely as the "Apostles' Creed" is attributed to each of them:

Peter: "I believe in God, the Father almighty, creator of heaven and earth"
Andrew: "and in Jesus Christ, his only-begotten Son, our Lord"
James the Greater: "who was conceived by the Holy Spirit and born of the Virgin Mary"
John: "suffered under Pontius Pilate, was crucified, died and was buried"
Thomas: "he descended into hell, on the third day rose from the dead"
James the Lesser: "ascended into heaven, where he sits at the right hand of God the Father almighty"
Philip: "whence he shall come to judge the living and the dead."
Bartholomew: "I believe in the Holy Spirit,"
Matthew: "the holy catholic Church, the communion of saints,"
Simon: "the forgiveness of sins,"
Jude Thaddeus: "the resurrection of the flesh,"
Matthias: "and the life of the world to come."

The apostles were thus perceived not only individually but also as a single body and as an image of the Church itself and of Christ its head. This union among them arose from experiences both common and individual. We see them all united in the Upper Room, and this on four occasions: on the Passover that saw the institution of the Eucharist, at the first appearance of Jesus on Easter Sunday when Thomas was absent, eight days later when Thomas was present, and at the descent of the Holy Spirit. We find them together again at the ascension of Jesus and at the "dormition," or "falling asleep," of Our Lady; all of them were around her or rather around her empty tomb that was filled with roses. All of them were to be martyrs: this union in task and in destiny is given narrative expression in the various representations of the above mentioned events, and symbolic expression in the many images that show them all gathered at the feet of Christ or at the *Etoimasia* ("preparation"), that is, the throne prepared for the return of Christ, or at the feet of the Virgin. In this kind of representation they are not infrequently shown in symbolic form, for example, as sheep at the feet of their shepherd as in the basilica of SS. Cosmas and Damian in Rome or in Sant'Apollinae in Classe in Ravenna.

Additionally, the group of Peter, James, and John is singled out from among the other apostles. As chosen witnesses of the transfiguration on Mount Tabor and of the prayer of Jesus in the Garden of Olives, the three have their special roles: Peter will be the first among the apostles, James will be the first martyr among them, and John will write an especially profound Gospel. In images of the apostles their number is not a matter of indifference: it is the number of the tribes of Israel, of the precious stones on the breastplate of the high priest, and of the minor prophets. Twelve is an ideal number derived from three and four. The number three, which foreshadows the Trinity, is the number of perfection, the key to the universe, and a sym-

Christ Receives SS. Cosmas and Damian.
In the horizontal band (the fascia) beneath the scene of SS. Cosmas and Damian being presented to Christ by SS. Peter and Paul, Felix IV, and Theodorus, there is a symbolic image of Christ as the Lamb, who stands on the mountain from which issue the paradisal rivers of grace. To his right and his left are other lambs, symbols of the apostles, who are both his contemporaries and his successors.
Mosaic, 6th cent., church of SS. Cosmas and Damian. The two saints, who hold the crown of martyrdom in their hands, are presented to Christ, who is seated on clouds and surrounded by SS. Peter and Paul, along with Theodore and Felix IV, who offers him the Church.
On a palm tree to the left is the phoenix. This indestructible mythical bird, which arises again from its own ashes, was regarded by the Fathers of the Church as a symbol of Christ and of the soul's immortality.

The Apostles at the Feet of Jesus.
Detail of a 14th-cent. fresco, church of Loreto Aprutino, Italy.

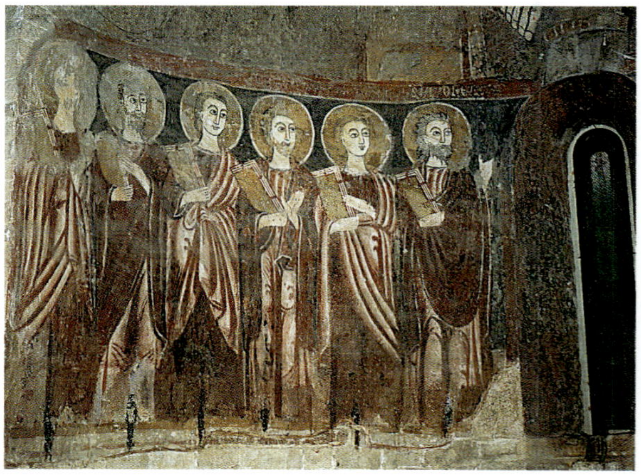

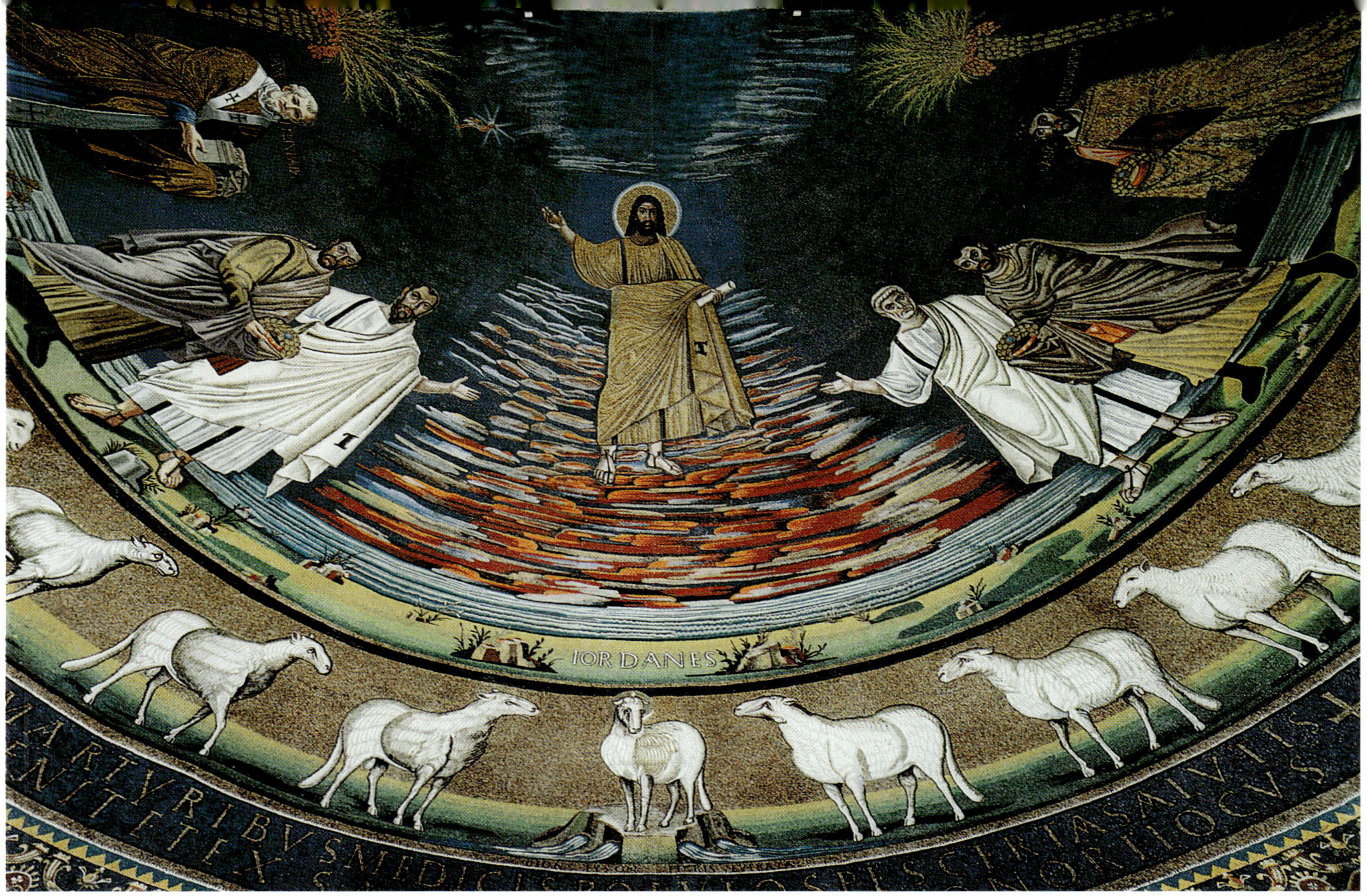

bol of God; thus three angels visited Abraham. The structure of Indo-European societies was based on three categories of persons: priests, warriors, and producers, and thus tended to represent the entire universe. The fact that beginning, middle, and end are events and elements that mark every creature, whereas the Creator contains them all, makes three the divine number par excellence. There are three ages of life, there were three races: white, olive-complexioned, and black; there were three known continents. Christ arose at dawn on the third day, and in prophecy of this Jonah spent three days in the belly of a fish. Finally, the human being has a fourfold structure: front, back, left, right; and four cardinal points define the earth.

Four times three makes twelve, a number that combines the divine and the human, and also leaves its mark on life in many ways. There are twelve hours in the day and twelve in the night, twelve months, and twelve signs of the zodiac. There were twelve rungs in the ladder of which Jacob dreamed, and twelve gates of Jerusalem. The number of the elect is twelve times twelve thousand (144,000), and it is a number representing the "entire Church."

After the betrayal of Judas eleven apostles remained, and eleven is the number of sin and betrayal. In images of the apostles there are eleven only when the intention is to stress the beginning of the passion of Jesus. Judas Iscariot is usually replaced by Matthias, the one who, in order to restore the number intended by Jesus, was chosen by the other apostles, or by Paul, who is often regarded as an apostle.

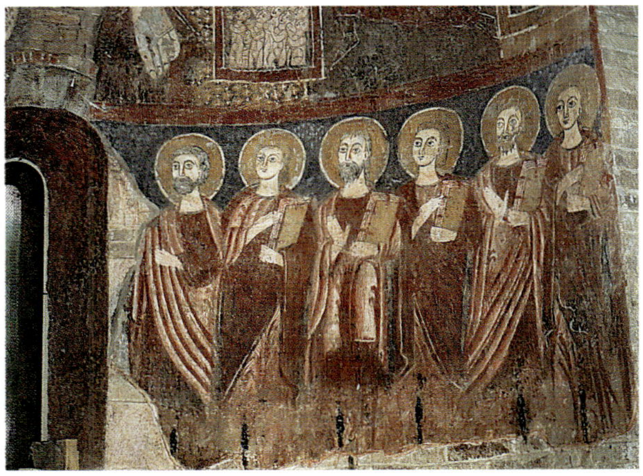

▷▷ There has been a rather homogeneous iconographical tradition for each of the apostles and especially for Peter and Paul. Even the features of their faces have always been the same ever since the images formed by early Christianity.

Tradition has it that the then-known world was divided up as follows with a view to its evangelization: Italy went to Peter, Asia to John, Achaia (Greece north of the Peleponnesus) to Andrew, Cilicia (today part of Turkey) to Bartholomew, Spain to James the Greater, Judea to James the Lesser, Palestine to Matthias, Ethiopia to Matthew, Persia to Simon, Mesopotamia to Thaddeus, and India to Thomas. At one time the chosen country was indicated in the nimbus of each apostle and in images of the *Divisio apostolorum* (the

Scattering of the Apostles); this last image was connected with a special feast introduced into the liturgy in the eleventh century and celebrated on July 15. However, this iconographical theme, which became widespread at the end of the fifteenth century in Germany and the Netherlands, disappeared after the seventeenth century.

▷▷ The apostles are represented with **bare feet**, in accordance with the instruction to travel without purse, bag, or sandals (Luke 10:4), and in the dress of their time. In the iconography the sign of their task as teachers is a **book** or, more rarely but more accurately, a **scroll**, which alludes to the proclamation of the Gospel and is their stable and constant attribute, as it is also for bishops, along with the pastoral staff and any special attributes of the individual.

The mission of the apostles has been represented by showing them as they scatter two by two or else as they approach the four cardinal points in groups of three.

Sometimes the apostles are represented in **episcopal vestments**.

Peter and Paul, Apostles

Solemnity: June 29

Peter is remembered as son of Jonah and brother of Andrew and as the first of the disciples to confess that Jesus is the Christ, the Son of the living God. Tradition says that he was crucified head downward and was buried in the Vatican gardens along the Triumphal Way. Paul is remembered as the Apostle of the Gentiles or the nations; he was beheaded and buried along the Ostian Way. Both apostles are equally venerated throughout the world. It is a fact that, according to a tradition born with Clement of Rome, the third successor of Peter (88–97), and continued in the *History of the Church* by Eusebius of Caesarea († 339; see *History* 2, 25, 8; 3, 1, 2), the testimony of Peter and Paul was perceived as being one and the same. The feast of June 29 commemorates the martyrdoms of both, which occurred rather closely in time. It was a documented certainty that veneration of them followed immediately on their deaths, the date of which can only be forever uncertain. Some scholars place them in the time of Nero, in 64, while others, more reliably, date them to 67.

Peter and Paul met in Jerusalem and in Antioch where they clashed on the question of whether or not converts to Christianity had to follow the prescriptions of Jewish Law. Despite Paul's strictly Jewish training, he never succeeded in evangelizing the Jews, while Peter had greater success among them. Just as Paul was the apostle of the *gentes,* the nations, that is, the pagans, and traveled extensively among them, so Peter was the apostle of the Jews. Peter's name is nevertheless attached to his mission to Rome, where he arrived perhaps in 44 or a little later and whose first bishop he became. It is probable that he met Paul during the latter's first imprisonment in Rome, but we have no information about this. They probably met again in Rome during their final years or even their final days.

The entire Christian tradition, and therefore the iconography too, thinks of them together and sees Paul as an apostle, so much so that he often edges out Matthias and takes his place among the Twelve.

In light of the documented historical facts the two apostles are viewed and represented as two pillars that combine to support the entire Church, Paul by his teaching, which is systematically set down in his letters, and Peter by the authority given by his assigned task of protecting the flock of the faithful and of binding and loosing, that is discerning who belongs to the Church.

▷▷ The iconography translates the traditions into an image that sees the two apostles together. Peter receives from Jesus the two keys of the kingdom, of which we shall speak later; this is known as the *donatio* or *traditio clavium* (the "giving" or "handing over" of the keys). Paul receives the scroll of the law, that is, of doctrine; this is described as the *traditio legis.* The image is one derived from classical art, in which the commitment of an office to an imperial civil servant was depicted in the same way. This same theme is found later in a synthetic form for Peter. Peter and Paul appear on each side of Christ, at the sides of altars, at the base of triumphal arches: they are distinct from each other but clearly paired as columns supporting the church, according to a pattern that is connected with the *donatio clavium* and the *traditio legis.*

SS. Peter and Paul, Apostles.
Bas-relief, 4th cent., Museum of Paleochristianity, Aquileia.

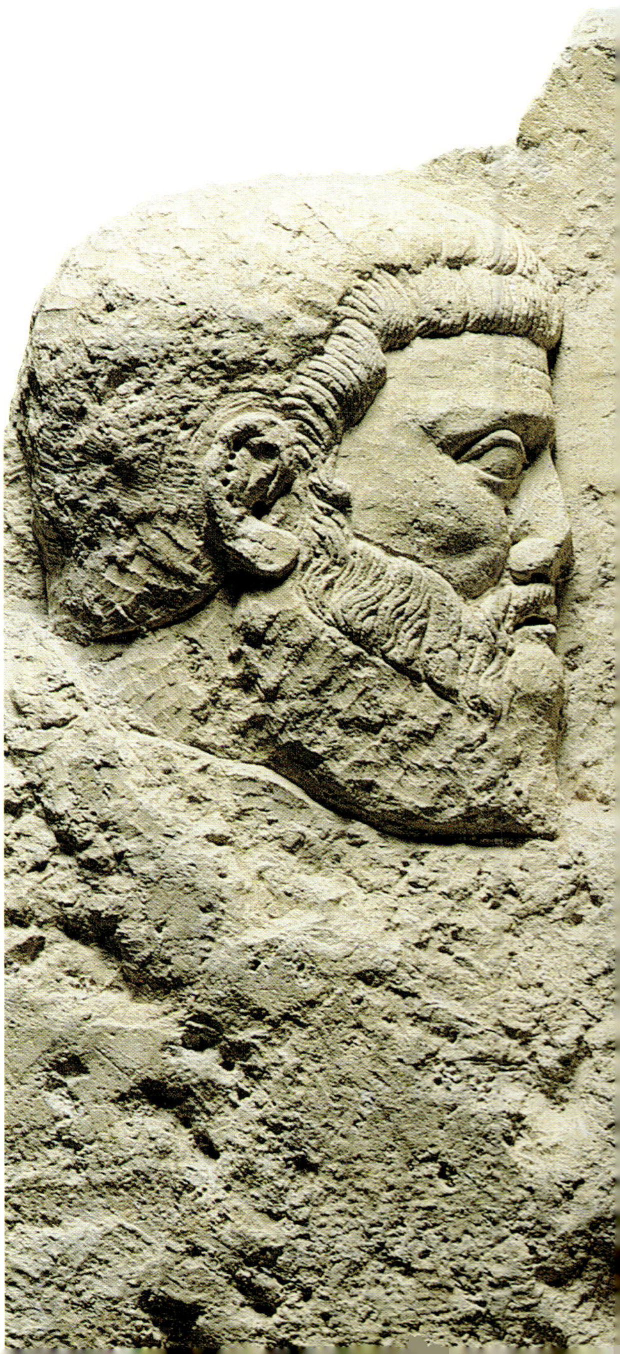

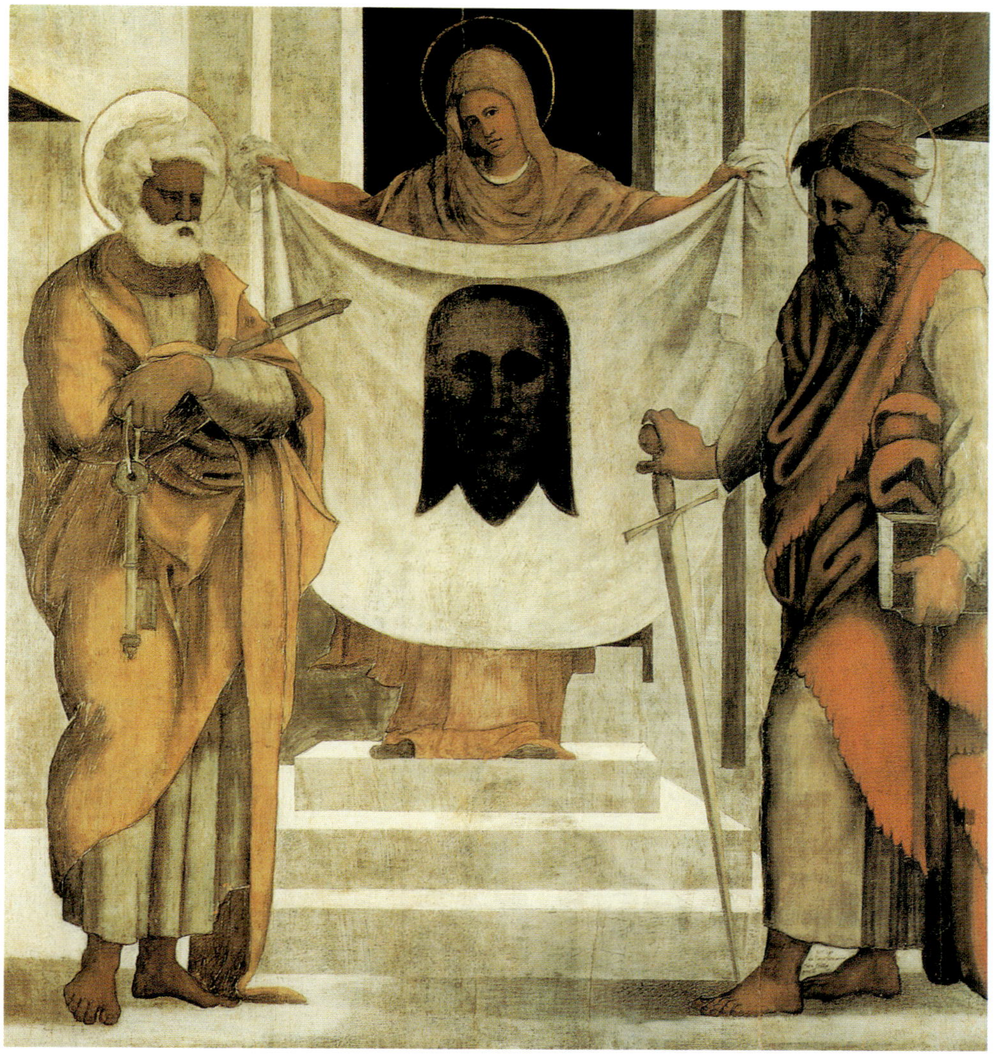

Veronica between SS. Peter and Paul.
Ugo da Carpi, 16th cent. in the Archivio Storico della Fabbrica di San Pietro in Vaticano, Rome. The "Veronica," that is, the "true icon" of Christ, is the relic that is preserved at St. Peter's, Rome, and consists of the image of the face of Christ that was miraculously imprinted on the cloth with which a devout woman wiped the face of Christ on the way to Calvary; the woman takes her name from the image.

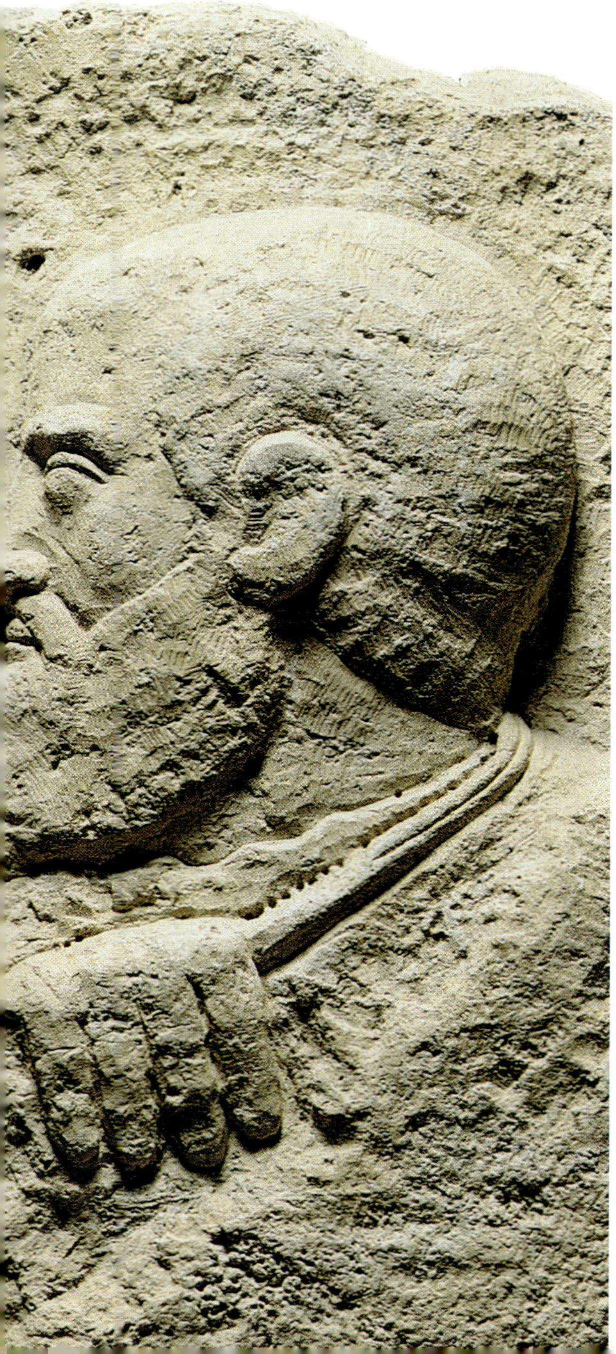

Peter, Apostle, Prince of the Apostles

Solemnity of his martrydom: June 29; Feast of the Chair of St. Peter: February 22
Gr.: Petros; Lat.: Petrus; It.: Pietro, Piero, Pierino; Fr.: Pierre, Pé, Pey, Père, Peyre, Pernet, Peronet, Pernot, Perronot, Perrin, Pierret, Pierrot; Sp.: Pedro, Petrillo; Ger.: Petrus, Peter; Russ.: Piotr.

February 22 is the feast chiefly of Peter's primacy. It is called the feast of *Cathedra Petri,* the "Chair of Peter," the chair here being the chair of one who teaches; Peter is placed on it because on him Christ willed to build his Church.

Peter was a fisherman, no longer very young, married, and the head of what we today would call a cooperative of fishermen at Bethsaida beside the "sea" of Galilee, or Lake of Gennesaret. Like his brother Andrew and his friends, he was perhaps a disciple of John the Baptist. After the death of the Baptist, Jesus definitively called him while he and his brother Andrew were working their **nets**: "Follow me and I will make you fish for people" (Mark 1:17). His life was characterized by enthusiasms and failures, as when he ran to meet Christ on the water of a stormy sea, but then hesitated and would have drowned had Jesus not reached out a hand to him.

He was the spokesmen of the other apostles in asking questions of Jesus, but he was also the only one to give an answer dictated by the Holy Spirit: "You are the Christ, the Son of the living God." This reply won him the assignment of a lifelong task: "You are Peter, and on this rock I will build my church, and the gates of Hades will not prevail against it. I will give you the **keys of the kingdom of heaven**, and whatever you bind on earth will be bound in heaven, and whatever you loose on earth will be loosed in heaven" (Matt 16:18-19). These words introduce the theme of Peter's primacy, which will be confirmed after the

Resurrection (see John 21:15-17), and, with it, the iconographical theme of the keys and of Peter as guardian of the gates of paradise, the entrance to which he controls.

Peter was certain that he could without any hesitation follow Christ; he drew his sword and cut off the ear of Malchus, servant of the high priest, but shortly afterward he denied Jesus three times within the space of a few minutes and before the **cock** crowed, as Jesus had foretold. But Jesus did not therefore deny Peter his love; indeed in that very prophecy he expressed it with great mercy. Peter's subsequent bitter tears are exemplary. He, like all the apostles except for John, remained at a distance from the cross and even from the burial of Jesus; with the younger disciple he hurried to the tomb when the women told him that the body of Jesus had disappeared. It was he who entered the tomb and, later on, it was he who received the mandate to lead the flock of Jesus, at the time when Jesus foretold his future martyrdom and urged him to follow him without question (John 21:15-23).

Peter was the first to recognize the fulfillment of Scripture in the death and resurrection of Jesus (Acts 1:16) and to suggest the election of another, twelfth apostle. It was Peter, again, who spoke first on Pentecost (Acts 2:14-36).

At that point, his courageous witnessing began. His was the first miracle after the Resurrection, when he went up to the Temple with John and cured a cripple: "In the name of Jesus Christ of Nazareth, stand up and walk" (Acts 3:6). From then on we see him preaching lengthy sermons, working miracles, and finally being imprisoned by Herod Agrippa, an imprisonment he faced with incredible serenity and confidence. In fact, while his friends were praying for him, "Peter, bound with two chains, was sleeping between two soldiers" (Acts 12:6). Then an angel appeared to him and led him out of the prison. After this, Scripture says little more about Peter, but the tradition of his coming to Rome and his martyrdom is very ancient and well founded. To it may be added the episode of his meeting with Jesus on the Appian Way, not far from what is now the catacombs of St. Sebastian. As Peter was fleeing from Rome, Jesus appeared to him. When Peter asked him: *Domine, quo vadis?* ("Whither are you going, Lord?"), Jesus answered that he was on his way to Rome in order to be crucified a second time. Peter understood and turned back. At the place of the apparition there is a small church known as the *Domine, quo vadis?;* in it is preserved a stone bearing the imprint of two feet: tradition has it that they are the feet of Jesus.

St. Peter probably suffered martyrdom during the persecution of Nero (64–68), which followed upon the well-known fire; he was **crucified**, but he wanted to die **head downward** out of humility, in order not to be like Jesus. The place was the Circus built by Caligula (37–41) in the *Ager Vaticanus,* that is, the Vatican gardens; he was buried in a nearby cemetery.

His cult began immediately. Pope St. Anacletus (or Cletus) (76–88) had an *aedicula,* or small shrine, over his tomb. From as early as about 200 C.E. we have the testimony of Gaius, a presbyter, who boasted: "I can point out the monuments of the various apostles. If you will go as far as the Vatican or the Ostian Way, you will find the monuments of those who founded this church" (Eusebius of Caesarea, *History of the Church,* 2, 25, 7; trans. Williamson, 105).

In 324 Constantine turned the shrine into a basilica *ad corpus,* that is, "near the body" of the saint; at the tomb of Peter the pope used to baptize while sitting on a wooden chair said to be that of the apostle. Pilgrims constantly met at this place, and here Pope Nicholas V (1447–1455) established the papal residence.

▷▷ Because of his former occupation Peter is the patron of anglers and, in particular, of freshwater anglers (since he himself fished in the Lake of Gennesaret) and of weavers of nets. Because of the chains he wore, he protects foundry workers and foundries, as well as locksmiths. He is the patron of harvesters and basketmakers because, like them, he "ties/binds/fastens." Because he has the keys, he protects locksmiths and watchmakers, since, like locks, watches are precision instruments; in addition, the cock was like a living clock of his own. Due to his very name Peter is patron of masons. As keeper of the keys to paradise, he is the patron of doorkeepers.

▷▷ He is invoked against fevers, bouts of madness, snake bites, and rabies; in his confrontation with Simon Magus he put to flight the dogs Simon had loosed against him.

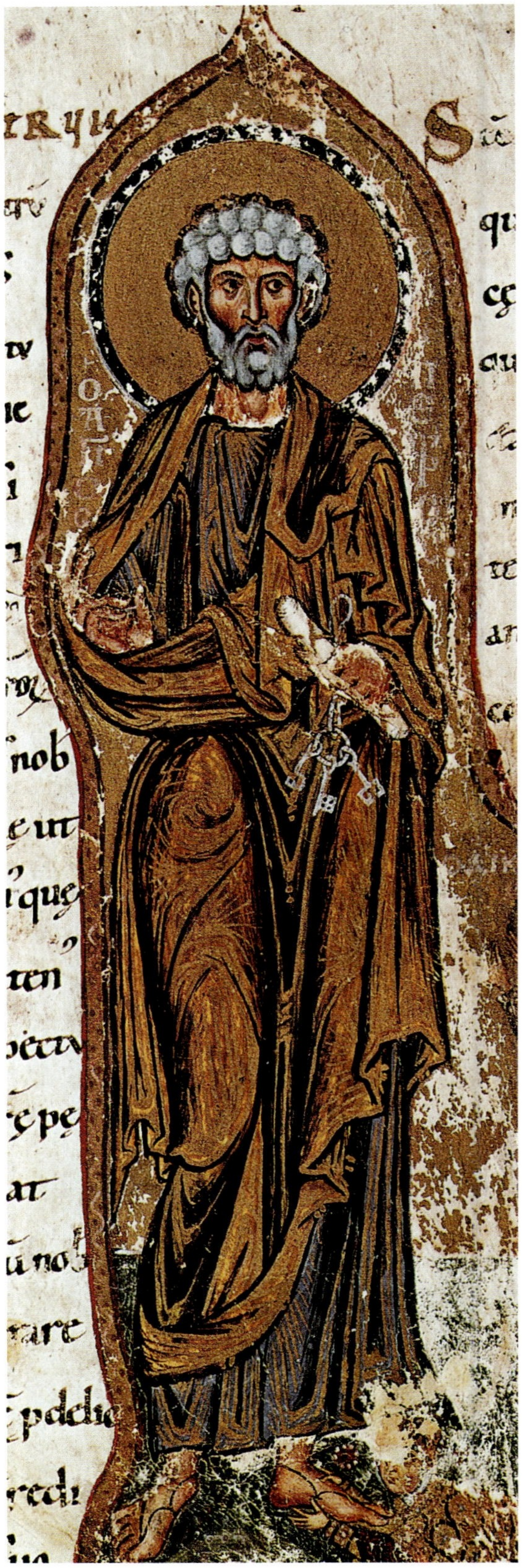

St. Peter.
Codex of Egbert, 10th cent., in the Sanctuary of Triers, Germany.

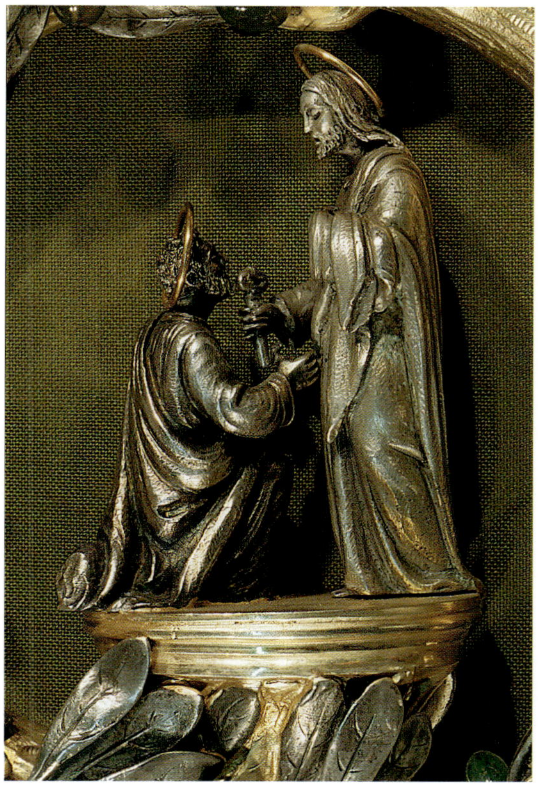

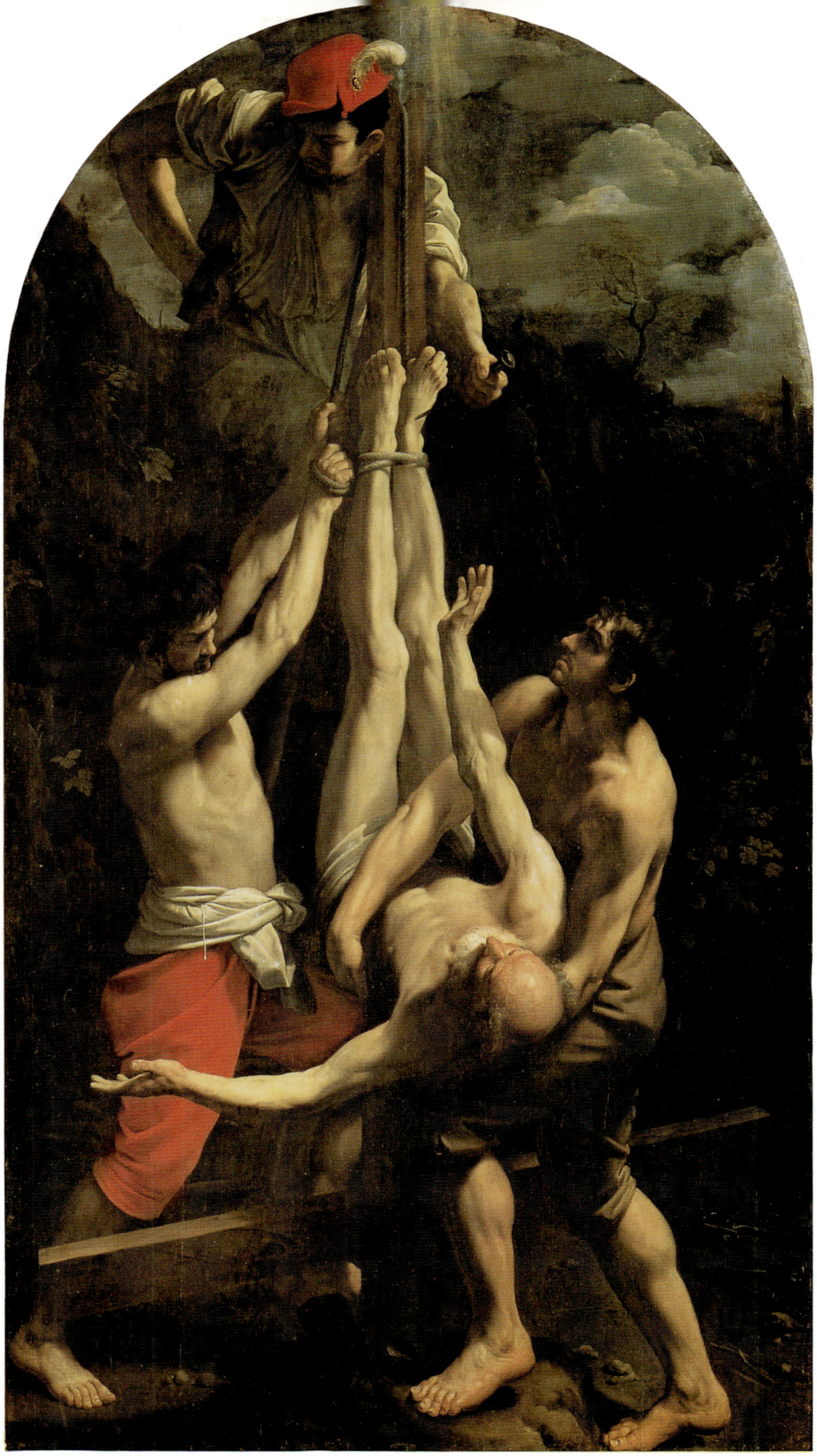

Christ Gives the Keys to Peter.
Detail from the staff of Blessed Tavelli of Tossignano, 11th cent., in the Treasury of the Cathedral, Ferrara.

Crucifixion of St. Peter.
By Guido Reni, 17th cent., Vatican art gallery.

▷▷ He is always represented with a beard and with hair that is tended and gathered up and that is dark or white, depending on the age that is being emphasized; most often he is advanced in years. All the incidents of his life are found in his iconography, which is very rich; to these incidents must be added the *traditio fidei* already mentioned. His principal attribute is the **keys**, one of gold, the other of silver; they are the keys of paradise and hell, of binding and loosing (that is, of absolving and excommunicating), or of spiritual power and temporal power (depending on the interpretations). The keys may also be three in number, to signify authority in heaven, on earth, and in hell. The keys are tied or linked together because the authority is one; this last point can also be made by showing only one key.

Other attributes are **nets** and **tools for fishing**; the **cock**, which crowed after Peter had denied Christ; the **chains** from which an angel freed him; the **boat** of which he is the helmsman, that is, the Church (in some cases, the main mast consists of the cross of Christ). Still other attributes are the **inverted cross**, the **tiara** with its three bands that refer to temporal, spiritual, and royal power; and the **papal cross** with its three transverse bars.

Paul of Tarsus, Apostle to the Nations

Solemnity of his martyrdom: June 29; Feast of his Conversion: January 25

Lat.: Paulus; It.: Paolo, Polo; Fr.: Paul, Pal, Pau, Pol, Poul, Pou, Paulet; Sp.: Pablo, Apostol de los Gentiles; Port.: Paulo; Ger.: Paulus, der Völkerapostel, Weltapostel; Dutch: Pauwel; Russ.: Pavel.

Saul was born in Tarsus, capital of Cilicia, of a Jewish family that gave him the name of Saul, the first king of the Hebrews. It is not certain whether from birth he was also called Paul, according to the Jewish practice at that period of having two names, one Jewish and the other derived from Greek or Latin and to be used mainly in dealing with pagans. He completed his education in Jerusalem in the school of Gamaliel and was a Pharisee.

In his zeal for persecuting Christians he was on the way to fomenting persecution against them in Damascus, but at the gates of the city Jesus himself revealed his glory to him and chose him for the proclamation of the Gospel to the nations. By asking Saul "Why are you persecuting me?" Jesus overwhelmed him with the revelation that Christ lives in the Church. The light and power of the Lord struck him and caused him to **fall from his horse**, while at the same time blinding him temporarily. This "thunderbolt on the road to Damascus" has become a synonym for an unexpected and decisive conversion. Convinced in this way of the living presence of Christ in his Church, a theme he would develop extensively in his letters, Paul obeyed the instructions given by the divine voice: he entered Damascus, went to Ananias' house, and was baptized. After a first attempt to evangelize his former companions, he spent three years in study and then returned to Damascus, but he was forced to flee again (being let down from the city wall in a basket).

He then went to Jerusalem and made the acquaintance of Barnabas, who had great respect for him and introduced him to the apostles. The time was 37–39 C.E. On leaving Jerusalem he went back to Tarsus. Barnabas went off to evangelize Antioch and sent word to Paul to come to that city, where the disciples of Jesus were first called "Christians" (Acts 11:26). Shortly afterward, the Holy Spirit made himself known to the prudent men of Antioch when they were gathered in prayer, and he asked that they "set aside" Saul and Barnabas for a special task. Then, after hands had been laid on them, the two men departed on a first mission. From this point on in Acts, Saul is always called Paul, from the Latin *paulus,* "little," out of humility.

When the question arose of whether converts had to become Jews and be circumcised before baptism, Paul and Barnabas went back to Jerusalem to discuss the question with the apostles and elders. After taking part in this "Council of Jerusalem" the two men continued to work together and completed their first apostolic journey in the years 45/46 to 49. They disagreed, however, on whether it was appropriate to take with them Mark, the later evangelist, and so they went their separate ways, Mark remaining with Barnabas. Paul went on his second journey from 50 to 53, his third from 53/54 to 58. At Caesarea he received prophetic foreknowledge of his imprisonment and death (Acts 21:10-14).

When he returned to Jerusalem, the Jews accused him of having profaned the Temple, and they stirred up the anger of the crowds against him. The Romans saved him from being lynched, but they imprisoned him. Subsequent attempts to explain his position were unsuccessful: the more Paul spoke, the angrier the Jews became and the less the Romans understood. By declaring himself to be a Roman citizen, Paul escaped being scourged. When a Jewish plot to kill Paul was discovered, the Roman tribune had him transferred to Caesarea and Felix the governor. Paul remained Felix's prisoner for two years, while hoping to

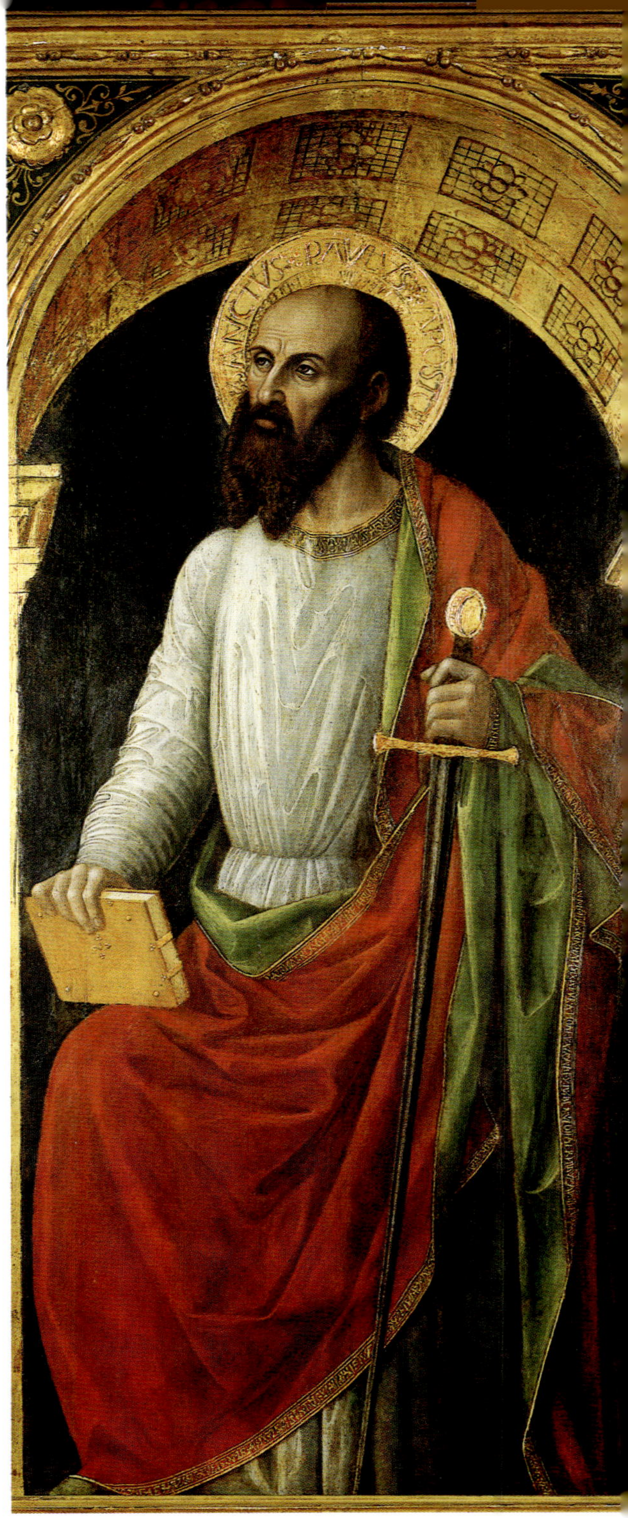

St. Paul.
By Vincenzo Foppa, ca. 1500, in the Isaac Delgado Museum of Art, New Orleans.

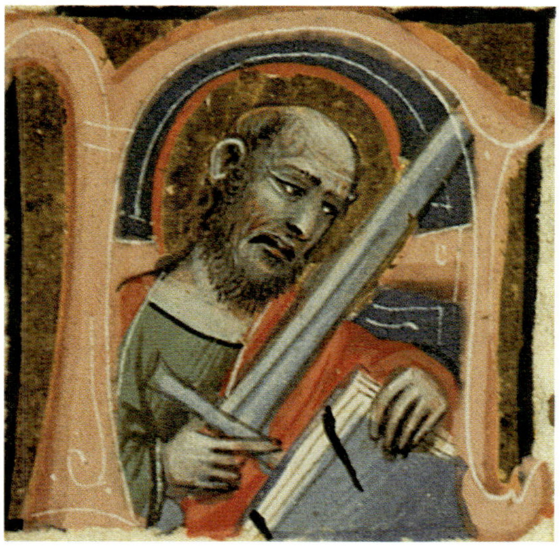

St. Paul.
Miniature from a handwritten gospel of the 15th cent. belonging to Blessed Tavelli of Tossignano, now in the parish church of Fontanelice, Italy.

be rescued; then Felix was succeeded as governor by Festus, and the Jews renewed their accusations. This time, Paul appealed to the judgment of Caesar, that is, the emperor, and Festus decided to send him to Rome. The journey was marked by a dramatic shipwreck, but the ship reached Malta (whose patron Paul therefore became); the voyage was resumed after three months and ended at Rome in 61. The accusers were obliged to present themselves again here, and while they were awaited, Paul was allowed to live by himself and receive whomever he desired, although under the eye of a guard; this situation lasted for two years. At this point, Acts ends its story of Paul and indeed its entire record.

From other sources and from the letters in particular we infer that Paul was probably set free because his accusers had failed to present themselves. After having been away from Rome during the persecution of Nero, he was imprisoned again and taken to Rome; this time his captivity there was much more difficult. He was far from his faithful friends, except for Luke (2 Tim 4:11), and suffered a painful isolation. A reliable tradition that is both literary and archeological says his martyrdom took place in 67 and at the present-day Tre Fontane on the Laurentian Way; he was beheaded with a sword because this was the only death worthy of a Roman citizen. His head bounced three times when separated from his body and gave rise to the three springs from which the place takes its name.

He was buried in the basilica on the Ostian Way, where we can read the inscription: "To Paul, apostle, martyr."

▷▷ Paul is the protector of Greece, whose patron he was proclaimed to be by Pius X on July 14, 1914, and of Malta. He was thrown from his horse at his conversion and has therefore become the patron of horsemen. By reason of his systematic presentation of Christian teaching he is the patron of theologians. He is the patron of tentmakers either because he supported himself by making tents, which were woven of twisted cords from the skins of Cilician goats, or because the cords were twisted, allowing a word play with the term "to convert" (the Latin verb *convertere* can have the Christian meaning of "to convert" but can also mean "to turn one thing into another"). He was also let down the wall of Damascus in a basket and by ropes; he is therefore the patron of basketmakers. He was killed by a shining sword and is therefore the patron of polishers and sword makers.

▷▷ He is invoked against storms because he himself escaped from a shipwreck, and against poisonous serpents and snakebites because he was not killed by a viper's bite on Malta. He is also invoked against blindness, from which he himself was healed after being blinded at the gates of Damascus.

▷▷ His iconography represents the important episodes of his life, especially his conversion and his beheading. He is depicted as mature or elderly, with beard and mustache, and with hair circling a broad, bald head. The earliest images show him with the scroll of doctrine, while the **sword** of martyrdom became his fundamental attribute from the thirteenth century on. He may have as another attribute the **basket** in which he was let down.

St. Andrew.
Miniature in the Oscott Psalter (England), ca. 1270, in the British Museum, London.

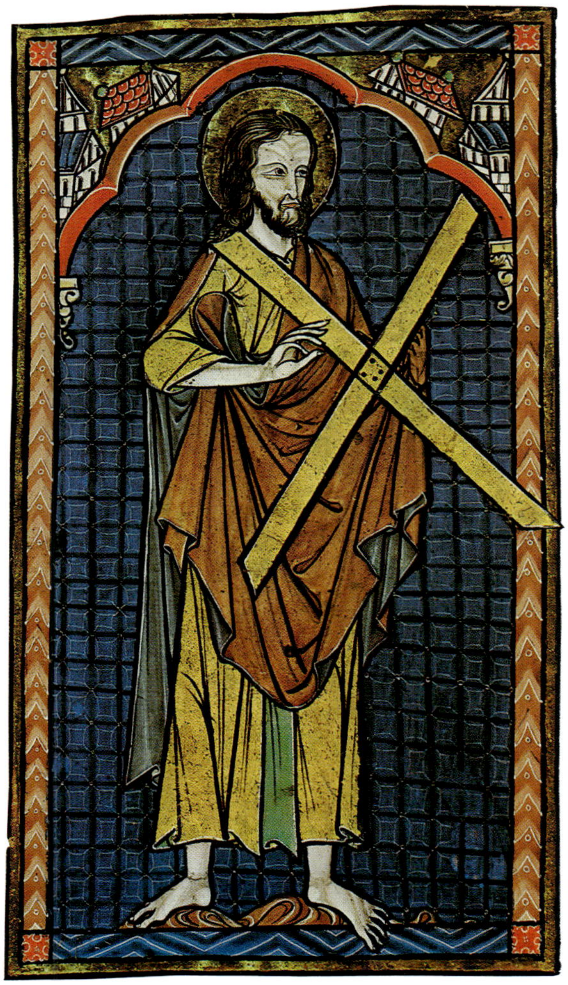

Andrew, Apostle

Feast: November 30

Lat.: Andrea; Gr.: Andreas; Fr.: André, Andrieu, Drouet, Druot; Sp.: Andrès; Ger.: Andreas, Ander (whence Andersen and Anderson in Denmark and England); Flem.: Andries; Russ.: Andreï.

This brother of Peter is remembered as the first of John the Baptist's disciples to be called by Jesus. His name means "virile," from the Greek *anêr, andros,* "a male person." Together with the apostle John he had been a disciple of the Baptist, but when the latter pointed Jesus out as the Lamb of God, Andrew and John followed him. Andrew then told his brother, Peter, that they had found the Messiah, and led him to Jesus. His immediate following of Jesus and his relationship with Peter won him a special place, and in iconography he often appears together with Peter, Paul, and the evangelists. It was Andrew who brought to Jesus the boy with the loaves and fishes.

When the apostles split up to undertake their separate missions, Andrew was appointed evangelizer of Scythia, that is, present-day Russia. As he was preaching, an angel appeared to him and sent him to Matthew in Ethiopia; he reached there in a miraculous fashion, but found Matthew blinded and thrown into prison. The gates of the prison opened to Andrew, who went in and knelt beside Matthew, praying there until the latter's sight was restored. He then went to Greece and Asia Minor where he worked various miracles: he delivered Nicaea from seven demons who had transformed themselves into dogs, and he put out a fire in Thessalonica.

He was next imprisoned by Quirinus, governor of Macedonia, on the charge that he was inciting people to destroy the temples and turning them away from the worship of the gods; Quirinus condemned him *ad bestias* (to the beasts), but a wild boar, a bull, and a tiger all spared him. He then went to Patras in the Peloponnesus, when he cured Maximilla, wife of Egeas the proconsul; the latter nevertheless had him flogged for disobedience to the emperor, then had him **bound to a cross that was in the form of an X (the crux decussata)**. Andrew died after two days of great suffering. Maximilla buried him, and Egeas was strangled by two demons. Andrew's crucifixion is reported in the Gnostic *Acts of Andrew*.

▷▷ In the East Andrew is patron of Greece and of Russia; one tradition says that he planted a cross where Kiev later rose and where one of the principal churches is dedicated to him. In the West, his cult is quite widespread in Scotland, Italy, and France.

Tradition has it that in the fourth century his relics were taken from Patras to Scotland; where the ship debarked, the university city of St. Andrew's was built. The *St. Andrew's Cross* was introduced into Scottish coats of arms; on the Union Jack of the United Kingdoms it had its place beside the *Cross of St. George*.

Andrew is patron of Amalfi, to which his relics were carried from Constantinople at the beginning of the thirteenth century.

Gregory of Tours reports that manna came forth from Andrew's tomb in Patras. The same phenomenon was repeated in Constantinople where a liquid was collected that flowed from his relics, a liquid that is today collected in Amalfi. The manna is produced in greater or lesser measure, especially during his feast on November 30; a scarcity of manna is interpreted by the people of Amalfi as a summons to penance.

Andrew is the patron of Burgundy in France, because the Burgundians thought they came originally from Scythia, which was evangelized by Andrew. Philip the Good placed the Order of the Golden Fleece under his protection, and its knights wore an X-shaped cross as a badge.

Having been a fisherman, he is the protector of fishermen and fishmongers. He is patron of rope makers both because he was tied to his cross by ropes and because rope makers supplied fishermen with rope for their nets.

▷▷ Andrew is invoked against gout, cramps, stiffness of the neck, erysipelas, and dysentery, which is known as "St. Andrew's sickness."

▷▷ Andrew is often represented in his martyrdom. When he appears with the group of apostles he stands beside his brother Peter. His principal attribute is the **X-shaped cross**; other attributes are an **angler's net** and the **rope** with which he was tied to the cross.

James the Greater, Apostle

† 42/44
Feast: July 25
Lat.: Jacobus Maior; It.: Giacomo, Jabopo, Jacobo; Fr.: Jacques le Majeur, Jacques le Grand, Jacquinet, Quinet, James, Jaumes, Jayme, Diègue; Sp.: Santiago (from San Jago el Major), Iago, Jaime, Jaume, Diego; Port.: Diogo; Ger.: Jakobus der Ältere, der Grössere, Dutch.: Jacob de Meerdere.

James, the first martyr among the apostles, was the son of Zebedee and Mary of Salome and the brother of John. He is called the Greater to show that of the two Jameses he was the first to be called along with his brother John and that he left everything to follow Jesus (Matt 4:21ff. and par.). We find him, along with his brother and Peter, at the raising of the daughter of Jairus (Mark 5:37), at the Transfiguration on Mt. Tabor (Matt 17:1ff.), and in the Garden of Olives, where the three men could not resist sleep (Matt 26:37).

When Jesus chose the Twelve, he called James and John *boanerges,* an Aramaic word meaning "sons of thunder," because of their boldness. When, for example, they were rejected by the Samaritans, they asked Jesus: "Lord, do you want us to command fire to come

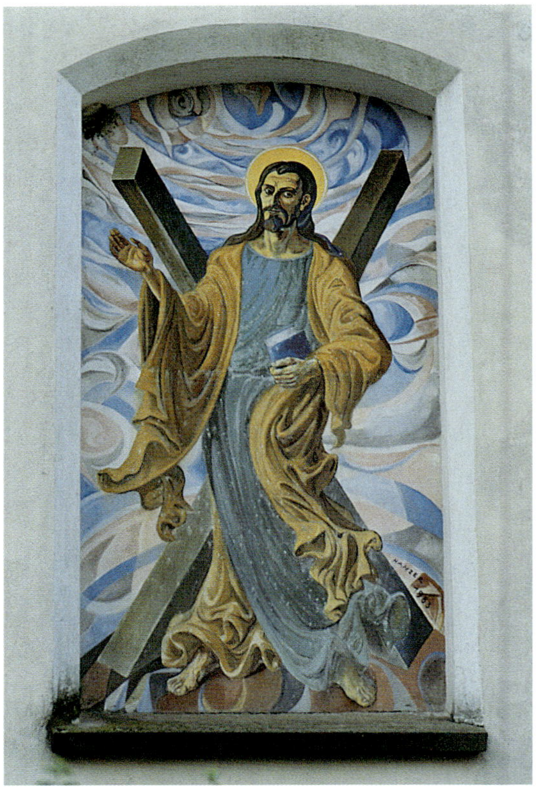

St. Andrew.
Fresco in a votive shrine, 20th cent., Melk, Austria.

St. James Transports Two Pilgrims.
Book of the Society of St. James of the Bridge, in the Biblioteca Palatina, Parma.

St. James.
Statue on the 17th-cent. facade of the cathedral of Santiago de Compostela, Spain.

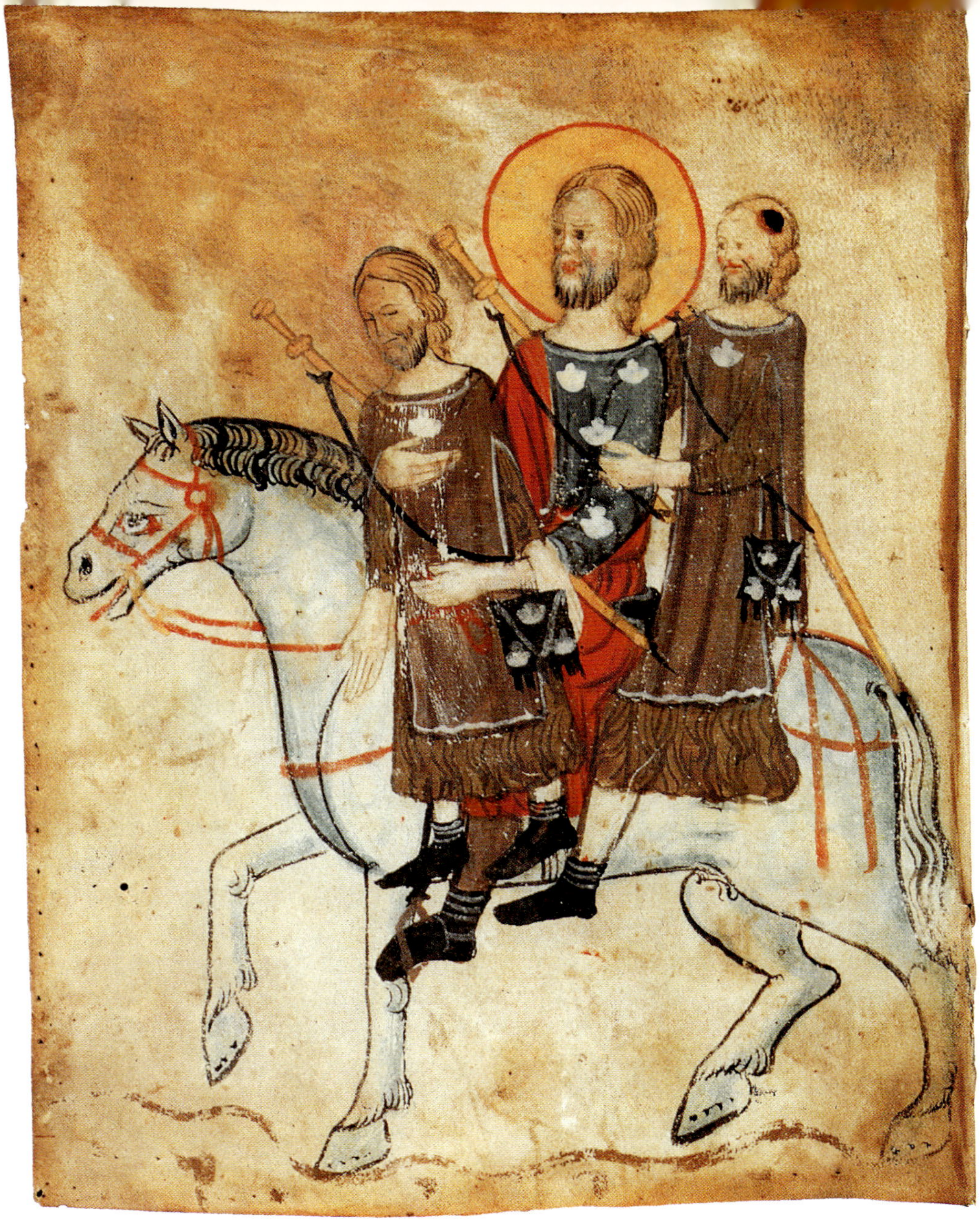

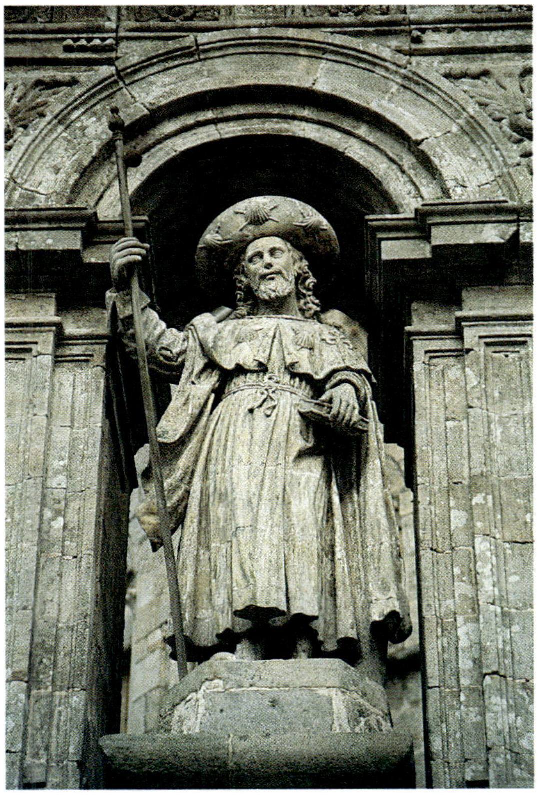

down from heaven and consume them?" (Luke 9:52-56), but he rebuked them. Their mother, a cousin of the Virgin, asked Jesus that her two sons might sit, one on his right, the other on his left, that is, that they might share in his royal dignity. Jesus in turn asked the two brothers: "Are you able to drink the cup that I am about to drink?" When they answered, "We are able," he replied with a prediction of their martyrdom, and in fact they were the first and last of the apostles to be martyred. After that incident, Scripture speaks of James again when it reports his martyrdom in Jerusalem (Acts 12:2) in the time of Herod Agrippa, who thought he would please the Jews by beheading James.

Tradition, however, which is repeated in the *Golden Legend,* says that the lot fell to James to evangelize Spain. Disappointed there by the poor results of his preaching, he started his return to Jerusalem before the date agreed on with the others, but on January 2, 40, near the present-day Saragossa, the Virgin Mary appeared to him atop a column *(pilar)*. She urged him not to be concerned about the seemingly paltry results of his preaching, and asked him to build a house of worship on that spot: the column would remain to the end of the world, and worshipers of Jesus would never be lacking in that city.

James had a church built there that is still to be seen within the great cathedral of Saragossa. He remained a while in Spain, preaching in Galicia, and then, at the appointed time, returned to Jerusalem, where he suffered martyrdom and was buried. But his only two disciples, Theodomirus and Athanasius, did not resign themselves to losing their teacher. They stole his body and carried it to Jaffa, where they boarded a ship that had miraculously berthed there, and entrusted themselves to Providence. The ship was steered to pass Gibraltar and run up the coast of present-day Portugal until it reached the Roman port of Iria Flavia where the rivers Sar and Ulla met. The body was taken from the ship and placed on a stone that melted like wax to form a coffin; after some marvelous incidents, the apostle's relics were finally placed in a mortuary chapel; the two disciples were also buried there.

A period of forgetfulness followed, and there remained only a faint tradition about the location of the tomb. But in 812–814, when Spain had been recovered from the Muslims and the little Christian kingdoms of the north were offering fierce resistance to them, a hermit named Pelayo received instruction by means of a vision of lights and discovered the tomb; this was interpreted as a divine approval of the Christian reconquest of Spain. St. James did not withhold his protection but appeared during the decisive battle of Clavijo. There a giant horseman on a white horse, carrying a banner with the cross on it, was seen descending onto the field of battle and routing the Moors. Whence the name Santiago Matamoros (St. James, killer of Moors), and the iconography inspired by the event.

On the place of St. James' tomb arose the present-day city of Santiago de Compostela (from *Campus Stellae,* "Field of the Star," a reference to the light that led the hermit to the place); it is the "City of the Apostle," which has been the goal of pilgrimages ever since the ninth century. On the "Road to Santiago," a route that was established over the centuries, the cultures of the countries of Europe have fused, and still are fusing, thus building a Christianity that defines the identity of Europe.

▷▷ James is the patron par excellence of pilgrims. Due to his image as a horseman in battle, he is also the patron of crusaders, cavalrymen, and all who travel by horse. He is the patron of those on the point of death and of the hanged, this because he restored to life a young man who had been unjustly hanged. He is the patron of pharmacists, merchants selling chemical and pharmaceutical products, and grocers who assist pilgrims. Because of the large pilgrim's hat (the *petasus* or wide-brimmed hat) that he wears, he is the patron of hatters and, because of his link with shoes and pilgrimages, of makers of shoes and clogs. He is the patron of the Order of Cluny, which he protected and which promoted pilgrimages to his tomb.

James is the principal patron of Spain and Spanish chivalry, which invokes him as "Santiago Chevalier"; of Guatemala, of The Hague in the Netherlands, and of Coimbra in Portugal. He is venerated in France, England, Belgium, and Germany, while all of Europe is furrowed by roads that lead to his tomb. In the Americas he has given his name to San Diego in California, Santiago in Cuba, and Santiago in Chile.

Pius X declared him patron of Nicaragua on May 15, 1914.

▷▷ James is invoked against rheumatism, the reason being that pilgrims sleep on the ground and are exposed to rain and, as a result, easily suffer rheumatism. He is petitioned for an abundant apple harvest, of which the early kinds mature in time for his feast on July 25. Because the hay is brought in at this time, shepherds celebrate a feast in honor of James. Among the animals he protects partridges and ptarmigans.

▷▷ The iconography of this saint shows him in various ways: as apostle with his book and the **sword** of his beheading. As pilgrim, in pilgrim's garb, with **cloak**, **staff**, **flask** or gourd for water, and **shell**; this last is his principal attribute, and is also the emblem of pilgrimage to Santiago and, consequently, of all pilgrimages; pilgrims use the shell to collect offerings and pin it to their clothing as a sign that they have been to Santiago. James is shown, finally, as a horseman, **on horseback, with a white banner marked with a cross**, a **whirling sword**, and the **decapitated heads** of Moors at his feet.

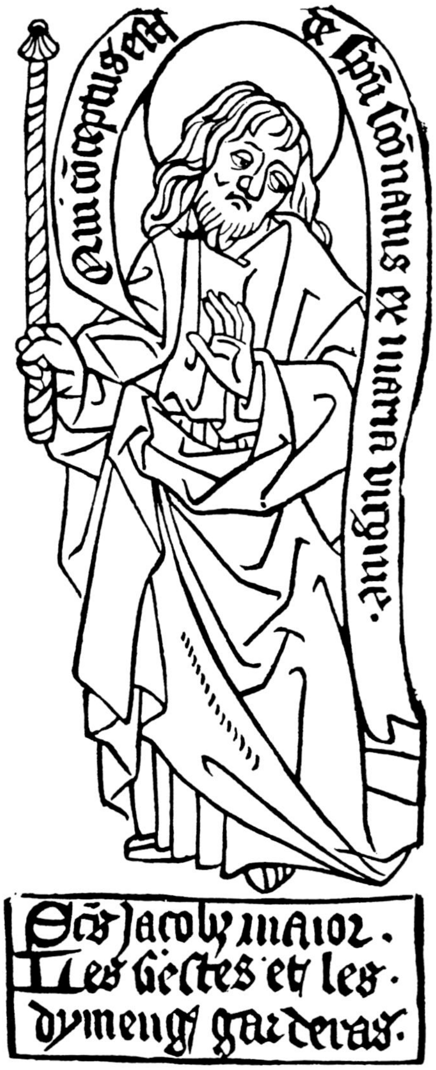

St. James.
15th-cent. woodcut. On the scroll surrounding the saint is written: "Conceived by the Holy Spirit, born of the Virgin Mary," which was the section of the Apostles' Creed that was assigned to James.

John, Apostle and Evangelist

Feast: December 27

Lat.: Johannes Evangelistia; Gr.: Ioann Theologus; It.: Giovanni, Vangelista, Teologo; Fr.: Jean l'Évangeliste, le Divin, le Théologien; Sp.: Juan Evangelista; Ger.: Johannes Evangelist, der Theologe; Pol.: Jan Evangelist; Russ.: Ioann Bogoslov; Hungarian: János.

John was a witness of the Transfiguration; later, at the foot of the cross, Jesus entrusted Mary to him as his mother. In his writings he proved himself a theologian, proclaiming the

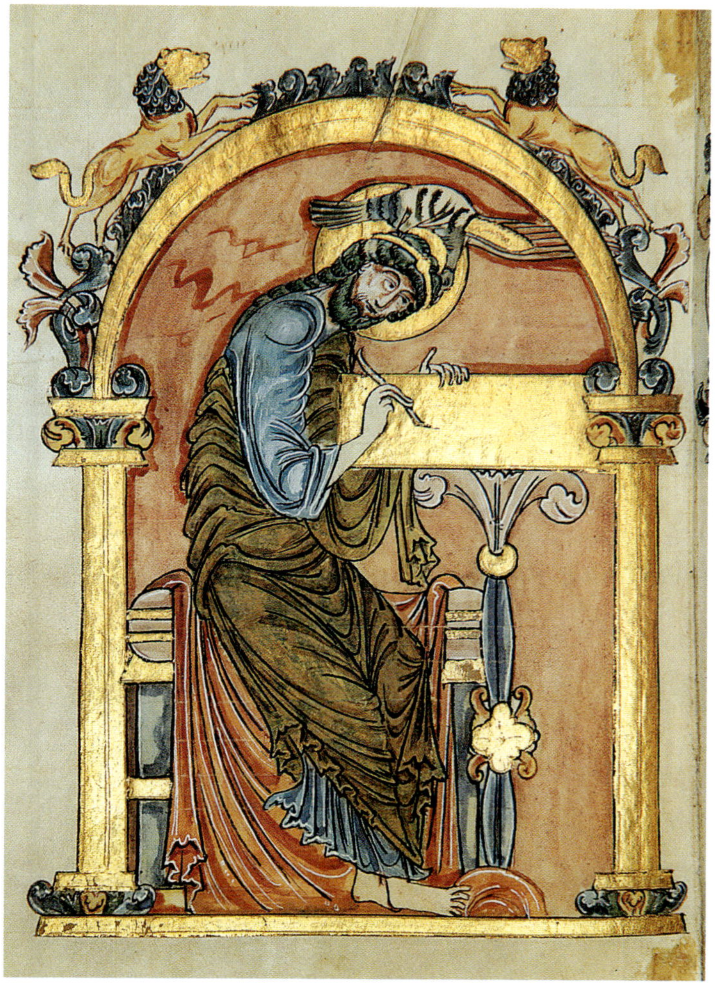

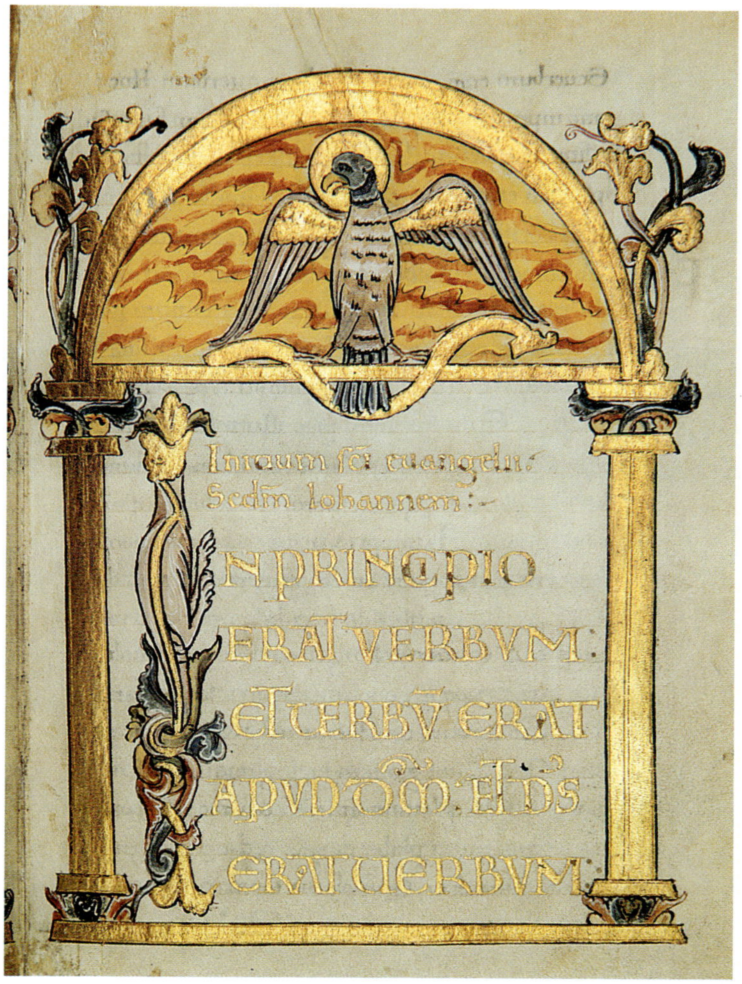

St. John the Evangelist.
11th-cent. miniature from an Evangeliary owned by Judith of Flanders, in the Archivio della Badia, Montecassino.

Gospel *incipit* with an eagle, the symbol of St. John.

glory of the Word Incarnate whom it was his privilege to contemplate. He is called the Evangelist, the Theologian, and in France "the Divine," because of the profound character of his Gospel, in which he fixed his gaze on the depths of the divinity, just as an eagle (it was believed) could fix its gaze on the sun. As a result, his principal attribute is an **eagle** and is often found, along with the symbols of the other evangelists, carved on pulpits and ambos. According to the *Golden Legend,* John himself said: "The eagle flies higher than any other bird and fixes its eye on the sun."

After having been previously a disciple of John the Baptist, this John, together with James, his older brother, appears at the most important moments in the Gospels (see above on James the Greater); we find him, alone of the apostles, at the foot of the cross, where Jesus entrusted his mother to him. We see him running with Peter to the tomb and then halting to let the older disciple enter first. Later on, he took Mary with him to live in Ephesus. In the mission of evangelization he received Asia Minor as his sphere. At the passing of Mary, he was charged with placing before her bier a palm branch picked by an angel in paradise.

He suffered in the persecution of Domitian around 95; at Rome he was thrown into a tub of boiling oil and on this account, although he survived, he is regarded as a martyr. Accused of practicing magic, he was exiled to Patmos, one of the Sporades islands, seventy kilometers from Ephesus. According to a legend, John brought about the collapse of the temple of Diana by his prayers. Aristodemus, a priest of the goddess, challenged him, promising to convert if John could drink without harm a cup containing a poison so strong that two men condemned to death and forced to drink it as a test died immediately. The apostle not only escaped the danger by making the sign of the cross but also raised the condemned men to life. Aristodemus converted and was baptized. For this reason John is represented with a **cup from which is emerging a serpent**, a sign of poison and evil. Many

Assumption of the Virgin, with Thomas Receiving Mary's Cincture.
Miniature, 2nd half of the 14th cent., from Antiphonarium notatum 7, in the Museum of the Studium Biblicum Franciscanum, Jerusalem.

miracles are told of John; for example, he raised various dead persons and changed straw and pebbles into gold and precious stones; as a result, he was invoked by alchemists.

In the Scriptures his writings consist of a Gospel, three letters, and the Apocalypse. He was over a hundred years old when he died, perhaps in 104, under Trajan.

▷▷ John's traditional patronage of Turkey and Asia Minor, which was connected with his sojourn in Ephesus, was confirmed by Benedict XIV on October 26, 1914. Jesus entrusted the Virgin to his care; as a result he is the patron of virgins and widows. But his patronages arose chiefly because of his writings and because of the sufferings he endured in the tub of boiling oil. As an evangelist, he is protector of theologians, writers, and artists. Because of his sufferings, he is the patron of all who are exposed to the danger of being burned or who have to deal with oil, such as fullers (fulling mills were hydraulic machines). He is the patron of gunsmiths, of candle-makers (because they used to boil the flesh of swine in order to collect the fat), of producers of oil for lamps, and of owners of crushing machines. He is also the patron of printers and typographers (who use a thick ink comparable to oil), of booksellers and bookbinders, copyists, scriveners, and engravers; of papermakers (because the rags are placed in a tub to steep) and stationers. The tub from which John is seen emerging halfway like a vintager, suggested him as patron of vine dressers and also of fullers. Finally, because he transformed straw into gold and pebbles into jewels, he is patron of alchemists, who dreamed of finding the philosopher's stone.

▷▷ He is invoked against burns, poisonings in general, and food poisoning in particular.

▷▷ John's principal attribute is the **eagle**; others are the **cup from which a serpent is emerging**, the **palm branch**, and the **four horsemen of the Apocalypse**, who are depicted as skeletons on horseback and who represent conquest, war, famine, and death. As an evangelist, John is depicted with an opened **scroll**.

Thomas, Apostle

Feast: July 3
Lat.: Thomas, Geminus; Gr.: Didymos; It.: Tommaso, Tomaso, Maso, Masaccio, Masolino; Fr.: Thomas; Sp.: Santo Tomás, Tomé; Ger.: Thomas der Zwilling, der Zweifler, Thoma.

St. Thomas.
18th-cent. bas-relief on the portal of the church of Ort, Austria.

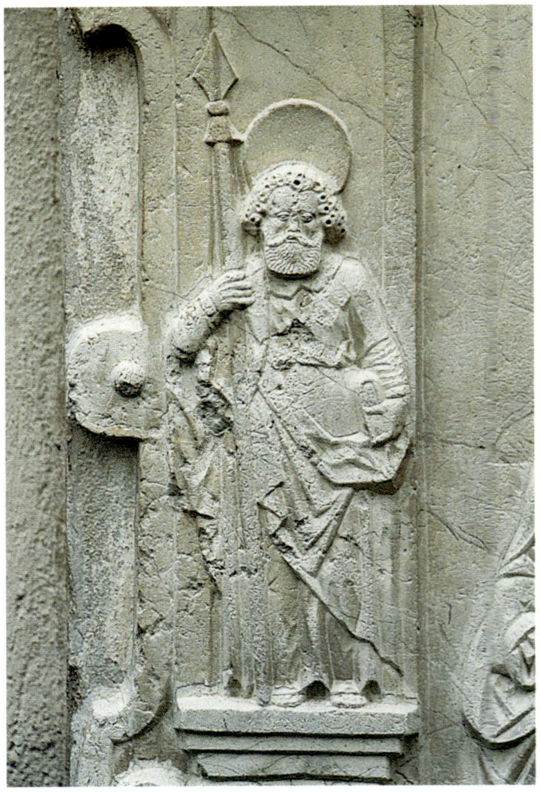

Thomas, whose name in Aramaic, Toma, meant "twin," was for this reason called "Didymus" in Greek. He was a fisherman (John 21:2). It is John who tells of the incidents involving Thomas. When Jesus decides to go the home of Lazarus, Thomas courageously says: "Let us also go, that we may die with him" (John 11:16). His words were courageous, because Jesus was being sought by his enemies and it was dangerous for him to travel openly to Bethany where he could be easily found. Later on, Thomas asks Jesus where the latter is going, so that he might follow him: "Lord, we do not know where you are going. How can we know the way?"; this elicited the well-known and basic answer: "I am the way, and the truth, and the life" (John 14:5-6). Still later, Thomas proved skeptical when his friends told him of the visit of Jesus on Easter evening: "Unless I see the mark of the nails in his hands, and put my finger in the mark of the nails and my hand in his side, I will not believe." But when he in turn met the risen Jesus eight days later he was ready to say: "My Lord and my God!" (John 20:24-29).

Tradition, as recounted in the *Golden Legend,* had him unbelieving once again in regard to the assumption of the Virgin. At the death of Mary, all the apostles except Thomas were present, having been miraculously summoned from the various parts of the world where they were preaching the Gospel. Mary died and Jesus himself was the first to receive her soul as it left her in a manner free of suffering just as she had been free of sin; then he had the apostles place her body in a tomb, and he himself returned after three days to ask the apostles what honor should be given to her who had been his mother. In keeping with their answer, the soul of Mary, accompanied by St. Michael, was reunited with her body and ascended to heaven.

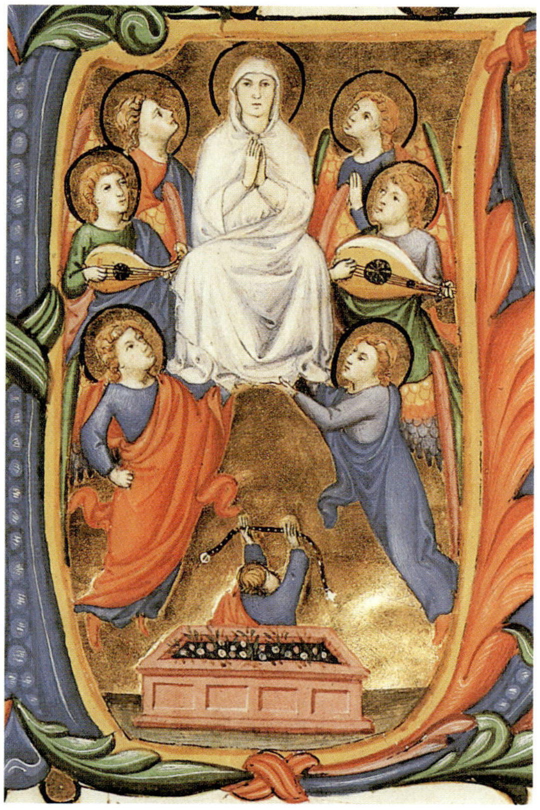

Thomas who had not been present refused to believe. But Mary's sash, intact and (in some depictions) tied, fell into his hands, in order that he might understand that the Mother of God had been taken up bodily (St. Jerome reminds us that incident has symbolic value).

In the apocryphal *Acta* Thomas is said to have been entrusted with the evangelization of Persia; the *Golden Legend* later reports his journey to India, marked by wonderful episodes.

Jesus himself introduced Thomas to an envoy of Gondofer, king of India, who had sent him to find a good architect. On reaching India, Thomas converted the king's daughter and her husband. Thomas then drafted a very beautiful plan for a palace and received in turn riches he gave to the poor. Thus he built a palace for himself, not on earth but in heaven. He then devoted himself to the evangelization of the Indians, but this dissatisfied the king who imprisoned him with the intention of burning him at the stake. But one of the king's brothers, a man whom Thomas had raised from the dead, made Thomas's power known to the king. After a long period of preaching and many miracles, he once again angered the king by reaching marital chastity. The king began to torture him (white-hot iron plates on which Thomas was to walk; a heated furnace), but Thomas emerged unharmed. A pagan priest then killed him by running him through with a sword (or a spear).

Until 1969, Thomas's feast fell on December 21.

▷▷ The most widespread image of Thomas shows him in the act of placing his finger in the wound in Jesus' side; we also see him receiving the Virgin's sash, showing it to the other apostles, and baptizing the Magi.

Because of the legitimate element in his unbelief, that is, because he wanted tangible proof, Thomas is the patron of judges. Because of his help in the building of a palace for the king of India, he is patron of engineers, architects, masons, carpenters, builders generally, and stonecutters. Because of the square he used as a builder, he is also the patron of surveyors, who use the square.

▷▷ He is invoked against afflictions of the eye, because Jesus healed him of his blindness of heart.

▷▷ Principal attributes: the **square** and the **spear**; another attribute: the **Virgin's sash**.

St. James the Lesser.
Painting by Georges de la Tour, 17th cent., in the Musée Toulouse-Lautrec, Albi.
The saint is recognizable from the piece of wood by which he was finally killed after having been thrown down from the walls of Jerusalem, the city whose first bishop he was.

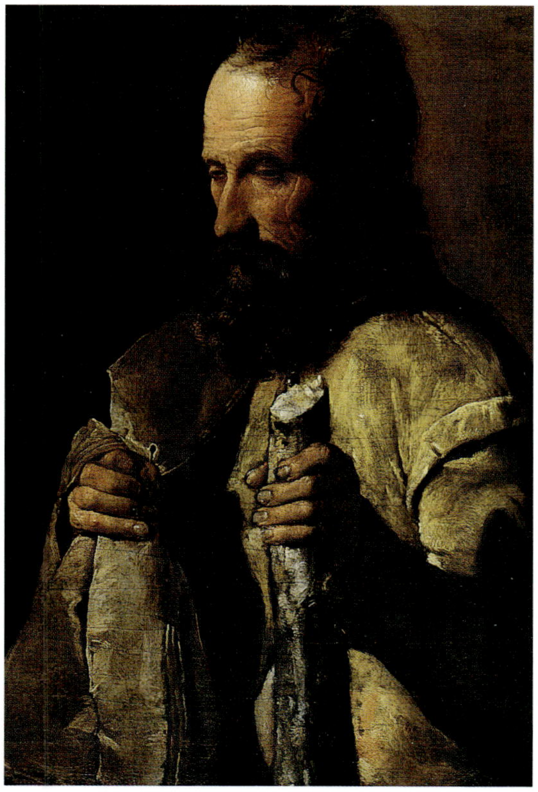

James the Lesser, Apostle

Feast: May 3

Lat.: Jacobus Minor; Fr.: Jacques le Mineur, le Jeune, le Juste; It.: Giacomo il Minore; Sp.: Santiago el Minor, Jaime Alfeo, Jaime el Menor; Ger.: Jakobus der Jüngere, der Kleinere; Dutch: Jacobuis de Mindere.

In the celebration of his feast James the Lesser is associated with Philip; both were disciples of John, were called at the same time, and followed Jesus. This James, known as the Just, was the first bishop of Jerusalem; he intervened in the disagreement over circumcision and maintained that the ancient prescriptions of the Law ought not to be imposed on pagans coming to Christ. He was the son of Alpheus and of Mary of Clopas and was called "Lesser," because he was called by Jesus after James the son of Zebedee. He too, therefore, was a cousin of Jesus, whom he seems to have resembled greatly, so much so that he earned the title "brother of the Lord" (in Greek, *adelphos tou kuriou*).

We have little information about him, in addition to the letter he wrote probably between 57 and 62. The *Golden Legend* contains the tradition about him. It says that he was the first of the apostles to celebrate Mass, this after he became bishop of Jerusalem. After the death of Jesus, he vowed to eat no more food; then Jesus in person appeared to him, had a table prepared, took the bread and blessed, and gave it to James, so that he might begin to eat again.

In 62, in the thirtieth year of his episcopate, the Jews determined to kill him; they tried in every way to make him deny the Lord; failing this, they hurled him from the walls, stoned him, and finished him with a blow from a club.

▷▷ James is the patron of fullers, because he was killed by a fuller's club, and of hatters, because they work with the fulled cloth.

▷▷ He is at times represented as a bishop, and his principal attribute is a pastoral **staff**.

Philip, Apostle

Feast: May 3
Lat.: Philippus Apostolus; Gr.: Philippos; It.: Filippo, Filippino, Lippo, Pippo; Fr.: Philippe, Phelippe, Philippot, Flipot, Flipo, Pot; Sp.: Felipe Apostol; Ger.: Philippus Apostel.

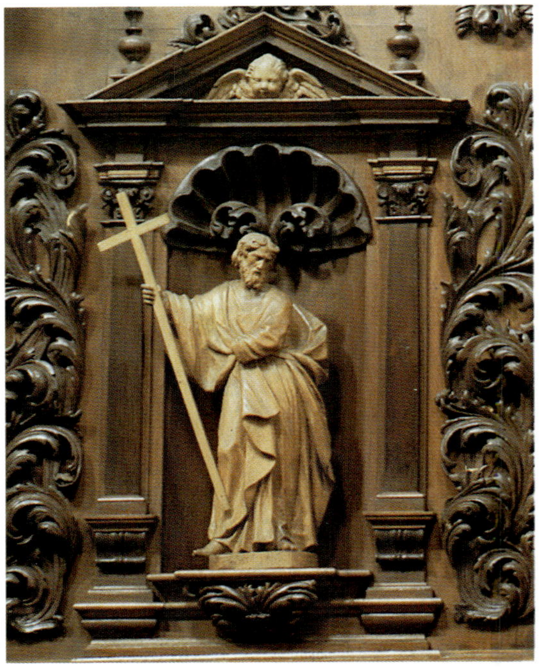

His feast is celebrated together with that of James the Lesser. His name, in Greek, means "friend of horses." He too lived in Bethsaida and it was he who, when calling Nathanael (Bartholomew), first declared Jesus to be the one of whom Moses and the prophets had written (John 1:45). It was he whom some pagans approached in their desire to know Jesus (John 12:21), and it was he who, after the last supper, asked: "Lord, show us the Father, and we will be satisfied" (John 14:8). After this point Scripture says nothing more about him.

Tradition has it that he evangelized Scythia and Phrygia. According to the *Golden Legend,* when he was imprisoned in Scythia by pagans who demanded that he offer sacrifice to the statue of Mars, a dragon emerged from the pedestal of the statue and terrified the bystanders. Philip exhorted them to faith, drove the dragon into the wilderness, healed those who had been wounded, and raised those killed; everyone was converted. Philip's two holy and chaste daughters collaborated with him in his mission. Foretelling that he would die seven days later, he called priests and bishops together in order to instruct them. Seven days later, the pagans imprisoned him; he was crucified, perhaps tied to the cross head downward, and was finished off by blows with stones. His daughters were buried beside him; this happened at Hierapolis in Phrygia.

▷▷ He is represented both bearded and beardless and is often associated with James the Lesser, both men being celebrated on the same day. His principal attribute is a **cross**, sometimes turned upside down; other attributes are the **dragon** and the **stones** by which he was killed.

Bartholomew, Apostle

Feast: August 24
Lat.: Bartholomaeus or Nathanael; It.: Bartolomeo, Bartolo, Baccio, Meo; Fr.: Barthélemy, Barthole, Bartholomé, Bartholomieu, Berthomé, Barthélemy, Berthomieu; Sp.: Bartolomé; Ger.: Bartholomaeus, Barthel, Bartel, Barth; Dutch: Bart.

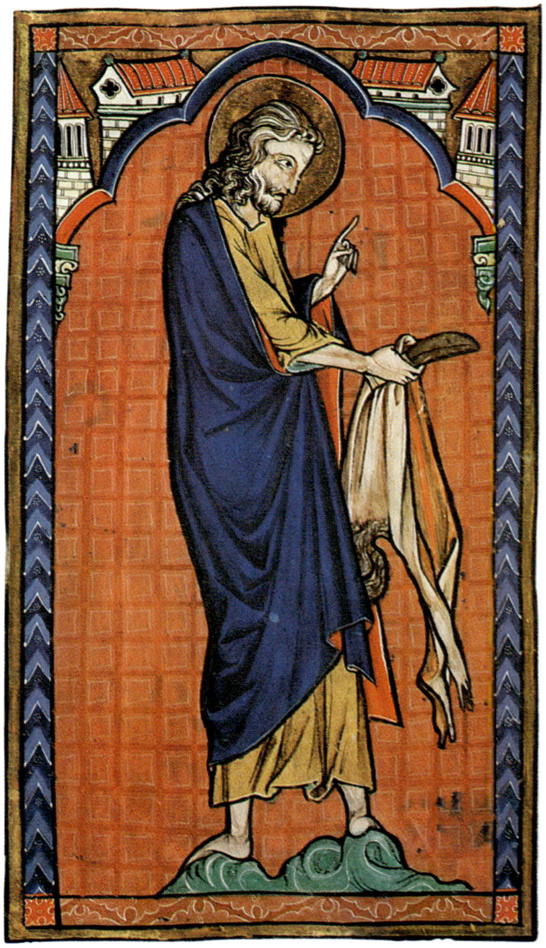

Bartholomew is identified with Nathanael; his name is a patronymic = Bar-Tholomaeus, "son of Tholomaeus." Philip called him and brought him to Jesus, who said to him: "Here is truly an Israelite in whom there is no deceit!" Nathanael asked him: "Where did you get to know me?" and when Jesus said that he had seen him under the fig tree before Philip called him, Nathanael responded: "Rabbi, you are the Son of God! You are the King of Israel." To this, Jesus replied: "You will see greater things than these" (John 1:43-50). Jesus then invited him to follow and made him one of the apostles.

After the ascension, he is supposed to have preached Christ in India. The Gospels say nothing more about him, but a reliable tradition ascribes to him an intensive evangelizing activity in Asia Minor, Mesopotamia, Parthia, and Armenia. In the last-named country he converted the brother of King Astyages and exorcized his daughter. The king was angered by the conversion and had him crucified. Such is the tradition maintained in the East; Western texts claim he was beheaded, while other writers, such as Isidore of Seville and Venerable Bede in his *Martyrology,* claim that he was flayed alive; this last tradition has been the most widespread and the most widely accepted.

▷▷ Because of the martyrdom he suffered, he is protector of all who work with skins or with knives: therefore butchers, tanners, bookbinders, glove makers, shoemakers, and makers of belts. Because he is often represented in the act of carrying his own skin on his arm as though it were a cloak, he is the patron of tailors.

▷▷ He is at times represented as an apostle giving a blessing, a man with dark beard, mustache, and hair, but he is more often shown in his martyrdom. As his principal attribute, he carries **his own skin** on his arm and, to remove all doubt, his face appears on the skin. As a result, he seems at times to be one of the head-carrying saints, that is, one who carries his decapitated head. Another attribute is the **pain-inflicting knife**.

St. Philip.
Statue on an 18th-cent. wooden choir stall, in the cathedral of SS. Cyril and Methodius, Velehrad, Czechoslovakia.
Philip, who was crucified, perhaps upside down like Peter, is distinguished in the series of apostles by a smaller cross.

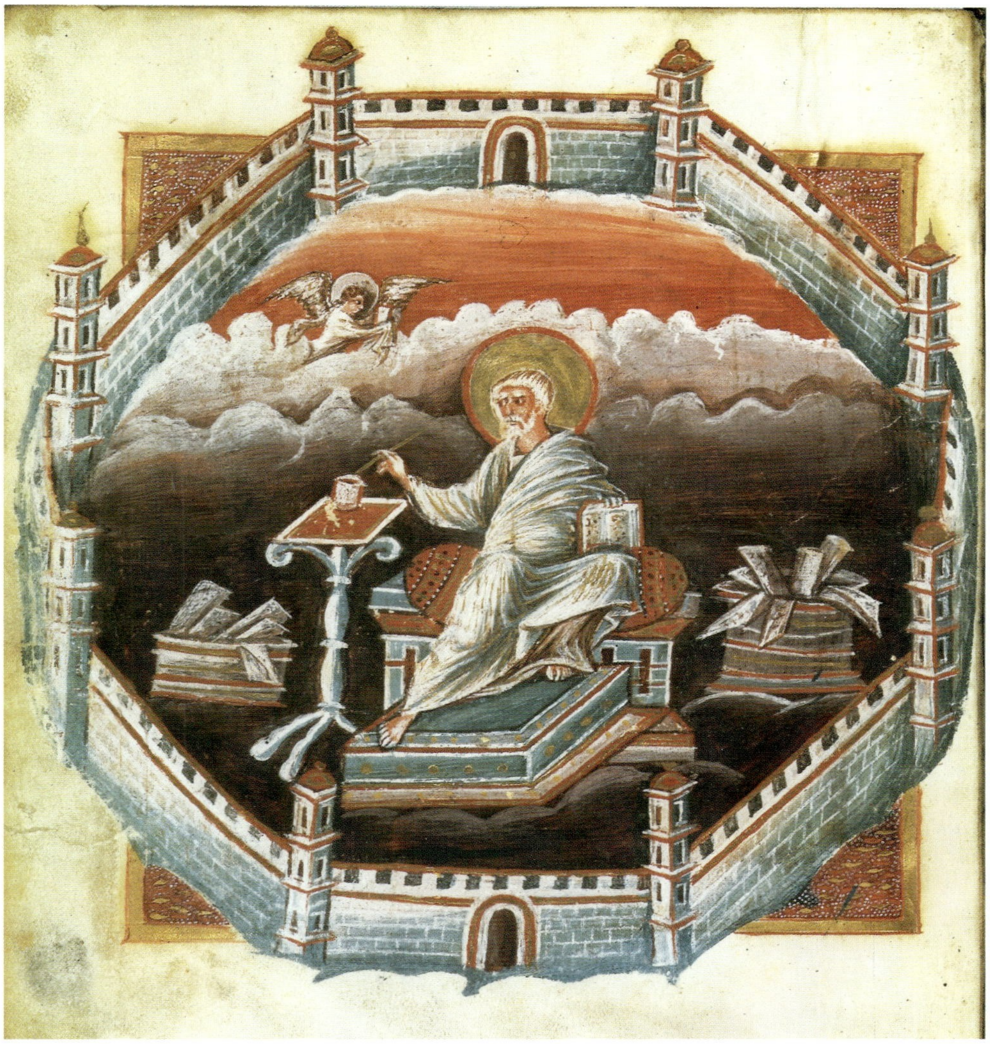

St. Matthew the Evangelist.
Miniature from the 9th-cent. Evangeliary of Santa Aura, in the Bibliothèque de l'Arsenal, Paris.

Matthew, Apostle and Evangelist

Feast: September 21
Lat.: Matthaeus, Mateus; It.: Matteo, Maffeo, Maiolo; Sp.: Mateo; Fr.: Matthieu, Macé, Mahé, Mahieu, Mathé, Mathey, Matthiez, Mathis, Mayeul; Ger.: Matthäus der Zöllner; Dutch: Mattheus de tollenaer.

Levi, son of Alphaeus, known as Matthew, deserted his job as tax collector or "publican," when he was chosen as an apostle. In his Gospel he proclaims that in Jesus Christ, of the line of David, the old covenant found its fulfillment. His Gospel differs from the others in that it opens with the human genealogy of Jesus, and it is this fact that yields Matthew's special emblem, namely, a **human or angelic face**. He is known primarily by the name Matthew, a variant of "Matthias" and a Greek name derived from Hebrew "Matthanja," which means "Gift of God" or "Faithful one." The use of two names can also be seen in Saul-Paul and John-Mark. Matthew's call is narrated in his own Gospel (9:9-13) and in that of Mark (2:13-17). He was a "publican" (Greek: *telônês*), that is, a collector of taxes (in Latin the state treasury was the *publicum*). He lived in Capernaum, where Jesus saw him and called him; Matthew immediately stood up and followed him.

We do not know which region he evangelized after Pentecost; perhaps he went to Ethiopia, perhaps to Syria, Macedonia, or Ireland.

Some say he died a natural death; others, disagreeing about the kind of death, make him a martyr. In fact, he converted King Hegippus of Ethiopia and restored his daughter Iphigenia to life, after which she consecrated herself to God. But Hirtacus, the king's successor, wanted to marry her; when Matthew supported Iphigenia in her refusal, Hirtacus had him slain by the sword as he was celebrating Mass. Others maintain that he was beheaded or burned alive.

St. Bartholomew.
Miniature, ca. 1270, in the Oscott Psalter in the British Museum.

▷▷ By reason of his former occupation, Matthew is the patron of bookkeepers, moneychangers, tax collectors, customs officials and those who pay or redeem a pledge, financiers, bankers, and accountants. On July 27, 1964, Paul VI proclaimed him the patron of all who deal with taxes.

▷▷ His martyrdom is rarely depicted; his calling by Jesus often is, and even more often his role as an evangelist, intent on writing under the inspiration of an **angel**: an **angel** or a **winged man** is his principal attribute. Others, though little used, are those connected either with his work as tax collector, namely, a **money bag** or **scales** for weighing gold or with his martyrdom, namely, the **sword** that killed him.

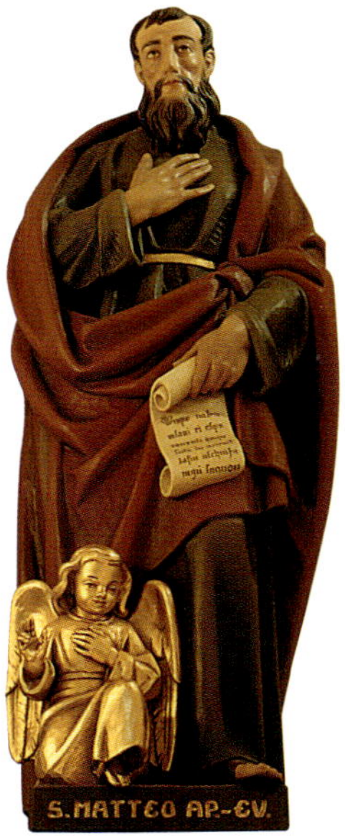

St. Matthew the Evangelist.
20th-cent. processional statue, Savigno, Bologna.

Jude Thaddeus, Apostle

Feast: October 28
Lat.: Judas Thaddaeus, Addaeus; It.: Giuda Taddeo; Fr.: Jude Thaddée; Sp.: Judas Tadeo; Ger.: Judas Thaddäus; Pol.: Tadeusz.

"Thaddeus" in Hebrew means "great hearted"; according to other versions the name is "Lebbeus," which means "courageous." The feast of Jude Thaddeus is celebrated together with that of St. Simon. At the Last Supper Jude asked Jesus why he was manifesting himself only to the apostles; Jesus replied: "Those who love me will keep my word, and my Father will love them, and we will come to them and make our home with them" (John 14:22-23).

Some believe Jude was the bridegroom at the wedding feast of Cana. According to tradition, his mission was primarily to Palestine and neighboring areas. Some assign him a calm death in Edessa; others would have him martyred in Arado, near Beirut.

It was the *Revelations* of St. Bridget that spread devotion to him as a advocate in difficult cases. His cult is very popular in Austria and in Poland, where his name is very widely given to children.

According to the *Golden Legend,* Thomas sent Jude to Abgar, king of Edessa. The latter had written to Jesus, acknowledging his divinity and offering him a refuge from his enemies. In his answer, Jesus had called Abgar blessed for believing without seeing; but since he could not come until he had completed his mission he would send a disciple who would restore him to health. From this letter Abgar understood that he would not see Jesus; he therefore sent a painter who would paint a portrait of Jesus. The painter was unable, however, to capture the features of Jesus, and Jesus therefore helped him: he took a piece of linen, pressed it against his face, and left his image on it; Jude was to take this to Abgar. When Jude reached Abgar, he explained that he was the disciple sent by Jesus; the king saw Jude's face full of resplendent life and recognized him as sent by Jesus to cure the king's leprosy. Jude then took the letter Jesus had sent to Abgar, passed it over the king's face, and cured him. According to tradition, he was later killed, at the age of 70, by a blow from a club at the foot of a statue of Diana.

▷▷ Jude is invoked against the fires of purgatory and in desperate cases. He is therefore the patron of conscripts, since the latter are forced to accept their call.

▷▷ The **cloth with the image of Jesus**, known as *acheiropoietos,* that is, "not made by a [human] hand," has become the principal attribute of Jude Thaddeus, together with the **club** that killed him. He is also represented with a **hatchet** or a **halberd** or a **square**, or even with a **cross on a long shaft**, signifying that he died by crucifixion.

St. Jude Thaddeus.
By Georges de la Tour, 17th cent., in the Musée Toulouse-Lautrec, Albi, France.
The saint is recognizable by the halberd.

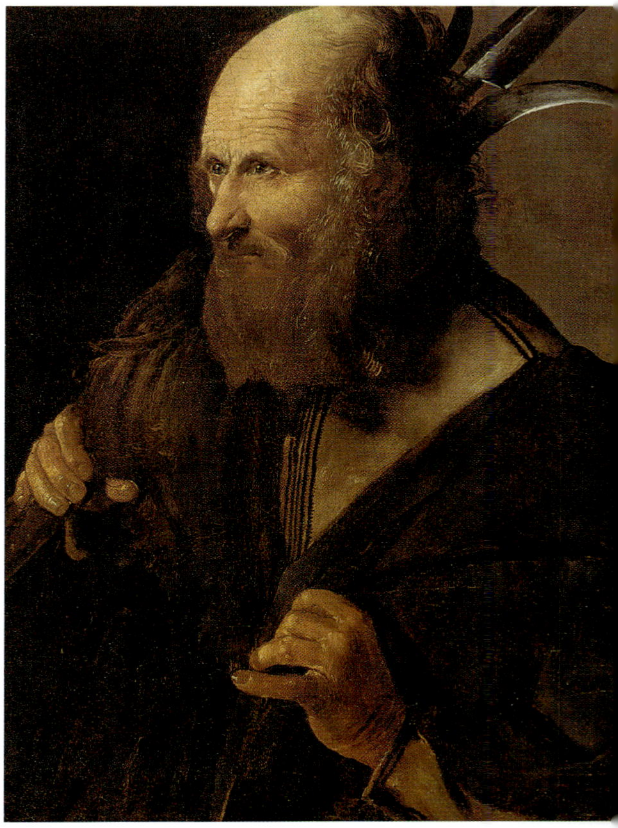

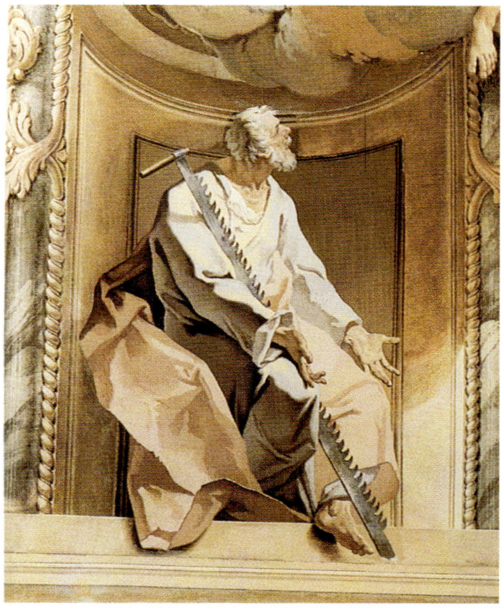

St. Simon.
18th-cent. fresco in the sanctuary of Maria Regina Montis Regalis, Vicoforte, Italy.
According to tradition, Simon was sawn in half; a saw is therefore his attribute.

Simon, Apostle

Feast: October 28
Lat.: Simon Cananaeus; It.: Simone; Fr.: Simon, Simenon, Simonet, Simonin; Ger.: Simon Zelotes; Dutch: De Apostel Simon, de Zelot.

Simon, known as the Canaanite or the Zealot, succeeded James the Lesser as bishop of Jerusalem; in the *Golden Legend* and in the Roman Breviary he is associated with Jude Thaddeus with whom he shares a feast day and with whom he preached the Gospel in Egypt and Mesopotamia.

There is very little known of him. He is depicted with the other apostles around Jesus in the upper room and with them also at other shared moments: Pentecost and the *Dormitio Virginis*.

The *Golden Legend* tells of the life and death of Simon together with Jude Thaddeus; according to other traditions, he was sawn in half.

▷▷ He is patron of those skilled in the cutting of wood, marble, and other materials.

▷▷ His principal attribute is the **saw** of his martyrdom.

Matthias, Apostle

Feast: May 14
Lat.: Matthias apostolus; It.: Mattia; Fr.: Matthia, Mathias, Mathis; Sp.: Matias, Macián; Ger.: Matthias.

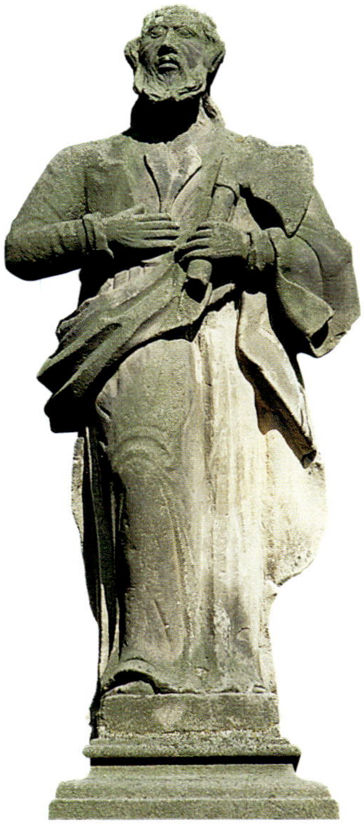

St. Matthias.
18th-cent. statue, Cracow.
An axe was the instrument of his martyrdom.

Matthias was Jewish; the Acts of the Apostles speak of him when they tell how he was chosen to replace Judas Iscariot (Acts 1:15-26). He was one of the disciples who had followed Jesus from the beginning.

His attribute is an axe; the stoning he suffered as an enemy of the Mosaic Law did not kill him, and a Roman soldier beheaded him with an axe.

Several apocryphal works are attributed to him: *The Gospel According to Matthias, The Traditions of Matthias,* and *The Secret Discourses of Jesus and Matthias,* of which we know only a very few passages cited by the Fathers.

▷▷ Because he was beheaded with an **axe**, Matthias is the patron of butchers, of woodworkers and carpenters who use this tool, and of those who make it. Being patron of carpenters, he became patron of engineers as well.

He is invoked against bad coughs.

▷▷ His principal attribute is an **axe**, which is sometimes replaced by a **halberd** or a **sword**.

Mark, Evangelist

Feast: April 26
Lat.: Marcus; It.: Marco; Fr.: Marc Évangéliste, Marc, Mard, Marz, Maz; Sp.: Marcos; Ger.: Markus, Marx.

The Gospel of Mark, written in Greek, is the shortest of the four and gives evidence in its form of containing the observations of an eyewitness, namely, Peter, whose spokesman Mark was. Mark was Jewish, but like many of his period, he had a second name for dealings with non-Jews; this name was John. We saw this phenomenon earlier in Levi-Matthew and Saul-Paul.

His conversion seems to have taken place after the ascension; he was a friend of Paul and Barnabas and had been baptized by Peter, whose secretary he was according to tradition.

Peter sent him to evangelize northern Italy; in Aquileia Mark converted Hermacora. After leaving that city he took to the sea and was overtaken by a storm but reached the Rialtini islands. There he fell asleep and an angel appeared to him with the greeting: "Peace be yours, Mark, my Evangelist," and promised him that he would sleep in these islands as he awaited the last day. This episode is depicted in the lunette over the main door of the basilica of St. Mark; it shows the angel appearing to St. Mark. Another story has it that St. Mark baptized Hermacora and took her to Rome. There St. Peter ordained him a bishop and put him in charge of Aquileia. For this reason, Mark is regarded as the first evangelizer of the Veneto.

Traveling across the sea, Mark became the first bishop of Alexandria in Egypt; there he was martyred in the year 68, and his faithful followers barely managed to save his body from the flames.

From its initial burial place not far from Alexandria, Mark's body reached Venice due to the "pious theft" of it by two Venetian merchants, Buono da Malamocco and Rustio da Torcello. The relics entered the city on January 31, 828, and as early as 829 there was talk of building a basilica in honor of the saint. However, knowledge of the location of the relics was somehow lost. In 1094 Doge Vitale Falier asked that a three-day fast be undertaken in order to find them. At the end of the Triduum, on June 25, the episcopal Mass was followed by a lengthy procession; after a few hours, the marble of one of the columns cracked and made visible the box containing the relics, which filled the entire basilica with perfume. From then on, Venice annually celebrated the translation and the discovery; this came to be known as the *Santa Apparizione di San Marco all'acqua di rosa.*

▷▷ Mark is invoked as a patron in Albania, Dalmatia, present-day Croatia, and, of course, Venice, on whose coat of arms appears a winged lion holding an open Gospel with the words "Peace be yours, Mark, my Evangelist." As an evangelist, he is a patron of painters. In his role as secretary of Peter, he is a patron of interpreters, copyists, clerks of the court, and notaries. Because he had St. Anianus, a shoemaker, adjust his sandals and because he healed Anianus of a wound inflicted by his awl, Mark is the patron of shoemakers and tanners. As patron of Venice, he is also patron of glass makers and therefore, too, of spectacle makers and opticians. Since his relics were hidden in a basket, he is the patron of basketmakers. He is invoked against scabies.

▷▷ Mark is represented mainly as an evangelist, and his principal attribute is a **lion**, sometimes winged, because he begins his Gospel by speaking of John the Baptist, whose voice was like the roar of a lion in the wilderness.

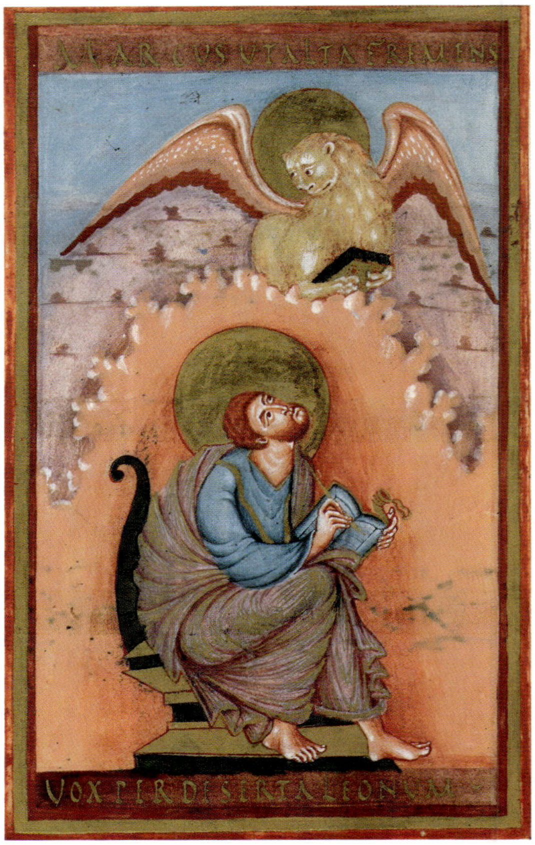

St. Mark the Evangelist.
Miniature, 849–851, from the Evangeliary of Lothar, Tours; now in the Bibliothèque Nationale, Paris.

Luke, Evangelist

Feast: October 18
Lat.: Lucas, from Lucanus; Gr.: Loukas; It.: Luca; Fr.: Luc l'Évangéliste, Laux, Lu; Sp.: Lucas; Ger.: Lukas Evangelist.

Luke was a Hellenized Jew, born in Antioch and converted by St. Paul, whom he accompanied on his travels and with whom he remained until the latter's martyrdom. He was a physician, an educated man, and able to paint; he wrote the Third Gospel, which is the one most attentive to the person and role of Mary. He begins his Gospel with the sacrifice offered by Zechariah, and for this reason his emblem is an **ox**. In the Acts of the Apostles he describes the life of the early Church. After Paul's death, Luke continued to evangelize Egypt and Greece. One tradition has him crucified at Patras, along with Andrew. Another has him meeting death in Damascus.

A tradition that goes back to at least the second century says that Luke painted a portrait

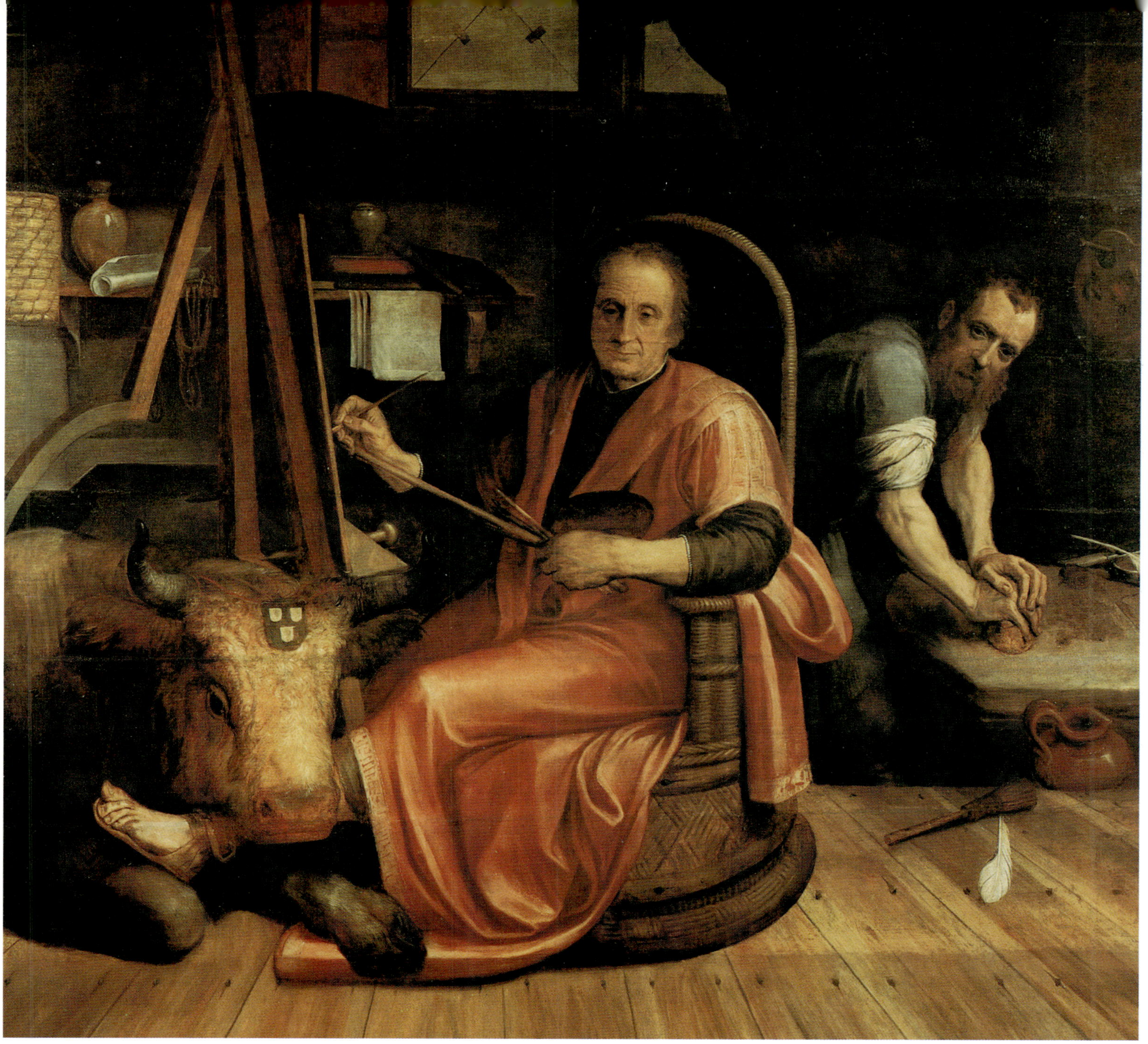

St. Luke Paints the Madonna.
By Floris de Vriendt, 15th cent., Antwerp. In the Royal Museum of the Fine Arts.
The viewer is looking at this picture through the eyes of the Virgin as she faces the evangelist who is painting her portrait.

of the Virgin and that she herself approved of his work and extended her blessing to all who paint and to those who contemplated this and other pictures.

▷▷ Luke is the patron of physicians. Because he painted a portrait of the Virgin, he is the patron of artists, painters, sculptors, and miniaturists. Because of the ox at his feet, he is the patron of butchers and also of tanners, who use the skins of oxen.

▷▷ The tradition that Luke was a painter not only provided a foundation for the defense of images but also determined one of the most common representations of Luke, that in which he is shown **in the presence of the Virgin and in the act of painting** on a canvas set on an easel.

He is also shown in the act of writing his Gospel; in these instances his principal attribute is always present, namely, an **ox** (because his Gospel opens with the sacrifice offered by Zechariah).

Other attributes are the **portrait of Mary with the infant** and a **physician's instruments**.

Barnabas of Cyprus

Memorial: June 11
Lat.: Barnabas Cyprius; It.: Barnaba; Fr.: Barnabé de Chypre; Sp.: Bernabè; Ger,: Barnabas.

The Bible describes him as a good man, filled with faith and the Holy Spirit; he was a Cypriot by origin and was called an "apostle" by reason of the authority he exerted and his relationship with Paul. He was one of the seventy-two disciples of Jesus; his baptismal name was Joseph, and it was the apostles who called him "Barnabas," which means "son of consolation" and also "son of preaching." It was he who introduced the newly converted Paul to the apostles and who prepared him for his mission; he himself became Paul's disciple and followed him on his first journey.

▷▷ Barnabas was very closely connected with Matthew and worked miraculous cures simply by placing on the sick person's head or chest the **book** of the Gospel of Matthew, which became his principal attribute.

He returned to Cyprus and preached Christ there; in 63 he was stoned and, when this did not kill him, was burned alive at Salamis in Cyprus.

When his remains were discovered in 458, the manuscript of Matthew's Gospel was with them.

▷▷ He is invoked against hail, an allusion to the stones by which his death was attempted.

▷▷ He is represented as an elderly or mature man, and his principal attribute is the **book of Matthew's Gospel**; another attribute is the **stones by which his death was attempted**.

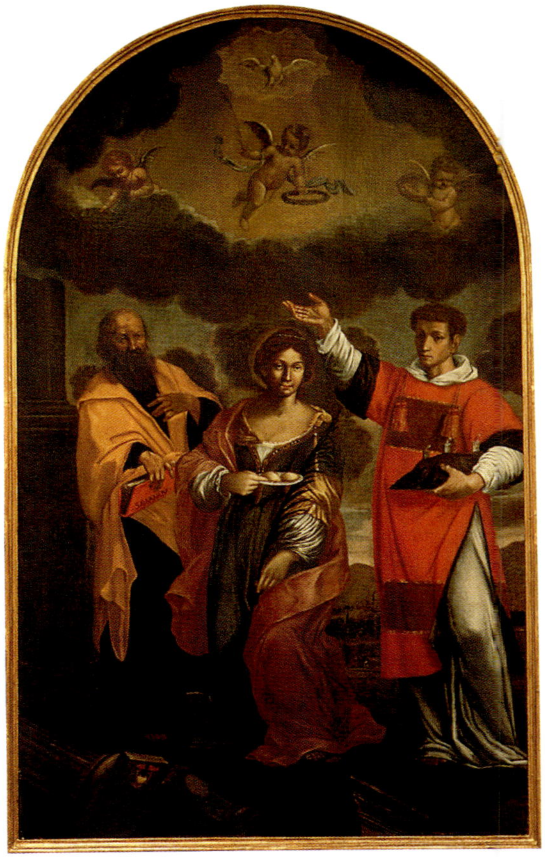

Stephen, the First Martyr

Feast: December 26
Lat.: Stephanus Protomartyr; Gr.: Stephanos; It.: Stefano; Fr.: Étienne, Estèphe, Estève, Estien, Estienne, Stapin, Stéphane, Thévin, Thévenot; Sp.: Esteban, Estevan; Port.: Estevaõ; Ger.: Stephanus der Erzmärtyer, Steffel, Steff; Hung.: István; Russ.: Arkchidiakone Stenka.

In Greek the name Stephen means "crown," and he was the first to wear the crown of martyrdom in Jerusalem; he also contemplated Christ in glory, seated at the Father's right hand. In Acts (6:5-15), when it became necessary for the apostles to devote themselves full-time to preaching and to leave *diakonia* or service, that is, caritative works, to others, the apostles chose for this task seven men "of good standing, full of the Spirit and of wisdom." Those chosen were Stephen, "a man full of faith and the Holy Spirit," along with six others. Among the seven, Stephen stood out as a man "full of grace and power," who "did great wonders and signs among the people"; no one could "withstand the wisdom and the Spirit with which he spoke." He was falsely accused of blasphemy against Moses and against God, was taken prisoner and dragged off for judgment; but all who looked at him "saw that his face was like the face of an angel."

Stephen then (Acts 7) delivered an impassioned discourse in which he linked Christ with the witnesses in the Scriptures; this only infuriated the onlookers all the more, and when he said: "Look! I see the heavens opened and the Son of Man standing at the right hand of God," they dragged him outside the city, to the very place where Christ had been crucified, and stoned him. Like Jesus, Stephen prayed for his executioners. "Devout men buried Stephen and made loud lamentation over him" (Acts 8:2).

Tradition has it that Gamaliel buried him; four hundred years later Stephen revealed, in a vision, the place of his burial. In fact, his relics were discovered in 415 and distributed throughout the Christian world, thereby expanding a cult that was already practiced and giving rise to many churches in his honor.

▷▷ Stephen is listed among the saints who are healers. People used to place flowers on his altar that were later placed on the sick to alleviate their sufferings, just as the linens from his altar were used to heal illnesses affecting the marrow and bones.

He is the patron of slingers (those who threw stones from slings) as well of stonecutters and masons.

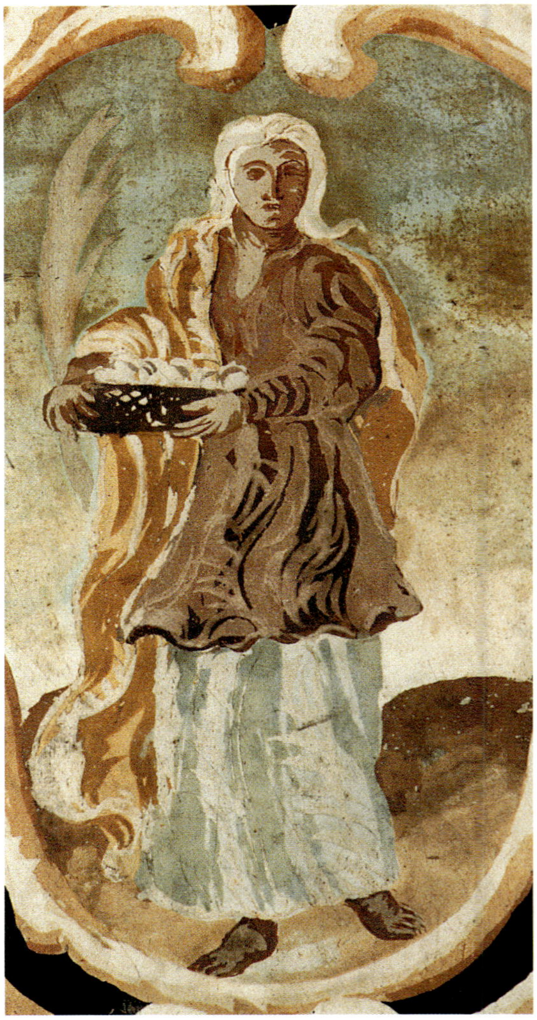

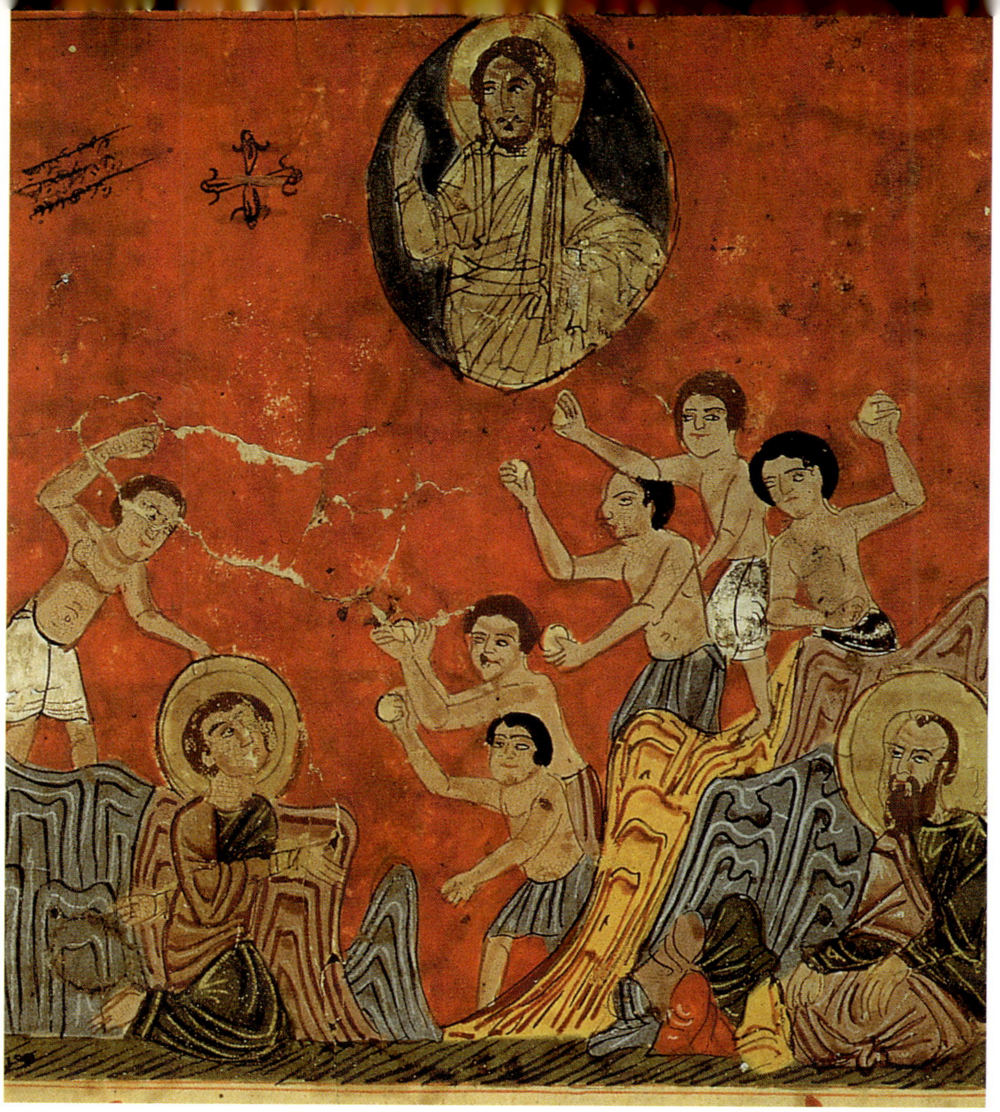

The Stoning of St. Stephen.
Miniature from a medieval Syriac Evangeliary in the Vatican Library, Rome.
The work faithfully reflects the passage in Acts; note also the presence of St. Paul, who is recognizable by his features and who holds the clothing of the persecutors (see Acts 7:57).

St. Barnabas with St. Agatha and St. Marinus.
By Girolamo Cialdieri, 1622, in the Church of St. Paul, Faetano, Republic of San Marino.
St. Barnabas is identified by the Gospel of Matthew, which he is holding in his hands and by which he worked miracles.

St. Stephen, Protomartyr.
Altar frontal in plaster, 18th cent., in the church of San Nicolò di Villola, Bologna.
The stones with which he was killed are the principal attribute of St. Stephen, but they can be variously arranged; here he holds them as in a basket for offerings.

One legend made him an equerry of Herod; he therefore became the patron of horses, coachmen, and grooms. He is invoked against ringworm (French: *teigne*), simply because of the resemblance in sound of *teigne* and *Étienne*.

Because he was stoned, he is invoked against illnesses involving stones, against headaches, and against illnesses of the spinal marrow.

▷▷ He is depicted as young and beardless, wearing a **dalmatic** (because this later became the liturgical vestment of deacons). His principal attribute is the **stones** hurled at him.

Eustachius, Martyr

2nd century
Commemoration: September 20
Lat.: Eustachius, Eustacius, Eustathius, Eustasius; Gr.: Eustathos; It.: Eustachio, Eustazio, Stae (Venetian dialect); Fr.: Eustache, Eustace, Eustasse, Eustathe, Huistace, Vitasse, Wistace; Sp.: Eustaquio; Ger.: Eustachius, Stachus.

Eustachius is listed among the Helpers, and his history is part of a family history. His original name was "Placid," and that probably was a good description of the man. He was a general under Trajan (53–117) and in character was generous and kindly.

In the story of his conversion we hear an echo of that of Paul. While he was out hunting and pursuing a beautiful deer, the animal suddenly halted, turned, and addressed him: "Placid, why do you pursue me? I am Jesus, whom you honor without realizing it."

Placid promptly had himself, his wife, and his sons baptized, and the four changed their names to, respectively, Eustachius, Theopista, Theopistus, and Agapius. When he returned to the place of this marvelous occurrence, a mysterious voice told him that he would be tried as Job had been. While he and his entire family were emigrating to Egypt, the captain

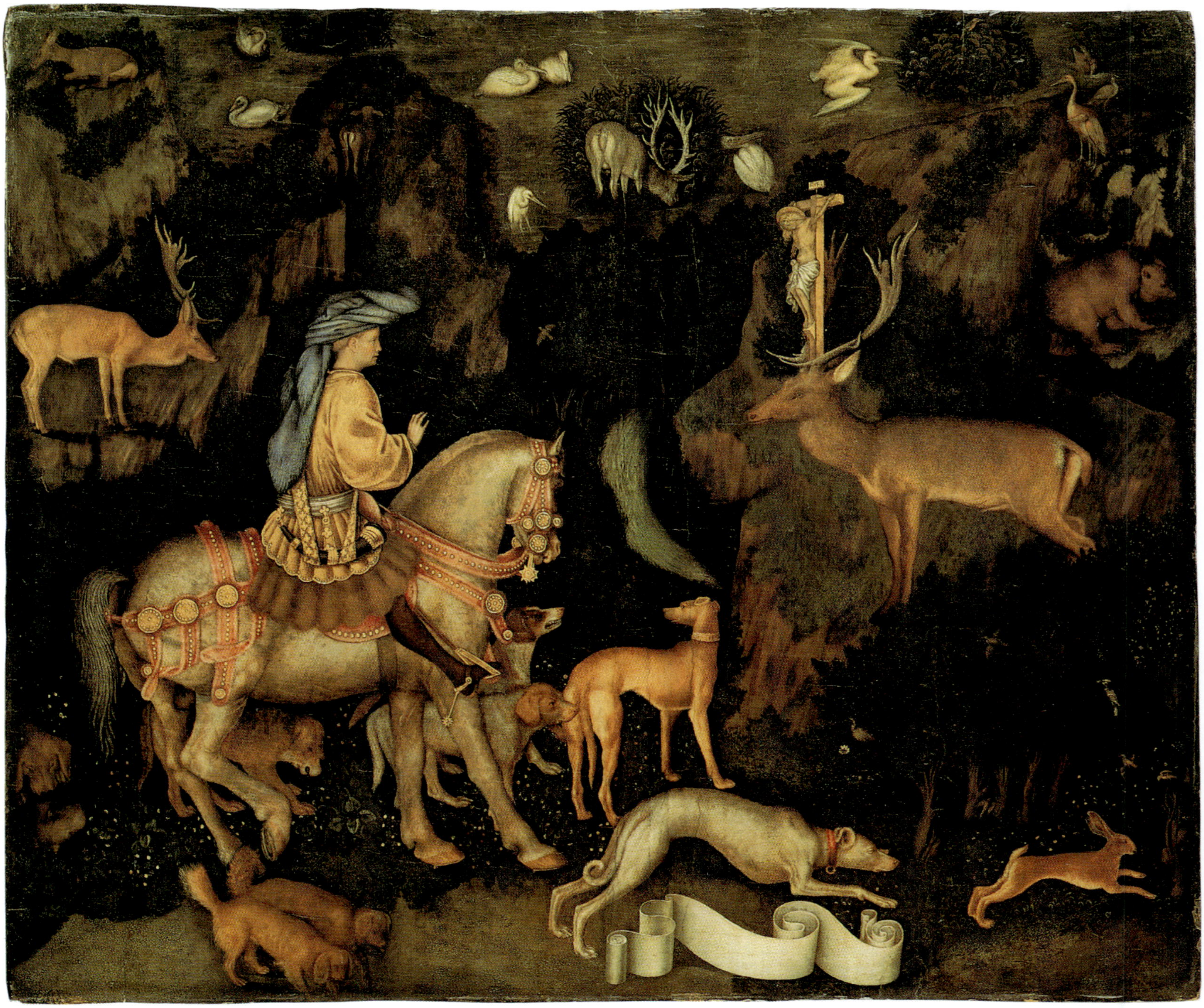

of the vessel took his wife from him because he did not have the money to pay the fare; hardly had they disembarked when a lion and a wolf seized his sons, who were subsequently rescued by people of the place, and they grew up in the same village without knowing one another. Fifteen years passed, and the barbarians were threatening the borders of the empire. At this point, Trajan remembered his former skilled and experienced general; he had him sought out and brought to Rome, where he was placed at the head of the imperial troops. He attempted to add new recruits; among the latter were his own sons, whom he did not recognize but who seemed to him to be so effective that he made them noncommissioned officers and his companions at table.

After the victory over the barbarians, Eustachius halted with his troops near the village in which his wife was living after the death of the sea captain. It was of her that the two young men asked for hospitality; soon, as they told one another their stories, the two realized that they were brothers; the mother did not reveal herself to them but on the following

Vision of St. Eustachius.
From the studio of Pisanello, 15th cent., in the National Gallery, London.

day she went to ask the commander that she might return to her native land; she then recognized him as her husband, and the family was reunited.

Eustachius was welcomed as victor by Hadrian, who had meanwhile succeeded Trajan. But when Eustachius refused to offer sacrifice to Apollo, they were all condemned to be devoured by the wild beasts in the circus. But the beasts were unable to touch them. They were then placed inside a bronze ox that was heated red-hot; they died immediately, but their bodies were not burned.

On the spot where Christians gave them their initial worthy burial a chapel was built in the time of Constantine, and their *dies natalis* was celebrated on November 1.

▷▷ From this lengthy and complicated history the iconographers selected, for emblematic treatment, the miraculous hunt of Eustachius, who is seen garbed as a warrior or hunter and kneeling before a large deer in whose horns the cross is enthroned; less frequent are depictions of his martyrdom, in which the heads and shoulders of the martyrs are seen emerging from the back of a bull.

Historical criticism has declared the story of Eustachius to be without foundation, but the man himself is very well known; his cult is alive and widespread throughout central Europe. Even the picture simply of an **cross-bearing deer** is an allusion to him.

▷▷ The extraordinary spread of his cult is due to the fact that he represents, above all else, the possibility of a miraculous occurrence leading to conversion (this being made easier in his case by his natural goodness), while he also reminds us that the blessing of conversion is often followed by numerous tribulations, for the greater glory of God. For this reason, he is invoked in "difficult cases."

His reputation spread chiefly in France in the twelfth century; in the medieval world, the scene of the hunt, early in his life, became the source of numerous patronages.

▷▷ Eustachius is the patron of hunters, watchmen, and foresters, and, because of the connection with hunting and skins, he is the patron also of furriers, drapers, and shoemakers. His principal attribute is the **cross-bearing deer**; others are **instruments of the hunt** and the **hunting horn**.

St. Lawrence.
Statue, from the 18th cent., on the bridge over the Otava river in Písek, Czech Republic.

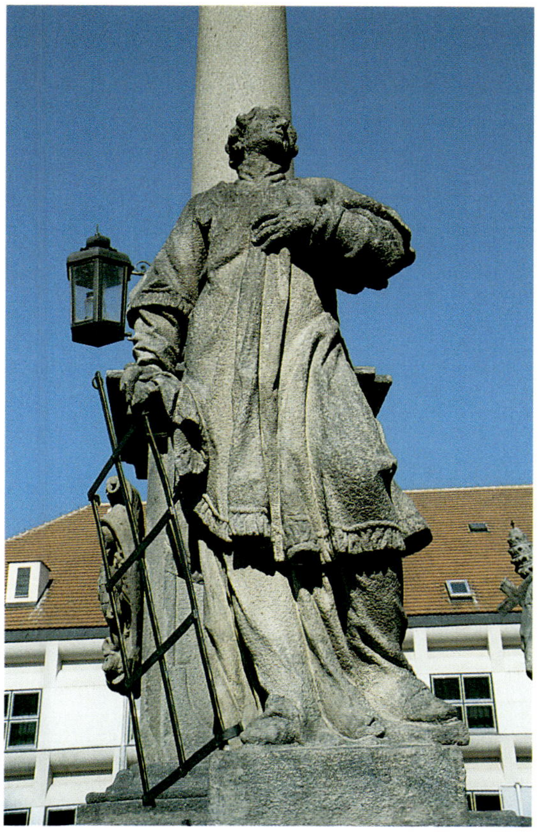

Lawrence, Deacon and Martyr

† August 10, 258
Feast: August 10
Lat.: Laurentius; It.: Lorenzo; Fr.: Laurent diacre, Laurens, Lorens, Lorint; Sp.: Lorenzo; Port.: Lourenço; Ger.: Laurentius, Lorenz; Swed.: Lars; Pol.: Wawrzyniec; Russ.: Lavrentii.

The falling stars that cleave the heavens on the night of August 10 are known as "the tears of St. Lawrence."

Lawrence was a young deacon; his task, like that of St. Stephen, was to help the poor from offerings made by Christians. According to one tradition, he was a native of Huesca in Spain, but later became known to Sixtus II, who brought him to Rome and appointed him an archdeacon. Later, Lawrence met Sixtus II when the latter was being led to martyrdom, and he wanted to follow the Pope but Sixtus exhorted him instead to follow him in virtue. The prefect, knowing that the archdeacon was in charge of the Church's treasures, ordered him to hand them over to him; Lawrence asked to be spared for three days. He sold the valuables, distributed the proceeds to the poor, then gathered these poor together, and presented them to the prefect: "Here are our treasures; you can find them everywhere." He was then led out to be tortured; his martyrdom made a deep impression and became tinged with legend. Pope Damasus spoke of floggings, torturers, flames, burning coals, and other torments. Tradition has it that he was placed on a **grate** over burning coals. After a while, he turned to the executioners and said: "I'm well done on this side; turn me on the other." The day was August 10, 258.

Lawrence is the Roman equivalent of St. Stephen: his name figures in the earliest lists of martyrs; his body was secretly carried to the cemetery on the Tiburtine Way; Constantine himself later had Lawrence's tomb embellished.

Another legend claims that every Friday Lawrence descends from heaven into purgatory and takes a soul back to heaven with him.

▷▷ He is the patron of the poor. Because as deacon he safeguarded the sacred books, he is the patron of librarians, bibliophiles, and booksellers. Because of the care he took of the poor, he is the patron also of innkeepers and hoteliers.

Because of his sufferings he is the patron of those whose work puts them in danger of being burned: firemen, coalmen, bakers, cooks, glassblowers, and pressers, who at one time used to fill their irons with coals. In Sicily, an image of Lawrence is applied to burns.

He is invoked against fires, burns, lumbago (because a symptom of this is a burning sensation in the kidneys), and against the fires of purgatory. In France he is invoked against a form of eczema known as "St. Lawrence's fire."

▷▷ There are many depictions of his martyrdom; he is almost always shown as a young, beardless man, wearing a **dalmatic**; his main attribute is the **grate** on which he suffered martyrdom.

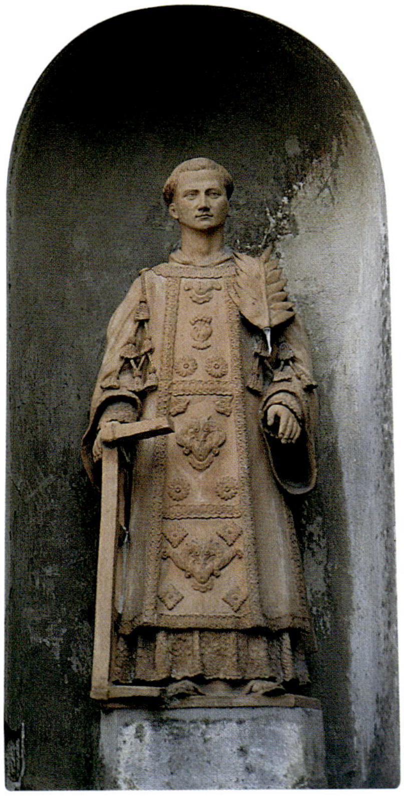

St. Lawrence.
A 17th-cent. statue in the Charterhouse of Galluzzo, Florence.
The statue clearly shows the dalmatic that distinguishes the saint. The dalmatic is the liturgical vestment, often of richly woven cloth, that was proper to deacons, that is, to those in charge of serving their brothers and sisters.

Cecilia, Virgin and Martyr

3rd century
Memorial: November 22
Lat.: Caecilia, Ceciia; Fr.: Cécile; Sp.: Cecilia; Ger.: Cäcilia, Cilli, Zilli.

Cecilia, a Christian, was engaged to Valerian, a young pagan; on her wedding night, Cecilia told her husband that an angel of God was protecting her virginity, and she urged him to convert; then he would be able to see the angel. She urged him to go out on the Appian Way, to the third milestone, where the poor would point out holy Pope Urban to him. The Pope instructed Valerian and baptized him; he then returned to Cecilia, and the angel crowned them both. Valerian asked the angel for the favor of the conversion of his brother, Tiburtius; when this took place, the two brothers devoted themselves to burying the victims of persecution. For this they were denounced and were executed by beheading. Cecilia placed their bodies in a sarcophagus and was in her turn condemned; she avoided the flames, however, and was to be beheaded, but, despite being struck three times, she survived for three days, during which she distributed her possessions to the poor and urged the Pope to turn her home into a church. The Pope saw to her burial.

▷▷ Cecilia has been regarded as the patron of singers and musicians, because we are told in her *Passion,* or account of her sufferings, that while she was preparing to celebrate her marriage, "as the musical instruments were being played, she sang in her heart to God alone" *(decantantibus organis, in corde suo soli Domini decantabat).* In the first antiphon for Matins on her feast day we read: "While the musical instruments were playing, the virgin Cecilia sang in her heart to her only Lord, 'May my heart, O Lord, and my body be immaculate, that I may not be put to shame.'"

According to tradition, after she had been buried by Pope Urban, her body was rediscovered by Pope Pascal I (817–824); the saint is said to have appeared to him and showed him where to look for her body. The Pope then placed the body in a church dedicated to her, but he put the head in an urn that was transferred to the church of the Four Crowned Saints.

In 1599 an investigation was carried out, and the saint's body was found to be intact and lying on its side. A statue by Stefano Maderno, commissioned by Clement VIII, shows the scene as it appeared at the time.

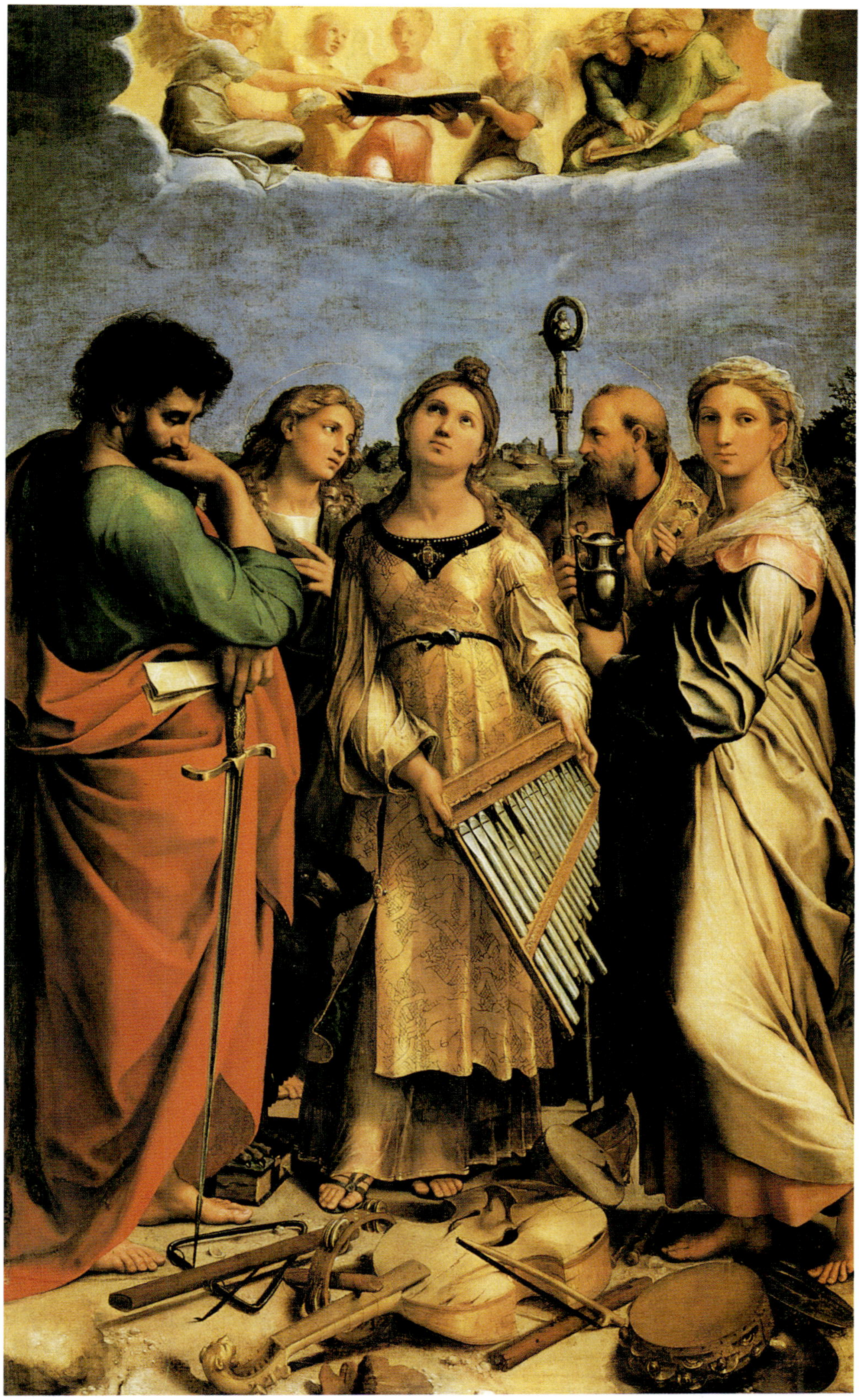

Ecstasy of St. Cecilia, Who Is Accompanied by SS. Paul, John the Baptist, Augustine, and Mary Magdalene. Altar piece by Raphael Sanzio, 1515, for the church of San Giovanni in Monte, Bologna, where a copy may now be seen. The original is in the Art Gallery of Bologna.

▷▷ Cecilia is patron of musicians and of the makers of any kind of musical instrument, as well as of poets.

▷▷ She is depicted in cycles that tell her story, as well as that of Valerian and Tiburtius. Mainly, however, she is shown holding a **musical instrument**, which is her principal attribute. Other attributes are a **crown of roses and lilies** and a **wound in her neck**.

Columba of Sens, Virgin and Martyr

† 273
Memorial: December 31
Lat.: Columba Senonensis; Fr.: Colombe de Sens, Colomme, Coulombe; Sp.: Columba, Coloma, Comba; Port.: Comba; Ger.: Kolumba.

Columba, whose original name was perhaps Eporita, came from a noble pagan family of Saragossa; she fled to Vienne and was baptized, receiving the baptismal name of Columba. She continued on to Sens, where she underwent martyrdom in 273, in the time of Aurelian, who wanted her to marry his son.

She was locked up in a brothel in the amphitheater, but when a man approached her, a **she-bear** defended her and forced him to acknowledge that she was adoring the true God.

Aurelian wanted both the she-bear and the young woman to be burned alive, but the bear managed to escape and a providential rain put out the fire. Finally, Columba was condemned to be beheaded. A man who had prayed to her and had recovered his sight saw to her burial.

▷▷ Although the story was hardly historical, the cult of Columba spread, and she became the patron of Andorra. By reason of her name she is protector of doves. She is invoked to obtain rain and avoid drought.

▷▷ Her principal attribute is the **she-bear**. The palm of martyrdom is sometimes replaced by a **peacock's feather**.

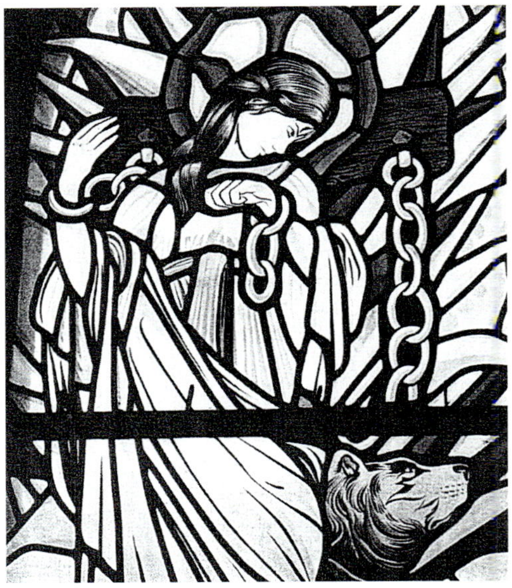

St. Columba of Sens.
Stained-glass window in the church dedicated to the patron saint of the city; 20th cent.
The she-bear can be seen that defended the martyr.

Apollonia of Alexandria, Virgin and Martyr

† 249
Commemoration: February 9
Lat.: Apollonia; Fr.: Apolinne, Apollonie, Pollonie, Polline; Sp.: Apolonia de Alejandria, Santa Polonia; Ger.: Apollonia, Ploni.

Eusebius speaks of this saint in his *History of the Church;* her *Passion* describes her as an "elderly virgin," but, like all the holy virgins, she is depicted in the bloom of a symbolic youthfulness. There are two stories of her martyrdom. One is that during a violent uprising against Christians she was, despite her blameless life, attacked by a mob; when she refused to offer sacrifice to idols she was struck in the mouth with stones so that her teeth were knocked out. The other is that an executioner pulled out her teeth, one by one, with pincers. When threatened with death at the stake, she refused to blaspheme and finally threw herself into the flames.

▷▷ Her cult is widespread throughout the world. She protects against toothache and is patron of dentists and of those who suffer from their teeth.

▷▷ Her principal attribute is the **pincers**, which are often shown holding a **tooth**.

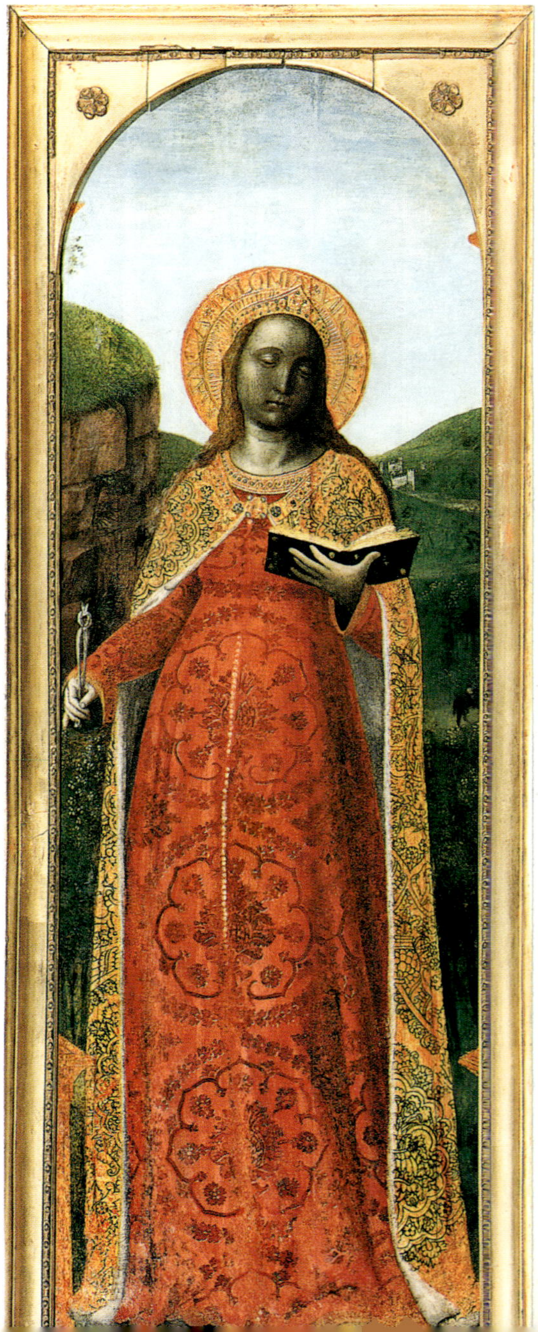

Cyprian of Carthage, Bishop and Martyr

ca. 200 to 258
Memorial: September 16
Lat.: Thacius Caecilius Cyprianus Carthaginiensis; Fr.: Cyprien de Carthage, Civran, Cybranet, Subran, Subrin, Syvran; Sp.: Cebrian; Ger.: Cyprian von Karthago.

This bishop of Carthage was one of the most important saints of Christian Africa in the third century; he is patron of North Africa. Cyprian was born in Carthage, around 200, of a family that was perhaps originally from Cyprus; he was a teacher of rhetoric and led a dissolute life until he was almost twenty-five years old or perhaps even until he was forty. He did not believe that he could change and was completely astonished by his own conversion, which he thought of as a rebirth that made him say: "Everything we are able to do comes from God." His was a radical conversion: he practiced a strict poverty, chastity, and obedience, distributed his possessions among the poor, and devoted himself to the study of Scripture and the works of Tertullian.

Ordained a priest in 248, he became bishop of Carthage in 249 by popular acclamation. His pastoral activities were interrupted by the persecution of Decian (250), which occurred after twenty years of peace for Christians. He became involved in the controversy over the readmission to the community of the "fallen" *(lapsi),* that is, those who out of fear had denied their faith. This question was one that plagued the Church for a long time and led to

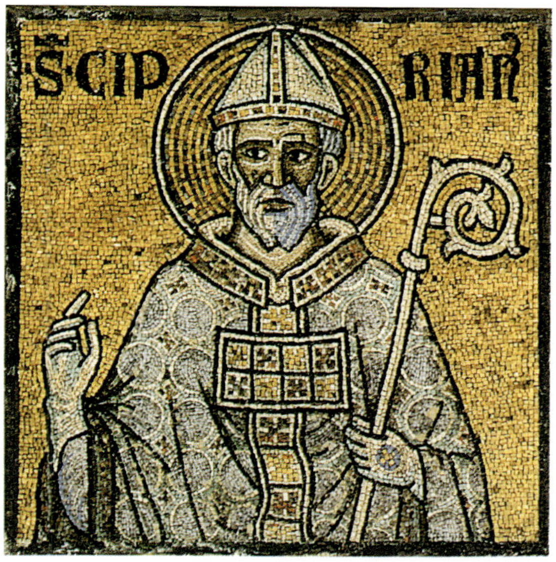

St. Cyprian of Carthage.
Mosaic by the Master of St. Cecilia's, 1300–1310, in the Baptistry of San Giovanni, Florence.

schisms and defections. Cyprian also had to deal with the tragedy of the serious plague that spread through Africa in 252–254: he exhorted all to show charity, helped the sick, whether Christian or pagan, and skillfully organized the steps to be taken.

In 257 came the persecution under Valerian: Cyprian was interrogated and exiled a short distance from the city; in the following year an edict was promulgated prescribing the death sentence for Christians. The persecution was aimed especially at the hierarchy, and Cyprian was recalled, questioned, and condemned to be beheaded. He himself put aside his dalmatic, tied the blindfold over his eyes, and gave the executioner twenty-five gold pieces; his disciples then tied his hands. After his martyrdom, the faithful removed his body during the night and buried it beside the road to Massalia. His relics are venerated today in Lyons and in the abbey of Compiègne.

▷▷ Cyprian was declared the patron of North Africa by Pius X on July 6, 1914, by Pius XII on January 10, 1958, and by John XXIII on July 27, 1962. On March 25, 1949, Pius XII proclaimed him the patron of Algeria. He is invoked against plagues.

▷▷ Cyprian is depicted with a short beard and white hair and, sometimes, seated at a writing table. He is singled out by his **episcopal garb**, and his attributes are the **sword** by which he was beheaded, and the **crown of martyrdom**.

Dionysius (Denis) of Paris, Bishop and Martyr

3rd century
Memorial: October 9
Lat.: Dionysius Parisiensis; It.: Dionigi, Dionigio, Dionisio; Fr.: Denis de Paris, Denys, Dyonis, Danis, Daunes, Denizot, Nisard; Sp.: Dionisio; Ger.: Dionysius von Paris, Dionys.

St. Apollonia.
By Vincenzo Foppa (1447–1515).
The saint holds a tooth in the pincers of her martyrdom; she is reading the gospel, thereby showing that she found her strength in Christ.

This Dionysius was at one time erroneously identified with Dionysius the Areopagite. In fact, according to Gregory of Tours, he was a monk whom Pope Fabius sent to evangelize Gaul around the middle of the third century. He was beheaded in Paris, together with his companions, Rusticus and Eleutherius.

Such is the historical basis of the tradition claiming that Dionysius was converted by St. Paul, who appointed him bishop of Athens, from where he later went off to preach in Paris. He was imprisoned there by the Roman prefect and brought for judgment along with Eleutherius, a priest, and Rusticus, a deacon. He was flogged and then roasted like St. Lawrence; with the sign of the cross he drove away the wild beasts; he was thrown into a fire and crucified. Despite all this, he did not die, but was led back to prison; there Jesus himself came and gave him Communion through the bars of his cell. Finally, on the hill known as Montmartre (Hill of the Martyrs), Eleutherius and Rusticus were beheaded by an axe and Dionysius by a cleaving sword. Dionysius, however, stood up, took his head, and walked two kilometers to the place of his burial.

Critics today tend to see in Eleutherius and Rusticus personifications of two adjectives applied to Dionysius: "eleutheros," which means "free," and "rusticus," which means "of the fields/countryside." They also see in the description of Dionysius picking up his head and walking away a translation into legend of images in which, in order to say he was beheaded, he was shown with his **head in his hands**.

His cult spread after St. Genevieve decided to build a church over his tomb. In 639 King Dagobert transferred his relics to a majestic abbey church which became a temple of the French monarchy, whose patron Dionysius was.

▷▷ As just said, Dionysius was the patron of the royal house of France. He is invoked against headaches and against venereal diseases and syphilis, which caused baldness (the Germans thought that water from the spring arising from the saint's tomb would cure syphilis, which they called "the French disease" and from which the saint was thought to have freed France). He is also invoked against bites by rabid dogs (the chains preserved in Saint-Dénis-de-la-Chartre used to be applied to these wounds).

▷▷ The saint is depicted in **episcopal robes**; as his principal attribute he holds **in his hands his own head on which is placed the bishop's miter**; in some instances he has two heads, one on his neck, the other in his hands. Other attributes are the **chains** of his prison.

St. Dionysius and His Companions, Rusticus and Eleutherius, Undergo Martyrdom.
Miniature from the Passion of St. Dionysius, ca. 1000, commissioned by Abbé Odbert for the abbey of Saint-Bertin; now in the library of Saint-Omer.

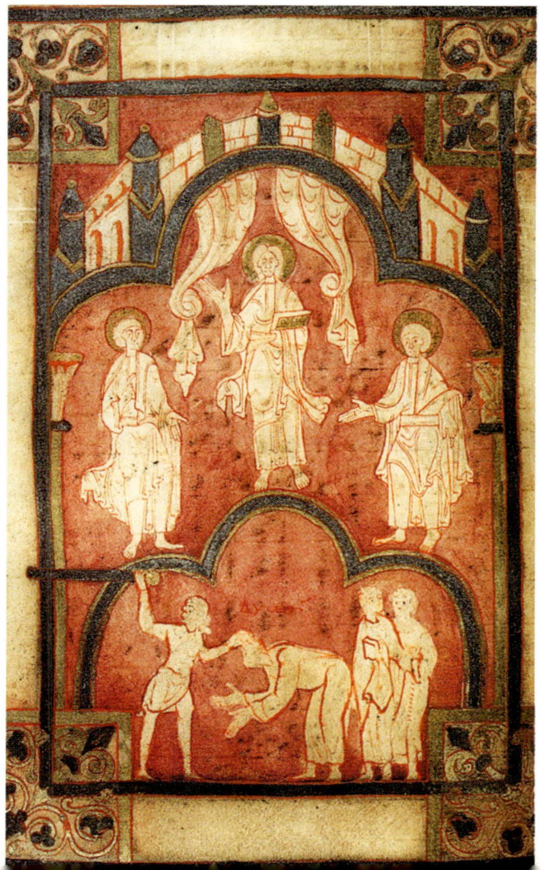

Sebastian, Martyr

3rd–4th century
Memorial: January 20
Lat.: Sebastianus; Gr.: Sebastos ("venerable"); It.: Sebastiano, Bastiano; Fr.: Sébastien, Bastien; Sp.: Sebastian; Ger.: Sebastian, Bastian, Bast, Basch, Nasti, Bastel.

Sebastian, who is regarded as Rome's third patron, after Peter and Paul, was born in Milan (or in Narbonne). Due to his faithfulness and loyalty he advanced rapidly in his military career and found favor with Diocletian and Maximian, who made him a member of the imperial guard.

It was this position that enabled him to encourage imprisoned Christians and to spread the Gospel, thereby effecting many conversions. This activity finally drew attention, and he was tried, especially for having buried the Four Crowned Saints; when he refused to yield in any way, he was condemned to die by being pierced with **arrows**. The executioners left him for dead and abandoned his body, bristling with arrows. In the night, Christians, including a woman named Irene, came to bury him but found him still alive. Irene nursed him, and the young man was miraculously healed.

Instead of fleeing, however, as his friends urged, he confronted the emperors when they came to offer sacrifice in the temple of Hercules, and he proclaimed his faith. He was again imprisoned and then killed by flogging in the hippodrome on the Palatine Hill; to keep his body from being found, it was thrown into a sewer. But Sebastian appeared in a dream to a matron named Lucina and showed her the place where his body was to be found; he ordered her to bury him close to the tomb of Peter and Paul on the Appian Way; Lucina faithfully obeyed the order and placed Sebastian's body in the catacombs.

▷▷ Sebastian became the model of a courageous confession of faith. Because of the wounds left by the arrows, wounds that resembled the sores caused by the plague, he, along with St. Roch, was invoked against plagues. His cult spread throughout Europe and his image is found everywhere, often together with that of St. Roch. Because of the torment inflicted on him, he is the patron of archers and harquebusiers. Because the arrows resembled tapestry needles, he became the patron of tapestry makers, of the makers of needles and of laces requiring ornamental stitching, as well as of ironmongers. He is also the patron of Pest (in Budapest).

The arrows that opened wounds in his body have been associated by analogy with contagious infections, which used to be regarded as divine punishments. As a result, the saint pierced by arrows became an emblem of those suffering from contagious diseases.

▷▷ The saint is depicted as young, tied to a pillar, **seminaked**, and wounded by **arrows**.

Christina of Bolsena, Virgin and Martyr

2nd–3rd century
Memorial: July 24
Lat.: Christina; Fr.: Christie; Ger.: Christina von Bolsena

Christina, daughter of a Roman military official, lived on the shore of Lake Bolsena. She was only fourteen when she converted to Christianity, and her very name tells us that she thought of herself as belonging to Christ. She refused to sacrifice to the gods and endured many harsh afflictions: her own father had her thrown into the lake with a **millstone** tied to her feet. Tradition says that she made her way back to the shore using the stone as a support on which to walk; the stone retained the imprint of her feet. On this stone, it is said, was erected the altar known as the "altar of the footprints."

After her father died, others attacked Christina, who suffered numerous torments. She survived being thrown into boiling oil and then into a hot furnace; when closed in with **snakes and adders**, these surrounded her but did not harm her; the torturers tore away her breasts and cut out her tongue. But the torture that became part of the iconography was the **arrows** which, when shot, turned back against the archers. She was finally killed by the sword; according to others, however, her skull was cleft and her brain pulled out.

Bolsena, where she came to be venerated, is on the pilgrimage route to Rome, so that the cult of Christina became widespread.

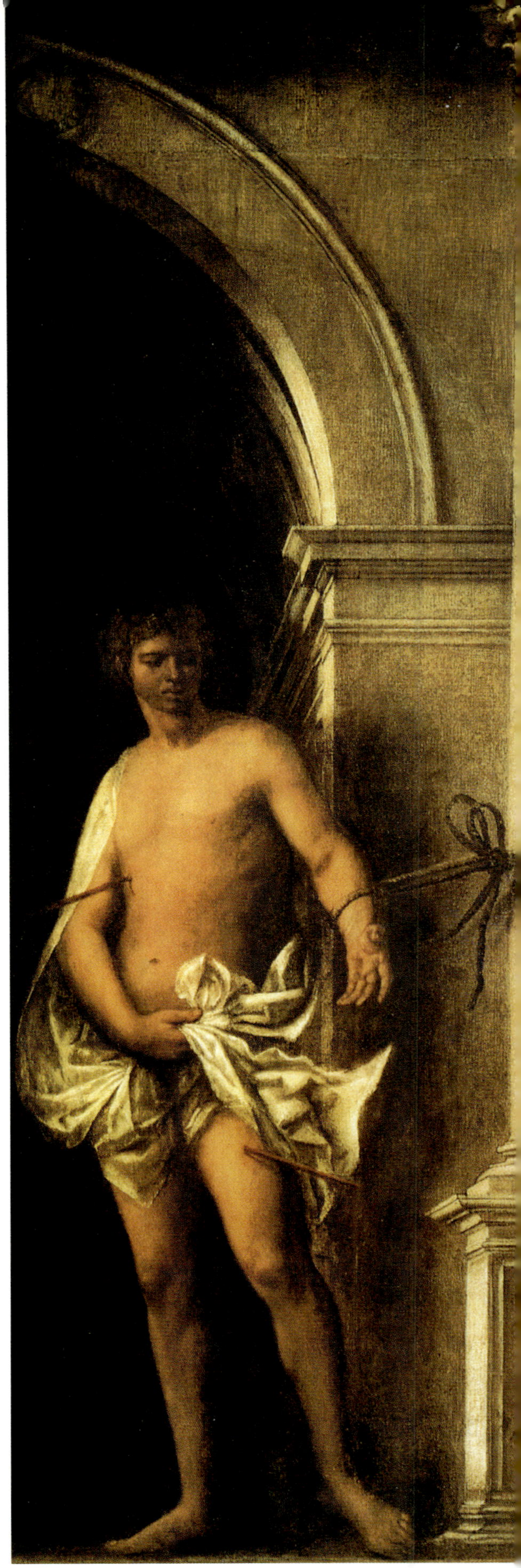

St. Sebastian Bound to a Pillar.
By Sebastiano del Piombo (ca. 1485–1547), on an organ pilaster. Now in the Gallerie dell'Accademia, Venice.

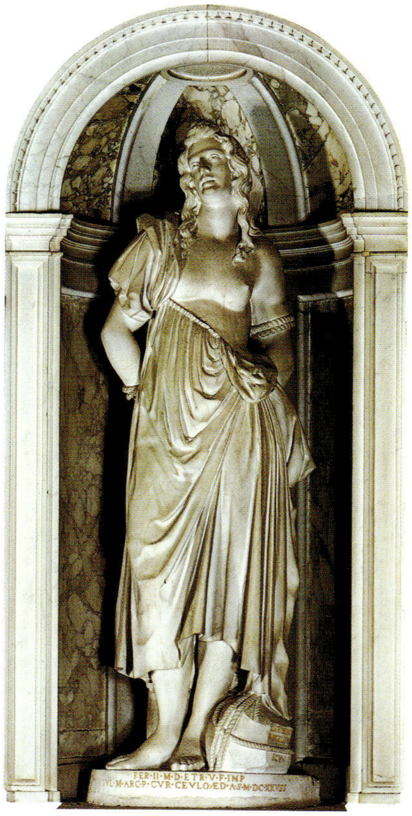

St. Christina of Bolsena.
Statue by Chiarissimo Fancelli, 1622–1625, in the Blessed Sacrament chapel (formerly: chapel of the Annunciation) of the cathedral of Pisa. The millstone to which the martyr was tied is clearly shown in this image.

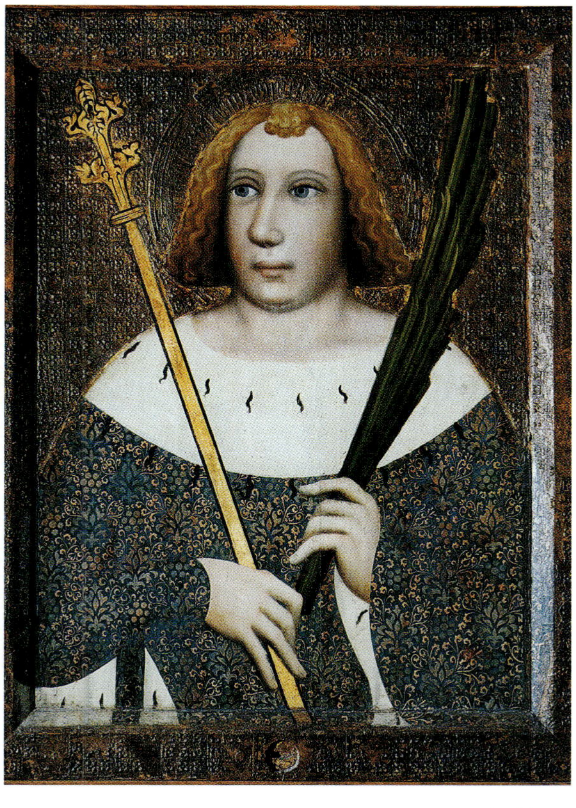

St. Vitus.
By Master Theodoric, 14th cent., in the Castle of Karlstein, Czech Republic.

▷▷ Because of the millstone tied to her feet, Christina became the patron of millers.

▷▷ Her principal attribute is an **arrow**, together with a **millstone**, which she sometimes carries around her neck. Other attributes are **pincers** and **snakes**.

Vitus, Martyr

† 303
Memorial: June 15
Lat.: Vitus; It.: Vito, Guido; Fr.: Guy, Gui, Guidon; Ger.: Veit; Pol.: Wit.

The cult of Vitus is attested since the end of the fifth century, but information about his life is meager and hardly trustworthy. In the *Martyrology* he is said to have been from Lucania, but the *Golden Legend,* which spread his cult further, appeals to third-century texts and says he was a Sicilian. His own father, a pagan, imprisoned him when he was still a child; but the father then saw seven angels in the cell with the child; he went blind and regained his sight only through the intercession of Vitus. The orphaned Vitus, who had been converted by Modestus, his teacher, and Crescentia, his nurse, worked miracles: he fled to Lucania, but was then called back to Rome, where he cured the possessed son of Diocletian. The latter thanked him by having him immersed in a **cauldron of boiling pitch**, then thrown to the **lions**, who licked his feet, and finally hanged from a tower along with Modestus and Crescentia. An angel set them free and transported them to the river Sele, in Campania, where they died.

▷▷ The cult of Vitus was widespread, and he was listed among the Intercessors. In the German world many places bear his name. Patronages and representations are connected with his youthfulness, since he was martyred as a child, and with the **cauldron**. He is invoked against epilepsy and chorea, a disease of the nerves which, because of the uncontrollable movements it causes, is known as "St. Vitus' dance." He is invoked also against the excessive need of sleep, against catalepsy, and even against insomnia, as well as against the bites of rabid dogs.

He is the patron of Bohemia, because his relics were given to the cathedral of Prague, where a splendid chapel holds them. He is invoked for the cure of epilepsy; he protects the mute, the deaf, also dancers, who appear to be imitating the movements of epileptics, and, by extension, actors. He also protects the insane in their indeliberate movements. By reference to the cauldron from which he emerged and which in representations resembles a chamber pot, he is the protector of incontinent children. Again because of the large cauldron, he protects tinkers, coppersmiths, and coopers, as well as brewers and vintners, who use large cauldrons and barrels. Since the cauldron resembles a mortar, he is protector also of pharmacists.

▷▷ Vitus is depicted as a youth whose head and shoulders are emerging from a **cauldron**. Other attributes sometimes shown are a **lion**, an **earthenware lamp**, referring to the theme of light, and a **white rooster**, since the sanctuary at which he is venerated in Lucania used to be known as Alecterius Locus, that is, place of the white rooster.

Marinus, Deacon and Hermit, Founder of the Republic of San Marino

† 301
Memorial: September 4
Lat.: Marinus; It.: Marino

Marinus is regarded as the founder of the Republic that derives its name from him and celebrates him on September 3. According to tradition, he came from Dalmatia to Rimini in 257, that is, before persecution had ceased completely, but during a period of relative tranquility.

Being a stonecutter, he was called to Rome to repair the fortifications of the city and went there with his friend Leo. He was respected by all, lived in peace, and spread the Word of God. But a woman from his native country, who was possessed by a demon, came to Rimini looking for him and claiming to be his wife; she wanted to force him to fulfill his conjugal duty. The saint withdrew to a hermitage in a cave on nearby Mount Titan and lived an ascetic life there for about a year, until some swineherds discovered him and spread the news of his presence. The woman immediately went to him, but he withdrew into the depths of the cave and resisted her through prayer. After six days the woman

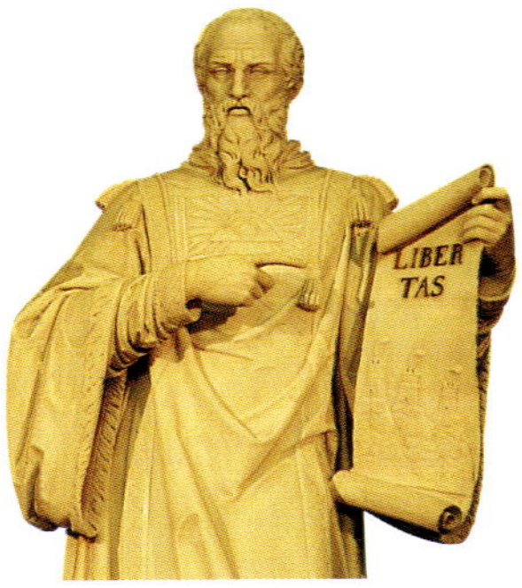

St. Marinus.
Statue by Adamo Tadolini, 1830–1831, in a parish church of the Republic of San Marino.

SS. Cosmas and Damian.
Detail from the painting "Virgin of the Medici" by Rogier van der Weyden, ca. 1400–1464. Now in the Städtelches Kunstinstitut, Frankfurt.

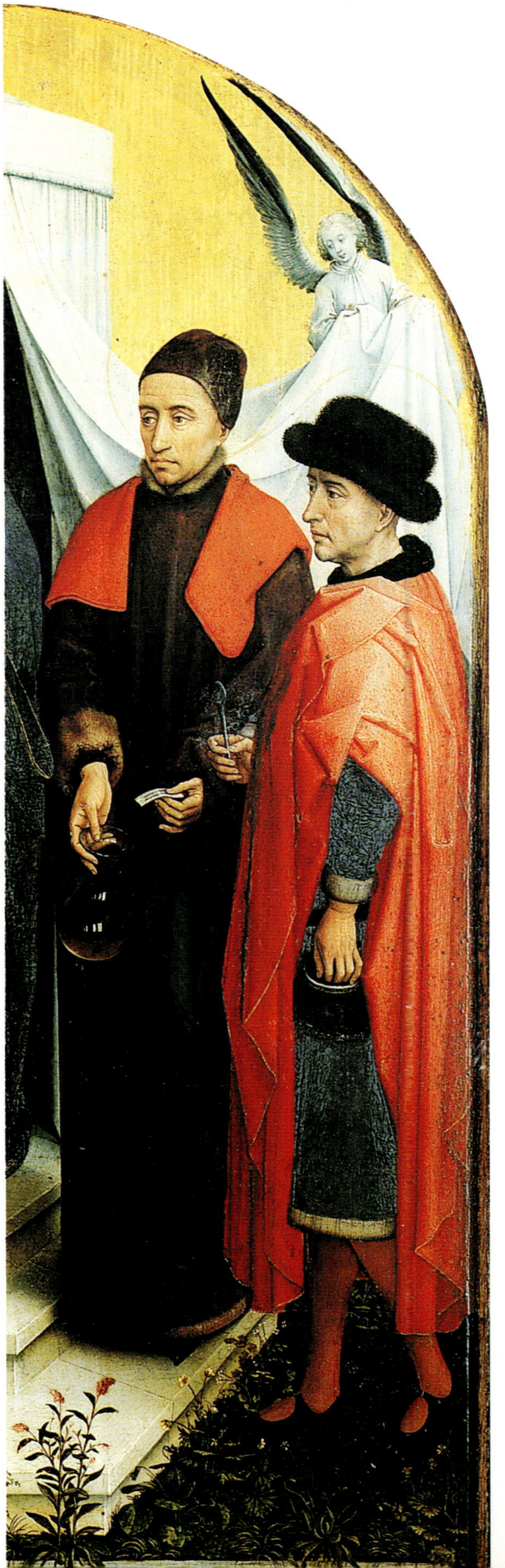

realized that she had been acting as a tool of the demon; she returned to Rimini where she confessed this and was killed by the evil one.

Marinus withdrew to the top of the mountain. Here a young man tried to taunt him but fell to the ground crippled; his mother called upon the saint to heal him; the saint did so. In gratitude the woman, who owned the entire mountain, gave it to the saint and was baptized with her entire family. Marinus settled on the mountain top with his followers, to whom he gave whatever he had. These followers were the nucleus of the community that later became the independent state called the Republic of San Marino.

When Bishop Gaudentius came to Rimini, he wanted to make the acquaintance of Marinus (and of Leo, who meanwhile had settled in the place named after him, St. Leo) and ordained him a deacon.

As Marinus was dying in 301, he supposedly said to his followers: "I leave you free from every human being," that is, from every civil and religious authority, a conception summed up in the inscription *Libertas*.

▷▷ Marinus is patron of the republic he founded; because of the work he did, he is also patron of stonecutters and masons.

▷▷ Marinus is depicted both as a young man and as an old man; in a deacon's dalmatic or in the garb of a hermit and of a stonecutter. As patron of the Republic, he is depicted holding **Mount Titan with its characteristic three peaks** (or three feathers, since *penna,* "feather," also means "peak"); this is his principal attribute, to which may be added others, e.g., the inscription *Libertas* or the tools used in his work (**hammer**, **chisel**, and **square**), or a **bear** he tamed.

Cosmas and Damian, Martyrs

† 303
Memorial: September 26
Lat.: Cosmas et Damianus, martyres medici, sancti medici; Gr.: Kosmas, Damianos; It.: Cosmo e Damiano, i santi medici anargiri, Cosma, Cosimo, Cosimato; Sp.: Cosme y Damian, los santos medicos; Eng.: also, the apothecary or medical saints, the moneyless physicians, the physicians without fees; Ger.: Kosmas und Damian, die Geldlosen; Dutch: Cosmus en Damianus; Russ.: Kosma, Kouzma.

The two are called, in Greek, *anargiri,* that is, "who did not accept money." The twin brothers were in fact physicians in Egea, a city of Cilicia, who healed both human beings and animals, but accepted no payment; they made converts among those who turned to them. They were arrested during the persecution of Diocletian, were tortured for a long time, and were finally beheaded. Their fellow believers rushed to take and divide their remains, but the camel who was carrying them said: "Do not separate them at their burial, since they were not separated in merit." As a result, they were buried together at Cyrrhus in Syria, where Emperor Justinian, who had received healing through their intercession, built a basilica in their honor. Their tomb drew pilgrims and the sick; from there their cult spread throughout the East.

Pope Symmachus (498–514) built an oratory for them, and Pope Felix IV (526–530) had their relics brought to Rome, where he built a basilica for them in the Roman Forum.

A basilica was dedicated to them in Constantinople. Here, as in Rome, the ritual of incubation was practiced; that is, the faithful needing favors slept on the floor of the church and in the morning woke up healed, often with the marks of surgery on their bodies. In Rome, a man with a gangrened leg found this replaced by the healthy leg of a recently buried black man.

▷▷ The two saints are patrons of Prague, Florence, and Bitonto, and of the Medici family of Florence. As physicians, they are the protectors of hospitals, physicians, surgeons,

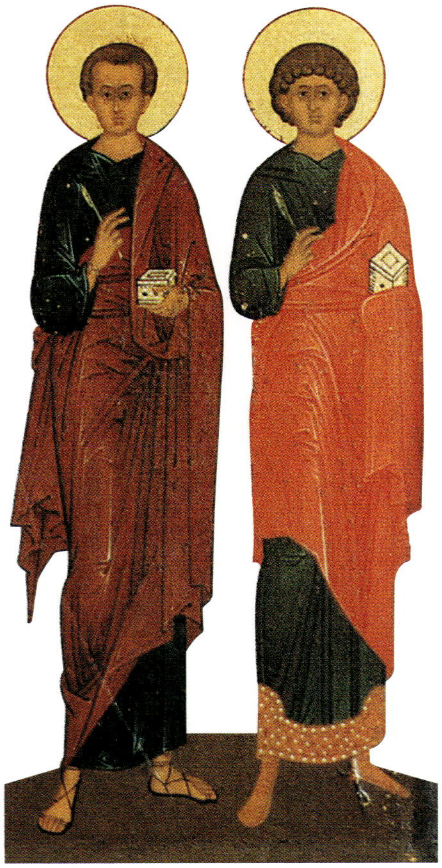

SS. Cosmas and Damian.
Detail from the icon known as "The Holy Hierarchs," 18th cent., Central Russia. In a private collection in Lebanon.

orthopedists, dentists, pharmacists, dealers in chemical and pharmaceutical products, midwives, barbers (who at one time were surgeons), and of the clients of all of these.

They are invoked against plague, gangrene, milk scab, ringworm, kidney diseases, indigestion, enteritis, and glandular inflammations. A urinal being one of their attributes, they are invoked against nocturnal incontinence in children and also against distemper.

▷▷ They came to be represented in Renaissance garb, because their image was widespread in the time of the Medici. Their principal attributes are **vials** and **surgical instruments**, a **pharmacist's mortar**, **box of ointments**, **scalpels**, a **spreader** for salves. Other attributes are: **urinal**, but also, because they are protectors of barbers, **combs** and **shears**.

Erasmus of Gaeta, Bishop and Martyr

† 303
Memorial: June 2
Lat.: Erasmus; It.: Erasmo di Gaeta, Erasmo di Formia, Ermo, Elmo, Telmo (from: Sant'Elmo); Fr.: Érasme de Gaëte, Agraopard, Arrache, Arras, Elme, Erme, Telme; Sp.: Erasmo, Elmo, Telmo; Ger.: Erasmus, Rasmus, Asmus.

Erasmus was bishop of Formia. His *Passion,* which has no historical basis, has him a native of Antioch and a bishop of that city, where persecution sought him out; as a result, he hid for seven years in a cave on Mt. Lebanon. When he returned to the city, he was arrested and tortured in many ways, but he did not yield and was imprisoned. After being miraculously freed, he went to Illyricumn, where he worked a great many conversions: four hundred thousand individuals, a great many of whom were immediately martyred. He himself suffered many torments: **nails** were thrust under his fingernails, he was burned with hot irons and sprinkled with boiling oil; finally he was imprisoned once again. Michael the archangel set him free and transported him to Formia, where he died in peace seven years later.

▷▷ In 842, the Saracens destroyed Formia, and the relics of Erasmus were transferred to Gaeta, where they were rediscovered in 917. At that point, Erasmus was proclaimed patron of the city. He was listed among the Fourteen Helpers and invoked against epidemics. Sailors venerated him under the name of Elmo. They speak of a long-standing tradition according to which, while he praying one day, lightning struck nearby even though the sky above him was clear; sailors invoke him in order that the masts may not draw down lightning. They give the name "St. Elmo's Fire" to the little *ignes fatui* that run along the masts and foretell a storm.

Torment of St. Erasmus.
Miniature, ca. 1400, in a Book of Hours, Ms. 822 (a.c. 513), fol. 101, in the Municipal Library of Arras.

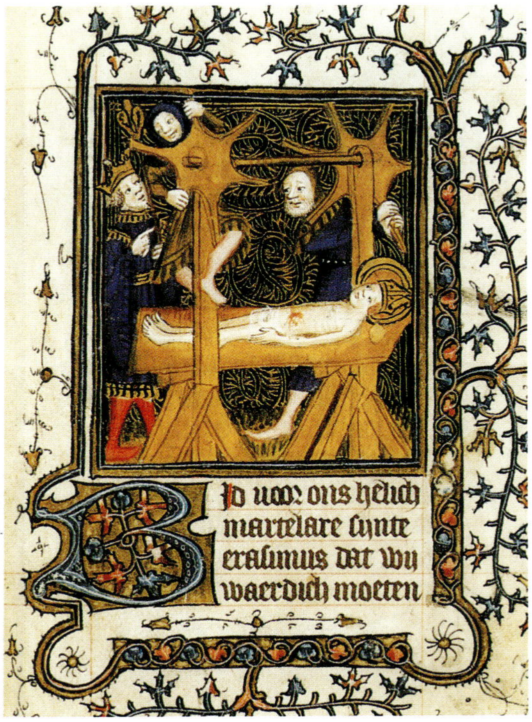

▷▷ As patron of sailors, Erasmus' emblem is a **windlass** with a rolled-up cable. This caused people on land, who were not familiar with a windlass, to think that with this instrument the saint removed intestines by rolling them up.

In any case, after the fourteenth century the particular torture suffered by Erasmus provided the most common way of representing him. He is patron of Compagna in Italy and the protector of sailors. Because of the nails, he is patron of those who manufacture them. The strings of musical instruments are at times made of gut, that is, the intestines of some animals; Erasmus is therefore the patron of lute-makers and the makers of other stringed musical instruments. Because of the movement of the windlass he is the patron of wood turners and weavers. Because of the torments inflicted on him, he is invoked against the pains of birth. He is invoked against all pains of stomach and abdomen (from upset stomach to colic) and against childhood exhaustion.

▷▷ Erasmus is depicted as a bishop, and his principal attributes are the **episcopal vestments** and the **windlass**; another attribute is the **nails** thrust under his fingernails.

Florian of Lorch, Martyr

† 304
Memorial: May 4
Lat.: Florianus; It.: Floriano; Fr.: Florian, Florien; Ger.: Florianus von Lorch, Florian.

Florian is one of the most popular saints of central Europe and is not to be confused with another Florian whose historical status is doubtful. He was an Austrian, a Roman soldier who voluntarily presented himself as a Christian to the prefect of Lorch, although he knew that forty of his fellow soldiers had been imprisoned. When he refused to sacrifice to idols, he was thrown into the river Enns with a millstone around his neck. An eagle kept watch over his body, which had run aground on a rock, and a pious woman buried him at the place where the Augustinian convent of St. Florian now stands.

▷▷ Florian is the patron of Austria. Because of his death in the river, whose waters extinguish fires, he is invoked against both floods and fires, lightning, burns, and the fires of purgatory. He is therefore protector of firemen, who extinguish fires, and of chimney-sweepers who deal with chimneys and fires. Because he puts out the "fire" of thirst, he is protector of brewers.

▷▷ He is depicted in **military uniform** with helmet, sword, and standard, or intent on throwing water on burning houses with a **bucket**, which became his principal attribute. Other attributes are the **millstone of his martyrdom** and a **nest of storks**, because it was thought that storks protected people generally and therefore also against fires, inasmuch as they often made their nests on the chimneys of the house on which they settled.

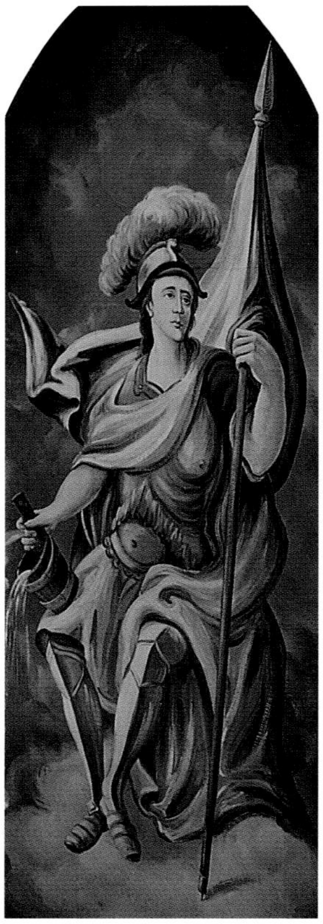

St. Florian of Lorch.
Fresco in a votive shrine, beginning of 20th cent., in St-Andrä, Austria.

George of Lydda

4th century
Memorial: April 23
Lat.: Georgius; Gr.: Georghios; It.: Giorgio, Jorio, Giorgione, Zorzo; Fr.: Georges. Jeux, Joire, Jorioz, Juéry, Juire, Jurs, Jurson, Yors; Sp.: Jorge; Ger.: Georg, Görg, Görres, Jörg, Jörigen, Jürgen; Dutch: Joris; Swed.: Göran, Orjan; Pol.: Jerzy; Russ.: Velikomoutchenik Georgii, Georgii Pobêdonosets (the Victorious), Igor, Iouri.

George's tomb is venerated at Lydda (Diospolis) in Palestine. In Greek, his name means "tiller of the soil," and it is not an accident that in many places rituals connected with the fields are celebrated on his feast day, for example, the blessing of farm machinery.

George is one of the soldier saints of Cappadocia. As a Roman legionary he went to Libya where, in the city of Silene, a dragon was killing all who approached it; the poor citizens tried to domesticate it by feeding it two sheep each day. When not enough sheep were left, they fed it a sheep and a human being, whose name was determined by lot. The lot fell to the king's daughter who could not escape her fate, and she approached the dragon. St. George was passing through the place, heard the whole story, and promised help in the name of Christ. An angel gave him a **white banner with a cross on it**; the **dragon** was defeated and was carried into the city tied by the sash of the **princess**. St. George announced that he had been sent to save this people in order that they might be converted. All were baptized, and the dragon was killed. The king had a large church built, from whose altar a spring flowed that healed every ill.

Later on, during the persecution of Diocletian, George put off his military garb and preached to encourage those who were tempted to abandon Christianity out of fear of torture. He was imprisoned, but miraculously survived terrible sufferings: they tore at his body with hooks, they put red-hot shoes on his feet, they suspended him head down over a brazier. He thwarted the attempt to poison him by making the sign of the cross over the deadly cup; angels broke the hook-covered wheels that were to tear his flesh; immersion into molten lead, accompanied by his sign of the cross, gave him refreshment instead. Not only that: he converted many who were present, and even pretended to them that he was ready to sacrifice to the gods, in order that he might then cause the temple to collapse and the priests to perish. He was finally beheaded; his martyrdom took place in 303.

Tradition tells that at the time when Christians were about to besiege Jerusalem, a handsome young man appeared in Antioch, wearing white armor with a shining red cross on it.

St. George and the Dragon.
Painting on a wooden panel, Ethiopian art, 18th–19th cent. In a private collection in Paris.

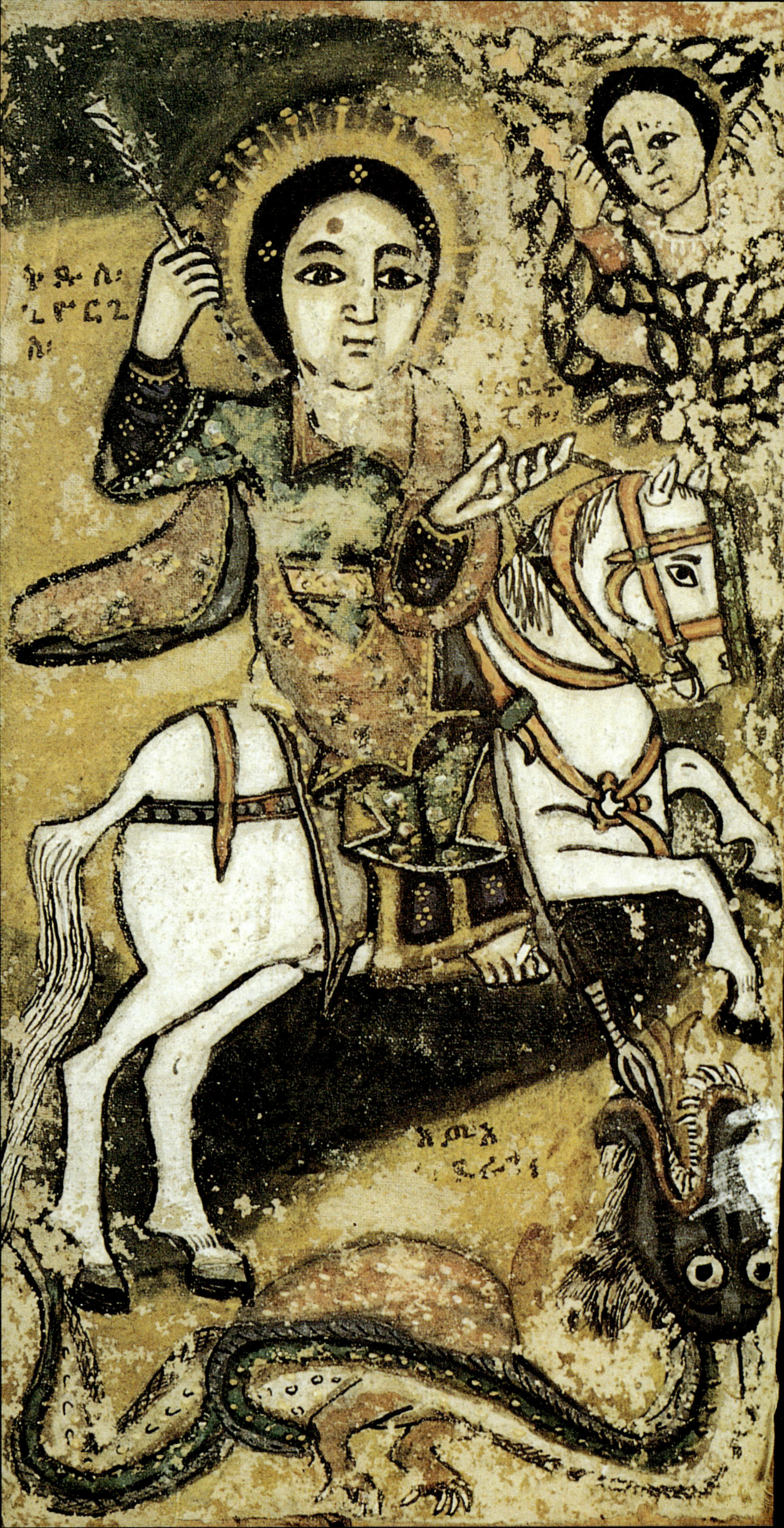
ቅዱስ፡ ጊዮርጊስ፡

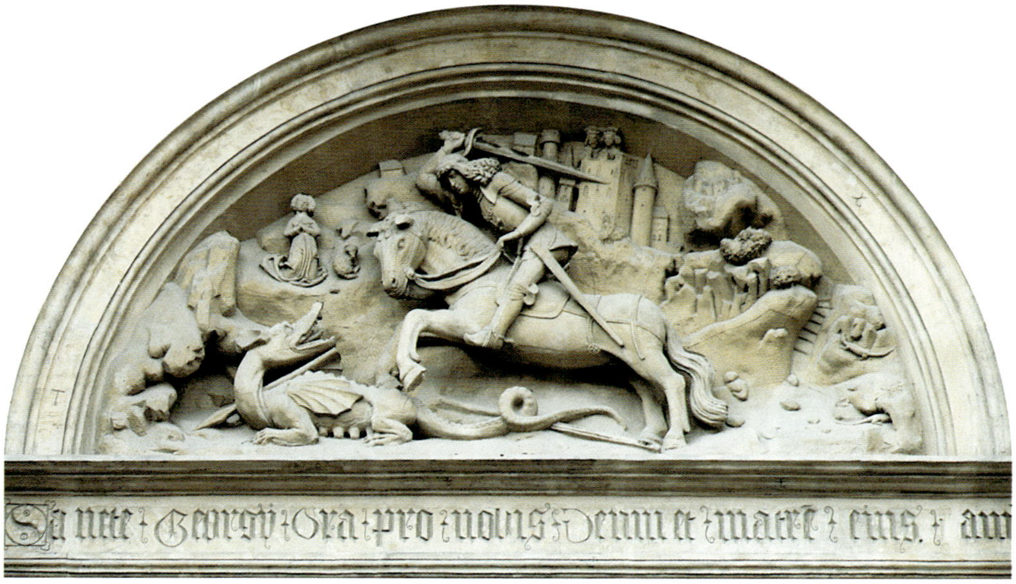

St. George and the Dragon.
Lunette in the cathedral of St. Vitus, Prague.
Beginning of 20th cent.

He revealed that he was St. George, and he promised that he would take part in the siege provided that the Christians carried his relics with them. They did and took Jerusalem.

Historical criticism does not know what to make of George. He is, however, one of those saints whose cult, approved by Pope Gelasius in 494, is very ancient, very widespread, and unbroken in its continuity. In the knight who fights to defend a young girl from a dragon it is easy to see Christ himself defending the Church from heresies.

▷▷ George is numbered among the Fourteen Helpers. He is patron of the ancient seafaring republics of Venice and Genoa. He became the national patron of England in 1222, and when King Edward III established the Order of the Garter, he placed it under George's protection; this patronage was renewed by Pope Pius XII on December 11, 1962. He is patron of all who travel on horseback and therefore of cavalrymen, archers, halberdiers, armorers, and makers and sellers of saddles and armor. His plumed helmet made him patron also of makers of feathers. Because of what his name means in Greek, he is patron of farmers. His role as patron of the crusades was strengthened by his standard, which almost always shows a red cross on a white background. Because he slew the dragon, he is invoked against snake poison. He is also patron of the Scouts.

He is also invoked against plague and syphilis, two diseases to which soldiers were exposed.

▷▷ George is depicted very attractively as a handsome young man in shining armor on a white horse, in the act of killing a **dragon**, which became his principal attribute (and recalls Michael the archangel), while the princess is off to the side. George offers a fine image of Christ defending the Church and orthodoxy. Other attributes are the **standard with the cross**, the **princess**, and the **white horse**.

Martyrdom of St. Agatha.
18th cent., in a private collection in the Republic of San Marino.
The depiction of the martyrdom is realistic and not symbolic, and is intended to arouse compassion and emotional participation. Quite often, nevertheless, even in the bloodiest scenes, the martyrs are distinguished by a calm composure that contrasts with the grim executioners.

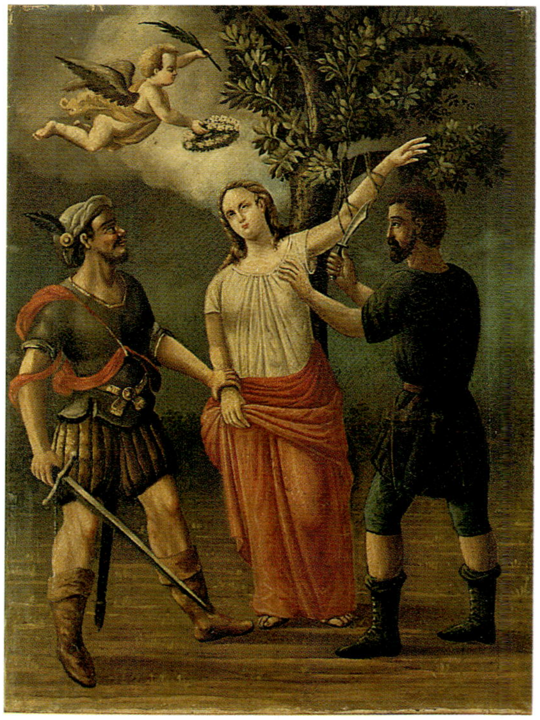

Agatha, Virgin and Martyr

† 251
Memorial: February 5
Lat.: Agatha Catanensis; Gr.: Agatha; It.: Agata, Gada; Fr.: Agathe, Aphte, Chapte, Chaptes, Chatte, Gaetta, Ogotta; Sp.: Agüeda, Gadea; Ger.: Agata.

Agatha is a Greek name that means good, capable, brave. This young woman was martyred in 251 during the persecution of Decius and was able to keep her body unblemished and her faith undiminished as she bore witness to the lordship of Christ.

Governor Quintian, a greedy, vainglorious, and lustful man, attacked her furiously and handed her over to a prostitute. Agatha and the other young Christian virgins were taken to a brothel both as a form of punishment (Tertullian described this in a play on words: she was condemned to a *leno* [brothel-keeper] rather than to a *leo* [lion]) and as a necessity if the executioners were to kill her, since it was regarded as a sacrilegious act to kill a virgin. When they were unable to destroy her virtue, they cut off one of her **breasts**; then they had her locked up and gave orders that no one was to tend to her. But an elderly man appeared in her cell, along with a young man who carried a lamp, and offered to heal her; when Agatha refused human care, the old man revealed himself as the apostle **St. Peter** and healed her.

Quintian then had her rolled over **sharp shards** and **hot coals**, both of which became elements in her iconography. As his command was being carried out, Catania was shaken by an earthquake; the fearful inhabitants tried to stop Quintian but he sent Agatha back to prison and fled; he drowned in the Simeto River, and, according to popular tradition, the lament of the cruel governor could still be heard in the river. Meanwhile, Agatha died in prison on February 5. Beside her tomb an angel placed a tablet containing the initials "M. S. S. H. D. E. P. L." = *Mentem sanctam spontaneam, honorem Deo, et patriae liberationem,* that is, "[Agatha had] a mind that was holy and spontaneous [her intellect was spontaneously directed toward holy things], [she] gave honor to God and [sought] the liberation of her native land."

Her protection of her country was confirmed in 252 when Catania was threatened by an eruption of Etna: the people halted the flow of lava with the **veil** that covered the saint's tomb. In the eleventh century her relics were taken to Constantinople. Agatha then appeared to two young soldiers of the Byzantine imperial guard and inspired them to steal the relics, which were then taken back to Catania.

Another saying having to do with Agatha recalled that when Catania rebelled against Frederick II (1194–1250), he decided to destroy the city and kill its citizens. According to tradition, the citizens asked as a final favor that they might celebrate a Mass the sovereign himself would attend. Then, on every page of his missal these words appeared: "Do not do harm to the native land of Agatha, because she avenges injuries" *(Noli offendere patriam Agathae quia ultrix iniuriarum est)*. This sentence became a motto of the saint and appears on the facade of her cathedral. The cult of Agatha soon spread through all of Europe.

▷▷ In the eighteenth century Agatha became one of the patrons of the Republic of San Marino, where her cult was already practiced. On February 5, 1740, the Republic was able to regain its lost freedom with the help of the papal legate, Cardinal Giulio Alberoni, and to experience the recovery of its rights.

Agatha is the patron of wet nurses and nursing mothers, and is invoked against every disease of the breast and against pulmonary diseases. She also protects against burns, volcanic eruptions, fire (including the fire of purgatory), flames, and earthquakes. Because of suffering from burning coals, she is patron of workers in brass and of glass blowers, due to the heat in which they work. Because bells used to sound a warning of fires, and because bells turned upside down resemble breasts, and because the hot metal used in casting bells is reminiscent of lava, Agatha is protector of those who make bells, the bells themselves, and those who ring them. Her image is often found on bells. Because of her veil, she protects those who produce and sell cloth.

▷▷ Agatha is depicted in prison or during her torments, and in her visitation by St. Peter and the angel. Her principal attribute is one or two **severed breasts**, placed on a dish; other attributes are the **shears**, **knife**, or **pincers** of her martyrdom, the **fire** and the **shards** on which she was rolled, **Etna** erupting, the **veil**, the two **sayings**, and even **St. Peter**.

Lucy, Virgin and Martyr

† 304–305
Memorial: December 13
Lat.: Lucia; It.: Lucia; Fr.: Lucie de Syracuse, Luce, Luche; Ger.: Lucia, Lutz, Litzen.

Lucy is an exemplar of the prudent virgin who awaits the bridegroom with lighted lamp; after being led to death for Christ, she was admitted to the wedding and the possession of a light never to be dimmed. Lucy herself, of Syracuse, took for her model Agatha of Catania and used to go to this saint's tomb in order to pray; she became a martyr in 304, in the time of

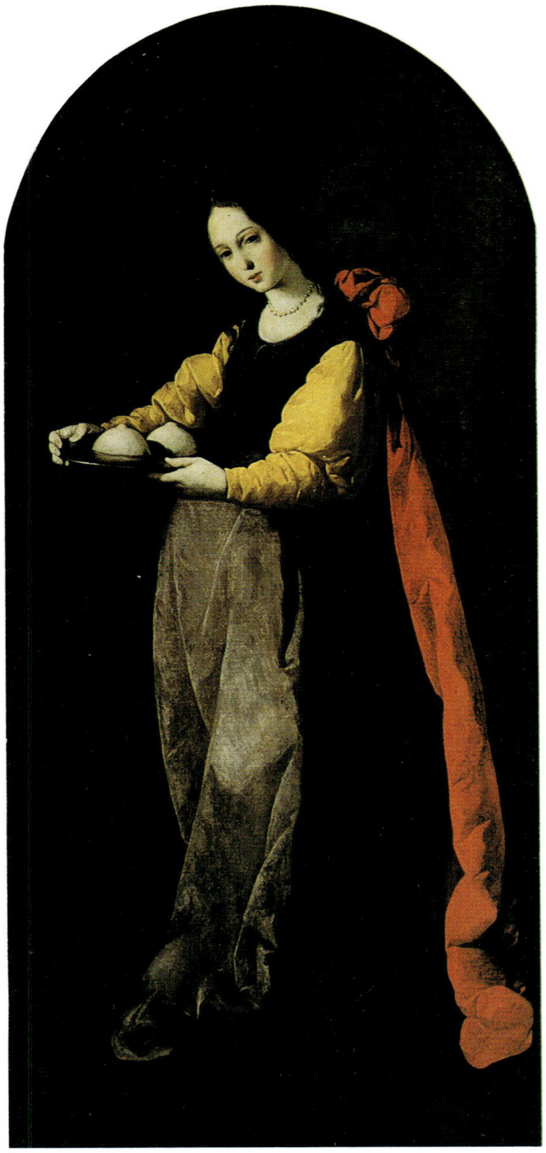

St. Agatha.
By Francisco de Zurbaran, 1598–1664, in the Musée Fabre, Montpellier.

Diocletian. Lucy is connected with light by her very name; in addition, due to the discrepancies between the calendar and the solar year at that time, the solstice ended up being celebrated on December 13 and so it was said that "the longest of nights [or: the shortest of days] belonged to St. Lucy." We must remember that in the Julian calendar, which preceded the Gregorian (introduced by Pope Gregory XIII in 1585), the solstice occurred on December 13, with the result that Lucy was linked to all the traditions involving the solstice. (Even today, moreover, December 13 is one of the days on which the sun sets early.) Thus it was said of Lucy that "she shed the light of her eyes on the long night of the solstice."

There is the entirely legendary story that her **eyes** were plucked out and sent to a suitor who, when rejected, had denounced her as a Christian in 304, during the persecution of Diocletian. In her *Passion* it is said that Paschasius, the official who interrogated her, wanted her placed in a brothel so that she could no longer claim that her body was a temple of the Holy Spirit. But even a **team of oxen** was unable to move her. The official then had **fagots** soaked in oil and resin piled up around her in order to burn her alive. But Lucy prayed to the Lord that fire might not harm her, saying: "I shall cause believers in Christ to see the power of martyrdom, and from nonbelievers I shall remove the blindness caused by their pride." Finally, Paschasius had her beheaded or, according to another version, had her throat cut. Because her time had come, Lucy allowed herself to be led to her martyrdom.

▷▷ The cult of Lucy spread rapidly. She is invoked as protector of bodily and spiritual sight. She is connected with gifts to children by an incident that took place in a Sicilian village in the twelfth or thirteenth century: an epidemic was causing blindness in children; their parents turned to the saint and went barefoot to her shrine along with their children; she assured them that when they returned home they would find their shoes filled with gifts. Lucy hastened not only to heal the children but also to keep her promise. From that time on, in the traditions of many countries it is she who brings gifts to children (this is attested in many places in Europe). It is said that the saint travels on a donkey for which the children prepare a dish of bran and flour and leave it on a windowsill; the donkey eats and Lucy leaves games, sweets, and fruits on the empty dish. For naughty children she leaves a small whip as a warning.

▷▷ Lucy's patronages have to do with light; thus she is the patron of the blind and of oculists, as well as of electricians. But she is also a patron of farmers, because in the unsuccessful attempt to remove her, oxen were used. She is invoked against diseases of the eyes and blindness, and, because she was killed by having her throat cut, against diseases of the throat.

▷▷ Her principal attribute is her **eyes on a dish**, offered up as were the breasts of St. Agatha; other attributes are a **sword** or a **dagger**, the **oxen** who were unable to move her, **flames**, a **lighted lamp**, a **candle**, and also the **starry background** of the illustrations.

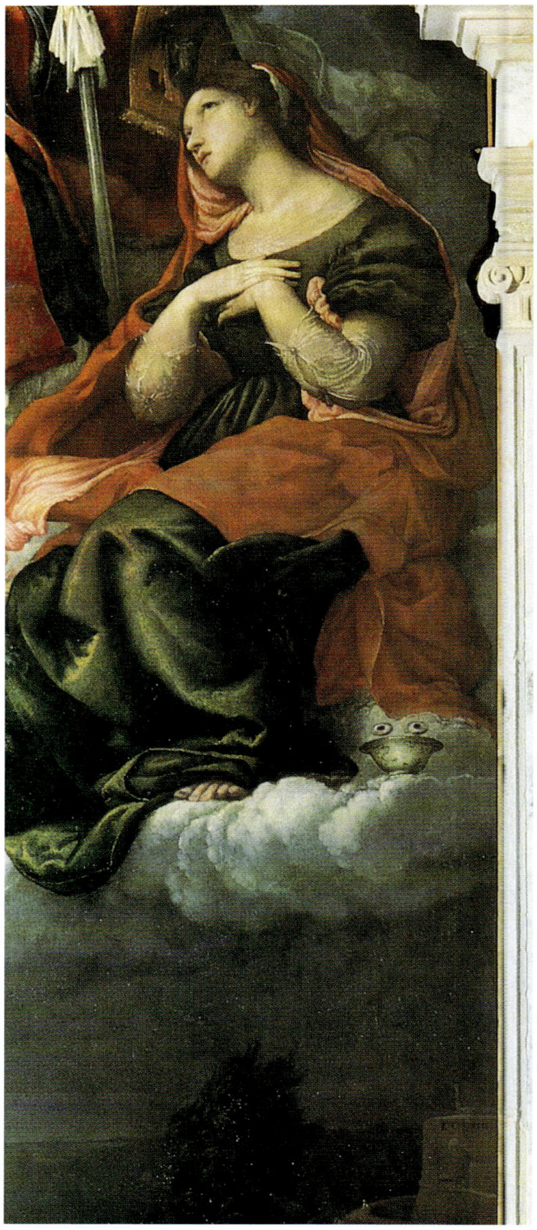

St. Lucy.
Detail of a painting of St. Nicholas in glory together with St. John the Baptist and St. Lucy, by Lorenzo Lotto, ca. 1480–1556, in the church of the Carmine, Venice.

Agnes, Virgin and Martyr

3rd–4th century
Memorial: January 21
Lat.: Agnes; It.: Agnese; Fr.: Agnès, Agnet, Anne, Annès; Sp.: Inés; Ger.: Agnes.

While still a child, Agnes overcame both the weakness of her tender age and a tyrant by bearing witness to the faith. She is regarded as the female image of the Lamb of God. Her name occurs in the Roman *Chronograph of 354,* which locates her memorial on January 21; she had been martyred during the persecution of Diocletian, that is, around 303–305.

In Greek the name "Agnes" means "chaste," but the similarity in sound between Greek *(h)agnê,* "chaste," and Latin *agna,* "lamb," led to the introduction of the gentle image of a **lamb** and of the idea of sacrifice. Of her St. Augustine said: "Agnes in Latin means 'lamb,' in Greek 'chaste.'" The saint was about thirteen years old. St. Ambrose emphasized her youthfulness and said that she died by being slaughtered like a lamb as she called upon her God: "Agnes is called a lamb, because she was meek and humble like a lamb."

The Greek tradition describes her as a very young adult and emphasizes her refusal to offer sacrifice. When she was taken to a brothel, the young man who approached her in order to

St. Agnes.
7th-cent. mosaic in the apse of the church of St. Agnes, Rome.
In images such as this one, holiness shines out in a timeless splendor. Yet it is not disconnected from the circumstances of the saint's martyrdom, the flames of which are seen starting up at her feet. The scroll she carries emphasizes the principal reference point of her life, namely, Christ and his Gospel.

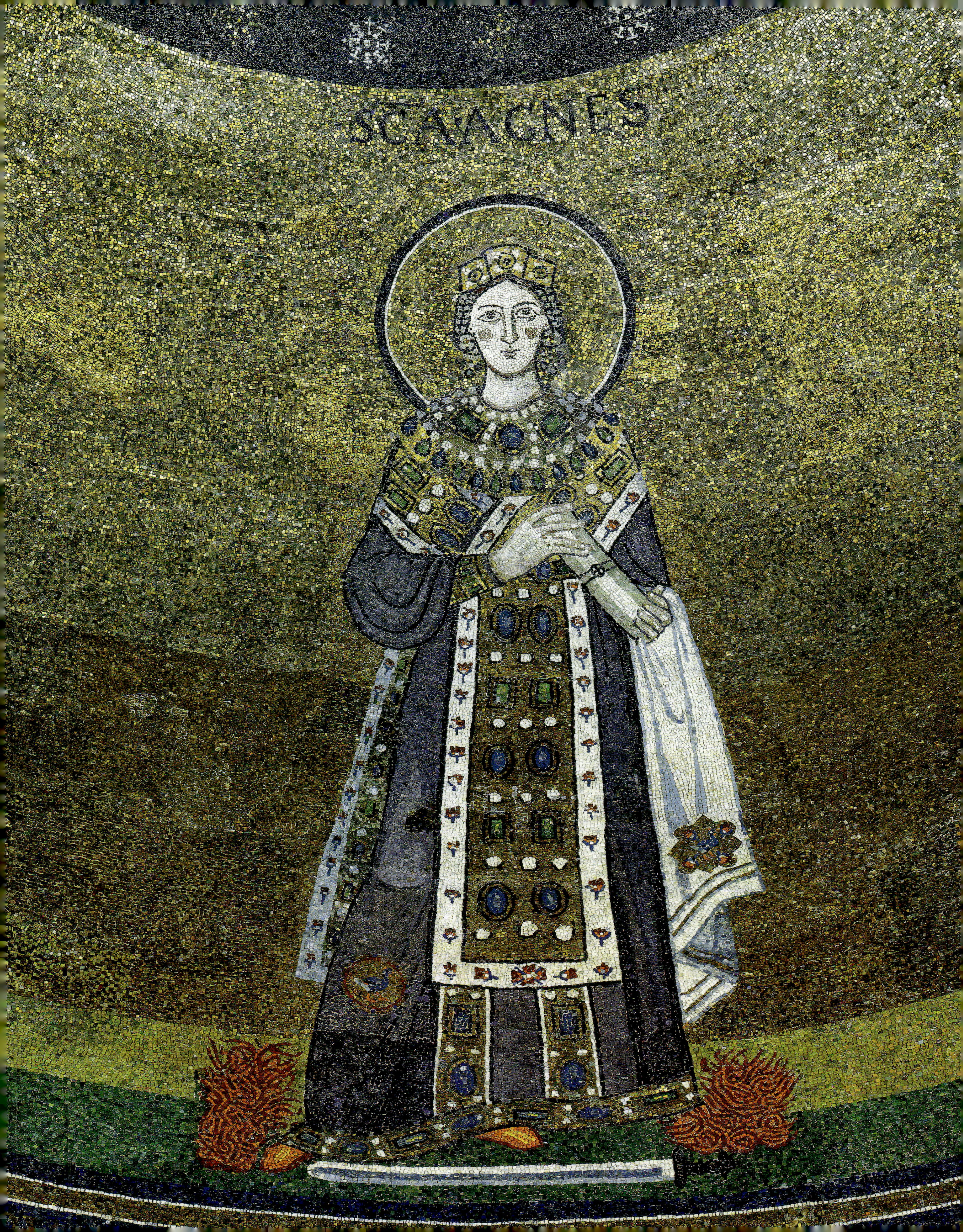
SCA AGNES

rape her, he dropped dead; when questioned, Agnes answered that she had been protected by an angel. A different version, which contributed to the iconography, says that she rejected the prefect's son, who fell ill of sadness; in order to persuade her, the father had her taken nude in a cart through the streets of Rome to a brothel, but her **hair grew** to the point of covering her **like a cloak**. The young man who was following her in order to take advantage of the situation was strangled by a demon, but the saint restored him to life. Agnes was then condemned to be burned as a witch, but the **flames created a space around her**; her throat was then slit.

Eight days after her death, she appeared to her parents with a **lamb** at her right side and consoled them.

The wool of the lambs that are blessed on her feast day is used to make the pallium that the pope gives to archbishops.

▷▷ The cult of Agnes spread throughout Europe. She is patron of the Trinitarians because their Rule was approved on the octave day of her feast. She protects the virgins of Rome, engaged women (because Christ was her fiancé), and gardeners (because virginity was compared to a *hortus conclusus,* a garden enclosed).

▷▷ In images of Agnes her principal attribute is a **lamb**; other attributes used are the **flames of the pyre** that moved away from her body, the **dagger** that cut her throat, and **the hair that concealed her entire body**.

Margaret (or Marina) of Antioch, Virgin and Martyr

3rd–4th century
Memorial: July 20
Lat.: Margarita; It.: Margherita, Rita; Fr.: Marguerite d'Antioche, Margaux, Margeride, Margerie, Marguarite, Margot, Margoton, Goton; Ger.: Margareta, Margret, Gretchen; Flem.: Greet, Griet; Pol.: Melgorzata.

Margaret dedicated her body to Christ through virginity and martyrdom. She is also called Marina; from her tradition are derived those of Marina and Pelagia; her name Margaret means "pearl," but both "Marina" and "Pelagia" provide a link with the sea (in Latin: *mare* and *pelagus*).

She was the daughter of a pagan priest of Antioch; after her mother died, she was entrusted to a foster-mother who brought her up in the faith; she was baptized, and when she came to know the courage of the Christians persecuted by Maximian and Diocletian, she wanted to imitate them. As she was watching over her foster-mother's flocks, she was seen by Olibrius, the governor, who became infatuated with her and wanted her for a wife or a concubine. He had her brought to him, but the girl immediately declared herself a Christian and resisted both enticements and threats. Olibrius had her flesh torn by **iron combs**. When she was thrown into a dungeon, the devil, too, tormented her; he appeared to her as a **dragon** surrounded by serpents but with a sign of the cross she freed herself. In other versions, the dragon devoured her, but she pierced its belly with a **cross** or the sign of the cross. For this reason, she is invoked by women in childbirth.

She then underwent other tortures: she was first hung over hot flames and then immersed in a vessel of cold water; but a **dove** appeared who blessed the water and baptized her again. She was finally beheaded.

▷▷ She is patron of shepherds and of laundresses, of pregnant women, of women in labor, and of midwives.

▷▷ She is invoked against hemorrhages and floods, against storms (because of the association of her name with the sea), against the pains of childbirth, and against conjugal sterility.

▷▷ Everywhere venerated, Marina is depicted as a young **crowned** woman, who is subduing a **dragon**, which is her principal attribute, and brandishing a **lance with a cross on it**. Other attributes are **torches** and **iron combs**.

St. Margaret (or: Marina) Strikes the Devil.
Fresco from 1541 in the church of the Beheading of St. John the Baptist in Arbore, Rumania.

Martyrdom of St. Agnes.
Juan Vicente Masipo, 1475–1550, in the Prado Museum, Madrid.
The large number of instruments of martyrdom is in contrast to the serenity of the saint, who, as her gaze shows, draws her strength from heaven. The bystanders, often present at scenes of martyrdom, are witnesses and guarantors of what is happening.

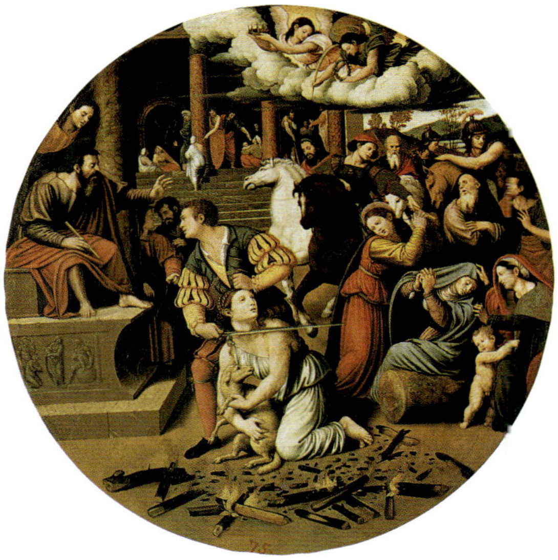

Martyrdom of St. Margaret (or: Marina) of Antioch.
By Hans von Egkel, ca. 1470, Melk Abbey.
The tragic aspect of the scene is tempered by the smiling Margaret as she emerges from the cauldron, hands joined in prayer. She holds on a leash the dragon that sought to swallow her up and which is clearly a symbol of the devil.

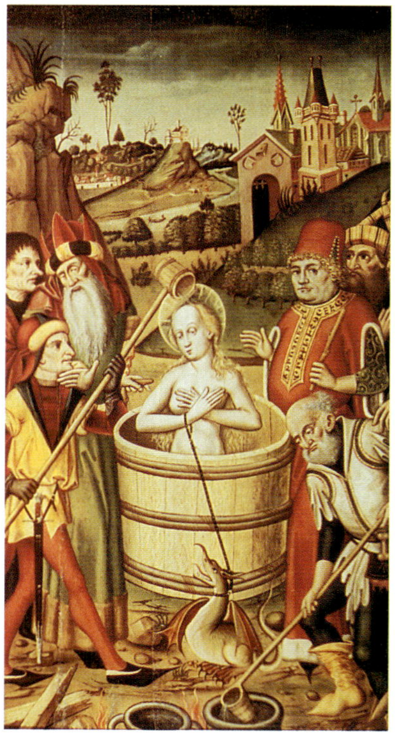

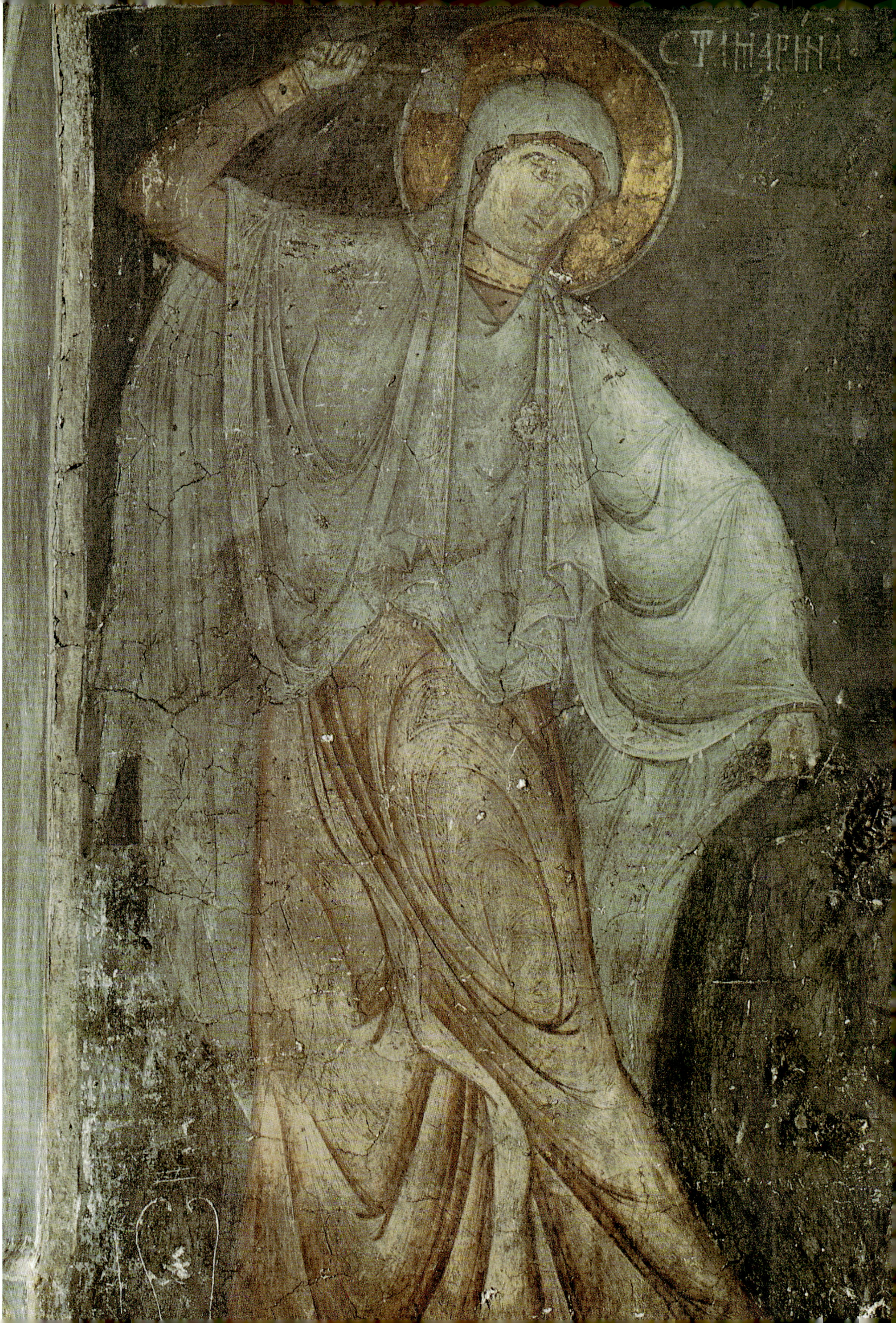
СТА МАРИНА

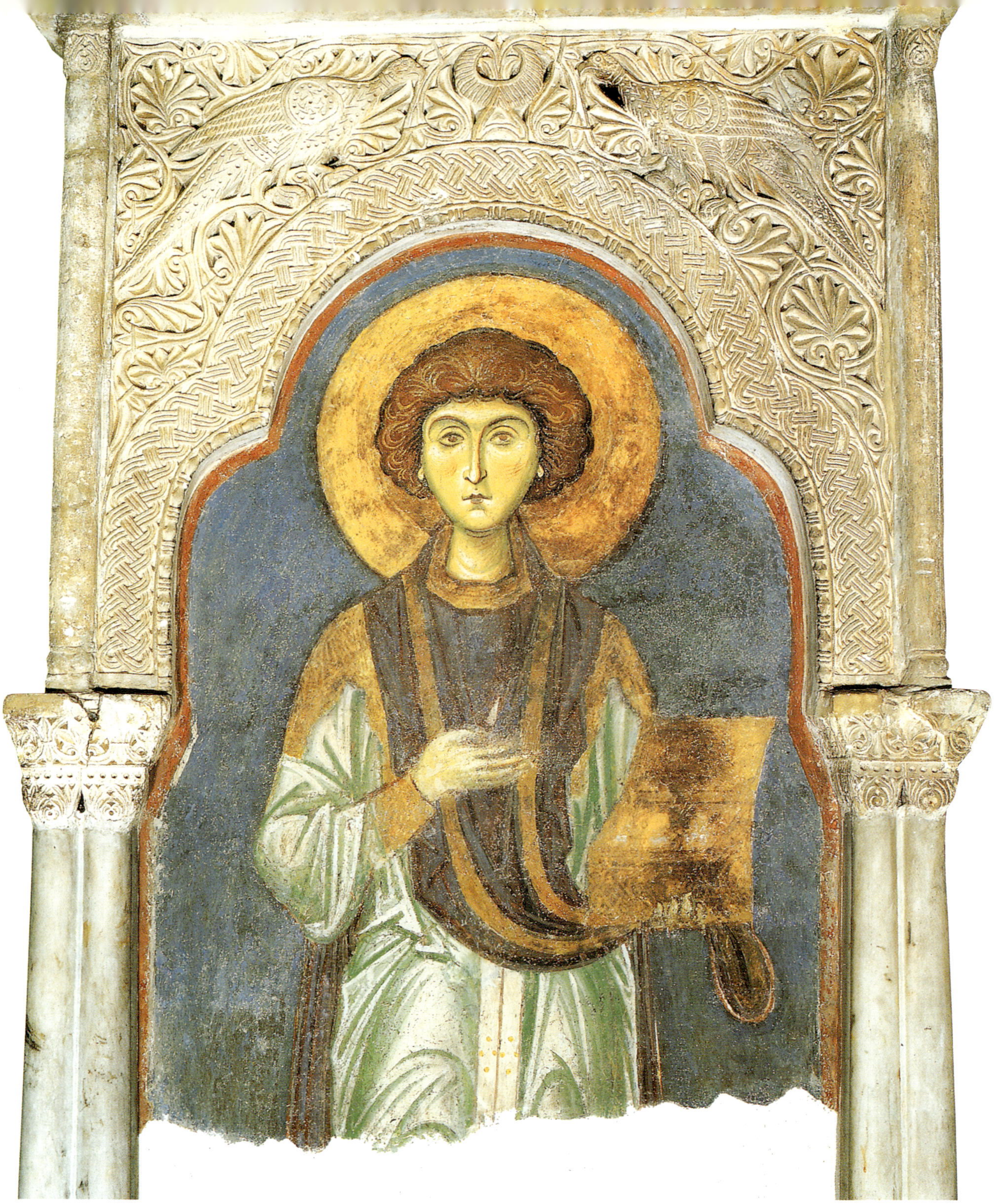

Pantaleon of Nicomedia, Physician and Martyr

† 305
Memorial: June 27
Lat.: Pantaleo Medicus; Gr.: Pantaleimon, "the merciful"; It.: Pantaleone, Pantalemone; Fr.: Pantaléon de Nicomédie; Pandelon, Pantaly, Plantaire; Sp.: Pantaleón; Ger.: Pantaleon.

Pantaleon is venerated as one of the *anargyroi* physicians, that is, those who healed without asking for any compensation. Born of a pagan father and a Christian mother, Pantaleon, who had not yet been baptized, became a disciple of the famous physician Euphrosinus; he acquired great skill and was admitted to the imperial court of Maximinian Galerius. He came to know Hermolaus, who was a secret Christian and taught the young man that Christ is the true physician and that prayer is effective medicine. In fact, through prayer Pantaleon obtained the **resuscitation of a child** who had been bitten by a snake. He then received baptism, converted his father, and healed a blind man with the sign of the cross.

St. Pantaleon of Nicomedia.
12th–13th-cent. fresco in the church of St. Pantaleon in Nerezi, Macedonia.
The saint holds the instruments of his work as a physician.

The saint roused the envy of his fellow physicians and ended up being delated to Maximinian. Despite the miraculous healing of a paralytic, Maximinian was not convinced and had Pantaleon suffer many tortures. He survived them all because Christ always delivered him and even appeared to him in the likeness of Hermolaus. When Pantaleon was imprisoned, Jesus appeared to him in his cell and gave him the name by which we know him, that is, Pantaleon, "he who is merciful." He suffered many torments: he was put on the rack, burned with torches, immersed in molten lead, and finally thrown into the sea with a millstone around his neck. But Jesus came walking on the water and led him back to shore. He was then thrown to the wild beasts as their food, but they licked his feet; his torturers tried to tear him to pieces by means of a toothed wheel, but this broke; they tied him to the trunk of an olive tree and nailed him to it by means of a **nail through his head, which was first covered with his own hands** (this torment appears in his iconography). Finally, he was beheaded, and from his torso flowed a great deal of milk, because of which he is patron of wet nurses.

Before dying, the saint asked for forgiveness for his executioners; at this, a voice from heaven proclaimed that his name was not "Pantaleon" but "Pantaleemon," that is, "He who has pity on all."

▷▷ His mercifulness won him fame in both East and West, and we find him numbered among the *anargyroi* physicians, like Cosmas and Damian, and among the Fourteen Intercessors. He is patron of physicians, midwives, and wet nurses, and is invoked against headache and consumption or tuberculosis.

▷▷ He is depicted either in the garb of his time or in Renaissance clothing, with his **hands nailed to his head** (the **nail** became his principal attribute). Other attributes are his **physician's instruments**, such as a **urinal** or an **ampoule of ointment**; he is also shown in the **act of healing a child**.

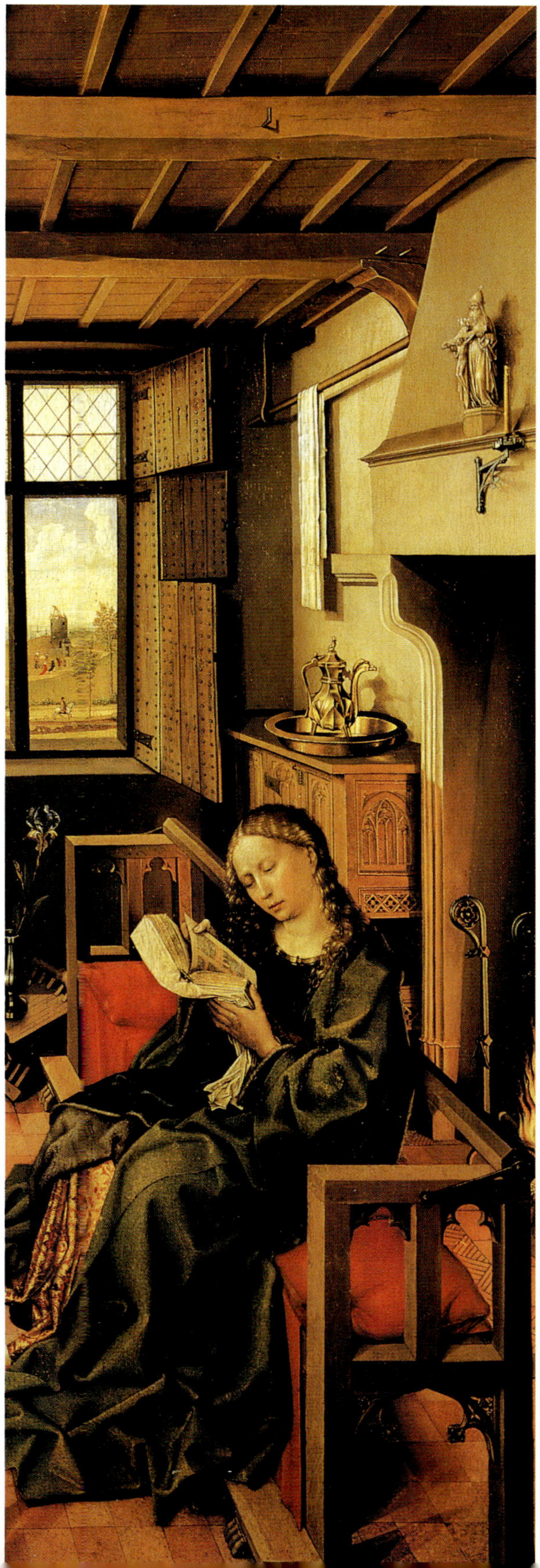

St. Barbara of Nicomedia.
By Robert Campin (1375–1444), formerly known as the Master of Flémalle; work now in the Prado Museum, Madrid.
The tower that was to mark the saint's fate and iconography appears on the horizon outside the window.

Barbara, Virgin and Martyr

† 306
Memorial: December 4
Lat.: Barbara; It.: Barbara; Fr.: Barbe, Babette; Sp.: Barbara; Ger.: Barbara, Bärbele; Russ.: Varvara, Varia, Varvenka.

The cult of St. Barbara was established and widespread from very early times, but we have only vague information about her. She was martyred between the middle and the end of the third century. Tradition says she was born in Nicomedia as the daughter of Dioscurus, a satrap. In order to remove her from the reach of suitors, he had her locked up in a **tower**. She wanted baptism, and before entering the tower she immersed herself three times in a nearby pool. To the two windows her father wanted the tower to have, she had a third added in honor of the Trinity. When Dioscurus learned that she was a Christian, he decided to put her to death. Barbara managed to escape by passing through the walls of the tower, but a shepherd betrayed her hiding place; in punishment, his sheep were changed into grasshoppers.

Barbara was then taken before the magistrates, who had her body wrapped in cloths so rough that they drew blood. After being healed during the night, she was tortured with white-hot plates. When taken naked around the city, she returned healed and clothed. The rods with which she was beaten turned into **peacock feathers**. Finally, she was beheaded by her own father, who was then incinerated by a deafening **lightning bolt.**

▷▷ Barbara is numbered among the Fourteen Intercessors. The list of her patronages is long and, like her iconography, these become connected, in successive linkings, with the themes of the tower and its construction, her imprisonment and desire to learn about Christianity, the lightning that struck her father, and the thunder that followed it, and the three windows, as well as with her name.

As a virgin who at a very early age applied herself to the study of Christian teaching, she is the patron of students and scholars. Because of her imprisonment, she is patron of prisoners. Because of the **tower** in which she was locked up, with its **three windows** in honor of the Most Holy Trinity, she is the patron of engineers, architects, masons, and builders generally. The thunder linked her with explosions in general; she is therefore protector of artillery men, miners, and those who dig and work on oil wells; she is protector also of those who work with saltpeter, as well as harquebusiers, armorers, soldiers generally. She is connected with these last also by the fact that in her iconography the tower had been replaced by a **cannon barrel**. The similarity between the cannon balls of the artillery and those used in games made Barbara the patron of ballplayers. She protects stonecutters because the walls of her prison opened up before her.

By reason of the fire and lightning she is invoked against fires and protects firemen. Because firefighters are summoned by bells, which also ring out when lightning and thunder are present, she is protector of bell-ringers, carillon players, and casters of bells, all of whom also face unexpected dangers in their work. By reason of her very name, Barbara, which suggests beards and therefore hair, she is patron of upholsterers and makers of tapestries and brushes, rackets, and, similarly, embroidery frames, as well as felt hats. She is invoked for the gift of curly haired children. In remembrance of the punishment inflicted on the shepherd she is invoked against invasions of grasshoppers and other harmful insects. Because the stones of the tower did not prevent her from fleeing, she is invoked against the illness of stones. By reason of her very name, she is invoked against uncouthness and diseases of the tongue. Because of the "unexpected" crash of thunder she is invoked by all who live in danger of sudden death, as, for example, roofers, who are in danger of deadly falls. She is therefore patron of the confraternities that pray for a happy death; as a result, the **chalice** of viaticum became part of her iconography.

▷▷ Her principal attribute is a **tower with three windows**; other attributes are a **peacock's feather**, a **cannon** and **cannonballs**, a **chalice and host**; sometimes she is depicted with her **father** and **executioners at her feet**.

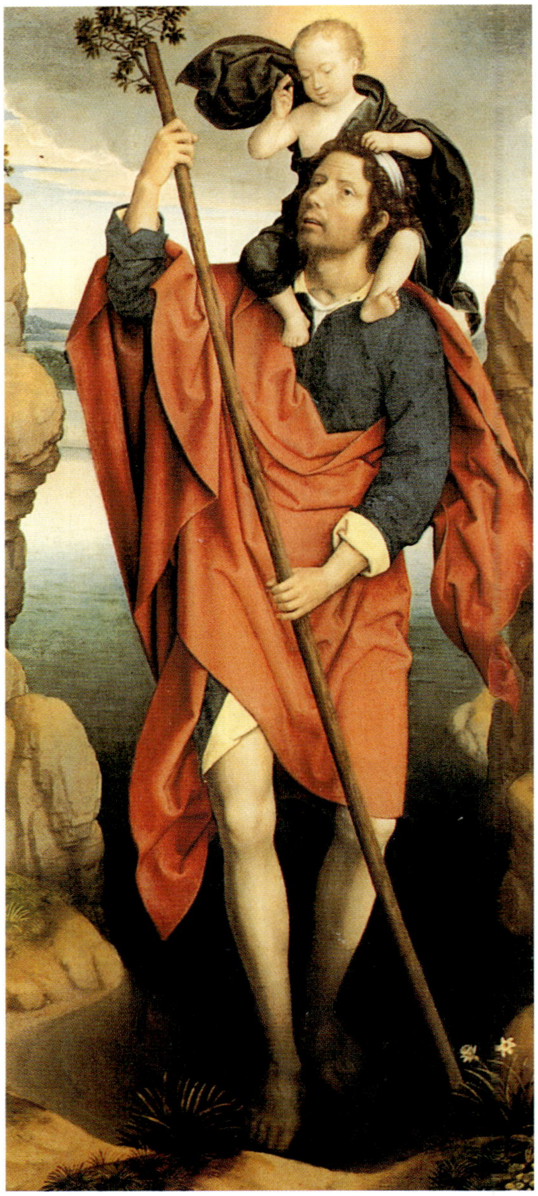

St. Christopher.
By Hans Memling, 1435/40–1494, in the Musée Communal des Beaux-Arts, Bruges.

Christopher, Martyr

4th century
Memorial: July 25
Lat.: Christophorus; Gr.: Christophoros; It.: Cristoforo, Crisofano; Fr.: Christophe, Christofle, Christol, Christoly, Christau, Christaud; Sp.: Cristobal. Ger.: Christoph, Christoffel, Stoffel, Christusträger, Stromträger; Russ.: Kristofor.

"Christopher" means "Christ-bearer." His real name was "Reprobus," and he was a gigantic Canaanite of fierce appearance. He was in the service of the king of his country, but he was overcome by a desire to serve the mightiest king of the world. He found a mighty king, but discovered that he was afraid of the devil; he then served the devil, but found that he was afraid of Christ. One day, when Reprobus and the devil were walking along together, they came upon a cross, and the devil fled; Reprobus questioned him and learned that one day a man named Christ had been nailed to a cross and that this sign terrified the devil. He realized, then, that he must search for Christ.

A hermit preached the gospel to Reprobus and suggested that he serve Christ through fasting and prayer. But Reprobus told him that these would not do in his case. The hermit then indicated to him a river in which many people drowned as they tried to cross it, and suggested that, given his height and strength, he help travelers to cross. This, he said, would greatly please Jesus, who perhaps would appear to him. Reprobus realized that this was something he could do, and he became a ferryman.

One day, a child asked him to be taken across; he put the child on his shoulders and entered the water. The river became swollen and turbulent, and the child became heavier and heavier, until Reprobus feared for his life. When he reached the other bank, the child told him that he had carried on his shoulders not only the world but its Creator. The child also promised him a sign: his **staff** would put forth flowers and fruit. Reprobus stuck the staff in the ground, and the next morning found it **leafy** like a palm tree and full of dates. He then had himself baptized under the name of Christopher, "Christ-bearer," and, in order to serve Christ, went off to Lycia. Here, after receiving the gift of understanding the language of the place, he undertook to strengthen Christians who were being led to martyrdom. He in his turn faced martyrdom: arrows were shot at him that turned back on the archers, and one of them blinded the prefect. Christopher died when he chose, after suffering many tortures without harm and not before having converted, through prodigies of preaching and charitable works, those who had tried to persuade him to sacrifice to the gods. By a miracle after his death he also converted the king who had had him put to death.

▷▷ St. Christopher is a holy martyr and a Helper. Because he carried Christ, he is patron of all who serve in transport and all travelers, including civil and military aviators: motorists and drivers, and therefore motor mechanics as well; boatmen, ferrymen, railway workers, tramway employees, porters, stevedores, stretcher-bearers, postal workers and couriers, as well as pilgrims, voyagers, and sportsmen; and, because of his flowering staff, patron also of gardeners and fish farmers, as well as fruit growers and fruit venders. Due to his great height and to the great weight he carried, he is patron of athletes. Because of the isolated life he lived as a ferryman, he is patron of hermits. He also protects those whose work exposes them to the danger of sudden death, such as harquebusiers and alpinists, whose staff resembles that of the ferryman. He is invoked against sudden death, plague, hurricanes, and hail; against diseases of the teeth, whitlow, and diseases of the eyes (this last because of the blindness that struck one of the archers). One who invokes him may find hidden treasure; as a ferryman he is also invoked against floods.

▷▷ Christopher is shown bearded or beardless; he is represented as a **man of giant size** and in **large scale** images outside churches, so that anyone who sees these is safe that day from a sudden death and a death without the consolation of the sacraments. This aspect of Christopher's charity was especially important for pilgrims who, coming from afar and meeting the dangers and difficulties of the journey, could see the image and have the strengthening assurance it conveyed. He always carries the **Child Jesus** on his shoulders (this is his principal attribute); other attributes are the **flowering staff**, which is almost always present, the **river with its fish**, and a **monk** in the distance.

St. Emidius.
By Ubaldo Gandolfi, 1728–1781, in the church of San Giuliano, Bologna.

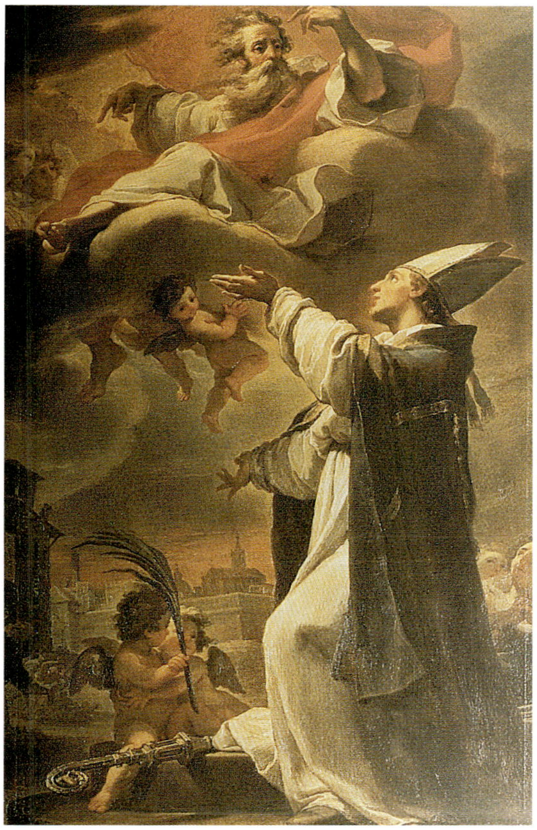

Emidius of Ascoli, Bishop and Martyr

† 303
Memorial: August 5
Lat.: Emigdius Asculanus, Emidius; It.: Emidio; Fr.: Émigde, Émygde; Ger.: Emygdius von Ascoli.

Emidius was born in Trier and lived there initially, but after his baptism he fled to Italy with his companions, Euplus, Garmanus, and Valentinus, and was ordained a priest by Maternus, bishop of Milan. Later on, he was consecrated a bishop in Rome and was sent to Ascoli, whose first bishop he was. Here he effected many conversions, among them that of the daughter of the Roman prefect. He was beheaded in 303. Information about him dates from only after the eleventh century. When in 1703 a terrible earthquake did not affect Ascoli, which regarded Emidius as its first bishop, his cult spread throughout many cities that chose him as one of their patrons.

▷▷ Emidius is the patron of Ascoli and is invoked against earthquakes.

▷▷ He is depicted in **episcopal garb and holding up a building that is wobbling**. Other images show him **carrying his head** or in the act of displaying a **model of the city**.

Catherine of Alexandria, Virgin and Martyr, Doctor of the Church

† 305
Memorial: November 25
Lat.: Catharina Alexandrina; Gr.: Aikaterinê; It.: Caterina d'Alessandria, Caterina della ruota; Fr.: Catherine d'Alexandrie; Sp.: Catalina de Alejandria; Ger.: Katherina von Alexandria, Käthe, Käthchen; Russ.: Ekaterina, Katenka, Katia; Hung.: Katalin.

This courageous and wise woman is venerated in a famous monastery on Mount Sinai. Her name in Greek means "pure." According to tradition, she was of royal blood and is depicted quite often wearing a royal crown. Emperor Maxentius or Maximinianus called upon his subjects to sacrifice to the gods; Catherine went to the place intending to encourage Christians in bearing witness; there she boldly exhorted them to acknowledge the true God. She was taken to the palace and ordered to offer sacrifice; she refused and, when **the wise men were summoned** to confound her, not only did she refute them she also converted them and convinced them to the point of martyrdom. When imprisoned, she was fed by a dove and visited by Jesus. The empress visited her, along with an officer and two hundred soldiers; Catherine converted them all. Then the emperor ordered her subjected to the torture of **hooked wheels**, but these **broke** and killed the torturers. The empress was converted and suffered martyrdom. Finally, Catherine was taken outside the city; there she prayed to God for her disciples and God himself answered; she was then beheaded.

From her neck gushed milk, and her body was immediately taken by angels to Mount Sinai. From her tomb, too, miraculous milk and oil flowed that healed every ill.

▷▷ Catherine is one of the Fourteen Helpers. She is patron of apprentice seamstresses (known in Italian as *caterinette*), milliners, and, as one espoused to Christ, of young girls. Because of her learned discussions, she is a patron of the liberal arts, notaries, lawyers, and attorneys, as well as of theologians, philosophers, university students, and schoolchildren. Because of her sufferings, she is a protector of the dying. She is protector of all trades that involve wheels, from cartwrights, millers, turners, and potters to spinners, knife-grinders, barbers, carters, and cyclists. She protects all who deal with blades, because the hooks of the wheels were sharpened like razor blades. Because of the milk that gushed from her neck, she is protector of nurses and wet nurses, and, because she was decapitated, she is invoked against migraine and diseases of the tongue.

Catherine is patron of Cyprus, Venice, Mantua, Sabbioneta, Guastalla, and Scala.

▷▷ Catherine is shown disputing with the wise men even as she is being martyred; she is shown also at the moment of her mystical marriage with Jesus: the Virgin holds Catherine's hand while Jesus places a ring on her finger.

Her principal attribute is a **broken wheel**; others are a **crown**, **princely garb**, a **book**, which alludes to her learned disquisitions, the **sword** that beheaded her, and the **ring** of the mystical marriage.

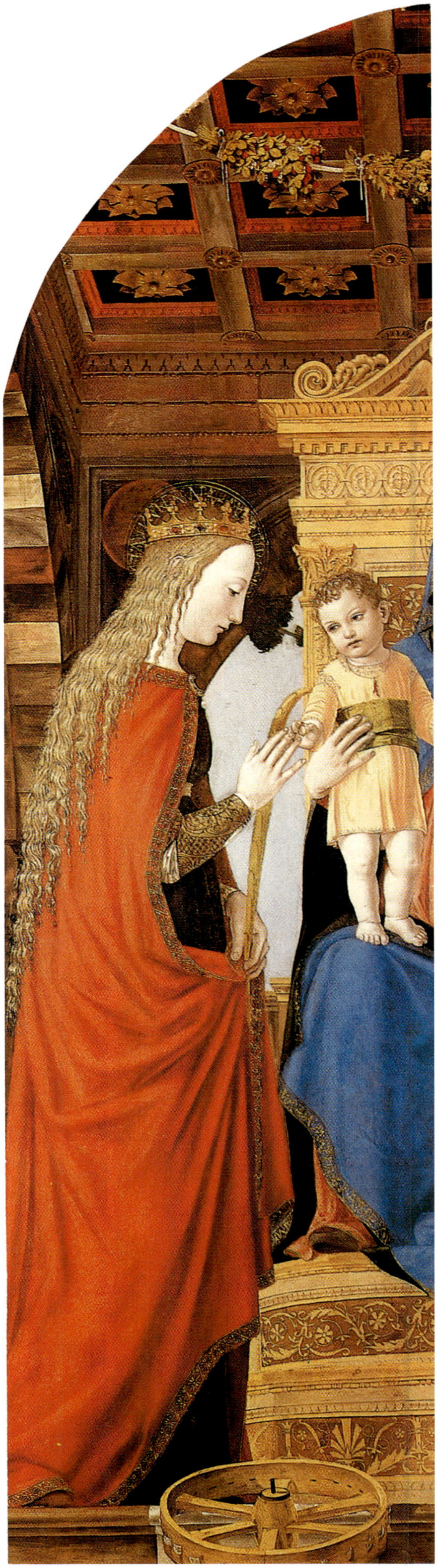

Blaise of Sebaste, Bishop and Martyr

† 316
Memorial: February 3
Lat.: Blasius Sebastenus; It.: Biagio, Blasio; Fr.: Blaise, Balu, Blais, Blaive, Blay; Sp.: Blasco, Velasco (from which is derived the patronym Velásquez = son of Velasco); Port : Braz, Vasco; Ger.: Blasius, Blas; Russ.: Vlas; Slav.: Vlaho.

Blaise was bishop of Sebaste (Sivas) in Armenia and, perhaps because of his gifts as a wonderworker, was thought to have been a physician. When a persecution broke out (probably that of Licinius, 307 and 323), Blaise took refuge on a cave in a nearby forest, where he used to heal sick animals with the sign of the cross; these animals remained with him.

Some hunters discovered him among the bears, lions, and tigers and delated him to the Roman magistrate; he was captured and locked up, but continued healing people with the sign of the cross. The most famous person among those he healed became part of his

St. Catherine of Alexndria and St. Catherine of Siena.
By Ambrogio da Fossano, known as "Il Bergognone," died 1552; in the National Gallery, London.

iconography: **a little boy who had choked on a fishbone stuck in his throat, and whose mother brought him to the saint**; the boy was immediately saved. While Blaise was in prison and suffering torments, a woman whose suckling pig had been carried off by a wolf asked for his help, and the wolf immediately brought the piglet back. The woman offered the saint food and **candles**. Blaise urged her rather to offer a candle every year to the church; this was to be put on an elevated stand and dedicated to him; if she did so, she would lack for nothing but would have every good thing.

After being cruelly tortured with **carders' combs**, Blaise was finally beheaded, but before dying he asked God to cure everyone with an illness of the throat who appealed to him.

His cult spread slowly but surely, and today is worldwide. He is celebrated on February 3, but in the East the date may be February 11 or 15.

▷▷ Because of his healing of the boy who choked he is invoked against all maladies of the throat and neck; in Germany, also against stones and maladies of the bladder, this because of the similarity of sound between *Blase* (= bladder) and the saint's name. In fourteenth- and fifteenth-century Germany, "St. Blaise's water" (water blessed on his feast day) was sprinkled on poultry, in order that they might be spared by the wolves.

Because of the miracle of the piglet Blaise is patron of pig-keepers. Because he tamed wild animals, he is invoked as protector of livestock; pig-keepers carved his name on their staves; in Abruzzo and Molise they tied a red string around the necks of the livestock.

Blaise is patron of Croatia and, more specifically, of Ragusa; Dubrovnik is called "St. Blaise's City." In Italy he is patron of Naples.

Because of the carders' combs with which he was tortured, he is patron of Yorkshire, England, which was a center of wool production. He is also patron of carders and mattress makers. Because the carder's comb resembles a mason's tool (the serrated chisel), Blaise is their patron as well. Due to the incident of the fishbone, Blaise is protector of laryngologists and is invoked against all maladies of the throat and against hiccups. Because *blasen* in German means "to blow," Blaise is protector of players of wind instruments. For the same reason, he is invoked against storms and protects windmills and therefore millers. Again because of the similarity of sound (in Italian) between "Biagio" and "bacio" (kiss), in many parts of Italy and in French Savoie Blaise is the saint of engaged couples: girls ask him for husbands, and a saying in Brescia has it that "the first one met is to be kissed."

Blaise is protector of carpenters and also of stonecutters, because the iron hooks of the combs recall the toothed tool with which they set up blocks of stone.

Tradition has combined in a gesture of devout prayer the themes of the **candles** and the **healed throat**. On the saint's feast day it is customary to apply to the neck two candles tied together in the form of a Y. In Germany, the last person to be blessed in the line of devotees used to be called *der Bläse* and was mocked for the rest of the year. In other places, the saint's altar has a white cord tied around it, and the devout advance on their knees to press their throats against the cord, while asking for the favors they want.

In some churches, special "St. Blaise rolls" are distributed (*Bubenschenkel* in German; *Cannaruzzeddi di san Brasi* in Sardinian), attesting to a widespread practice: if properly made, these rolls should represent the affected part, namely, the throat, and preserve it from illness. In Rome there is a church known as "San Biagio alla Pagnotta" (of the loaf); in Milan it is the custom to keep a slice of panettone to be eaten on February 3.

The saint's name in French patois, "Bla," suggests the word for grain, "blé"; as a result, he is invoked by peasants for a good harvest. At one time, in rural areas, a handful of grain was brought to the church; when blessed and mixed with the seed to be sown, the grain ensured a proper germination and a good harvest. In France and in Istria, at least until the war of 1914–1918, there were processions of decorated carts carrying groups of people in costumes.

▷▷ Blaise is depicted in **episcopal garb**, and stories of his miracles are represented: the scene most frequently shown is that in which **the woman brings her lifeless son to the saint**. His principal attribute is a **carder's comb**. Another is **candles**.

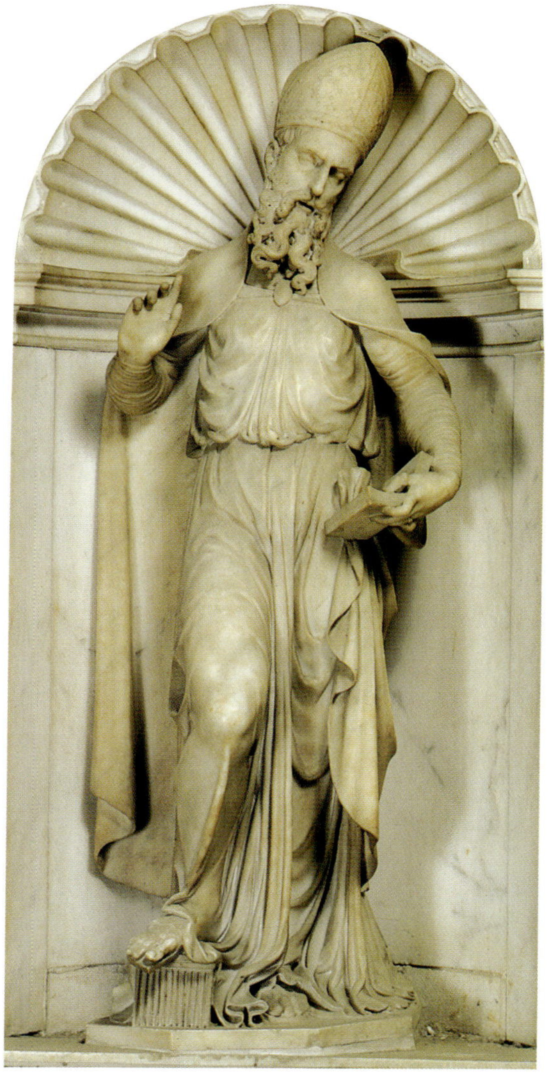

St. Blaise.
Statue by Pandolfo Fancelli, 1523/1526, in the cathedral of Pisa.

Helen, Mother of Emperor Constantine

250–329
Memorial: August 18
Lat.: Helena; It.: Elena; Fr.: Hélène, Elne, Helaine, Helayne; Sp.: Elena; Ger.: Helena, Lena; Swed.: Elin; Rum.: Ileana; Russ.: Olga.

Helen was a hotel keeper when she married Constantius Chlorus, and she already had one son, Crispus. Later on, she had to step aside when Constantius, on becoming emperor, was obliged, for political reasons, to marry Theodora, daughter of Maximian Herculeus.

By Constantius, Helen had a son, Constantine, who on becoming emperor brought her to his court, gave her the title of Augusta, and greatly honored her. She took advantage of her son's generosity in order to do good; thus wherever she went, she aided the poor, whom she invited to her table and served with her own hands; she set prisoners free and brought exiles home. At the age of 78, she set out from Naples in 326 on a pilgrimage to the Holy Land. It was perhaps a penitential pilgrimage to atone for the two murders which, it was said, were ordered by Constantine himself (Crispus and his wife had been killed).

Tradition has it that in the Holy Land she discovered the true **cross** on Golgotha and that she persuaded her son to build the basilica of the Anastasis (Resurrection). St. Ambrose refers to her with admiration because she made a gift of the discovered **nails** of Christ's crucifixion to her son, having one of them shaped as a horse's bit and having another inserted into a crown that would become famous and be venerated as the Iron Cross (now in the cathedral of Monza). The queen's obvious intention was to urge moderation on her son and to make him realize that there is no earthly ruler who is not subject to Christ.

With Constantine at her side, Helen died around 329 in some unknown place, but her body was taken to Rome and placed in a mausoleum on the Labican Way "near the two laurels" (now Torpignattara).

On her feast day in Russia people sow flax, with the hope that it may become as long as her hair.

▷▷ Helen is patron of the Knights of the Holy Sepulcher. Because she found the true cross, she is invoked in the search for lost objects. Because the holy cross caused demons to flee, she is invoked against demons and the harm they cause (epilepsy, for example) and also against tumors. She protects nail-makers, because she also found the nails that pierced Jesus, and of dyers, because she discovered the tunic of Jesus that was dyed purple. France and the cities of Paris and Madrid invoke her as their patron.

▷▷ She is depicted as a Roman matron, wearing an imperial **crown** and cloak. Her principal attributes are, first, the **cross**, and then the **crown of thorns** and the **nails**.

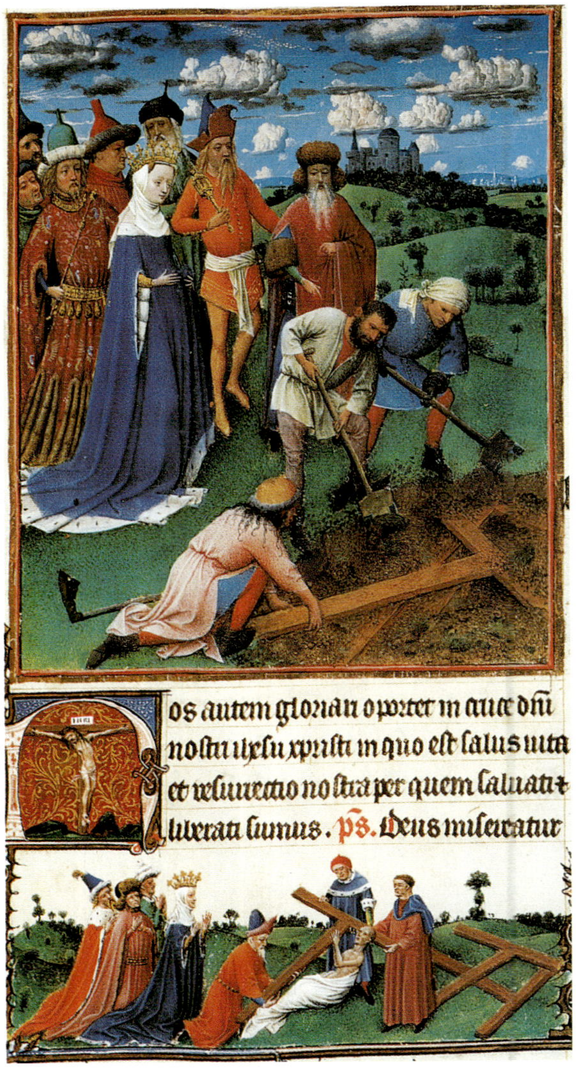

St. Helen Discovers the True Cross.
Miniature in the 15th-cent. Milanese *Book of Hours,* in the Musei Civici, Turin.

Anthony Abbot, Hermit and Wonderworker

251–ca. 356
Memorial: January 17
Lat.: Antonius; It.: Antonio, Tanzio; Fr.: Antoine l'Ermite; Sp.: Antonio Abad, de Viana (i.e., of Vienne or Viennois), Antón; Ger.: Der Heilige Antonius Abt, Eremit, der Einsiedler, der Grosse, Antoni, Toni, Tönnies, Tüns, Túenes; Dutch: Antonius de Heremiet, de Kluizenaar.

The cult of St. Anthony Abbot, who died in 356 without ever having left Egypt, became universal; he is a good example of the way in which the history of a saint does not end with his earthly life but continues in his active relationship with human beings and with God, leaving traces in his iconography.

Anthony was one of the founders of monasticism, a word whose Greek root is *monos* = "one"; a monk is a man who belongs to One alone, that is, to God, and lives alone. We see him depicted, therefore, in the monastic habit; he is called "abbot," that is, "father," because a monastic superior is a father to his monks.

After his parents died, Anthony distributed his possessions to the poor and withdrew into the solitude of the Thebaid in Egypt. He lived according to the rule "Pray and work,"

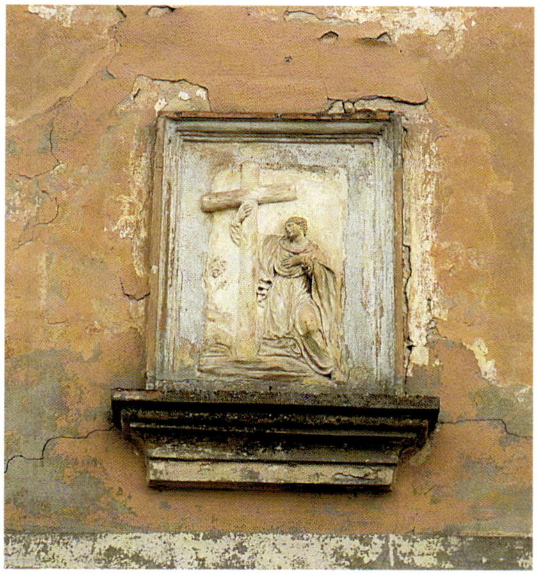

St. Helen Adores the Cross.
19th-cent. devotional plaque in the parish church of Sacerno, Bologna.

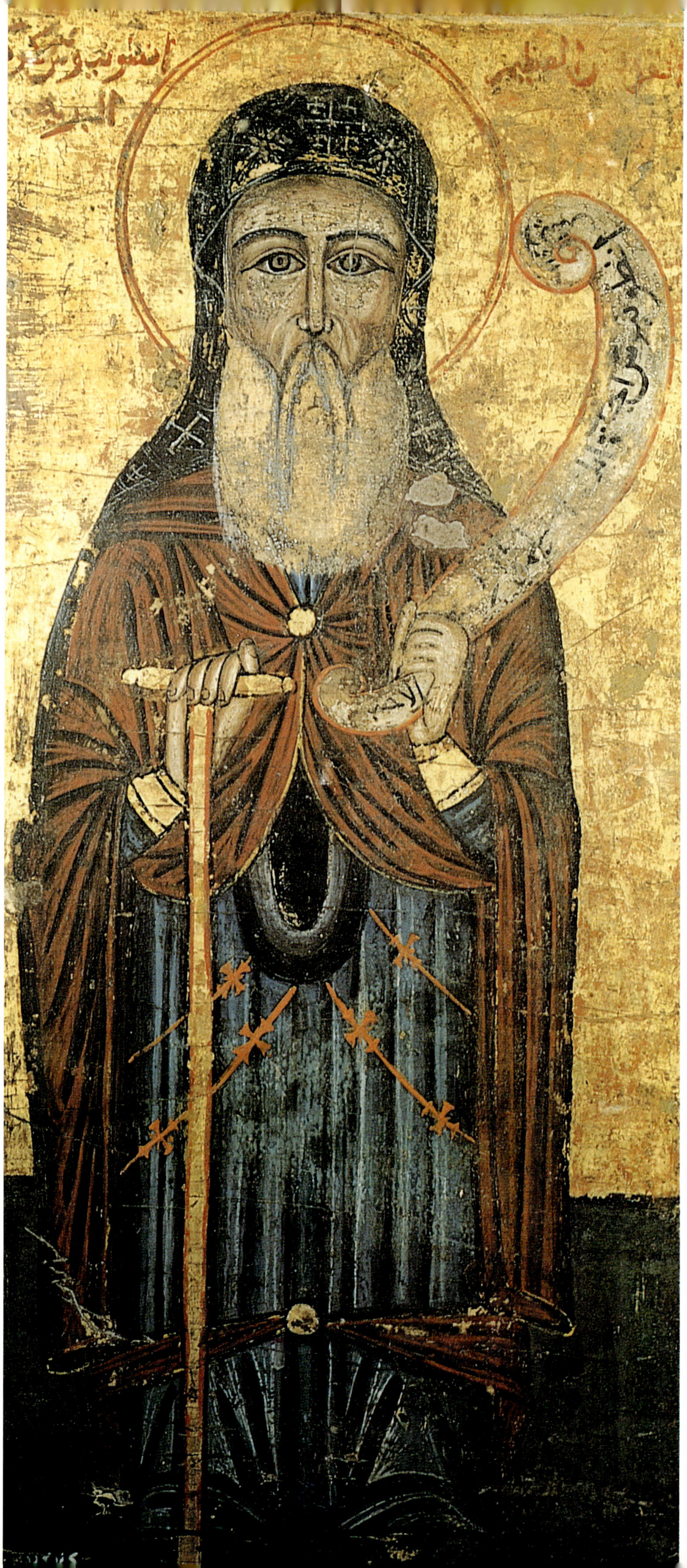

St. Anthony the Great.
18th-cent. icon in the Museum of Coptic Art in Old Cairo.
St. Anthony Abbot, one of the fathers of monasticism, is a saint venerated in both the East and the West.

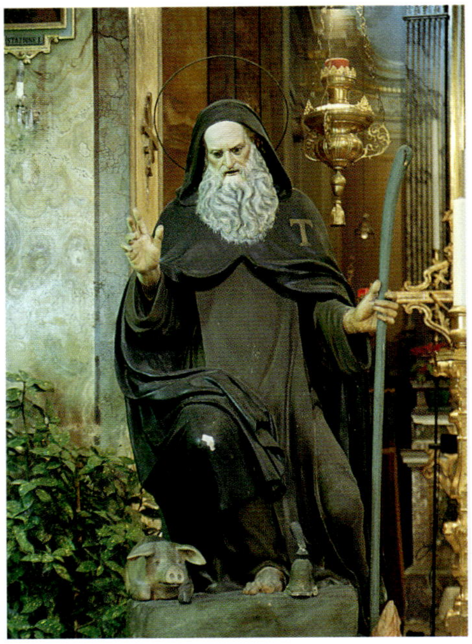

St. Anthony Abbot.
Processional statue by Angelo Piò, 1690–1770, in the church of St. Magdalene of Cazzano, Bologna. The feast of St. Anthony Abbot, on which stables and domesticated animals are blessed, is highly esteemed in the rural areas of Europe, and the traditions about this saint are kept alive through processions and festivals. In the cities, too, the practice of bringing domestic animals to the church for a blessing is now spreading.

which an angel had taught him. The devil tempted him cruelly in the desert by obscene thoughts and by thoughts only seemingly spiritual. For this reason, legends presented him as frequently doing battle with the devil for the souls of recently deceased Christians. The devil appears often in his iconography. Thanks to prayer, he resisted temptations, and the Lord allowed him to comfort the afflicted, free those possessed, heal the sick, and instruct those who desired to devote themselves to the ascetical life. A pleasant legend claims that Anthony went down into hell to steal the devil's fire and that while he distracted the devil, his **piglet** ran into hell, stole a firebrand, and carried it away to give it to human beings.

Anthony's reputation as healer of shingles (which was therefore known as "St. Anthony's fire") brought the sick to the French village that took its name from him: Saint-Antoine de Viennois. It was to this place that his relics came; a hospital was built there, run by a confraternity of religious men who later became the Hospital Order of the Antonians. This order took as its emblem the T, "tau," a traditional attribute of the saint. The T is a very ancient sacred symbol of the center of the world; it is the last letter of the Hebrew alphabet and therefore alludes to the last things and to destiny; it was the form taken by monks' staves. The Antonians raised **pigs** that wore a **bell** and had the privilege of grazing freely throughout the countryside.

▷▷ Anthony is the patron of hermits. Because, with a lion's help, he buried Paul the Hermit in the desert of the Thebaid, he is patron also of gravediggers. By way of the piglet not only did the bell become an element in the saint's iconography (he is also called "St. Anthony of the Bell"); in addition, the saint became the protector of pigs and their keepers, as well as of domesticated animals generally, in particular those kept in stables; he also became the patron of many trades having to do with pigs and pig products. Tradition had it that during the night of the eve of January 17 animals were heard to speak in their stables; the blessing of stables on that day is a deeply rooted and lively tradition. Animals, ranging from large dogs to little fish, are taken from the countryside into the cities for a blessing.

Again because of the piglet Anthony is protector of butchers and grocers, shearers and makers of brushes (made with pigs' bristles), weavers and cloth merchants, tanners and glove makers. He is patron of basketmakers because he himself wove baskets in the desert. He healed the "fire" of shingles and is therefore patron of firefighters; he is invoked against the fire of hell and against conflagrations, as well as against every kind of infection, especially all diseases of the skin, such as mange, itch, scabies, scurvy, leprosy, syphilis, and other venereal maladies, and also against simple boils and varicose veins. Because of the piglet's bell, he is the patron of bell ringers. He is also invoked in time of plague because the T-shaped staff recalls the Hebrews whose lives were spared when the brazen serpent was raised on high to combat an epidemic: whoever looked on it would be saved. This cross is a clear image of Christ.

▷▷ Anthony is depicted either in the **garb of a monk** or hermit or as a **mitered abbot** in episcopal dress. His principal attributes are the **T-shaped staff**, the **piglet**, and fire; secondary attributes are the **bell** and **animals** that are kept in stalls, such as **horses**, **dogs**, and **pigs**.

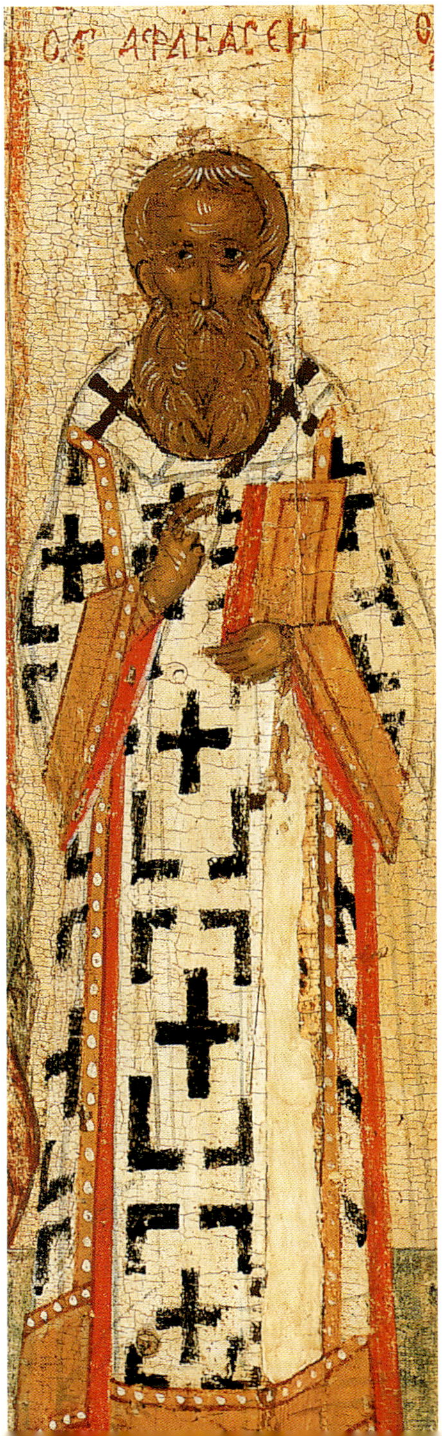

Athanasius the Great, Bishop and Doctor of the Church

298–373
Memorial: May 2
Lat.: Athanasius Alexandrinus; It.: Atanasio di Alessandria; Fr.: Athanase; Sp.: Atanasio; Ger.: Athanasius der Grosse.

Athanasius was one of the Greek Fathers of the Church. He was born in Alexandria in 298, became that city's bishop in 326, and took part in the Council of Nicaea as an opponent of Arius and the latter's heresy (Christ possessed only a human nature).

Athanasius is one of those saints whose greatness consists in an abundance of works and of teaching; his relatively simple life was not marked by sensational incidents, and images of him are not numerous in the West. He was a child during the persecutions of Diocletian; he became a disciple of Anthony Abbot in the desert, and it was there that he began to write his books. He saw the rise of heresy in the preaching of Arius, attended the Council of Nicaea, and succeeded the bishop of Alexandria in 328. But he did not exercise his authority in an atmosphere of tranquility, for while he was supported by the Catholics, throughout his life he had to endure the hostility of the Arians, who were often backed by the emperors. He was forced several times to take refuge among the hermits of Egypt, who loved him greatly, and was several times exiled, despite the protection of Popes Julius and Liberius. The final years of his life were fairly tranquil, although he continued to devote himself to the defense of orthodoxy against the Arian heresy. He died in 373.

His books are very numerous; he was one of the first nonmartyr bishops to be venerated. His relics are venerated in the Church of the Holy Cross in Venice, to which they were transferred from Constantinople in the middle of the fifteenth century.

▷▷ He is invoked against headaches.

▷▷ He is depicted as a Greek bishop and therefore does not wear a miter. His principal attribute is a **light-filled triangle**, a symbol of the Trinity, which he defended against heresy; another is a **ship**, which is a reminder of how he once fled on a ship from the violence of his enemies.

St. Athanasius the Great.
Icon from the second half of the 15th cent., Novgorod.

St. John Chrysostom.
Royal door, in the Tret'jakov Gallery, Moscow.

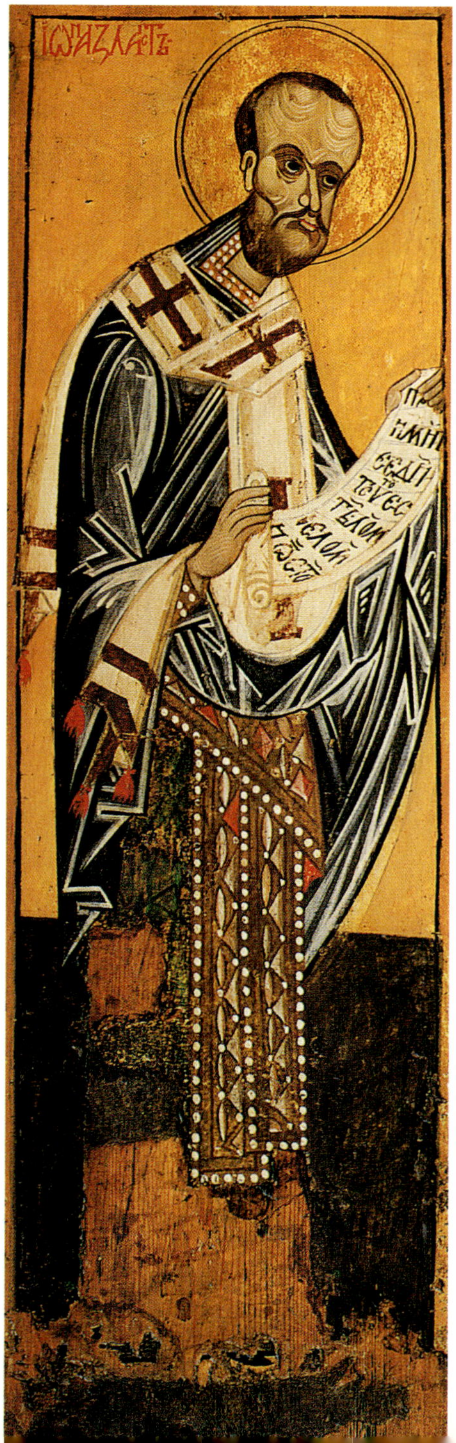

John Chrysostom, Bishop and Doctor of the Church

344–407
Memorial: September 13 (January 27)
Lat.: Johannes Chrysostomus; It.: Giovanni Crisostomo, Giovanni Cristomi, Gio Crisostome Bocca d'oro; Sp.: Juan Crisostomo Boca de oro; Eng.: (also) John of the Golden Mouth; Ger.: Johannes Chrysostomos, Goldmund; Pol.: Jan Zlotousty; Russ.: Ioann Zlatooust.

John was born in Antioch in 344 and owes the name "Chrysostom" (= "Golden Mouth") to his eloquence. He was a fellow student of Basil, was baptized in 368, and embraced the eremitical life after his mother's death. He spent two years in a cave without ever lying down to sleep and while being tormented by the cold; he fell ill and had to return to the city and to pastoral activities. He was consecrated a bishop in 385 (386); in that office he devoted himself to preaching and had the ability to fascinate crowds of hearers. He was consecrated patriarch of Constantinople in 398 but was banished due to the intrigues of Empress Eudoxia, whose vices he had castigated. He died in exile in 407.

▷▷ His role as patron of preachers was confirmed by Leo XIII on July 4, 1884, and by Pius X on July 8, 1908. He is a patron of Turkey, and his patronage of European Turkey (now Bulgaria) was confirmed by Pius X on January 7, 1914.

▷▷ John is depicted wearing a **dalmatic**, and his principal attribute is a **beehive** placed at his feet (as in the case of St. Ambrose). Another attribute is a **parchment scroll** which he holds in his hand and which sometimes lengthens out into a stream from which the faithful drink.

Martin of Tours, Bishop

316–397
Memorial: November 11
Lat.: Martinus Turonensis; It.: Martino di Tours; Fr.: Martin de Tours; Sp.: Martín; Port.: Martinho; Ger.: Martin von Tours; Dutch: Maarten.

Martin is, as it were, a spiritual bridge across Europe between France and Hungary, where this saint was born. He is one of the most popular and beloved saints, especially in rural areas, because of his humility and generosity. A great many churches are dedicated to him, and the picture of him sharing his cloak with a poor man has always been a familiar one. It is no accident that we very often find it along pilgrimage routes, because the poor man was soon identified with a pilgrim (an image of Christ), in keeping with the words of Jesus at the final judgment: "Whenever you did it to even one of these, my least brothers, you did it to me" (Matt 25:40).

Martin was born in Pannonia (present-day Hungary) to a very loyal officer of the army, who dedicated him to Mars, the god of war. When Martin was a still a child, his father was assigned to Pavia; it was here that the boy came to know Christianity and became a catechumen, much to the disapproval of his father, who, in order to turn him from his purpose, started him on his military career at the early age of fifteen.

The incident of the cloak occurred when Martin was about twenty-one or twenty-two. During a nocturnal patrol, a poor seminaked man came before him; Martin had no money, but **he shared his cloak**; the poor man appeared to him the following night in a dream and revealed that he was Jesus, who praised him for having helped him even before he became a baptized Christian. Martin was baptized during the following year but was unable to win a discharge from the army until 354. He withdrew to Poitiers in order to be near St. Hilary, leaving only to return to Pannonia, where he converted his mother. When he returned to Poitiers, he was authorized by the bishop to evangelize the rural areas while living as a hermit. He settled at Ligugé, which became the first monastery in France and in Europe. In 371 the Christians of Tours elected him their bishop by acclamation. He wanted to avoid the appointment and to this end fled to the countryside where he hid in the midst of a flock of **geese**, but these made his presence known by their cackling, so that he could not escape the election. For this reason a fat **goose** appears in his iconography.

As a bishop, he never wearied of traveling through rural areas, the needs of whose inhabitants he knew; he thus Christianized a region that was still Celtic, rather than Roman, in its customs and religion. By this activity he also began the custom of pastoral visitation; at Marmoutier, he established the first center of clerical formation.

It is told of him that at the gates of Paris he healed a leper with a kiss. On one occasion he determined to fell a pine tree sacred to pagans; in order to show how baseless their cult was, he placed himself where the tree would fall and then, with a sign of the cross, caused it to fall in the opposite direction. When he went on a pilgrimage to Rome together with Bishop Maximinus, a bear devoured the donkey who was carrying the baggage; Martin then loaded the baggage on the bear, which served him until they reached Rome.

During a pastoral visitation, he felt death approaching and made ready for it by lying down on a plank that was covered with ashes, and remaining there in prayer. He died on November 8, but his feast is celebrated on November 11, the day on which he was carried to Tours, where his friend St. Ambrose, by a feat of bilocation, was present at his solemn funeral. In the Middle Ages Tours became a major goal of pilgrimage and a rallying point for those going and coming from Santiago de Campostela.

▷▷ Martin was so popular that he was spoken of as "the thirteenth apostle" or as "the equal of the apostles." He is the patron of beggars and the oppressed, as well as of soldiers and cavalrymen, tailors and furriers (because he gave the beggar part of his cloak as a covering); of tanners and leather workers (because of the belt on which he hung his sword and because when he was a soldier he was humble enough to take care of his own uniform); of cloth merchants (because of his cloak). He is patron also of innkeepers (because on one occasion he turned water into wine); of potters (who make pitchers); of drinkers, and even of drunkards. His patronage of vine growers and vintners is due to the time of year when his feast is celebrated and because on that date, in many places, the new wine is drunk and

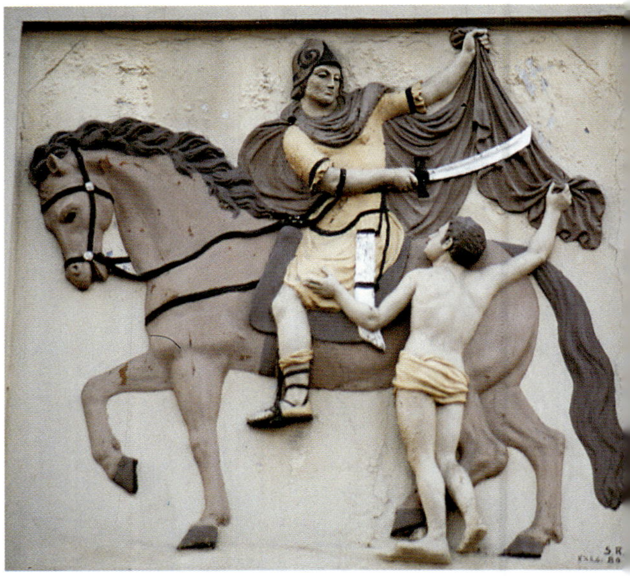

St. Martin Shares His Cloak with a Poor Traveler. 19th-cent. devotional plaque in the church of St. Martin of Bertalia, Bologna.

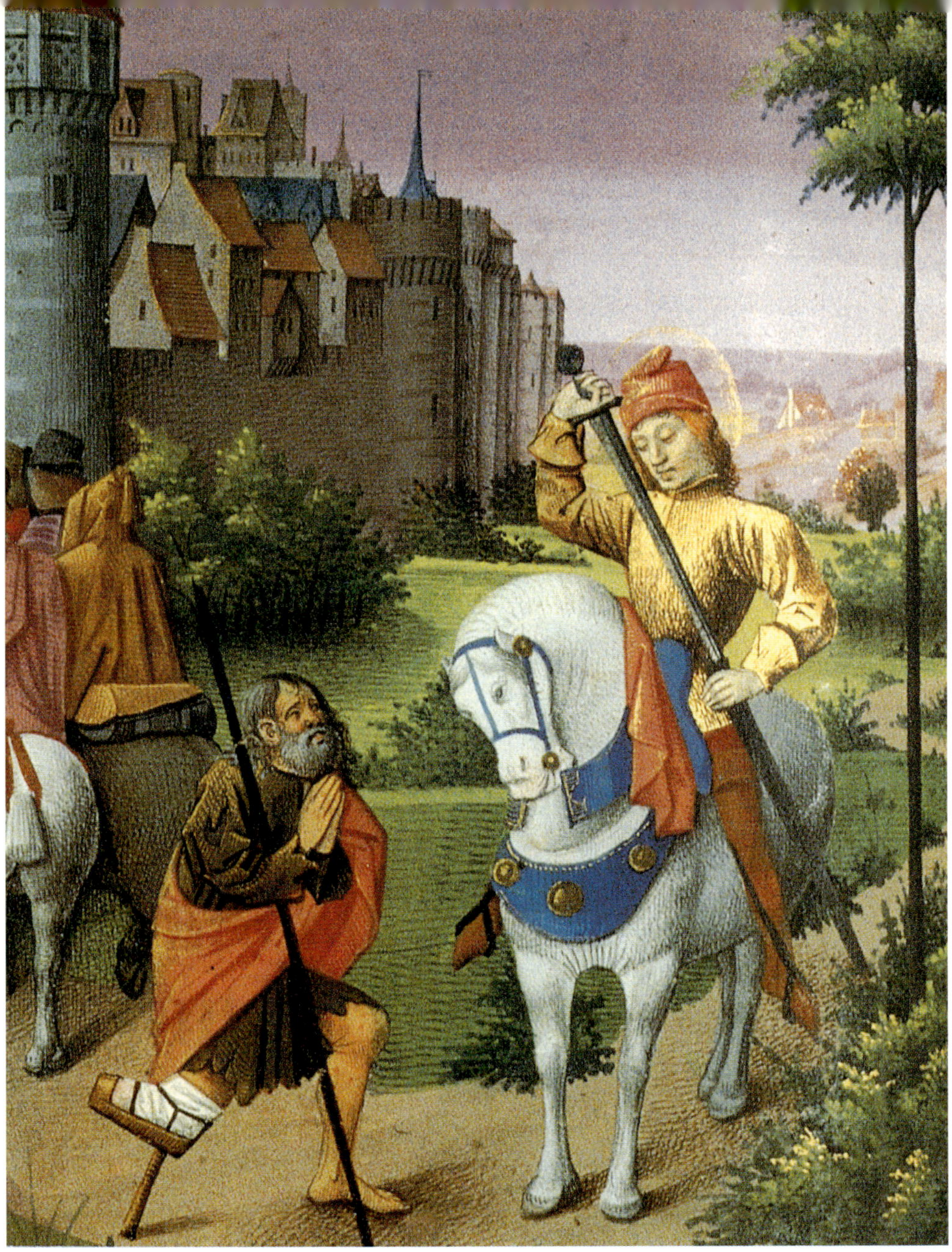

roast chestnuts are eaten. As a cavalryman, he is patron of horses and also protects the geese that enabled the faithful to find him.

▷▷ There are two typical images of Martin: as a soldier and as a bishop. The most common representation shows Martin **as a soldier on horseback, who resolutely cuts his cloak into two parts**. The image was a very effective one, but in fact the two pieces would not have been adequate for both Martin and the poor man. It is much more likely that, instead, Martin removed his cloak and gave away the interior fur lining of the red cloak worn by Roman officers and kept the outside, cloth part for himself.

Martin's cloak subsequently became part of the history of architecture in the word **cappella**. *Cappa* was the Latin word for a protective garment; it became common in the fourth century. That word yielded the French *chape* and its diminutive *capelle,* which came to mean also the physical place in which the Merovingian kings preserved a piece of the *cappa,* that is, St. Martin's cloak. It was added to the royal treasury in perhaps the seventh century and was so favorite a relic that oaths were taken on it. Moreover, in keeping with the custom of the Merovingian kings, who liked to be accompanied by protective relics, it went along with these kings on their travels. It was used in battle as a defensive banner; nothing now remains of it. In the images of Martin as a soldier, the **poor man** is the principal attribute.

St. Martin and the Poor Man.
A miniature from the Book of Hours of Luis de Laval, produced in the studio of Fouquet, 15th cent.
Now in the Bibliothèque Nationale, Paris.

When Martin is represented in **episcopal garb**, the principal attribute is the **goose**. In German-speaking countries, Martin the bishop sometimes replaces St. Jerome on pulpits that originally depicted the four Doctors of the Western Church.

Ambrose of Milan, Bishop and Doctor of the Church

340–396
Memorial: December 7
Lat.: Ambrosius Mediolanensis; It.: Ambrogio, Ambrosio, Ambrogiotto; Fr.: Ambroise, Ambreuil, Amborix; Sp.: Ambrosio; Ger.: Ambrosius von Mailand; Russ.: Ambrosii Mediolanski.

When Ambrose was still in his cradle, a **swarm of bees** lighted on his mouth, and the bees went in and out of it, carrying their honey, which at that time was likened to ambrosia, the mythical sweet food of the gods. Ambrose was born in Triers, where his father was the prefect; on his father's death Ambrose returned with his mother to Rome where, on Christmas day of 353, he was present at his sister Marcellina's profession of virginity. After finishing his literary studies, he began, as magistrate in Sirmio, a brilliant career that led him to the post of *consularis* in the provinces of Liguria and Emilia, which included present-day Lombardy. He resided in Milan, which was in upheaval due to the struggle between Arians and Catholics; he ruled with equity and kindness.

Upon the death of Auxentius, bishop of the city, the community gathered in a church to elect a new shepherd; due to the disagreement between Arians and Catholics, the meeting was a tumultuous one, and Ambrose, as an imperial official, went to it in order to quiet things down. A little boy shouted: "Ambrose for bishop!" and the people in agreement proclaimed their beloved official their new bishop; the story may not be a true one, but it shows the authority Ambrose enjoyed. He was still a catechumen and not eligible to be a bishop, but such was his prestige that both Emperor Valentinian and the other bishops agreed that the popular will was a divine sign, and his consecration took place on December 7, the day on which the Church still commemorates him. Ambrose found himself in the position of having to teach before he himself had learned (*De officiis* 1, 1, 4); he therefore prepared carefully for a pastoral activity that left its mark and turned him into one of the great episcopal "defenders of the city"; the community, both civil and religious, formed around him and felt safe. Augustine, still a young teacher of rhetoric, felt the power of this community when he came to Milan; Ambrose eventually baptized him in the cathedral, in the octagonal baptistery that still stands. During his episcopate, Ambrose also promoted the rediscovery of the relics of Gervase and Protase, the holy protomartyrs of Milan.

Throughout his life Ambrose enjoyed great authority and had a good relationship with the emperors; he was also very decisive in judging relations between religious authority and civil authority. He made it explicitly clear that the emperors had no standing in religious matters; in face of the Arians who said they wanted him to leave the city, he asserted that "a priest of God cannot entrust his temple to anyone else" (Letter 20, 1). In 390, at Thessalonica, Emperor Theodosius permitted a massacre of unarmed citizens who had gathered in the circus; this was in reprisal for the murder, by a band of fanatics, of a military commander who had dared to imprison a charioteer who was an idol of the impassioned crowds who attended the chariot races. Ambrose excommunicated the emperor, and even left the city so that he would not have to meet him; thus arose the famous image of Ambrose imposing penance on Theodosius, whom he stopped at the door of the church. The scene never took place as described but it is in substance accurate, because it shows how Theodosius yielded and acknowledged the bishop's authority. Ambrose was in fact a great friend of Theodosius, who revered him; when the emperor died prematurely, Ambrose delivered a moving eulogy of him.

Ambrose's own death, which is remembered on the Thursday after Easter of 396, did not end his love of the Milanese, whose patron he became. He was buried in the crypt of the basilica that is named after him, alongside the bodies of Gervase and Protase. Tradition has it that in 1338, when the city was threatened by the army of Emperor Louis of Bavaria, Ambrose appeared on horseback and put the enemy to flight with a **three-corded whip**, which became an element in his iconography.

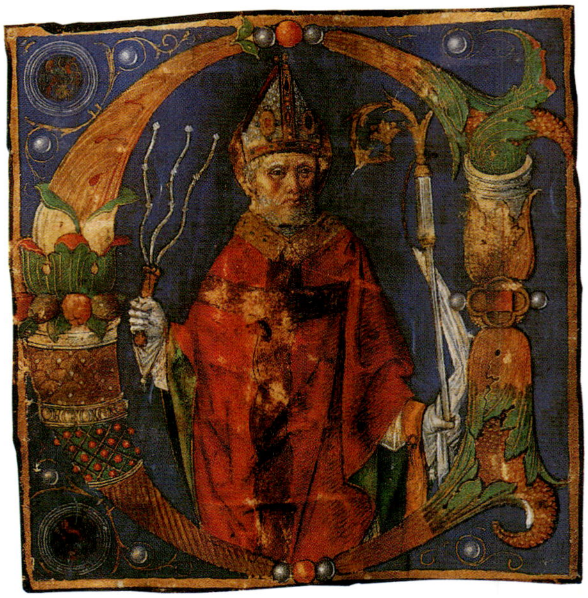

St. Ambrose.
Miniature from Hymnal 13, a codex of the 17th cent. The three-corded whip alludes to the intervention of this patron saint on behalf of the Milanese in 1338 and, symbolically, to the mystery of the Most Holy Trinity.

St. Ambrose.
18th-cent. statue in the church of the Trinity, Dresden.
Here the beehive that appears in the folds of the cope alludes to the saint's name (Ambrose—ambrosia), which is understood as foretelling his skillful and persuasive oratory.

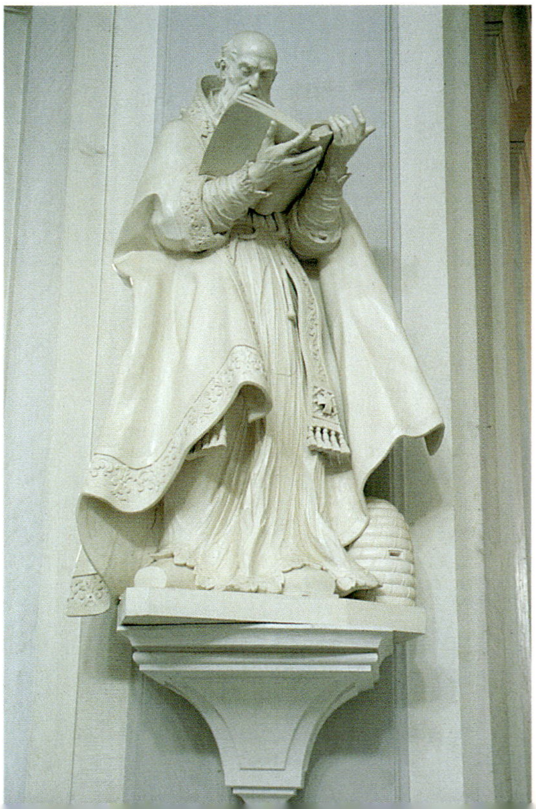

Ambrose's literary works were extensive, and he is regarded as one of the four Doctors of the Western Church. For this reason his image often appears on pulpits, along with those of the other Doctors.

▷▷ Ambrose is patron of persons and things connected with bees: beekeepers and workers with wax, and also of bakers of a particular kind of bread known as "honey-bread"; he is, of course, protector of bees.

As patron of Lombardy, he is patron also of stonecutters, who at one time came from that region.

▷▷ Ambrose is depicted in **episcopal garb**, with pastoral staff and book. To these are added, as his principal attribute, a **beehive** and the **bees** that visited him as an infant and to which his name alludes. Other attributes are a **baby in a crib**, that is a reminder of the boy who acclaimed him, and a **tricorded whip**, which is perhaps also an allusion to the Trinity, which he defended against the Arian heresy. More rarely **bones** are shown, a reminder of the rediscovered relics of the protomartyrs.

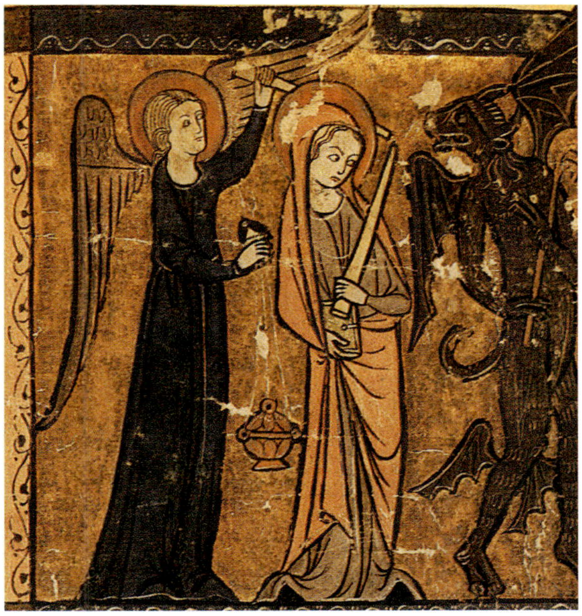

St. Genevieve.
Miniature from the tax records of the abbey of St. Genevieve.
As the saint walks to the basilica, she has a candle in her hand and is being protected by an angel, while the devil is blowing on the candle in order to extinguish it.

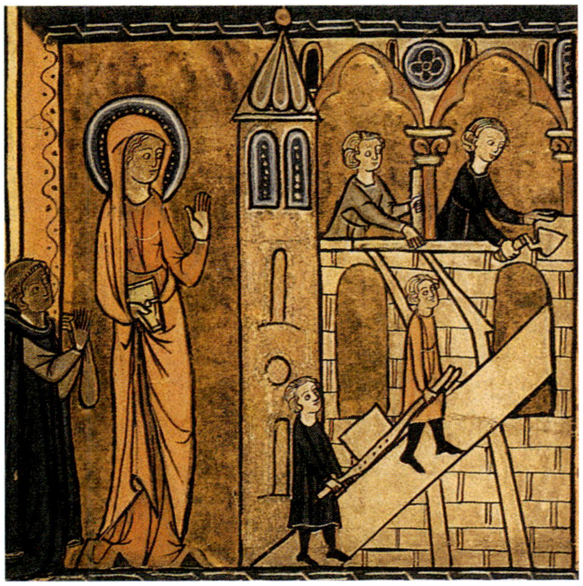

St. Genevieve.
Same source.
The saint oversees the construction of the basilica of St-Denis in Paris.

Genevieve of Paris, Consecrated Virgin

422–500
Memorial: January 3
Lat.: Genovefa Parisiensis; It.: Genoveffa di Parigi; Fr.: Geneviève de Paris, Genevièvre, Genevote; Ger.: Genovefa.

Genevieve was born in 422 in Nanterre, not far from what would later be the city of Paris. Tradition claims that when she was six years old and tending to her flock, she was seen by St. Germanus of Auxerre (378–448). He was struck by her obvious piety and consecrated her to God by placing a **medal with a cross on it** around her neck. When her mother slapped her for going to church despite having been forbidden to do so, the mother was struck blind and recovered her sight only when Genevieve had her wash her eyes in water the child had blessed. Here are some of the stories: At the age of fifteen, after her parents died, she took the veil when urged to do so by Bishop Germanus, and lived a life of the most harsh penance in the home of her godmother in Paris. She took food only on Thursdays and Sundays and remained in seclusion from Epiphany to Holy Thursday. In 451, when Attila's Huns were advancing on Paris, she persuaded the residents of the city to pray instead of fleeing, and she promised that the city would be spared, as in fact it was.

She then petitioned King Childeric to spare some condemned men; during a siege which the king himself laid against Paris, she went by boat to Arcis-sur-Aube to find grain and thus managed to save the city from starvation. After Childeric died in 481, she had a good relationship with Clovis, who often granted her pardon for those condemned to death. She had a church built over the tomb of St. Dionysius; and she went on pilgrimage to Tours in order to venerate St. Martin.

It is said that while she was walking to the church at night, her candle went out and she relit it with a simple gesture; another version of the story has it that a **devil** extinguished her candle and an **angel** relit it. She died on January 3, in about 500.

After her death a church was built in her name on the hill that dominates the Latin Quarter; today this church is the Pantheon and is dedicated to the glories of France. During the plague of 1130, Paris was saved by her intercession.

▷▷ Genevieve is the patron of Paris and of France, she is also patron of candlemakers and of shepherds and shepherdesses. She is invoked against plague, leprosy, and fevers, for an end to excessive rain and to drought, and for the healing of kings.

▷▷ She is depicted in two ways: as a consecrated virgin who is carrying, as her principal attribute, a **candle**, and is accompanied by an **angel** and a **devil**, the latter puffing to put out the candle and the angel relighting it; or else as a **shepherdess** with a **crook** or in the **act of spinning**. Another attribute is a **medal with a cross, around her neck**.

Augustine of Hippo, Bishop and Doctor of the Church

354–430
Memorial: August 28
Lat.: Augustinus, Hipponensis episcopus; It.: Agostino d'Ippona; Fr.: Augustin, Austin, Outin, Utin; Sp.: Agustín; Port.: Agostinho; Ger.: Augustinus, Augustin.

Augustine was born in 354 at Thagaste near Hippo (Bona) in North Africa. He studied rhetoric in Carthage and then in Rome, where we find him in 383. In every respect his youthful years were far from exemplary and were tormented by doubts. His mother Monica was very worried about him, especially since he was so attracted to Manicheanism. He moved on to Milan, in the diocese of St. Ambrose, who seemingly had little time for the rather conceited young teacher of rhetoric; Augustine's conversion came unexpectedly in 387.

He was lying under a fig tree one day when he heard a voice saying to him: *Tolle, lege,* that is, "Take it and read it." He had at hand the letters of St. Paul and opened it at random; he read: "Live not in debauchery and licentiousness. . . . Instead, put on the Lord Jesus Christ" (*Induite Dominum Jesus Christum:* Rom 13:13-14). The text was a lightning bolt. He received baptism from St. Ambrose. His mother, Monica, consoled now by the baptism of her son, died at Ostia, just before embarking for the return to Africa. When Augustine returned home, he was consecrated bishop of Hippo in 395 and died there in 430, as the city was being besieged by the Vandals. He had written *City of God,* his most famous work, and a very large number of other works on every aspect of Christian doctrine. Another famous work of his is *The Trinity,* the fruit of profound meditation; traces of it can be seen in his iconography.

He is shown with his **mother**, who holds him by the hand and seems to be presenting him to God and begging for his conversion. Other scenes show his conversion, his baptism, and, above all, his meditation on the mystery of the Trinity. This last subject is represented by **a little boy on the seashore, trying to pour the sea into a hole with a shell or a spoon**. This episode, which has become part of his iconography and nicely reflects his long study of the subject, did not appear until the thirteenth century in a collection of *Exempla* for preachers, compiled by a Rhenish Cistercian, Caesar of Heisterbach, who connected the story with *scholasticus quidam*. It was Thomas of Cantimpré who thought of assigning it to Augustine, in connection with the latter's treatise on the Trinity. Thomas placed the scene on the African shores of the Mediterranean; others placed it at Civitavecchia. The story with its accompanying illustration became very popular; it is indeed characteristic of Augustine and clearly conveys the idea of the ineffable depths of the mystery.

Liutprand, king of the Lombards, took Augustine's body to Pavia and built a tomb for it in the church of San Pietro in Ciel d'Oro.

Augustine is credited with founding the Hermits and the Canons Regular of St. Augustine; these religious are distinguished from the Franciscans by wearing a leather belt over a black habit, instead of a rope.

Augustine's *Rule* was adopted by the Antonians, the Premonstratensians, the Servites, the Trinitarians, and the Brigettines.

▷▷ Augustine is patron of these orders, as well as of theologians, biologists, typesetters, and printers. He is invoked against diseases of the eyes and against coughs, this because of the sound of his name in French and German: *Augustin-oeil-Auge,* and (for coughs) *Toux-Husten*. He is also invoked, as "the African," against grasshoppers and harmful animals.

▷▷ He is depicted mainly in **episcopal vestments**; rarely as a **monk with a black habit and a leather belt**. His principal attribute is a **heart** he holds in his hand, a heart sometimes pierced by three arrows; *Cor caritate divina sagittatum,* "A heart pierced by divine love."

Augustine is often seen in the ornamentation of pulpits, where he is associated with the other Doctors of the Church: Ambrose, Gregory, and Jerome (or Martin). Other attributes are: a **book**, which alludes to his copious writings, and, in others kinds of representation, his **mother** and **the child pouring water into a hole with a shell**.

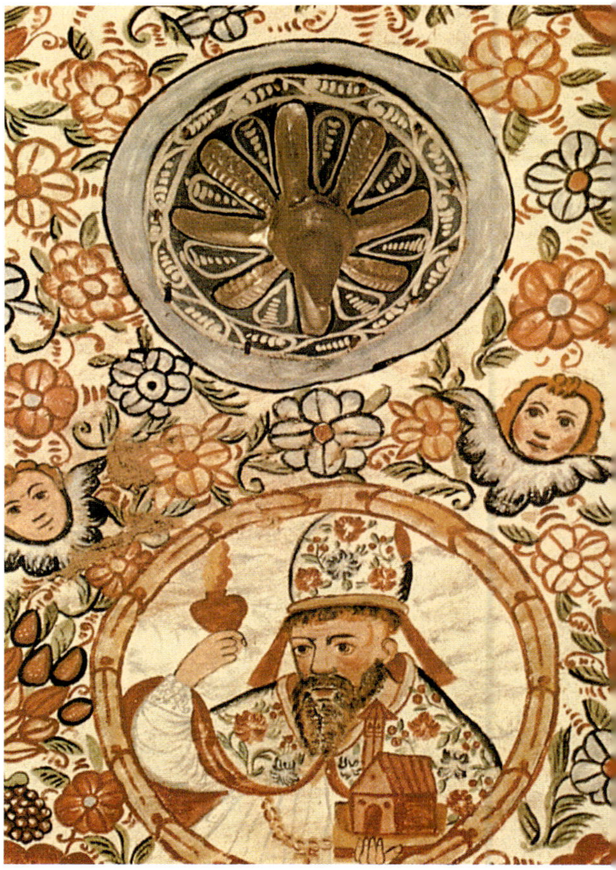

St. Augustine of Hippo.
18th-cent. fresco in the vault of the church of Ocongate, in Cuzco, Peru.
The saints crossed over to the New World with their images and symbolic attributes. Here the heart alludes to the famous words: "My heart is restless until it rests in You."

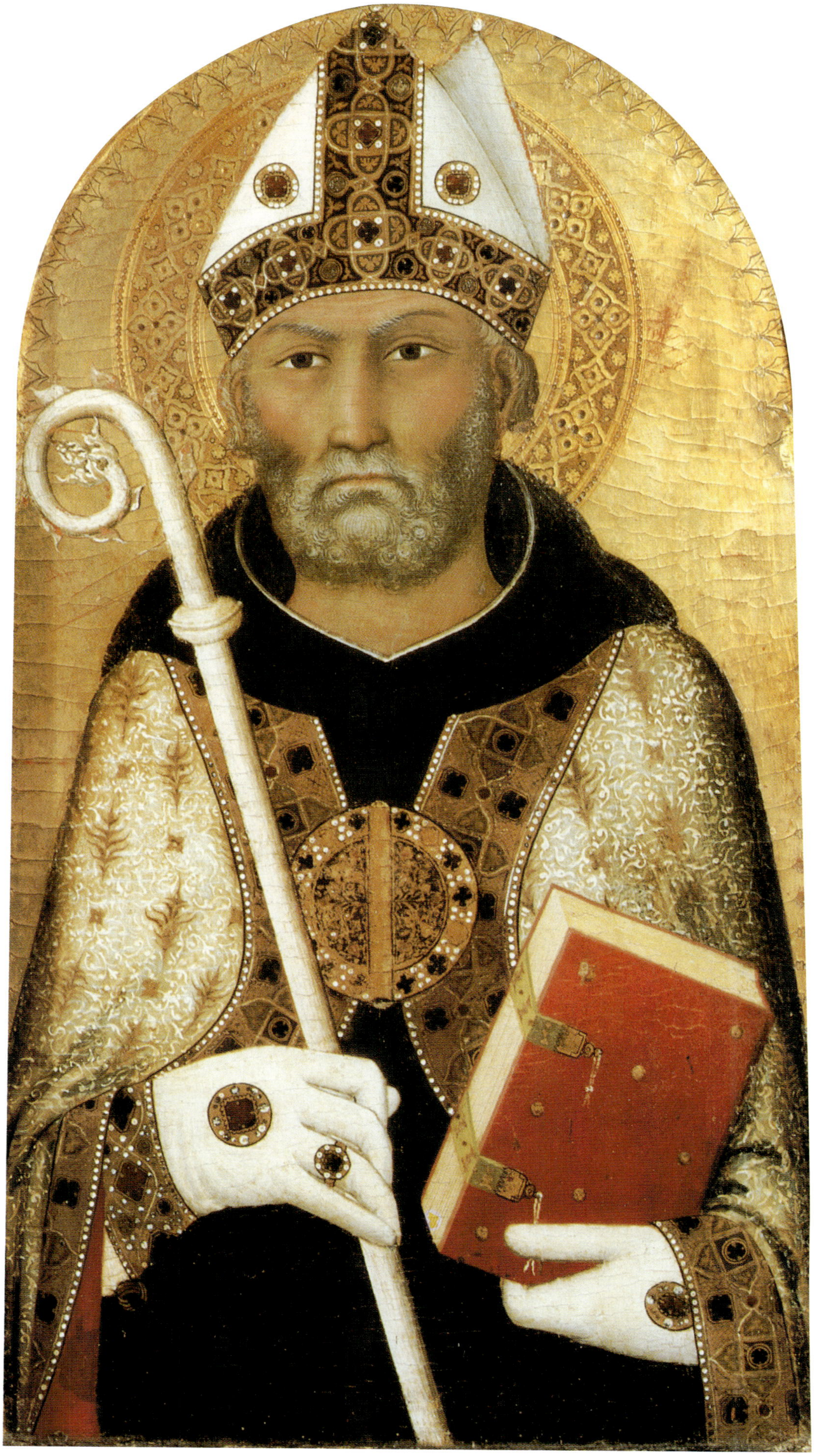

St. Augustine of Hippo.
By Simone Martini, 1284–ca. 1344, in the Fitzwilliam Museum, Cambridge.
The saint is seen here in his episcopal robes. Note the gloves, the ring, the book, the pastoral staff, and the miter.

Basil the Great, Bishop and Doctor of the Church

328–379
Memorial: January 2
Lat.: Basilius Magnus; Gr.: Basileios ho Megalos; It.: Basilio Magno; Fr.: Basile le Grand; Sp.: Basilio el Grande; Ger.: Basilius der Grosse; Russ.: Vasili Veleki.

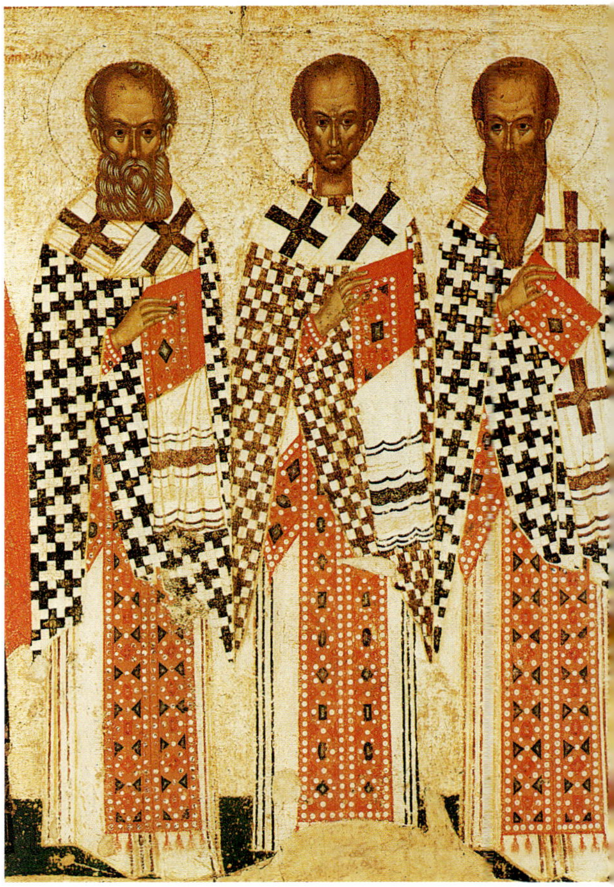

Basil is remembered together with Gregory Nazianzus; so deep was their friendship that Gregory could describe as follows the grief he felt when they had to separate: "It was though a body were cut in two and both parts died" (*Discourse in Honor of St. Basil* 6–7; PG 36:500-504). Basil was the Church's first great orator and his works are of great importance for the history of Christianity. He was born at Caesarea in Cappadocia, but during the persecution of Maximinus he and his paternal grandparents had to flee into the mountains of Pontus, where they survived miraculously on game. The entire family was a holy one, says Gregory of Nazianzus: grandmother Macrina, parents Basil and Emmelia, older sister Macrina, and brothers Gregory and Peter, who became bishops of Nyssa and Sebaste respectively.

Now an orphan, Basil distinguished himself in his studies at Caesarea; later on he went to Constantinople and then to Athens, where he struck up a friendship with St. Gregory of Nazianzus and vied with the latter in learning, wisdom, and virtue. The two were also the center of a select group devoted to study and prayer. Basil left the group in order to devote himself to the monastic life; after various travels and after receiving baptism from the bishop of Caesarea, he withdrew to a hermitage, where he was joined by St. Gregory. While there, the two men collected the finest passages from the works of Origen.

But Arianism was on the rise, and Basil had to leave his hermitage and devote himself to the defense of orthodoxy. He was ordained a priest by Bishop Eusebius of Caesarea, who drew Basil into his own ministry and was succeeded by Basil in 360. The latter was opposed by Emperor Valens, an Arian, but he refused to be intimidated. It was said that the pen with which Valens wanted to sign the order for Basil's exile broke three times and that Valens' ill son felt better after a visit from Basil but died after being blessed by Arian priests.

Basil was especially moved by human illness and misery, and wanted a hospital to be built in each ecclesiastical territory; in Caesarea he built a large hospital, known as the Basiliad. The remainder of his life was troubled by the struggle against Arianism and against the divisions to which this struggle gave rise in the Eastern Church. In fighting this division he several times asked for the support of Rome, but his relationship with the latter was marked by ambiguities and misunderstandings. When, at last, Valens, an Arian, died, Arian persecutions of Catholics came to an end, but Basil, worn out by the difficulties of the apostolate and the Arian struggle, was unable to enjoy the new tranquility: he died in 379, when he was only fifty years old.

Among his writings is a treatise on the Holy Spirit, in which he defends the equality of the Spirit with the other Persons of the Trinity.

When Basil died, the monks of the Orient lost a defender and a father. He provided a rule of life for them when he wrote his Rule for his own Basilian monks, a rule St. Benedict later drew upon to some extent.

▷▷ Veneration of Basil is very widespread among the Orthodox. On the evening of the vigil of his feast they devoutly light candles and spend the night in entertainment and games; they also eat a special cake named after him. He is a patron of schools, and his feast day is also one for children.

Together with St. Gregory Nazianzus and St. John Chrysostom Basil is celebrated on the feast of the Three Ecumenical Hierarchs or Doctors (January 31). In the Eastern Church he was also celebrated individually on January 1, even after the feast of the Circumcision of Jesus was assigned to that date.

His relics are in Bruges, whither they were taken in 1098 by Robert II, Count of Flanders (1093–1111); one of his relics is venerated today in the little church of Saint Basilis.

▷▷ We have some descriptions of Basil that depict him as pale, thin, and bald (the few hairs he has are brown), with a black, pointed beard, and hollow temples. He is shown with the **pallium**, a **red cross with three crossbars**, and the **dove of the Holy Spirit** on one shoulder.

The scene in which he resists Emperor Valens has a parallel in the relationship between Ambrose and Theodosius.

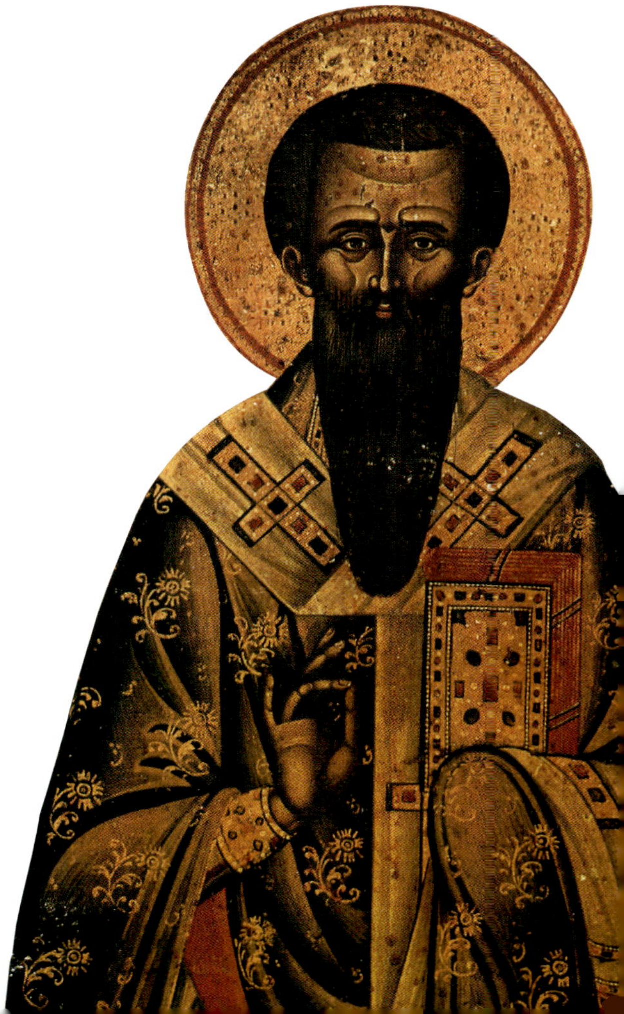

SS. Gregory Nazianzus, John Chrysostom, and Basil the Great.
15th-cent. icon in the Tret'jakov Gallery, Moscow

Brigid of Kildare.
Detail of the painting The Glory of Mary by the master who derives his name from this painting: second half of the 15th cent.: in the Wallraf-Richartz-Museum, Cologne.
Brigid is depicted with a cow, her principal attribute, at her feet.

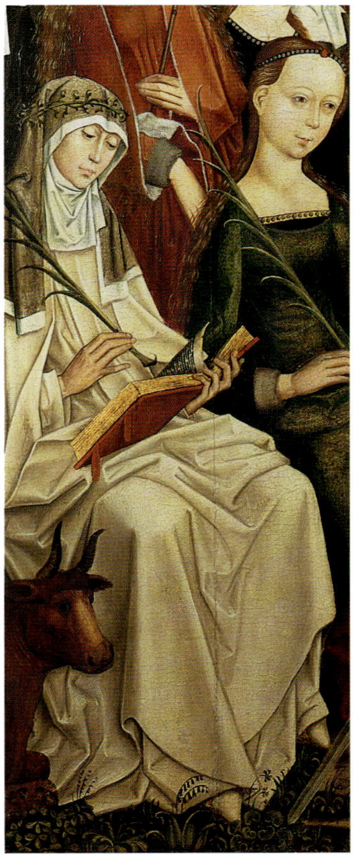

Brigid of Kildare, Abbess

ca. 453–525
Memorial: February 1
Lat.: Brigida Hibernensis; It.: Brigida di Kildare; Fr.: Brigide d'Irlande, Bride, Berchet; Ir.: Brigit, Brighid, Brìd; Ger.: Brigida, Brida.

Brigid founded the monastery of Kildare in Ireland, where she continued the evangelizing activity of St. Patrick.

She is also known as Brigid of Scotland. She seems to have been born on the eastern coast of Ireland, known as the land of the Lagin; she is therefore also known as Brigid Lagen or Brigid of the Lagin, although her own people belonged to the line of the Priteni, the earliest inhabitants of Britain and Ireland.

She has been called "another Mary" or "Mary of the Hibernians" (i.e., the Irish). One tradition has it that her birth was prophesied by a druid, who said: "She will be like Mary, the Mother of the Lord." She was born around 453 and was baptized by St. Patrick. At the age of fourteen she built a cell for herself under an oak tree. This developed first into a monastery of women and later into a double monastery, of men and women, and became one of the monastic centers of Ireland. Brigid died on February 1, 525.

Her life was passed in silence, but miraculous incidents were not lacking. After being surprised by a storm one day when she was watching her sheep, she hung her garments on a ray of the sun to dry. She changed the water of her bath into beer; geese and ducks followed her to her monastery. Like Mary, she was a compassionate woman and distributed to the poor moulds of butter she herself had churned; an angel returned them to her. One day many bishops came to visit the monastery. In order to receive them properly, she milked her one **cow** three times, and it gave her as much milk as three milk cows.

▷▷ She is the second patron of Ireland and is very popular in Wales and Brittany, in Holland and along the Rhine.

Because of the miracle of the milk, she is regarded as protecting women in childbirth, dairyers, cows and chickens, and, more generally, animals of the farmyard. She is invoked against misfortunes and persecutions.

▷▷ She is depicted chiefly as an **abbess**, a mature but not elderly woman, wearing a white robe and black veil, and with a tongue of fire on her head. There are also some images that show her as a peasant woman churning butter or watching over animals in the fields. Her principal attribute is a **cow** at her feet.

Nicholas of Myra and of Bari, Bishop and Wonderworker

270–345/352
Memorial: December 6
Gr.: Nikolaos; Lat.: Nicolaus Myrensis; It.: Nicola, Niccolò di Mira, Mirense, di Bari; Fr.: Nicolas de Myra et de Bari, Niclausse, Nicolle, Cola, Colin, Colesson, Colinet; Sp.: Nicolás Taumaturgo, Nicolau; Ger.: Nikolaus der Wundertätige, Niklas, Nickel, Santa Klaus; Dutch: Niklaas. Klaas, Sinter Klaas; Dan. and Swed.: Niels, Nils; Hung.: Miklos; Russ.: Nikolaï, Tehoudotvorets (= Thaumaturgos), Kolia.

Anyone visiting the churches of Europe can easily see how greatly this saint is loved and how widespread the cult of this holy wonderworker is; he is a true bridge between East and West. The addition, "Wonderworker," acknowledges the power of his intercession. His name is made up of two words: Greek *nikan* = to conquer, and Greek *laos* = people, and means "Victor among the people." In the first and second millennia he was well known everywhere and loved to the point of calling him *allos sotêr,* "another Savior." The pious theft of the saint's body, in April 1087, by the people of Bari, who had already greatly venerated him and dedicated five churches to him, as well as the subsequent building of a great basilica for him, confirmed the fact that Nicholas was truly a bridge between East and West, and added a further wonder to those worked by the saint.

Nicholas was born around 270 in Patara on the coast of what is now western Turkey; his parents were Epiphanius and Joanna. His family was well-off, and he himself was generous but also shy. An incident during his youth shows a style of action that was both attentive and

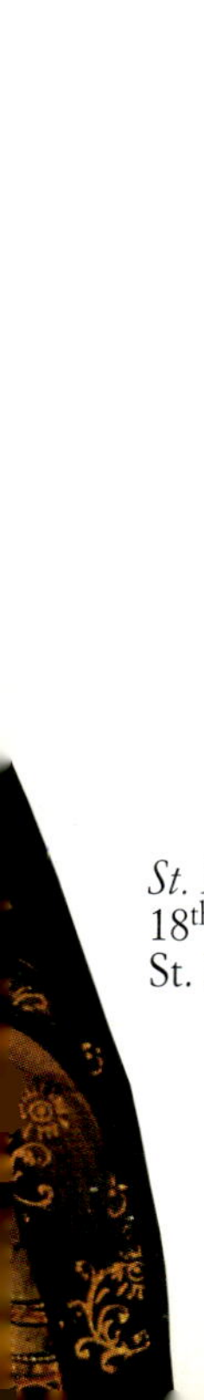

St. Basil the Great.
18th-cent. icon by John of Jerusalem, in the church of St. Nicholas, Tripoli, Lebanon.

reserved. He found out that a neighbor had fallen on hard times and was unable to provide a sufficient dowry for his three daughters; he decided therefore to make prostitutes of them, and the three young women were desperate. Nicholas decided to intervene, but secretly: on three successive nights he threw into their house, through a window, **three packets of money**, which provided dowries for the three girls and changed their lot.

The election of Nicholas as bishop of the nearby city of Myra on the coast of Lycia was marked by a wonder that showed a divine intervention. When the former bishop of the city died, the community gathered to pray and choose a successor; they were joined by some bishops of neighboring communities. The most authoritative of these bade the people pray and fast; during the night he was also divinely inspired to take a position at the door of the church at dawn and to consecrate the first man to enter, whose name was Nicholas. The bishop did so and, when he saw Nicholas approaching, asked him his name and led him to the bishop's chair, on which the saint sat in an attitude of wonderful humility.

Another incident: during a serious famine, when no one had any food left, Nicholas learned that some ships laden with grain were in the harbor; he went in person to ask the sailors for a hundred bushels. The sailors hesitated because the cargo had been carefully measured for the city of Alexandria. Nicholas promised that the customs officers would not find any shortage and so it happened; the grain thus obtained lasted for two years, and some of it could be sown.

Various sources tell of how Nicholas encouraged Christians during the persecution of Diocletian. He took part in the Council of Nicaea in 325 and humiliated Arius; for this reason he was stripped of his episcopal robes and imprisoned, but Christ himself and the Virgin appeared to him and restored his robes. He continued his pastoral ministry for many years, before dying at some time between 345 and 352. Countless miracles have been attributed to him; from his relics there used to flow (and still flows) a miraculous liquid known as "St. Nicholas' manna" (Greek *manna* and Hebrew *mn,* a resinous substance).

Sailors from Bari, after leaving a cargo of Grain in Antioch and pretending to be on a commercial journey, came to Myra and stole the body of the saint; on Sunday, May 9, 1087, the remains of St. Nicholas entered Bari in triumph. It took only two years to build a suitable basilica. On October 1, 1089, Pope Urban II placed the relics under the altar in the crypt, where they remain to this day.

The number three, an obvious symbol of perfection, runs through the traditions about Nicholas. In particular, it is said that he won the freedom of three Byzantine officials who had been unjustly accused of treason and had been condemned to death. The stories speak of the men as "innocent," and because children are par excellence innocents, the three men in stories about Nicholas and images of him became **three children**. This accounts for the legend of the three children who were cut to pieces and placed in brine by a wicked innkeeper; this supposedly happened on Christmas night. Nicholas found out about this and restored the children to life. Among all his miracles this is certainly the one connecting him most closely with the world of children; moreover, in many countries of central and eastern Europe, it is Nicholas who brings gifts to children, sometimes accompanied by Rupert, a black-faced and terrifying horseman or by Krampus, a big devil, either of whom chastised naughty children.

In France, students at the college of Saint-Nicolas-du-Louvre had a holiday on the saint's feast day, December 6; one of them dressed as a little bishop and went around bearing gifts in imitation of the saint. This child with the red episcopal garment became Santa Claus: Sankt Nikolaus, then Sanct Klaus, then Sancta Klaus, and, finally, the Santa Claus of the Anglo-Saxon world, when in 1863 Thomas Nast changed the image of the bishop into that of a good-natured, bearded old man, clad in a red garment trimmed with white fur.

▷▷ Nicholas' traditional patronage of Russia was confirmed by Pius XI on October 28, 1932. He is also a patron of Greece. He is patron of students, choristers, girls of marriageable age, girls in danger, and, in general, the oppressed and the poor. Due to his journeys by sea, he is protector of sailors, ships' carpenters, and all who travel by sea or fear shipwreck. Because of the cask in which the three children were to be pickled, he is protector of barrel-makers, wine venders, and those involved in the transportation of wine. Because he punished some dishonest

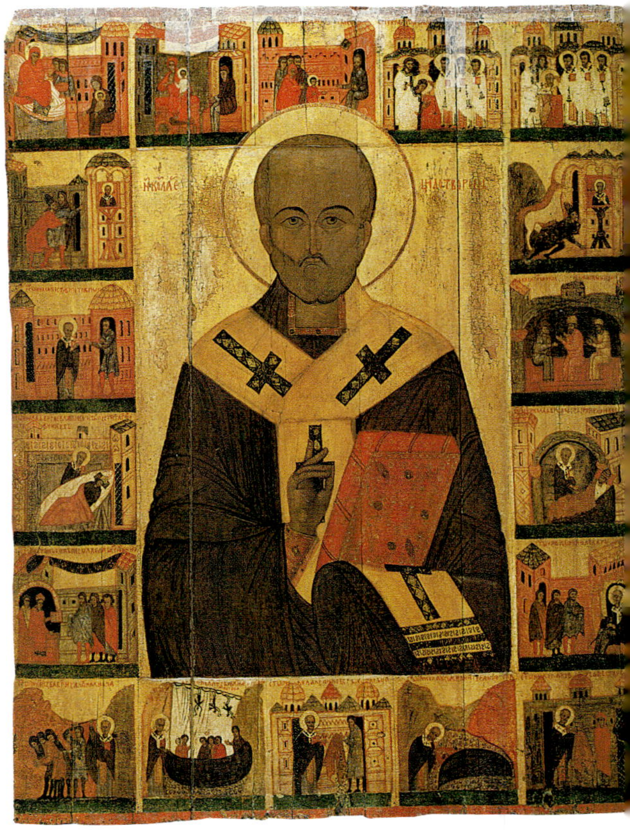

St. Nicholas the Wonderworker, with Scenes from His Life.
A 14th-cent. icon in Novgorod.

St. Nicholas in Glory with St. John the Baptist and St. Lucy.
By Lorenzo Lotto, 1480 ca.–1556, in the Chiesa del Carmine, Venice.

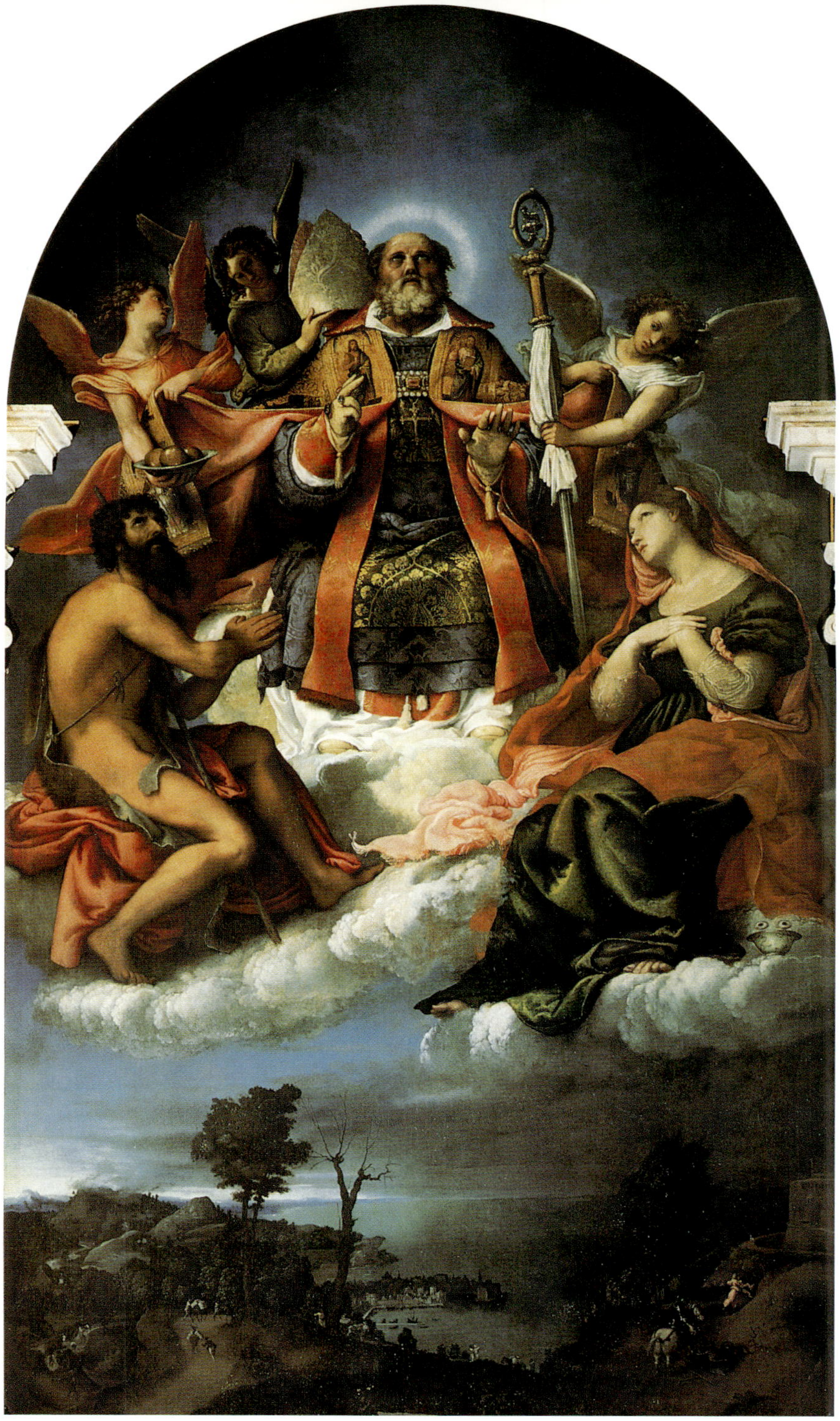

lenders, he is patron of pawnbrokers. Because of the manna, he is patron of producers of oil, perfumers, pharmacists, and druggists. Because of three young men condemned unjustly, he is patron of prisoners, victims of judicial error, lawyers, and solicitors. Because of the children cut to pieces, he is patron of butchers. Because of the three bags of money given as alms suggest loaves of bread, he is patron of bakers. Because of the miracle of the grain that was unloaded from the ship without being lost, he is patron of longshoremen and grain merchants.

He is invoked against judicial error and thieves and for happy marriages that are blessed with children. Those who sought favors through his intercession used to sleep on the floor of his basilica. We refer the reader here to the example of the parents of St. Nicholas of Tolentine.

▷▷ In the East are to be found cycles of stories about his life. In the West he is depicted as **elderly, bearded, and dressed as a bishop**, with the **pallium** in clear sight, and with **miter and pastoral staff**. His principal attribute is **three spheres** referring to the bags of money given as alms; these usually lie on a book of gospels or on a dish held by an angel, or simply at the feet of the saint. Other attributes are the **three children** who are emerging from a barrel in the folds of the bishop's cloak, and the **three young women**.

St. Nicholas Raises the Three Boys to Life.
Miniature, 15th cent., in Jean Brandon, Chronodromen seu cursus temporum, in the Bibliothèque Royal Albert I, Brussels.

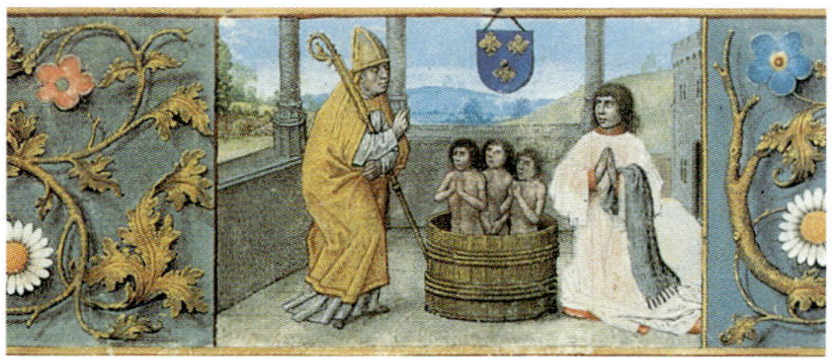

Jerome, Priest and Doctor of the Church

340/345–420
Memorial: September 30
Lat.: Hieronymus; It.: Girolamo, Geronimo; Fr.: Jérôme, Hierosme; Sp.: Jerónimo; Ger.: Hieronymus; Russ.: Ieronim.

Jerome was born into a Christian family in Dalmatia, went to Rome to complete his studies, and was baptized there when about nineteen years old. Desirous of living an ascetical life, he left for the East in 374 and stayed in Antioch, where, in a dream, he was rebuked for his love of the Latin classical writers and accused of being a Ciceronian rather than a Christian. He withdrew into the desert, where he endured illnesses and temptations. There, too, he studied Greek and Hebrew and began an intense activity as a translator, his most notable work being the *Vulgate,* a Latin translation of the Bible, the greatest part of which, if not the whole, came from his pen. In Laodicea he accepted ordination as a priest, on condition that he remain an independent monk.

He accompanied Pope Damasus at the council of 382, and after the latter's death withdrew to Bethlehem; here Paula, a Roman matron, and her daughter Eustochium provided him with the means of founding a monastery for men, another for women, and a hospital for pilgrims. From his retreat in Bethlehem, where he died in 420, he intervened in all the controversies of the time, defended the perpetual virginity of Mary, wrote a great many letters, composed commentaries on the texts of the Bible, and translated valuable works such as the *History of the Church* by Eusebius, for which he wrote a continuation.

▷▷ From his monastic life comes the **lion** that almost always appears in images of him and is his principal attribute. The saint had in fact extracted a thorn from the paw of a lion who approached him. The lion remained with him and willingly protected his donkey when it was out in the pastures. It is also told that when thieves stole the donkey, the lion was suspected of having eaten it; the lion would not rest until it found the thieves, retrieved the donkey, and led it back to the monastery, thereby winning exoneration.

This last story is probably one borrowed from the life of another hermit named Gerasimus, but in any case the lion is always present in images of Jerome. It has been suggested that the lion's presence was due to the fact that Jerome, being linked with the Doctors of the Church to the four Gospels, was paired with St. Mark, whose symbol was a lion; the lion was then attributed to Jerome, the justification being the story of the thorn.

There are three main images of Jerome; all show him as **elderly**, with a long beard and white hair, and with other symbols that became other attributes. One image depicts him as a hermit, **clothed in skins**, kneeling before a **crucifix**, holding a **stone** with which he beats his breast, a **skull** to remind him of death, a **rosary**, a clay **lamp**; in this image also appears the theme of temptation, of which he spoke in a letter recalling his prebaptismal life in Rome, and in which were **dancing girls** and the **devil** in monstrous forms. The second image shows him as writer and founder, wearing the **robe** and **hat** of a cardinal, surrounded by **books** and intent on study and the collation of texts, and sometimes wearing **eyeglasses**. The third image shows him supported by his disciples as he receives his **final Communion**.

▷▷ Jerome is patron of Dalmatia, where it was thought he had been born, and of Rome and other cities. Because of his translation of the Bible into Latin and his great learning, he is a patron of translators, scholars, learned men, humanists, students, archeologists, booksellers and bookbinders, librarians and bibliophiles, as well as of the Jeronimites and the Gesuati. Because his sight was weakened during the work of translation, he is a patron of the short-sighted and is invoked on behalf of weak vision.

St. Jerome Removes the Thorn from the Lion's Paw. By Zanetto Bugatto, 15th cent., in the Accademia Carrara, Bergamo.
In the case of Jerome, as elsewhere, the tame lion is a symbol of instincts under control and of mastery of natural forces, such as was attributed to hermits, among others. Note the cardinal's robes and hat, which in fact the saint never wore.

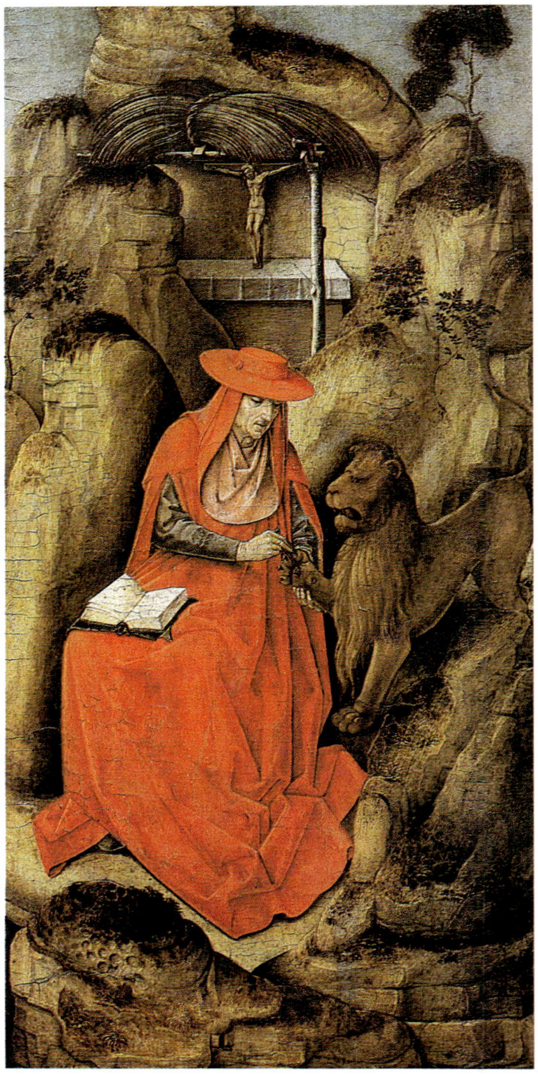

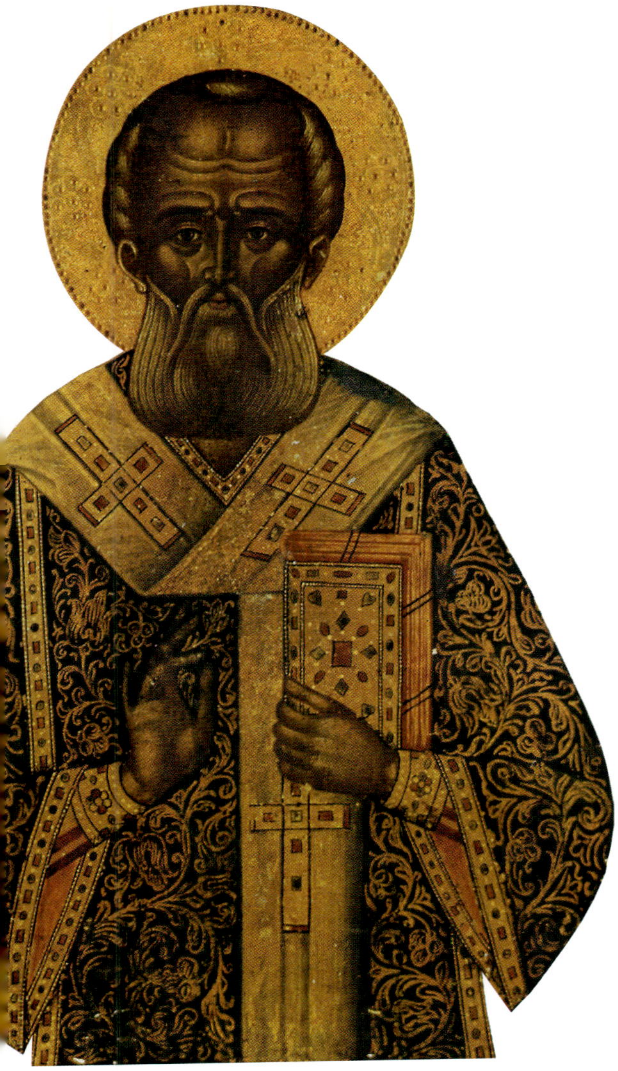

St. Gregory of Nazianzus.
18th-cent. icon by John of Jerusalem, in the church of St. Nicholas, Tripoli, Lebanon.

Gregory of Nazianzus, Archbishop of Constantinople and Doctor of the Church

ca. 330–389
Memorial: January 2
Gr.: Gregorios ho Theologos; Lat.: Gregorius Nazianzenus, Theologus; It.: Gregorio di Nazianzio; Fr.: Grégoire de Nazianze; Sp.: Gregorio Nacianceno, de Nacianzo; Ger.: Gregor von Nazianz; Russ.: Grigorii Bogoslov.

Gregory was born in the village of Arianzus, near Nazianzus in Cappadocia, as the son of the bishop of Nazianzus. He began his studies at Caesarea in Cappadocia, where he came to know Basil and went with him to Athens. He received baptism in Byzantium in 355, while on his way back to his homeland. He taught for a while but then felt called to a contemplative life and therefore withdrew into solitude along with his friend Basil. His father called on him for assistance in governing the diocese; Gregory was unwillingly ordained a priest and, as soon as he could, returned to Basil and the eremitical life. He was several times called to exercise pastoral offices, but always returned to the contemplative life. Finally, he had to accept the call to Constantinople, whither he went in 379; he gladly left the capital in 381 and withdrew for the last time to his native place, Arianzus, where he died on January 25, 389.

Although he did give himself to pastoral work, his inclination was entirely to the contemplative life. His work as writer of homilies and poems is impressive. They testify to a ceaseless search for God and a passionate worship of Christ.

▷▷ Because of his poetical works he is patron of Christian poets; he is invoked also against gout.

▷▷ He is depicted as a **bishop of the Greek Church**, that is, without a miter; he is often depicted with **his friend Basil**.

Ursula of Cologne, Virgin and Martyr, and the Eleven Thousand Virgins

4th century
Memorial: October 31
Lat.: Ursula; It.: Orsola, Orsa; Fr.: Ursule, Ourse; Sp.: Ursula con las oncemil virgenes; Ger.: Ursula, Urschel, und die elftausend Jungfrauen; Dutch: Ursula en de elfduizend Maagden; Pol.: Urszula.

In the church of St. Ursula in Cologne there is an inscription, dated to the fourth/fifth century, according to which Clematius, a man of senatorial rank, had a vision leading him to rebuild this church at his own expense, on the spot where "the holy virgins shed their blood for the name of Christ." This was probably the historical nucleus of the story of St. Ursula.

The story has it that Ursula, daughter of a Breton king, and a woman consecrated to God, was asked to be the wife of Etherius, a pagan king. At the advice of an angel and in order to avoid a war, Ursula asked for a delay of three years, promising meanwhile that she would marry him provided he converted and would accompany her on a pilgrimage to Rome. When the three years had elapsed, Ursula, along with **ten noble young women**, each of them (Ursula and the ten) accompanied by a thousand virgins (**eleven thousand** in all), took flight on eleven triremes, faced the sea, traveled up the river Waal to Cologne, and continued on to Basel. From there the young women went to Rome on foot as pilgrims. Pope Cyriacus received Ursula and her promised husband.

On the return journey they stopped in Cologne, which had by now been conquered by the Huns. When Ursula refused to marry their king, she was pierced by an arrow, and her companions were likewise all slain. After this, however, an army of eleven thousand angels

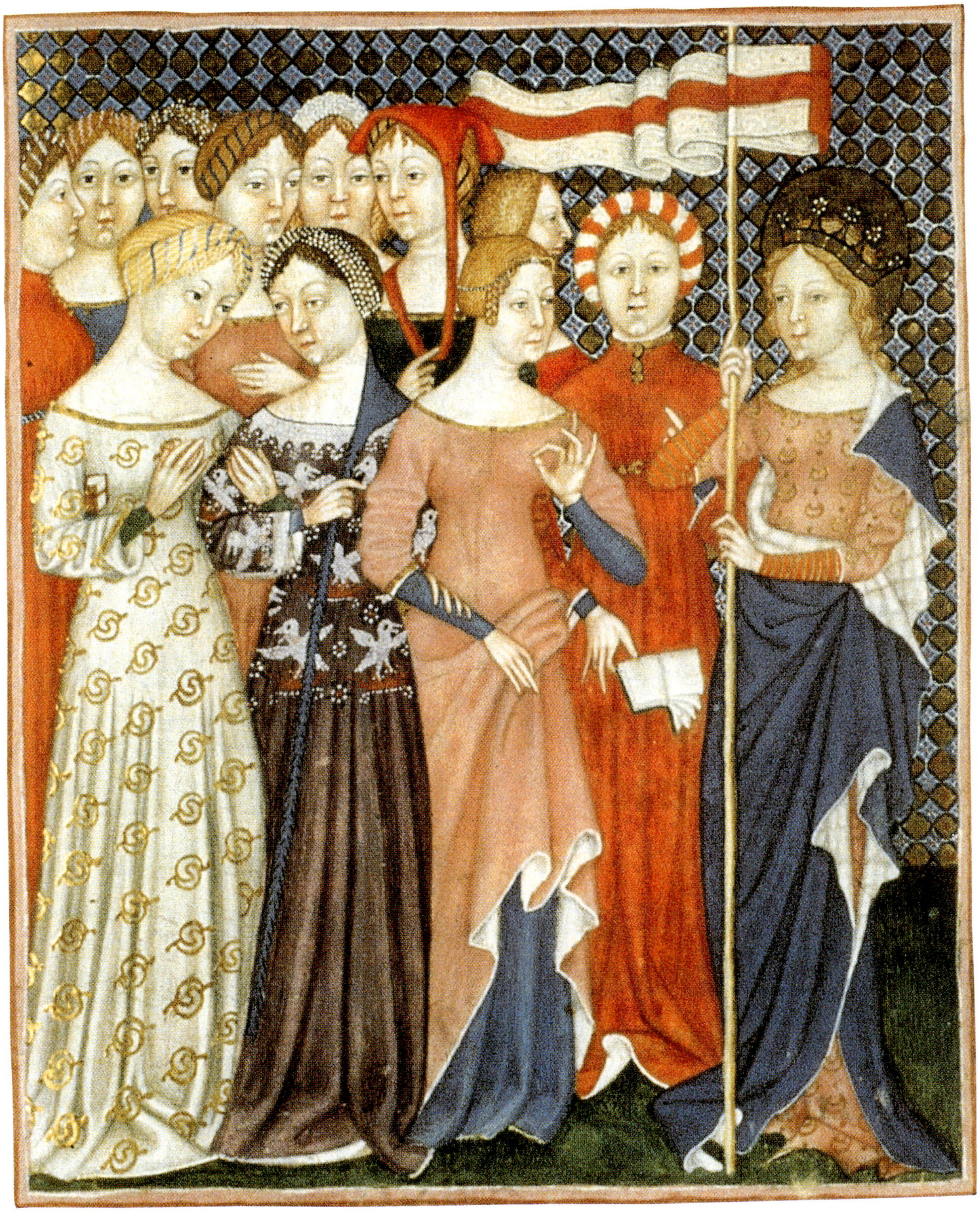

St. Ursula and Her Companions.
15th-cent. miniature by the Master of the *Book of Hours,* Latin no. 757, in the Bibliothèque Nationale, Paris.

put the Huns to flight, and Cologne was free again. The inhabitants then recovered the remains of the young women, and Clematius, who had come from the East, rebuilt a church and consecrated it to the martyrs.

Be all that as it may, the cult of Ursula goes back at least to the eighth century. In 1535, St. Angela Merici founded the Society of St. Ursula (the Ursulines) for a contemplative life of penance and virginity. Later on, congregations arose that took their name from St. Ursula but had education and instruction as their purpose; this explains why the saint is the patron of teachers.

▷▷ Ursula is patron of Cologne and of Delphi, and a secondary patron of England. Because of the arrow that struck her down, she is a patron of archers. She is protector of the

Order of the Ursulines. Because her companions are shown under her **cloak**, she is the patron of orphans as well as of drapers. She is protector of the Universities of the Sorbonne, Coimbra, and Vienna.

▷▷ Petitioners invoke her for a good death, using the "Litany of Ursula for a happy death." Because of the indulgence shown by her promised husband, she is invoked for a good marriage. She is invoked also against burns and scalding, against headaches, and against shipwrecks on rivers, especially on the Rhine.

▷▷ She is always depicted as a beautiful young woman, often with a **spacious cloak** beneath which, as at Bordeaux, she gathers her **companions**; the resultant image resembles that of a Madonna of Mercy. Her principal attributes are her **companions** and a **standard with a cross**.

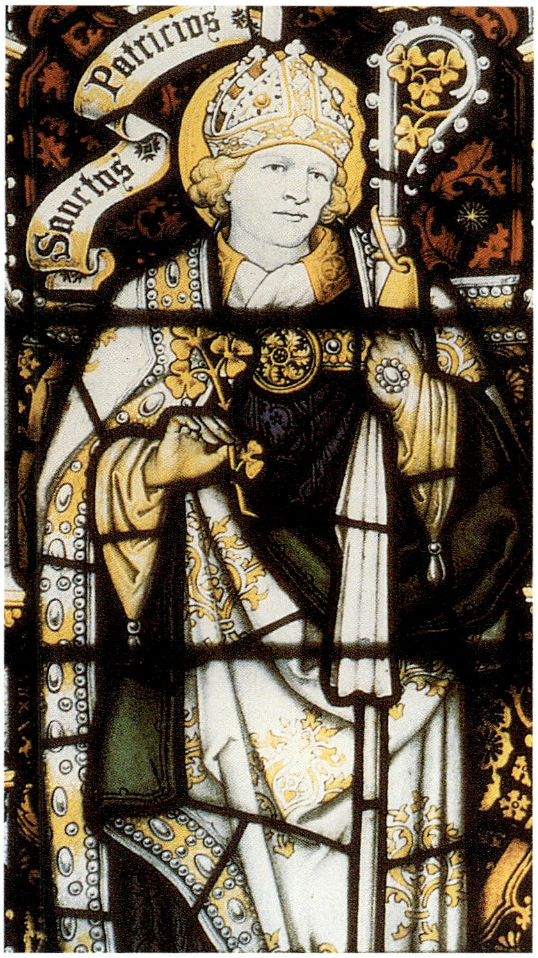

St. Patrick.
Stained-glass window, early 19th cent., in the parish church of Chilham in Kent, England. The saint is clearly indicated by the shamrock he used in explaining the mystery of the Trinity.

Patrick of Ireland, Bishop

390–461
Memorial: March 17
Lat.: Patricius; It.: Patrizio; Fr.: Patrick, Patrice, Parize; Sp.: Patricio; Ger.: Patricius.

Patrick was the apostle to the Irish, to whom he explained the Trinity by means of the shamrock; as a result the shamrock is the symbol of Ireland, where it grows in abundance.

Patrick was born in Roman Britain. At the age of sixteen he was captured by Irish pirates who took him as a slave to their island and sent him to shepherd flocks. He thus had the opportunity to know and love the Irish; as a result, when, six years later, he was able to escape to Gaul, he devoted himself to study in order that he might return to Ireland as a missionary. After being ordained a priest, he joined Bishop Palladius, whom Pope Celestine I had sent on a mission to Ireland; at Palladius' death Patrick succeeded him. From the hill of Croagh Patrick, the saint used the sound of a **bell** to rid the island of **serpents and poisonous animals**. Images of Patrick show him piercing a **serpent** with his **pastoral staff**; this is clearly a metaphor for evangelization, but it does not deny that Patrick also really got rid of serpents. He won over the people and established monasteries, from which came such monks as St. Columbanus, who in turn reevangelized Europe and founded monasteries that followed the Rule of St. Benedict while adapting it. Patrick died in 461, but some traditions claimed he died at the age of 120, in 493.

Tradition has compared him to Moses and Joshua. In fact, on the occasion when he spoke to an angel concealed in a thorn bush, and on the day of his death, the sun did not set. Popular tradition says of him that his fingers were illumined like torches and that the drops of water that fell from his hands were changed into fire; he set icicles on fire and changed snow into milk and butter.

▷▷ His tomb is venerated at Downpatrick in Ulster. His traditional patronage of Ireland was confirmed by John XXIII on December 3, 1962. To the Irish he is not only a patron but a national hero; Patrick asked and was granted that he should be their supreme judge at the final judgment. He accompanies the souls of the deceased. In order to convince unbelievers, he dug a hole in the earth from which the flames of purgatory leaped up and the wailing of the damned could be heard. God granted him the privilege of freeing some souls momentarily from the torments of hell: seven souls every Thursday and twelve every Saturday. He is invoked to escape the torments of hell and against serpents and rabies.

▷▷ He is depicted as a **mitered bishop**. He thrusts his **pastoral staff** (which, along with the **shamrock**, is his principal attribute) into the earth and the **flames** of purgatory shoot up from the spot. Other attributes are **serpents** and the **flames** of purgatory leaping up from the earth.

Remigius, Bishop

ca. 437–ca. 533
Memorial: October 1
Lat.: Remigius (Remmigius, Remedius, Romedius) episcopus Remensis; It.: Remigio, Romedio, Romeo; Fr.: Remi, Arromeux, Remy, Remède, Remège, Reèze, Rhémy, Romède, Rommé; Sp.: Remigio; Ger.: Remigius, Remeis.

Due to his great reputation as a healer, the name Remigius was changed into "Remedius" (= healer). His first miracle occurred at his birth: a blind hermit told his mother, already elderly, that she would bear a son, and he asked that while nursing the infant she would bathe the hermit's eye in milk, so that he might regain his sight. The little child, sitting on his mother's knees as she nursed him, touched the blind man's eyes with a drop of milk and restored his sight.

Remigius became bishop of Rheims when he was probably only twenty-two years old. He governed that church for about seventy years, and it was he, having close ties to Queen Clotild (a Christian princess from Burgundy), who baptized her husband, King Clovis, previously a pagan, and thus gave France a Christian destiny.

Remigius was buried in an ancient cemetery in a chapel that took its name from him and became the focal point of the first abbey; the latter burned down and was replaced by a new cathedral. The latter was called the "archmonastery" and also the "leader of France," and remained standing until the French Revolution.

It is also told of Remigius that at the climactic moment in the baptism of Clovis, king of the Franks, the crowd prevented the priest with the chrism from reaching the bishop; at that point, a **dove** came down and, in its beak, brought a **cruet** of chrism to Remigius. In the eyes of the bishop of Rheims this incident gave approval to the practice of anointing the kings of France, of which Remigius is one of the principal patrons. The feast of the saint is celebrated on October 1: when the schools open on that day, the children who are just beginning their education are called "Remigians."

▷▷ The saint is depicted in **episcopal robes**; his principal attribute is a **dove with a cruet in its beak**; other attributes are a **book** and a **lamp**.

St. Remigius Prepares to Baptize Clovis. Statue on the western facade of the cathedral of Rheims. The cruet brought by the Holy Spirit is clearly shown.

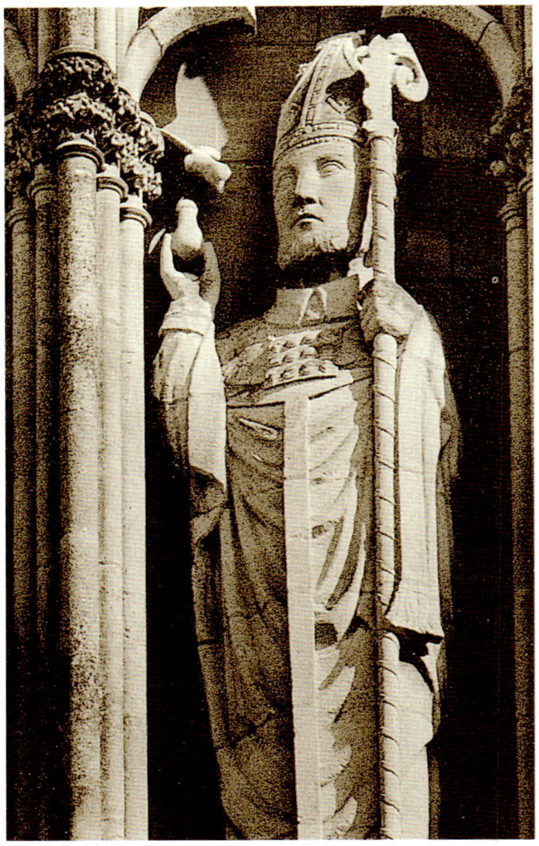

Benedict of Nursia, Abbot and Patron of Europe

ca. 480–547
Feast: July 11
Lat.: Benedictus Cassinensis; It.: Benedetto da Norcia, Benozzo, Betto; Fr.: Benoît de Nursie, Benezet, Benêt, Benezech, Benezit; Sp.: Benito; Ger.: Benedikt, Benedictus von Nursia.

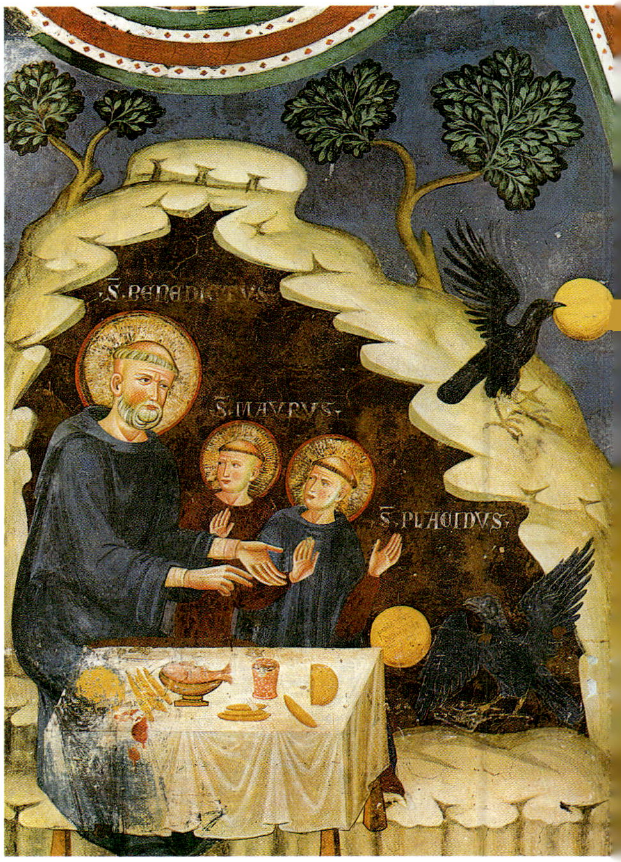

Benedict is the patriarch of the monks of the West. He introduced eremitical life in the area of Subiaco, had many disciples, founded the famous monastery of Monte Cassino, and composed a *Rule* that is the basis of all the Western monastic rules. The source for the history of St. Benedict is the second book of the *Dialogues* of St. Gregory the Great, who was able to consult Benedict's first disciples and the eyewitnesses of his life.

Benedict and his twin sister Scholastica were born around 480 in Nursia into a well-to-do family that sent him at an early age to complete his literary and juridical studies in Rome. While devoting himself to his studies there, he was troubled by the quarrels between factions supporting different claimants to the office of pope (Symmachus and Lawrence) and was disgusted by the dissolute life of young men there. He left the city, together with his foster-mother, and took refuge at Affile, along with some other young men. He miraculously put together an **earthenware sieve** that had fallen to pieces, and thereby attracted curiosity. He then moved to Subiaco and to a cave that would later be known as the Holy Cave; there he was clothed in a monastic habit by Romanus, a monk who also took care of bringing him food.

The saint lived there for about three years; he did not escape diabolical temptations, which he overcame by throwing himself into thorn bushes. His reputation spread, and the monks of Vicovaro asked him to be their leader. They were unable, however, to put up with his austerities and they even tried to kill him with a **poisoned cup**, which Benedict shattered by a sign of the cross that he made before drinking. He then returned to his cave but was drawn from it again by many requests from those who wanted him as a guide in the

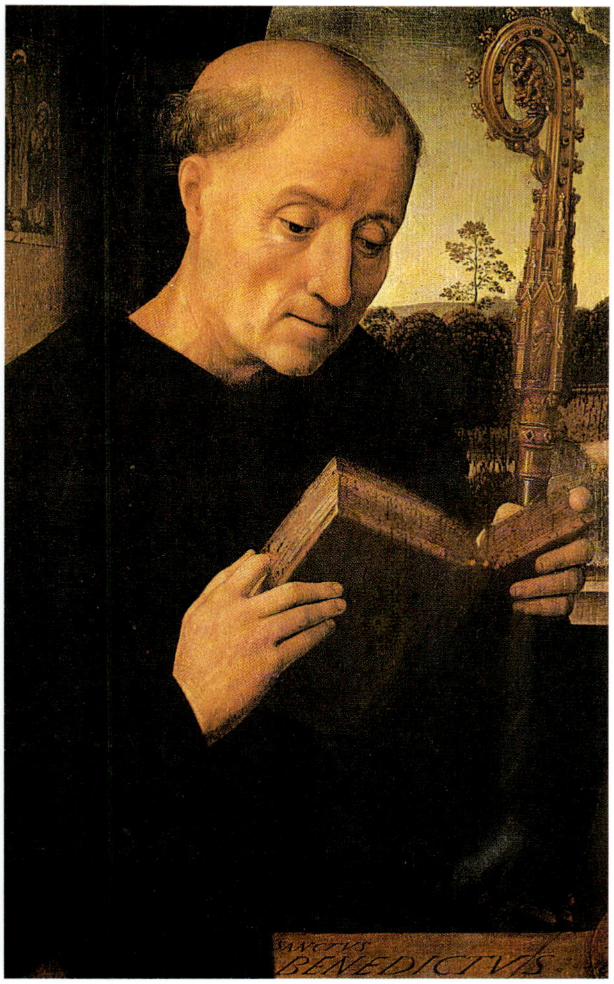

St. Benedict.
By Hams Memling, from the left-hand panel of the triptych for Benedetto Portinari, 1487.
The praying and meditating saint is wearing a black habit and holding the pastoral staff that was the usual attribute of abbots.

monastic life. As a result, there sprang up on those hills twelve small monasteries, each with twelve monks, and all of them under the leadership of Benedict.

Life there was marked by miracles that confirmed the rightness of the undertaking. Benedict made water spring up on the top of a mountain. He brought up from the bottom of a lake a **bill hook** that had been dropped by a Goth and that reattached itself to its handle. He drove away a devil who was tempting a young monk. When a little boy named Placid, whose family had entrusted him to Benedict, was in danger of drowning in the lake, Brother Maurus immediately obeyed Benedict and ran to save the child; only after having pulled him to the shore, did Maurus realize he had walked on the water.

Everyone admired Benedict, but he did arouse the enmity of Florence, the priest of the locality, who even tried to poison him with a **loaf a raven snatched from the saint**. Florence's enmity was providential, since when he tried to harm Benedict's disciples as well, the saint decided to move away and went to a mountain on which stood the citadel of ancient Cassino. There, where an episcopal see had once been, pagan cults had been revived, and temples of Apollo and Jove stood on the hill. Yet Benedict chose this spot, to which he was accompanied by **three ravens and two angels** as protectors. He settled there between 525 and 529, precisely in order that work of God might be more evident. He built his monastery to be a city of God in opposition to the city of the devil; after cutting down the groves sacred to the gods, he consecrated to St. Martin, regarded as the founder of monastic life in the West, the temple formerly belonging to the gods. He also built a chapel to St. John the Baptist, who was thought of as an ideal model of a Christian hermit.

In the new monastery, which had become a center of the active and contemplative lives and of the apostolate, Benedict had a vision one night: in the depths of the night light dissipated the darkness around him and he was able to contemplate the entire universe brought together under a single ray of the sun.

Benedict's sister, Scholastica, had followed his example and become a nun. The two used to meet once a year outside the monastery. At what was to be their final meeting, Benedict was on the point of saying goodbye to her when she asked him to stay with her that night. Her brother said the rules did not allow this. The nun then joined her hands and bowed her head; when she raised it, such a cloudburst ensued that Benedict and his monks had to stay in her house that night. Scholastica explained that she had asked God for that which Benedict had refused, and God had granted her prayer. The two spent the night in edifying conversation and then took leave of one another. Three days later, Benedict had a vision of a dove flying up into the heavens and realized that his sister had died. He then had her placed in the tomb intended for himself. Not long after, Benedict learned the date of his death and had the tomb reopened six days in advance. When the end came, he had himself carried to the chapel of St. Martin; there he took Communion and, held up by his disciples, raised his hands to heaven and died.

Benedict's work endured because of his *Rule,* so-called because it "regulates" the conduct of those who profess obedience to a father, the abbot, who leads them on to holiness. The *Rule* unites, to a marvelous degree, common prayer (the *opus Dei* or "work of God," over which nothing is to take precedence), study, and manual work, these three being equitably distributed throughout each day. The motto *Ora et labora,* "Work and Pray," is not in the *Rule,* although it has become a summary of it, because the spirit of the motto fills the *Rule*. The *Rule* became the real foundation of a new western religious life; as practiced in monasteries down the centuries, it proved so fruitful that on October 24, 1964, Paul VI proclaimed Benedict to be the patron of Europe.

▷▷ In Italy Benedict is the patron of Subiaco, Monte Cassino, and Palermo. Because of the restored bill hook of the Goth, which stood as a metaphor of the fact that the Benedictines taught peoples to work the fields, he is a patron of farmers. Because of his work of material and metaphorical "construction," he is protector of engineers and architects, and, because he made poison harmless, of chemists as well. He also protects coppersmiths, schoolchildren, and speleologists. Because his monks were reclaimers of the soil, John XXIII, on July 12, 1961, proclaimed him patron of officials and associations dealing with land improvement.

St. Benedict and the Miracle of the Poisoned Bread.
13th-cent. fresco by Master Conxolus, in the interior church of the Holy Cave, Subiaco.
With the sign of the cross St. Benedict thwarts the attempt to poison him with a loaf of bread, which a crow then providentially carries off.

Benedict's feast was celebrated on the day of his death, March 21, leading to the popular saying: "On St. Benedict's day, the swallows nest in the roofs." The saying is no longer valid, however, since his feast has been moved to July 11.

▷▷ The saint is invoked against stones, because he healed Emperor Henry II of Germany of this affliction. Because of his exemplary death and because he knew in advance the day of his death, he is a patron of the dying.

He is invoked against poison and poisoning, as well as against those who commit this crime; against diabolical temptations; among illnesses, he heals erysipelas and stones.

▷▷ Benedict is depicted in the **black habit** of a monk, but he may also be seen in a white habit, when the intention is to stress the idea that he is also the "founder" of other Benedictine Orders, such as the Cistercians and Olivetans, who wear a white habit. There are many cycles of stories about his life, but in the emblematic images we see him always in a **monk's robe with a cowl, a scapular, and the pastoral staff** that tells us he was an abbot and is his principal attribute. He is often accompanied by a **raven with a piece of bread in its beak**, to remind us of the raven that saved him.

His fundamental attributes are the **pastoral staff, miter, and book of the Rule with the inscription "Pray and Work"**; secondary attributes are the **raven with bread in its beak**, the **cup with the two serpents**, the **scourges** that point to the need of punishment for violation of the **Rule**, and the **broken sieve**.

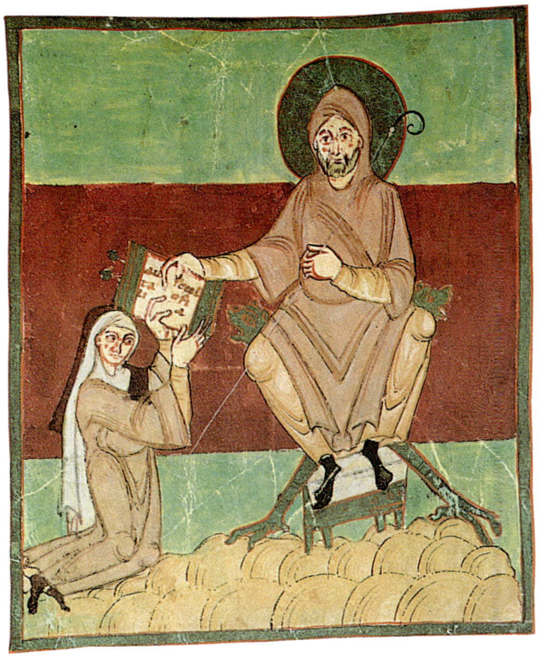

St. Benedict Gives the Rule to Abbess Aelika. Miniature from the frontispiece of a manuscript (1025) containing the *Rule* and belonging originally to the abbey of Ringelheim. Now in the State Library of the Prussian Cultural Heritage, Berlin; ms. theol. lat. qu. 199.

Gregory the Great, Pope and Doctor of the Church

ca. 550 to 604
Memorial: September 3
Lat.: Gregorius Magnus; It.: Gregorio Magno; Fr.: Grégoire le Grand; Sp.: Gregorio Magno; Ger.: Gregor der Grosse; Dutch: Gregorius de Grote; Russ.: Grigori Veliki, Dvoiéslov (from Greek *Dialogos*).

Gregory was born at Rome around 550 and served as an official of the Byzantine government in Rome. After the death of his mother, St. Sylvia, he turned his home on Monte Celio into a monastery named "St. Andrew's," and he built another six monasteries in Sicily. On Monte Celio he lived some happy years devoted to prayer and to study of the Bible and the Fathers. He spent a lengthy period in Constantinople as an official of Pope Pelagius II, and was then recalled to Rome in 585/586 to be the Pope's personal secretary. At the death of Pelagius II in 590, Gregory was elected Pope as the unanimous choice of the clergy, the senate, and the people.

Rome had been devastated by a plague. A week after his election, he decreed a solemn procession, the "sevenfold litany" *(litania septiformis),* in which the entire population took part, as seven different processions departed from seven different churches, all leading toward St. Mary Major, where Gregory delivered his first sermon. On this occasion, he had a vision of the archangel Michael standing atop the mausoleum of Hadrian, which is today known as Castel Sant'Angelo; the angel sheathed his sword, indicating that the epidemic was now over.

In the city of Rome Gregory revived the practice of the stational liturgies, held at the basilicas of the martyrs on the major feasts; on these occasions he gave instructive homilies. He reorganized the Roman Curia and opposed extravagance and simony. Without interfering with the proper autonomy of the bishops, he kept watch over their behavior. He promised to evangelize Great Britain and to that end sent Augustine, a monk, there. Gregory died in 604.

To Gregory we owe the biography of St. Benedict, contained in the second book of his *Dialogues*. We also owe to him the description of the writing of music and chant, as well as the codification of the prayers of the Mass (the Canon) and of the antiphons.

The image of Gregory is often found with those of the other Doctors of the Church, a foursome that is set in parallel with the four evangelists. Among the subjects of representations of Gregory are some that have become iconographical. The depiction of a supper at which Gregory and thirteen guests are present, one of them an angel or a pilgrim, recalls the fact that he was accustomed to invite twelve poor men to supper and that one evening Jesus himself sat at table as a thirteenth guest.

St. Gregory in Ecstasy, with His Secretary Eavesdropping.
Miniature in a codex of the Dialogues from the second half of the 12th cent., in the abbey of St. Lawrence, Liège.

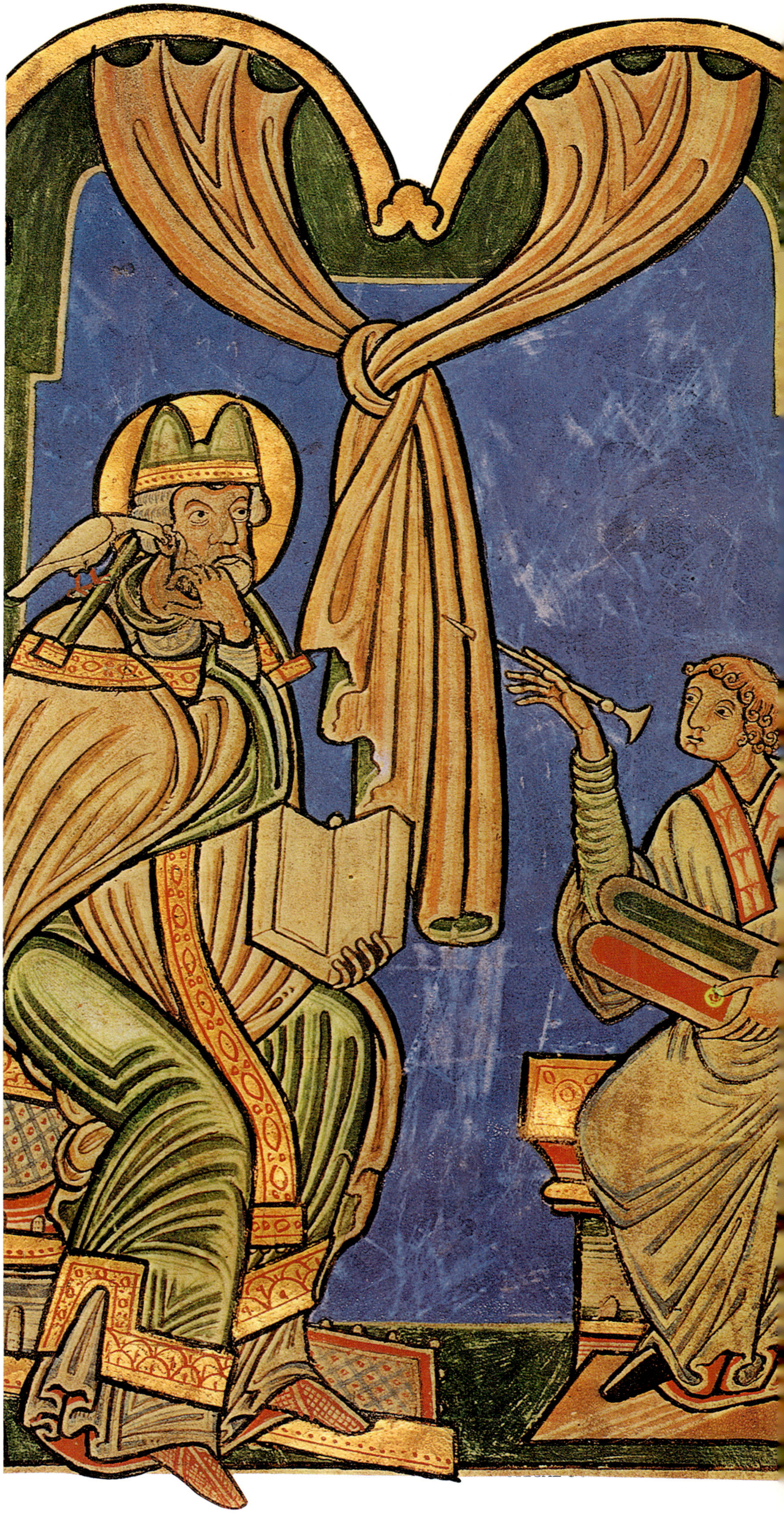

St. Gregory The Great.
Miniature from the Breviary of Blessed Tavelli of Tossignano, now in Fontanelice, Italy. The saint can be identified by the dove of the Holy Spirit and by the papal tiara.

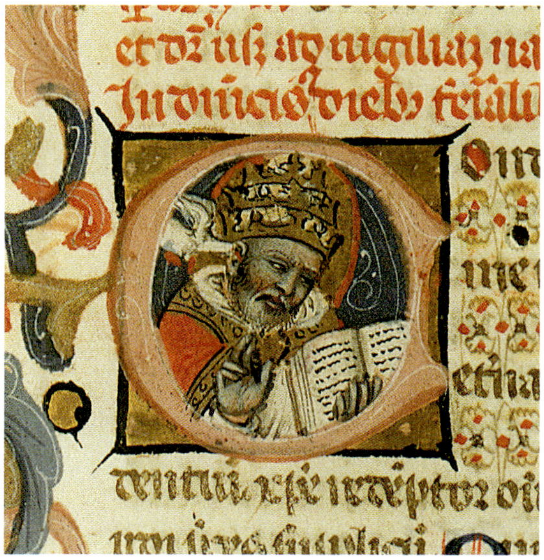

The scene of Gregory at prayer in the presence of the naked body of Trajan, recalls how the saint obtained the deliverance of the emperor's soul from purgatory. A widow had asked Emperor Trajan for justice for her son, who had been murdered by the emperor's son. The emperor gave her his own son in exchange, but he also had to pay a penalty in purgatory. Gregory had the emperor's body exhumed and found that the emperor's tongue was intact. By his prayers Gregory obtained the liberation of Trajan's soul from purgatory.

In prayer St. Gregory saw a monk among the flames of purgatory. An abbot had denied this brother the Office of the Dead after finding three coins in his cell; Gregory liberated the man's soul by celebrating thirty Masses. This story led to the pious practice of praying for the liberation of a soul that is being purified by having a priest celebrate thirty Masses on thirty successive days.

Another representation shows Gregory intent on elevating the Host at Mass, while on the altar Jesus appears, displaying the signs of his passion and being supported by angels. This recalls the incident in which Gregory found an unbeliever among the faithful at Mass and asked for a sign, which was granted to him by the appearance of Jesus on the altar.

Again, Gregory is shown causing blood to flow from a piece of linen. The Empress Constantia had asked Gregory for a precious relic and had received a *brandeum,* that is, a piece of cloth sanctified by contact; she scorned it and returned it to him. But Gregory showed her blood flowing from the piece and thereby demonstrated the value of this "indirect" relic.

▷▷ Due to his own extensive culture, Gregory is the patron of the wise and the learned. Due to Gregorian chant he is the patron of musicians, choral cantors, and singers. He protects the souls in purgatory and is invoked for their salvation; he is also patron of confraternities devoted to praying for these souls. He is invoked against the fires of purgatory, plague, and gout.

▷▷ He is depicted as a **mature man**, with the **papal insignia, the tiara, and the papal cross**, and the **dove** representing the Holy Spirit; this last is his principal attribute. Other attributes are a **stole** and the **papal keys**.

Augustine of Canterbury, Bishop

† 604
Memorial: May 27
Lat.: Augustinus Cantuarensis; It.: Agostino di Canterbury.

Augustine enters the historical record only in 596, when he was abbot of the Benedictine monastery of St. Andrew on Monte Celio in Rome. In that year, Pope Gregory the Great sent him, together with about forty monks, to preach in England. His first journey ended at Aix-en-Provence, where Augustine received such discouraging information about the country that awaited him that he returned to Rome. But the request for Christian preaching had been made. Before and after 313 the British Isles were inhabited by Romanized and Christianized people: Bretons in present-day England, Scots in Scotland, and Gaels in Ireland. The decline of the Roman Empire had opened the way to the invasion of the British Isles, in part by Germanic peoples (Angles, Saxons, and Jutes) who had not been touched either by Roman civilization or by Christianity. The Romanized and Christianized people then retreated into Wales and Cornwall, and several small states arose.

Canterbury, formerly *Durovernum Cantionum* (Latin transcription of the Celtic name), which around 200 C.E. already had walls and a theater for its citizens, was called "Cantwabyrig," "city of the people of Kent." It was the capital of the Jute kingdom of Ethelbert, who was master of all England at the end of the sixth century. This king married a Frankish princess, Bertha, who was a Christian and asked, as a wedding gift, for a church and Catholic priests. Pope Gregory again sent Augustine, who reached the mouth of the Thames on Easter, 597, and began the second evangelization of England. Though Bertha was a Christian, Ethelbert was still distrustful, but he was convinced by the activities and holiness of Augustine and, together with many of his followers, was baptized on June 1, 597.

Augustine was consecrated a bishop and received the pallium from Pope Gregory, who wanted the establishment of two metropolitan sees, at Canterbury and at York. Augustine chose Canterbury as his see and there founded a cathedral and a Benedictine abbey of

St. Columbanus.
Devotional image, beginning of 20th cent.

St. Columbanus Displays the City of Bobbio.
Panel on the tomb of the saint in the basilica of St. Columbanus, Bobbio.

St. Columbanus Writes His Rule under Inspiration.
Panel on the tomb of the saint in the basilica of St. Columbanus, Bobbio.

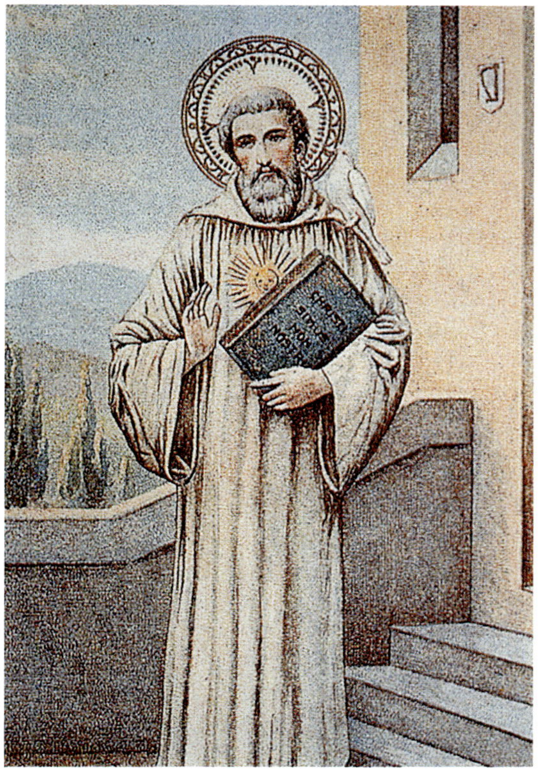

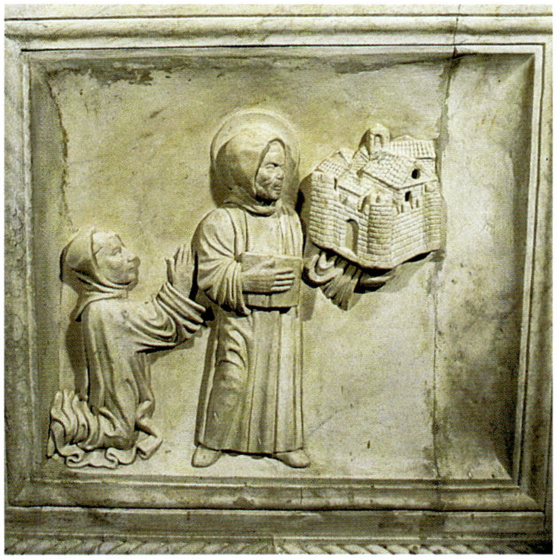

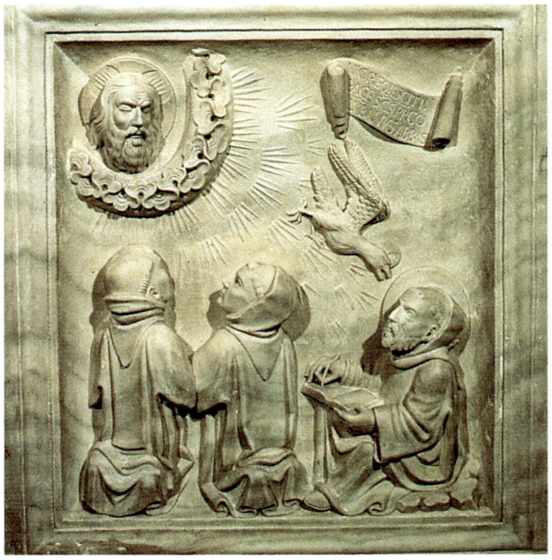

which he was the head until his death. Before that death he succeeded in converting all of Kent and completed his work by establishing the sees of London and Rochester. He died on May 26, 604/605. It is on his chair, preserved in the cathedral of Canterbury, that the archbishops of this see are enthroned.

▷▷ Augustine is one of the patrons of England.

▷▷ He is depicted with **episcopal insignia** and seated on his **throne**.

Columbanus of Bobbio or Luxeuil, Abbot

543–625

Memorial: November 23

Lat.: Colombanus Luxoviensis; It.: Colombano di Bobbio o di Luxeuil; Fr.: Coloman de Luxeuil, Colban, Cloman, Colum, Colombai, Colombin, Koulm; Sp.: Columan; Ger.: Columban.

The date of birth of this unwearying founder of monasteries is uncertain, but can be placed between 525 and 543 (depending on different computations). He was born in the kingdom of Leinster, in east-central Ireland. In a vision, his mother saw herself carrying a radiant sun in her womb. The young man soon experienced a monastic vocation and went to stay in the monastery of Bangor under the guidance of Abbot Comgall, who sent him and twelve disciples to the continent in order to begin a new evangelization of Europe.

The group landed in France near the present St-Malo, and Gontran, king of Burgundy, assigned them a dilapidated Roman fortress on the upper Saone. The monks wore a **white scapular** and a **tonsure in the form of the cross**, and proved to be skilful builders who soon became famous. Columbanus was a stern leader and increased his personal strength in solitude, spending his nights in a cave that had been yielded to him by a **bear**. When a fellow monk complained about how far they had to go for water, Columbanus said to him: "Dig up the rock!" A **fountain** sprang up that is venerated even to this day. He used to call the **birds** and they would fly to his shoulders and take food from his hand; the squirrels used to play in the folds of his garment; a **crow** brought to him a glove he had lost; a **bear** did not tear a deerskin intended for the monks' sandals.

Because his disciples became so many, Columbanus established a new foundation at Luxeuil, a city of hot springs that had turned into a swamp and had to be drained (this is why he is invoked against floods). Then he founded a third house at Fontaine. Columbanus also composed a **Rule** that was geared to these men of the wild forests, men rough and easily yielding to their senses; it said, without any equivocations, that the monks must fast, pray, work, and **read** every day. Disagreements arose, however, between Columbanus and the king who was their protector, and the saint was eventually forced to leave Luxeuil. On his journey, people thronged to him, and Columbanus continued his work of evangelization by curing illnesses and driving out demons.

The journey was a long one, and Columbanus stayed for a good while at Bregenz, which became a monastic center. He later set out from there as a pilgrim to Rome, moving through an Italy that was in the hands of the Lombards and engaged in a great struggle against the Arian heresy. He was received by King Agilof and was given Bobbio, where he settled and founded a monastery that became a great cultural center and possessed a very extensive library. Here a **bear** appeared once again in the saint's life: the bear tore to pieces one of the oxen that was pulling a beam for use in the building; the saint made the bear accept the yoke in place of the ox; from then on, the bear served the convent until its death.

Columbanus himself died at Bobbio on November 23, 615; a tradition had it that a **sun** appeared to him before his death. His relics consist of his head, which is kept in a silver bust, his wooden bowl, and his **knife**. It is on this image that mothers rely: they cut a loaf of bread and eat it in order that they may give milk more abundantly.

▷▷ Columbanus is a patron of Ireland, Scotland, Cornwall, and Bobbio.

▷▷ He is depicted in monk's garb with a **white or black scapular**. His principal attributes are a **bear** and the motto "We belong to Christ and not to ourselves." Other attributes are a **sun** on his breast, a **dove** on his shoulder, a **whip** for use in correction, and the **fountain** he caused to spring up.

Constantine of Cornwall, King of Scotland and Martyr

End of 6th century
Memorial: March 11
Lat.: Constantinus imperator, martyr.

This man, who is remembered as a disciple of St. Columba in the Irish and Scottish martyrologies, is Constantine, king of Dummonia (present-day Cornwall), who led an evil life until 587, the year of his conversion. He then left his kingdom and did penance for his sins in the Irish monastery of Rathan in Offaly. After seven years he was ordained a priest and was sent to preach in Scotland, where he was under the direction of St. Columba. He was slain there by idolaters.

▷▷ His cult spread in Scotland, of which he is a patron, and in Ireland and Cornwall.

▷▷ He is depicted as a **warrior king** who grasps a **sword** and carries the **cross**.

Eligius, Bishop

ca. 590 to 660
Memorial: December 7
Lat.: Eligius (from *electus* = "chosen"), Elogius, Eulogius Noviomensis; It.: Eligio, Alò, Lò; Fr.: Éloi, Alar, Aloy, Elouis, Hilloine, Alar and Eeler (Breton); Sp.: Eloy; Ger.: Eligius, Loyen, Loy.

Eligius was born in the Limousin (France) into a family of modest means. He first became a blacksmith and farrier and was then sent to Lyons as an apprentice to a goldsmith, who coined money for the king. He then went to Paris, where he became acquainted with the treasurer of the king, Clotar II, and was introduced to the latter. Tradition has it that the king gave him gold with which to make a throne; because the material was so abundant, Eligius presented the king with two thrones and amazed him with his honesty. Eligius then

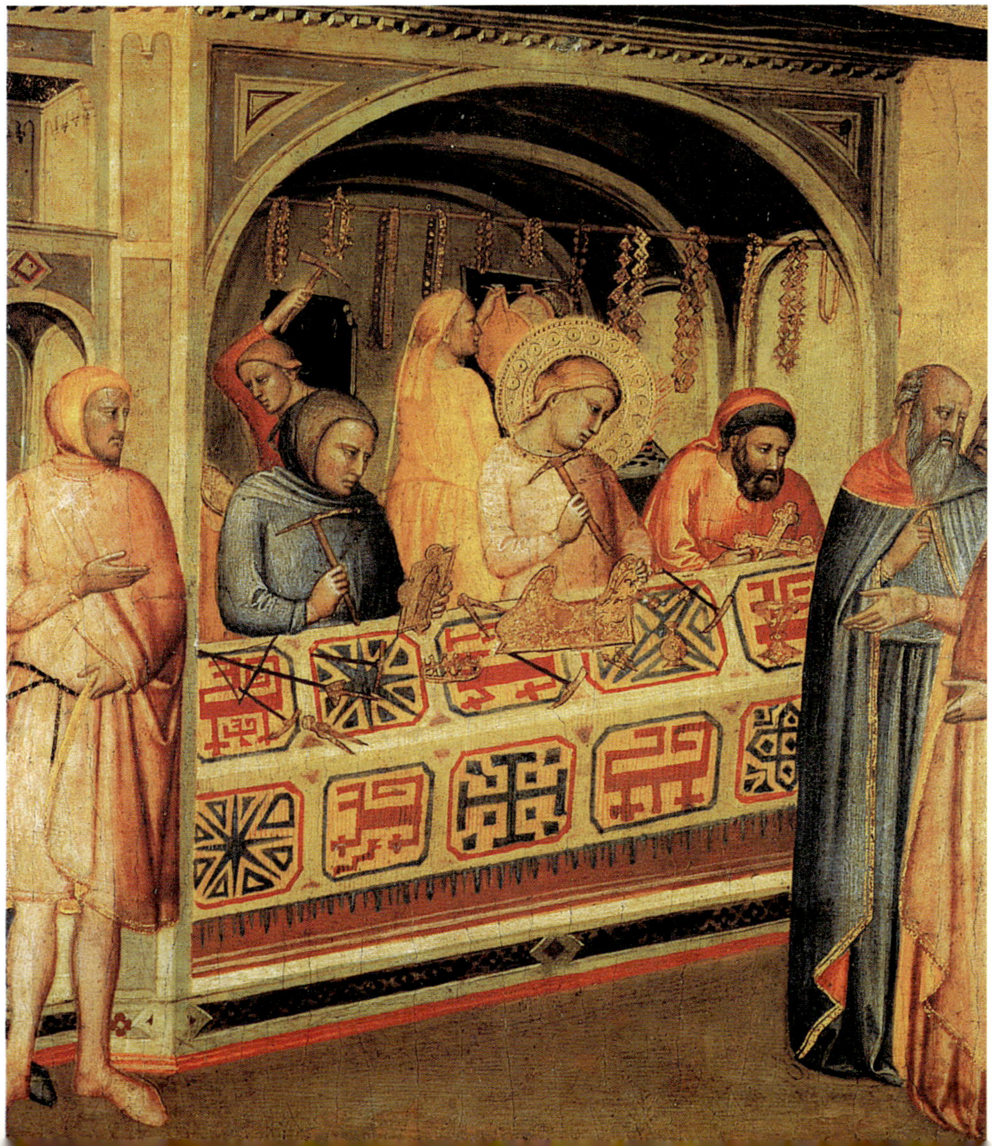

St. Eligius Working as a Silversmith.
Tempera on a panel by the Maestro della Misericordia, 3rd quarter of the 14th cent.
The saint is depicted here working alongside other artisans, whose patron he would later become.

became director of the mint in Marseilles, while continuing to work as a goldsmith; numerous works were attributed to him, among them the tomb of St. Martin of Tours.

When Dagobert I succeeded his father, Clotar II, in 623, he gave Eligius some responsible tasks. Eligius was a charitable man and the seaside city gave him opportunities to ransom and liberate prisoners of war.

Amusing incidents were not lacking. In order more easily to shoe a recalcitrant horse, he cut off a foreleg, worked on it, and then reattached it. On one occasion, the devil took the form of a beautiful young girl in order to tempt Eligius, but the latter twisted the girl's nose with his fiery pincers.

In 632 he founded an abbey for men at Solignac, imposing the Rule of Luxeuil; a year later, he founded a monastery for women in Paris. At the death of Dagobert, he withdrew into religious life, but in 641 was elected bishop of Lyons-Tournai. He founded some monasteries in his diocese and made apostolic visitations. He died in 660, perhaps on December 1; his cult spread rapidly, since he had combined an active life with a noteworthy skill displayed in the work he did to enhance the worship of God and in his pastoral ministry.

▷▷ Eligius became patron of the Limousin, northern France, Germany, and Italy. He is protector of blacksmiths, goldsmiths, and jewelers, tinsmiths, gilders, and embellishers of leather, makers of luggage, workers in the mint, makers of bells and trumpets, toolmakers, makers and sellers of knives and locks, saddlers, farriers, carters and muleteers, horse traders, makers of harnesses, saddles, and spurs, renters of carriages and coachmen, and therefore of automobiles, mechanics, and garage owners. Because of his skill in shoeing horses, he became patron of veterinarians and horses, which in many parts of France are blessed on his feast day. He is also protector of grooms. Because he cured a lame person, he is patron of the crippled and of hospitals and hospital workers. He is patron also of makers of candles and of oil for lamps.

▷▷ Because he saved the Church of St. Martial in Paris from being burned down, he is invoked against fires and, oddly enough, against floods. He is also invoked against mesenteric tabes, ulcers, and enteritis in children, and against lameness and boils.

▷▷ Eligius is depicted as a bishop wearing **episcopal insignia**, as well as with **hammer, anvil, and tongs**. The latter are his principal attributes and appear also in images showing him as a blacksmith at work. He is also depicted as a goldsmith with **scales** and **chalice** or **ring**, which are further attributes.

St. Giles (Egidius), Abbot.
Detail from the Moreel Triptych by Hans Memling, now in the Musée Communal des Beaux-Arts, Bruges (photograph by Joseph Martín, Collado Villalba, Madrid).
The saint, wearing his black Benedictine habit, holds the book of the Rule. His arm has been wounded by an arrow intended for the deer, which is frightened but trusts in the saint's protection.

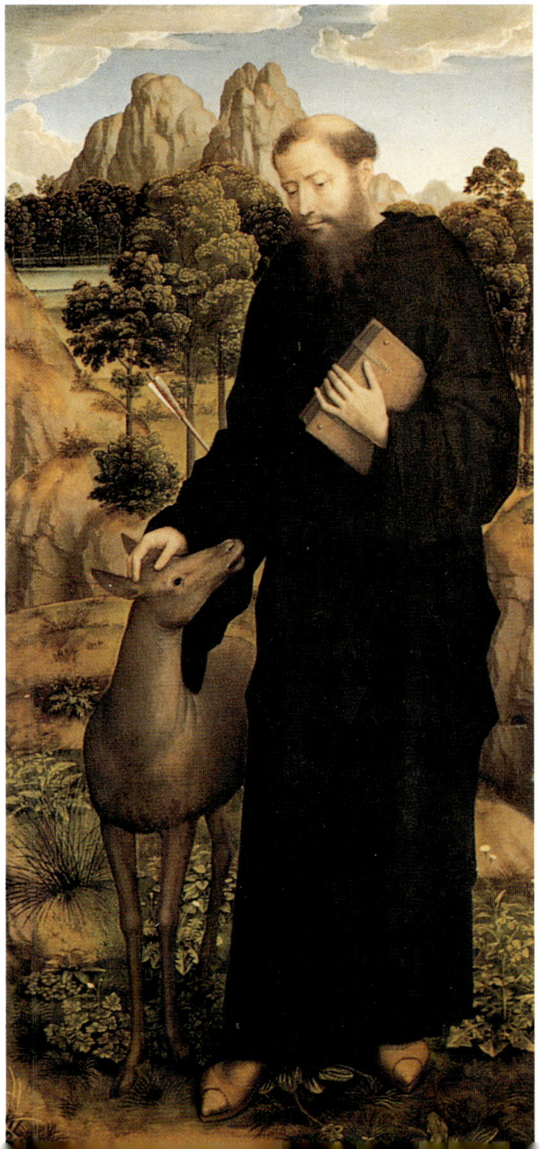

Egidius, Abbot

ca. 650–ca. 721
Memorial: September 1
Lat.: Aegidius, Gidius; It.: Egidio, Gillio; Fr.: Gilles, Egide, Gide, Gile, Gély, Gilly, Gillet, Gilson, Gire; Sp.: Gil, Egidio; Ger.: Aegidius, Aegid, Gilg, Gilgen, Ilgen, Igels; Dutch: Gillis; Swed.: Ilian; Hung.: Egyed.

Egidius was probably born in Athens, and his parents were Theodore and Pelagia, aristocrats noted for their piety. He was quickly baptized and then given a Christian education. He became "the wonder of the city of Athens," for he healed a poor, sick man by throwing his own cloak around him. He healed an unfortunate man dying of a serpent's bite and healed one who was possessed.

When his parents died, Egidius gave all his possessions to the poor, in order to avoid the admiration of the crowds, he set sail for France. During this voyage he calmed a storm by his prayers; the ship came to land at the mouth of the Rhone near Arles, and here he healed a sick person who had been tormented by fevers for three years. Egidius continued on toward the Alps and came to rest in the valley of Baume de Sanillac, where he became a disciple of a holy hermit; the two lived on roots, herbs, and the milk of a **deer**. One day, Wamba, king of the Goths, was out hunting and followed the deer to Egidius' cave; the saint was wounded in the hand by an **arrow** meant for the **deer**, which had taken refuge close by him. Wamba, struck with admiration of the hermit's life, gave him a large piece of land, known as Valle Flavia, and wanted a monastery built there. Following the will of God thus manifested, Egidius went over to a life lived in common with other monks. The monastery was quickly built and filled with fellow monks and those of the faithful who wanted guidance from the saint; the latter was compelled to let himself be elected abbot. The abbey was dedicated to St. Peter and given over to Pope Boniface II, who took it under his direct jurisdiction.

Baptism and Martyrdom of St. Boniface.
Miniatures from a Missal, beginning of the 11th cent., in the cathedral treasury, Fulda.

When the Muslims threatened these lands, Egidius and all his companions took refuge with Charles Martel in Orléans. One day, during the celebration of Mass, as Egidius was praying for the king, an angel appeared to him and gave him a **scroll** on which was written a sin the king did not dare to confess, and also forgiveness already granted for the sin, provided the king would repent of it. After the Mass Egidius spoke to Charles Martel; when the latter saw the scroll that had thus come to the saint, he repented and made his confession. The king then offered the means of rebuilding the monastery in Valle Flavian that the Muslims had destroyed. Here, after prophesying his own death, Egidius died peacefully on September 1, 721.

▷▷ Egidius is the patron of Provence (known as "the land of St. Egidius"), France, and the city of Graz. Devotion to him became widespread throughout Europe by way of the pilgrimage routes, and villages are everywhere to be found that bear his name and have churches dedicated to him. He is listed among the Fourteen Intercessors; by reason of his monastic life he is a protector of hermits; because he confessed the faith he is a protector of confessors and sinners, as well as of archers, the ill, the lame, nursing mothers, hunters, weavers, foresters, furriers and glove makers, drapers, and shoemakers; because the king was on a horse, Egidius is protector of harnessers. By reason of the milk received from the deer, Egidius is patron of wet nurses and, of course, protector of deer.

Because he welcomed the terrified deer, he is patron of the mad, because fear has caused their madness; he is invoked against fear and nightmares. In the Touraine region he is invoked against cancer, in Normandy against convulsions and epilepsy, which is known as "St. Egidius' illness." Because of the wound in his hand, he is invoked against wounds of the hand; people also pray to him for conjugal fertility.

▷▷ Egidius is depicted in the **black robe of the Benedictines**, and his principal attributes are an **abbot's pastoral staff** and a **deer**. Other attributes are an **arrow** and a **lily**.

St. Gudula.
Wooden statue, 16th cent., in Antwerp.
St. Gudula experiences, along with St. Genevieve, a nocturnal attack by the devil, who puts out the light (in this case a lantern).

Boniface of Mainz or of Fulda, Bishop and Martyr

671–754
Memorial: June 5
Lat.: Bonifacius Maguntinus, Germanorum Apostolus; It.: Bonifacio; Fr.: Boniface; Ger.: Bonifaz, Bonifacius, Bonifazius, Bonifatius, Apostel der Deutschen.

This evangelizer of Germany was born near Exeter in England, perhaps in 672, and was named Winfrid or Winfrith. In 719, he took the meaningful name of Boniface, "he who does good *or* who brings the good news." He studied at the abbey of Exeter and dedicated himself to the evangelization of Europe.

In 716 he landed in Frisia and joined St. Willibrord in Utrecht. Pope Gregory II gave him charge of Thuringia, and he was consecrated a bishop in 722. In 732 Gregory III bestowed the pallium on him and appointed him an archbishop and the papal vicar for the whole of Germany. There he began a vast work of organization, established dioceses, and appointed bishops, thereby placing Catholicism on a firm foundation. He then went to the regions of Hesse and Thuringia, where he established the episcopal see of Erfurt. In 744 he founded the monastery of Fulda and in 745 became archbishop of Mainz.

Codex Ragyndrudis.
In the cathedral treasury, Fulda.
According to tradition, the cuts in the pages came from the blows of the sword inflicted on St. Boniface, who, at the moment of his martyrdom, defended himself against his assailants armed only with his Book of the Gospels.

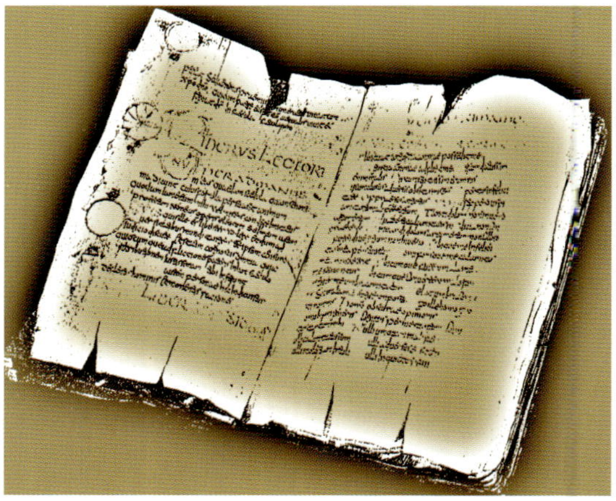

During the difficult period of the transition between the Merovingian dynasty and the Carolingian, he devoted himself to the reform of the Frankish Church, a reform that was crowned by a general council in 754, over which he presided. Here the organization of the

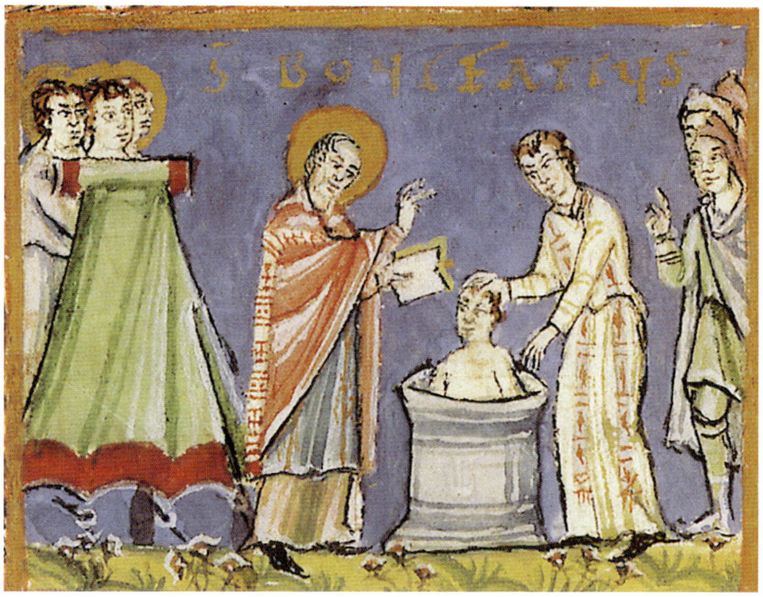

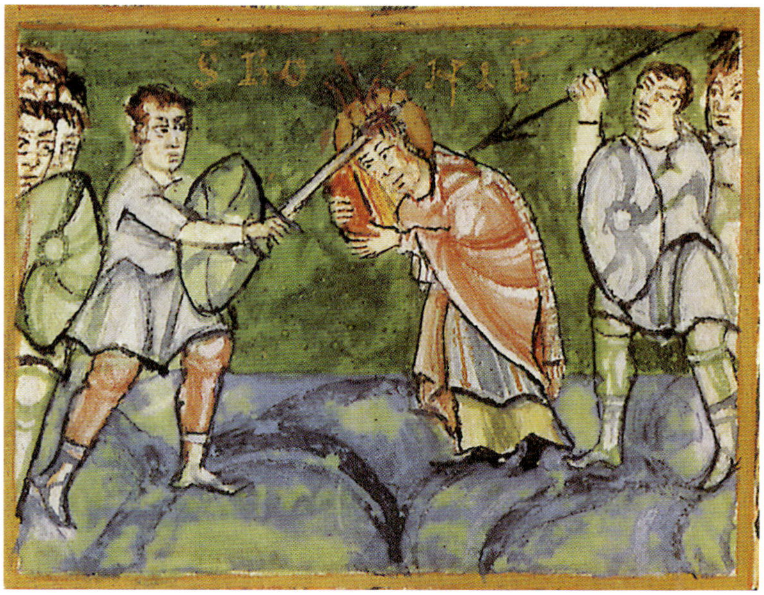

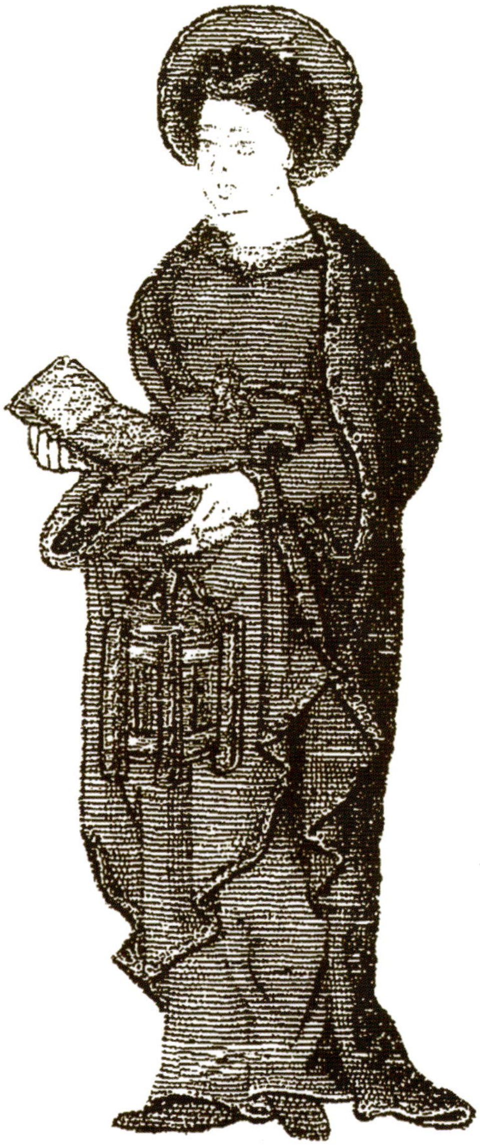

Church was determined, pagan superstitions were rooted out, and the observance of the Benedictine Rule was prescribed for monasteries. He wanted to evangelize the Frisians, and for this purpose he sailed down the Rhine toward the Zuiderzee; when he was about to administer the sacraments to neophytes gathered around him, a group of pagans assaulted his camp at Dekkum and killed him and his fifty-two companions. His head was pierced by a spear as he raised on high his Book of the Gospels. His body was buried in the crypt of the cathedral of Fulda.

Some episodes of his life are depicted in images of him: his preaching in Frisia, the foundation of the monastery at Fulda, how he cut down with an **axe** an oak dedicated to the god Thor, how he caused a fountain to spring up by pushing the shaft of his episcopal cross into the ground, and how he used the Evangeliary to defend himself against his murderers.

▷▷ Boniface is patron of Germany and especially of Mainz, Erfurt, and Fulda. In the Netherlands he is venerated, along with Willibrord, as "the apostle to the Frisians," because he completed Willibrord's work. Because of the similarity between his name and the German word *Bohnen* ("beans"), these legumes are planted on his feast day.

▷▷ His principal attributes are his **episcopal vestments**, along with **miter** and **staff**, the **Book of the Gospels, pierced by a spear**. Another attribute is the **axe** with which he cut down the sacred oak.

Gudula of Brussels, Virgin

650–712
Memorial: January 8
Lat.: Gudula, Gudila, Guodila, Bruxelliensis; It.: Gudula; Fr.: Gudule de Bruxelles, Goële, Gouidèle, Goule, Ergoule, Tergoule; Sp.: Gudula de Bruseles; Ger.: Gudule, Goude, Gudrum; Flem.: Goedele.

This patron of Brussels devoted herself to charitable works and prayer; she liked to go off at night to pray in peace in the church of Moorsel, a little distance from her own village. It was this fact that determined her iconography: when she walking along at night with a **lantern**, a demon extinguished it, but at her prayer it was relit.

▷▷ Gudula is a patron of Belgium and Brussels. In the diocese of Malines and Ghent, her feast is celebrated on January 19.

▷▷ She is depicted as **a young woman with a lantern** (her principal attribute), which **a demon extinguishes and an angel relights**.

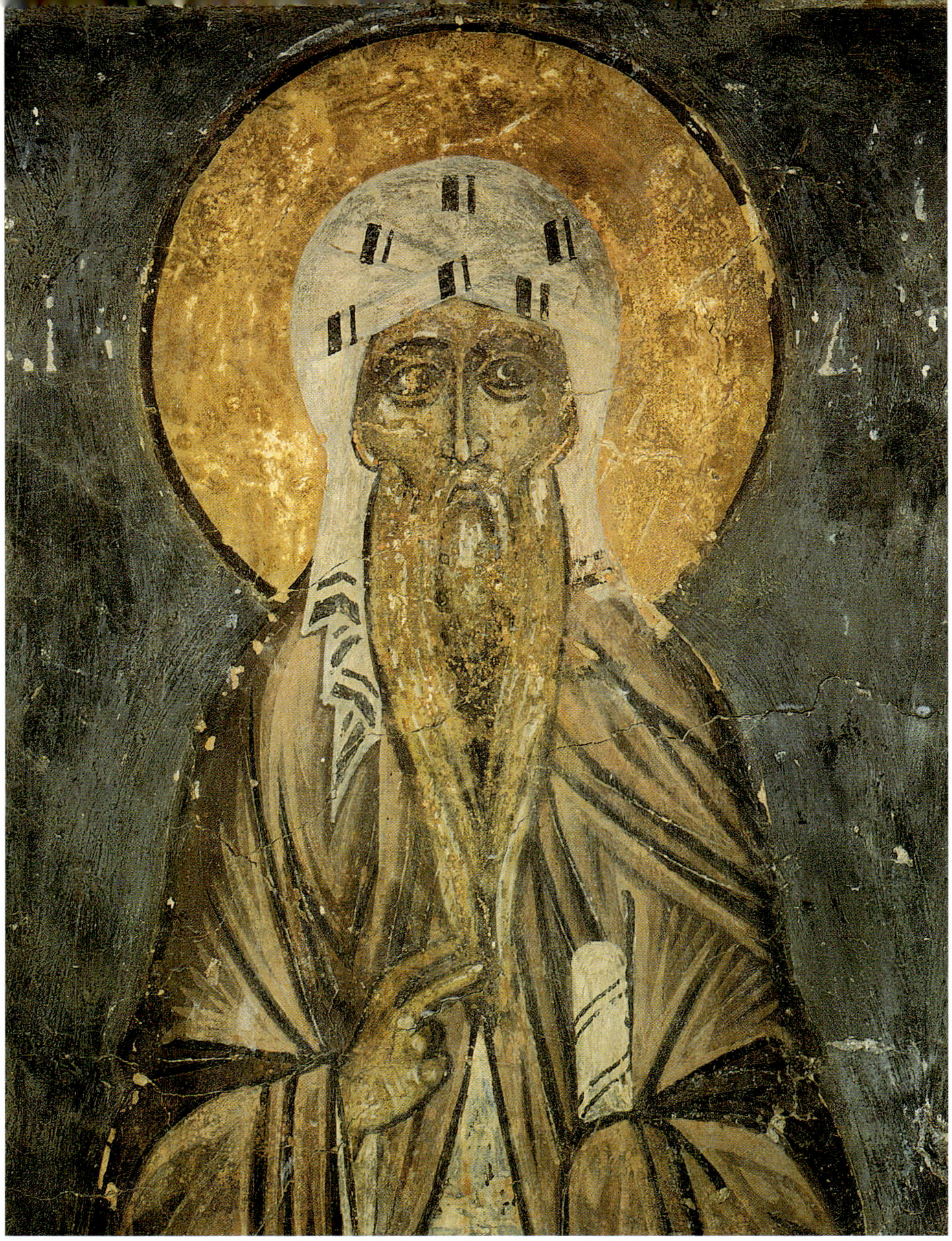

John Damascene, Priest and Doctor of the Church

675–749
Memorial: December 4
Lat.: Johannes Damascenus; It.: Giovanni Damasceno; Fr.: Jean Damascène, de Damas, Jehan le Damassien; Sp.: Juan Damasceno; Ger.: Johannes von Damaskus, Damascenus; Russ.: Ioann Damaskine.

This valiant defender of the veneration of sacred images was born into a Christian family of Damascus; his father worked at the Ommayad court as the imperial collector of the taxes Christians owed the caliph. After a solid literary and philosophical education he withdrew to the Laura of St. Sabas in Palestine. In the controversy over images he resolutely defended the iconodules in a treatise that is his best-known work. We owe to him one of the first expressions of consecration to the Virgin as the Mother of God who leads us to him.

His iconography was influenced by a tradition that had little basis: in order that Emperor Leo the Isaurian might avenge himself on John for the latter's defense of images, he denounced him to the caliph, who had **one of John's hands cut off**. But the Virgin, who was grateful for the defense of images of her, reattached his hand, but left as a remembrance **a red mark on his wrist** in the form of a bracelet.

▷▷ John is a patron of Belgium and protector of iconographers. Because his hand was reattached by the Virgin, he is patron of one-armed persons, and because the Madonna healed him, patron of pharmacists.

▷▷ His principal attributes are a **hand cut off** and, in honor of his Syrian origin, a **turban**.

St. John Damascene.
Fresco, Monastery of Zverinec, Novgorod; and lunette over the north door of the church of St. Simeon.

Hubert of Liège or of Maastricht, Bishop

† 727

Memorial: May 30 (November 3)

Lat.: Hubertus Leodiensis, Higbertus, Hogobertus, Hupertus; It.: Uberto, Umberto; Fr.: Hubert de Liège, Humbert, Imbert, Heubert; Sp.: Huberto; Ger.: Hubert von Lüttich, Hubrecht, Umbrecht, Huprecht; Dutch: Huybrecht, Huygebaert.

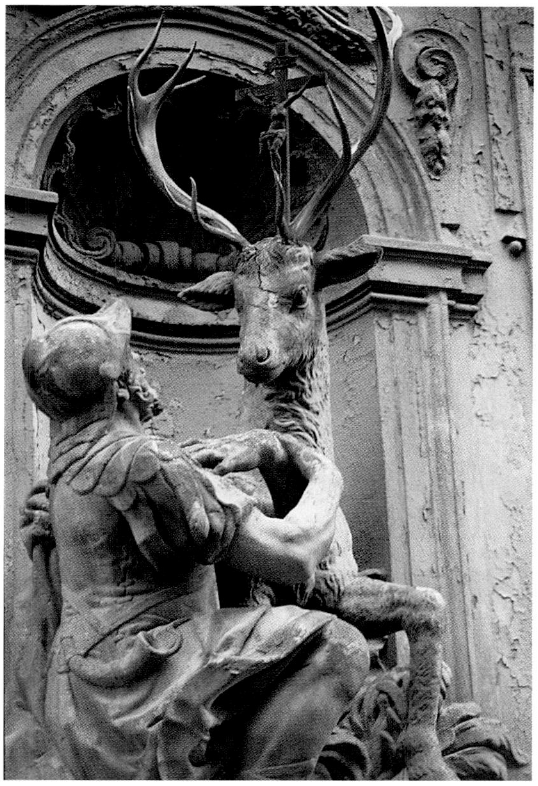

St. Hubert of Liège.
18th-cent. statue in a private building, Prague. The saint is shown in a scene from the early part of his life, when his meeting with a cross-bearing deer leads to his conversion. The garb of a Roman soldier confirms the theory that the legend of St. Eustachius provided images for St. Hubert. In fact, in northern Europe, beginning with the 11th cent., the story and vision of St. Eustachius, a Roman general, was assigned to St. Hubert.

Hubert, who probably belonged to a noble family, became bishop of Tongres-Maastricht in 703/705, succeeding St. Lambert, whose relics Hubert transferred solemnly to Liège in 717/718. Hubert was the evangelizer of the last pagans left in the forest of the Ardennes and of Brabant. He died as the result of a wound caused by a clumsy servant using a fish hook. When he felt that his end was near, he wanted to consecrate a new church in Héverlé (now Louvain) and arranged that he himself should be buried in Liège, in the church dedicated to St. Peter; his body was taken there after his death on May 30, 727.

When his tomb was opened sixteen years later, his body and clothing were intact and sweet-smelling. Beginning in the ninth century, his cult spread and he was venerated especially in Belgium, Holland, and Luxembourg. But his memory also spread throughout Europe, due to the image of him with a **deer that bears a cross on its forehead**; many scholars, however, maintain that this aspect of Hubert's story, as told in the *Golden Legend,* was simply copied from the life of St. Eustachius. The legend has it that Hubert went hunting on Good Friday and, on spotting a gigantic deer, pursued it all day long, until the deer came to a halt and a luminous cross could be seen on its forehead. The deer then spoke to Hubert, who had fallen on his knees: "Why are you pursuing me? So greatly has your passion for hunting made you forget your salvation! Go to my servant Lambert in Maastricht, and he will tell you what to do."

As a result, Hubert went to Lambert, bishop of Liège, and there devoted himself to God; when he became a widower, he withdrew into the forest. While at Rome on a pilgrimage, an angel appeared to Pope Sergius, telling him that Lambert had died and ordering him to consecrate Hubert a bishop. When the latter hesitated to accept, an angel brought to him St. Lambert's **pastoral staff and pontifical vestments**, while the Virgin gave him a **stole woven by her own hands**. St. Peter appeared to him on the day of his consecration and gave him a **golden key**; a golden key and a stole are in the treasury of the abbey of St. Hubert and of the church of the Holy Cross in Liège. One of the miracles he worked during his life was to extinguish, with a simple sign of the cross, a fire threatening the episcopal palace; another was to cause a flood that rendered the dried-up Meuse navigable; still another was to cure a poor fellow infected with rabies.

▷▷ The story as a whole dates from after the fifteenth century, but even before that hunters had chosen Hubert as their patron, and the monks of the abbey of St. Hubert raised hunting dogs. This perhaps became the source of the later tradition.

Hubert is one of the Healer saints: those infected with rabies used to go to the abbey of St. Hubert in the Ardennes, where a priest would make a small incision on the person's forehead; for nine days the person had to keep a black bandage on his forehead, while a hot iron, known as "St. Hubert's **key**," was applied to his body.

Hubert is a patron of Liège, as well as of hunters, foresters, hunting dogs, wood turners (because of the branching horns of the cross-bearing deer), and also foundry workers.

The saint is invoked against rabies (known as "St. Hubert's illness") and against the bites of mad dogs and poisonous serpents.

▷▷ Hubert is depicted in two ways: as a **bishop** and, especially, as a **hunter kneeling** before **the cross-bearing deer**; the latter is the saint's principal attribute.

Other attributes are the **stole** and the **key**, as well as other elements of a hunt: **horse**, **dog**, **hunting horn**, and a **falcon on the arm**.

Willibrord, Bishop

658–739
Memorial: November 7
Lat.: Willibrordus Trajectensis; It.: Willibrordo; Fr.: Willibrord d'Utrecht and d'Echternach; Ger.: Willibrord, Welwert.

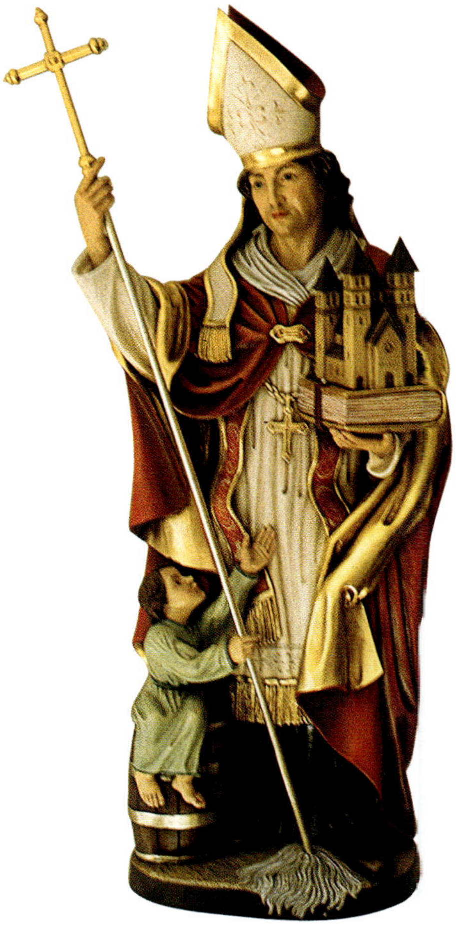

The future "apostle of the Frisians" was born in Northumbria and as a very young man entered the Benedictine abbey of Ripon, while his father, whose wife had died, withdrew to the life of a hermit. Willibrord made his vows at the age of fifteen, completed his studies in Ireland, was ordained a priest in 690, went with eleven companions to Frisia (now Holland), and was confirmed in his mission by Pope Sergius. When the mission had yielded its first fruits, Willibrord was appointed bishop of the new diocese of Frisia; he received his consecration in Rome in 695 and took up his residence in Utrecht. From there he went on many missionary journeys, one purpose being to found monasteries following the Benedictine Rule; one of these was at Echternach in Luxembourg, to which he subsequently withdrew until his death.

Willibrord was a man of both prayer and action; he was a clear and persuasive preacher and possessed great organizational skills (it was due to him that the office of auxiliary bishop was introduced into the West). Among his relics there is a rare portable altar, now in Trier, which bears witness to his missionary activity. It is told of him that he caused a **fountain** to burst forth and that by means of his **pastoral staff** he filled a **cask** with wine.

▷▷ His traditional role as patron of Holland and Luxembourg was confirmed by Pius XII on September 29, 1950, and October 4, 1956.

The centers of his cult are Utrecht and Echternach; in 751 the abbey of Echternach became a royal abbey. The pilgrimage to the saint's shrine at Echternach is marked by an unusual dancing procession that lasts for several hours and during which, at one time, the participants took five steps forward and then three backward. This ritual arose in thanksgiving for the end of an epidemic of St. Vitus' dance, an illness of the nervous system that is marked by rapid, uncontrollable movements.

Willibrord is invoked against the forms of herpes (cutaneous inflammations of a viral kind) and against convulsions, epilepsy, and chorea.

▷▷ The saint is depicted in **episcopal garb** and thrusting his **pastoral staff into a cask**.

Anskar or Oskar of Corbie, Bishop

801–865
Memorial: February 3
Lat.: Anscharius, Ansgarius; It.: Anscario; Fr.: Anschaire, Ansgaire, Anschar, Oscar; Sp.: Ansgario; Ger.: Ansgar, Oskar.

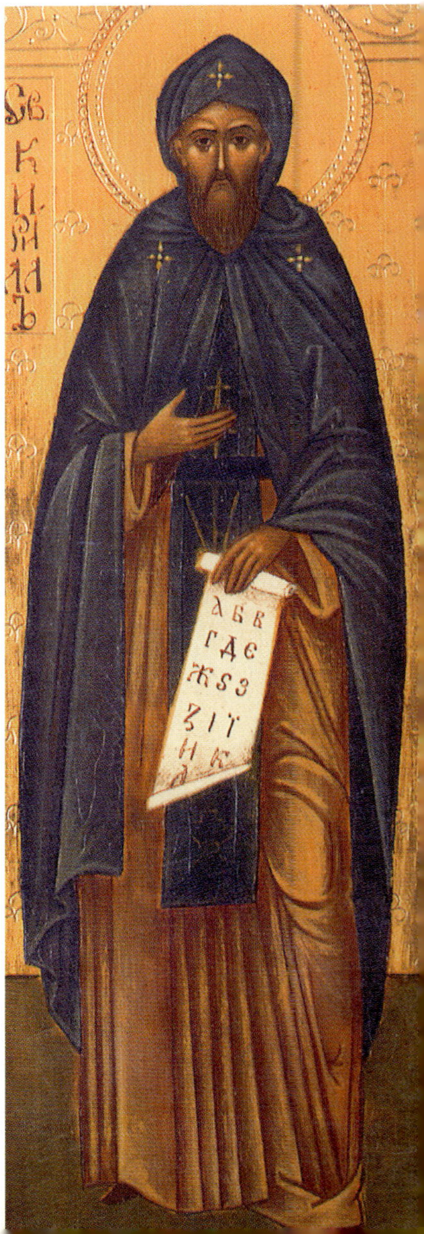

Anskar was born in 801 at Corbie on the Somme in northern France; he was bishop of Hamburg and apostle of the North and especially of Denmark; he died in Bremen on February 3, 863. He was described as "exteriorly an apostle, interiorly a monk" *(foris apostolus, intus monacus),* because he combined in himself the characteristics of both monk and apostle.

Anskar was educated in the Benedictine monastery of Corbie, where, at the wish of Charlemagne, young Saxons such as Anskar were prepared for the apostolate among their own people. In 822 Anskar was sent to Corvey or New Corbie as teacher in the monastery recently founded at the imperial court of Höxter on the Weser. His reputation won him the task of accompanying, on his homeward journey, Harold, claimant of the Danish throne, who had come to Mainz to be baptized.

Anskar's work in Denmark did not yield the expected fruits, whereas in Sweden he succeeded in building, at Birka, the first church erected in the Scandinavian countries. In order to consolidate the work of evangelization, he returned to Saxony and obtained from an imperial council permission to establish at Hamburg a diocese that would be the vital center for the evangelization of the Scandinavian countries. He was the first bishop of this diocese and received both the pallium and the approval of his work when he went to Rome in 831/832. On this occasion he was appointed apostolic legate for Denmark, Sweden, and all the northern Slavs.

Anskar devoted himself to organizing the new diocese while leaving local missionary work to his companion Gausbert. He took special care in the training of young Danes, whom he formed in a monastery, given to him by Louis the Pious, at Turnhout near Bruges,

Saint Willibrord.
Painted wooden statue by Andre Demetz; 20th cent.: in the Church of Bettendorf, Luxembourg. Willibrord is shown holding a model of the basilica of Echternach.

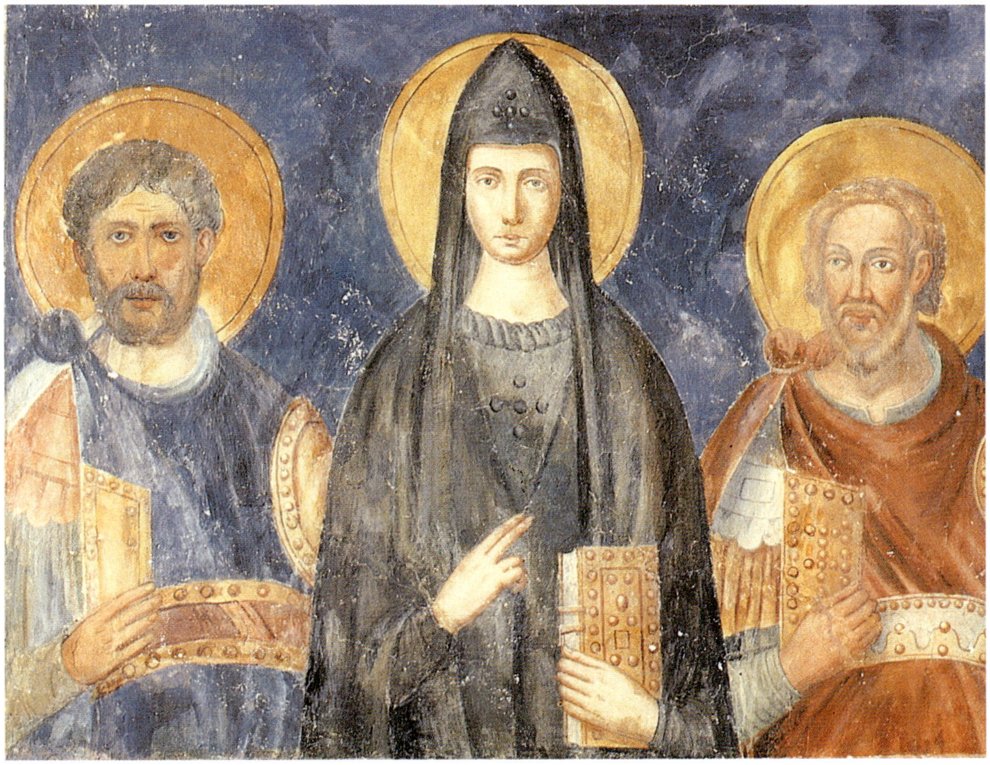

St. Benedict between SS. Cyril and Methodius.
14th-cent. fresco in the basilica of St. Francis. Cyril and Methodius were regarded as patrons of Europe. Here they flank St. Benedict, all three being bringers of the Gospel, which is at the foundation of European culture.

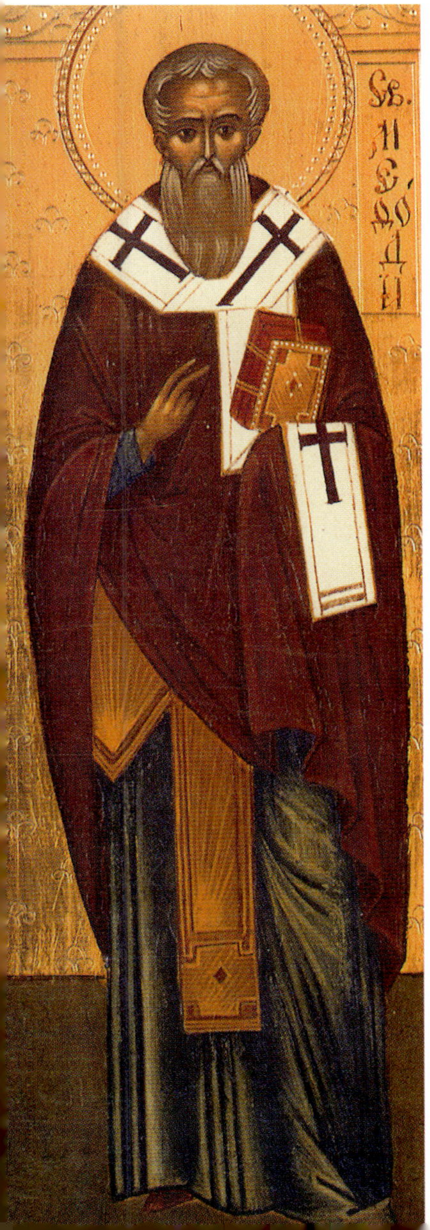

SS. Cyril and Methodius.
A modern portable icon in a private collection. Cyril is depicted as a monk and Methodius as a bishop.

whither he summoned the Benedictines of Corvey. But this convent was taken away from him by Charles the Bald after the Treaty of Verdun (843), and the Benedictines returned to Corvey. Then, in 844, Vikings sacked Hamburg, and Anskar's work was destroyed.

Louis the Pious intervened once more and entrusted to Anskar the episcopal see of Bremen, which at that time was combined with Hamburg. From Horik, king of Denmark, Anskar won freedom of worship for Catholics, and he built churches in Jutland, in Schleswig, and at Riba. He then went over to Sweden, from which Gausbert had been expelled, and managed to win permission from King Olaf to preach Christianity. Before returning to Hamburg, he turned over to Rambert the continuation of his work.

By the time Anskar died in Bremen in 863, the faith was solidly established in the city of Birka, on the shores of Lake Mälar, in Schleswig, and in Riba.

▷▷ Anskar is patron of Sweden; he was officially proclaimed a patron of Denmark, Germany, and Iceland, by Pius X on June 22, 1914, who thereby confirmed past tradition.

▷▷ Anskar is depicted in **episcopal garb** with an **episcopal cross** and the **church of Birka** in his hand.

Cyril, Monk, and Methodius, Bishop, Patrons of Europe

827–869 and ca. 815–865
Joint memorial: February 14
Lat.: Cyrillus et Methodius; It.: Cirillo e Metodio; Fr.: Cyrille et Méthode; Sp.: Cirilo y Methodio; Ger.: Kyrillus und Methodius; Russ.: Kiril i Metodii.

These brothers, known as "the apostles of the Slavs," were born in Thessalonica and, before becoming monks, were named Constantine and Michael (or Manuel). The younger, Constantine, was born in about 827. Upon the death of his father he was summoned to Constantinople, where he was raised with Emperor Michael, then still very young.

Here Constantine-Cyril applied himself and learned all the arts; he became the patriarch's librarian and later a deacon. Desirous of solitude, he withdrew to a monastery on the Bosphorus and later joined his brother, Michael-Methodius, as a monk in Bithynia. In 861 he was charged with a mission to the Chersonnesus, where he remained for a long time along with his brother;

while there, he discovered the body of Pope St. Clement I, who had been exiled there and whose body had been thrown into the sea. In 863 he was sent to Moravia and to King Rostislav who had asked for missionaries who could speak the Slavic language. Here the two brothers invented an alphabet, the Glagolithic (from Slavic *glagol* = "sound"), from which was derived in turn the Cyrillic alphabet, which took its name from St. Cyril and which they used in translating the Sacred Scriptures and the liturgical books; they also trained disciples.

The brothers then went to Hungary, then Venice, and finally Rome, where they gave Pope Hadrian II the relics of St. Clement. The Pope ordained Methodius a priest. The books in Slavic were placed on the altar of St. Mary Major's and the liturgy was celebrated in Slavic in the churches of St. Peter, St. Petronilla, St. Andrew, and St. Paul.

In December 868, Cyril fell ill; anticipating the end, he donned the monastic habit, took the name of Cyril, and died fifty days later, at the age of only forty-two. He was buried in the basilica of St. Clement in Rome, where he is still venerated.

Cyril had asked Methodius not to return to a monastic life and not to abandon the mission they had shared. Methodius was consecrated a bishop and installed as bishop of Pannonia and Moravia. He died on April 6, 885, and was buried in his cathedral, which popular tradition locates in Velehrad, where devotion to the two brothers is strong. However, we do not know the precise place in which Methodius was buried.

▷▷ The brothers are patrons of Bohemia and Bulgaria. Their traditional role as patrons of Moravia was confirmed by Pius X on May 18, 1914, and by Pius XI on March 25, 1936. Leo XIII extended their cult to the entire Church in his encyclical *Grande munus* (September 30, 1880), which proclaimed them patrons of what was then Yugoslavia. This role was confirmed by Benedict XV on August 8, 1917, and by Paul VI in his apostolic letter *Pacis nuntius* of 1964. John Paul II, in his apostolic letter *Egregiae virtutis* (1980), proclaimed them joint patrons of Europe; the same Pope devoted his encyclical *Slavorum Apostoli* to them.

The brothers are invoked as patrons of professors, teachers, and schoolmasters; because of the Cyrillic alphabet, this is especially true in Bohemia, Slovakia, and Bulgaria.

▷▷ The brothers are almost always depicted **together, bearded** and carrying a **cross**; Cyril holds a **book on which is written** *bonum certamen certavi* ("I have fought the good fight"), which repeats the words of St. Paul and refers to the difficulties encountered and to the work of translation. Methodius wears **episcopal garb**, Cyril the **monastic habit**.

Wenceslas, Duke of Bohemia, Martyr

† 935
Memorial: September 28
Lat.: Wenceslaus; It.: Venceslao; Fr.: Venceslas; Ger.: Wenzeslaus, Wenzel; Czech: Václav; Pol.: Waclaw; Russ.: Viatcheslav.

Wenceslas received his life and his title from his father, Vratislav I. He was raised as a Christian by his grandmother, Ludmilla, wife of Duke Borivoj, and acquired an education noteworthy at that time. Being still a minor at the death of his father, he took power only later on; he was quite different from his younger brother, Boleslav. He introduced order into the rural areas and promoted a flourishing religious life, of which he himself was an example. Thus he took part in religious services, going barefooted as a sign of penance; he fasted often, and wore a haircloth; he also **personally prepared the bread and wine** of the Eucharist, to this end cultivating vines on the slope by the castle. In politics he was prudent and farsighted. He displayed an image of the crucified Christ on his helmet and his tabard. He was responsible for the building of the cathedral of Prague, which was dedicated to St. Vitus, a saint venerated among the Saxons, with whom Wenceslas was connected; he also procured relics of Vitus for some churches.

This spreader of Christianity had among his enemies his own brother Boleslav, who invited him to a banquet during which hired assassins were to kill him; but Wenceslas offered a prophetic toast to St. Michael the Archangel, and the ambush failed. When this attempt was unsuccessful, Boleslav tried another: when Wenceslas, according to his custom, went unescorted to the recitation of Matins, his brother and his accomplices attacked him; Wenceslas managed to fell Boleslas and then returned the latter's sword as a sign of forgiveness, but Boleslav's hired assassins **stabbed** the king to death. According to tradition,

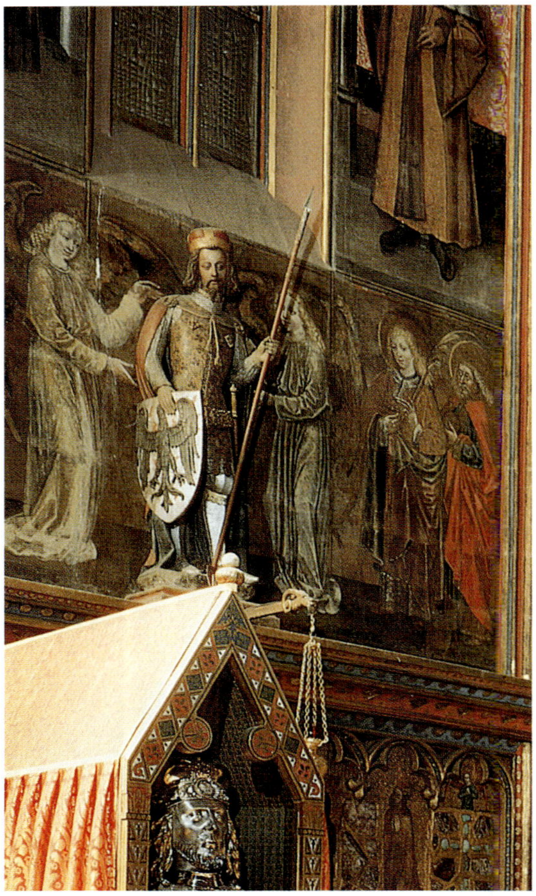

St. Wenceslas of Bohemia.
Renaissance statue in the chapel of St. Wenceslas in the cathedral of St. Guy, Prague.

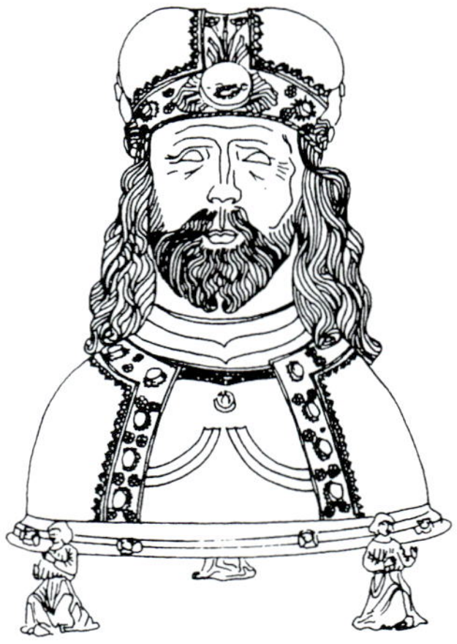

St. Wenceslas.
Sketch of the reliquary bust (1497–1500), in same place.

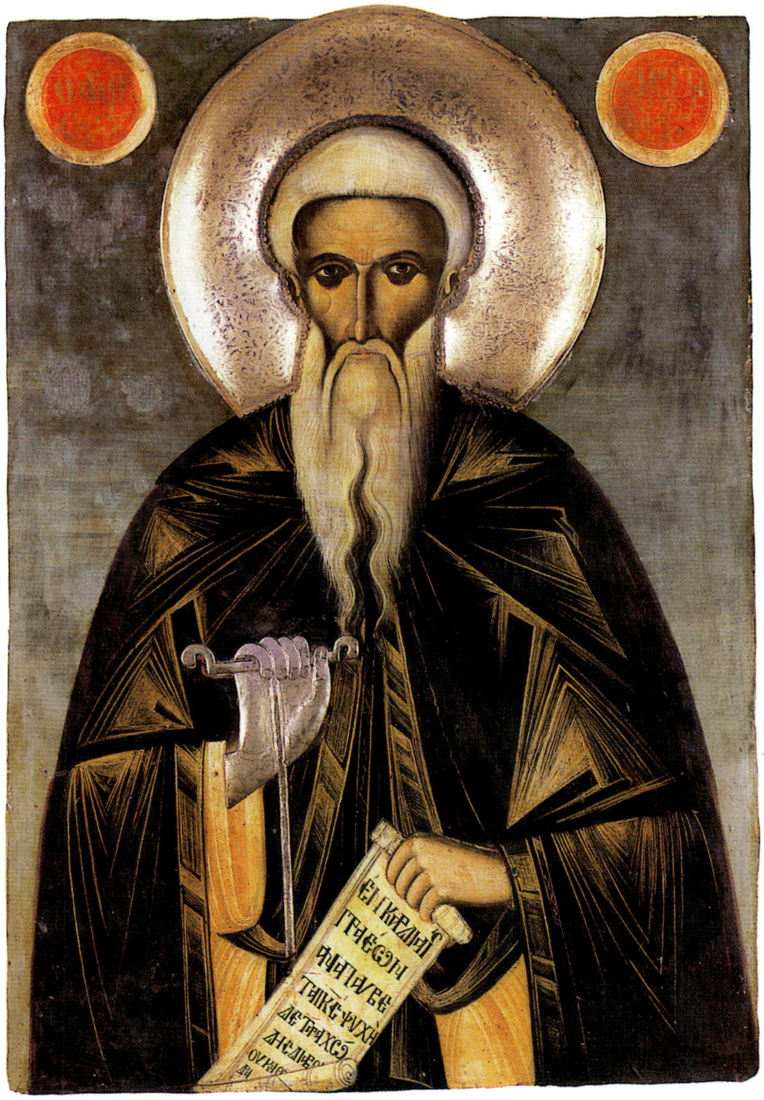

St. John of Rila.
Icon in the monastery of Rila.
John of Rila, a hermit monk, who is shown here in habit and cloak, founded a community that served as a model for all of Bulgaria. The monasteries founded by his followers, who soon became numerous, still exist today and keep alive the memory of this saint.

the blood that spilled on the wooden floor of the outside deambulatory of the church could not be washed away. The king's body was buried in the cathedral of St. Vitus. His reputation for a holy life was the source of a deep-rooted cult.

▷▷ Wenceslas is a patron of Bohemia and Moravia and of prisoners.

▷▷ He is often depicted together with other saints, such as Adalbert, Sigismond, and Ludmilla; he is shown wearing **knight's armor**, with a **ducal hat**, a **spear**, and a **shield displaying the imperial eagle**; his principal attribute is the **dagger** with which he was killed.

Another attribute is a **cluster of grapes and a wine press**, because he himself pressed the grapes for the Mass wine.

John of Rila, Hermit

876/880–946
Memorial: August 18 (August 31 in the Gregorian calendar)
Lat.: Johannes Rylensis; It.: Giovanni di Rila; Fr.: Jean de Rila.

John was born into a peasant family and as a boy worked in the fields. After his parents died, he realized his true calling, sold his possessions and gave the proceeds to the poor, and withdrew, at about the age of twenty, to a nearby monastery. Since he was hardly in a position to enter it, he went by himself to a hut, but bandits drove him from it. He visited several monasteries and finally chose the life of a hermit on Mount Rila, the highest mountain in the Balkans (3,000 meters) and one covered with woods and small lakes.

He made his dwelling in the hollow of a gigantic tree and lived on wild berries and chickpeas, which he offered to visitors. John was called to live as a stylite, and isolated himself atop a hundred-meter high rock, the identity of which has been forgotten. He was not spared the attacks of the devil but resisted them by means of prayer and penance. After shepherds discovered him, he became a center of attention and a teacher. A small community grew up around him, but John was nostalgic for the solitary life and became a deliberate recluse. He died on August 18, 946.

▷▷ John is a patron of Bulgaria, which commemorates him on the anniversary of his death and on the anniversary of the translation of his relics, October 19 (November 1 in the Gregorian calendar).

▷▷ John is depicted as a **hermit** with **habit** and **cloak** and holding a **cross** and an **opened scroll**.

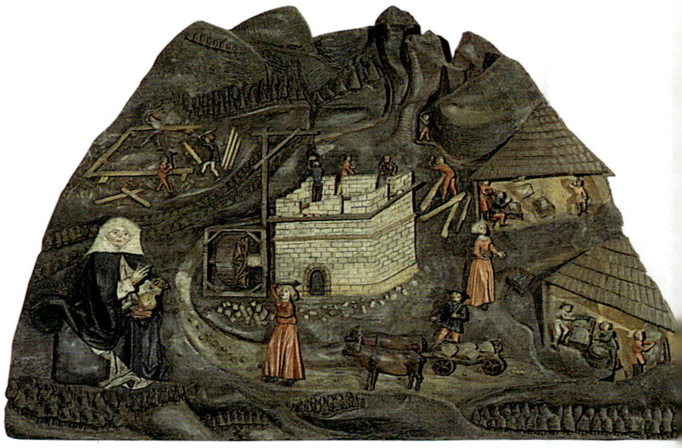

Emma of Gurk, Widow

ca. 980 to 1045
Memorial: June 29
Lat. and Ger.: Hemma.

Emme was the **widow** of the Count of Sann in Lower Styria; when her son was killed in 1036, she inherited a sizable fortune she used to help the poor and for the **founding of two monasteries**, that of the Benedictine nuns of Gurk in Carinthia, and that of the Benedictine monks of Admont in Styria. Her body rests in the crypt of the abbey of Gurk.

▷▷ Emme is a patron of Austria and of Carinthia in particular. Devotion to this saint is rather well established in Austria, where she is invoked against diseases of the eyes and for a safe childbirth.

▷▷ She is often depicted wearing the **veil of a widow or a nun**, holding in her hand a **model of the monasteries she founded** and a **purse of money**, which recalls her almsgiving.

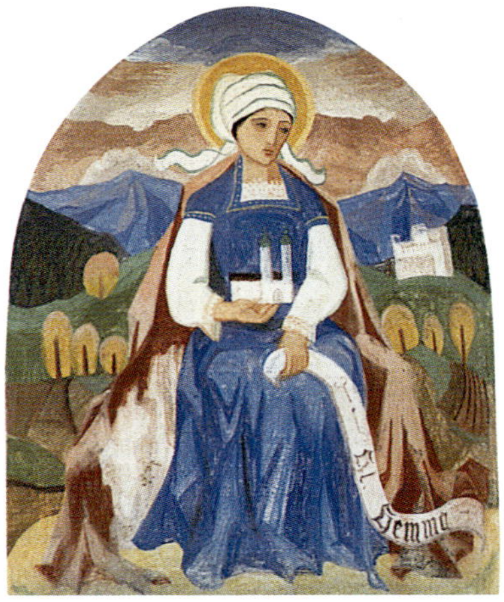

St. Emma of Gurk.
High relief sculpture from 1500, in the abbey of Gurk, Austria.
St. Emma, a widow, is shown supervising the building the abbey of Gurk.

St. Emma of Gurk.
20th-cent. fresco in a votive shrine.
The saint holds in her hands a model of the abbey she founded.

Vladimir of Kiev, Prince of Russia

960 ca.–1015
Memorial: July 15
It.: Vladimiro; Fr.: Vladimir de Kiev; Ger.: Wladimir der Heilige, der Apostelgleiche; Russ.: Vladimir Sviatof, Volodia, Volodimier.

This tenth-century Russian prince has been called the Constantine or Clovis of Russia, because he converted Russia to Christianity. He was probably reared by his grandmother Olga, who had visited Constantinople and been converted there. Vladimir became prince of Kiev in 979. He was still a pagan, but received baptism in connection with his marriage to Anna, a princess of Constantinople; at that time he took the name of Basil; Boris and Gleb were his sons. Influenced again by his wife, he devoted all his efforts to spreading Christianity and organizing the life of the Russian Church. For this reason the Greek Church speaks of him as "equal to the apostles" *(isoapostolo)*. He was in contact with Olaf of Norway and Stephen of Hungary.

▷▷ He is a patron of Russia.

▷▷ He is depicted as a **mature man, seated on a throne with a crown and a cross**.

Boris and Gleb, Princes and Protomartyrs of Russia

† 1015
Memorial: May 2, July 24 (Boris), September 5 (Gleb)
Ger.: Die heiligen Dulder Boris und Gleb; Russ.: Boris i Gleb.

These sons of Vladimir, Grand Duke of Kiev and first Christian Prince of Russia, were baptized Romanus and David respectively.

When Vladimir died on July 15, 1015, he had divided his lands among his twelve sons, but Svyatopolk, who had inherited the Grandy Duchy of Kiev, went against his father's will and had his brothers murdered. Nine days after the death of his father, Boris, Prince of

SS. Boris and Gleb.
Icon from the beginning of the 14th cent., in the Museum of Russian Art, Kiev.

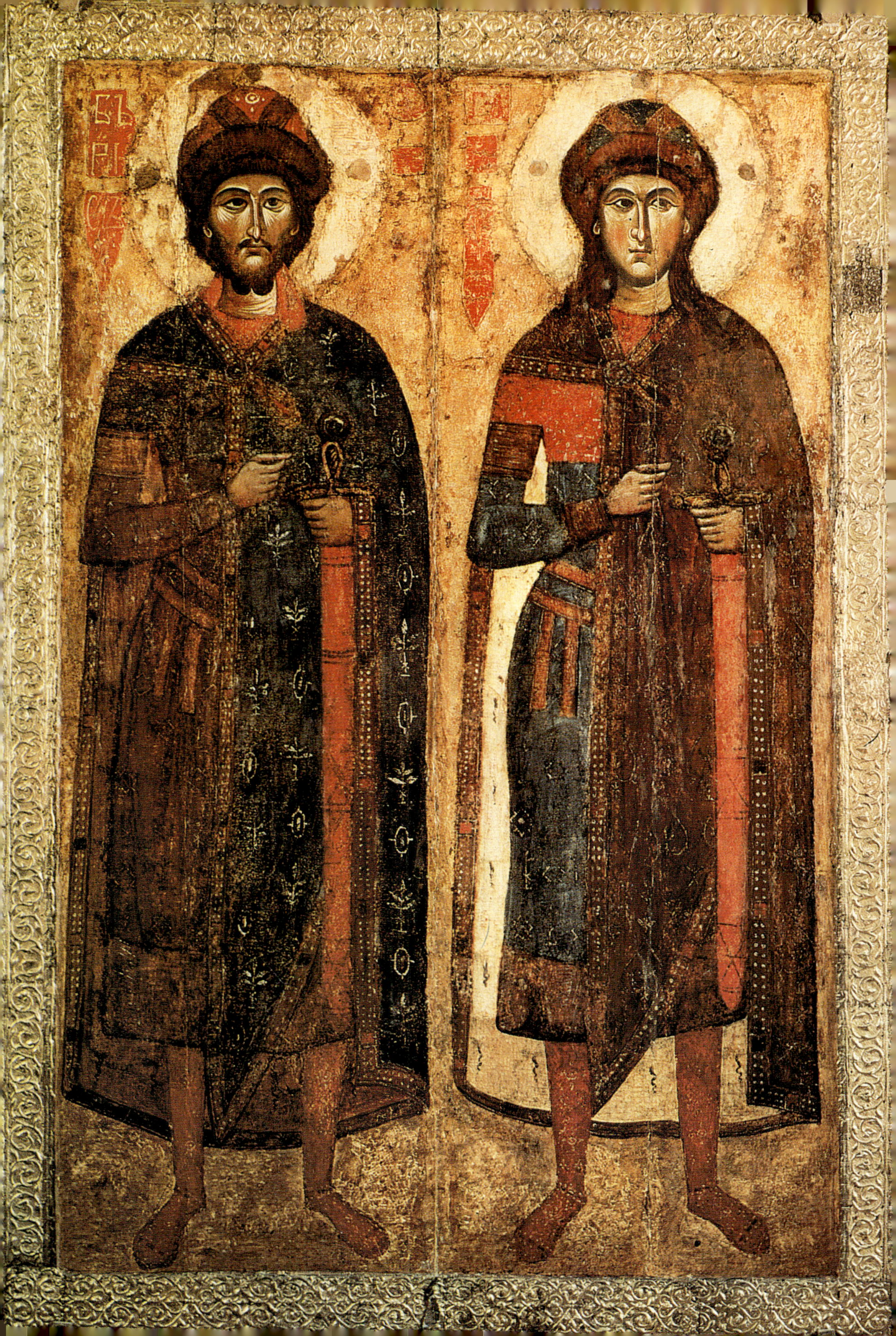

Rostov, was killed as he was returning from a victorious campaign; he refused to let his men defend him against his older brother, whom he looked upon as a father. On September 5, Gleb in turn, as he was sailing up the Dnieper on his way back to Kiev, was slain by the ship's cook, one of his elder brother's hired assassins. In 1019, Yaroslav, Vlamidir's eldest son, defeated Svyatopolk and captured Kiev; he had the bodies of Boris and Gleb interred in the church of St. Basil in Vysgorod and thereby gave rise to their cult. The brothers were venerated together on May 2, the anniversary of a solemn translation of their relics in 1072. They are also venerated separately on July 24 and September 5 respectively.

They are venerated together as protomartyrs, to the point where monasteries and villages in Russia took the name "Borisoglèbsk."

▷▷ The brothers are principal patrons of Russia and secondary patrons of Poland. They are protectors of horses and their riders.

▷▷ The two are depicted together, sometimes on horseback, **Boris being bearded and Gleb unbearded**; they carry **swords** and wear **conical fur hats**; sometimes they carry **Russian crosses with their three crossbars**.

Olaf of Norway, Martyr

995–1030
Memorial: July 29
Lat.: Olavus, rex Norvegiae; It.: Olav; Fr.: Olaf de Norvège; Norw.: Olav Haraldsson; Swed.: Olov.

St. Olaf II, son of Harold, was born in 995 to Harold Harfager. He took part in Viking expeditions to England, where he came to know Christianity; he converted and was baptized at Rouen in 1014.

On returning to his native land in 1015, he contested the throne, which had been taken over by usurpers, and he conquered the country in 1016. Then his brother Harold demanded the throne; according to one tradition, the two decided that the throne would go to whoever reached Norway first. Harold had a very swift ship named *The Serpent,* while Olaf had a heavier and slower ship named *The Ox;* but God favored Olaf, who won the race because he was a Christian while Harold was a pagan.

Once he mounted the throne, Olaf introduced Christian customs and laws into Norway, as well as Anglo-Saxon canon law. He was regarded as the destroyer of paganism.

In order to deal with his enemies, he allied himself with his brother-in-law James and fought also against Canute of Denmark; at that period, Scania, a region in southern Sweden, was under Danish rule. But his enemies got the better of him and in 1028 he left Norway and went to Gardarike on the island of Gotland, where he was welcomed by Yaroslav, another brother-in-law. The party opposed to Olaf's policies won out in Norway and chose Canute of Denmark as their king. After Olaf had tried in vain to reconquer the kingdom in 1030, he was slain on July 29, in the battle of Stiklestad, near Nidaros (today Trondheim).

It is said that on one occasion when Olaf was thirsty, he was given a **jug** of water that had been blessed by the bishop; but when he raised it to his mouth the water changed into beer, and Olaf refused to drink it, because that was a day of fast; he also refused the honey offered to him. They brought him more water, which this time turned into wine, but now Olaf drank it with the consent of the bishop.

▷▷ Olaf is regarded not only as the organizer of the Norwegian Church but also as the founder of the kingdom and its first lawgiver. On the spot of the battle in which Olaf died, a wooden chapel was first built and then, in 1073, a church of stone; finally a cathedral was built there, in which his relics were kept in a silver sarcophagus. The place immediately became the goal of numerous pilgrimages. The miracles that took place at Olaf's tomb fired devotion to him as a martyr, a status approved by Bishop Grimkel in 1031.

In the Middle Ages the cathedral was the most visited place of pilgrimage in Norway, and among its people Olaf replaced the mythical figure of the god Thor. Despite his lack of success, he was venerated as the founder of the kingdom, and his cult spread throughout the North. His feast was celebrated in Trondheim with great solemnity and the presence of

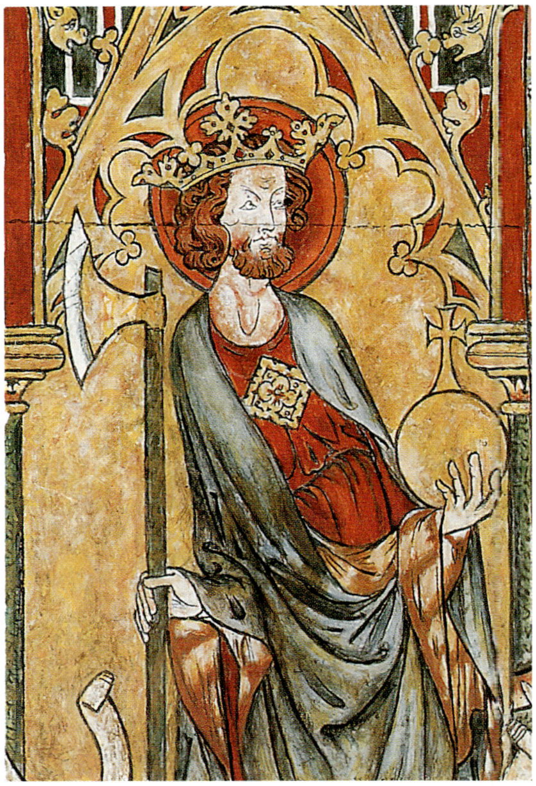

St. Olaf, King of Norway.
Medieval fresco from the Katolske Stift in Trondheim, Norway.

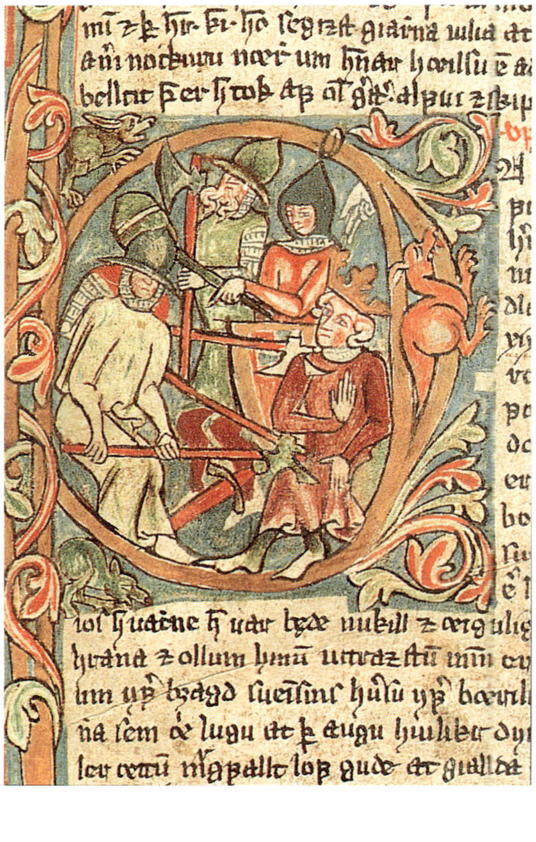

Death of St. Olaf, King of Norway.
Miniature from the Flateyjarbók, written in Iceland ca. 1387. GKS 1005 fol.

throngs of pilgrims. Celebrations on the vigil of July 29 were known as "Olavsvaka"; the memory of Olaf is still alive today, and the Catholic feast brings many pilgrims. July 29 itself is a national holiday. The silver urn containing the saint's relics was carried in procession on his feast day and, when a new king was to be elected, it was taken to Öreting as a sign of the collaboration between the civil and the religious authorities. After the Reformation his sarcophagus was taken to Denmark and melted down.

The Norwegian custom of drinking a toast that strengthened bonds with the gods and with the ancestors was known as *minnesdrickning,* "drink of remembrance." It was practiced on the feasts of the Trinity, the Virgin and the saints, and therefore on that of Olaf.

▷▷ Representations of the saint show a **boat**, which is a reminder of his competition with his brother; he is shown with a **jug** in his hand and, at his feet, a **dragon** or **monster**, which represents his defeated pagan brothers and is a symbol of evil. In some statues, the saint holds an **axe**: this was rubbed, nine times, to any diseased part of a body, and each time the axe returned to the saint's hand as if to renew its wonderworking powers.

▷▷ Olaf's principal attributes are: a **crown** in his hand, along with a **two-edged axe**, and at his feet a **chained dragon**, a symbol of the idolatry which Olaf eradicated.

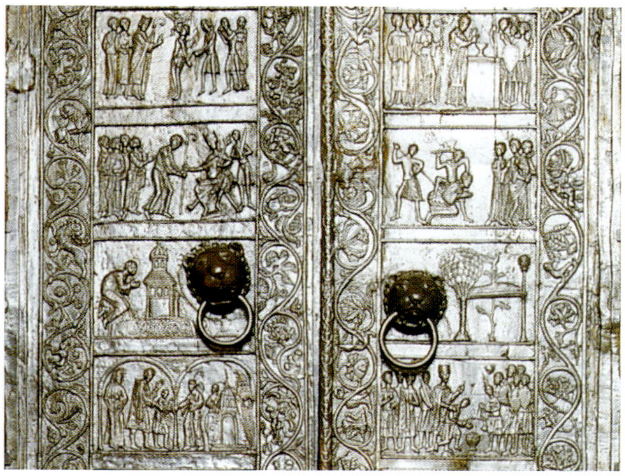

St. Adalbert of Prague, Bestowal of His Staff and His Martyrdom.
Details from the bronze door (ca. 1175) of the cathedral of Gniezno, Poland.
The panels of the door tell of episodes in the saint's life.

Adalbert of Prague, Bishop and Martyr

956–997
Memorial: April 23
Lat.: Adalbertus (Albertus) episcopus Pragensis; It.: Adalberto, Adalbero, Alberto, Berto, Betto, Bettino; Fr.: Adalbert, Albert, Aubert; Ger.: Adalbertus, Adelbert; Albrecht, Bertel; Czech.: Vojtsch; Pol.: Wojciech; Hung.: Béla.

Adalbert, who is regarded as the Apostle of Prussia, was born into the noble Bohemian family of the Slavnik; he was ordained a priest in Prague in 981 and consecrated bishop of that city in 983. He entered the city barefooted and shared his meals with the poor. As a way of bringing the inhabitants of the city to lead a more Christian life, he practiced penances and fasts and slept on the bare ground. He twice abandoned his see and withdrew to a convent in Rome where he prayed for his city, whose way of life was growing increasingly worse. At Rome he was entrusted with the education of the young Stephen of Hungary.

Finally Adalbert devoted himself to the evangelization of regions still pagan. To this end he sailed up the Vistula to Danzig, where many were converted. But the Prussians were hostile to him: he was assaulted at Tenkitten, where Prussian idolaters ran him through with a spit, cut off his head, and scattered his limbs, although according to tradition these were guarded by an eagle until King Boleslav gathered his remains and placed them in Gniezno. Here they remained until the people of Prague stole them in 1639 and took them back to their city, where he exercised a posthumous pastoral activity; the pious theft is celebrated in Prague on August 25.

▷▷ Adalbert is a patron of Poland.

▷▷ He is depicted in **episcopal garb**, and his principal attribute is a **seven-pronged spit**. Another attribute is a **cruet of wine** that fell without breaking when it was discovered in the monastery of St. Alexius in Rome.

Stephen, King of Hungary

975–1038
Memorial: August 16; *dies natalis:* August 15
Lat.: Stephanus rex Hungariae; Gr.: Stephanos, "crowned"; It.: Stefano; Fr.: Étienne, Estèphe, Estève, Estien, Estienne; Stapin, Stéphane, Thévenin, Thévenot; Sp.: Esteban, Estevan; Port.: Estevaõ; Ger.: Stephan, Steffel, Steff; Hung.: István; Russ.: Stenka.

Stephen was born in 975 as son of Duke Geza, and, as an infant, was baptized Stephen in honor of the protomartyr. He was a direct descendant of Prince Árpád Vajk, conqueror of Pannonia, which is the present-day Hungary.

His father converted to Christianity and called the Benedictines to Pannonhalma in 996, but he also continued pagan rites and customs. Stephen was the real Christianizer of his

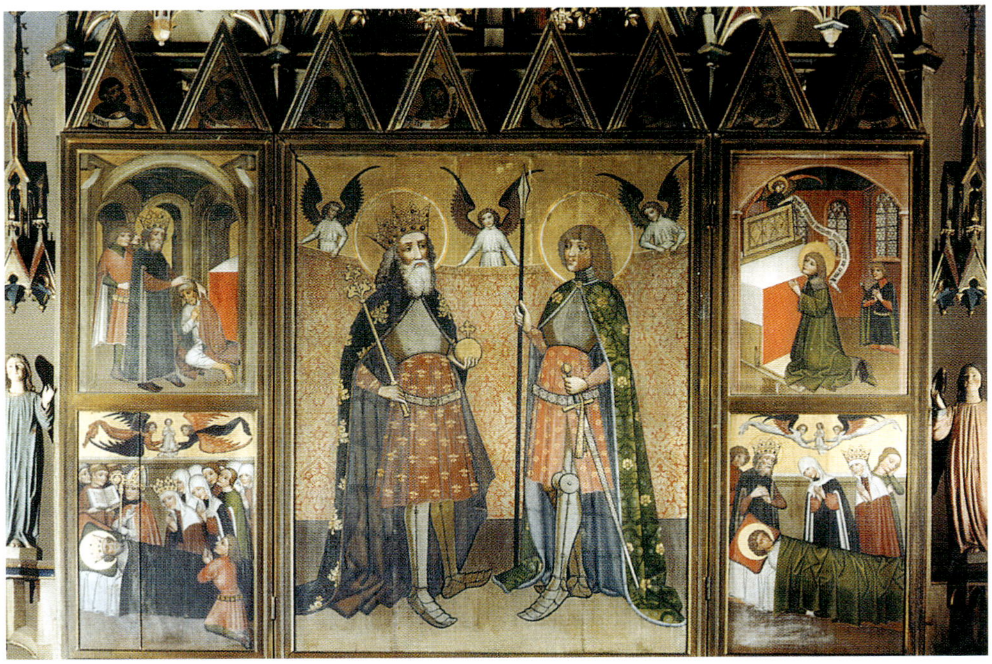

St. Stephen of Hungary and St. Wenceslas.
15th-cent. altar-piece in the church of St. Matthew, Budapest.

people, because he was the first to be fully Christian. He married Giselle of Bavaria in 995; he was anointed on Christmas eve of 1000 and crowned with a crown sent by Pope Sylvester. He organized the religious and political life of the realm, dividing it into ten dioceses, building churches and monasteries, ensuring the position of the clergy, and launching a Christian culture, to which end he invited French, Italian, and German Benedictines and bishops. He died on the feast of the Assumption in 1038 and was buried in the cathedral of Szekesfehérvar. He was the first Christian sovereign to be canonized, when in 1083 Gregory VII ordered the *elevatio corporis* of all who had worked for the conversion of Pannonia. Stephen's work earned him the title *Miles Christi.* His son was St. Emerich.

▷▷ Stephen is the principal patron of Hungary. His feast, which had earlier been assigned to September 2 in order not to coincide with the Assumption, was moved to August 16.

▷▷ Often represented are Stephen's baptism and his dedication of Hungary to the Virgin. In his person he is frequently depicted as a **thoughtful older man, with white hair and a gray beard**; he is wearing a **crown**, holding a **scepter** and a **globe topped by a cross**: these are his principal attributes.

Anselm of Aosta or of Canterbury, Bishop and Doctor of the Church

1034–1109
Memorial: April 21
Lat.: Anselmus Cantuarensis, abbas Beccensis; It.: Anselmo; Ger.: Anselmus von Canterbury.

St. Anselm of Canterbury Gives Matilda of Canossa a Prayer-Book.
From the *Orationes sive Meditationes* in the Bodleian Library, fol. 18v, initial S.

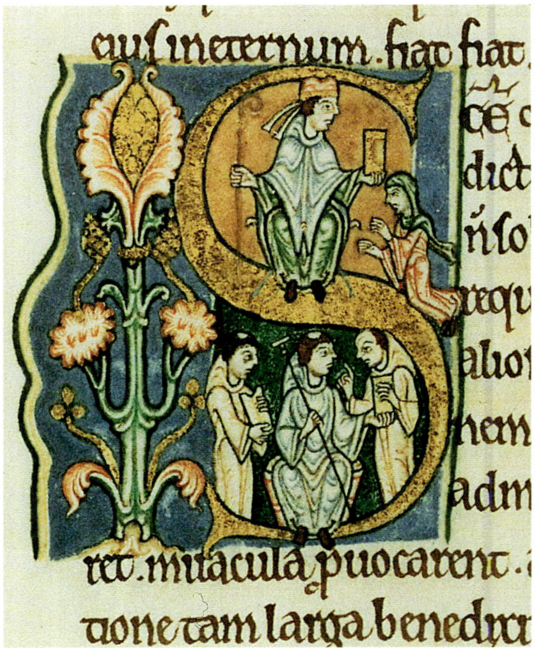

Anselm, a Benedictine monk and a Lombard by birth, was born in Aosta in 1034. He made his religious profession in 1060 at the abbey of Bec in Normandy, to which he had been drawn by the reputation of Lanfranc, whom he succeeded first as abbot of Bec, then as archbishop of Canterbury and primate of England.

He became involved in lengthy and bitter controversies with the English kings, against whose interferences he had to defend the rights of the Church. He was exiled in 1097 and returned to England in 1100, after the death of William Rufus. Anselm wrote many noteworthy theological works; in one of them we find the ontological proof of the existence of

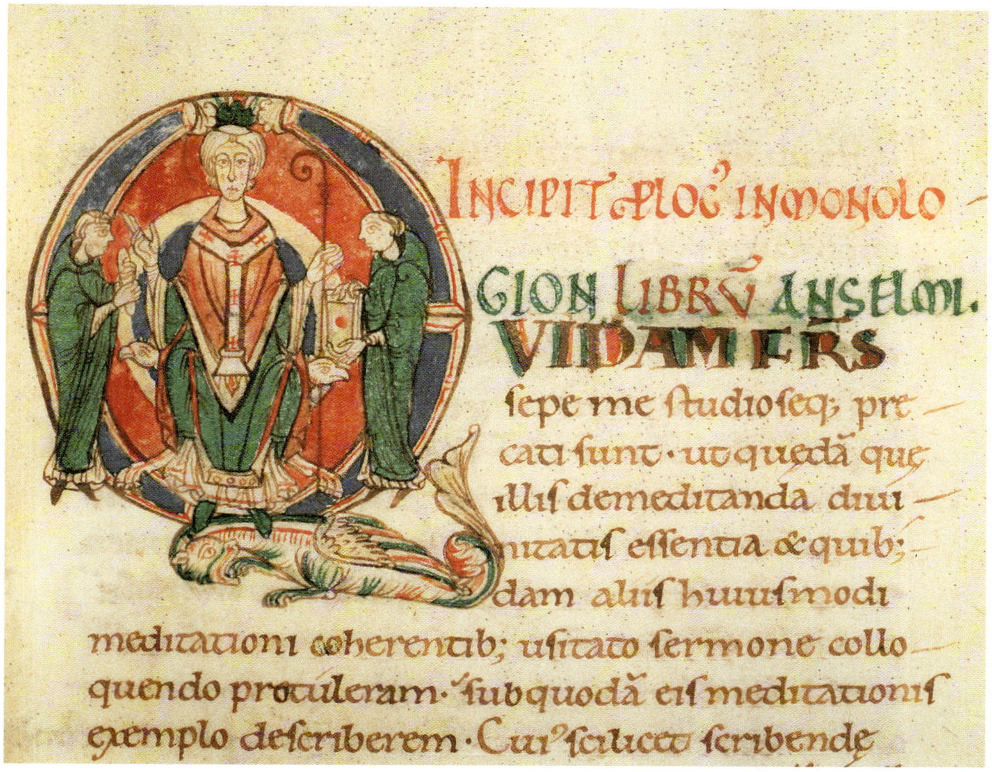

St. Anselm of Canterbury with Two Monks. Miniature from fol. 38v of the Bolton Book of Hours, Ms. Add. 2, in the York Minster Library. The dragon at the saint's feet represents conquered heresy.

God. He also defended belief in the Immaculate Conception of Mary and, for this reason, is numbered among "the Virgin's chaplains."

▷▷ Anselm is depicted as a **mature man, in episcopal garb** and with the customary **episcopal insignia: miter and pastoral staff**. His principal attribute is a **book which he is shown writing**; a secondary attribute is **heretics lying at his feet**.

Canute IV, King of Denmark, Martyr

1040–1086
Memorial: July
Lat.: Canutus martyr in Dania; It.: Canuto; Fr.: Canut; Sp.: Canuto; Ger.: Kanut der Heilige; Dan.: Knud den Heilige.

Ecstasy of St. Canute. Popular print from an etching of Christian Paynoi, 18th cent.

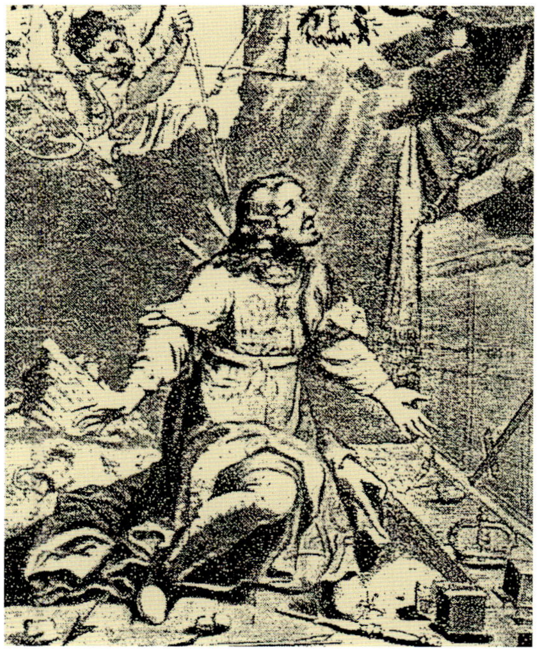

When Sven Estridsson, king of Denmark and Canute's father, died in 1076, the Danish barons preferred Canute's younger brother Harold; Canute had to abandon his estates and take refuge in Sweden. When Harold died in 1080 Canute was at last elected king.

He was a devout and zealous man who practiced penances and fasts. As ruler, he brought about a noteworthy improvement in his country: he fostered the organization of the Church, giving equal power to the bishops and the feudal lords, removing the clergy from the jurisdiction of the civil courts, and, in general, making his own the reforms of Gregory VII. He established the cathedral chapter of Lund (now in Sweden), began building the cathedral of Odense, repressing paganism, and protecting strangers and slaves that had been freed.

In his desire to implement the new order, he overplayed his hand by forcing the people to pay tithes to the Church; to the discontent this caused he added a further reason, the scattering of his fleet due to imprudent action.

The people rebelled, and Canute had to flee. He took refuge at Odense in the church dedicated to the English martyr, St. Albert. His men defended him but he was nevertheless pierced by a spear hurled through a window; shortly after this, his enemies broke into the church and finished him off with arrows on July 10, 1086.

Canute's brother Olaf, who had led the rebellion, saw in the drought that followed a punishment for the murder of Canute; in 1100 another brother, Henry Ejegord, received permission from Pope Paschal II to venerate Canute's relics, an act that amounted to canonization. Canute's relics still rest in the cathedral of Odense.

▷▷ Canute is venerated as a national patron of Denmark and as a patron of southern Sweden.

▷▷ He is depicted in **royal war dress**; **a spear, an arrow**, and a **royal crown** at his feet are his principal attributes.

Casilda of Burgos or of Toledo, Virgin

† 1075 (1087)
Memorial: April 9
Lat.: Casilda; It.: Casilda; Fr.: Casilde de Burgos; Ger.: Casilda von Burgos.

Casilda, who is greatly venerated in Spain and Latin America, was the daughter of the emir of Toledo and was brought up in the Muslim religion. She always felt compassion for Christians, and it is to this sentiment that we owe her iconography, the main element of which is **loaves transformed into roses**. When she was going out to bring bread to Chris-

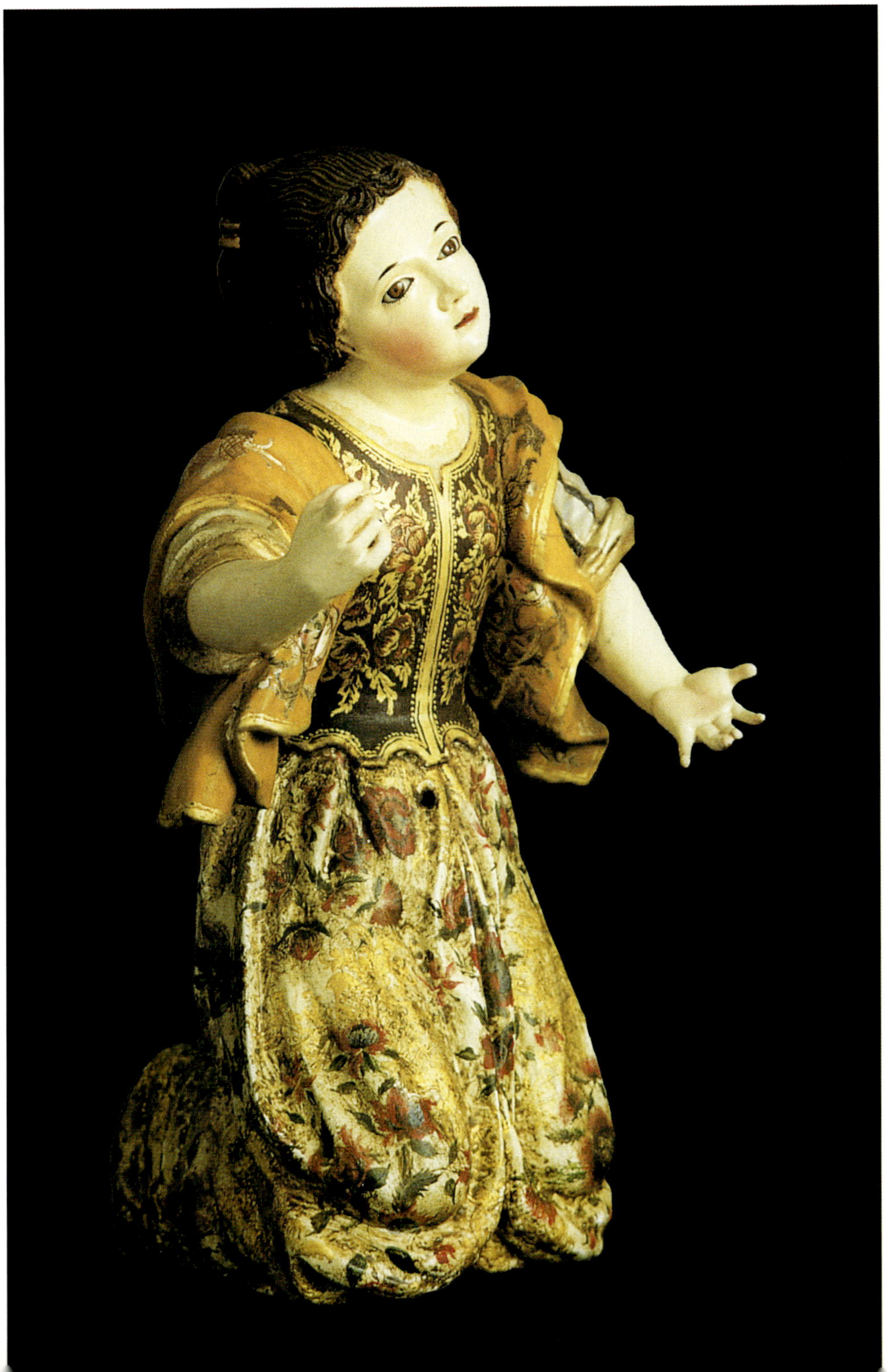

St. Casilda of Burgos.
Baroque popular small statue in the Colección Oswaldo Flores Bermeo, Quito, Ecuador.
The roses, which are the saint's attribute, are here embroidered on her dress.

tian prisoners, her father asked what she was carrying, and she replied "Roses"; he asked to see them, and roses miraculously appeared. This is a trait she has in common with St. Elizabeth of Hungary, St. James of Alcalà, St. Rosalia of Palermo, and others.

When she fell ill, she had no confidence in the Arabian doctors, but went on a pilgrimage to the sanctuary of St. Vincent of Briviesca, in the Diocese of Burgos, a shrine famous for the miracles wrought by its waters. She was healed, became a Christian, and decided to lead an eremitical life near the springs, to which her name was later given. She died in 1087, at perhaps the age of one hundred, and was buried in the sanctuary.

▷▷ Casilda is a patron of Burgos and Toledo. She is invoked against uterine hemorrhages and against conjugal barrenness.

▷▷ Her principal attribute is **roses in the folds of her robe**.

St. Bruno of Cologne with a Benefactor of the Carthusians.
Detail of a diptych by an anonymous Dutch painter, 1515–1535.
The miter and pastoral staff that have been set aside refer to the ecclesiastical dignities which Bruno renounced.

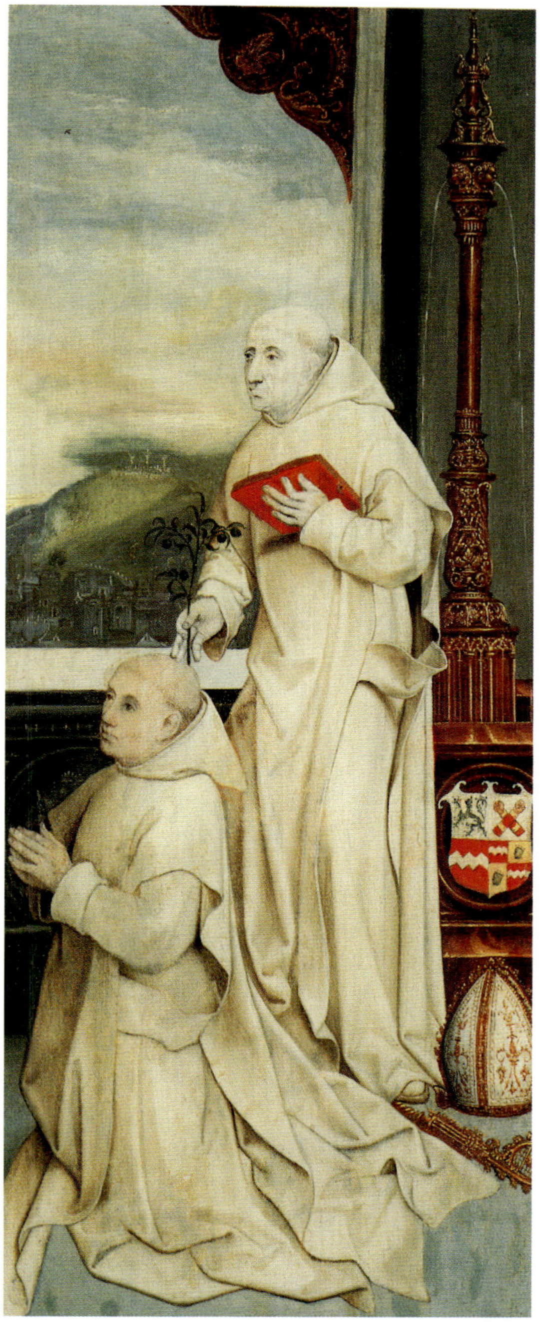

Bruno of Cologne, Monk and Founder of the Carthusians

1035–1101
Memorial: October 6
Lat.: Bruno coloniensis eremita, Carthusianorum institutor; It.: Bruno di Colonia, Brunone di Colonia, certosino; Fr.: Bruno, Brun, Brunon; Ger.: Bruno, Braun von Köln, der Kartäuser.

Bruno, founder of the Carthusians, was born in Cologne; he studied literature in Rheims and philosophy in Tours; on returning to Cologne he devoted himself to the study of theology and was ordained a priest in 1055. He was then called back to Rheims, where he was director of its famous school for twenty years. He was forced to leave Rheims because of conflicts with the new archbishop, whose simony he had condemned. He was able to return in 1080, but by then he had chosen to retire to a private life, due in part, a tradition says, to having seen a deceased friend rise up three times from the bier and announce his own damnation.

He gave away his possessions and, together with his disciples, Peter and Lambert, traveled to Molesme to ask advice of St. Robert, founder of the Cistercian Trappists. Finding Bruno to be inclined to the eremitical life, Robert offered him the hermitage of Séche-Fontaine, a dependency of the abbey. Bruno was not completely satisfied there and in 1084 found a spot more agreeable to him near Grenoble in the Dauphiné Alps, having been taken there by St. Hugo, bishop of the city. As a result of a vision Hugo had of **seven stars** that were leading seven pilgrims to a solitary place, he accompanied Bruno and his six companions to an inaccessible valley known as Chartreuse, which was 24 kilometers northeast of Grenoble and lay at an altitude of 1200 meters.

Here, before winter settled in, Bruno and his companions built their separate huts, one beside another and all forming a square; they also built some other needed structures. This was a model for all the "charterhouses," which derived their name from the Chartreuse. The order underwent an extensive development: 271 charterhouses throughout its history; in 1514 there were 196, containing 3,000 monks and nuns.

Bruno wanted for himself and his followers a wholly contemplative life lived in their cells, joined to such manual work as would serve for the upkeep of each; the cells were joined together by a single cloister. The Carthusians begin their day at 2:45 a.m., and end it at 6:45 p.m.; it consists of a sequence of prayer, meditation, study, penance, abstinence, fasting, and silence. St. Bruno wrote to a friend: "Here, as a recompense for the battles they have fought, God gives his athletes the reward they desire: peace, of which the world knows nothing, and the joy of the Holy Spirit."

Bruno was called to Rome in 1088 by his former student, Otto of Châtillon, who had become Pope Urban II; there Bruno's companions asked and received permission to return to their charterhouse. When Urban II was driven from Rome by antipope Gilbert of Ravenna, Bruno followed the Pope to Calabria, where he refused to be elected archbishop of Reggio. Desirous of the peace of the cloister, he asked permission to leave the papal court, and this was granted, provided that he settle in Italy; he then chose La Torre, another solitary and high-lying place near Squillace in the province of Catanzaro. Here he built a monastery, dedicated to St. Stephen, which soon proved inadequate for the great number of disciples who came. When he felt death approaching, he called his disciples together and made a solemn profession of his faith in the Trinity and the Eucharist. La Torre and St. Stephen's Monastery are now contained within the commune of Serra San Bruno in the province of Catanzaro; St. Bruno's relics are preserved at La Torre.

▷▷ St. Bruno is depicted as a **mature man with an ascetic face and a monastic tonsure**. His principal attributes are the **white habit** of the Carthusians, a **black cloak**, and a **star** on the breast. Other attributes: a **miter** and a **pastoral staff**, but these are lying at his feet to show his rejection of the honors of the episcopate; a **skull** on which he is meditating; a **crucified Christ on a wooden cross** (wooden to show that the cross had been carried into the forests where the Carthusians had their origin); an **olive branch**, which refers to the great expansion of his order, for it echoes Psalm 51:10 (LXX): "I am like a fruitful olive tree in the house of God."

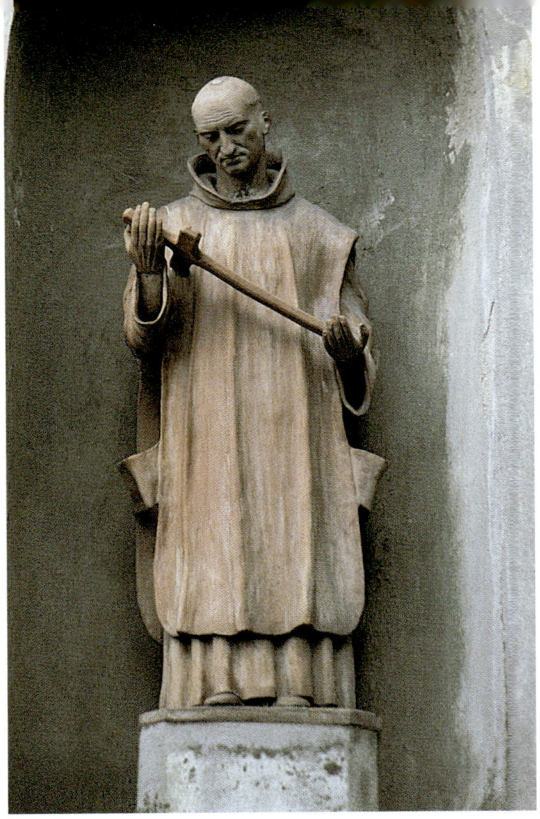

Ladislas, King of Hungary

1041–1095
Memorial: June 27
Lat.: Ladislaus rex Hungariae; It.: Ladislao d'Ungheria; Fr.: Ladislas de Hongrie, Lancelot, Lalo; Ger.: Ladislaus von Ungarn; Pol.: Wladyslaw; Hung.: Laszló.

Ladislas was king of Hungary, Poland, and Croatia. After reaching the throne in 1077 (not without opposition), he married the daughter of Rudolf of Sweden. He worked for the canonization of his predecessors, King Stephen and his son Emerich. During his reign in Hungary he set Christianity on a firm footing and extended it to Croatia; by means of his laws he supported the salutary changes introduced by the Gregorian Reform. Ladislas was a benefactor of the Benedictine abbey of St. Egidius in Hungary; while in Croatia he established the diocese of Zagreb. Stories are told of his being levitated during prayer. Another has to do with **gentian**, "the herb of St. Ladislas": as a plague was spreading, the king won by his prayers this favor, that the disease would be cured by whatever herb would be hit by an arrow the king would shoot into the air. The arrow landed on gentian.

During a siege, in order to save men and animals from thirst, the king prayed and then his horse struck the earth with its hoof and a spring gushed up. On another occasion, when his army was unable to shake off its pursuers, the king prayed and this time, when the horse struck the ground with its hoof, a gorge opened up in a mountain, enabling the army to escape its enemies. After his death, the horses drawing the cart with his corpse turned, by divine inspiration, toward Nagyvarad (now Oradean in Romania). Ladislas was canonized in 1192. After his death, he appeared at the head of his army, as St. James had done.

▷▷ Ladislas is a patron of Hungary and is invoked against plagues.

▷▷ He is depicted as a **mature, bearded man**. His principal attributes are a **royal crown** and a **long sword**; or else he is shown **on his knees before a deer**. Other attributes are **two angels** and a **banner**.

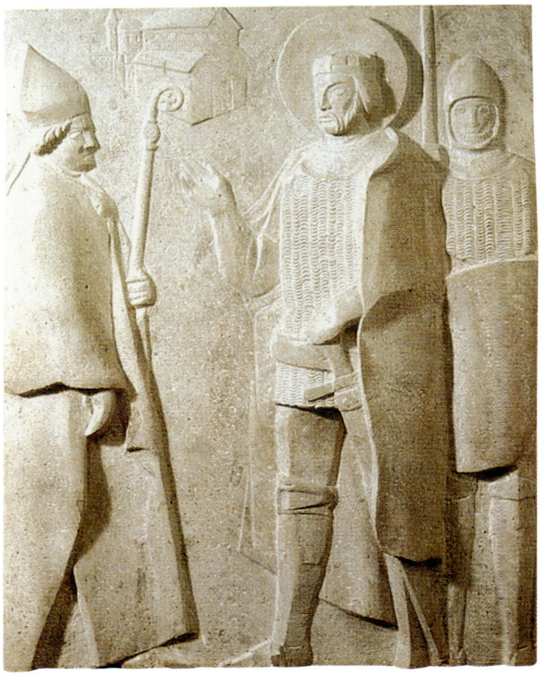

Margaret of Hungary or of Scotland

1046–1099
Memorial: November 16
Lat.: Margarita de Hungaria; It.: Margherita; Fr.: Marguerite.

This daughter of an exiled heir to the English throne was born in Hungary. After returning with her father to England, they were forced to take refuge in Scotland, where in 1070 she married the Scottish king, Malcolm III, and had eight children by him. Her life was spent in Edinburgh and Dumferline and was marked by penance and fasting; a cave in Dumferline, to which she withdrew for the sake of an eremitical life, is still a goal of pilgrimage. The pilgrimage of the Scots, whose patron she is, takes place on a Sunday in June that is decided upon each year. Margaret devoted herself to restoring the Scottish Church along the lines of the Cluniac Reform; in this she was supported by her children, whom she had raised in a Christian manner.

▷▷ Margaret is depicted in **royal dress**, with **crown and scepter**; and also in **a quasi-monastic habit**, and with a **cross in her hand**.

St. Bruno.
Statue in the porch of the sanctuary at Fatima, beginning of the 20th cent.

St. Ladislas.
Bas-relief sculpture by A. Kiss Nagy, 20th cent., in the Hungarian Chapel of the Vatican, Rome.

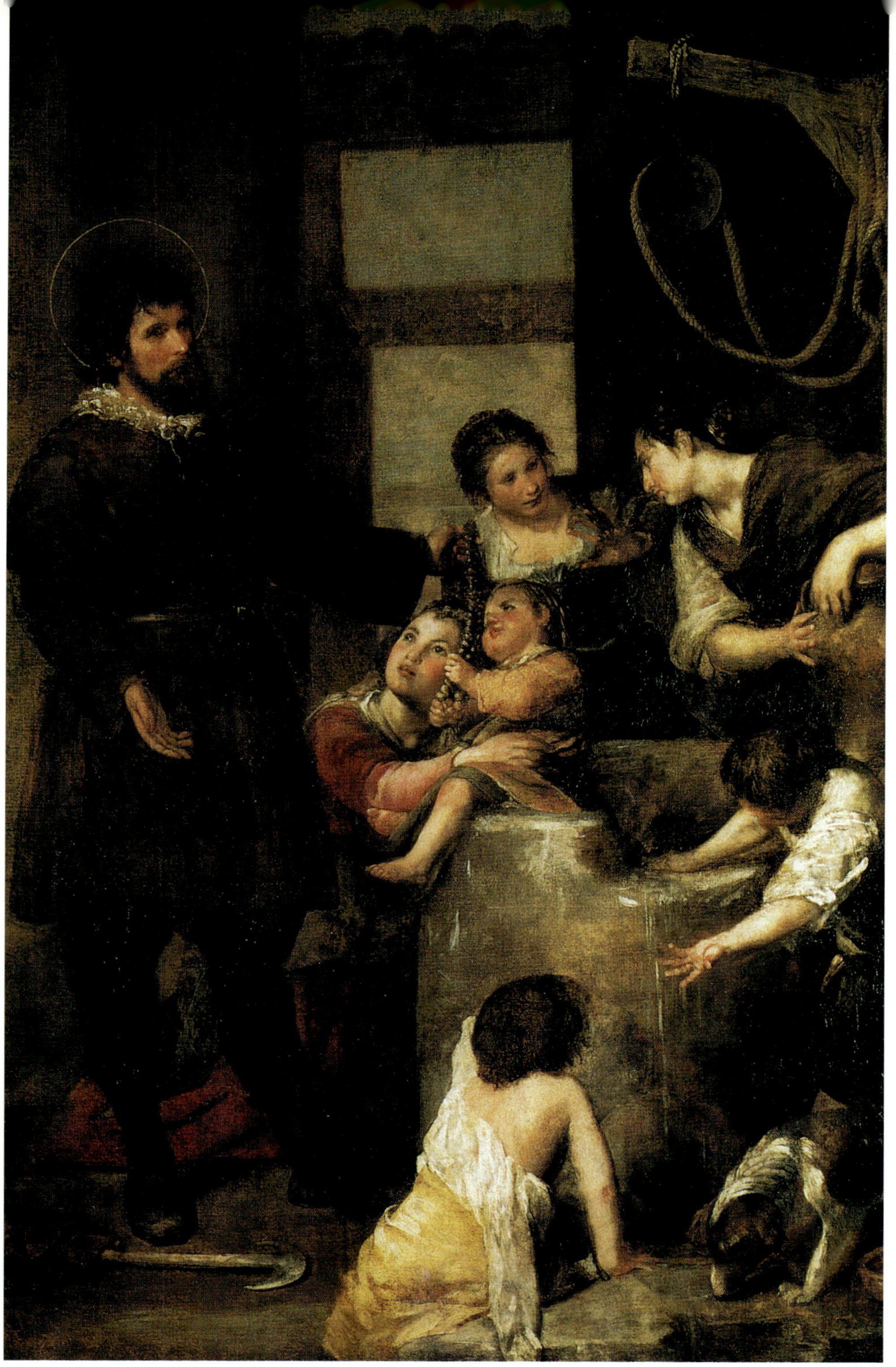

St. Isidore the Farmer and the Miracle of the Well. By Alonso Cano (1601–1667), in the Prado, Madrid. The image depicts the miraculous rescue of a child who fell into a well and is shown here with its mother and two other babies. At the saint's feet is a reaping hook that points to his work in the fields.

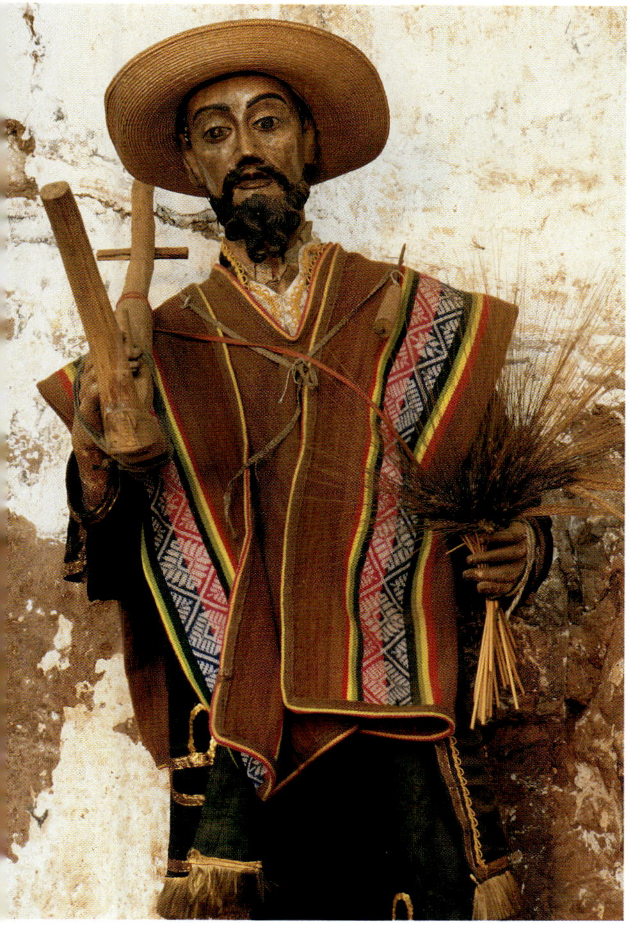

Statue of St. Isidore. In this statue, which is in the church of Chinchero, Peru, the saint is clad in traditional peasant garments.

Isidore of Madrid, Farmer

1070–1130
Memorial: May 15
Lat.: Isidorus Agricola Matritensis; It.: Isidoro di Madrid; Fr.: Isidore le Laboureur de Madrid; Sp.: Isidro el Labrador; Ger.: Isidor der Bauermann, der Landmann, der Pflüger.

Isidore was born in Madrid and after being orphaned became a laborer on an estate, where envious fellow workers accused him of neglecting his work. When Madrid was taken by the Arabs, Isidore took refuge in Torrelaguna, where he married Maria, a devout young woman. He worked as a tenant farmer for a landowner who wanted to give Isidore a greater return than he did others, but Isidore went so far as to give these others all the grain from his holding; in recompense God multiplied the little that remained for himself. After returning to Madrid, he worked on the estate of John of Vargas; the latter spied on Isidore to see whether he was praying instead of working; he found **the angels ploughing the fields while Isidore prayed**. Isidore is also said to have made **a fountain spring up with his spade**.

▷▷ Isidore is a patron of Madrid, of several French provinces, of Austria, and of Bavaria. In addition, he protects farmers and tenant farmers. He is invoked for the protection of harvests.

▷▷ In images his manner of dressing varies, because he is depicted in the peasant dress proper to the many and varied regions to which his cult had spread. He is shown as an **adult man and in peasant garb**, while **a pair of white oxen are guided by an angel**. Other attributes are a **farm cart**, a **scythe**, a **sheaf of grain**, and a **spade that causes a fountain to spring up**.

Leopold III, Margrave of Austria

1073/75–1136
Memorial: November 15
Lat.: Leopoldus Pius; It.: Leopoldo; Fr.: Léopold d'Autriche; Ger.: Leopold der Heilige, Luitpold.

Leopold was born at Melk and became margrave of Austria during the Babenberg dynasty. He was educated by the holy bishop Altmann of Passau († 1090) and married Agnes, daughter of Henry IV of Germany, who gave him eighteen children. He governed from 1095 to his death and did so zealously and in fear of God, while showing great benevolence to his subjects. He protected churches, monasteries, and abbeys, especially the abbey of Melk. Upriver from Vienna he founded the **abbey of Klosterneuberg**, which at that time became a convent of the Canons Regular of St. Augustine. Behind the founding was this incident: after his marriage to Agnes the two showed themselves on a balcony, where a gust of wind carried away her veil; nine years later, while riding in the woods around Vienna, Leopold and his wife found the veil intact, hanging from a branch of an elder. There they had the monastery built; this was only one of the many they built for various orders. Leopold lived in the monastery for a long time and was buried there after his death in 1136.

▷▷ Leopold was proclaimed a patron of Austria by Pius X on December 17, 1913.

▷▷ He is depicted **in royal robes**, **as either a young man or an old one**, **with cloak and crown**, often with his children. His principal attribute is a **model of the abbey** he founded. Another attribute is **two baskets** that show him as a father to the poor.

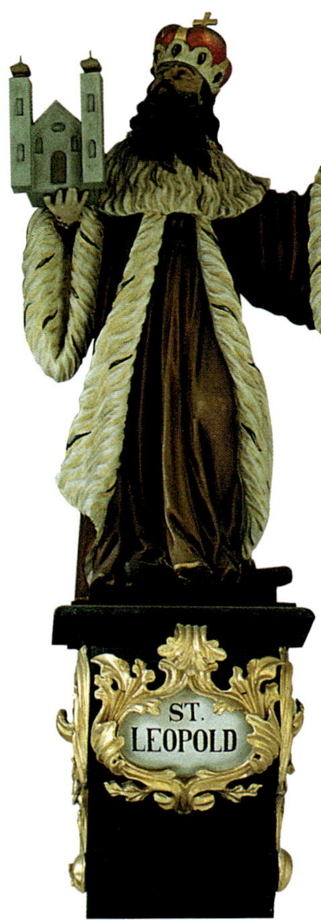

St. Leopold III.
17th-cent. statue in the abbey of Gurk, Austria. The saint is shown with a model of the abbey he founded.

Magnus, Martyr

1075–1116
Memorial: April 16
Lat.: Magnus martyr.

This great-grandson of Earl Sigur, first Christian governor of the earldom of Orkney (the Orkney Islands of Scotland), lived his youth amid the wars and plundering that were part of "political" life in that age; but he became disgusted with all this and was converted. When Magnus Barefoot, the king of Norway, attacked his family in order to conquer the Orkneys, Magnus refused to fight and sat on the bridge of a ship singing the psalms while the battle raged around him; yet he suffered no wound. This behavior did not please his family and earned him exile at the court of Edgar the Peaceful, a Scottish king. When the earldom of Orkney was restored to Magnus ten years later, he governed it in peace by sharing it with a cousin, until the cousin claimed it all and attacked him. Magnus refused battle, spent the night in prayer, received Communion, and went to meet the enemy but did not allow his men to fight. One of his cousin's servants killed him with an **axe**.

▷▷ Many miracles took place at his tomb in Christ Church in Birav, which was at that time the cathedral of the realm. In 1135 his body was transferred to beneath the main altar. He was one of the first northerners to be canonized. His relics were spread abroad in northern lands, in Iceland and the Faroes, and in various European countries.

▷▷ Magnus is depicted as a **Viking noble**. His principal attributes are the **axe** with which he was slain, and a **fish**, for he is a patron of fishmongers. He is a patron of Norway.

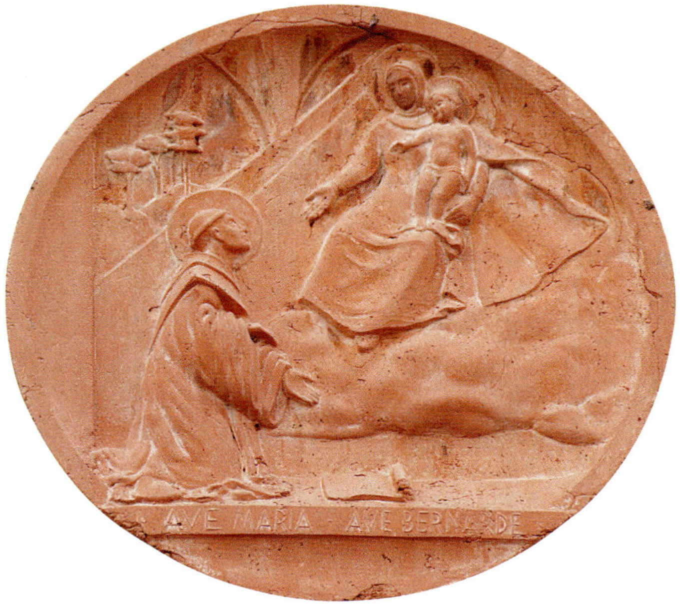

Dialogue between the Virgin and St. Bernard.
Devotional plaque in the Trappist monastery of Viterbo.
The dialogue *"Ave Maria, Ave Bernarde"* brings out the deep devotion of the saint to the Virgin.

Bernard of Clairvaux, Abbot and Doctor of the Church

1090–1153
Memorial: August 20
Lat.: Bernardus Claravallensis, Claraevalis abbas, Doctor mellifluus; It.: Bernardo di Chiaravalle; Fr.: Bernard, Barnard, Bènard, Nénart, Béraud; Sp.: Bernardo de Claraval, Bernat, El Doctor Melifluo; Ger.: Bernhard von Clairvaux, Bernward, Bernt, Benno; Dutch: Bernaert, Barend, Bernardus von Clairvaux; Russ.: Bernard Lervosski.

Bernard was born at Fontaine-les-Dijon in Burgundy. In 1112, along with thirty companions, he entered the monastery of Citeaux, birthplace of the Cistercian Reform, which at that time was governed by St. Stephen Harding, himself the heir of Blessed Alberigo and St. Robert of Molesme, who had begun the reform of the order.

In 1115, Bernard, with twelve fellow monks, founded the monastery of Clairvaux *(Clara Vallis),* of which he became the first abbot and remained in office until his death. Life there was so attractive that it drew many young men; in Bernard's lifetime a good sixty-eight foundations sprang from Clairvaux. Bernard intervened in all questions of ecclesiastical life in his time, and in all of them he was regarded as an authority, so much so that even while urging the monks of Cluny to a stricter observance he became a close friend of Abbot Peter the Venerable. He traveled throughout Europe defending Innocent II as legitimate pontiff, whose right to the papacy was challenged by Anacletus II. He preached the Second Crusade that ended in failure. He supported the Templars, who derived their Rule from him. He fought heresies, especially Catharism.

Endowed with a very charming personality, he was a great teacher for his monks and left behind him many works on theology, asceticism, and mysticism, as well as a collection of sermons, the most popular of which were those on the Virgin. He was in fact profoundly devoted to **Mary** and, due to his influence, all Cistercian churches were dedicated to her. It is not by chance that in the *Divine Comedy* (canto 33 of *Paradise*) it is he who presents Dante to the Virgin in a prayer that begins with the words: "Virgin Mother, daughter of thy Son," which from then on became a prayer used by many.

His teaching is marked by a strong Christocentrism, by devotion to the Incarnate Word and his mysteries (infancy, name, passion), and by emphasis on the theme of Mary as co-redemptrix.

He was directly responsible for the foundation of many abbeys, and it was he who defined Cistercian architecture, which avoids ornaments, decorations, and sculptures (this out of respect for monastic poverty) and relies entirely on the careful harmonization of space and light.

Bernard died on August 20, 1153; in 1174 Alexander II canonized him, while in 1830 Pius VII declared him a Doctor of the Church. His relics, which were preserved at Citeaux, were scattered in 1793; the sole remaining relic is his head, which is venerated at Troyes.

Christ Embraces St. Bernard.
By Francisco Ribalta, 1565–1628, in the Prado, Madrid.
This incident is often found in images of the saint.

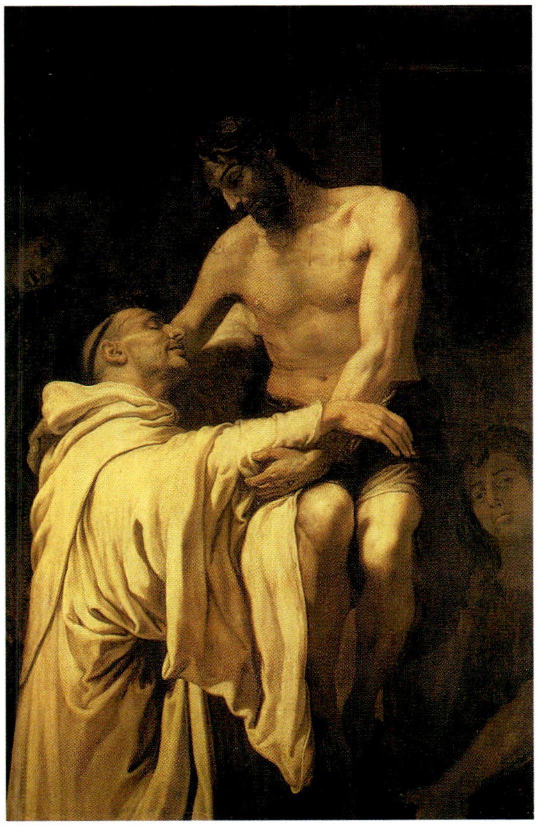

▷▷ The cult of Bernard spread everywhere. He is a patron of Gibraltar, of the part of Burgundy from which he came, and of Liguria. He is a patron of preachers and, because he was called *Doctor mellifluus,* also of beekeepers and workers in wax; because he came from Burgundy, a land of vines, he is patron also of vine dressers. He is invoked against nightmares, demoniacal forces, misfortunes among animals, and bad weather.

▷▷ In images of him, Bernard always wears a **white scapular** (white cloth was the cheapest kind when the monks of Citeaux chose their habit). Tradition has it that Alberic, second abbot of Citeaux († 1108), had a vision of the Virgin, to whom he was very devoted, and who told him that his monks should wear white robes; it was Alberic who introduced devotion to the Virgin among the Cistercians. In representations of Bernard, the Virgin, with or without her Son, is almost never absent; many images carry the words *Ave Maria* and *Ave Bernarde,* suggesting a loving dialogue. Bernard is often shown kneeling at the feet of the Virgin; a **pastoral staff** and a **miter**, insignia of abbots, are **on the ground**, showing his submission to the Mother of God; sometimes he is leaning over a book, which suggests both the Gospel and the *Rule* or other writings of the saint.

One image that is especially popular in Spanish surroundings is known as the *lactatio* ("breast feeding"): Mary, seated with the child in her arms, causes a stream of milk to flow from her breast onto Bernard's lips. This scene, together with the motto *Monstra te esse matrem* ("Show yourself a mother [to all]"), which derives from the hymn *Ave, Maris Stella,* emphasizes the theme of Mary's mediation.

Another image, less widespread but derived from Bernard's writings, especially the *Exordium Magnum Cisterciense,* shows him praying before Jesus crucified, who releases his arms from the cross in order to embrace Bernard.

Bernard is, therefore, recognizable by his **white scapular** and by his principal attribute: his **pastoral staff laid at the feet of the Virgin Mary**.

Other attributes: a **beehive** that suggests honey and the sweetness of Bernard's preaching (this is an attribute he shares with St. Ambrose); a **chained dragon** that reminds the viewer that Bernard vanquished heresy; **three miters**, a reminder that he refused the episcopate three times; **pen** and **book**, which allude to his teaching. Other attributes that are to be seen: the **instruments of the passion of Christ**, on which Bernard meditated; a **cart wheel**, which compelled a devil to protect him; and a **white dog**, which appeared to his mother in a dream while she was pregnant with him.

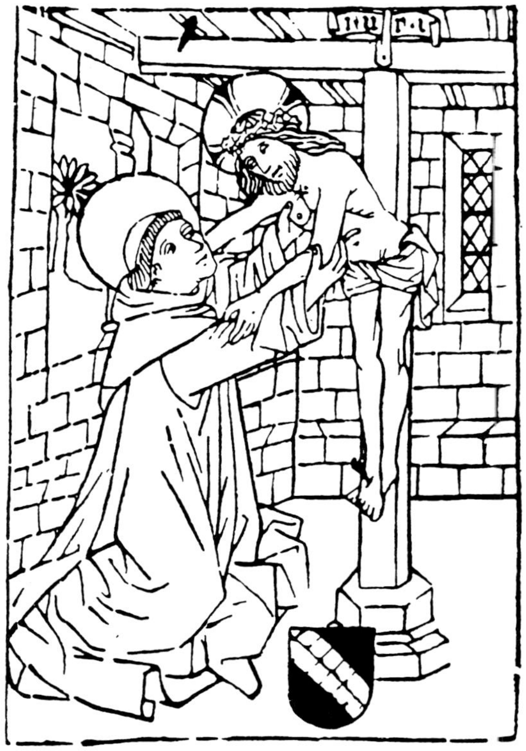

Christ Embraces St. Bernard.
15th-cent. print.

Helen of Skövde, Widow

† 1160
Memorial: July 31
Lat.: Helena vidua; It.: Elena; Fr.: Hélène, Elne, Helaine, Helayne; Sp.: Elena; Ger.: Helena, Lena; Swed.: Elin; Rom.: Ileana; Russ.: Olga.

This widow is regarded as a martyr. Information about her is very limited but significant. She was from a noble and well-to-do family and, after being widowed, remained in that state and spent her life in prayer and penance. Her daughter unfortunately married a violent man; one day this son-in-law fell into a rage against the daughter and then became furious with the servants for defending her; he attacked them, and they in turn became incensed and killed him. Helen was accused of playing at least some part in the killing. In order to avoid the quest for revenge by the relatives of the son-in-law, she went on pilgrimage to the Holy Land. She returned a year later; on July 31, while she was traveling to the consecration of a church in Götene, she was killed in an ambush, about two kilometers distant from Skövde.

A short time later, a blind man being led by a child passed by the spot of the crime; the child saw a rosebush that seemed full of light, and in it he found a **severed finger** belonging to Helen and still holding a ring from the Holy Land. The blind man bent down and touched Helen's blood; when he put his hands to his eyes, he recovered his sight. In that spot a spring gushed up, subsequently known as "Helen's spring." In 1596 a Lutheran archbishop tried to force the spring back into the ground, but no matter how much earth he heaped on it, the water did not stop gushing. The people venerated Helen as a saint, a martyr, and a pilgrim, and many miracles occurred at her tomb. In Denmark, too, she is greatly venerated. On the coast, near Kattegat, which at one time was a village of fishermen, there was another "Helen's spring" that cured the sick, especially those who visited it on the vigil of the feast of St. John, that is, on June 23. Helen was canonized by Pope Alexander IV in 1164.

▷▷ Helen is a patron of Sweden.

▷▷ Her attributes are the **sword** that pierced her, and the **severed finger lying on the Gospel**.

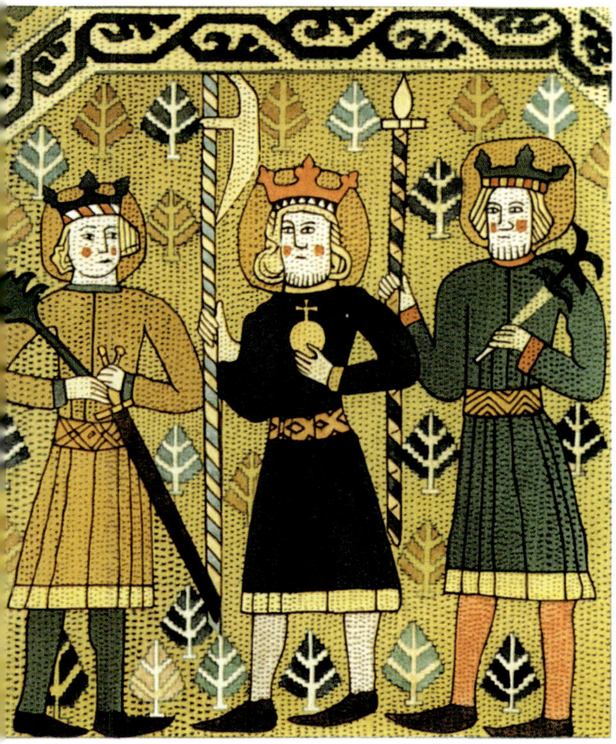

The Scandinavian Royal Saints: Eric of Sweden, Olaf II of Norway, and Canute IV of Denmark. Drawing by Lorenzo Cecchi after a piece of 18th-cent. Swedish embroidery, in the State Historical Museum, Stockholm.

Eric of Sweden, King and Martyr

Reigned 1150–1161
Memorial: May 18 (13)
Lat.: Ericus, a variant of Henricus, Upsalensis; It.: Erico; Ger.: Erich von Upsala; Swed.: Erik.

Information about Eric is scarce: he was king of Sweden and Gothia from 1150 to 1161, ruled his people wisely, and defended the rights of women. Seven years after ascending the throne, he undertook an expedition for the conversion of the pagans of Finland. He defeated them and left a holy bishop, also named Eric, to carry on the mission.

Eric died on May 18, 1161: as he was attending Mass, he was attacked by Danish prince Magnus Henriksson, who challenged his rule, and in the melee was killed by a blow to the throat. He was buried in the cathedral of Uppsala and was immediately venerated as a saint and a martyr. At one time, every king taking possession of the throne had to take his oath on the relics of Eric. When the ancient city was destroyed and rebuilt, the relics were transferred to the new cathedral. Every year, Eric was celebrated in a solemn procession through the fields, in a circuit that linked the old city and the new. This custom ended with the coming of Lutheranism.

▷▷ Eric is a patron of Sweden and Finland and a protector of farmers. He is considered a protector of farmers because in May the ears of grain begin to grow. A popular motto was: "Eric [May 18] gives the ear and Olaf [July 29] gives the bread."

▷▷ Eric is depicted as a **beardless young king**, with the **royal insignia** and the **sword** that killed him.

Henry of Uppsala, Bishop and Martyr

† 1156
Memorial: January 19
Lat.: Henricus episcopus Upsalensis; It.: Enrico.

Henry, an Englishman by birth, appears on the scene as bishop of Uppsala in the middle of the twelfth century. There he consecrated the new cathedral that had been built by Eric, patron of Sweden. When Eric returned home from his expedition to Finland, Henry remained there and, first of all, baptized Kuppis, leader of the defeated pagans. In the district of Kumo, people still point out today the remains of the house in which the missionary bishop supposedly preached. His earthly mission did not last long; in fact, barely a year later, a man on whom he had imposed a penance for murder killed him with an axe. This man, named Lalli, then cut off the bishop's thumb, the finger on which the episcopal ring was worn at that period. In the following spring the finger with the ring and its episcopal seal was discovered, and a blind man who touched it regained his sight.

Henry's thumb became an emblem of the cathedral chapter of Abo (now Turku). Tradition has it that when Henry predicted his death he asked his disciples to have his body drawn by a pair of never-before yoked oxen and to bury it where the animals stopped. The disciples did so, and today in the place known as Nousis there is a church dedicated to St. Henry. When the cathedral at Abo was completed, the saint's relics were transferred there; Tsar Peter I had them taken to Russia and all trace of them was lost.

▷▷ Henry is regarded as the apostle of Finland and is venerated as its patron (he was proclaimed such by John XXIII on February 24, 1961) and, in particular, of the city of

Abo, which celebrates him on January 20 and June 18, whereas his feast is celebrated on January 19 throughout the rest of Scandinavia.

▷▷ He is depicted with the **episcopal insignia and in the act of trampling on an assassin armed with an axe.**

Sabas of Serbia

1174–1275
Memorial: January 14
Serb.: Sava

Sabas was the third son of Serb ruler Stephen Namanja (1159–1196), founder of the dynasty named after him. He had succeeded in shaking off the influence of Bulgaria and Byzantium and in establishing a vast kingdom known as "Greater Serbia," which lasted until the middle of the fourteenth century. The man who was to become the first archbishop of the Serbian Church and patron of Serbia was given the baptismal name of "Rastko" (from Serbian *rastjeti,* = Latin *crescere;* thus "Crescentius"). When he was only fourteen his father intended to entrust the government of a region to him, but the youth had other plans: at the age of sixteen he fled in the company of a monk of Mt. Athos, the Sacred Mountain, and took refuge there unknown to his father. He entered the Russian monastery of St. Pantaleon; his father sent men to look for him but he refused to return and took the monastic habit and the name Sabas in honor of St. Sabas the Great (439–532), founder of monasticism in Palestine.

Sabas completed his education by learning Greek and deepening his knowledge of the Church Fathers, Byzantine literature, and the liturgy. He did so at Vatopedi, a very important monastic center. His parents' enticements proved useless, as they endeavored to induce him to abandon monastic life by sending him a great deal of money. In the end, the father followed the example of the son: he left the kingdom to his son Stephen Protocoronatus and became a monk with the name Simeon; he remained in Serbia, however, and founded the monastery of St. Nicholas. Two years later, at the suggestion of Sabas, Simeon moved to Vatopedi, at the foot of Mt. Athos, together with a large retinue of servants and nobles, many of whom became monks.

Sabas was dispatched to Alexius III Angelus, emperor of the East, and obtained from him three Golden Bulls that allowed him, with his monks, to occupy the monastery of Chilandari, a dependency of Vatopedi but abandoned at this time, and to rebuild it as a house for Serbian monks who wanted to live a monastic life on Mt. Athos. There Sabas, who had received a cenobitical training (that is, in communal monastic life) but had a propensity for an eremitical life (a life of solitude), took his inspiration from the rule of a monastery in Constantinople and wrote a new *Rule* in the Serbian language; this served as the *typicon,* that is, the founder's rule, of the new monastery. In fact, he wrote three rules, one of them on the wall on his cell in Kareia, in the center of the Mt. Athos peninsula, that it might remain there for those who might later occupy the cell.

Simeon, Sabas' father, died around 1200, and Sabas took steps to have him canonized. At that time, Sabas himself was ordained a deacon and then a priest and finally was proclaimed archimandrite, that is, superior, of Mt. Athos by three bishops and the metropolitan of Salonica.

When the Crusaders brought about the fall of Constantinople in 1204, Stephen Protocoronatus, king of Serbia and Sabas' brother, invited Sabas to return to Serbia. Sabas brought with him the relics of his father St. Simeon and settled at Studenica in Serbia, where he became higumen. In Serbia he pushed the construction of Zizha, to which he then transferred the seat of the Serbian archiepiscopate. In 1219, at Nicaea, which had become the capital of the Byzantine Empire, he was consecrated archbishop of Serbia by order of Emperor Theodore I Lascaris; this action established the autonomous Church of Serbia. Having settled in Zizha, Sabas saw to the organization of the diocese and convoked a synod of the Serbian clergy. As did his brother the king, Sabas maintained good relations with Honorius III, the Roman Pontiff, who sent Bishop Methodius in 1220 to bless Serbia and crown the ruler; Sabas himself then crowned his brother and anointed him king in the

St. Sabas of Serbia and St. Simeon Nemanja.
Medieval icon in the National Museum, Belgrade.
Father and son are shown together.

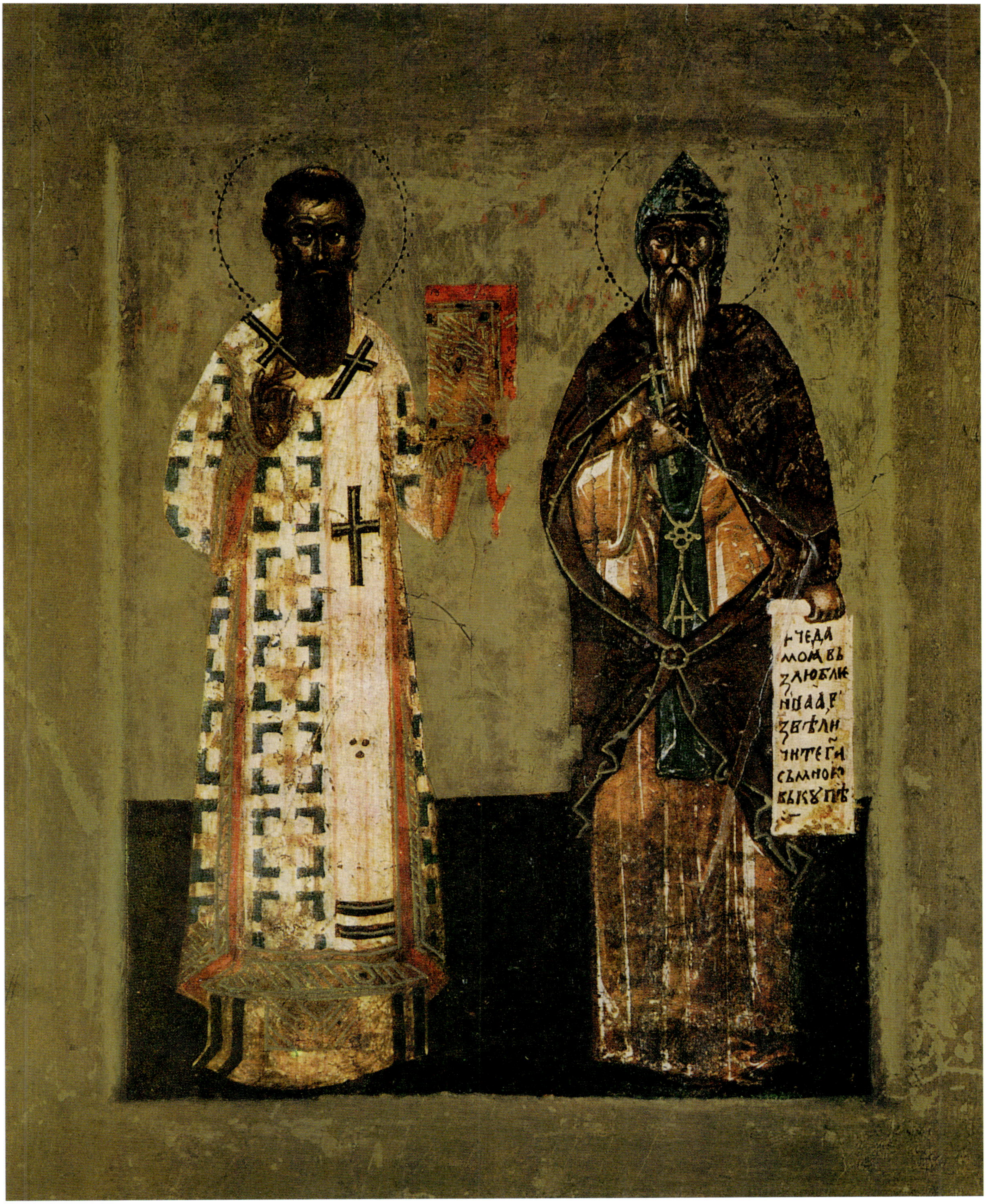
ЧЕДА
МОѦ ВЪ
ЗЛЮБЛЕ
НАА, Р
ЗВѢЛИ
ЧИТЕ ГА
СЪ МНОЮ
ВЪКУПѢ

presence of a synod convoked for the purpose. After 1220 Sabas composed a *nomocanon* or general rule regulating the life of the Serbian Church.

Subsequent events, however, led to Bulgaria's becoming the major power in the Balkans, and the Serbian Church became dependent on the Bulgarian episcopal see of Ochrida, which was in the hands of the Byzantine clergy. In 1233 Sabas renounced his office as head of the Serbian Church and passed it on to his disciple Arsenius I (1234–1264), who became a saint. Sabas then went to the Holy Land; he met the patriarchs of Jerusalem, Alexandria, and Antioch and visited the monks of the Thebaid; he then went on to Constantinople. A result of his lengthy journey was that he obtained the restoration of the Bulgarian patriarchate of Trnovo (1235); this led in turn to the liberation of the archiepiscopal see of Ochrida from the influence of the Byzantine clergy and promoted the independence of the Serbian Church.

In 1234–1235 Sabas went to Mesembria on the Black See and from there to Trnovo, where he was welcomed by his relative, King John II Asen. Here he fell ill, died on January 14, and was buried in the church of the Forty Martyrs; two years later, his remains were solemnly taken back to Serbia, but were burned by the Turks in 1594. He was canonized shortly after his death, and a lively veneration of him has lasted to our own times. In his *Rules (typika)* he gave the norms for monastic life in the Balkans.

▷▷ Sabas is a patron of Serbia.

▷▷ He is shown in **episcopal garb, with the Book of the Gospels or of the Rule**, and quite often **together with his father, St. Simeon, who is always depicted as a monk**.

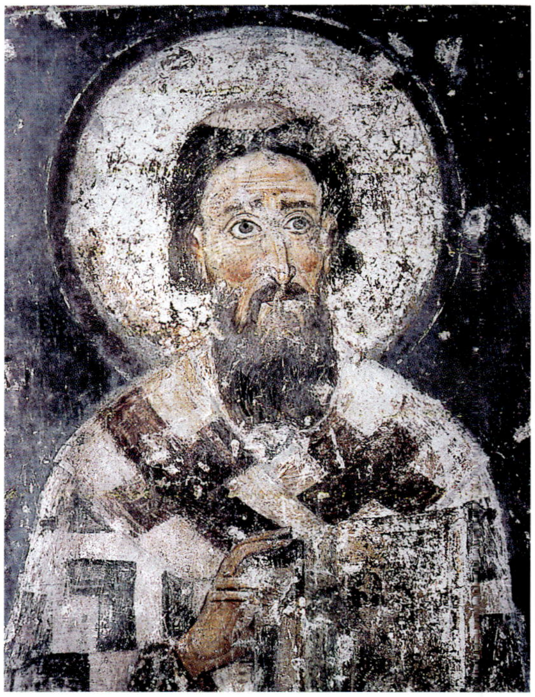

St. Sabas.
Medieval fresco in the monastery of Milesevo in Serbia. The saint is shown in episcopal garb.

Thomas Becket, Bishop and Martyr

1118–1170
Memorial: December 29
Lat.: Thomas Cantauriensis; It.: Tommaso Beckett; Fr.: Thomas le Martyr, Thomas l'Anglais de Cantorbie; Sp.: Tomás Cantauriense, Tomé.

Known as Thomas of Canterbury and also as Thomas the Martyr, Thomas Becket was born in London of Norman parents. He studied at the abbey of Merton, but then the archbishop of Canterbury himself sent him to complete his studies in Paris and Bologna. On his return, he was appointed archdeacon of Canterbury. Meanwhile, King Henry II appointed him chancellor of the realm and made him his adviser and a companion in his adventures. Henry did not fully trust the power of the Holy Spirit and insisted that Thomas be successor of the archbishop of Canterbury. The king was expecting that in Thomas he would have an ally in the Church, even though Thomas told him that he, Thomas, would acknowledge but one master. The Spirit descended on him at his ordination to the priesthood on June 3, 1162, and again at his consecration as bishop on the following day.

Thomas changed from a dissolute man of the world to an austere and zealous pastor, and he did penance for a life of pleasure by means of hair shirt, disciplines, and vigils. His friendship with the king did not prevent him from refusing to yield to Henry, and he did not recognize the Constitutions of Clarendon (1164), which revived illegal interference by the king in the affairs of the Church. Since he was alone in defending his position, he avoided the king's anger by taking refuge for six years in a French Cistercian monastery. After Pope Alexander III had advised him not to intensify his opposition, he returned and received a triumphal reception from the faithful, but he knew that he had returned in order to die in their midst. Though warned of the danger, he refused to flee: on December 29, 1170, wearing his episcopal garments, he faced his assassins at the altar, saying: "I accept death in the name of Jesus and for the Church." The assassins slew him there. The people acclaimed him as a saint, and three years later Alexander III canonized him. Pilgrimages to his tomb began immediately.

The *Canterbury Tales* of Chaucer, one of England's best loved authors, have as their background these pilgrimages to the tomb of the martyred bishop. Fifty years after the martyrdom, on the occasion of the translation of Thomas's relics, Stephen Langton († 1228), his successor in the see of Canterbury, established a kind of spiritual jubilee. In

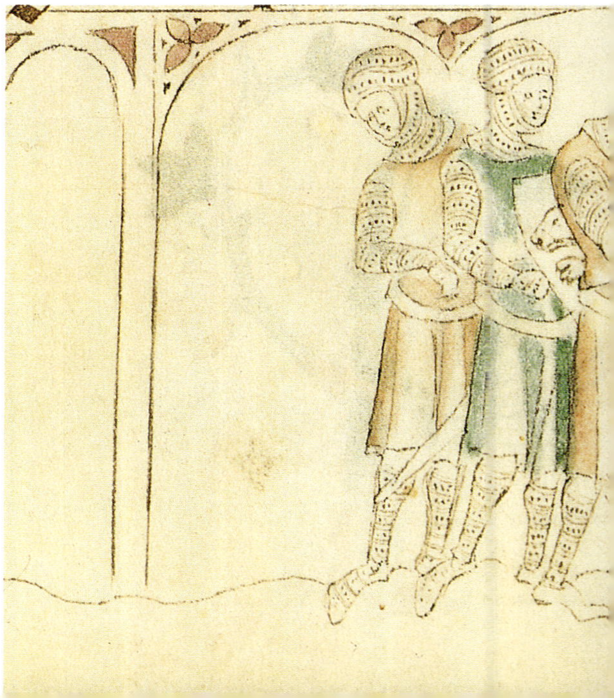

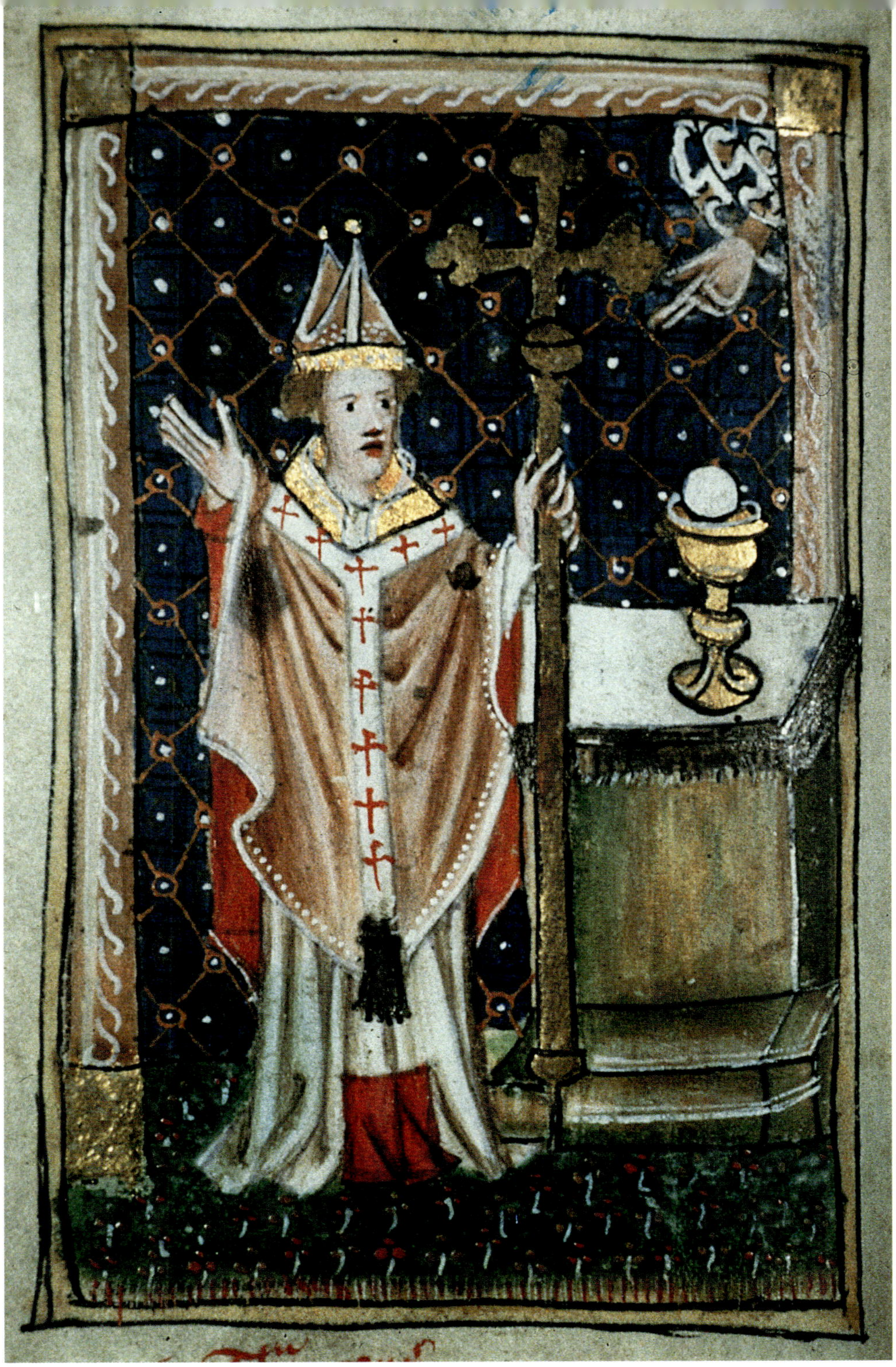

St. Thomas Becket Celebrates Mass.
From the Bolton Book of Hours = Ms. Add. 2, fol. 38v, in the York Minster Library.
The red chasuble alludes to his martyrdom.

Martyrdom of Thomas in the Cathedral.
From Ms. Royal 2. B. vii in the British Library, London.

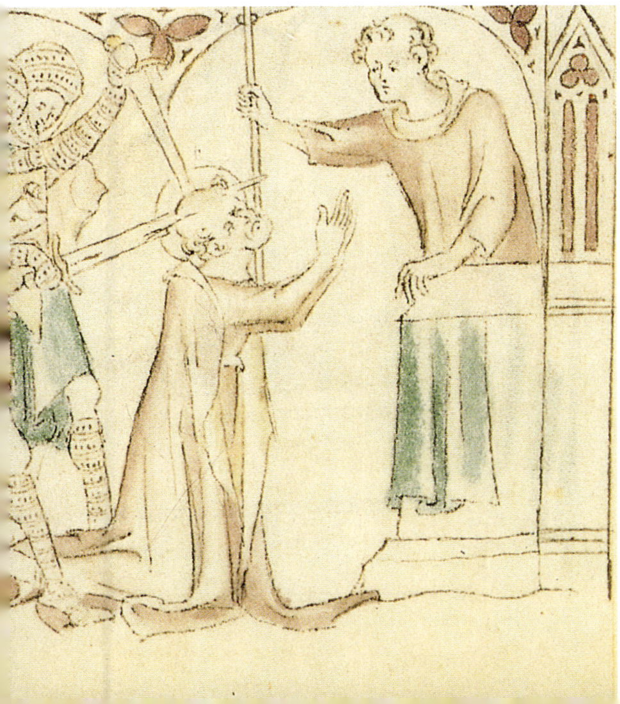

1220, in a sermon on compunction, Langton compared the jubilee indulgence connected with Becket to that of the Crusaders. By order of Henry VIII the tomb of Becket was destroyed and his relics were scattered; this king also ordered images and the very name of Becket to be removed from the liturgical books.

▷▷ Becket is a patron of England and, because of the manner of his death, patron also of butchers; of coopers in Venice and brewers in London; and also of Kent, by reason of the cultivation of hops, widespread throughout that region.

▷▷ Various cycles of images tell of the incidents of his life, showing him not only at the moment of martyrdom but also as an exile and a returnee to his native land; as he distributed goods to the poor and as he received from the Virgin a **red chasuble** that foretold his martyrdom. This chasuble is his principal attribute, together with the **sword** that killed him by **piercing his head**. He is depicted as a **mature man, a bishop with miter, pallium, and pastoral staff**.

Francis of Assisi, Founder of the Friars Minor

1181–1226
Feast: October 4
Lat.: Franciscus Assisiensis; It.: Francesco, Cecco, Ciccio, Poverello di Assisi; Fr.: François d'Assise, Francisque; Sp.: Francisco de Assis; Ger.: Franziskus von Assisi, Franz; Pol.: Franciszek z Assyzu; Russ.: Frantsisk Assizski; Hung.: Ferenc.

Portrait of St. Francis.
13th cent., in the Sacro Speco, Subiaco.

St. Francis is thought of as being an *alter Jesus,* because of the manner in which he followed Christ.

His *Rule,* which was approved by Pope Honorius III in 1223, was essentially this: "to observe the gospel of the Lord Jesus Christ by living in obedience, owning nothing of one's own, and in chastity." Francis understood and welcomed the desire for the renewal of the Church, a desire many people were voicing at that time in movements that often departed from orthodoxy. Francis channeled his desire for renewal into an order practicing strict obedience; he thus became an authentic innovator.

Francis was born in Assisi to Pietro di Bernardone, a cloth merchant, and Giovanna, known as Pica, who was of Provençal origin. In homage to the birth of Jesus, this mother wanted to give birth in a stable, which was improvised on the ground floor of the paternal house. This "Stallette," or "little stable," became a place of worship; a pilgrim asked to see the infant and predicted its holiness. In the father's absence the mother baptized the child "John" in honor of the Baptist; when the father returned, he added the name "Francis" because of his own frequent trips to France.

Francis was a light-hearted young man, although also a skillful merchant like his father. His friends proclaimed him "king of banquets." He took part in the struggles of the city, and as a result spent a year as prisoner in Perugia. He was ill for a long time; his outlook changed, and in his quest of glory he thought of becoming an armed knight, but in a dream he was urged to follow "the master rather than the servant." He returned to Assisi, abandoned his former companions, and spent his time in meditation and pious practices; he even made a pilgrimage to the tomb of St. Peter in Rome. In 1205, in the church of San Damiano, Jesus spoke to him three times from a crucifix: "Francis, go and repair my church, which, as you see, is wholly in ruins." The young man withdrew to the neighborhood of that church and restored it materially; his father was, of course, disappointed. In 1206 Francis publicly stripped himself of his clothes and loudly renounced his inheritance in the presence of Guido II, bishop of Assisi (1204–1228); then he gave himself to God as a penitent.

He lived in solitude and restored the now vanished church of San Pietro alla Spina, as well as the church known as the "Portiuncula" or "Little Portion," as the area was described in the land register of Assisi. There, on February 24, 1208, he heard the passage of the Gospel in which Jesus sends the apostles, and he realized that his vocation was to live in complete poverty and humble abandonment to God and to become an itinerant preacher to the people. He then abandoned the solitary life and the hermit's dress with its leather belt, staff, and sandals. Instead he girded himself with a rope and fashioned for himself a coarse garment in the form of a cross, to which he added a hood of the kind worn by Umbrian peasants. He thus created the garb of the Minors and immediately began to preach as a man of great heart and simple words.

A year later, when Francis and his disciples numbered twelve, Innocent III approved the first **Rule of the Brothers known as Minors**, this last word signifying their humility and their service and submissiveness to all. The tonsure introduced them into the ranks of the clergy. Shortly afterward, Francis was ordained a deacon, but out of humility refused to go on to the priesthood. From that point on, Francis' activity was unwearying and everywhere brought him followers.

In 1216 Francis asked Christ himself for a plenary indulgence, promising paradise to all who on August 2 would visit the little chapel of the Portiuncula, dedicated to the Virgin. Around this chapel later arose the Basilica of St. Mary of the Angels. Later on, Pope Honorius confirmed the indulgence while he was in Perugia.

Together with Clare, Francis founded the Order of the Poor Ladies of San Damiano (later: Poor Clares). He then sought martyrdom in the Holy Land which, after vain efforts, he finally reached in 1219; there, near Damietta, he preached before Sultan Al-Malik al-Kamil. Back home, he organized his order into twelve provinces, which reached as far as

St. Francis.
Detail from *St. Francis and Twenty Scenes from His Life.*
13th cent., in the Cappella Bardi of the church of Santa Croce, Florence.

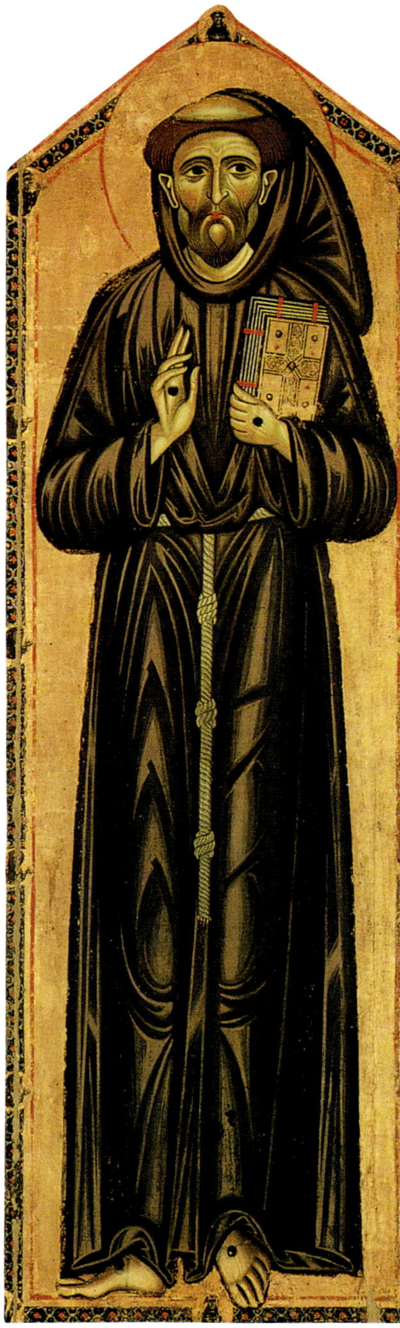

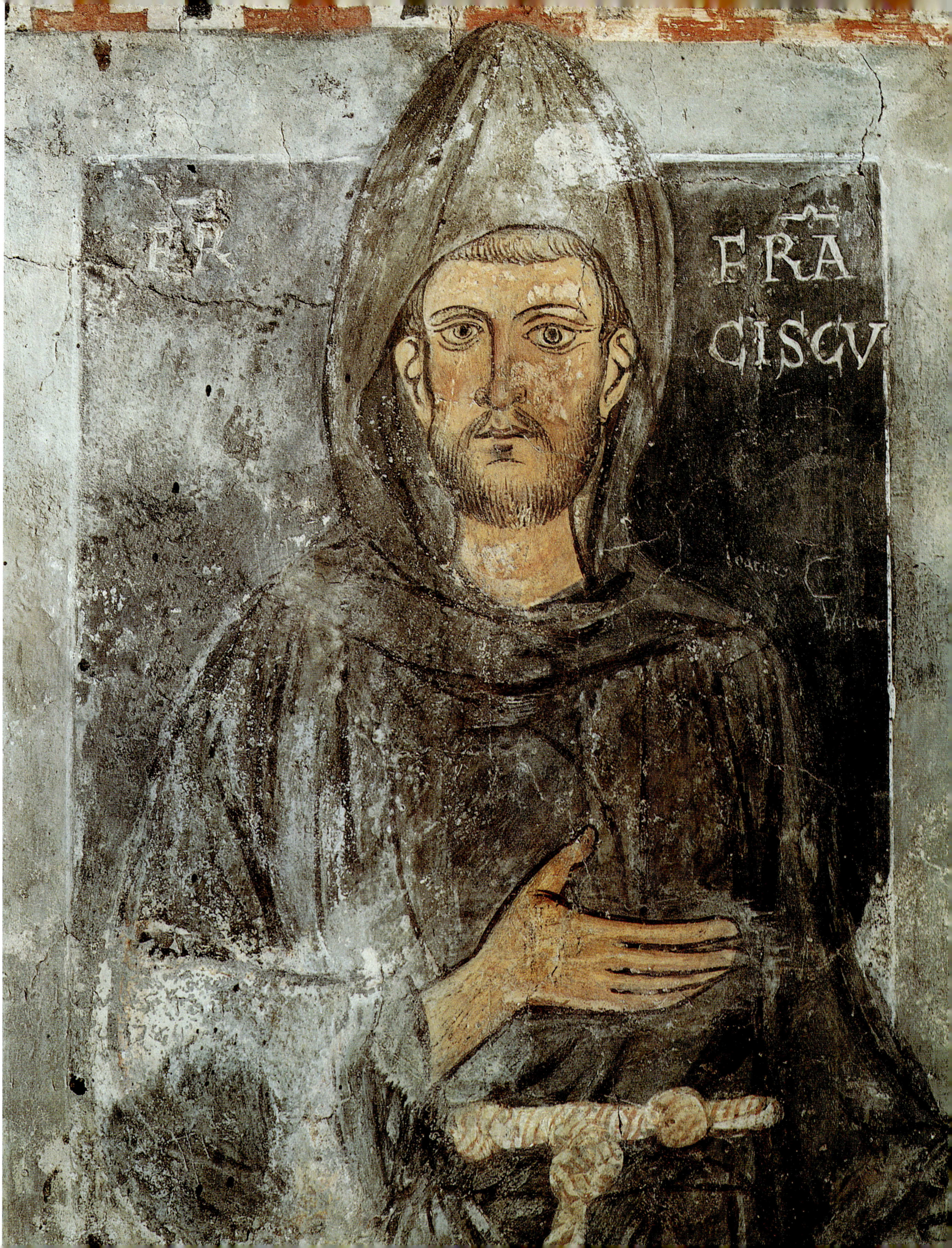
FR
FRA
CISCV

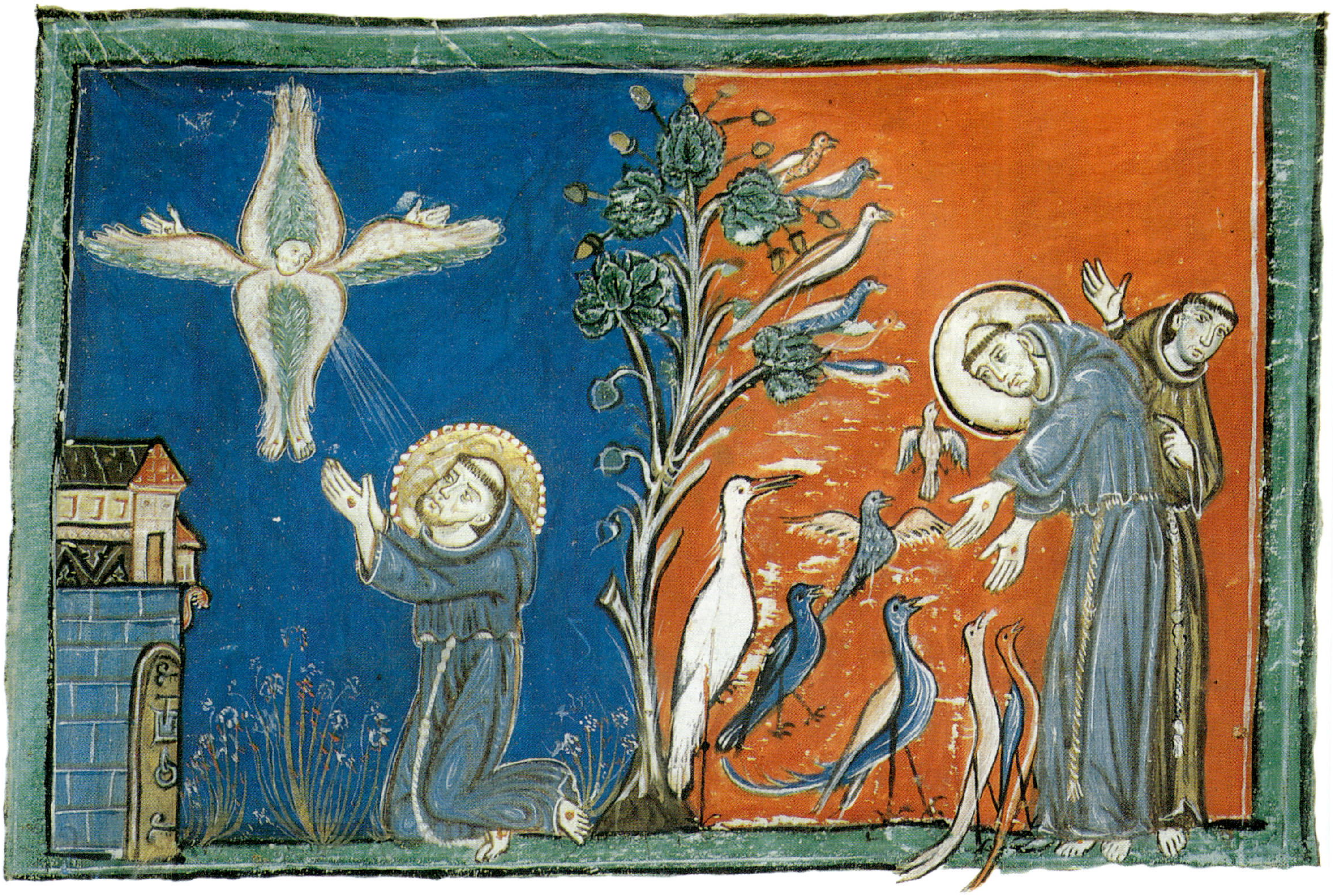

Stigmatization of St. Francis, and His Preaching to the Birds.
From a 14th-cent. Italian Breviary, in the Archivio San Pietro B27, Vatican Library, Rome.

Palestine and Morocco. In this last place, the first Franciscans were martyred in 1220; these were the ones whose bodies St. Anthony saw being brought to Coimbra.

In 1223, as a kind of summary of inherited Nativity representations, Francis established his own well-known commemoration of the birth of Jesus (the crèche), showing himself here again to be both a preserver of the past and an innovator. While he did not have any great esteem of knowledge, the risks of which he understood, he nevertheless approved of the study of Sacred Scripture and authorized the opening of a school of theology in Bologna (1223–1224). The first lecturer there was St. Anthony, whom Francis reverently called "his bishop."

After 1224 Francis lived a secluded life. While he was meditating on Mt. La Verna and preparing by a forty-day fast for the feast of St. Michael the Archangel, the crucified Jesus appeared to him in the form of a winged seraph and gave him the stigmata on the morning of September 14, 1224, the feast of the Exaltation of the Cross. This was the first time such a miracle had occurred in Christianity.

At the beginning of 1225 Francis composed his *Canticle of Brother Sun*. A year later, exhausted by diseases of the liver and spleen and almost blind, he dictated his testament to the brothers and had himself carried to the Portiuncula and laid on the bare earth; he died as the Psalm *Voce mea* (142 LXX) was being sung. It was Saturday, October 3, 1226.

Some episodes from his life have become part of his iconography, such as his preaching to the birds and his subjection of a wolf at Gubbio.

His cult became universal; his love of poverty won him the name "The Poor Man of Assisi."

▷▷ Francis was proclaimed the principal patron of Italy by Pius XII on June 18, 1939. He is a patron of Umbria and of many cities, among them the American city named after him: "San Francisco." As the son of a cloth merchant, he is patron of upholsterers and braidmakers, rug merchants, and weavers. He is invoked against poverty, headache, and plagues.

▷▷ He is depicted wearing a **brown habit** and a **cincture with three knots**, these alluding to the three vows of poverty, chastity, and obedience. His principal attribute, however, is the **stigmata**, often shown emitting rays of light.

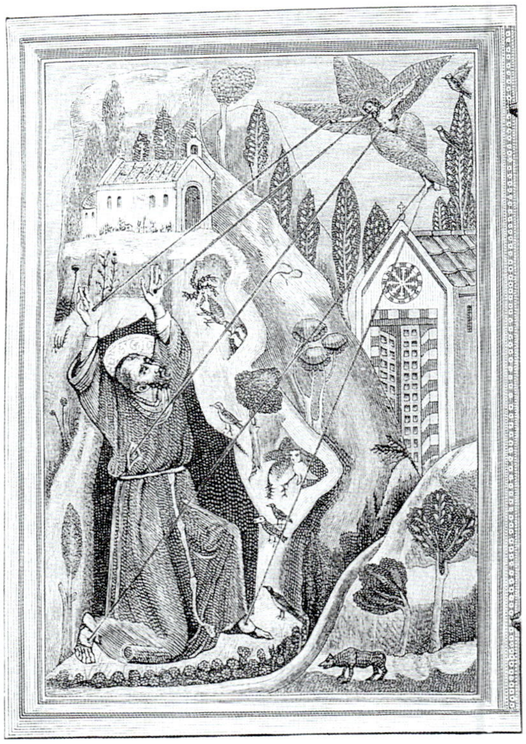

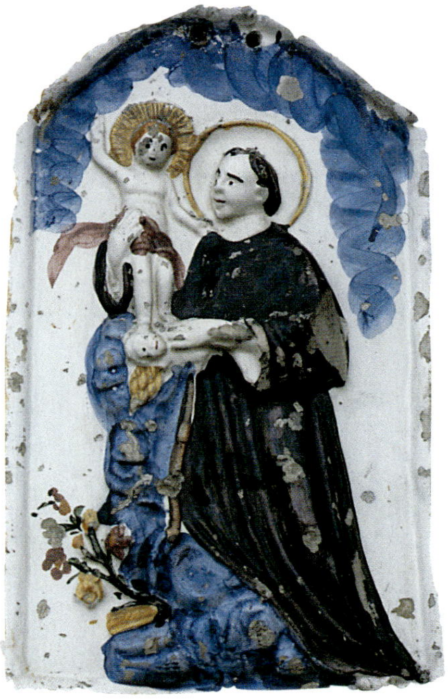

St. Anthony of Padua.
19th-cent. devotional plaque, Lizzano in Belvedere (Bologna).

Stigmatization of St. Francis.
15th-cent. devotional altar; etching after the original in the collection of Abbé Couissinier, in the Museo Francescano, Rome.

▷▷ Other attributes are: a **crucifix with rays** shining from the wounds, the **wolf** he tamed at Gubbio, and the **birds**.

Anthony of Padua, Priest and Doctor of the Church

1195–1231
Memorial: June 13
Lat.: Antonius Lusitanus (Ulysiponensis, Ilixibonensis) sive Patavinus, Paduanus; It.: Antonio da Padova; Fr.: Antoine de Pade, de Pave, Antoine le Portugais; Sp.: Antonio de Padua; Port.: Antonio de Lisboa; Ger.: Antonius von Padua, Kindltoni; Pol.: Antoni Padewski; Russ.: Antoni Padouanski.

It is difficult to find a church in Europe that does not have an image of this saint, often decorated with flowers and candles.

This great wonderworker, who is invoked on every kind of occasion, is claimed by Lisbon where he was born and by Padua where he lived and died. Paduans call him "Sant'Antonio mio bello" ("My noble St. Anthony"); he is indeed a Doctor of the Church and a wonderworker, but to the Paduans he is like an older brother, a family friend who intervenes in very serious cases but also on more ordinary occasions. For example, it is enough to recite *Si quaeris miracula,* and things lost are found. Strange it is, and yet meaningful, that this prayer brings together everything that torments human beings: leprosy, demons, the sea, and trivial distractions. To all of these is opposed a single certainty: *petunt et accipiunt,* "if you ask, you will receive." This is followed by the necessary testimony: *dicunt paduani,* "the people of Padua say so."

The sequence composed by Frate Giuliano da Spira (ca. 1232) for the rhythmic Office in Franciscan convents, takes its title from its first verse:

Si quaeris miracula, mors, error, calamitas, daemon, lepra, fugiunt; aegri surgunt sani.	If you're looking for miracles, look! death, error, calamity, the demon, leprosy, all flee; The sick rise up healed.
Cedunt mare, vincula; membra resque perditas petunt et accipiunt iuvenes et cani.	The sea is calmed, chains break; young and old seek and obtain health of body and things lost.
Pereunt pericula, cessat et necessitas; narrent hi qui sentient dicant paduani.	Dangers vanish, difficulty ceases; let those tell who experience it, let the Paduans speak.

Anthony was born in 1195 and received the name Fernando at baptism. He entered the Order of Augustinian Canons while still a youth, acquired a profound knowledge of Scripture, was ordained a priest, and took up residence in the monastery of Santa Croce in Coimbra. In that city was a group of Franciscans who gathered in the church of St. Anthony Abbot; Anthony became fascinated by their way of life. St. Francis had sent his friars to preach in Morocco; five of them were beheaded, and their bodies were brought to Coimbra. Anthony was moved by this martyrdom; he asked and obtained permission to become a Franciscan; in order to emphasize the radical character of this choice, he changed his name and took that of the holy abbot to whom the little church of the Franciscans was dedicated.

Desiring to be a missionary, he obtained permission to go to Morocco; he fell ill there and stayed for one winter; on the return journey constant winds unexpectedly carried the ship to Italy, where he took part in the chapter of the Franciscans in Assisi. He was sent to a hermitage in the Romagna; there, however, he was obliged to replace a preacher and showed that he was learned, eloquent, and persuasive, with the result that he was given the task of preaching and of teaching theology. From 1225 to 1227 he was in France, speaking against the Catharist heresy; from 1227 to 1230 he was superior of the Franciscans of northern Italy and was tireless in visiting all the convents. His period of teaching in Bologna, 1223–1225, marked the beginning of the Franciscan school of theology.

His residence, however, was in Padua; there he wrote his *Sunday Sermons* and, in the last year of his life, his *Sermons for the Feasts of the Saints*. This was also the period of his work for the poor and for the reconciliation of the social classes. After three years of traveling, and sick now with asthma and dropsy, he asked and received permission to retire to the convent of Santa Maria Mater Domini, near to the little church that would later be expanded over his tomb. He continued to hear confessions and to preach. Worn out by the Lenten preaching of 1231, he withdrew to Camposampiero, twenty kilometers from Padua, where his friend Count Tiso built him a small cell hanging from a walnut tree; here Anthony spent his days amid the foliage, because the open air gave him relief. In one of his last nights, when tormented by many pains, he had a **vision of the Infant Jesus** that has become part of his iconography; his friend Tiso was a witness to this vision.

On June 13, when he felt himself failing, he asked to be taken to Santa Maria Mater Domini; the only transport that could be found was an ox-drawn cart. On the outskirts of Padua his condition worsened, and the group stopped at the convent of Arcella, where he died. In the following year, on May 30, 1232, Pope Gregory IX proclaimed him a saint. Thirty-two years later, when Anthony's remains were being transferred, St. Bonaventure of Bagnoregio found the saint's tongue to be intact; this relic is still preserved in the Chapel of the Relics. The tongue, of course, was a physical instrument for his preaching.

The construction of the basilica *ad corpus,* that is, the basilica in which the remains were to be kept, began immediately. The people and the authorities wanted this church to be as beautiful as St. Mark's in Venice; in it different styles are combined—Romanesque, Byzantine, and Arabic—because, the Paduans say, "St. Anthony is everybody's saint." Two translations of the body are recorded: in 1263 from the little church of Santa Maria to the basilica, under the central cupola; in 1310 from there to a special Gothic chapel, which was later torn down because it was crumbling, and was rebuilt in 1500. The moulding of the chapel displays, in high relief, scenes from Anthony's life. The siting of the altar-tomb allows the faithful to circle it and to place their hands on the slab of dark marble that encloses the back of the tomb. The hands, clutching a rosary, a handkerchief, or a holy card, rest there for the time it takes to say a prayer or make a request; they pass on. On the balustrade of the altar are flowers, crutches, ex-votos, pictures of every size, photos, writings, enough of them to cover the altar; these attest to favors received. Pius XII named Anthony a Doctor of the Church on January 16, 1946.

▷▷ Anthony is patron of orphans, prisoners, shipwrecked seamen, and barren women; of draftees, who invoke him for a good number on the list; of potters and sellers of pottery; sellers of strawberries, because strawberries lie hidden beneath the leaves, just as Anthony was hidden amid the foliage of the walnut tree at the end of his life; and of messengers. Lisbon and Padua rival in claiming his name; tradition has made him a patron of both cities. His role as patron of Portugal was solemnly affirmed by Pius XI on June 13, 1934, and March 25, 1936. He is invoked in the search for mislaid or stolen objects and against conjugal barrenness.

▷▷ The earliest images of the saint show him holding only a **book** to indicate his learning; Gregory IX, in whose presence Anthony preached and who admired him for his profound knowledge of the Scriptures, called him "Ark of the Testament." The most common image shows Anthony with the **Child Jesus**; sometimes the saint is kneeling before the child, sometimes the child is standing or seated on **the Gospels** the saint holds in his hand, along with a **lily**, the symbol of purity. Jesus always displays affection for his Anthony.

This saint's many miracles are often depicted: a newborn child proclaims the innocence of its mother, who was accused of adultery; Anthony made it known that the heart of a miser was located not in his bosom but in his strongbox; he reattached a young man's foot, and raised several children to life. Once, in Rimini, where a small church in the center of the old city still preserves the memory of the event, he was challenged by a heretic: the man took a mule that had not eaten for three days and placed it between its fodder and a consecrated Host; after celebrating Mass, Anthony went, with the monstrance, to the place where the mule was, and the mule, paying no attention to food, knelt down before the Blessed Sacrament.

Again in Rimini, a gathering place of heretics, when people did not pay heed to Anthony's words, he turned to the fish, which thronged to his presence; this is the episode known as "The sermon to the fish." The saint's principal attributes are the **Child Jesus** and a **lily**; another attribute is a **book**.

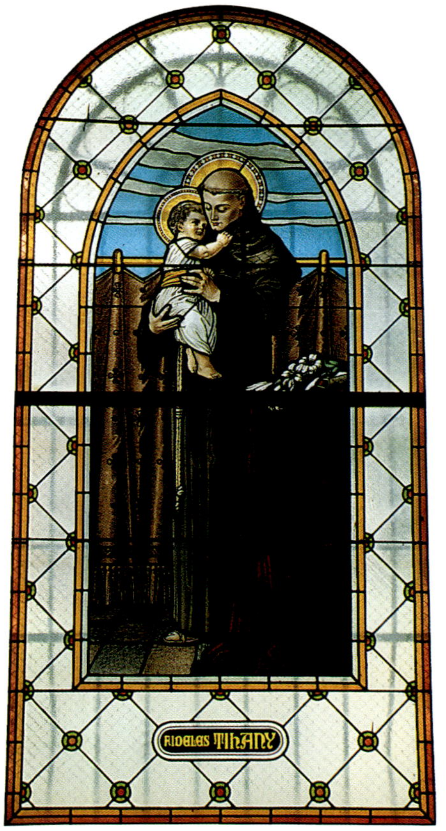

St. Anthony of Padua.
Stained-glass window, early 20th cent., in the shrine of the Assumption of Mary, Levoca, Slovakia.

St. Anthony and the Miracle of the Mule.
By the Master of the *Ancient Book of Prayers* belonging to Maximilian, ca. 1496. From the breviary of Queen Eleanor of Portugal, in the Pierpont Morgan Library, New York.

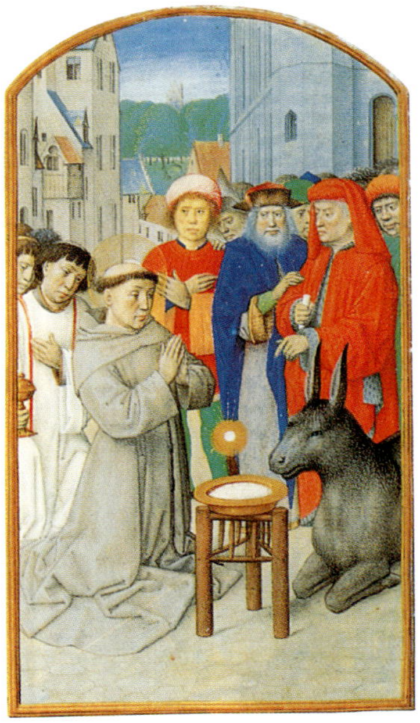

St. Dominic Guzmán and St. Vincent Ferrer. at the Feet of the Virgin and Child.
By Ubaldo Gandolfi, 1773, in the Museum of the Basilica of St. Dominic, Bologna.
The Virgin is giving the rosary to St. Dominic.

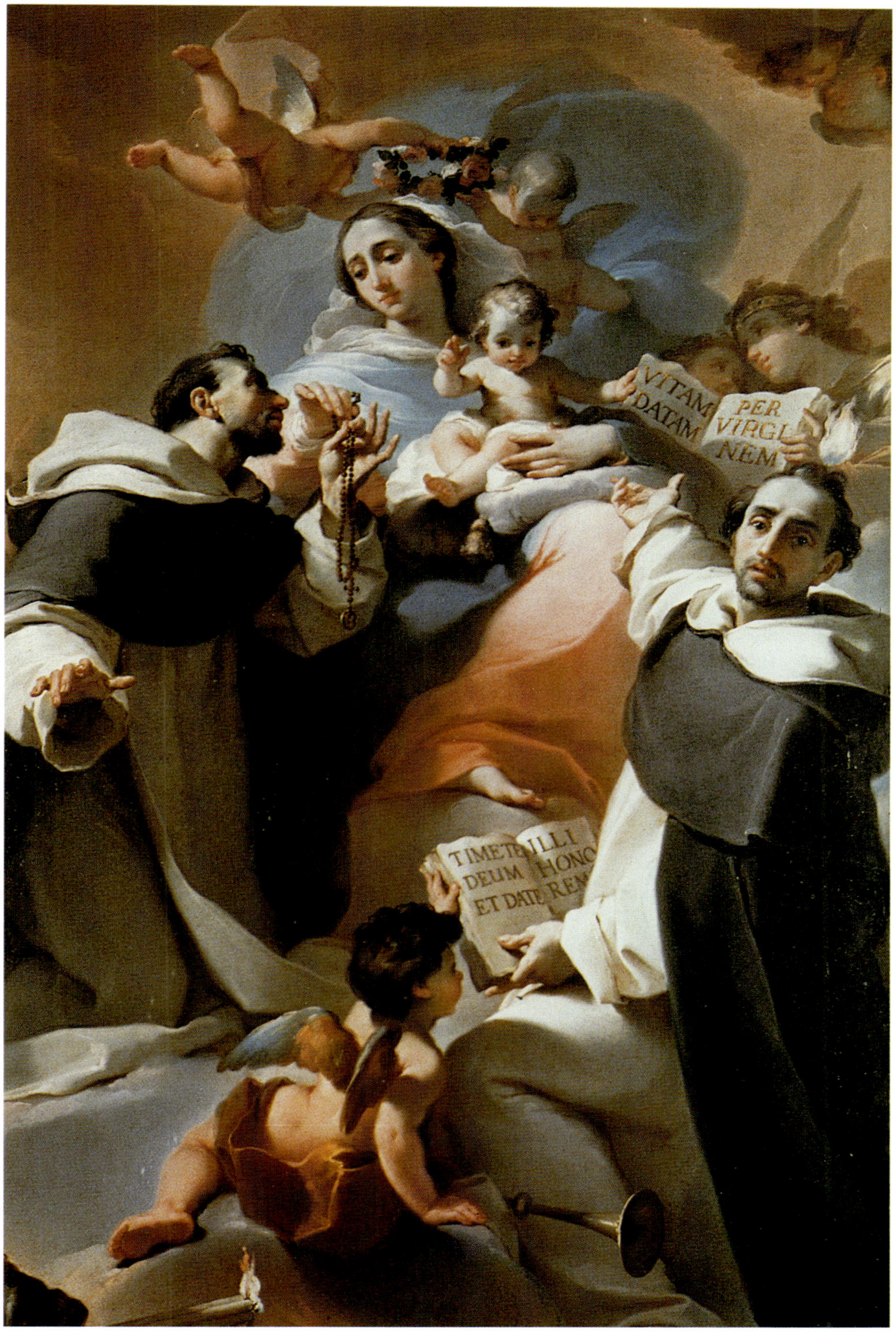

Dominic Guzmán, Priest and Founder of the Order of Preachers

1170–1221
Memorial: August 8 (date of death: August 6)
Lat.: Dominicus; It: Domenico, Mino, Minghin; Fr.: Dominique, Domange, Demenge, Demonge, Demonge, Domingue, Mangin (whence: Maginot, Monge); Sp.: Santo Domingo de Guzmán; Ger.: Dominikus.

The future founder of the Order of Preachers, known as the Dominicans, was born at Calaruega in Spain, not far from Burgos. His parents were Felix Guzmán and Giovanna, who was later proclaimed a blessed. Before he was born, his mother had a vision of carrying in her womb a **little dog** which, after emerging from the womb, seemed to set the whole world on fire with a **torch held in its mouth**; then his godmother had a vision of the child with a **star** shining from his forehead and shedding light over the entire world.

From the time he was a little boy he despised all luxuries and slept on the bare ground. He was educated first by an uncle who was an archpriest; he then studied in the best schools of the liberal arts in Palencia; finally, he studied theology for four years. Ever since his very young years he loved poverty and the poor; later, he aided them by founding a hospice and selling his own very valuable manuscripts. After ordination at Osma he spent some years as a contemplative. In 1203–1205 he accompanied his bishop, Diego, on a long journey through Europe and was struck by the spread of heresy, which at that time was resisted by means of excommunications and confiscations. He observed how the people were attracted by the moral lives of the heretics and how the ignorant clergy were unable to defend the faith.

Dominic then devoted himself to preaching, going from city to city, begging for his daily food, debating with heretics, and strengthening the faithful. This was a new manner of life and was approved by Pope Innocent III in 1206. For about ten years Dominic was almost alone in carrying on the work; then in 1215, after assembling some fellow workers, he submitted to Innocent III a plan for a new Order of Preachers. The approval came from Pope Honorius II in 1216. The order had a representative form of government, in which the chapter had supreme authority. Furthermore, he chose to send his brothers chiefly to universities, in order that Christianity might be seen as a source of culture. He also wanted his men to live on daily alms, and he constantly saw his trust in God confirmed. He had a special affection for Bologna, the seat of a great university, and held the first general chapter of the order there. There, too, he died, worn out by the labor of constant preaching, and there his relics are preserved; he was canonized in 1234.

Dominic was very devoted to the **Virgin**; to him is owed the great spread of the **rosary**, the practice of which he set down. As a result, in his iconography we find the **Virgin in the act of giving him the rosary**. Many stories of miracles have been handed down; the most famous show up in his iconography. For example, in Tolosa Dominic's works were subjected to a test: the flames spared his books and burned up those of the Albigensians; he raised to life a young man, Napoleon Orsini, who had fallen from a horse. In Bologna the convent lacked food; Dominic nevertheless offered praise and blessing before eating, and two angels came in carrying two baskets of bread and dried figs.

Dominic gave the Magi as a model for the brothers who were studying: "you ought to worship the God-man as the devout royal Magi did"; this subject is never missing from Dominican churches. His brother preachers are called "Dominicans" in the sense of "belonging to Dominic," but it was also said that Dominic himself, like all of his followers, was *Domini canis,* because a preacher is a "dog of the Lord," baying at the demons who are thieves of souls.

▷▷ Dominic is a patron of Tolosa where he preached, of Calaruega where he was born, of Naples where he preached, and of Bologna where he died. He is patron of the Dominicans, of orators and preachers generally, and of seamstresses and tailors.

Because he saved some pilgrims who were about to drown in the Garonne, he is invoked against drowning.

▷▷ He was very devoted to the Virgin; it was said that in 1530 Our Lady of the Rosary appeared to a Dominican and showed him how St. Dominic should be depicted holding a lily and a book bound in red. In the basilica of St. Dominic in Bologna there exists a reconstruction of his head, based on anthropometric measurements of his skull. He is depicted with a tonsure and sometimes with a beard. His principal attributes, in addition to the **Dominican habit**, are the **dog with the torch or candle**, the **star on his forehead**, the **lily**, and a **book**.

Other attributes are the **Virgin giving him the rosary** and an **angel** serving him.

Portrait Bust of St. Dominic Guzmán.
Polychrome terracotta by Nicolò dell'Arca, 1493, in the Museum of the Basilica of St. Dominic, Bologna.

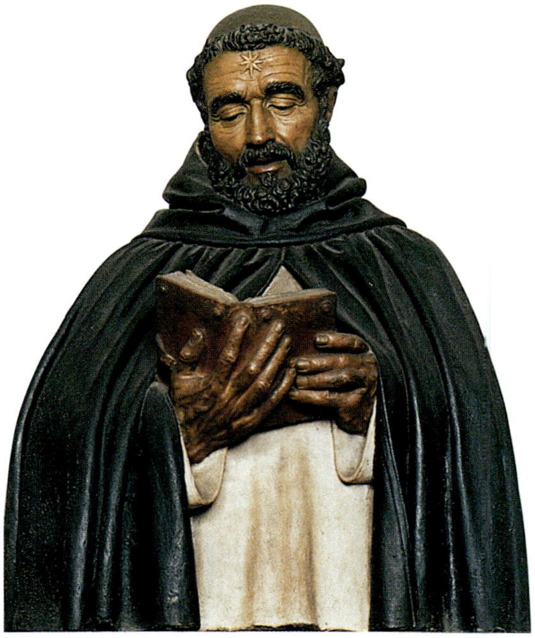

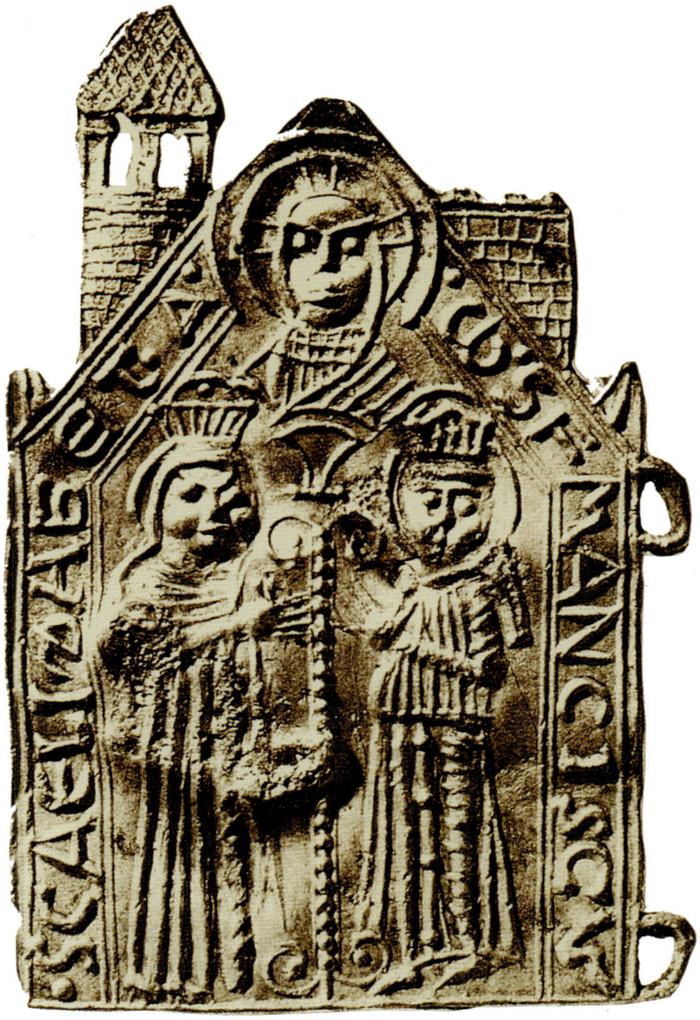

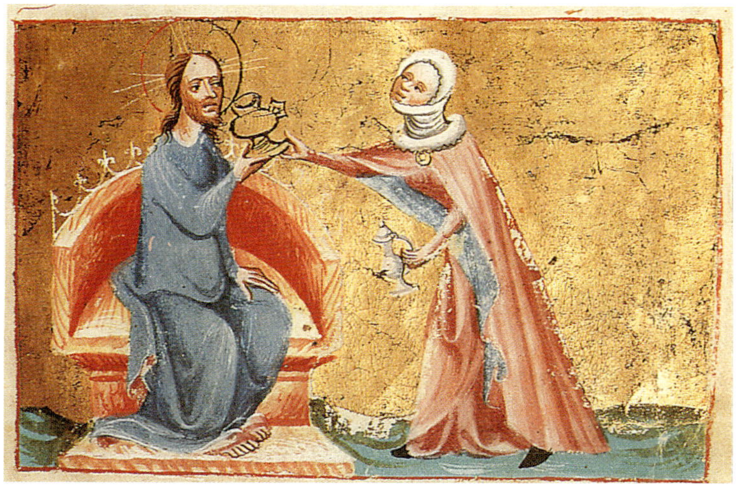

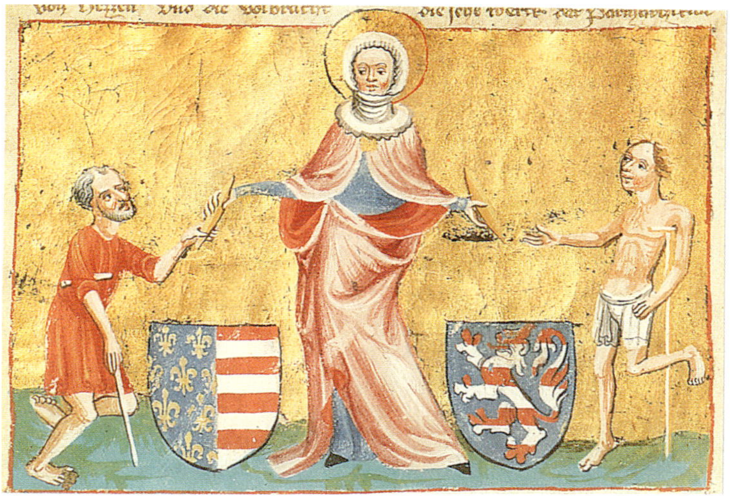

Pilgrim's Badge showing St. Elizabeth of Hungary and St. Francis.
In the Museum "Kulturen," Lund.

"I was a stranger and suffering, and you gave me a drink."
Scene from the life of St. Elizabeth, in the *Leitbuch des Nürnberger Heiliggeistspitals,* Nuremberg, 1410–1420, now in the Stadtarchiv D 2/II H-G-S/ Antsbücher 4 and 5.

"I was hungry and you fed me."
Same source.

Elizabeth of Hungary or of Thuringia, Religious Woman

1207–1231
Memorial: November 17
It.: Elisabetta d'Ungheria o di Turingia; Fr.: Élisabeth de Hongrie or de Thuringe; Sp.: Isabel; Ger.: Elisabeth von Ungarn, von Thüringen, Elsbeth; Dutch: Elisabeth von Hongarije; Hung.: Erszébet; Pol.: Elzbieta.

This daughter of King Andrew II of the Árpad dynasty was born in Hungary in 1207. At the age of four she was the promised wife of Louis IV, who was the Landgrave of Thuringia and only seven years older than she. The marriage took place in 1221. The combination of passionate love for her husband with dedication to Christ characterized her life; Louis understood this and fostered it. Elizabeth had a tender love for her husband, with whom she had grown up from infancy; by him she had three children: Herman, Sophia, and Gertrude, the last of whom died in the odor of sanctity. Elizabeth liked to take personal care of the poor, and it happened that her husband, or a relative, did not approve of this, thinking it to be beneath her dignity. One day, Elizabeth was carrying food to some abandoned individuals; her husband, or a relative, called to her and asked what she had under her cloak; "Roses," she answered, and the person ready to rebuke her saw **roses**. It is told, again, that, moved by charity, she had laid a leper on her bed; but when her husband drew back the covers, he saw Jesus crucified on the bed, for "the eyes of his soul" had been opened. These two incidents, which are not historically certain but the spirit of which is clear, have become part of the usual iconography of the saint. In 1224 Louis "took the cross" and devoted himself to preparations for the Crusade; but he died in 1227 at Otranto. Elizabeth then left the Wartburg and withdrew first to Eisenach, then to Pottenstein, and finally to Marburg. Conrad of

Marburg forbade Elizabeth to give away her dowry; Elizabeth was living in Marburg in poverty and doing works of charity; with the dowry she built a hospital for the most abandoned sick people and attended to them herself.

She died on November 17, 1231, when barely thirty-three, and was buried at Marburg on the nineteenth.

▷▷ Elizabeth is a patron of Germany and also of the Franciscan Tertiaries, the Franciscans, and the Knights of the Teutonic Order; of hospitals and hospital workers, as well as those sick with ringworm, whom she cured. Because she took bread to the poor, she is a patron of bakers and beggars; of charitable associations, Sisters of Charity, widows and orphans, and those persecuted without cause.

▷▷ The most common representation of Elizabeth has, for her principal attributes, the **roses in the folds of her cloak**, her **royal garb**, and a **crown.** She is also depicted surrounded by the sick, although this image appears only after the fourteenth century. She is often shown in the Franciscan habit, but she was never a Tertiary, even though her confessor was a Franciscan. At times she is shown holding a little model of the **church of Marburg**. Another attribute is a set of three crowns, which refer to her royal origin, her piety, and her continence.

Hedwig, Queen of Poland

1174–1253

Dies natalis: July 17

Lat.: Hedwigis regina Polonorum; It.: Edvige, regina di Polonia; Fr.: Hedwige, Avoye, Havoie; Sp.: Edwigis de Polonia; Germ.: Hedwigis, Hedwig von Schlesien; Pol.: Jadwiga.

Hedwig was the daughter of Louis, king of Hungary, and was espoused as an infant to William of Austria; but because she could not occupy the throne of Hungary, she was destined for the Polish throne. She arrived in Cracow on October 15, the feast of her holy patron, Hedwig, Duchess of Silesia and Poland. Her marriage to William was about to be celebrated, but the Poles did not want him as their king. Then, when Ladislas Jaggelon asked for Hedwig's hand and promised that he and the entire Lithuanian people would be baptized, her family agreed and the young woman, though very distressed, accepted in faith what seemed to her to be the divine will.

Ladislas was baptized in 1386 and the wedding was celebrated shortly afterward. William tried to oppose it, but even the pope approved of the marriage. Hedwig intervened actively and in an original way in the life of the state and influenced her husband, whose conversion she wanted to be more than a formality. She worked for a peaceful and thorough conversion of Lithuania and promised for those lands evangelizers who knew the local languages. She called for the founding of a Benedictine novitiate in Cracow as well as for the establishment of a theological school. She founded several hospitals and, in her charity, protected the peasants.

Tradition has it that a crucifix once spoke to her, saying "Hedwig, your prayer has been heard."

She died young, and her reputation for holiness spread far and wide.

▷▷ Hedwig is a patron of Poland and is very often shown together with the Polish saints; an image of her, now lost, existed on the arms of a crucifix in Wavel castle, Cracow, with the legend: "Blessed Queen Hedwig, wife of Ladislas Jagellon, died in 1399."

▷▷ Hedwig is depicted wearing **royal garb and a crown**, before the crucifix that is speaking to her, and with **cross in her hand**.

Blessed Hedwig of Poland.
Small devotional image, 20th cent., Poland.

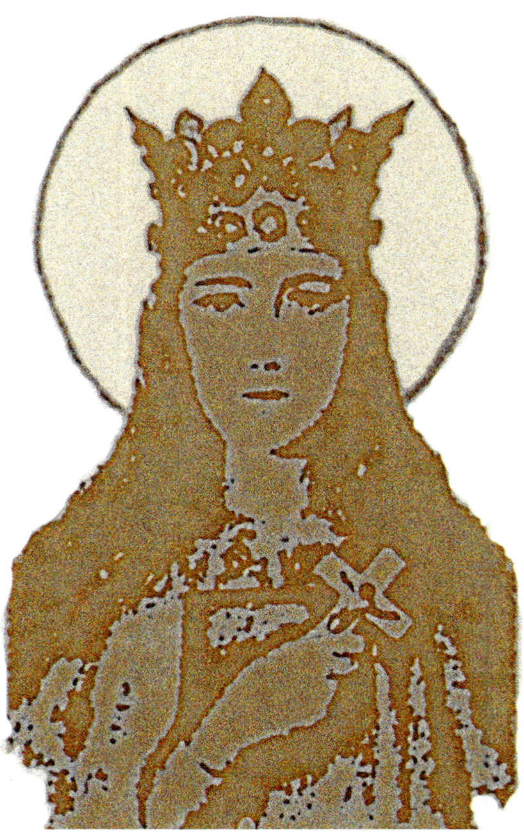

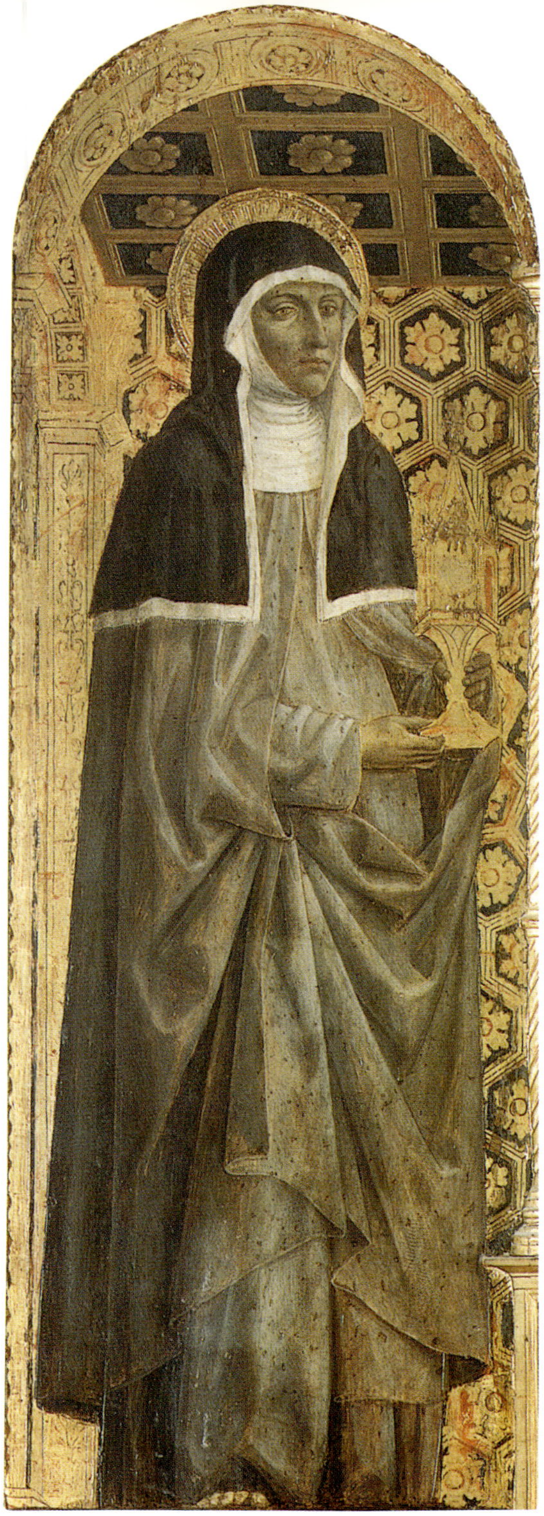

St. Clare of Assisi.
By Vincenzo Foppa (1427–1515).
The saint is shown with the monstrance she held up to the Saracens and which became her principal attribute.

Clare of Assisi, Virgin and Foundress of the Poor Clares

1193–1253
Memorial: August 11
Lat.: Clara Assisiensis, de Assisio; It.: Chiara d'Assisi; Fr.: Claire d'Assise; Sp.: Clara de Assis; Ger.: Klara von Assisi.

Clare, a follower of St. Francis and foundress of the Poor Clares (that is, the female branch of the Franciscans), lived a hard life that was filled with charity; she had a deep love of the poor.

Attracted by the clarity of Francis' ideal, during the night of Palm Sunday, March 28, 1211 (or March 12, 1212, according to some), Clare left her father's house and took refuge in the Portiuncula, along with her friend Bona di Guelfuccio. In the presence of his disciples, among whom were Rufinus and Sylvester, two relatives of Clare, Francis clothed her in a gray habit. She was then accompanied to Bastia and the Benedictine monastery of San Paolo; fifteen days later, she moved on to the Benedictine monastery of Sant'Angelo in Panso, where she was joined by her sister Agnella, who had likewise fled from her family. Francis settled the new religious family near the church of San Damiano, which he had restored. Clara was appointed abbess of the "Cloistered Poor Ladies of San Damiano," as they were called. Francis provided them with their first *Rule;* then in 1247 Clare herself composed one approved in 1252–1253. She also obtained from Pope Gregory IX the "privilege of poverty," that is, an obligation not to accept any property, even in common; this privilege had already been granted by Innocent III and was later confirmed by Innocent IV.

Clare mortified her body with harsh hair shirts, slept on the bare ground, and ate only sparingly, until finally Francis himself persuaded her to temper her austerity. Francis esteemed her and consulted her when he had to decide on the direction to be taken in his own order: toward the eremitical life or toward the apostolate? Clare urged him to preach and played a part in this activity by her prayers and sacrifices. In her monastery prayer and wonders abounded. For example, when the monastery had only one loaf left, she ordered half of it to be sent to the friars, yet from what remained she obtained fifteen slices; moreover the bread increased in the hands of the religious who was cutting it. On an occasion when they had no oil, Clare with her own hands washed the vessel that was to contain the oil and found it miraculously filled.

"Bright *(clara)* by name, brighter *(clarior)* in her life, brightest *(clarissima)* in her ways," is how Thomas of Celano describes her in his first *Life of Francis* (I, ch. 8). Clare had great devotion to the Eucharist. Thus, when the Saracens, serving Frederick II of Swabia as mercenaries, flooded into Assisi in 1243, Clare, even though ill, went to the door of the monastery with **the Eucharist in a monstrance**; in response to her prayers, a child's voice spoke from the monstrance, promising: "I will always guard and defend you." The Saracens hastily fell back; this episode became part of the saint's iconography.

Francis died before Clare, who subsequently spent the last years of her life immobilized on her bed. One Christmas night, as she grieved that she could not be in the choir with her sisters, she saw before her eyes the interior of the basilica of St. Francis and was able to enjoy the psalmody of the friars and see the Christmas crib.

She died on August 11, 1253, and during the final moments of her life had a vision of the saints and the Virgin.

▷▷ Only after Clare's death did the "Poor Ladies" take the name "Poor Clares." She was canonized by Pope Alexander IV in 1255; she is the patron of the Poor Clares, and her cult has spread all over the world.

She is a patron of Assisi, which she defended from the Saracens. Because of the **glass monstrance** she carried, she is the protector of painters on glass, while because of her vision of the

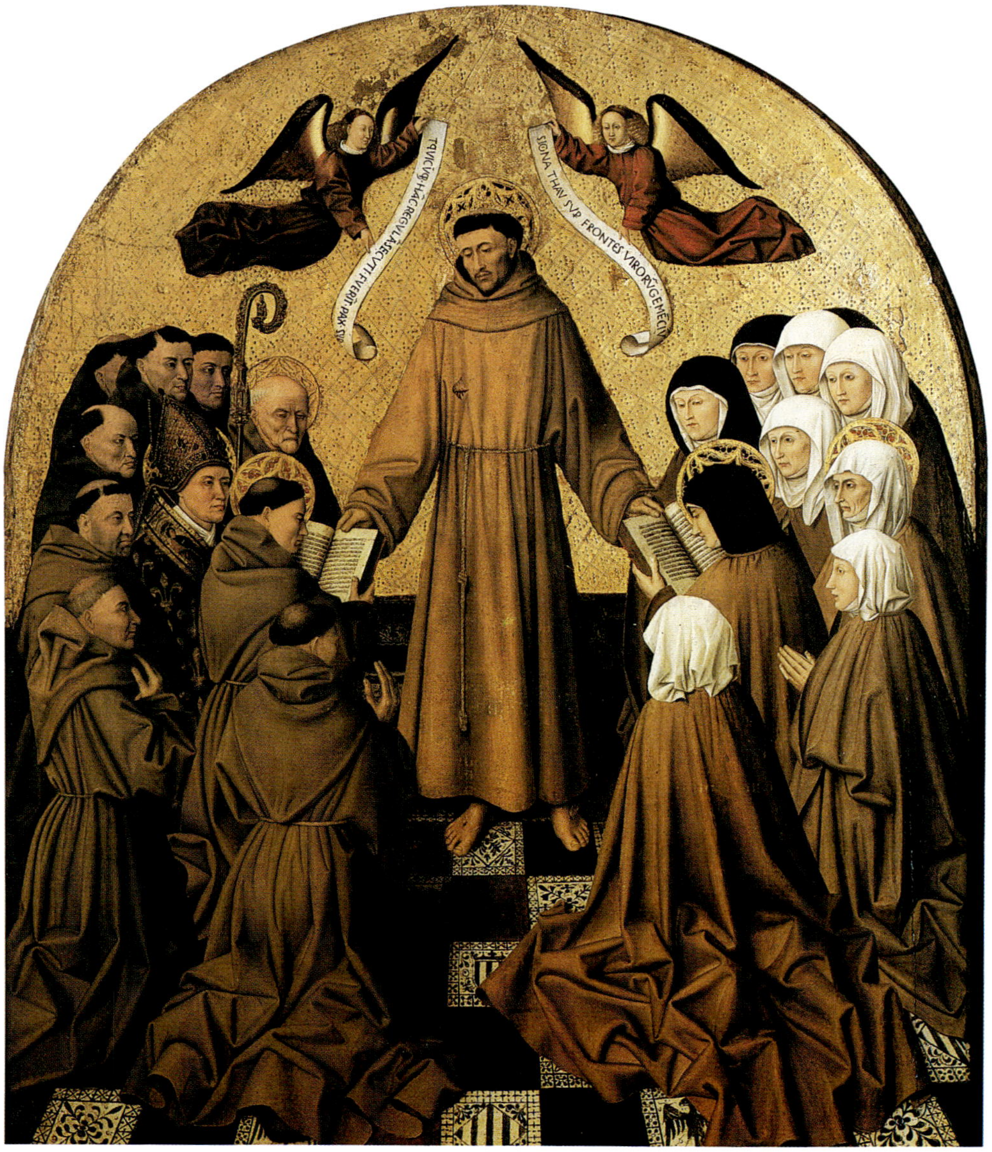

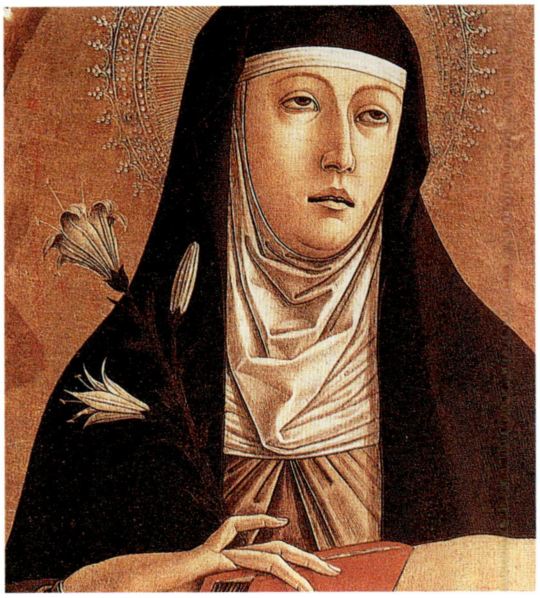

St. Clare.
Detail from a work by Carlo Crivelli, 1435–ca. 1500. Here the attribute is the lily.

St. Francis Gives the Rule to St. Clare and the Franciscans.
By Colantonio, 1445–1450, in the Museo di Capodimonte, Naples.

Christmas Mass, she is patron of the communications media and, in particular, of television; Pius XII declared her the matron of this medium on February 14, 1958. Her name brings to mind the dawn and light, and she is therefore patron of producers of lamps and mirrors, of laundresses, ironers, embroiderers, and makers of church furnishings, who work dressed in white. She is also patron of the blind and of oculists and opticians; of needle-makers and gilders. She is invoked against fever and blindness and for the gift of good sight.

▷▷ Clare is depicted in her **Franciscan habit with its three-knotted cincture of rope**. Her principal attribute is the **monstrance** by which she repelled the Saracens. Other attributes are a **cross, an olive branch, and a lily**, the three being often intertwined. Since she is a patron of the blind, she sometimes carries a **lamp**.

Ferdinand III, King of Castille and León

1198–1252
Memorial: May 30
Lat.: Ferdinandus rex Hispaniae III; It.: Fernando III, Ferdinando, Ferrante; Sp.: Fernando, Hernando, Hernan (whence the patronymics Fernandez, Hernandez); Ger.: Ferdinand.

This king was a lover of the sciences; he also proclaimed himself to be "Servant of St. Mary and standard bearer of the apostle St. James." Under him the kingdoms of León and Castile were united for the first time. By his first marriage, to Beatrice of Swabia, he had a son who would become Alfonso X the Wise. Once the realms were united he promoted the

Reconquest of Spain from the Arabs; in fact, he reconquered a great part of Spain, as far as Seville, and was called "the Reconquerer of Andalusia." In every place he was a great benefactor of the Church; such was his activity that the Roman Curia acknowledged him as patron of the reconstituted sees.

His greatness was more than military, for as a sovereign he was not only invincible but also magnanimous; he was unyielding toward heretics, and yet was generous toward the conquered, tolerant of the Jews, and submissive to religious authority. He was a man of pure life, prudent, generous, and gentle, and was wholly inspired by a desire to serve his people. He surrounded himself with twelve prudent men whom he continually consulted in order that he might be just toward his subjects. He promoted the sciences, the arts, and universities, and welcomed the rising religious orders: Franciscans, Dominicans, and Trinitarians.

He was a pious man and most devoted to the Virgin, and humble to the point of asking to do public penance. When dying in Seville, he wanted to receive viaticum on his knees, saying: "Lord, I came forth naked from my mother, the earth, and I offer myself naked to her; O Lord, receive my soul among the throng of your servants."

He was immediately recognized as a true model of a Christian king, and was canonized by Clement X in 1671.

▷▷ Ferdinand is a patron of Spain and, in particular, of Cordoba and Seville, as well as of rulers; he is also a protector of prisoners and the poor.

▷▷ He is depicted as a **sovereign with crown and scepter**, on horseback, and with a **Crusader's banner**; sometimes with a **key because of his motto** ("God will open, the king will enter in") and with a **small statue of the Virgin**, which he always carried with him.

Louis IX, King of France

1214–1270
Memorial: August 21
Lat.: Ludovicus nonus, Francorum rex, rex Galliae; It.: Luigi, Ludovico, Alvise, Luigino, Gino; Fr.: Louis roi de France, Loys, Loyset; Sp.: Luis; Ger.: Ludwig der Heilige, Aloisius; Dutch: Lodewijk; Hung.: Lajos.

Louis' faith was active in the defense of Christians. He was a just king, loved the poor, was constant in adversity, and spent all his energy and even his life in defense of the Holy Sepulcher.

Louis was born at Poissy, the son of Louis VII and Blanche of Castile; he became king in 1226, after his mother's regency. He married Margaret of Provence, restored order in the realm, and in 1248 went for the first time on a Crusade (the seventh); he was away for seven years. In 1267, he set out again and died during a plague under the walls of Tunis on August 25, 1270.

St. Louis in Royal Robes.
Detail from a miniature in the Missal of the Sainte-Chapelle, second quarter of the 14th cent. Now in the Bibliothèque Municipale of Lyons, Ms. 5122, f. 1420.

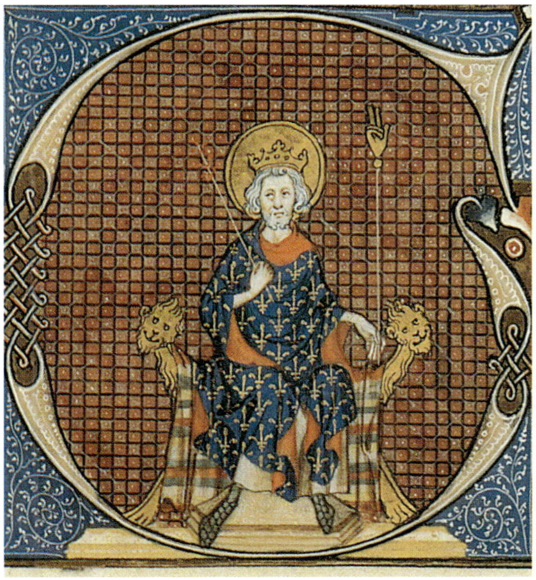

Louis was raised with a horror of sin and tried to instill the same horror in those around him. His ideal, as he himself used to say, was the "prudent man": this included balance, service of God and neighbor, piety, and conscientiousness in the exercise of power. This ideal was combined with an almost monastic way of life; thus he devoted a great deal of time to the liturgical Office (the Hours of the day), which he and a chaplain recited in a low voice as the clerics were singing it, as well as to the Office of the Virgin; to these two he added, in private, the Office of the Dead. He attended two Masses daily, sometimes three.

He loved the gift of tears of repentance and desired to have it even more intensely. Every evening he made fifty genuflections, each accompanied by a Hail Mary. He used to remain kneeling in prayer for long periods, to the point of no longer knowing where he was. He confessed his sins every Friday, and afterward received the discipline from his confessor. As was customary at that time, he received Communion six times a year: Easter, Pentecost, Assumption, All Saints, Christmas, and Purification, and prepared for each by the practice of continence. He fasted in Advent, Lent, between the Ascension and Pentecost, on the Ember Days, on vigils, and on Fridays. On many days he took only bread and water; he multiplied his abstinences. He sent to the poor the first fruits and first fish of each season, keeping for himself only what was cheaper. He wore a hair shirt on the Fridays of Lent, and used to deprive himself of what might give him pleasure.

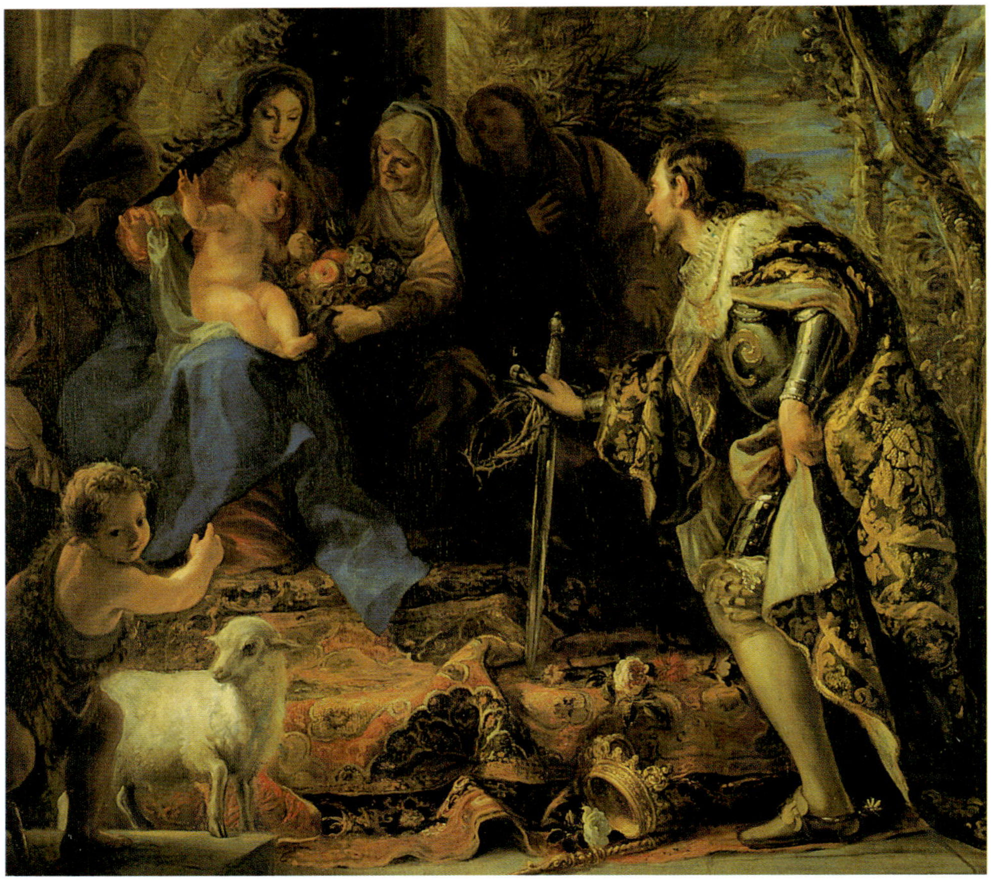

He had a tender love of his wife, and the two together imposed moderate periods of continence on themselves; he did not, however, allow her to play a part in politics. He trained his children by having them take part in his own life. The alms he gave were huge: every day he fed a hundred and twenty poor persons, washed the feet of three poor persons every Saturday, and always had three poor persons at his table. In the Cistercian abbey of Royaumont he used to serve the religious at their meals; he visited the sick, even visited a leper. In his exercise of royal power he was concerned with the souls as well as the bodies of his subjects. In his life he had a reputation for holiness, while the return of his remains from Tunis was marked by miracles. In order to prevent corruption, his remains were boiled to separate the flesh from the bones; the flesh was given to Charles of Anjou, while the bones were placed in the cathedral of St. Denis.

▷▷ Louis is patron of Paris and Poissy; he is protector of rulers generally and of the French monarchy in particular. All the kings of France from that time on were his descendants, and his name was hereditary in his dynasty. He composed a *Book of Trades* and for that reason he is, in France, the patron of a great many categories. Because he built the Sainte-Chapelle, he is patron of masons, marble-workers, stonecutters, and sculptors; of upholsterers; of the peddlers who had their business in the Palais de la Cité. Because of his generosity to the churches in which they worked, he was patron of embroiderers, tailors, makers of sacred furnishings, ornaments, and buttons, all of whom were members of the same group. Because his biographer says that his hair was always well-combed and that he shaved his beard before his First Crusade, he became the patron of hairdressers, wig-makers, and barbers. He became the patron of producers of linen because he gave them a place to practice their trade, namely, the Rue de Lingerie. It is not clear why anglers with their fishing rods invoke him as a patron. Having himself been on two Crusades, he became a patron of pilgrims. He is also a protector of the Jesuits.

He is invoked against deafness, because of the similarity of sound between Louis and *ouïe* ("hearing"); against blindness because he established the Hôpital des Quinze-Vingts; and against the plague from which he died.

▷▷ His principal attributes are the **royal garb**, with **crown and ermine cloak** and with the **lilies of France** on the cloak, and with a **cross** in his hand. Other attributes are the

St. Louis, King of France, Worships the Holy Family.
By Claudio Coello, 1665–1668. Now in the Prado, Madrid.
Clearly shown are the royal trappings and the crown of thorns, which is an attribute of the saint.

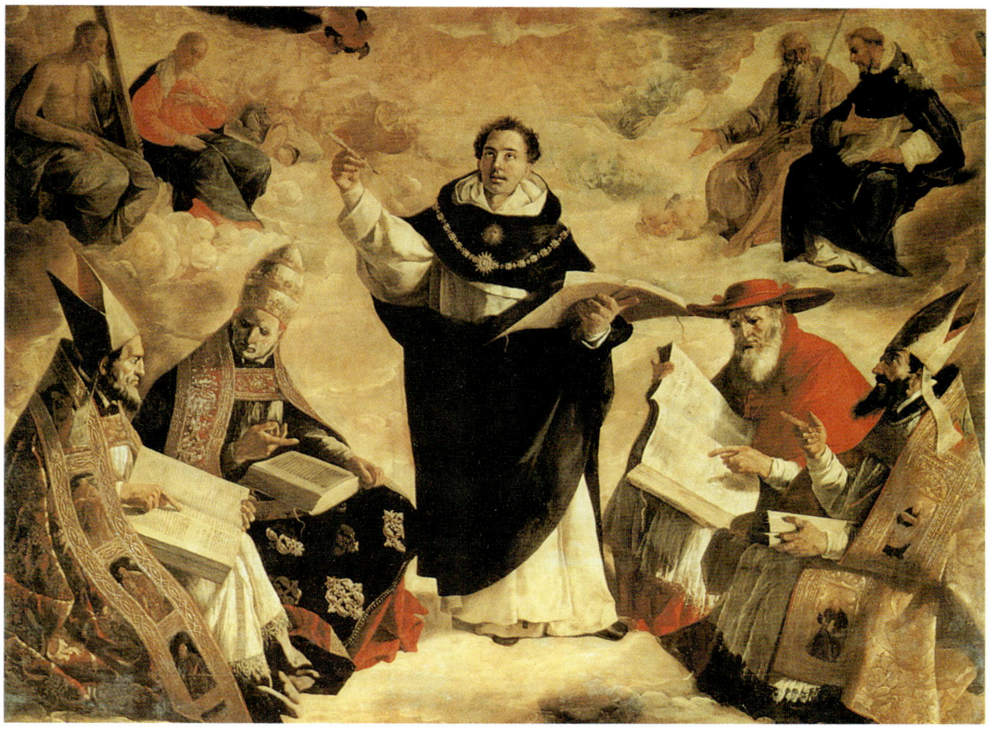

St Thomas Aquinas among the Fathers of the Church. B; Francisco de Zurbaran, 1598–1664, in the Museo Provincial, Seville. Note the star on the saint's breast.

crown of thorns, the **three nails** of the crucifixion, and a **model of the Sainte-Chapelle**. He had in fact acquired these relics of the crucifixion and had them placed in the Sainte-Chapelle, which thus became the place richest in relics of the passion of Christ.

Thomas Aquinas, Dominican Priest and Doctor of the Church

1225/27–1274
Memorial: January 28; day of death and translation, March 7
Lat.: Thomas de Aquino, Aquinas; It.: Tommaso d'Aquino; Fr.: Thomas d'Aquin; Sp.: Tomás de Aquino; Ger.: Thomas von Aquino; Russ.: Toma Akvinski.

Thomas was the son of Landulf, a nobleman of Lombard origin who was in the service of the emperor. While at the University of Naples, Thomas came to know Aristotelianism and the Dominican Order and took the Dominican habit in 1243/1244. The family was opposed to this action and had him locked up in the paternal castle; they tempted him in various ways, but Thomas resisted through prayer, which won him "the bond of perpetual virginity" *(perpetuae virginitatis vinculum)*. When set free, he spent time in Naples, Rome, and Cologne, where St. Albert the Great was his teacher. He was dubbed the "dumb ox," because he was large and taciturn; in response, St. Albert said of him "the lowing of his teaching will be heard throughout the world."

In fact, his gifts soon became evident. He finished his education in Paris, where he then began to teach. He then taught in Naples, too, where a center of studies arose that had long been desired by the Dominicans. His writing ceased in 1273; after celebrating Mass on the feast of St. Nicholas, he decided no longer to teach and dictate, saying: "All that I have written seems to me only straw." The secret reason for this decision was perhaps an ecstasy he experienced during Mass on Passion Sunday of 1273, in which Friar Romanus of Rome appeared to him.

During his final illness two of his fellow religious saw a **great star** come in through the window, rest briefly on Thomas's head, and then leave by the window. A short time later, after lengthy ecstasies, he made known the moment of his death, which occurred on March 7, 1274, in the Cistercian abbey of Fossanova, where he had broken his journey on the way to the Council of Lyons. Before dying, he received Communion and professed his devotion to the Eucharist and his submission to the Church. John XXII canonized him in 1323. Some of his brethren saw Jesus drawing near to Thomas as the saint was writing about the Eucharist; Jesus said: "You have written excellently about the sacrament of my Body."

Thomas was tall, large, pale, and bald, of a passionate and irascible temperament; yet he was utterly balanced in his writings, activity, teaching, and preaching.

His many works include commentaries on Scripture and the Fathers, but above all the *Summa contra Gentiles* and the *Summa Theologiae,* which lay the unsurpassed foundations of Christian philosophy. In them he combines a profound understanding of Aristotelian philosophy with a Christ-centered vision of the world, one of which he teaches his readers to give a rational, systematic account.

He has been named "the Angelic Doctor," "the Prince of the Schools," "the Light of the Church." To him we owe the splendid Office for the feast of Corpus Christ; this inspired composition has found a place in his iconography.

▷▷ His role as patron is connected with study and writing: thus he is patron of universities and especially that of Naples, of theologians and students of theology, of pencil-makers and booksellers.

On August 4, 1880, Leo XIII proclaimed Thomas the patron of Catholic schools and universities. He is invoked against lightning, thunder, and storms. As a model of chastity, he protects and is invoked against lust.

▷▷ The saint is depicted as a heavy man in a **Dominican habit**. One principal attribute is **a large ruby on his chest** that illumines the Church; this is in keeping with a vision given to a Dominican of Brescia in which the latter saw Thomas as a "light for the Church," alongside St. Augustine. Because of Thomas's Office for Corpus Christi, another principal attribute is the **Blessed Sacrament**. Other attributes are: **the dove of the Holy Spirit** that calls attention to the inspiration granted to Thomas; the **cincture of chastity** *(cingulum castitatis)* with which angels girded him in a dream; because of visions granted to two fellow religious, a **star** or a **sun** on his head, with, on one occasion, an inscription on his chest; a **lily**; more rarely, **wings**, suggested by the adjective "Angelic [Doctor]."

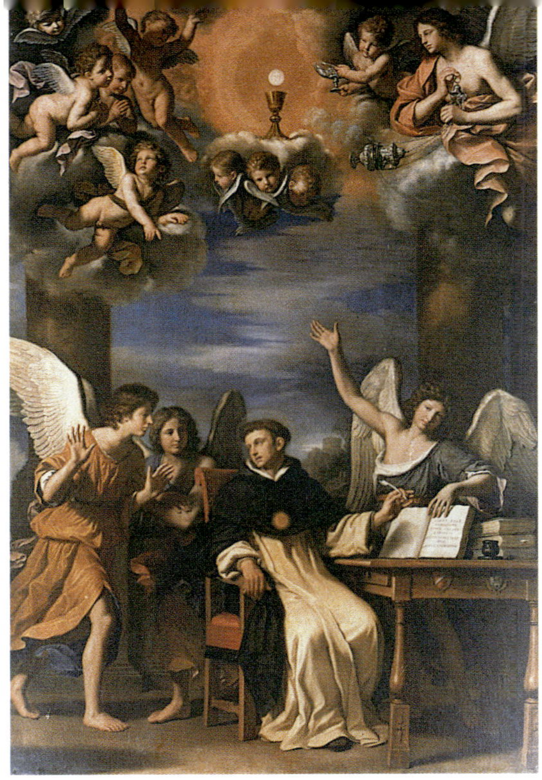

St. Thomas Composes the Office of Corpus Christi.
By Giovan Francesco Barbieri, known as "Il Guercino," 1591–1666, in the Basilica of St. Dominic, Bologna.
The presence of angels points up the saint's divine inspiration.

Nicholas of Tolentine, Augustinian Priest

1249–1305
Memorial: September 10
Lat.: Nicholas Tolentinus, presbyter Ordinis Eremitarum Sancti Augustini; It.: Nicola da Talentino, Niccolò di Tolentino, Nicola Tolentinate; Fr.: Nicolas de Tolentino, de Tolentin; Ger.: Nikolaus von Tolentino.

Nicholas of Tolentine is linked to St. Nicholas of Bari inasmuch as his parents, who wanted a child, were urged by an angel in a dream to go to Bari. They went from Castel Sant'Angelo in Pantano, their own town in the Marches, to Bari, where the couple, after praying, followed the custom of pilgrims and slept on the floor of the basilica. Nicholas of Bari appeared to them in a dream and promised them a son destined for religious life and holiness. The promised son was born, and a comet appeared in the sky over Tolentine to announce his birth; he became a great preacher and wonderworker.

His parents gave him the name Nicholas, and at the age of twelve he became an oblate in the convent of the Augustinian Friars in his town (these were the Hermits of St. Augustine). By divine inspiration Nicholas took up residence in Tolentine in 1275 and there became "the angel of the confessional" and of the poor. He reminded the rich of the social purpose of wealth and exhorted them to be charitable; he became the adviser of young aristocrats and students. He possessed only one habit and that was patched; his life was marked by fasting and abstinence, penance and prayer. By celebrating Mass for the souls in purgatory every day for a week, he won the deliverance of the soul of a deceased fellow religious and of many other souls being purified. For this reason, he is invoked against the flames of purgatory through the pious practice of "St. Nicholas' Septenary," that is, seven days of Masses and

Vision of St. Nicholas of Tolentine.
By Giangiacomo Barbelli, 17th cent., in the Chiesa Prepositurale di Sant'Andrea.
The vision of a star told the saint the date of his death; note the face in the sun on the saint's breast.

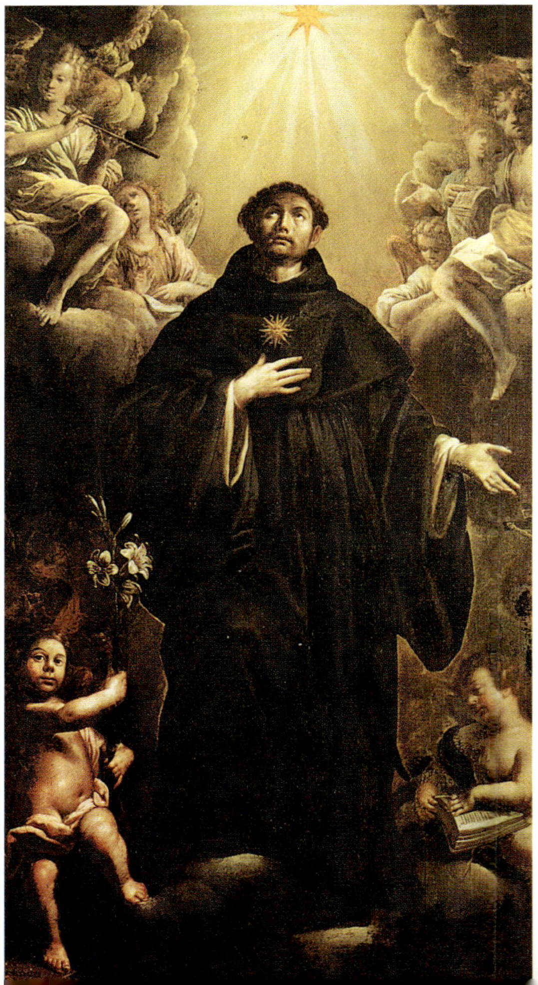

prayers. At Tolentine, the Sunday after his feast is celebrated as a "Sunday of Forgiveness." The Virgin herself healed him of an illness by giving him a **piece of bread** soaked in water; this gave rise to the devotion involving small blessed loaves, to which many miracles were due, among them, the rescue of his city from a plague against which he was invoked.

His imminent death was made known to him: he had a repeated vision in dreams of a star that came and stopped over the oratory of St. Augustine in Tolentine. He asked an elderly fellow religious to interpret the dream for him; the religious recognized in the star a symbol of Nicholas' holiness, which would be a source of grace for all, and in its stopping over the chapel a sign of the saint's imminent death. Nicholas then saw the **star** again while he was awake, and it went before him to the altar. Then, in a vision, Jesus, the Virgin, and St. Augustine told him the day of his death. He died on September 10, 1305. He was canonized in 1446 and, in the course of the process, he was recognized as having performed 301 miracles.

Noteworthy is the cult of the *Holy Arms*. Forty years after the saint's death, for reasons unknown to us, his arms were cut off, and a great deal of blood flowed out. Subsequently, the latter phenomenon occurred many times. Cloths soaked in the blood were carried in procession on the saint's feast day and on the fourth Sunday of Lent. Today the arms and body are located together in a silver urn in the crypt of the basilica that bears his name in Tolentine.

▷▷ Because Nicholas obtained the liberation of a prisoner, he is a patron of those treated unjustly; a patron also of the dying and the souls in purgatory, and he is invoked to avoid its flames. He protects mothers and children and is invoked against pestilence and fever. "St. Nicholas' bread" is given to the sick and to women in childbirth, after it has been dipped in water. In the animal world he is protector of partridges.

▷▷ The saint is depicted as a **young man with a tonsure and wearing the black habit of the Augustinians**. Because of the repeated vision he had, his principal attribute is a **star on his breast** with a **face** inscribed on it. Other attributes are a **skull**, an allusion to his meditation on death; a **crucifix adorned with lilies**, and a **basket of rolls**.

Gertrude of Helfta, Virgin and Cistercian Religious

ca. 1256–1301

Memorial: November 16; *died natalis* November 17

Lat.: Gertrudis Magna; It.: Gertrude di Helfta; Fr.: Gertrude la Grande; Sp.: Gertrudis la Magna, La Grande; Ger.: Gertrud die Grosse von Helfta; Flem.: Gertrudis de Groote, Geert, Geertryt.

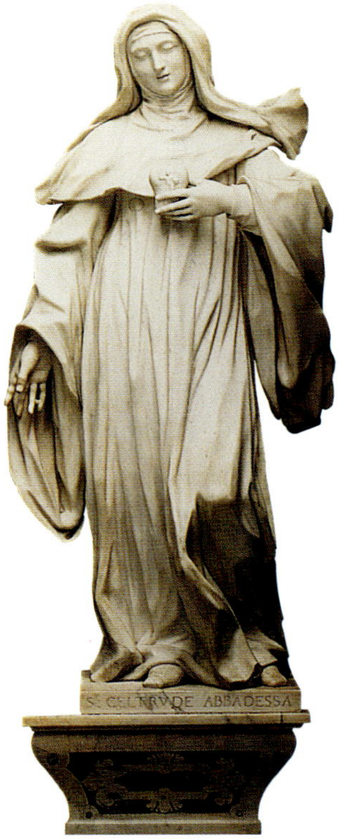

St. Gertrude of Helfta.
18th-cent. statue in the sanctuary of Maria Regina Montis Regalis, Vicoforte, Italy.
Clearly visible in the saint's heart is the image of the teenage Jesus that identifies her.

This Cistercian mystic, known as "Gertrude the Great" and the "Teresa of Germany," was an important forerunner of devotion to the Sacred Heart of Jesus.

She told her own story in her *Revelations:* she entered the Cistercian monastery of Helpede, that is, Helfta, in Saxony and devoted herself entirely to study for twenty years. The pleasure she derived from study dampened her fervor for religious practices and as a result she suffered the loneliness and anguish of a spiritual crisis. She emerged from this, however, as a woman renewed on January 27, 1281, when she had a vision of Jesus as a young man who comforted her and promised her salvation. After this event, which she called a conversion, she turned to prayer, contemplation, and meditation on the Scriptures and the writings of the Church Fathers.

In order to share the delight she found in these sources, she began to explain the Scriptures to everyone, using the vernacular. Her more than rigorous observance of the *Rule* undermined her health and in 1288 she entered into a period of illnesses and sufferings that led to her death on November 17, 1301.

In addition to her *Revelations,* her *Spiritual Exercises* have also come down to us.

Her cult began slowly and she was not canonized until 1677, but after that her reputation became widespread, reaching even Spain and Portugal. She is the only German saint to be called "Great."

▷▷ She is patron of Tarragona in Spain.

▷▷ She is depicted in the **white Cistercian habit** with a **pastoral staff** and a **flaming heart that contains an image of the teenage Jesus** and an inscription: "You will find me in the heart of Gertrude." Another attribute is a **crown held up by angels**.

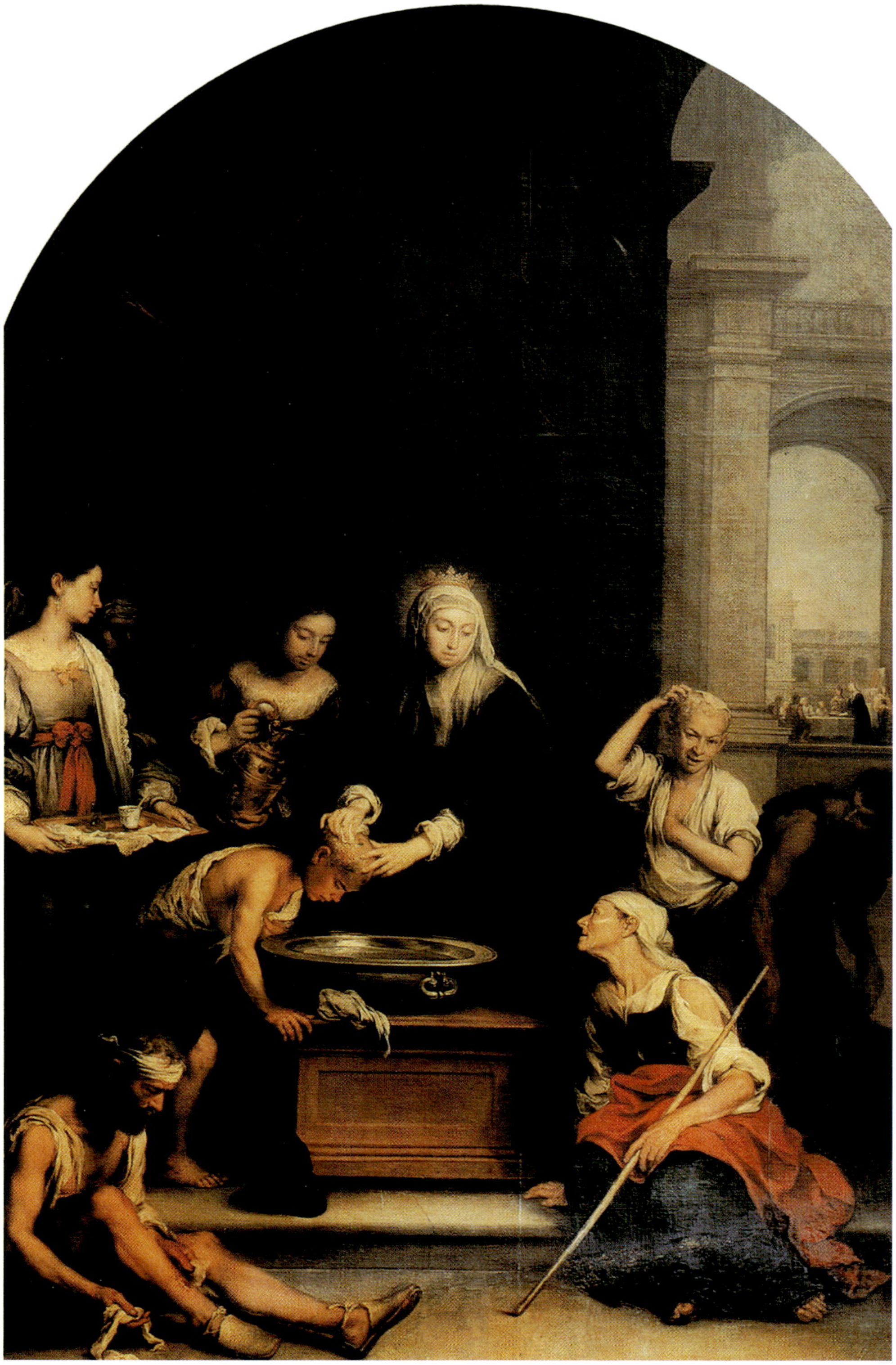

St. Elizabeth, Queen of Portugal, Tends to the Sick. By Bartolomé Esteban Murillo, 1618–1682, in the Prado, Madrid.

Elizabeth, Queen of Portugal

1271–1336
Memorial: July 4
Lat.: Elisabeth de Lusitania.

Elizabeth was a peacemaker and generous in her charitable works. She was married, at a very young age, to Denis, king of Portugal and bore him two children: Alfonso, who succeeded his father, and Constance, who married Ferdinand IV of Castile.

The marriage was not a happy one, due to the dissolute life of the king; Queen Elizabeth endured her lot without complaint and even took care of the children of her husband's mistresses, while living a life marked by austerity, works of charity, and mortifications. She was accused of taking Alfonso's side in a quarrel between father and son and was ordered into exile: she avoided this by taking up an immovable position between the supporters of the father, on one side, and the son on the other. The place is still pointed out today where she remained until the opponents settled their grievances. The king did not hold this against her and from that point on esteemed her highly; he came to love her and changed his way of life. When Denis fell ill, Elizabeth took care of him and led him toward a holy death.

Once she was widowed, Elizabeth devoted herself entirely to good works, sold her possessions in order to help the poor and support monasteries, became a Franciscan Tertiary, and went barefoot to Santiago de Compostela. Finally, she withdrew to the convent of the Poor Clares in Coimbra, a convent she had founded. She subjected herself to harsh penances. Her confessor wanted her to drink a little wine, but one day, when she insisted on drinking only water, the water in the **carafe** changed miraculously into the wine she really needed. She left the monastery only to bring peace between her son and her son-in-law. At the point of death, she made a religious profession; her tomb became the goal of pilgrimages. Urban IV canonized her in 1625.

▷▷ Her principal attributes are a **royal crown**, a widow's **veil**, the **knotted cincture of the Poor Clares**, and a **carafe** of wine.

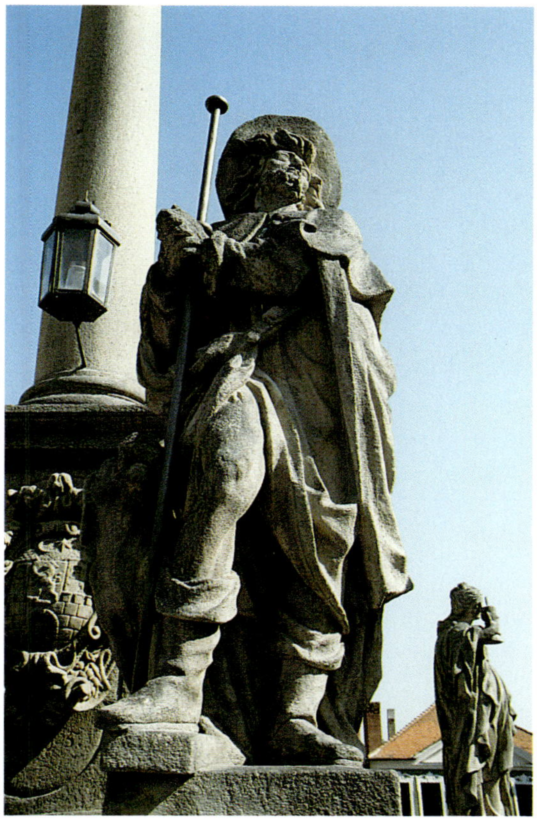

St. Roch.
Statue from 1754–1757 on a bridge over the Otava, in Pisek, Czech Republic.

Roch, Pilgrim

1350 to ca. 1379
Memorial: August 16
Lat.: Rochus de Monte Pessulano, Monspessulanus; It.: Rocco; Fr.: Roch de Montpellier, Roc, Reu, Roque; Sp.: Roque; Ger.: Rochus; Swed.: Rokh; Russ.: Rokh.

Roch's life was marked by pilgrimage and pestilence. He was born in Montpellier in 1350. He seems to have had a red cross on his chest; his name, therefore, would derive from *rubeus,* "red," and not from *roc,* "rock." When left an orphan while still young, he gave away his possessions, left his native Montpellier, and went on pilgrimage to Rome. A pestilence was raging when Roch stopped at Acquapendente, where he cured the plague-stricken with the sign of the cross. His power of healing took him to the Romagna, where he remained until the epidemic had passed. He reached Rome, where again he tended to the sick, and remained there for three years.

He then set out for his home but when he reached Piacenza, where the plague had broken out, he became infected. In order not to oblige others to take care of him, he fled to the river Trebbia at Sarmato and near a spring on the land of a nobleman, Gottardo Pollastrelli. One of this lord's **dogs** entered the cave that sheltered Roch, took a liking to him, and daily brought him a **piece of bread**; the lord became curious, followed the dog, and discovered the saint. He took care of Roch and began a new life.

Then Roch took to the road again but when he reached Montpellier, no one recognized him; he was imprisoned as a vagabond and died after years in prison. Above his head was found a **board** on which it was written that anyone who was sick of the plague and had recourse to Roch, would be immediately cured.

It is not known how his body reached Venice; there, in 1490, it was placed in the church that bears his name, near the Frari.

▷▷ Roch is one of the patrons of pilgrims and is very often associated with St. Sebastian in invocations against plagues and against infectious diseases in general, such as cholera, as well as against sores and wounds of the legs. His cult peaked in 1630, when every place in which the plague ended built him an oratory; the date of the dedication of these chapels tells us the year and month in which the plague ended in the various parts of Europe. He protects vines from phylloxera, "the plague of vines," and from natural catastrophes. Because he himself buried those who had died of the plague, he is protector of gravediggers; he also protects dealers in second-hand goods. Because his name suggests

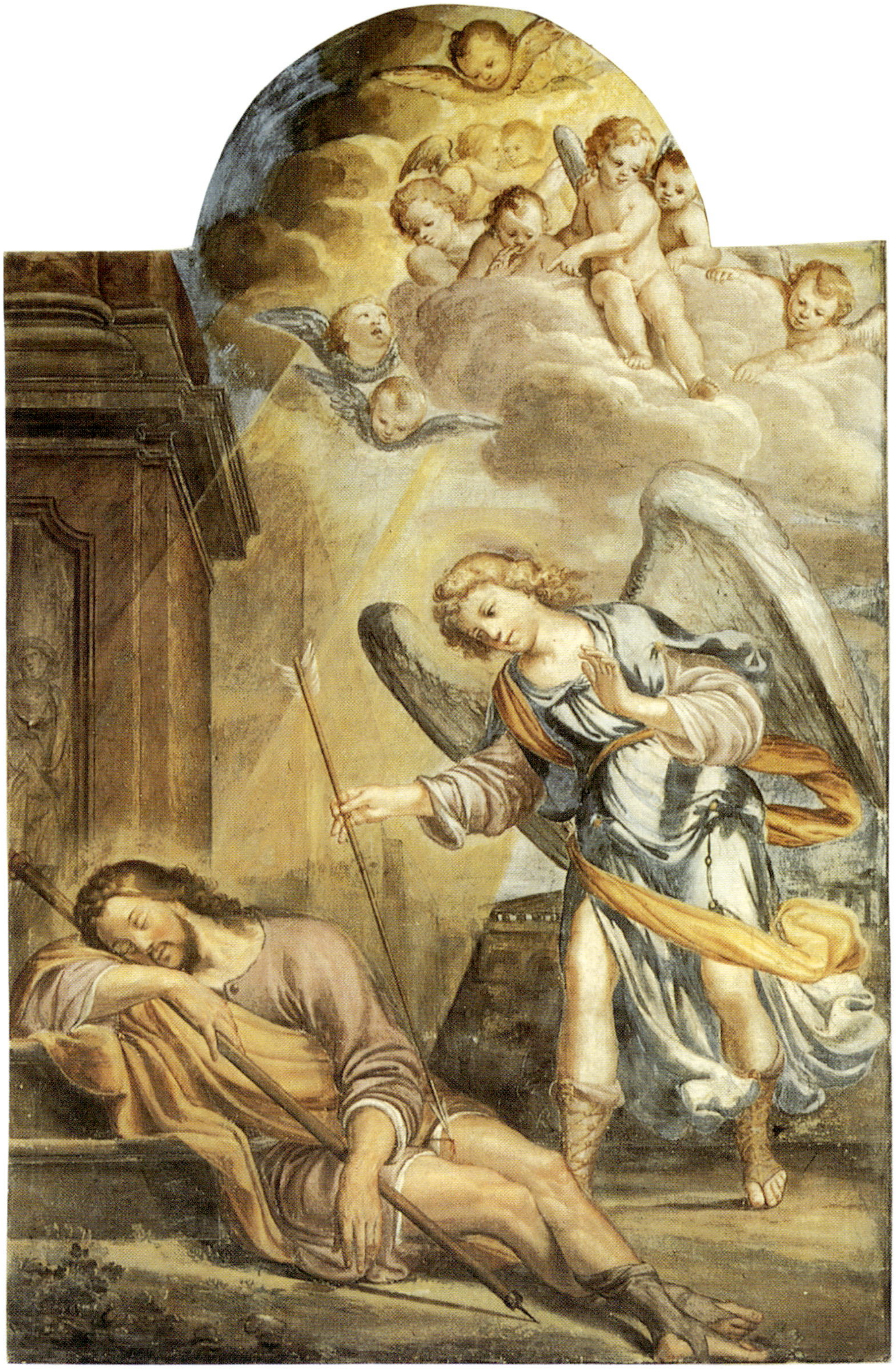

“rock,” he is invoked by those who used pieces of stone in their work: stonecutters, pavers, and masons.

▷▷ The episodes of his life are represented in cycles: distribution of possessions, care of the plague-stricken, the illness in which he was comforted by an angel and the dog, and his imprisonment.

He is depicted as a **young man**, **in pilgrim’s garb**, and in the act of **pointing out on his thigh an open bubonic sore** that looks like an arrow wound; a **crouching dog gives him a piece of bread**. Such are his principal attributes. Others are: the short **cape** or *sanrocchino* that takes its name from him; the **pilgrim’s staff** and the **wide-brimmed hat** of the pilgrim; and **the board with the inscription**.

St. Roch Is Stricken by the Plague.
By Sebastiano Razzali, 1640, in the Oratory of St. Roch, Bologna.
The emphasis here is on the providential character of the saint’s illness.

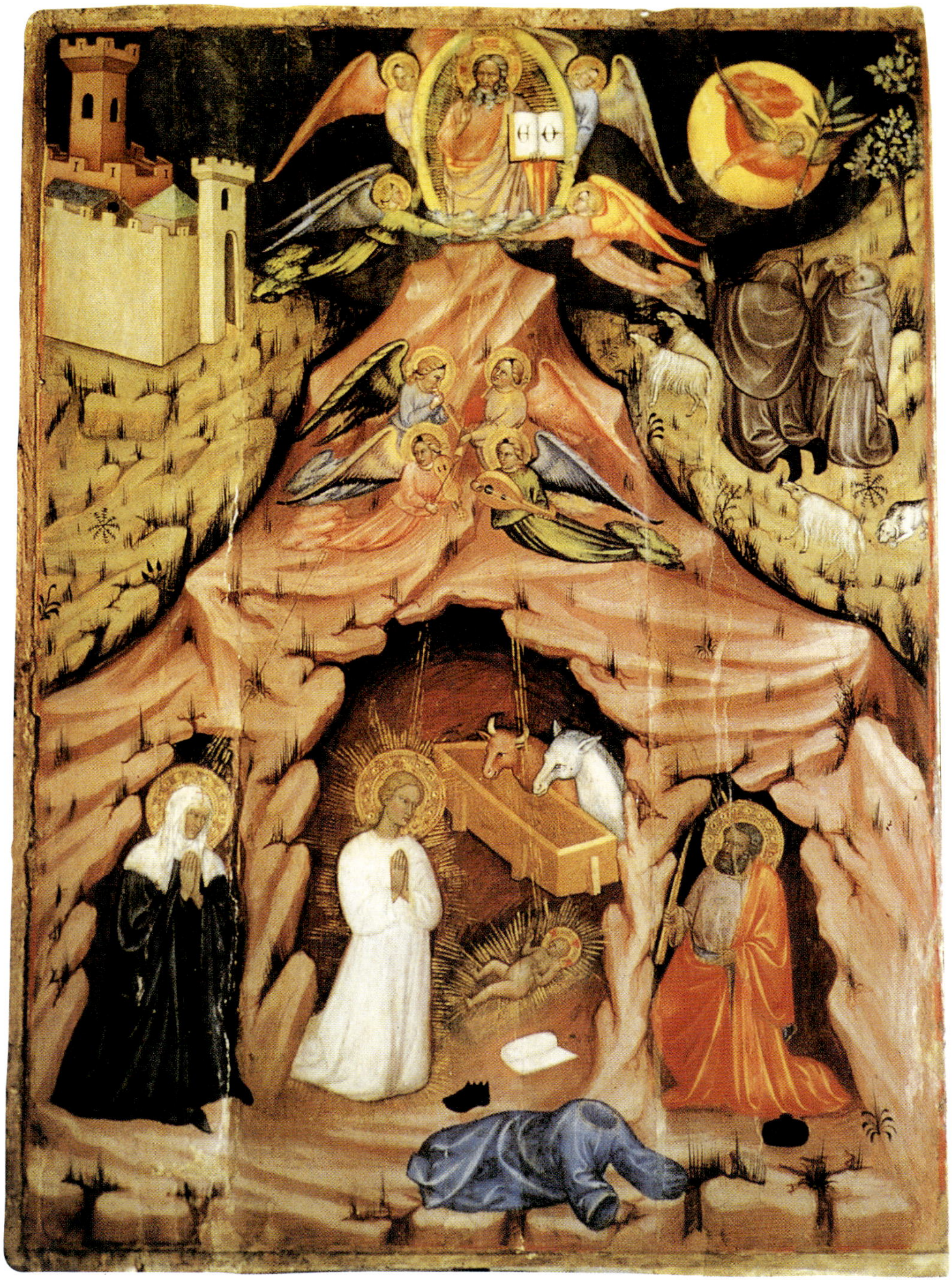

Vision of St. Bridget.
Pisan School, 14th cent., in the Museo Nazionale di San Matteo, Pisa.
The visions of the life of Jesus that St. Bridget recorded in her *Revelations* had a great influence on subsequent iconography.

Bridget of Sweden, Foundress of the Order of the Holy Redeemer, Patron of Europe

1303–1373
Memorial: July 23
Lat.: Birgitta Suedica, Vidua; It.: Brigida di Svezia; Fr.: Brigitte; Ger.: Birgitta von Schweden; Swed.: Birgitta.

This great mystic and foundress was born in 1302 near Uppsala, into an aristocratic family whose line gave Sweden many of its kings and which promoted the ideals of chivalry. At her baptism she was named after the holy Irish nun. At the age of seven she had her first vision of the Virgin, who placed a crown on her head; at the age of ten Jesus crucified appeared to her. Her early youth was marked by miracles: a riding whip with which an aunt sought to punish her unjustly broke into countless pieces; the Virgin helped her with a difficult piece of embroidery; the devil appeared to her as a hundred-footed monster she escaped by calling on the crucified Jesus.

At the age of fourteen she married eighteen-year-old Ulf Gudmarson, a good and devout young man, whom she herself then instructed and led to greater faith and to good works. She lived with him in complete chastity for two years and then in an exemplary Christian conjugal life. Together they went on pilgrimage to Santiago de Compostela, practiced fasting and abstinence, and did works of piety. She had eight children. She was then summoned to the court to educate and help the new young rulers of Sweden, on whom she had a beneficent influence.

Pilgrimages characterized her life. With her husband she went on pilgrimage in 1339 to the relics of King Olaf II, patron of Norway, at Nidaros (now Trondheim) and of King Erik, patron of Scandinavia. They went on pilgrimage to Santiago de Compostela, a journey that left its mark on their lives. When they returned, the couple decided to retire to a monastery, and Ulf immediately entered the monastery of Alvastra, where he died in 1344, nursed by his wife. For two years Bridget lived in a building near the monastery. It was here that the period of the great visions began. She came to grips with these with the help of her spiritual director, Master Matthias, her confessor, Petrus Olavi, and Petrus, a Cistercian, to whom she dictated her visions and who translated them into Latin as the *Revelationes sanctae Birgittae,* a work that notably influenced her iconography.

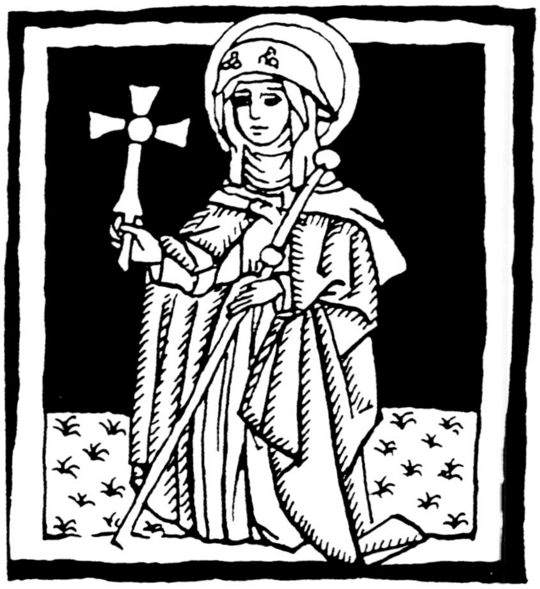
St. Bridget as a Pilgrim.
15th-cent. devotional image engraved on wood.

Bridget then devoted her efforts to the founding of a new order, which was distinguished by having monasteries of men and of women. She received in a vision the *Rule* of the new order, which was named "of the Holy Redeemer." The rulers of Sweden gave her the royal castle of Vadstena on Lake Vättern. The new order was devoted to veneration of the Passion; the emblem of the Brigettines, both men and women, was **five red flames resembling drops of blood**. These recalled the five wounds of Christ and were worn by the women on their head covering, by the men on their robe.

Bridget went to Rome in 1349 for the Jubilee and remained there permanently. At that point a new phase of her life began, one devoted to study, prayer, and the Scriptures. She aided pilgrims, experienced need and even begged alms, but she was sustained by her visions. Among these: in what is today the chapel of the Most Blessed Sacrament in the basilica of St. Paul's Outside the Walls there is a wooden crucifix, attributed to Cavallini, which spoke to Bridget, who often went there to pray. Today we see the saint depicted in a statue (by S. Maderno, 1576–1636) in which she faces the crucifix. Prophetic gifts guided her in admonishing and rebuking sinners and exhorting the popes residing in Avignon to return to Rome. She visited the major sanctuaries as a pilgrim. In 1370 she obtained approval of her order.

One of her practices of devotion left its mark in her iconography: every Friday, as a penance, she let a hot drop of wax from a **candle** fall on her hand, and reopened the wound it made if it healed over in less than seven days. Together with her daughter, she went on pilgrimage to the Holy Land in 1372 and again had numerous visions as she visited the holy places. After her return, she died in Rome on July 23, 1373, in her house near the Campo dei Fiori, having prophecied the return of the pope to Rome.

▷▷ Bridget is a patron of Europe and of pilgrims. Her role as patron of Sweden was confirmed by Leo XIII on October 1, 1891, and by Pius XI on March 10, 1926.

Because she knew in advance the day and hour of her death, she is invoked for the same favor by others.

▷▷ She is depicted in two ways. In the **dress of an abbess**, with a **pastoral staff**; she can be recognized by the **typical headdress of the Brigettines** in which two bands form a cross over the head, the arms being connected by a circular strip on which are five flames, one at the center and four around the edge, which recall the wounds of Christ. Or she is depicted in the **garb of a pilgrim**, with a **staff**, **a knapsack adorned with the keys of Rome and the palms of Jerusalem**, and a **broad-brimmed hat**. Other attributes are a **flaming heart with the red cross of Jerusalem**, a **cross**, the **crown** that signifies her rank, the **book** and **ink-stand** that recall her writings, the **monastic veil**, and, more rarely, a **shield with the lion of Sweden** on it.

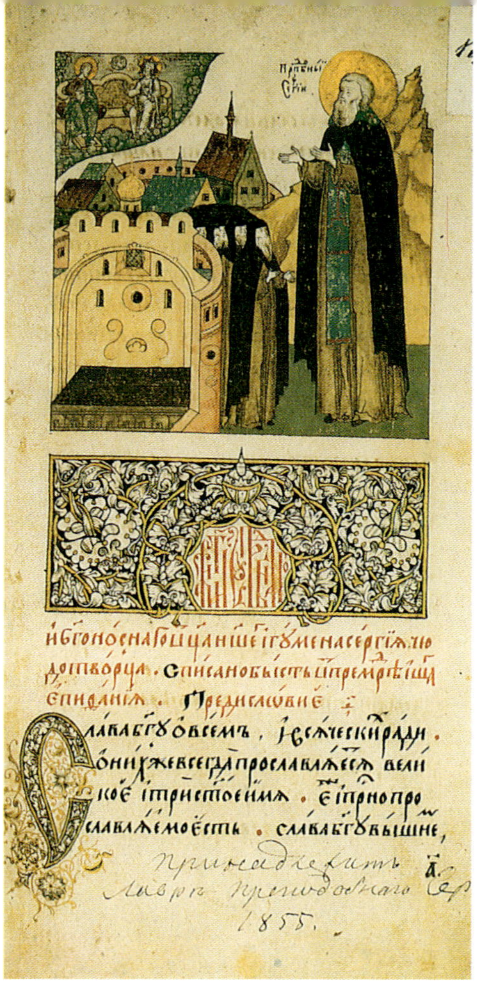

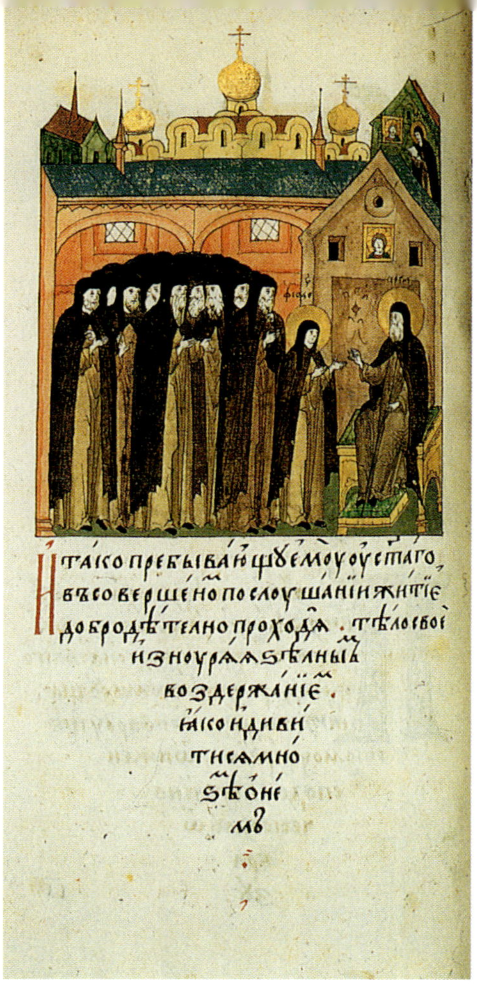

St. Sergius of Radonezh.
Miniature, end of 16th cent., from the codex *Life of St. Sergius of Radonezh,* fol. 230, in the Russian State Library, Moscow.

St. Sergius and His Brother Monks.
Ibid., fol. 75v.
Observe in the background of both scenes the buildings of the laura he founded.

Sergius of Radonezh, Hermit

1314–1392
Memorial: September 25
Lat.: Sergius de Radonez; It.: Sergio; Fr.: Serge; Ger.: Sergios von Radonesch; Russ.: Sergiei Radonejski.

This gentle man, adviser of princes and consoler of peoples, reformer of Russian monastic life, was born into a noble family in the area of Rostov. He was baptized Bartholomew and from his youth showed an inclination to the contemplative life.

When his family lost its estates, it moved to the village of Radonezh in the area of Moscow. When Sergius was twenty, his parents became monks, while he and his older brother, Stephen, entered a monastery and settled where now stands the laura named after him. The two brothers together built a little church dedicated to the Trinity, but Stephen could not tolerate the life of a hermit and went to a monastery in Moscow.

In 1337 Bartholomew took the **monastic habit** and the name Sergius and spent two years in complete solitude, his only companion being a domesticated bear. But then others came in order to imitate his life, and a community of twelve monks came into being. Their first higumen (abbot) was Metrophanes; when he died, Sergius replaced him. Other people came to live around the monastery and formed an inhabited area: the city of Sergiev, today Zagorsk. Donations and possessions came in and the monastery became a *scriptorium*. In addition, Sergius' brother Stephen returned, but then disagreements arose and Sergius left to found a second monastery, that of the Annunciation. When the monks of the Trinity begged him, he returned there.

Sergius was the founder of some ten monasteries, at the head of which he placed his disciples. For this reason he is regarded as the father of Russian monasticism. He died on September 25, 1392, and was canonized in 1448.

▷▷ He is a secondary patron of Russia.

▷▷ His principal attribute is a **bear** and, sometimes, the **laura he founded**.

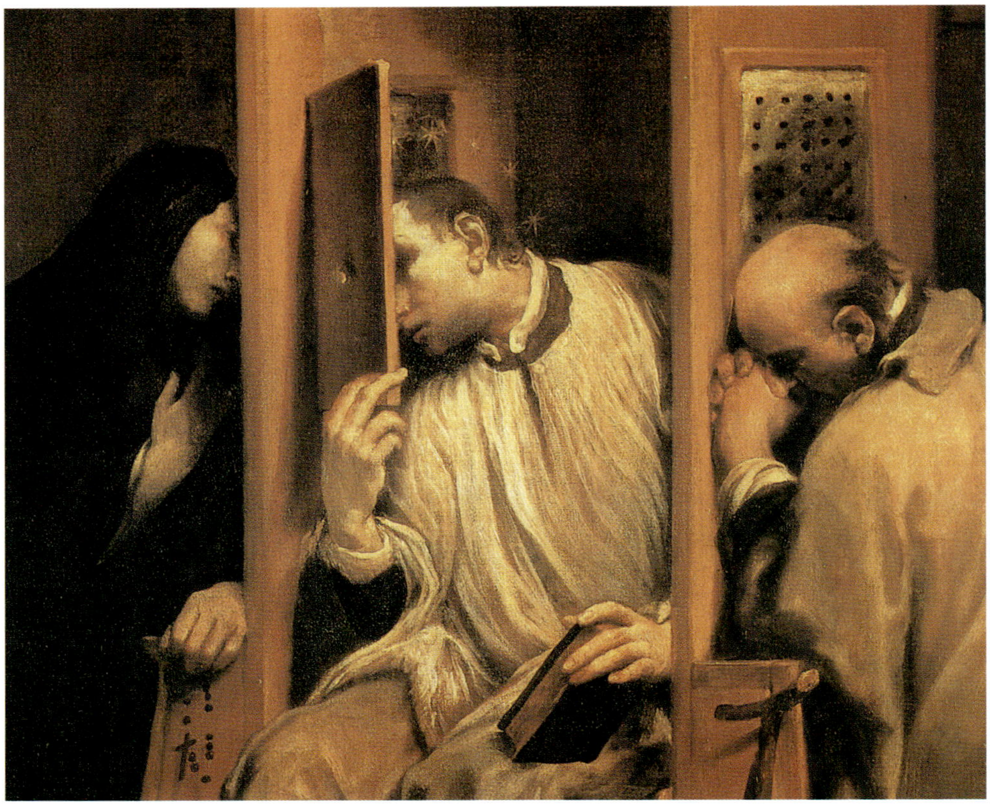

St. John Nepomuk in the Confessional.
By Giuseppe Maria Crespi (1665–1747), in the Galleria Sabauda, Turin.

St. John Nepomuk.
18th-cent. processional statue, Opele, Poland.

John Nepomuk, Priest and Martyr

1340/50–1393
Memorial: March 20
Lat.: Joannes Nepomucenus Pragensis, martyr Pragae; It.: Giovanni Nepomuceno; Fr.: Jean Népomucène de Prague; Sp.: Juan Nepomuceno; Ger.: Johann von Nepomuk; Czech.: Jan Nepomucky.

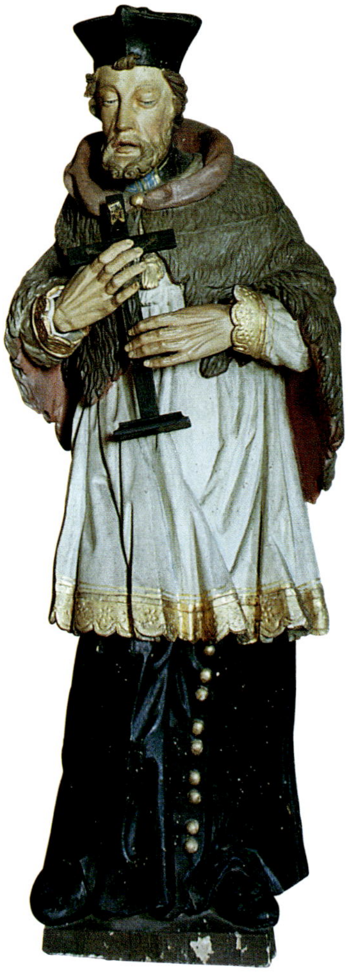

John was probably the son of the mayor of Pomuk (now Nepomuk) in Bohemia. He followed a usual career that saw him become a cleric and notary in Prague, a priest in 1380, pastor of St. Gall parish in Prague, and notary of the archbishop. He went to Padua to pursue his studies; there he was elected rector of the students "from beyond the mountains." On completing his studies, he returned to Prague where he became a Canon Regular of St. Augustine at the cathedral of St. Guy, archdeacon, and, finally, vicar general of Bishop Jenstejn in 1389. These years were marked by attempts of King Wenceslas IV, whose wife was John's penitent, to gain control in various ways of the possessions of the Church of Bohemia. As the struggle against the clergy grew bitter, the bishop admonished the king publicly. The latter then tried to arrest Jenstejn and his followers; the bishop fled, but John and others were imprisoned, then interrogated and tortured by the king himself. Then, while the other priests were set free, John was taken out at night and thrown into the river Moldau from the Charles Bridge.

A **crown of stars** marked the spot where the body came to rest, and it was finally buried in the cathedral. Four months after the priest's death, the bishop denounced his murderer to Pope Boniface IX, calling John a "holy martyr." The saint's miracles were described in a life written by the bishop's confessor. According to this life, John's death was due less to opposition between the king and the Church of Bohemia than to the fact that the saint refused to tell the king, who was suspicious of his wife, what she had said in confession.

John's cult immediately spread and was approved in 1720. During an investigation in 1725, the saint's **tongue** was found to be dried out and dark in color, but within three-quarters of an hour it regained its shape and became reddish in color; it is now preserved in a reliquary in the treasury of the cathedral of Prague. Benedict XIII canonized him in 1729 as a martyr for the seal of confession.

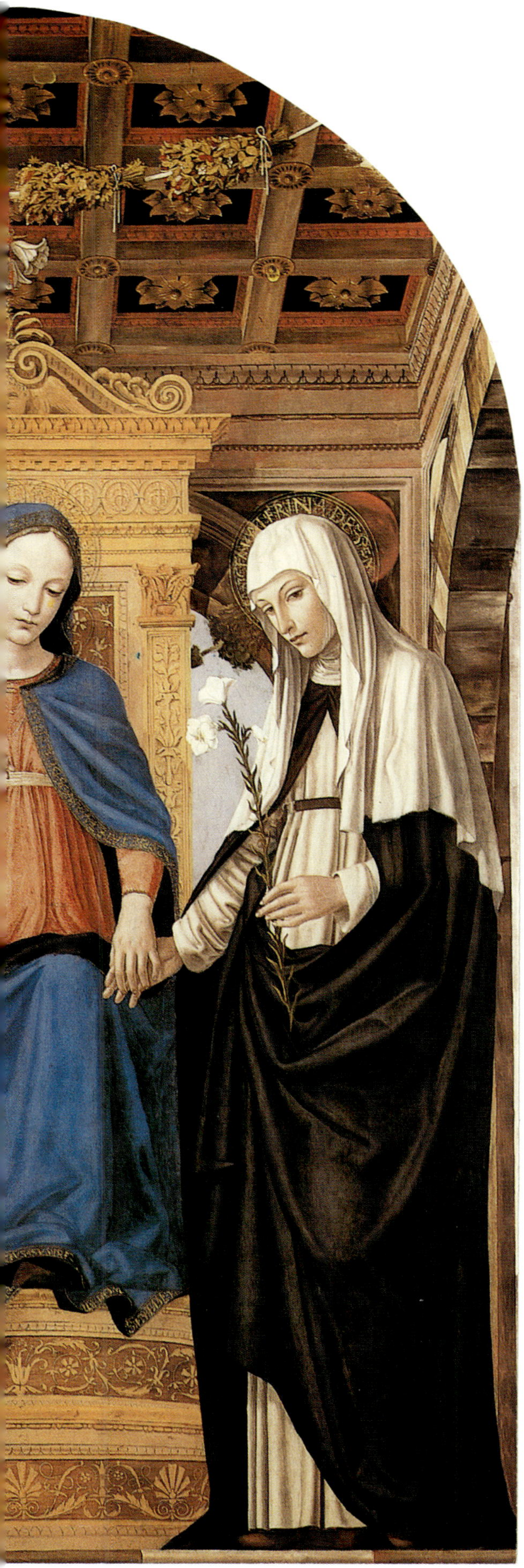

St. Catherine of Siena.
Detail from *The Madonna Enthroned between St. Catherine of Alexandria and St. Catherine of Siena,* by Anbrogio da Fossano, known as Il Bergognone (d. 1522), in the National Gallery, London.

▷▷ John is a patron of Bohemia, Prague, France, and Lorraine, as well as of confessors and canons. Pius X proclaimed him patron of Slovakia on March 28, 1914.

His statue is often found on bridges where it recalls his martyrdom. Consequently, he is protector of bridges, boatmen, and sailors; he is invoked against dangers in rivers. John died by drowning and therefore is invoked against drowning and floods, and, in contrast, in order to obtain rain. His tongue, which remained uncorrupted, appears glorified on pulpits, urging respect for the secrecy of the confessional. He is therefore invoked against abscesses and tumors of the tongue, and also against pestilences; furthermore, he is invoked in order to gain and preserve a good reputation.

▷▷ In Central Europe he is depicted in countless images on bridges and in town squares, as well as on pulpits: in the **habit of a canon**, with a **biretta** and **mozetta** or hooded cape. His principal attributes are a **halo of stars**, alluding to the stars that made known the location of his body, and a **crucifix**, which he contemplates.

Another kind of iconography shows John with a **finger on his lips** and the motto *Tacui* ("I remained silent"). Another attribute is a **water lily**, a reminder that he died of drowning.

Catherine of Siena, Virgin and Doctor of the Church

1347–1380
Feast: April 29
Lat.: Catharina Senensis; It.: Caterina da Siena; Fr.: Catherine de Sienne; Sp.: Catalina de Siena; Port.: Catarina de Sena; Ger.: Katharina von Siena.

Catherine's desire was to know God and be like Jesus. She worked for peace, for the return of the pope from Avignon to Rome, and for the unity of the Church. Tradition has it that she was born on March 25 to Jacopo Benincase, a dyer of skins, and Lapa Piagenti. She was their twenty-fourth child and was born with a twin, Giovanna, who died at birth. The saint was called "Euphrosyne" because of her good disposition, and she early showed a bent toward religious life. At the age of twelve she had her first vision: of Christ in pontifical robes and hovering in the air over the basilica of St. Dominic. In order to convince her family of her irrevocable decision, Catherine cut her hair, an unmistakable gesture at that time, and shut herself up in her room in order to devote herself to Christ. The family, however, obliged her to do wearying and menial tasks in order to keep her from recollection and penances. Catherine built herself a spiritual cell instead of a material, something she later advised her disciples to do.

When her father saw a **dove** come to rest on Catherine's head as she was praying, the family ceased its opposition. In 1363 Catherine was allowed to ask for acceptance into the Third Order of St. Dominic, among the Mantellate ("cloaked"), so-called because they wore a long black cloak over a white dress. She was accepted as a postulant. She was diligent in attending the church of St. Dominic, the Della Scala hospital, and the leprosarium of St. Lazarus; three times a day she disciplined her to the point of blood. Her ascetical life was accompanied by visions and ecstasies, but she was not without envious slanderers. She led a hidden life until, during the pontificate of Urban V (1362–1370), which interrupted the Avignon Captivity of the popes, she received, in a vision, an order from Jesus to give herself to the apostolate. She devoted herself to the care of the plague-stricken in 1374; in 1375, in order to support Pope Gregory XI in his effort to inspire a crusade against the Turks, she went to Pisa. There, on April 1, she received the **stigmata** while praying before the **crucifix** of Giunta Pisano in the church of St. Catherine on the Lungarno. On June 20, she assisted a young man unjustly condemned to death, an episode she describes in one of her most beautiful

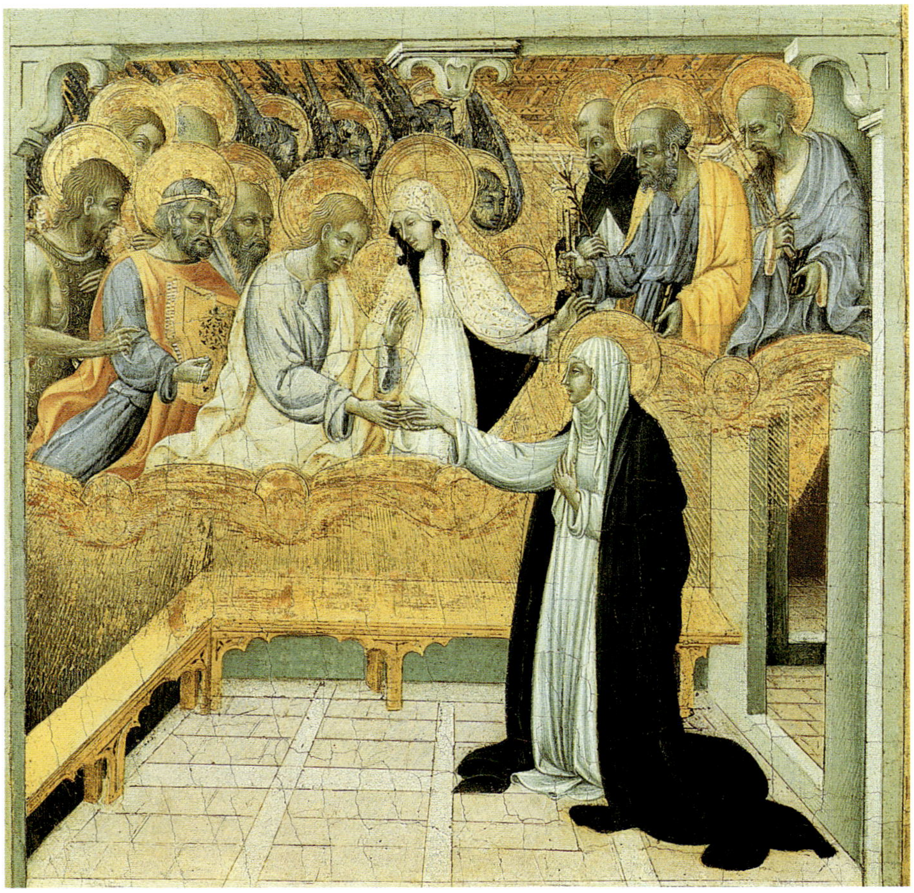

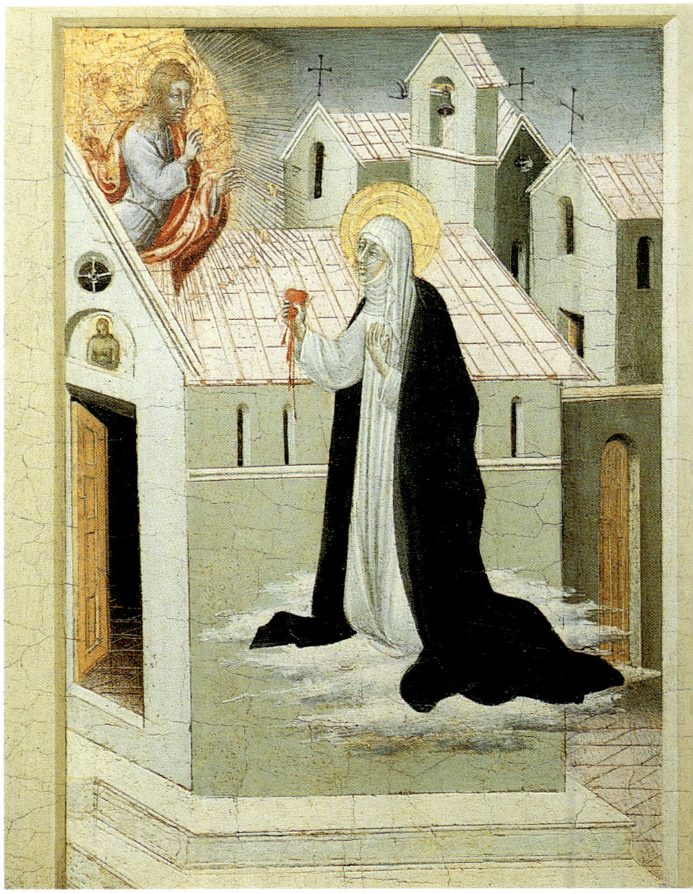

letters. She interceded with the Pope in Avignon in order to advance peace with Florence; she also obtained not only privileges for her own religious family but, above all, the Pope's return to Rome. She chose not to be present for this but returned to Siena. She devoted herself to bringing peace to souls and gave impetus to the reform of the Dominican Order. She died on April 29, 1380, surrounded by her disciples and in her own house in Siena.

She left several works taken down by secretaries: an extensive *Epistolary,* a *Dialogue on Divine Providence,* and *Prayers.*

▷▷ On September 27, 1970, Paul VI declared Catherine a Doctor of the Church. Because of her care for those condemned to death, she is a protector of the dying and is invoked for a happy death. Because she tended the plague-stricken, she is invoked against pestilence and also headaches. Because of her connection with the work done by her family, she is protector of washerwomen.

She is a patron of Siena and of Rome, but in addition she was proclaimed patron of Italy by Pius XII on June 18, 1939, and patron of Europe by John Paul II in 1999.

▷▷ Catherine's iconography is a very rich one: it displays her (often idealized) portrait, the episodes of her life, and the miracles she worked after her death. We also find the motif of the **mystical marriage**, as also in the case of the earlier Catherine of Alexandria.

Her principal attributes are the **white habit and black cloak** of the Dominican Order, a **lily** for purity, and a **book**, alluding to her writings. Other attributes are a **crucifix**, a **heart**, a **crown of thorns**, the **stigmata**, and the **dove** over her head.

Mystical Marriage of St. Catherine.
By Giovanni di Paolo, 1395/1400–1482, in a private collection, New York.

Christ and St. Catherine Exchange Hearts.
By Giovanni di Paolo, ibid.

Vincent Ferrer, Dominican Priest

1350–1419
Memorial: April 5
Lat.: Vincentius Ferrerius; It.: Vincenzo Ferrer, Ferreri, Ferrero; Fr.: Vincent Ferrier de Valence ou de Vannes; Sp.: Vicente Ferrer; Ger.: Vincenz Ferrer, Vincentius Ferrerius.

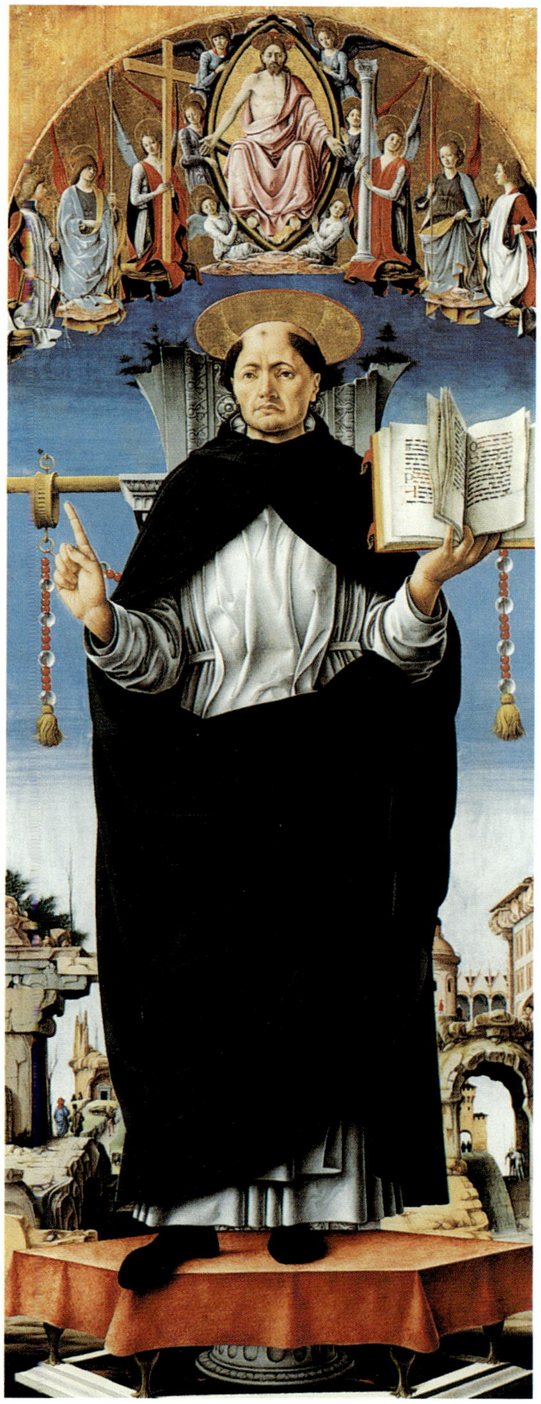

St. Vincent Ferrer.
By Francesco del Cossa, 1436–1478, in the National Gallery, London.

This great preacher and wonderworker was called "the greatest preacher of the divine word after the apostles" *(maximus post apostolos Divini Verbi praeco)* because of his eloquence, which became known throughout Europe. He was born in Valencia and died in Brittany. As a Dominican, the change that occurred in his life was due to a vision he had in 1398: when he was ill, Jesus appeared to him along with St. Dominic and St. Francis, healed him, and entrusted him with the task of evangelizing the world. He began his mission by becoming an itinerant apostle, stirred enthusiasm wherever he went, and worked miracles. Many persons followed him, and he gave them a white and black habit and a rule of life. He traveled through France, Spain, Italy, and perhaps England. At Constance, in 1415, he was coming to the end of his life but recovered in the space of a few moments and, as he had predicted, continued to preach and call for the unity of the Church, which at the time was divided by schism. The miracles that accompanied his preaching continued after his death; he was canonized by Pius II in 1458.

As a result of his preaching, which stirred hearers to the imitation of Christ, the model of all holiness, and of his miracles, his cult spread everywhere. The Dominican Ritual still contains the formulas of the blessings he gave.

▷▷ Many aspects of his cult are connected with the fields and with a particular episode: when a poor woman asked him for an alms and he had nothing but the straw hat that protected him from the broiling sun, he gave it to her, and the woman thenceforth found it to be always full of flour. From straw to fields and their needs is any easy step.

▷▷ Vincent is a patron of Valencia and of Vannes. He is protector of makers of bricks and tiles and therefore of roofs and those who construct them. He protects straw-hat makers. In Brittany he protects horses. He is patron of preachers. He is also invoked as protector of fields and vineyards and therefore of innkeepers. Because he is patron of fields, which must be safeguarded against lightning, and because he was inspired by the Holy Spirit, as is shown by a **tongue of flame over his head**, he is invoked against lightning strikes, earthquakes, and drought, and also against epilepsy and headache. Water is blessed in his honor.

▷▷ Vincent is depicted as a **adult, tonsured, in a Dominican habit** and with a **flame over his head**, a flame that recalls his fiery and inspired preaching and is his principal attribute. He is shown in the act of preaching: holding a **crucifix** in his left hand and with his **right hand held aloft** in the gesture of a preacher.

▷▷ Other attributes are connected with his preaching on the final judgment: **lightning in the background** and the **trumpets of the Judgment**, as well as a **banner** with the inscription: "Fear God and give him honor, for the hour of his judgment is coming." Sometimes a **baptismal font** is a reminder that he converted and baptized many Spanish Jews.

Bernardino of Siena, Priest of the Friars Minor

1380–1444
Memorial: May 20
Lat.: Bernardinus Senensis, de Senis; It.: Bernardino da Siena; Fr.: Bernardin; Sp.: Bernardino de Sena; Ger.: Bernardinus von Siena, Bernhardin.

This great Franciscan preacher evangelized Italy by spreading love of the name of Jesus. He was born in Massa Marittima, where he was soon orphaned and raised by his father's brother and sister in Siena. There, after finishing his literary and juridical studies, he devoted himself to the study of Sacred Scripture and theology. He obtained a licentiate in canon law and founded the Compagna dei Disciplinati "Beatae Mariae," whose aim was to reach perfection by helping the needy.

The illness of a relative and the help he gave her caused him to think of becoming a monk. In 1402 he entered the convent of St. Francis in Siena, made his novitiate on Mount Amiata, and at its end distributed his possessions to the poor. In 1403 he made his solemn profession, and in 1404 celebrated Mass and preached for the first time. He then withdrew to the hills of Capriola where he built a small convent for Friars of the Observance. There, from 1405 to 1417, he devoted himself to the study of the great Doctors of the Church, theologians, ascetics, and mystics, especially those of the Franciscan Order.

In 1417 he became vicar for Tuscany and began an outstanding preaching career; his voice, initially hoarse and weak due to an illness, became unexpectedly clear and musical. He traveled throughout Italy, composing hymns, establishing peace between factions, and stirring up vocations, and this in language that was precise but simple and often even colorful. To all he offered a single emblem: the graphic symbol for the name of Jesus, the **IHS** inscribed in a radiant sun. The symbol lent itself to varying interpretations. *IHS* or *JHS* is an acrostic for *Jesus Hominum Salvator* ("Jesus Savior of Humanity"). It can also be read as the first three letters of the name of Jesus in Greek (*H* is the capital form of long *ê*). It can also be taken as an acrostic for the Constantinian motto, *In Hoc Signo [vinces];* or even of the German *Jesus Heiland Seligmacher* ("Jesus Redeemer who renders blessed").

Bernardino himself planned the emblem and gave each part of it a meaning. The surrounding sun clearly alludes to Christ, who gives life as the sun does; the rays suggest the radiation of charity. The warmth of the sun is spread by its twelve twisting rays, which recall the twelve apostles and the twelve articles of the Creed. The mystical meaning of the twisting rays was expressed in a litany: 1. Refuge of penitents; 2. Banner of fighters; 3. Healer of the sick; 4. Strengthener of those who suffer; 5. Honor of believers; 6. Joy of preachers; 7. Merit of doers; 8. Help of the defective; 9. Inspirer of meditators; 10. Support of those who pray; 11. Delight of those who contemplate; 12. Glory of the triumphant. The eight lesser, straight rays represent the eight beatitudes. The band surrounding the sun represents the happiness of the blessed, which has no end. The heavens in the background are a symbol of faith, the gold a symbol of love. St. Bernardino also extended the left-hand upright of the *H* and added a cross-piece to form a cross. In some instances, the cross rises from the crossbar of the *H*.

This emblem is often found along with the emblem of Maria, that is, the letters *M, R, A* intertwined, the three letters being an acrostic of *Ave Maria* or *Maria Regina Angelorum* or *Ave Maria Regina*. This addition was not insignificant, since Bernardino was one of the most ardent supporters of the thesis of the universal mediation of Mary.

At the end of his sermons he had people kiss the trigram, which he presented to them on a small tablet.

The saint had to submit to as many as three trials, but from each his orthodoxy emerged as crystal clear. He also took a position on St. Joseph, defending the thesis that Joseph was already risen from the dead. He spoke on the fundamental principles of economics as maintained in Scholasticism; that is, the instrumental and social nature of wealth, and moderation in the acquisition of possessions, thereby giving an ethico-moral assessment of trade.

As a result of his preaching, the trigram spread everywhere and was used in devotion both private and public; Pope Eugene IV approved the public devotion in 1432.

In 1438 Bernardino became minister general of the Franciscan Order and devoted himself to renewing the spirit of the Franciscan *Rule;* his main concern was the formation of the friars, and to this end he provided courses in theology and law (he also forbade illiterate and ignorant friars to hear confessions). The liveliness of his excellent, clear sermons made him everywhere hailed and loved, for in them the hearers recognized their own world and their problems as Bernardino gave instructions for daily life on various subjects, including greed and usury. In his treatises he explained the dogmatic and moral truths of Christianity, gave methods for the spiritual and ascetical life, and made known the persons of Mary and Joseph.

Bernardino died at Aquila where, in the presence of his body which was shedding blood copiously, quarrels among the citizens were settled. He was canonized in 1450; his relics are now in the church dedicated to him in Aquila, a church designed by St. James of the March, one of his disciples.

▷▷ The saint is patron of Siena, of his native Massa Marittima, of Perugia, and of Aquila, which still preserves his relics. A city in California is named after him.

He is patron of preachers and of advertisers, because of the brilliant unity of the emblem he created; because he fed the spiritual flocks he became patron of wool-merchants (whose

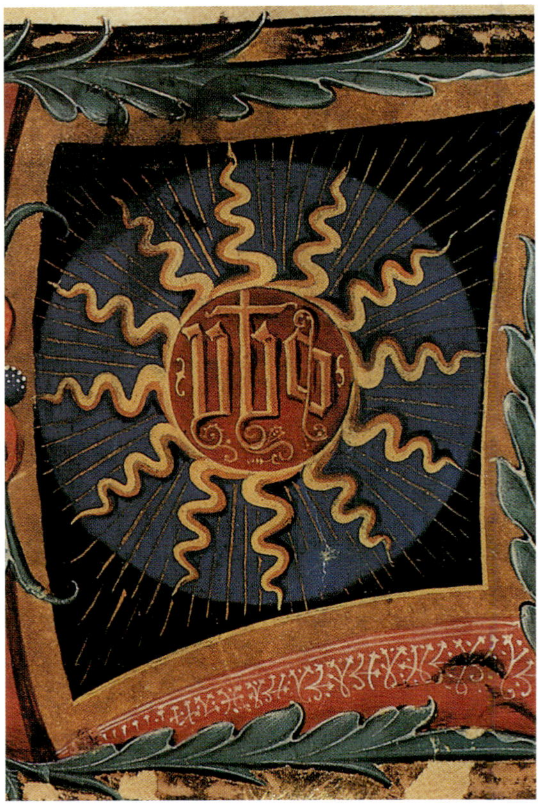

The Bernardine Monogram.
17th-cent. miniature in the museum of the Studium Biblicum Franciscanum in Jerusalem.

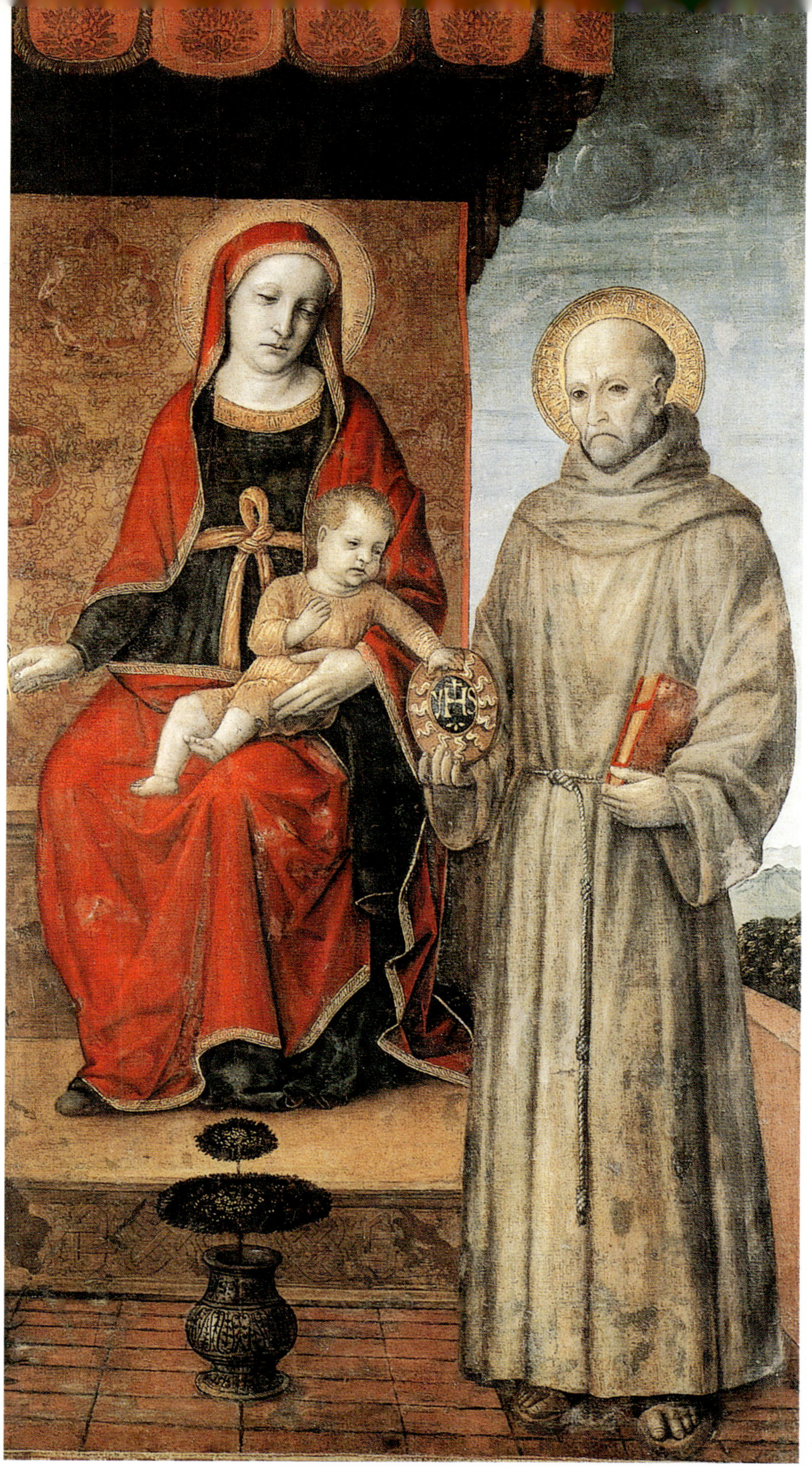

Madonna and Child with St. Bernardino of Siena. Detail from the reverse side of the Banner of the Orzinuovi, by Vincenzo Foppa, ca. 1514, in the Tosio Martinengo Gallery, Brescia.

guild flourished in Siena) and therefore of weavers. He was patron of pugilists because of his combative attitude.

▷▷ He is invoked against hemorrhages, hoarseness, tuberculosis, and all pulmonary diseases, because he himself at one time was hoarse from continual preaching.

▷▷ Bernardino is depicted in a **Franciscan habit**, **his face ascetical and hollow-cheeked**, one reason being that he had lost all his teeth, and accompanied by the indispensable **trigram**, which sums up his preaching and is his principal attribute. Other attributes are **three pastoral staffs** or three miters lying at his feet, because he had thrice refused the episcopate (of Siena, Ferrara, and Urbino); the **dove of the Holy Spirit** next to his ear and inspiring him; and the **city of Siena**, either in the background or as a model in his hand.

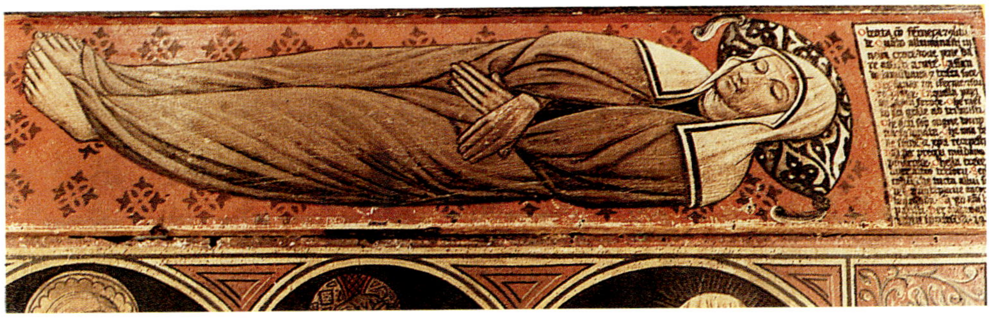

St. Rita of Cascia.
Cover of the saint's first coffin, 15th cent., in the sanctuary of St. Rita, Cascia.

Rita of Cascia, Religious

1378–1447
Memorial: May 22
It.: Rita da Cascia; Fr.: Rite de Cascia; Sp.: Rita de Casia.

Rita patiently put up with a violent husband; she mourned his death and that of her children. When widowed, she became a nun and, in all things, an example of patiently offering up everything to the crucified Christ.

Rita, whose name was an abbreviation of Margarita, was born at Roccaporena, a hamlet on the side of a dark hill, seven kilometers from Cascia. Tradition reports some unusual stories about her. When, as a very little child, her parents took her with them into the fields, a **swarm of white bees** was seen to go in and out of her mouth (bees symbolize zeal for the house of God). A peasant who raised his arm to scatter them was suddenly healed of a wound in his wrist due to reaping. Still very young, she obeyed her parents and agreed to marry a violent man by whom she had two children. She succeeded in making him calmer, but he had many enemies and these killed him in a vendetta. The children, filled with hatred, then tried to continue the vendetta. When Rita could not change their minds, she asked God that they might die before becoming murderers; the young men did die.

Rita then betook herself to the convent of the Augustinian nuns of Cascia, in order to pursue at last what had always been her true calling; she was not accepted, however, because the nuns feared becoming involved in a feud. She then prayed to St. Augustine, St. John the Baptist, and St. Nicholas of Tolentine, who took her in a miraculous manner to the monastery, where the nuns found her; they then accepted her. A less wondrous version has it that she was accepted when her relatives pardoned her husband's killers.

Her life was marked by miracles. Her desire to be identified with Christ was satisfied in 1432 by means of a **thorn from the crown of Jesus**, which stuck in her **forehead** and produced a painful and foul-smelling wound; this caused her to remain apart, but it closed up temporarily to let her travel to Rome with her sisters for the canonization of St. Nicholas of Tolentine.

One incident gave rise to the custom of distributing **blessed roses** on May 22: Rita, who was ill, asked a visitor to go and pick a rose in the courtyard of her house in Roccaporena; the woman did so and, even though it was winter, found **two roses in bloom**.

When Rita died on May 22, the bells of the surrounding villages rang by themselves. Her burial place became a goal of pilgrimages. At her death her corpse was eviscerated and filled with tow soaked in perfume; it was never buried and is preserved in the sanctuary that replaced the little church in 1947. She was canonized in 1900.

At midday on May 22, at the end of the "Fifteen Thursdays of St. Rita" (which commemorate the years in which she had the thorn in her forehead) the "Prayer to St. Rita" is recited in all the churches and before all the chapels dedicated to her.

▷▷ Rita is known as "The saint of the impossible" and is invoked in desperate cases; because of the wound in her forehead, she is invoked against smallpox and against wounds to the forehead in general. Grocers have chosen her as their patron.

▷▷ She is depicted as a **mature Augustinian nun**; her principal attributes are the **thorn in her forehead** and a **crucifix** she contemplates. Other attributes are **roses** and **bees**.

St. Rita of Cascia.
Side of the first coffin.
This is the oldest representation of the saint; it shows the thorn that wounded her in the forehead.

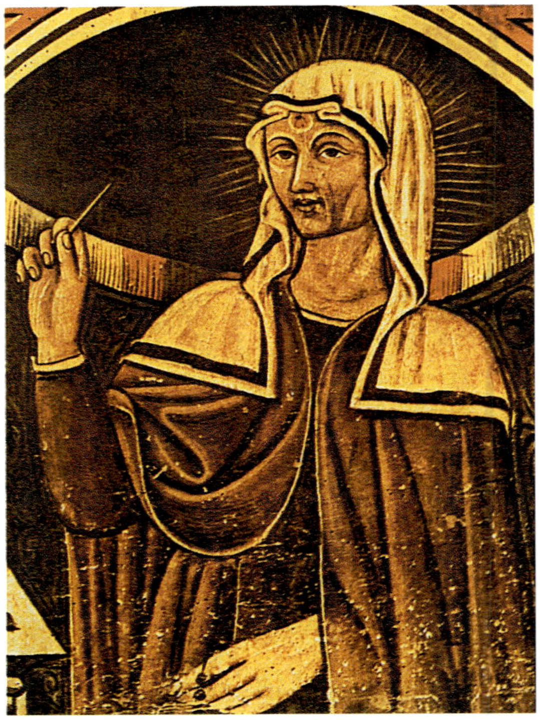

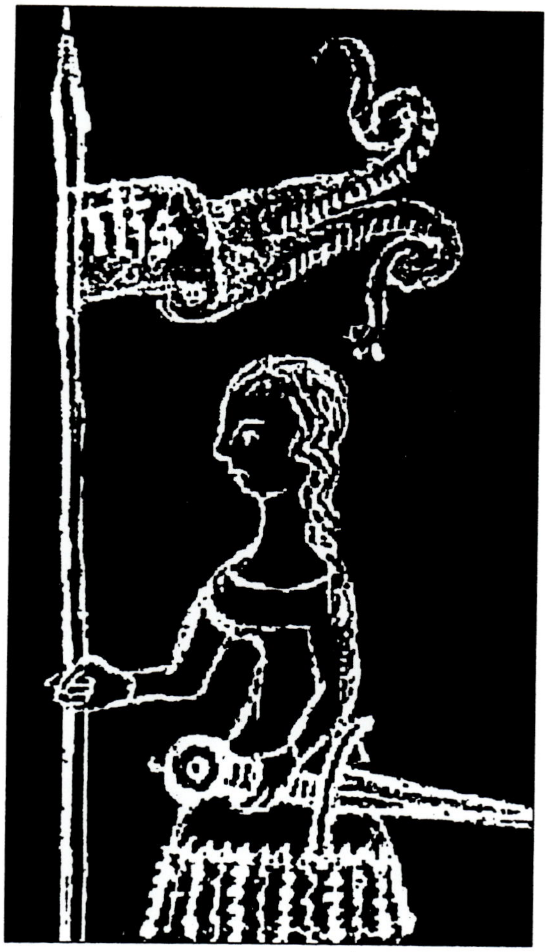

St. Joan of Arc.
Sketch made in the margin of the Register of the Parliament of Paris during a hearing in the process of nullifying the condemnation of the saint (1449–1456). This is the earliest representation of the saint.

Joan of Arc, Virgin

1412–1431
Memorial: May 30
Lat.: Johanna ab Arce, Puella Aurelinensis; It.: Giovanna d'Arco; la Pulcella, la Pulzella d'Orleans; Gianna; Fr.: Jeanne d'Arc, Joanne, Jouanne; Ger.: Johanna von Arc, die Jungfrau von Orleans, das Mädchen von Orleans.

The young girl of Orleans was inspired to fight for her country and save it, but was betrayed and handed over to her enemies, and finally burned at the stake after an unjust condemnation. When she was thirteen, Michael the Archangel, St. Catherine of Siena, and St. Margaret appeared to her and told her, "on behalf of the King of heaven," that her mission was to free France from England and to have Charles VII anointed as king. At the beginning of 1429 she managed to reach the king at Chinon, where she convinced prelates and jurists of her sincerity. She moved the king to organize an army, with which she succeeded in fighting off the siege by the English and their allies.

After defeating the English once again, she saw to it that the king was anointed on July 17, 1429, in the cathedral of Rheims, the traditional place of the anointing of the kings of France; this won the favor of the people for Joan.

Accepting bad advice, Charles VII hampered Joan, who was wounded in a clash outside Paris. In 1430 she intervened again to aid Compiègne, which was being besieged by the Burgundians, who at that time were allies of the English. During a sortie Joan was taken prisoner, moved from prison to prison, and finally, in December of 1430, was handed over to the English, who paid 10,000 pounds for her. She was tried for heresy, the intention being to do away with Charles VII's strongest supporter. The trial was a farce that ended with the condemnation of Joan as a recidivist who had again donned men's clothing. She was burned at the stake in Rouen on May 31, 1431.

The process of France's liberation from the English could not be stopped. Paris was reconquered (1436) and Charles VII ordered an inquiry into the trial and death of Joan, who in the end was solemnly rehabilitated in 1456.

Despite popular favor, Joan fell into obscurity due to the negative attitude of the Enlightenment toward the Middle Ages. She was beatified only recently in 1909 and canonized in 1920 by Benedict XV. She was tenacious of her virginity and was devoted to prayer even during battles; she carried the battle flag in order that she might not kill anyone, even an enemy. She seemed always to be listening to supernatural voices, which she heard every day. She showed that hers was a vocation to holiness in the temporal order. She ended her life with the name of Jesus on her lips.

▷▷ Pius XII declared her a patron of France on May 13, 1944, and that is the day of her feast. She is a patron of Orleans, where her feast is celebrated on the day of the city's deliverance, May 8 (1429), and of Rouen. She protects shepherds. Because of the voices she heard, she is patron of those who work in radio, and protects radio and wireless telegraph. She is invoked against fires in woodpiles.

▷▷ She is depicted principally in **armor** with **sword** and **standard**. Other images show her as a **shepherd** listening to the voices of the saints or, more rarely, at the **pyre**.

Joan on Arc on Horseback with the Royal Banner of France.
Miniature by Antonine Dufour, in *La vie des femmes célèbres* (1505), in the Musée d'Obrée, Nantes.

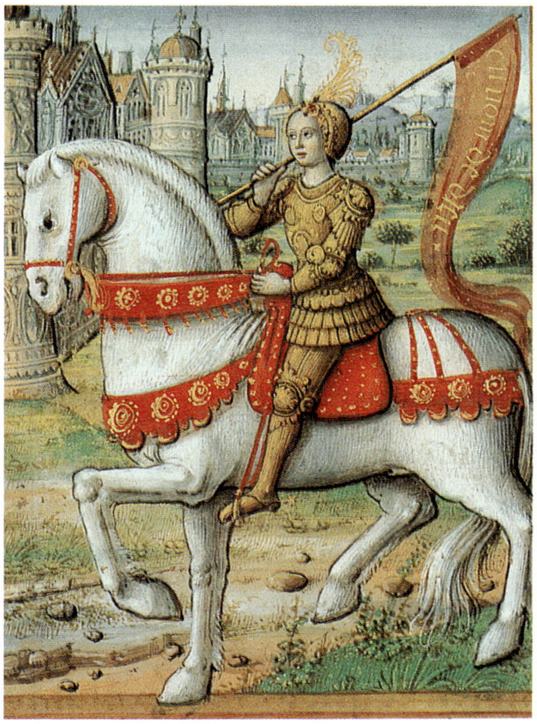

Francis of Paola, Hermit and Founder of the Order of Minims

1416–1507
Memorial: April 2
Lat.: Franciscus de Paula; It.: Francesco di Paola; Fr.: François de Paule; Sp.: Francisco de Paula; Ger.: Franziskus von Paola; Russ.: Framzisk iz Paoly.

This wonderworker, who wanted his followers to live on alms and in a perpetual Lent, was born in Paola, a small village of Calabria, where his parents lived. They had him when they were elderly, and had promised St. Francis to give the child his name. At the age of twelve, he was taken to the convent of San Marco Argentano, of the Conventual Friars Minor, in order that he might wear the habit for a year as his parents desired. Here the miracles began: he was seen to serve Mass and at the same time to appear in the refectory; the beans cooked even though the fire had gone out while he was absorbed in prayer; he went to the kitchen to obtain burning coals for the thurible and, having no other container, carried them to the church in a fold of his cassock, which did not catch fire. When the year was up, despite requests from the religious, Francis returned to his parents and with them made a pilgrimage to Assisi, Montecassino, Loreto, Monte Luco, and Rome. Here, seeing a cardinal's rich cortege passing by, he advanced to the window of the carriage and pointed out to the prelate the contrast with evangelical humility; the cardinal, Giuliano Cesarini, was not offended and made his excuses.

On returning to Paola, Francis immediately went off to live a hermit's life, just as Byzantine hermits had done nearby at one time. Prayer, fasting, contemplation, and work were his activities from 1429 to 1435. The first disciples arrived and soon numbered twelve; they became known as the Hermits of St. Francis. The archbishop of Cosenza gave his approval in 1436; cells were built and a small church, then a cloister. This was the first convent of a new mendicant religious order; Francis' father entered it after the death of his wife in 1450.

The building of new premises to accommodate new followers was accompanied by miracles: even today the area is known as "the area of miracles." Francis entered a blazing furnace without being harmed; with his staff he made a spring gush up, "the water of the spoons," for the workers; he stopped a falling rock, the "hanging rock," which even today remains extraordinarily balanced; on one occasion some hunters had cooked a **little lamb**, named Martinello, which was dear to him, but he raised it to life simply by calling it. Miracles also accompanied the building of other convents in Paterno, Spezzano, and Corigliano. Francis cured paralytics, lepers, the blind, and the possessed; he raised his sister's son to life; he worked wonders for the poor, laborers, and all the oppressed in a society in which the powerful escaped justice. He denounced the abuses of power by the mighty, called for justice for the poor, threatened with divine punishment those who abused their power, and spoke out fearlessly even to the king.

The miracles piled up, and the fame of the saint finally nettled the king, who threatened to destroy his convents on the pretext that they had been unauthorized, but the soldiers sent to look for the saint became the first witnesses of his miracles. He was called to Sicily and, when a seaman refused to ferry him over, he spread his cloak on the water and stepped on to it with his companions; they all knelt down and, making the sign of the cross, set out to sea and reached Messina. Here he raised a hanged man who had been dead three days and who then entered the order. Francis' *Rule* was definitively approved in 1474, and the order was called "Congregation of the Brother Hermits of Francis of Paola."

King Louis XI of France, who was seriously ill, called for Francis, but he refused to go until Pope Sixtus IV obliged him to do so. As the saint was passing through Naples, King Ferrante received him in the royal palace and sought to win favors from him by giving him gold coins in a richly decorated vessel. Francis refused it and, when the king insisted, he took one piece, broke it, and, when blood flowed from it, said to the king: "This is the blood of your subjects whom you oppress and who cry out for vengeance in the sight of God."

In France Francis delivered two cities from a pestilence. King Louis, who consulted him and took his advice, was not cured but he did obtain a good death after having made reparation for many abuses of power.

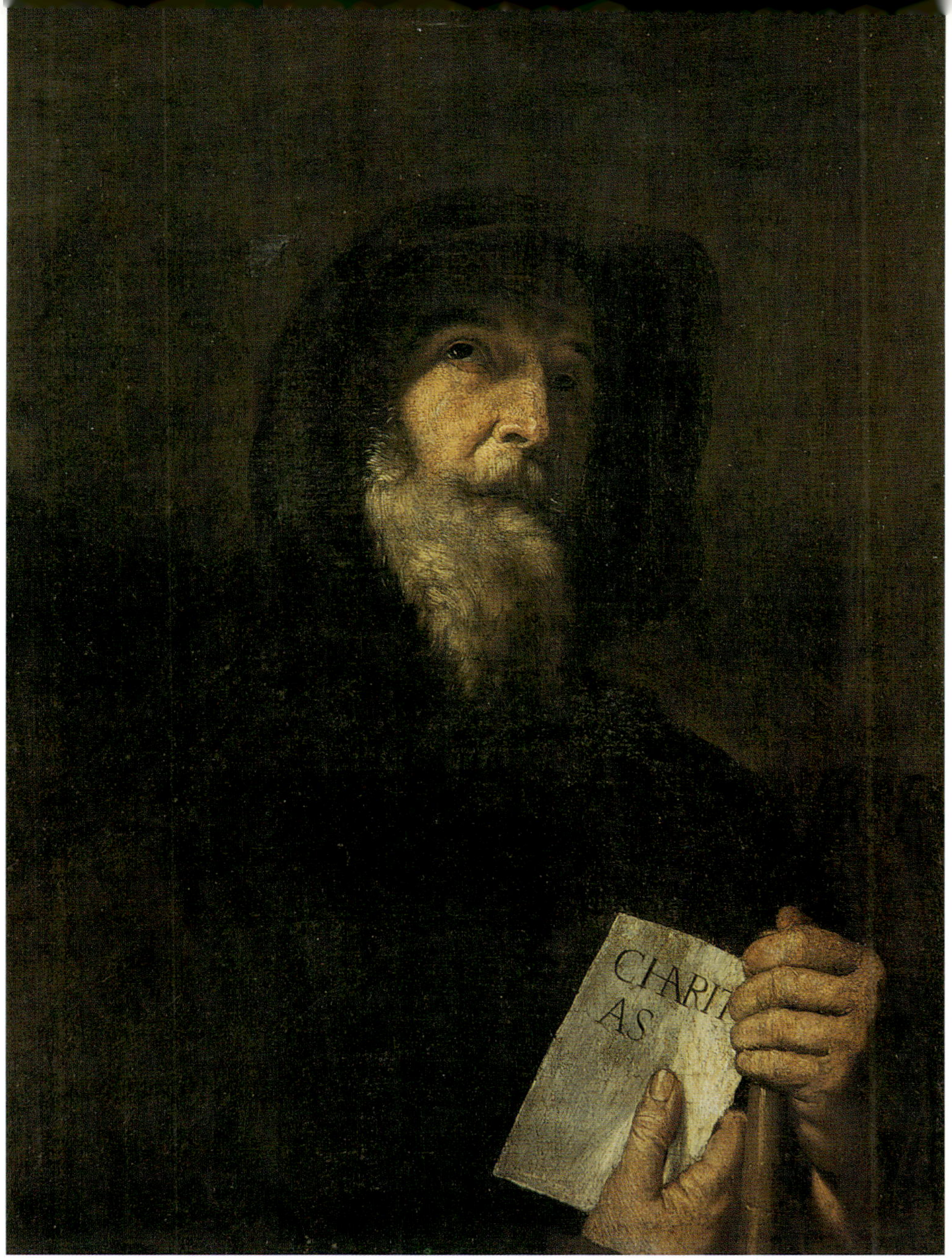

Francis asked and obtained permission for his monks to take a fourth vow, the vow of perpetual Lent, that is, to live a regime of Lenten penance every day of the year.

The saint's miracles were accompanied by a trusting abandonment to God.

The successors of Louis XI detained him in France, where he died at Plessis-les-Tours on April 2, 1507; the day was Good Friday and he died as he listened to the reading of the Passion. So many crowds came to see the saint that it was not possible to bury Francis for eleven days. Leo X canonized him in 1519.

We owe to Francis the devotion of the Thirteen Fridays of the Passion.

▷▷ Francis' cult spread everywhere, and he was venerated as a great wonderworker. He is a patron of the Calabria region, of Cosenza, Naples, and Tours, as well as of the Minims and of hermits generally, and also of mariners and missions to the people.

He is invoked against barrenness: many women obtained from him the favor of conceiving; he recommended to one of them that on every Friday of the year she recite, with her arms extended to form a cross, five Our Fathers and five Hail Marys in honor of the five wounds of Jesus. People turn to Francis to obtain eternal salvation and also to gain a good husband.

▷▷ Francis is depicted wearing a **brown habit with the hood pulled over his head**; his principal attributes are a **staff in his hand** and the word *Charitas* or, sometimes, *Humilitas* inscribed in a radiant oval. Another attribute is a **little lamb**.

St. Francis of Paola.
By Giuseppe Ribero, known as Spagnoletto, 1591–1625, in the Museo Nazionale delle Belle Arti, Valletta.

Nicholas of Flue, Hermit

1417–1487
Memorial: March 21
Lat.: Nicholas de Rupe; It.: Nicola di Flüe; Fr.: Nicolas de la Flüe; Ger.: Bruder Klaus von Flüe.

Nicholas was born in 1417 in Flüeli by steep Mount Ranft and near Sachseln in the canton of Obwalden. Inclined to contemplation from his youth, he came to know Matthias of Bolsheim, a hermit and prior of the Benedictine monastery of Engelberg; the latter told him of the Alsatian movement known as the "Friends of God" *(Gottesfreunde)*. Nicholas married, however, and had ten children.

He was appointed mayor of Sachseln and had to take part in several military campaigns; during these he did his utmost to see that conquered enemies were treated humanely and that churches, women, and children were spared.

He began to feel the call to an eremitical life more keenly, and with the consent of his wife withdrew to a spot near Ranft, an isolated crag below Flüeli. In 1468 the other peasants built him a cell and chapel there. Nicholas left his cell only to attend church and to save the peace of his country on several occasions: when threatened by Austria in 1473, when the civil war was going on in Switzerland in 1481, and when in 1482 the Swiss Confederation declared war on the city of Constance. The lasting peace he won on this last occasion gained him the title "Father of His Country" *(Pater Patriae)*.

During the nineteen years he lived in his cell Nicholas took no food and lived on the Eucharist alone; because of his reputation as a "living saint" the lowly and the mighty alike sought him out for strength and advice. After his death miracles multiplied and were recorded in the register of the local church in 1488. He was beatified in 1669.

▷▷ Later periods of political disorder hindered a quick canonization. In fact, he was canonized only on May 15, 1947; in that same year, on June 3, Pius XII confirmed his status as patron of Switzerland.

▷▷ He is depicted as a **hermit, barefooted**, with a **crutch**, a **rosary**, and a **cross**.

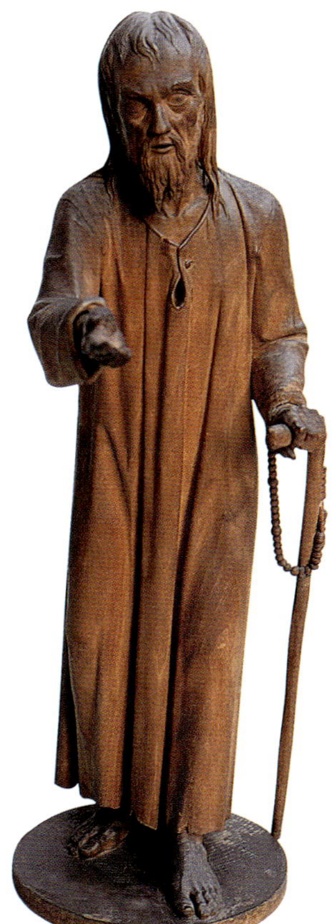

Nicholas of Flue.
Wooden statue by an anonymous carver; in the Nidwaldner Museum, Stans, Switzerland.

Casimir of Lithuania, Prince of Poland

1458–1484
Memorial: March 4
Lat.: Casimirus; It.: Casimiro; Fr.: Casimir; Pol.: Kazimierz.

Casimir was a man full of faith, a lover of chastity and penance, kind to the poor, and very devoted to the Eucharist and the Virgin. He was born in Cracow on October 3, 1458, as the third of the thirteen children of Casimir IV Jagellon, king of Poland and grand duke of Lithuania, and of Elizabeth of Hapsburg, daughter of Albert II. Elizabeth was also known as "mother of kings": of her sons Ladislas became king of Bohemia (in 1471) and of Hungary (1490–1516); John Albert was king of Poland from 1492 to 1501; Alexander was grand duke of Lithuania beginning in 1492 and king of Poland from 1501 to 1506; Sigismund was king of Poland and grand duke of Lithuania from 1506 to 1548.

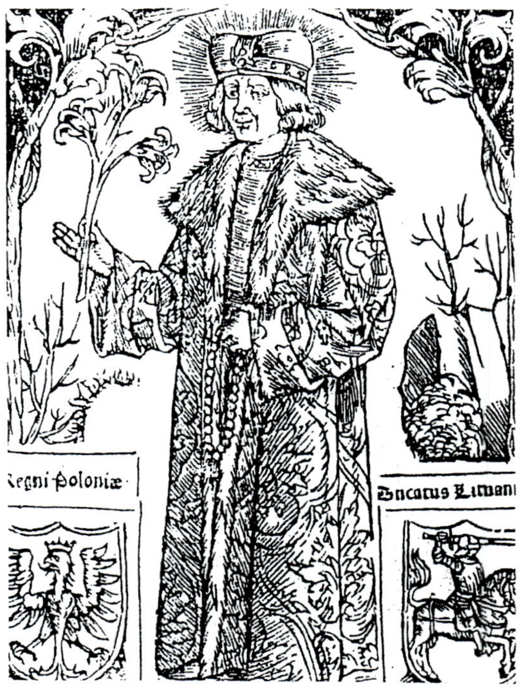

An attempt to place Casimir on the throne of Hungary in 1471 when he was only thirteen was a failure. Meanwhile he continued his education, on which Canon Jan Dlugosz had an important influence. Casimir had a delicate constitution but a cheerful temperament; being studious, he learned easily. From the age of seventeen on, he always accompanied his father on the latter's journeys and several times carried out administrative duties.

During the few years of his earthly existence, and even in the midst of this public life, he never abandoned the activities and rules of a solid piety that was marked by a deep devotion to the Virgin Mary and to Jesus in the Eucharist, a resolute chastity, an active charity, and an unwearying zeal.

Casimir fell ill with tuberculosis and died at the age of only twenty-five on March 4, 1484, in the castle of Gardinas at Grodno, Lithuania. His body was taken to the cathedral of Vilna, where his tomb soon became a goal of pilgrimage. The miracles attested there heightened the reputation of the young prince for holiness. The existence of a cult is attested by the granting of indulgences by Alexander VI as early as 1501.

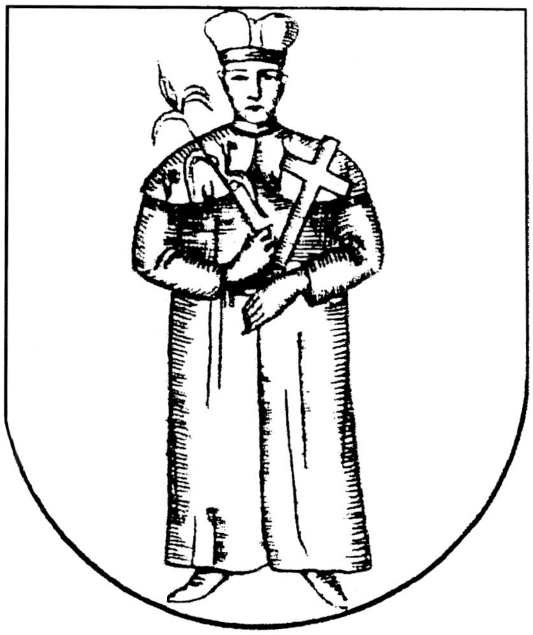

St. Casimir of Lithuania.
18th-cent. etching, showing the coat of arms of the Lithuanian city of Kvedarna.

The canonization process seems to have been begun by Pope Leo X in 1517, but subsequent documentation is full of gaps. In any case, on January 13, 1621, Pope Paul VI placed his feast in the Breviary and Missal of the Universal Church.

▷▷ Casimir is patron of Lithuania, Poland, and Bohemia, of chastity and the young, and is invoked against pestilence, against all the enemies of religion and of the fatherland, and against temptations of the flesh.

The Lithuanians, moreover, immediately adopted him as their protector, and on two occasions Casimir appeared to the Lithuanian army when it was engaged with the Russians: in 1518 during a battle near Polck, and in 1654 when Lithuania was threatened with invasion. Many churches were dedicated to him in Poland and Lithuania and in countries to which Poles and Lithuanians emigrated. The city of St. Casimir was founded in Venezuela in 1758, and St. Casimir is the name of a place in the province of Quebec, Canada.

Casimir became patron of the Order of the Knights of Malta, which in 1690 obtained some of his relics from the cathedral of Vilna. In 1948 Pius XII proclaimed Casimir the patron of Lithuanian youth (see *AAS* 42 [1950] 330ff.). He is invoked against lust.

Due to the efforts of Casimir, the hymn *Omni die dic Mariae* ("Daily say to Mary"), which was composed in the thirteenth or fourteenth century, became very widely known. When his tomb was inspected in 1604, a copy of the hymn was found in it.

▷▷ Casimir is depicted as a **young man**, in **royal garb**, with a **robe reaching to his feet**; he wears a **hat** or a **duke's crown** and has a **scepter**, a **lily**, a **rosary**, and from 1631 on, a **cross**, which he is holding in woodcuts that illustrate the texts in his liturgical Office. The crown and scepter are often at his feet, symbolizing his renunciation of the throne.

Thomas More, Martyr

1477–1535
Memorial: June 22; Martyrdom: July 6
Lat.: Thomas Morus; It.: Tommaso Moro; Fr.: Thomas More.

Thomas, the upright father of a family and an official at the court of Henry VIII, gave his life out of fidelity to the Catholic Church; he is remembered for the resolute Christian tranquility with which he accepted his misfortunes, and as "a man for all seasons." He shared his imprisonment and martyrdom with Bishop John Fisher.

Thomas was son of a common law judge, attended the University of Oxford, began the study of Greek, and completed his legal studies in London. He had a brilliant career and in 1529 was appointed chancellor of England. He was already a friend of Erasmus of Rotterdam, had studied St. Augustine, and had written *Utopia,* the book that made him famous.

His life as a successful lawyer and humanist was one of study as well. He rose at 2:00 a.m. and studied until seven; this was followed by Mass. To his daily morning and evening prayers he added the seven penitential psalms and the litanies of the saints. He often went, on foot, on pilgrimages to nearby shrines; he also did something unusual at that time: every time he had to face some test, he received Communion. During meals one of his daughters read passages from the Scriptures.

Thomas sang in his parish choir, served Mass, took part in parish life, was generous in works of charity, and, at his own expense, rented houses in which he took care of the elderly, the sick, and the poor.

In his writings, moreover, he opposed Luther and dealt with the "last things": death, judgment, hell, and paradise.

His social and cultural popularity did not prevent his being tried in 1535 for refusing to take an oath recognizing the supremacy of the king over the Church in England; he defended himself by silence. When the death sentence was pronounced, he responded to his judges in a noble speech of forgiveness in which he expressed his desire to meet them all again in paradise. He was spared the punishment of hanging and quartering, which was reserved for Catholics, and was beheaded on the hill of the Tower in London. During his time in prison he had written his *Dialogue of Comfort against Tribulation,* a *Treatise on the Passion of Christ,* and *A Devout Meditation*.

St. Casimir of Lithuania.
Engraving (1521) from Z. Ferreri, *Vita beati Casimiri confessoris* (Torun, Poland).

He ascended the scaffold with jokes on his lips, asked that those present pray for him, and attested that he was dying as a faithful servant of the king but, above all, as a faithful servant of God. He then recited the *Miserere* and had some humorous words of comfort for the executioner; he himself put the bandage over his eyes and placed his head on the block. It was July 6, 1535.

His severed head was displayed to the public for a month; his daughter Margaret prevented it from being thrown into the Thames by paying for it.

▷▷ Thomas was proclaimed the patron of public servants by John Paul II on October 31, 2000.

▷▷ He is depicted in a portrait as **a gentleman of that period**, a man of peaceful face, dressed in the **robes of a chancellor** and wearing an **honorary neck-chain**.

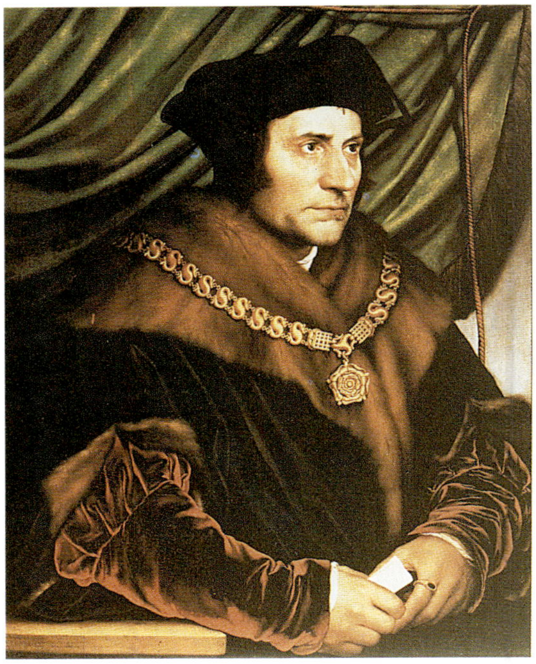

St. Thomas More.
By Hans Holbein, 1527, in the Frick Collection, New York.

Ignatius of Loyola, Priest and Founder of the Society of Jesus

1491–1556
Memorial: July 31
Lat.: Ignatius a Loyola; It.: Ignazio di Loyola; Fr.: Ignace de Loyola, Ignat; Sp.: Iñigo López de Loyola, Ignacio; Ger.: Ignatius von Loyola, Ignaz.

Ignatius was born into a noble family at Loyola in the Basque province of Guipuzcoa. He took his name from St. Iñigo, abbot of San Salvador at Oña, near Burgos. Destined by his father for a career in the Church, he received the tonsure when he was fourteen. This did not mean that he would then have gone on to become a priest, and in fact his first inclination was to the same military life undertaken by his brothers; his father consented. He spent his youth in hunting and jousting and in reading poems of chivalry. While in the service of the king of Navarre he was wounded in the leg and forced into inactivity. During this period he read the *Life of Christ* by Ludolf the Carthusian and the *Golden Legend* by Jacobus de Voragine. This key encounter took place in 1521, and from then on, as he himself wrote, "he could never again give the slightest consent to the things of the flesh."

He went on a pilgrimage to the Virgin of Montserrat and laid down his sword before her as an ex-voto. He served the sick at Manresa for a year, meanwhile practicing penances, self-scourgings, lengthy prayers on his knees, and reading the *Imitation of Christ*. Then as a pilgrim and beggar he went to Rome and then Venice, from which he embarked as a pilgrim to the Holy Land. On his return, he began to study and was admitted to the University of Paris. There he met a group of young men among whom was another Spaniard, Francis Xavier, with whom he professed vows of poverty and chastity in 1534. In Rome, the two were ordained priests and meanwhile brought to completion, and put into practice, the *Spiritual Exercises*.

In implementing this "spiritual manual," the exercitant spends about thirty days in silence and solitude, following a process that is divided into four weeks. In the first, he meditates on the end of the human person and awakens in his heart a detestation of sin. In the second, he meets Jesus as a king who calls us to follow him in the struggle against the world, and he thinks about the reform of his life; in the third week, he meditates on the Passion and strengthens his resolution to follow Jesus in trials and tribulations. In the fourth week, he advances to a life of unbroken union with God and learns to see and love him in all his creatures.

Ignatius was inspired to establish the Company, or Society, of Jesus, and in 1540 obtained the approval of Paul II. The first missionaries immediately set out for the countries of Europe and Asia. Ignatius himself remained in Rome and acquired the title of "apostle of Rome" for his dedication to healing the city of its social and moral wounds. In order that Rome might become a center of educational development in the service of the Pope, in 1551 Ignatius established the Roman College, which was later renamed the Gregorian University in honor of Pope Gregory XIII (1572–1585), who did a great deal to advance the Society. Ignatius also labored to promote charitable works in support of the poor, the sick, young people in danger, converted Jews, orphans, and whoever else needed help. He adopted the motto *Ad Majorem Dei Gloriam,* which, in the form *AMDG* was and still is used by many religious and priests. Ignatian spirituality, which is based on the Trinity, Christ, and the Mass is solidly rooted in the Church and in Catholic tradition.

St. Ignatius of Loyola.
Wood sculpture, ca. 1700, from the Reducción San Ignacio, in Guazu, Paraguay.

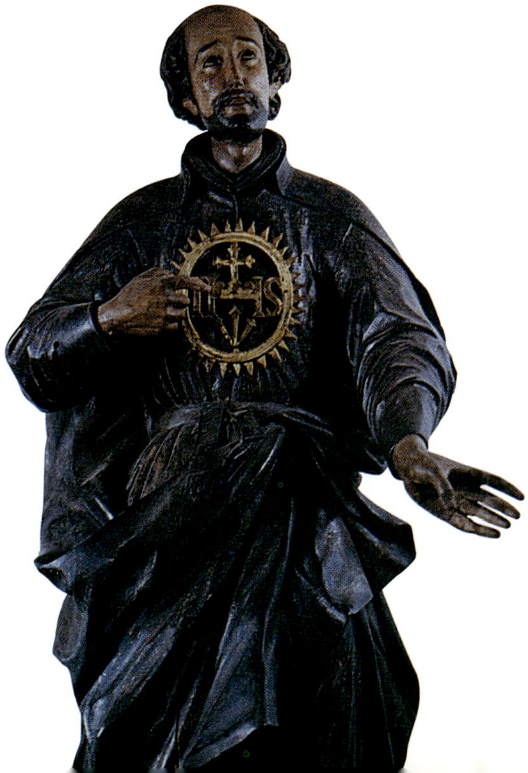

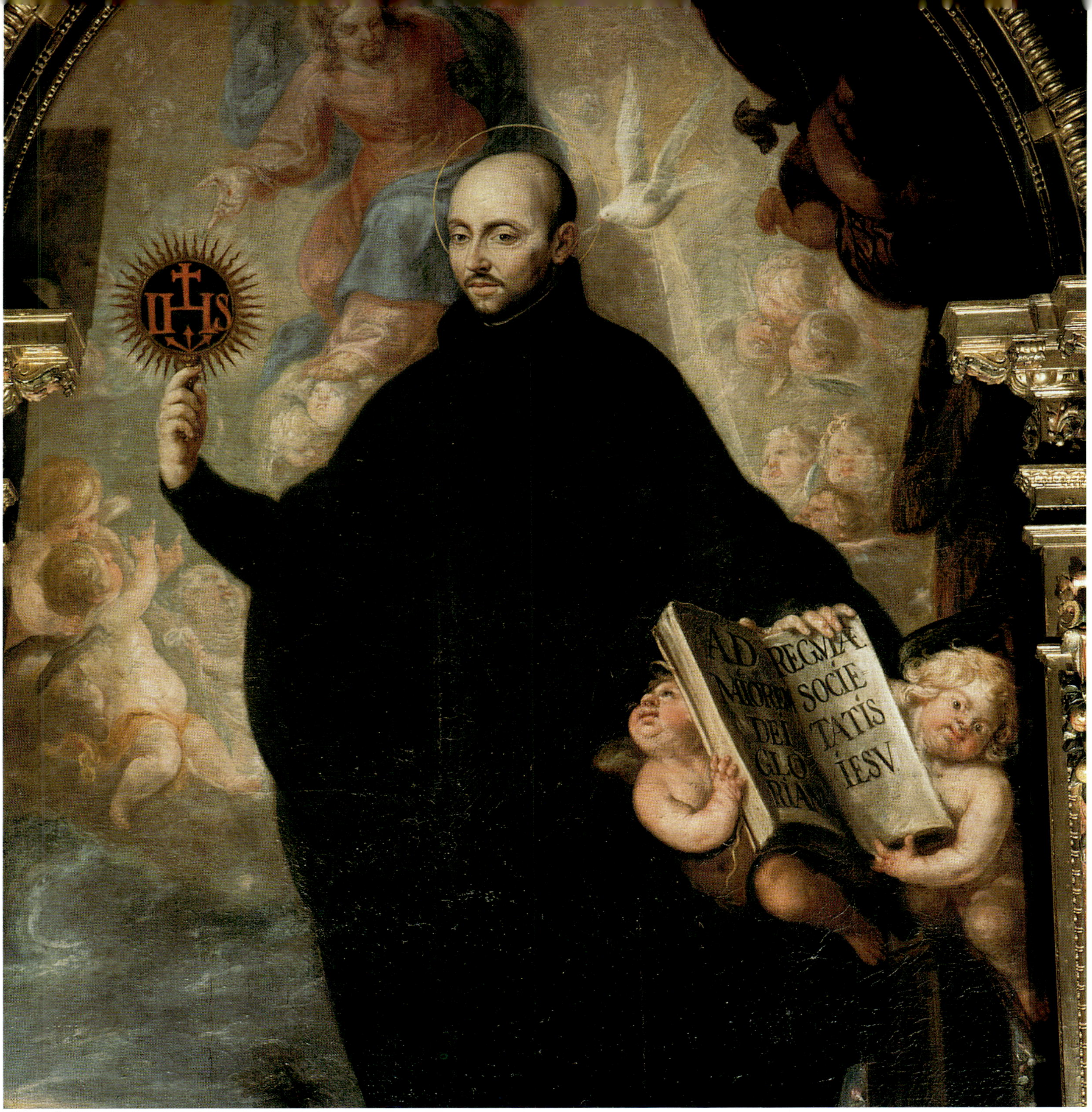

St. Ignatius of Loyola.
In the chapel of St. Ignatius, Hospital of Antezana, Alcalá de Henares.
St. Ignatius' motto, *Ad Majorem Dei Gloriam,* became very widespread and many individuals used it to mark the pages of their writings. Ignatius was also responsible for a further spread of St. Bernardino's monogram *IHS.*

Ignatius died in Rome on July 31, 1556, and was canonized in 1622.

▷▷ He is the patron of the Jesuits. Because of his own illness he is invoked against fever and against baleful influences and for the cure of the possessed; because of the similarity with his name López, he is invoked against wolves *(lobos)* and protector of flocks. He is also invoked against scruples.

▷▷ He is depicted wearing a **black cassock**, with a **bald forehead**, a **prominent nose**, and a **poorly shaved beard**.

His principal attributes are a **flaming heart of Jesus**, a **radiant IHS**, and the abbreviation *AMDG,* referring to the motto of the Society. Another attribute is the **book of the Rule** with the motto written on it. He is also depicted on pulpits along with allegorical figures representing the four parts of the world, an allusion to the missions of his order.

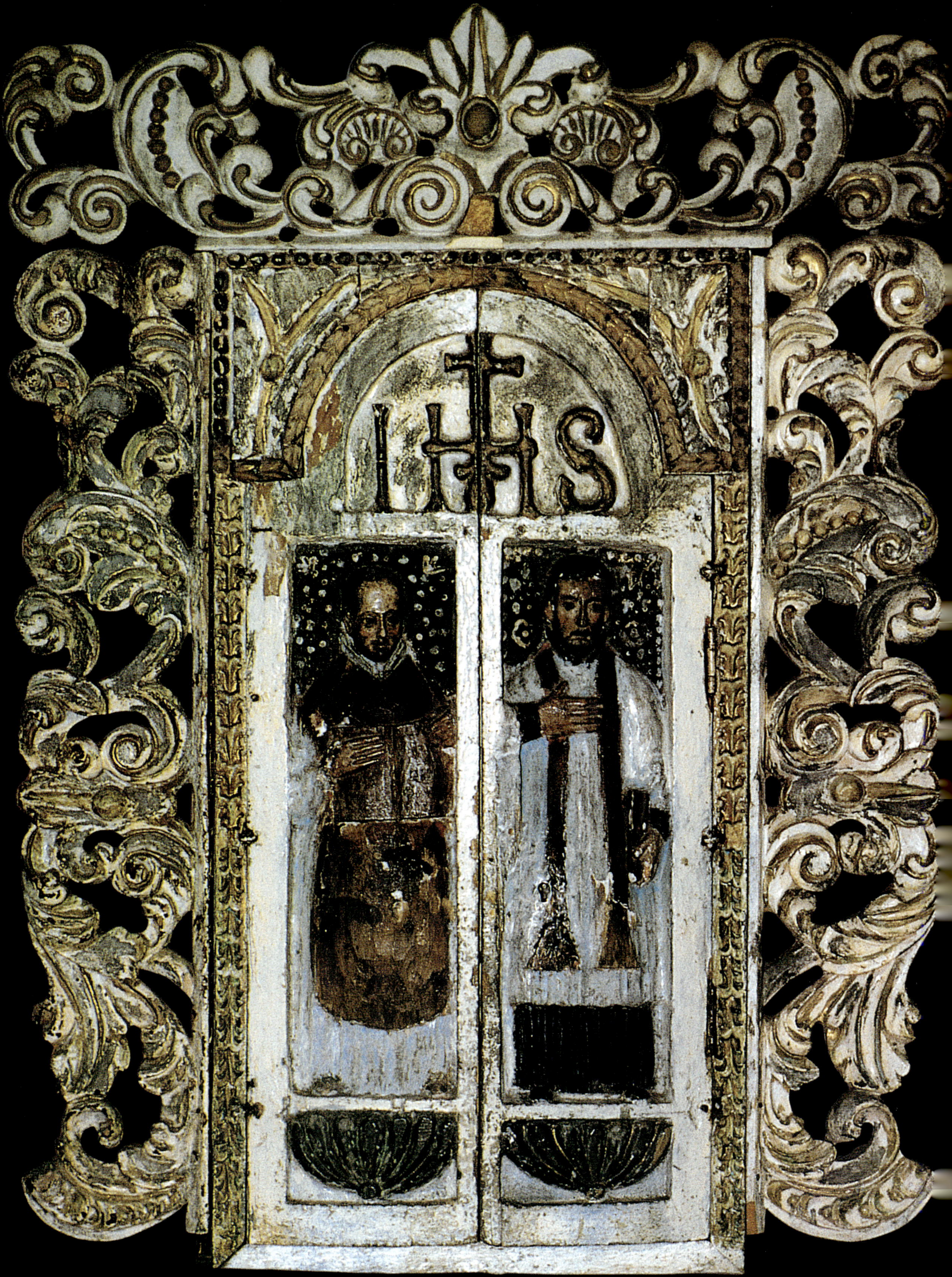
IHS

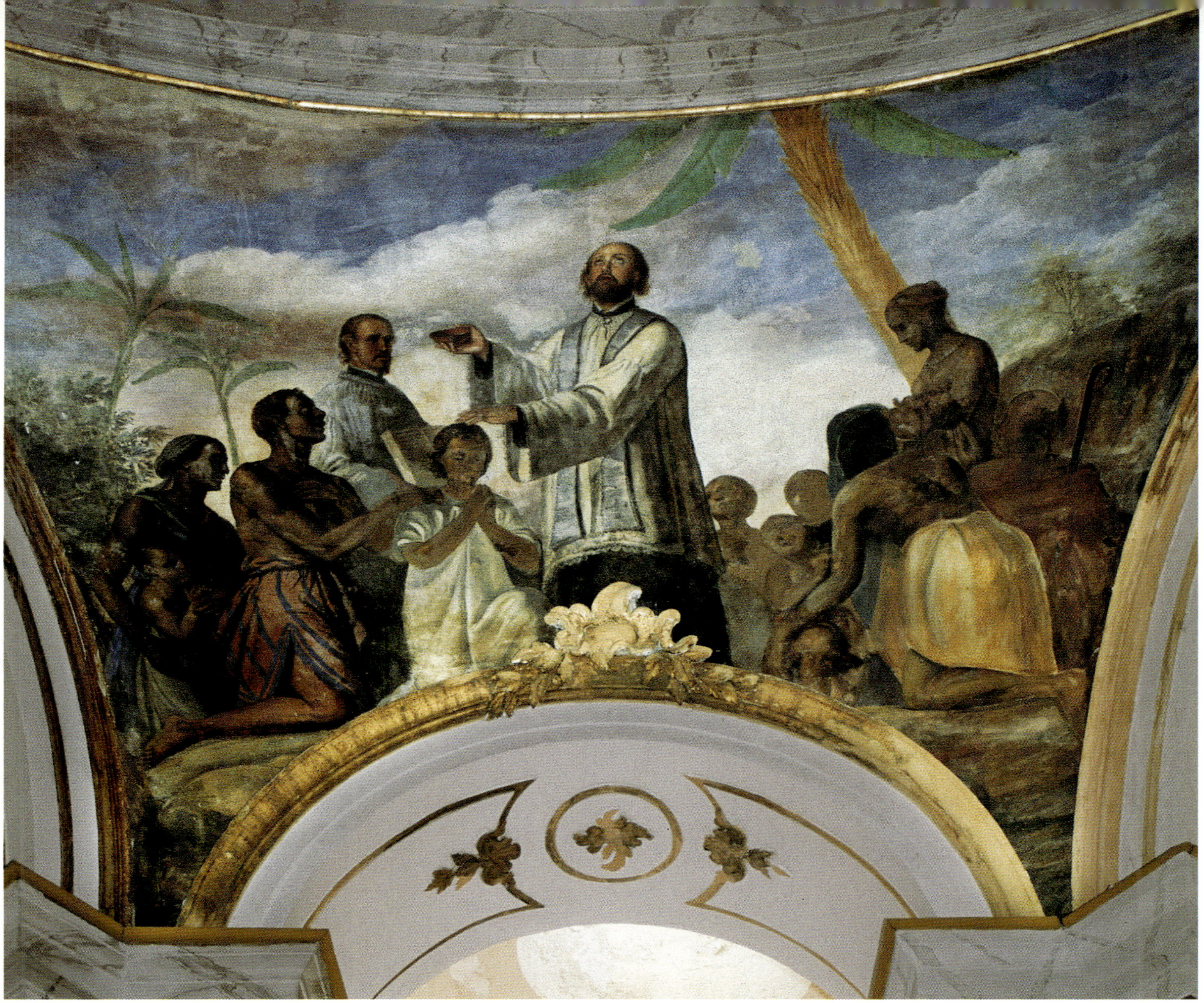

St. Francis Xavier Baptizes the Indian Princess Neachile.
Baroque Jesuit art in the church of St. Francis, Palermo.

Francis Xavier, Jesuit Priest

1506–1552
Memorial: December 3
Lat.: Franciscus Xaverius, Indiarum apostolus, Xaverius Japonicus; It.: Francesco Saverio; Sp.: Francisco Javier; Ger.: Franziskus Xaverius, Franz Xaver; Pol.: Franciszek Ksawey.

This Jesuit is regarded as the apostle of the Indies and Japan. He was born in Spain, in the castle of Xavier in Navarre. He studied in his native country and then in Paris, where he had Blessed Peter Favre and Ignatius of Loyola as roommates. With them and another four companions he made a vow to go on pilgrimage to the Holy Land, with the intention of living there a life of chastity and the apostolate. He made the *Spiritual Exercises* under Ignatius' guidance in 1535. He was ordained a priest in 1537, spent 1539 in Rome, and contributed to the founding of the Society of Jesus, which was approved in 1540. The king of Portugal asked Ignatius for missionaries to the Christians of southeast India; one of those appointed fell ill, and Francis became part of the mission.

He was able finally to set out for India in 1541 as a priest under Portuguese protection and as an apostolic nuncio. The distressful voyage took him to Brazil, then to Mozambique, where he fell seriously ill. He next reached the island of Socotra and finally Goa, the capital of the Portuguese empire in the East, where he devoted himself to the colonists, the

St. Ignatius of Loyola and St. Francis Xavier.
Doors of the 18th-cent. tabernacle in the church of St. Mary of Achao, Chiloé, Chile.

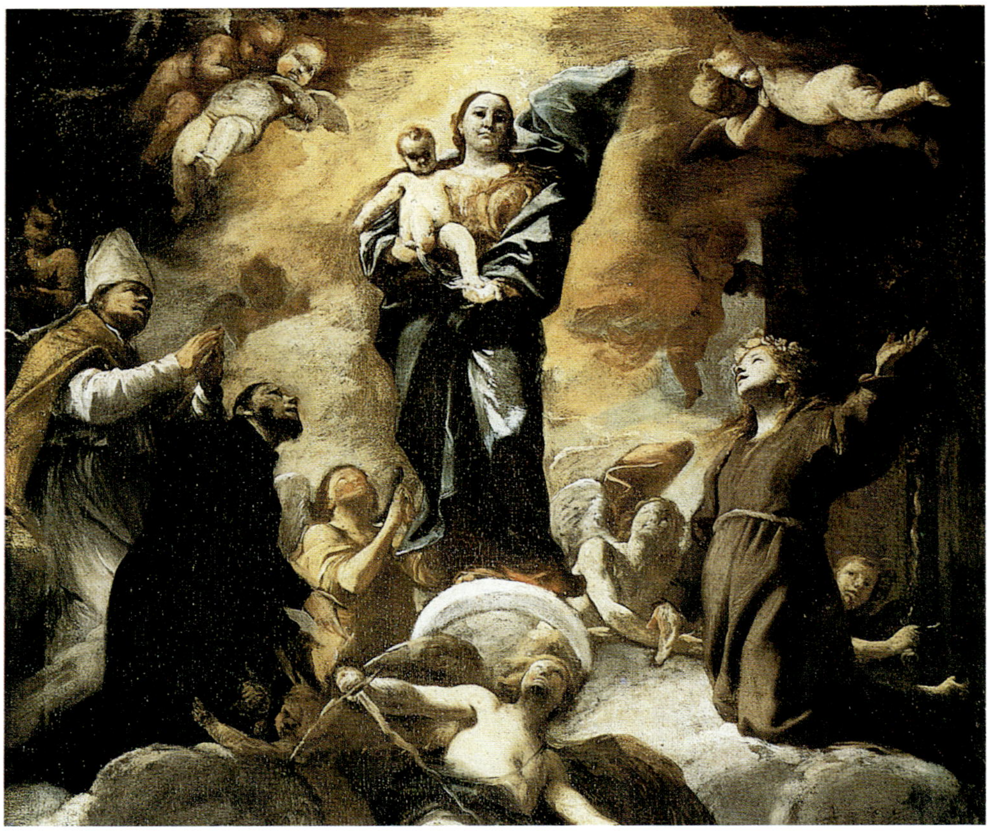

children, the slaves and the lepers. He then set out for southeastern India, where, in 1535–1537, he converted about 20,000 fishermen, but left them without any further guidance. Francis devoted himself to the instruction of the natives, suffered along with them when many neophytes were massacred, and made countless converts. He then set sail for Malacca, where there was hope of conversions; here he met a Japanese named Angero, who had fled there because of a murder he had committed. His stories made Francis determined to go to Japan, a country still ignorant of Christianity.

He set out with Angero, whom he had baptized as Paul; within a short time he was able to begin preaching and start a Christian community. He thought next of going from Japan to China but he had just reached the island of Sancien when he fell ill and died twelve days later; he was attended by a Chinese Christian named Anthony, who later told the story of the saint's last days. Francis' body, covered in quicklime, was taken back to Goa, where it proved to be uncorrupted and where it is preserved in the church of Bom Jesus, attached to the house of professed Jesuits.

Among the various episodes of his lengthy missionary work, one is to be mentioned here that influenced his iconography: during a voyage the sea became stormy, and Francis, probably hoping to calm the waters, dipped into them a little crucifix he carried on his breast, but he immediately lost it and was much grieved. The ship landed the next day at the island of Baranura; here, as the saint and his companions were walking on the beach, a **crab** came up from the sea, holding the crucifix aloft in its claws, and hurried toward Francis, who met it on his knees; after giving the crucifix to the saint, the crab returned to the sea.

St. Francis Xavier, St. Rosalia, and St. Januarius Intercede at the Feet of the Virgin.
Detail of an ex-voto (for deliverance from the plague of 1656) by Mattia Preti, in the Gallerie Nazionali di Capodimonte, Naples.
On Francis Xavier's robe can be seen a crab that is opening its claws.

In his preaching Francis was skilled in adapting himself to the situations he met; he also had the catechism and various prayers translated into the Eastern languages. Back in Europe, his letters would contribute to rousing great enthusiasm for the missions.

Francis was canonized by Pope Paul V in 1622.

▷▷ Francis is patron of the Indies, Japan, Pakistan, and Portugal, and of the cities of Bologna, Piacenza, Cremona, and Bastia. On December 14, 1927, Pius XI proclaimed him, together with St. Thérèse of Lisieux, to be the patron of all Catholic missionaries; he was proclaimed patron of Pakistan by Pius XI on August 16, 1933, and by Pius XII on March 1, 1940. He is patron of the Jesuits and of missionaries. He was proclaimed the patron of Propaganda Fide by Pius XI on December 5, 1922.

He is protector of sailors, especially in the Far East, and also of tourists, especially in that same area. He is invoked against hurricanes and plagues.

▷▷ He is depicted in the **Jesuit habit**; he turns his gaze to the radiant Host and pulls his habit aside to show his **fiery heart**; his principal attribute is a **crab at his feet**.

Other attributes are a **torch** and a **crucifix**; he is sometimes shown **surrounded by Indian and Philippino youths**.

Francis Borgia, Jesuit Priest

1510–1572
Memorial: September 30
Lat.: Franciscus de Borja; It.: Francesco Borgia; Fr.: François Borgia; Sp.: Francisco de Borja; Ger.: Franz von Borgia.

Francis was the son of the Duke of Gandia in Spain; he studied philosophy at Saragossa, and resided at the court of Charles V. He married Eleanora de Castro, a Portuguese lady, by whom he had eight children. He was so deeply moved by the death of his queen, Empress Isabella, whose body he had to accompany to Granada, that he determined not to serve "any lord who could die." In 1541 he became acquainted with the Society of Jesus and, when his wife died in 1546, he made the *Exercises* of St. Ignatius. He also made vows of chastity and obedience and a vow to enter the Society.

St. Francis Borgia.
Black and white panel in gesso showing allegorical scenes from the life of the saint; mid-17th-cent. work of craftsmen of Carpi, in the Collezione Bianchi, Florence.

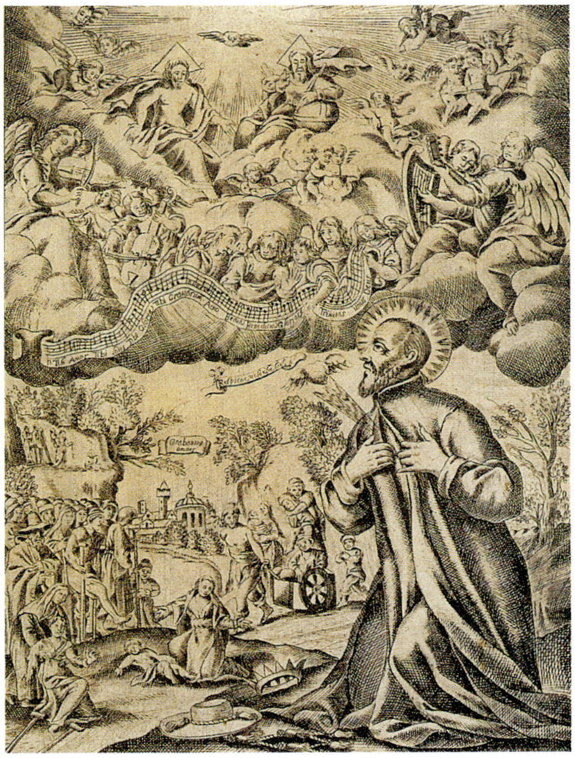

In Gandia Francis founded the first college of the Society, which was later made a university. In 1551 he renounced his dukedom, took the religious habit, and was ordained a priest. He devoted himself to preaching and to the writing of spiritual treatises. He was severely tested in 1559 when a book, falsely attributed to him, was placed on the Index by the Inquisitor General in Spain, to the detriment of himself and the Society; he suffered for a long time before the misunderstanding was cleared up. In this matter, however, he refused to defend himself and took refuge in Portugal. In 1565 he was elected superior general of the Society. In that office he worked for the preservation of the interior spirit of the Society, concerned himself with the formation of the novices, ordered an hour of meditation each morning, and had the church of the Gesù built in Rome. During one of his stays in Rome he met St. Stanislaus Kostka. After making a pilgrimage to Our Lady of Loreto, he died on September 30, 1572, in the rooms in which St. Ignatius had died.

He was especially devoted to the Eucharist; he venerated the Virgin and had many copies made of the image known as the *Salus Populi Romani,* which was revered in the Basilica of St. Mary Major. This lover of humility and mortification thought of himself as the greatest of sinners, and he devoted himself to continual prayer. He established the first overseas missions in the Spanish-speaking countries. He was canonized by Benedict XII in 1721.

▷▷ Francis is invoked against storms and plagues and also against earthquakes. He is a patron of Portugal, a fact confirmed by Pius XI on June 13, 1934, and again on March 25, 1936.

▷▷ He is depicted in **the black habit of the Jesuits**, with a **flaming heart on his breast**, often in adoration before a **crucifix** and a **monstrance**. A secondary attribute is a **ducal crown** lying **at his feet** and a **skull without a crown**; these show how important the sight of the corpse of Empress Isabella had been for him.

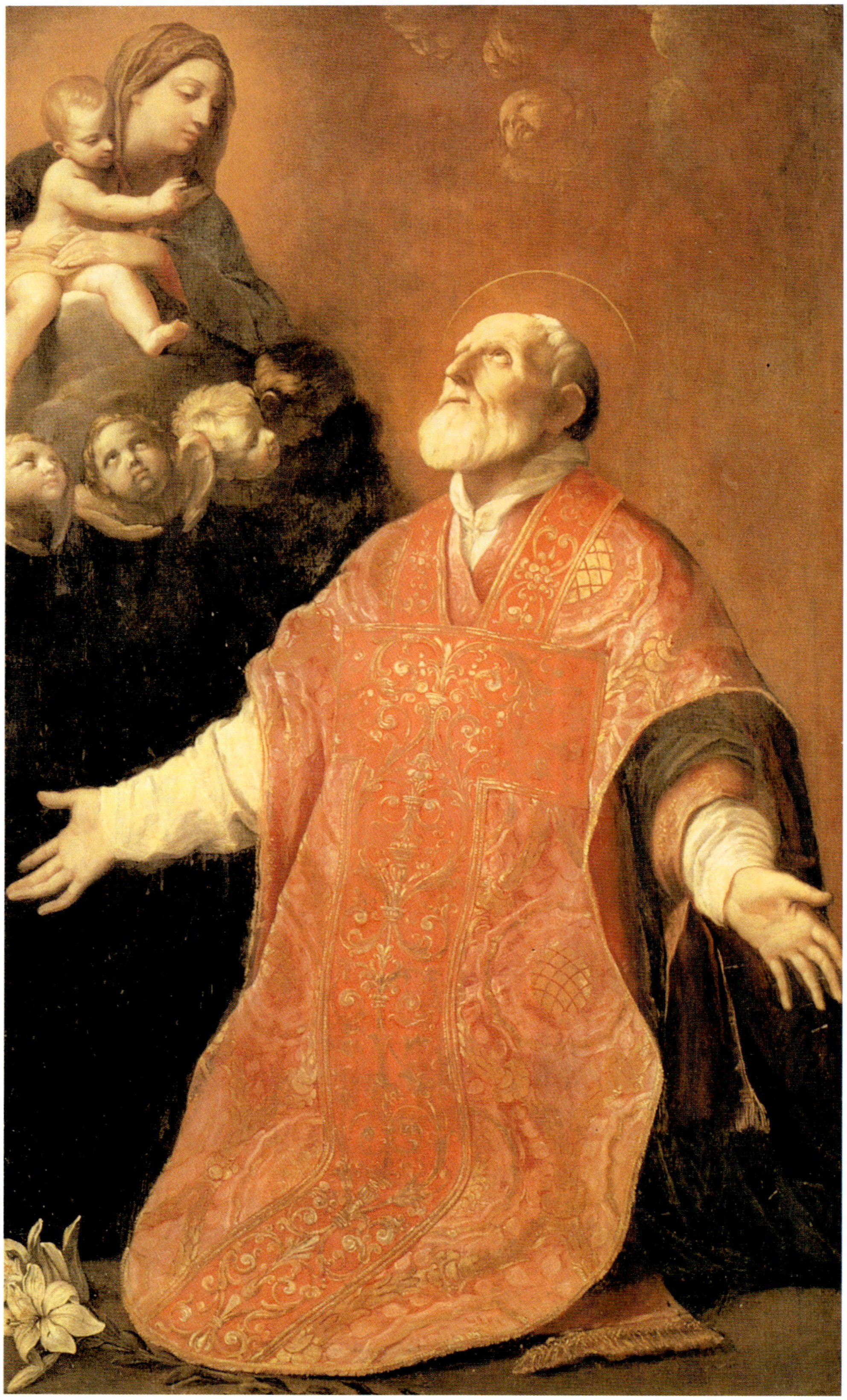

Vision of St. Philip Neri.
By Guido Reni (1575–1642), in the Chiesa Nuova, Rome.

Philip Neri, Priest and Founder of the Congregation of the Oratory

1515–1595
Memorial: May 26
Lat.: Philippus Nerius Florentinus, congregationis Oratorii fundator; It.: Filippo Neri; Sp.: Felipe Neri; Ger.: Philippus Neri,

This founder of the Oratories, the life of which consisted of teaching, singing, charity, and evangelical simplicity, is the saint of Christian joy.

He was a Florentine who was sent to Rome to learn business practices but instead attended the schools of theology. He soon felt a call to help both the sick and the well; he would say to the latter: "When shall we begin to do a bit of good?"

He spent many nights in the catacombs of St. Sebastian; there, in 1544, during an ecstasy, a ball of fire penetrated his breast, broke two ribs, and enlarged his heart, which at his death proved to be exceptionally large.

In 1548, with a view to the Holy Year of 1550, he and some other laymen established the Confraternity of the Trinity in order to assist sick pilgrims. Only in 1551 was Philip ordained a priest.

His inspired work was the Oratory, a meeting place for people of every kind who came to read together books on asceticism and lives of the saints and to pray and sing. The members of the Oratory then took turns helping the sick.

Philip then invented a new kind of pilgrimage to Rome: the Visit of the Seven Churches; its purpose was to make reparation for the excesses of the Roman Carnival. "Pippo bono," as he was familiarly known, had a motto: "Be good if you can": without setting any obligations he achieved a holy life for himself and for others. He died on May 26, 1595.

▷▷ Philip is the patron of the young and of musicians and anyone having to do with music. He is invoked against rheumatism and also against earthquakes.

▷▷ He is depicted wearing a **biretta and a black cassock**, along with the surplice proper to the Oratorians; his principal attributes are a **rosary**, a **lily**, and an angel who gives him a book with the **inscription "You have expanded my heart."**

He is also shown in priestly garb and a **chasuble**, in **ecstasy before the Virgin** who shows him the Child. This is the most widespread image of this saint.

Another attribute is a **wreath** of roses on his head.

St. Theresa of Avila.
Statue, from the beginning of the 20th cent., in the porch of the sanctuary at Fatima.

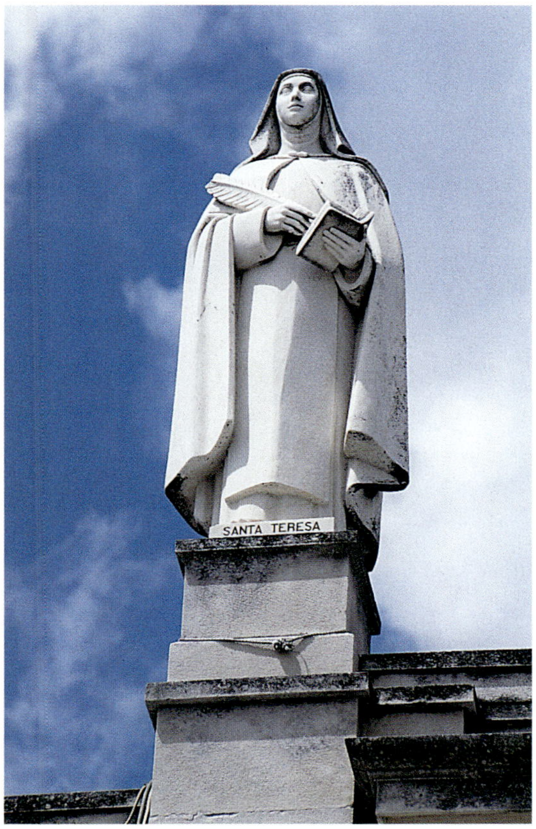

Theresa of Jesus, of Avila, Virgin and Doctor of the Church

1515–1582
Memorial: October 15
Lat.: Theresa Magna, a Iesu; It.: Teresa d'Avila di Gesù; Fr.: Thérèse; Sp.: Teresa de Jesús, de Avila; Ger.: Theresa von Jesus, von Avila.

This saint, usually known as Theresa of Avila, was the great reformer of the Carmelite Order. She was born at Avila in Castile on March 28, 1515, to Alonso Sánchez de Cepeda and Beatrice de Ahumada. Having been reared as a Christian, she was accustomed to reading the lives of the saints; as a result, she and her brother ran away to the territory of the Moors in order to become martyrs, but an uncle brought them home. Then the two children began to imitate the life of hermits outside the gates of the city.

During her adolescence, however, she fell into a tepidity for which others rebuked her. Then, against her father's will, she entered the Carmelite nuns and made her profession in 1537. She was subsequently afflicted with health problems and was paralyzed for three years; she was cured through the intercession of St. Joseph, to whom she always remained devoted. Until 1557, she went through periods of tepidity; her definitive conversion came about through an encounter with the suffering Christ and the direction she received from some Jesuits. Her mystical graces multiplied and were confirmed as authentic by St. Francis Borgia; she also had the support of St. Peter of Alcantara.

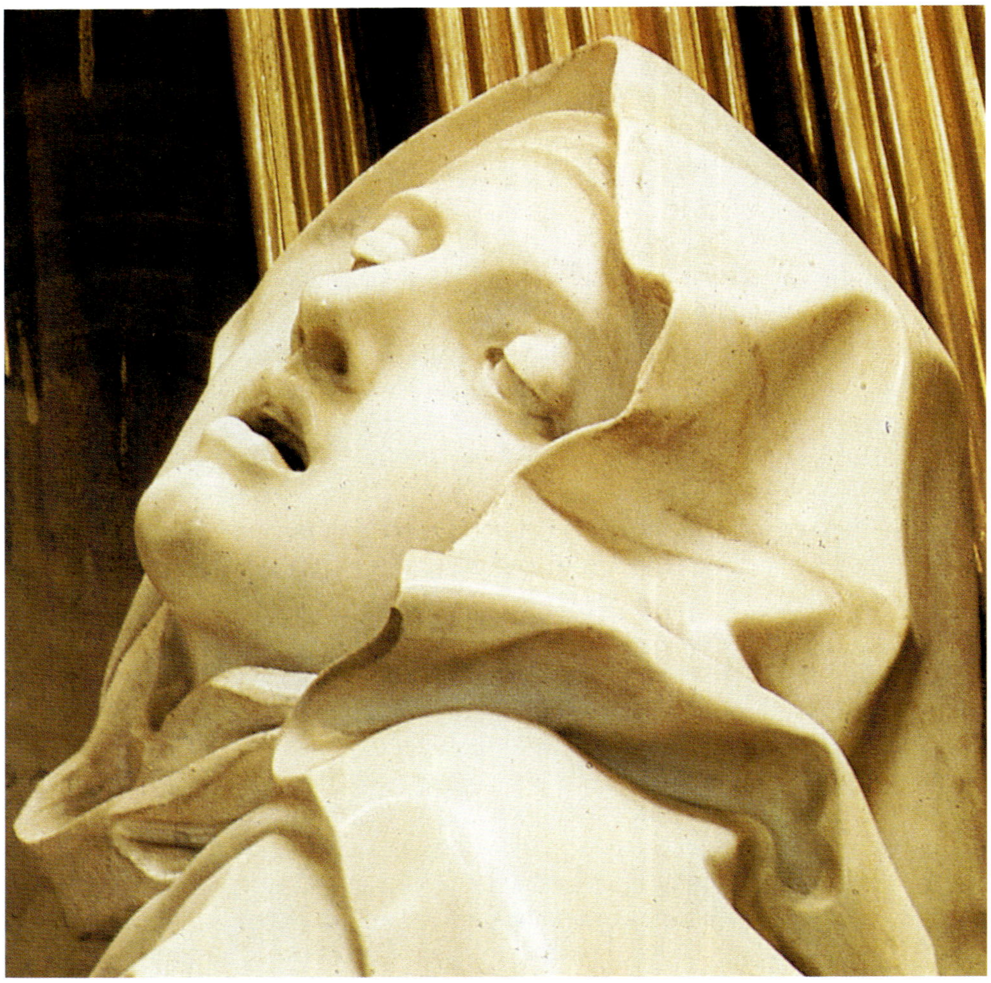

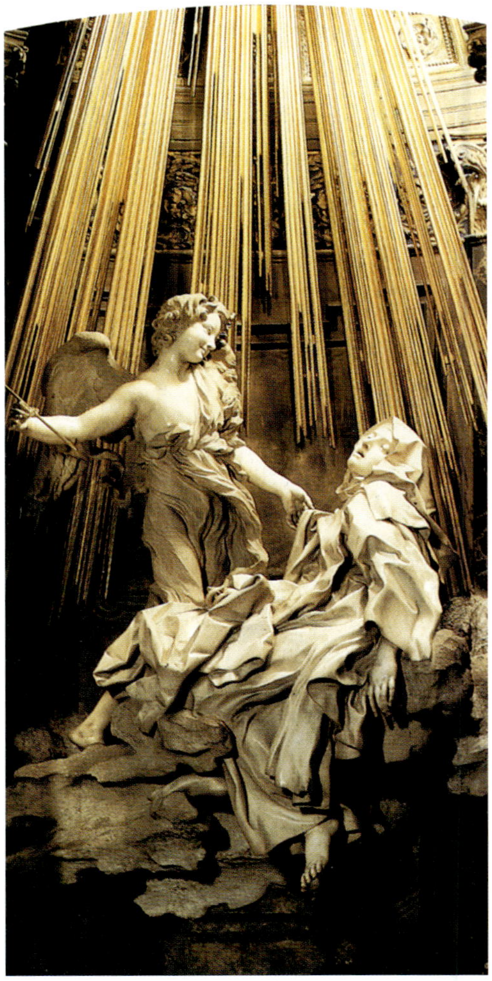

The years after 1557 were the years of her great visions, of **the piercing of her heart with an arrow hurled by an angel**, and of the vision of hell. As a result of this last, she determined to follow the *Rule* perfectly and gave thought to a monastery that would return to the primitive *Rule*. She worked toward this goal and on August 24, 1562, started the small monastery of St. Joseph by giving the veil to the first four novices. After obtaining permission to live in complete poverty, she became prioress in 1563. Her visions and ecstasies multiplied; love of God took complete hold of her and supported her in her work as reformer. In 1567, at Avila, the Father General of the Carmelites admired what she had done and authorized her to found other monasteries of nuns and two convents of contemplative men.

Thus began the years of travel, which were marked by, among other things, conflicts over jurisdiction. In Avila, as prioress of the monastery of the Incarnation, she had St. John of the Cross come as confessor. One day, as she received the Eucharist from his hand, she was lifted up to a spiritual marriage with Christ, who with his right hand gave her a nail. Henceforth she was granted a continual, peace-filled communion with God, in which she enjoyed the presence of the Trinity and of the humanity of Jesus.

The path of the reform was strewn with difficulties, yet it was during this time that Theresa wrote her masterpiece, *The Interior Castle*. She obtained the separation of the Discalced men and women from the other Carmelites, and in 1580 Gregory XIII promulgated new constitutions for the Discalced. Other foundations followed in the course of two years of obedient toil. After a brief illness, Theresa, now old and weary, died at Alba de Tormes, whither she had been sent in order to comfort the duchess; her death occurred on October 4, 1582, which became October 15 when the calendar was reformed. Her *Way of Perfection* was published in 1583.

Piercing of St. Theresa.
Sculpture by Gian Lorenzo Bernini, 1644–1652, in the Cappella Cornara of the church of Santa Maria della Vittoria, Rome.
Entire statue and a detail from it.

Her reputation for holiness spread before her death, and her relics became a source of miracles. In 1622 Gregory XV canonized her, together with St. Isidore the Farmer, St. Ignatius Loyola, St. Francis Xavier, and St. Philip Neri. Her body is now venerated in Alba de Tormes.

▷▷ Theresa is patron of many cities and dioceses in Spain, of the Archdiocese of Mexico City, of Naples, of Spanish Catholic writers, and, as a reformer, of the Spanish "Military Service Corps."

Because the Carmelite nuns embroidered cloths and linens for the churches, Theresa is protector of makers of lace and decorative trimmings. Because her heart was on fire with love, she is invoked on behalf of the souls in purgatory and against its fires; she is also invoked against diseases of the heart.

▷▷ Her principal attribute is a **flaming arrow** that transfixes her heart. In fact, the scene most represented is this **"piercing,"** which is described by the saint herself. Other representations: Jesus, crowned with thorns, shows her his wounds as she receives Communion; the Virgin bestows a golden garland on her; St. Joseph wraps her in his cloak, which is a symbol of purity. Another attribute is a **dove**, of which the saint had a vision that inspired her.

St. John of the Cross and the Miracle at Segovia. Print by Antoine Wiericx, 1591; in the Gabinetto delle Stampe, Bibliothèque Royal Albert I, Brussels. The image shows the dialogue from which the saint's identifying motto *Pati et contemni* is taken: "John, what reward do you want for your sufferings?" "Lord, to suffer and be scorned for your sake."

St. John of the Cross. Statue, from the beginning of the 20th cent., in the porch of the sanctuary at Fatima.

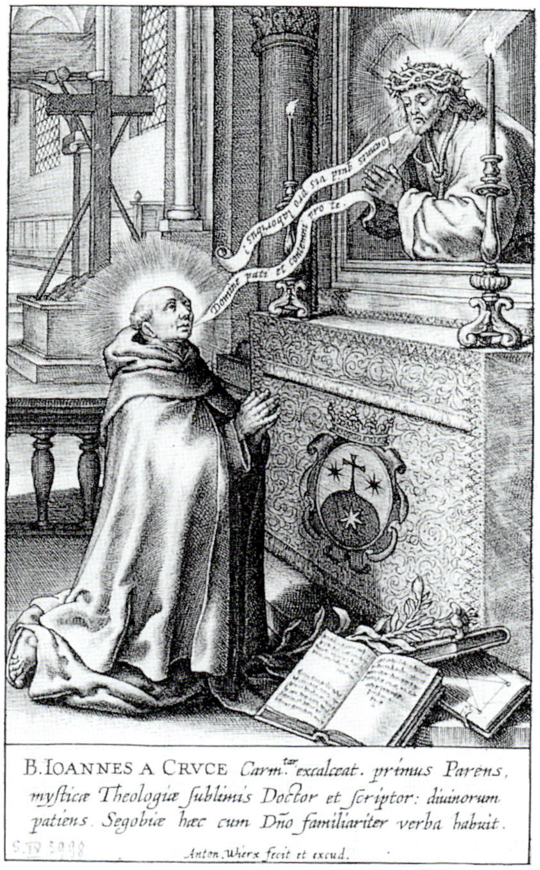

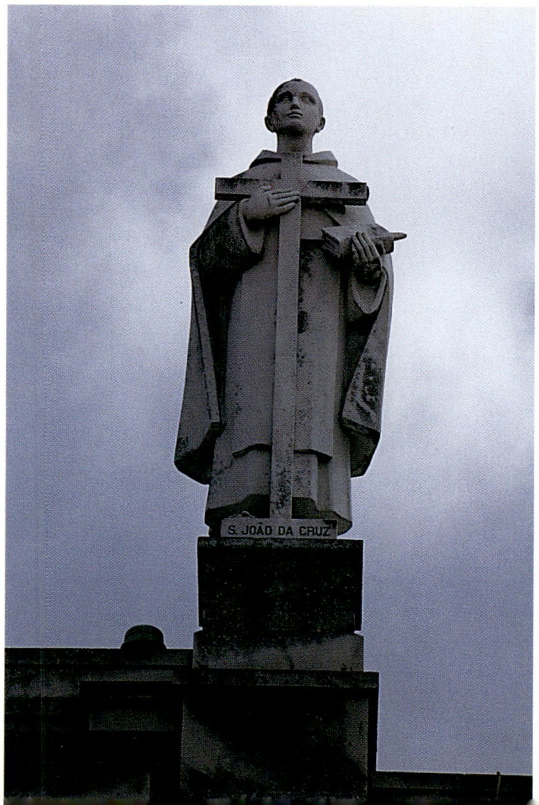

John of the Cross, Priest and Doctor of the Church

1542–1591

Memorial: December 14

Lat.: Johannes a Cruce; It.: Giovanni della Croce; Fr.: Jean de la Croix; Sp.: Juan de la Cruz; Ger.: Johannes vom Kreuz; Dutch: Jan van het Kruis; Pol.: Jan od Kryza.

John was the first Carmelite Discalced monk, though he never was part of the order's hierarchy; he was known as "of the Cross," because the only thing in his cell was **a cross**, and he spent whole nights with extended arms before the crucifix.

Juan de Yepes was born near Avila and experienced poverty as a youth. He entered the Carmelites in 1563 and was allowed to profess the primitive *Rule* of the order, taking as his name "John of St. Matthias." He was ordained a priest in 1567 and thought of becoming a Carthusian because he saw the Carmelite *Rule* being so poorly observed. His meeting with Teresa of Avila, whose confessor and spiritual director he became, persuaded him to follow her example and try to reform the order. As a result, he opened a first house of the Discalced Carmelites in Daruelo, near Avila; on this occasion he changed his name to "John of the Cross." But his "calced" brethren accused him of rebellion and shut him up in prison for nine months; it was there that he gained the experiences that turned him into a supreme mystic. After fleeing the prison, he took part in a meeting of the Discalced and became superior of the convent of El Calvario in Andalusia.

Only for a short time did he carry out general offices, and as he did so was tormented by the misunderstanding of many. When he was only forty years old, he died in the monastery of Ubeda, between July 13 and July 15, 1591. He had a very great influence on his age, on his spiritual sons, and on the people who came to him in the confessional, to which he devoted a great deal of his time. His works, including his poetry, show him to be a great mystic and a master of the asceticism needed for reaching the union (the spiritual marriage) of the soul with Christ, a union characterized by the union of wills. He gave the name "dark night" to the darkness in which divine wisdom along with love is communicated to the soul, and the soul is united with God.

▷▷ A cult of John began immediately, and he was canonized by Benedict XIII in 1726. Pius XI proclaimed him a doctor of the Church in 1926. He became patron of various dioceses in Spain, of the imperial house of Germany, and of the Duchy of Mantua.

▷▷ He is depicted with a **serious and dignified face, with handsome features, and in the habit of a Carmelite**, mainly with a **crucifix** in hand and the motto *Pati et Contemni* ("to suffer and be scorned"). But he is also shown at a table, **intent on his writing**.

Alphonsus Rodriguez, Jesuit Religious

1531–1617
Memorial: October 30
Lat.: Alphonsus Rodriguez; It.: Alfonso Rodriguez; Fr.: Alphonse; Sp.: Alonso Rodriguez; Ger.: Alfons.

Alphonsus, who is numbered among the great Spanish mystics, was born in Segovia and died on Majorca.

His was one of those simple, straightforward lives that hide treasures of asceticism and teaching. He married but lost his wife, his children, and all his possessions; he then became a lay brother of the Society of Jesus and served for forty years as doorkeeper of the College of Palma on the island of Majorca, where he died. His cult spread along with Spanish colonization, and he became popular in Colombia, Ecuador, and Venezuela. Leo XIII canonized him in 1888.

▷▷ He is patron of doorkeepers, janitors, and ushers.

▷▷ He is always depicted in the **garb of a brother who is a doorkeeper**, with **a key and a rosary hanging from his cincture**. He had a famous vision: Jesus and the Virgin Mary appeared to him in the act of pressing from their hearts, which they held in their fingers, two jets of blood the saint received on his breast. This scene was painted by Zurbaran in 1631; the painting is in the Academia de San Fernando in Madrid.

Charles Borromeo, Bishop

1538–1584
Memorial: November 4; *dies natalis,* November 3
Lat.: Carolus Borromaeus Mediolanensis; It.: Carlo Borromeo; Fr.: Charles Borromée de Milan; Sp.: Carlos Boromeo de Milan; Ger.: Karl Borromäus van Mailand; Dutch: Carolus Borromeus; Russ.: Karl Borromeiski.

Charles was born on October 2, 1538; his mother, Margarita de' Medici was the sister of Gianangelo de' Medici, who became Pope Pius IV in 1559. Tradition has it that an unusual light accompanied his birth.

The family was of Tuscan origin and owned a great landed estate in Arona. Charles had five siblings and was the second-born of the males. His father, a devout and charitable man, rejoiced to see signs of a vocation in this son. Charles was only seven when he was admitted to the clergy of Milan. He studied in Milan and graduated in jurisprudence in Pavia. His uncle, Pope Pius IV, called his nephews Frederick and Charles to Rome. There Charles received important dignities; he was his uncle's reliable adviser and took part in the Council of Trent, whose works he influenced. Meanwhile, however, his life, though blameless, was stamped with a brilliant and cultivated worldliness.

A change came with the death of his brother Frederick in 1562. Charles saw in this event a divine call, and he changed his way of life; he was ordained a priest in 1563, and in 1564 was consecrated a bishop and received the pallium of an archbishop. His life became austere; he intensified his theological studies and prepared himself for preaching; he studied Christian antiquities and is regarded, along with Philip Neri, as one of the inaugurators of these studies at a scientific level. His uncle, Pius IV, initially disapproved of him, but then imitated him and died in his arms in 1565.

Charles had already been appointed archbishop of Milan but was detained in Rome and had not yet taken possession of his see; only after the conclave in which Pius V was elected Pope, was Charles able to go to Milan.

Charles was one of the bishops who implemented the Catholic Reform by revising the organization of the Church. He rearranged the parishes, established a seminary for the formation of the clergy, and in 1566 began a lengthy pastoral visitation to which he devoted himself with great enthusiasm. He aided the poor and encouraged the formation of confraternities and pious sodalities engaged not only in works of mercy but in the spiritual building up of the brethren. He promoted cultural and social institutions and, among other things, supported poor university students. He won for himself and his successors the right to confer degrees in theology. He defended the Ambrosian Rite and pushed activities in the city that promoted devotion. When a plague reached Milan in 1576, Charles was absent but he returned and personally assisted the plague-stricken, although other authorities abandoned the city.

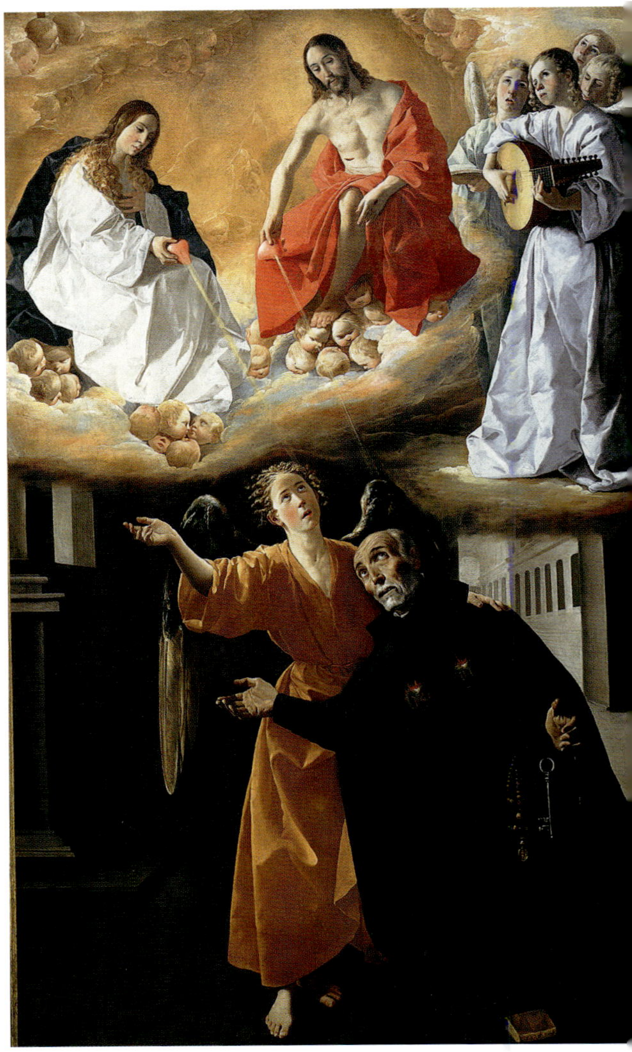

Blessed Alphonsus Rodriguez.
By Francisco Zurbaran; 17th cent.; in the Real Academia de Bellas Artes de San Fernando, Madrid. The work depicts the famous vision granted to Aphonsus: two jets of blood springing from the hearts of Jesus and Mary strike the saint's breast.

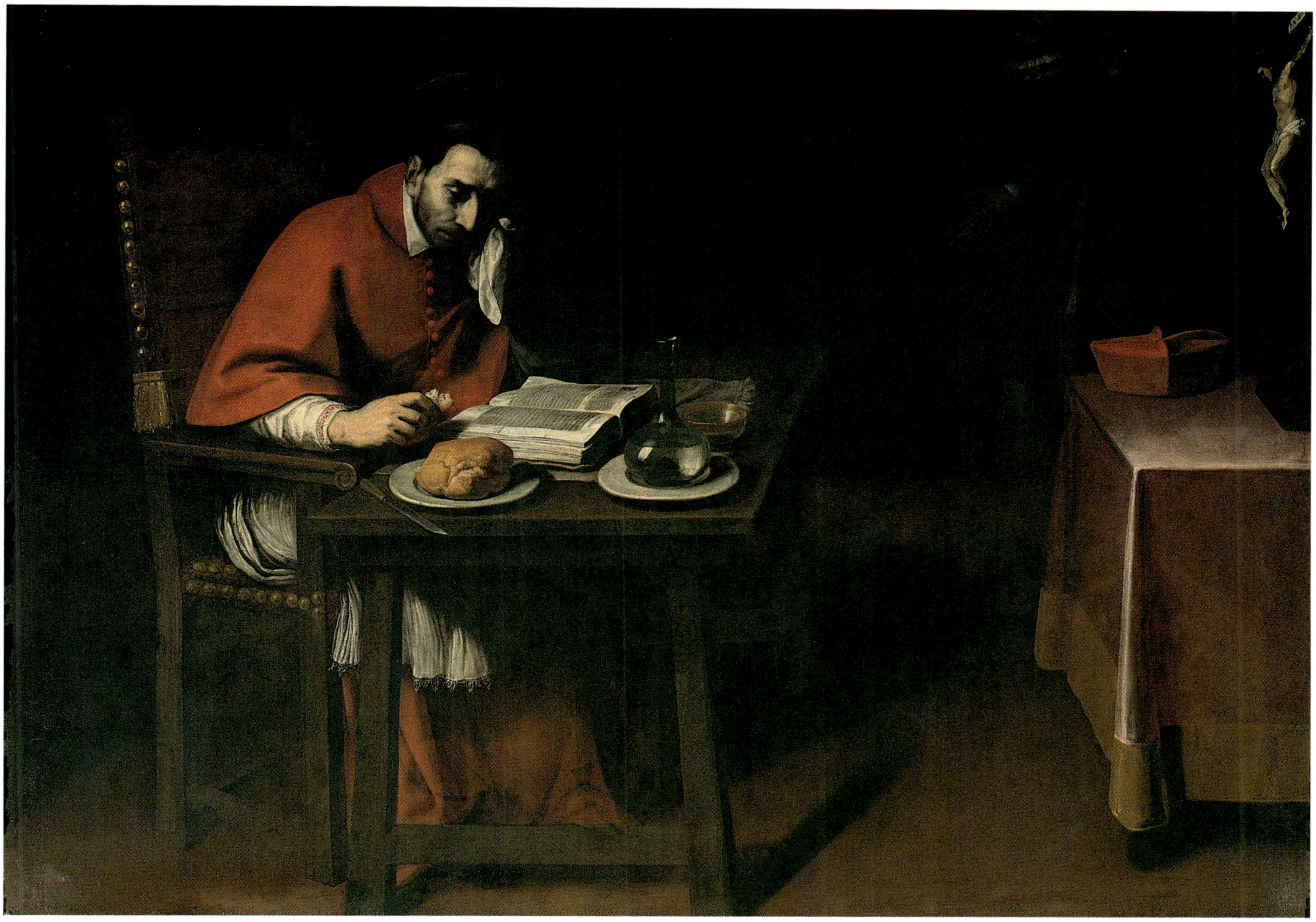

St. Charles Meditates on the Passion.
By Daniele Crespi (1598/1600–1630), in the church of Santa Maria della Passione, Milan.

Charles' life became increasingly austere: he ate only once a day. He devoted himself entirely to the care of souls and made it a primary goal to urge the faithful to adoration of Christ in the Eucharist. He also promoted the practice of the Forty Hours and perpetual adoration, as well as devotion to Jesus crucified; he himself went four times to Turin in order to venerate the Shroud. He instituted a famous procession with the Holy Nail, a relic of the Passion; he also fostered devotion to the Virgin and emphasized the feast of St. Ambrose on December 7.

His reforming activity did not please everyone, and a discontented friar, one of the Humiliati in the convent of Brera, shot him with an harquebus; he was miraculously unharmed, even though the shot penetrated his clothing.

He fell ill of a fever on October 20, 1584, while making a retreat at the Sacro Monte di Varallo. On his way back to Milan, he stopped at Arona, where he celebrated his last Mass on November 1. He reached Milan by canal but was a dying man, and death came to him at nine o'clock in the evening of November 3. The Church remembers him on the fourth, because Vespers had already been celebrated and according to the practice of the time it was already November 4.

▷▷ Charles is patron of Milan, Arona, Guastalla, Rocca di Papa, and Savoy. He is protector of the clergy generally, of catechists, teachers, and makers of starch. On April 26, 1932, Pius XI proclaimed him patron of catechetical activities and catechists. Because of the care he took of the plague-stricken, he is invoked against pestilences.

▷▷ He is shown distributing Communion and anointing the plague-stricken, or eating his frugal meals. Above all, however, he is shown **on his knees before the crucifix**, wearing

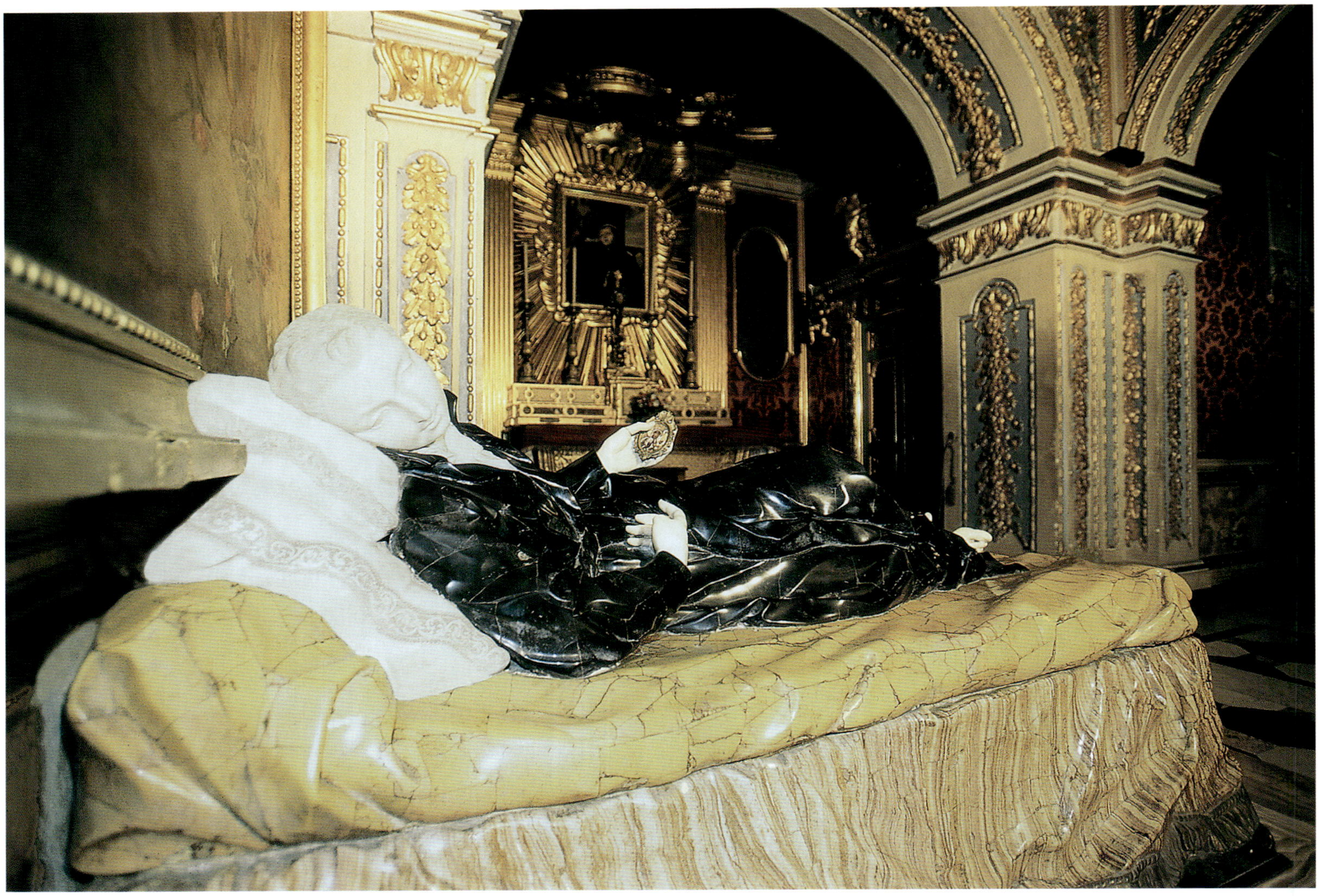

a **cardinal's cape**. His face is characterized by a rather prominent **aquiline nose**. His principal attributes are his **kneeling** in adoration and his **aquiline nose**. Other attributes are the **plague-stricken**, a **firearm**, and the **Holy Nail**.

Stanislaus Kostka, Jesuit Novice

1550–1568
Memorial: August 15
It.: Stanislao Kostka; Fr.: Stanislas Kostka; Sp.: Estanislao Kostka; Ger.: Stanislaus Kostka; Pol.: Stanislaw Kostka.

Stanislaus was born in the castle of Rostkovo, in Masovia in the kingdom of Poland, and was destined for a career as a diplomat. He was sent to the Jesuit College in Vienna, but when this college was closed by Maximilian II, an enemy of the Society, he continued to live in Vienna. He loved a life of recollection, prayer, and chastity, which enabled him to control an ardent and passionate temperament, but which also opened him to persecution by his brother and his tutor, both of which were frivolous and worldly men; meanwhile he devoted himself enthusiastically to study. When he fell seriously ill in December 1565, he had numerous mystical experiences. He was tormented by the devil in the form of a furious dog, but he also received Communion from an angel; the Virgin placed the Child Jesus in his arms and urged him to become a Jesuit.

He did not win permission to do so, and fled secretly from Vienna in 1567; he then took refuge in Augsburg with Peter Canisius, provincial of the Jesuits. After passing a test in a house of the Society in Dillingen, he asked that he might be sent to Rome. To reach the city he crossed the Alps on foot and was accepted as a novice by Francis Borgia. After a month

St. Stanislaus Kostka.
Sculpture by Pierre Legros, 1703, in the church of Sant'Andrea al Quirinale, Rome.

of doing the most menial tasks, he was transferred to the Jesuit house of Sant'Andrea in Quirinale, where he pronounced simple vows in May 1568. On August 5 he predicted his death, and died, as he had foretold, at dawn on August 15.

His motto was *Ad maiora natus sum* ("I was born for greater things"). He was the first Blessed of the Society of Jesus and was canonized in 1726, together with St. Aloysius Gonzaga.

▷▷ On August 31, 1962, John XXIII confirmed the tradition that made him a patron of Poland; he is also patron of the Jesuit novices, of youthful students, the dying, and those who are despairing of their salvation.

▷▷ Stanislaus is depicted as a **Jesuit novice, kneeling in adoration of the Blessed Sacrament**; in the act of receiving Communion; or with the **Child Jesus** in his arms, but his principal attribute is a **lily**, the symbol of purity.

Camillus of Lellis, Priest and Founder of the Ministers of the Sick

1550–1614
Memorial: July 14
It.: Camillo de'Lellis; Fr.: Camille de Lellis; Sp.: Camilo de Lelis; Ger.: Kamillus von Lellis.

This saint's father, John, was a colonel in the Spanish army; his mother, Camilla Compelli, was a holy woman who had lost her first child as a baby and had waited for Camillus for many years, during which she devoted herself to prayer and helping the poor and the sick. She was almost sixty when she conceived him; in a dream she saw the boy with a **cross on his breast** and, behind him, many others with the same sign.

Out of devotion, his mother decided to give birth to him in a stable. Little Camillus, future founder of the Ministers of the Sick (the "Camillians"), was born on Pentecost Sunday, 1550, at the Elevation of a Mass being celebrated in the church. The child was given his mother's name, which meant "minister of sacrifice." He lost his mother when he was thirteen and his father not long afterward. In 1571 he went to Rome in order to get healing for a wound in his right foot at the Hospital of San Giacomo degli Incurabili. He enlisted in the army, was in the pay of the Spaniards, and was finally discharged in 1574. He lost everything he owned while gambling and became a laborer in the factory of Capuchins in Manfredonia.

Glorification of St. Camillus of Lellis. 18th cent., attributed to G. B. Pittoni, in the church of Santi Gregorio e Siro, Bologna.

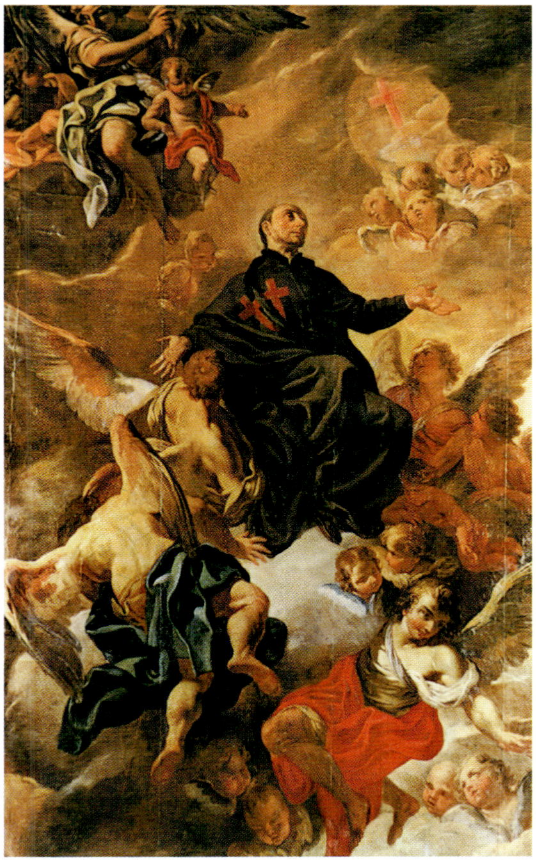

His conversion occurred on February 2, 1575; he then asked to become a Capuchin and was accepted. He had to return to the Incurabili because the wound in his foot reopened; he remained there for four years, attending to the other sick people. Once again he thought himself healed and returned to the novitiate, but was sent away for good when the wound reopened. He then made a vow to devote himself to the service of the sick in the Hospital of San Giacomo, where he remained thenceforth. He then considered forming a company of men who with him would devote themselves to the sick out of love for God and would have as their distinguishing external sign a **cross** that would be a sign of an interior disposition. An image of the crucified Jesus told him that such was indeed to be "his" work, and gave him the courage to overcome all obstacles. He resumed his studies, became a priest in 1584, and in 1586 obtained approval of his society, the Ministers of the Sick; these men were consecrated to the Immaculate Virgin and wore a black habit with a **red cross** on the breast; they were also called "the Fathers of a good death." Their activity was focused on care of the sick, who were often placed in the care of ignorant and indifferent servants.

He was tireless in helping the sick; his motto was *Haec est requies mea: reficere lassos* ("My rest is to refresh the weary"). His *Rule* called for tending to the sick with the affection and love of a mother for her only child. He died in Rome on July 14, 1614. His relics are in the church of St. Mary Magdalene near the Pantheon.

▷▷ Because of his care of the sick he is invoked against a painful death and for a good death in the spiritual sense. He is patron of Rome and Chieti. On June 22, 1886, Leo XIII proclaimed him patron of hospitals and the sick, and Pius XII declared him patron of nurses on August 28, 1930.

▷▷ He is depicted chiefly as a **mature man with an ascetical face**, intent on caring for the sick, or as hearing the crucified Jesus speak to him, or in glory. His principal attribute is a **red cross on the breast of a black habit and possibly on his cloak as well**. Other attributes are a **book**, representing his **Rule** and the rulebook of nurses; a **rosary**, an **angel**, and a **skull**.

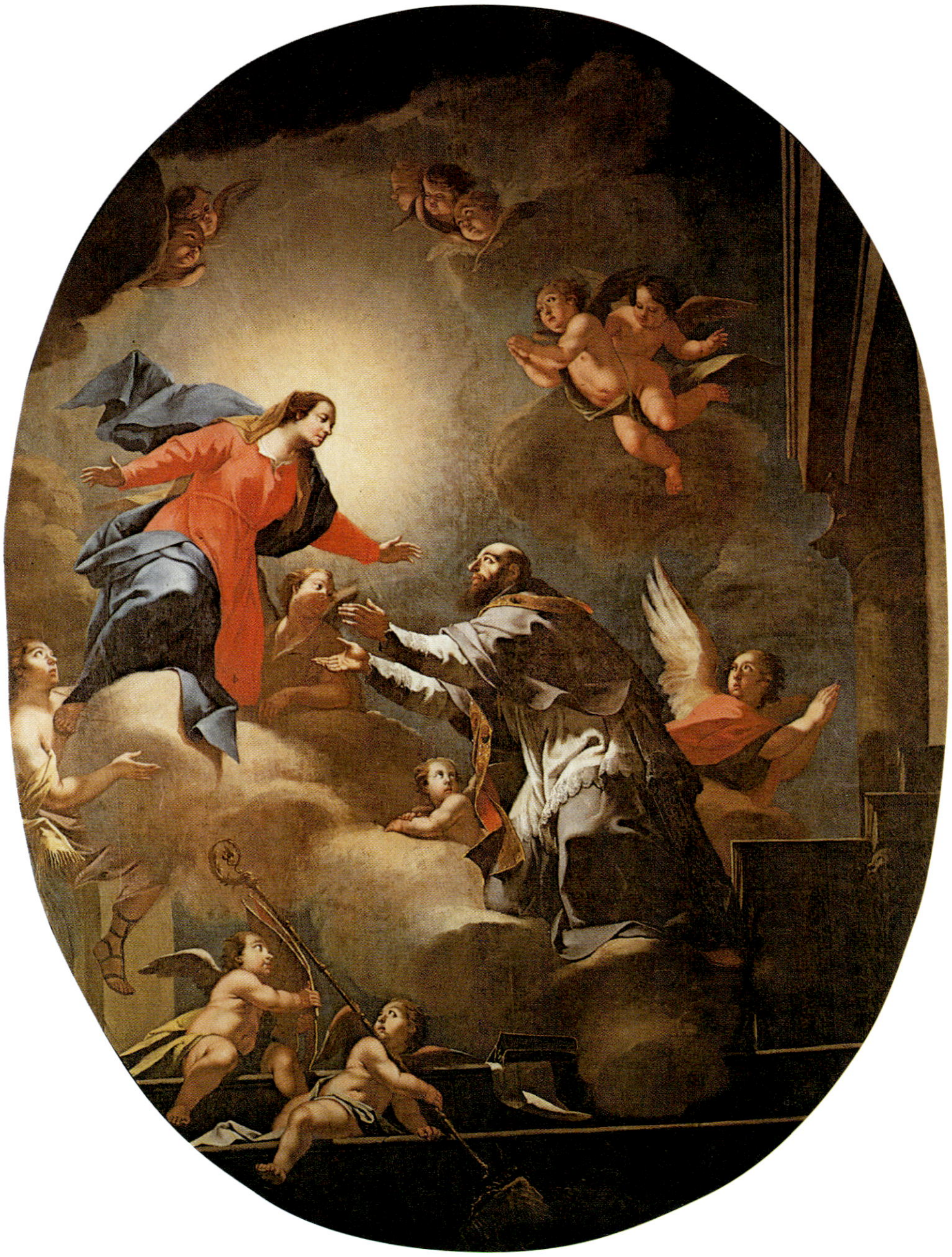

Apotheosis of St. Francis de Sales.
By Valentin Metzinger, 1755, in the National Gallery, Ljubljana, Slovenia.

St. Francis de Sales.
Statue, beginning of 20th cent., in the porch of the sanctuary of Fatima.

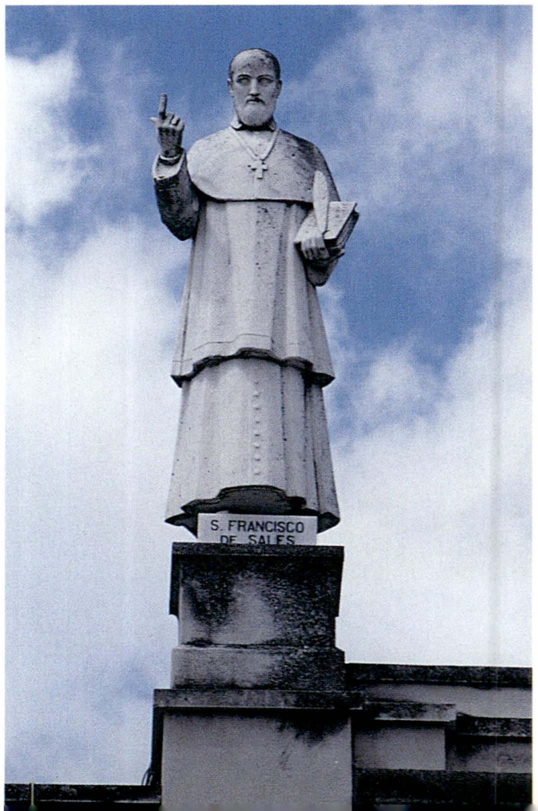

Francis de Sales, Bishop and Doctor of the Church

1567–1622
Memorial: January 24; *dies natalis:* December 28
Lat.: Franciscus Salesius; It.: Francesco di Sales; Sp.: Francisco de Sales; Ger.: Franz von Sales, Franciscus Salesius von Genf.

Francis was born at the castle of Sales, near Annecy, in 1567, to Catholic parents. He received a strict education in which he was inspired to practice mortification and love of the poor by his mother and to have courteous manners by his father.

As was true of many piously educated young boys of that period, he liked to build little altars and chapels and to "sing" Mass. He desired to receive tonsure at the age of eleven, and did his studies at the Jesuit College of Clermont in Paris, and then at Padua. He went to Loreto in order to fulfill a vow, and then to Rome. Finally, he became a priest and a simple and effective preacher against heresies. He was elected bishop of Geneva in 1602, but remained for good in Annecy, since Geneva was Calvinist.

While preaching Lenten sermons in Dijon in 1604, he made the acquaintance of Jane Francis de Chantal, a widow with four children, who was looking for a spiritual director. Under the guidance of the bishop and with methodical prudence, Chantal worked out her plan to found an order of women. This finally came into existence in June of 1610, in a section of Annecy known as "La Galerie." The new order consisted of only three sisters and had as its name: "Congregation of the Visitation of Our Lady," in honor of the meeting of Mary and Elizabeth. Its goal was to live a life of contemplation combined with an active life of charity toward the poor and the sick. The emblem of the congregation was a heart pierced by a sword and supporting a crown of thorns, over which were the names of Jesus and Mary.

Francis' *Introduction of the Devout Life* (or *Philothea*) was published in 1608; it was the most popular book of spirituality of the seventeenth century and had a great influence on Francis' own time. It consisted of letters by means of which Francis acted as spiritual director of many noble women, who in turn had a good influence on their husbands; thus it led to a noteworthy, even if hidden, social action. In order that his message might reach everyone, Francis had it printed on sheets of paper he himself slipped under the doors of houses.

Francis devoted himself to the clergy, whom he desired should be a cultivated body, convinced of their calling. He carried out the pastoral visitation of the 450 parishes of his diocese, where he took particular care of catechizing the very young, a work he engaged in personally. He found a lay "Confraternity of Christian Doctrine" and adopted the catechism of Cardinal Bellarmine for its manual.

He died in Lyons, cut off by a stroke on December 27, 1622. He was canonized in 1665 and proclaimed a Doctor of the Church in 1887. His great aim was to provide a rule for a life of meditation and charity that could be practiced by everyone without abandoning the world but rather remaining in it as active and creative Christians.

▷▷ On January 26, 1923, Pius XI proclaimed Francis to be the protector of Catholic writers and the Catholic press. He is patron of Annecy, Chambéry, and Geneva, and was proclaimed patron of India by John XXIII on June 27, 1962.

▷▷ He is depicted as **bald and bearded, wearing a surplice and without a miter**. His principal attribute is the **heart of Jesus**, sometimes inflamed, **surrounded by a crown of thorns**.

Aloysius Gonzaga, Jesuit Novice

1568–1591
Memorial: June 21
Lat.: Aloysius Gonzaga; It.: Luigi Gonzaga; Fr.: Louis de Gonzague; Sp.: Luis Gonzaga; Ger.: Aloisius von Gonzaga, Alois; Dutch: Lodewijk Gonzaga.

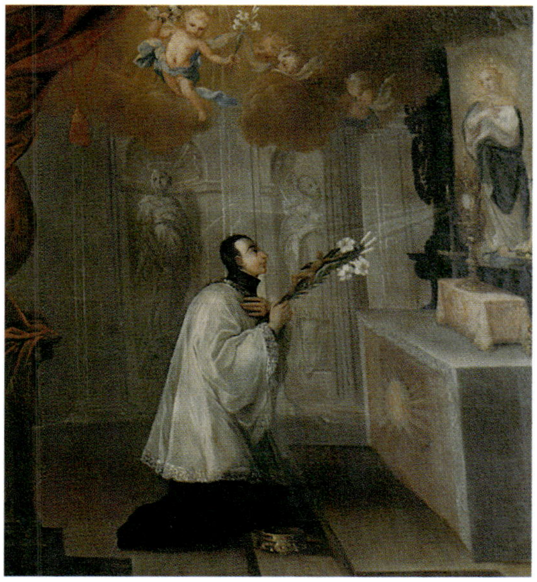

St. Aloysius Gonzaga. 18th cent., in the church of St. Gilgen, Sankt-Gilgen, Austria.

Aloysius died of the plague at the age of twenty-two. He was born into the Gonzaga family of Mantua, had a military career awaiting him, and frequented the courts of Tuscany and Spain. He was attracted, however, not by the life of the court but by veneration of the Virgin Mary. As a result, despite his father's anger, he renounced his hereditary title and on November 25, 1585, entered the Roman College of the Jesuits; his teacher there was St. Robert Bellarmine.

When the plague struck Rome in 1590, Aloysius devoted himself to the sick, caught the disease and died of it.

▷▷ Because of his precocious priestly vocation Aloysius is the patron of youthful students; in 1726 Benedict XIV proclaimed him patron of the students of the Jesuit College, and in 1926 Pius XI proclaimed him patron of Christian youth. Many parochial youth confraternities are named after him. He is invoked for help in choosing a state of life, and against lust and pulmonary diseases.

▷▷ His principal attributes are the **white surplice of a Jesuit novice**, a **lily**, and **contemplation of the crucified Jesus**. Other attributes are the **rosary**, a **skull**, the **discipline**, and the **ducal crown at his feet**.

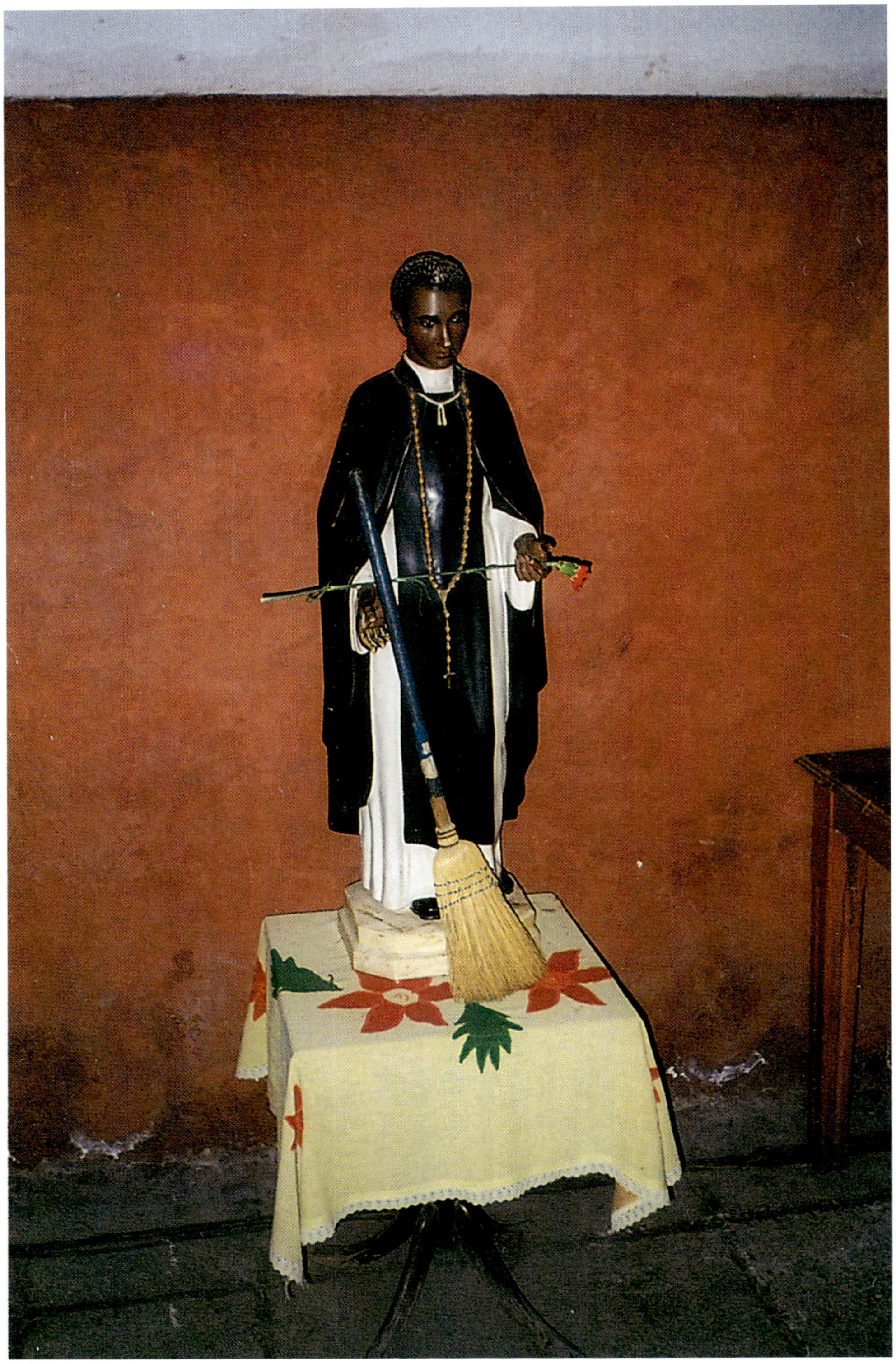

Martin de Porres, Dominican Religious

1579–1639
Memorial: November 3
Lat.: Martinus de Porres; It.: Martino di Porres.

Martin was born in Lima, Peru, to Juan de Porres, a Spanish knight, and Anna Vásquez, a black freedwoman of African origin. He was baptized in the same church as Rose of Lima. His father acknowledged him only years later; the color of his skin and his illegitimacy burdened his childhood, which was marked by poverty. But thereafter he spent some peaceful

St. Martin de Porres.
20th-cent. processional statue, in the church of Acatitlan, Mexico.

years with his father and mother and was able to study. He leaned toward a medical career and became a barber-surgeon, that is, a combined barber, surgeon, physician, and pharmacist, and was highly esteemed. But his path in life took a different turn, and he desired to enter the Dominican convent in Lima. He was accepted initially only as a tertiary, but the friars soon realized his gifts, and he was admitted to vows, making his solemn profession in 1603.

Martin spent hours in adoration of the Blessed Sacrament, disciplined himself at night, and meditated on the Passion. He was often seen in ecstasy and in a state of levitation in which he embraced the crucifix and kissed the wound in the Savior's side. He had the gifts of wisdom and knowledge, which he used to help the students of theology, and of prophecy and bilocation. He devoted himself entirely to the poor and the oppressed. Although he spoke of himself as a "mulatto dog," he was sought out by the archbishop and the viceroy who were eager to receive his advice; as a result, he became the patron of jurists.

St. Martin de Porres.
Small devotional image, 20th cent.

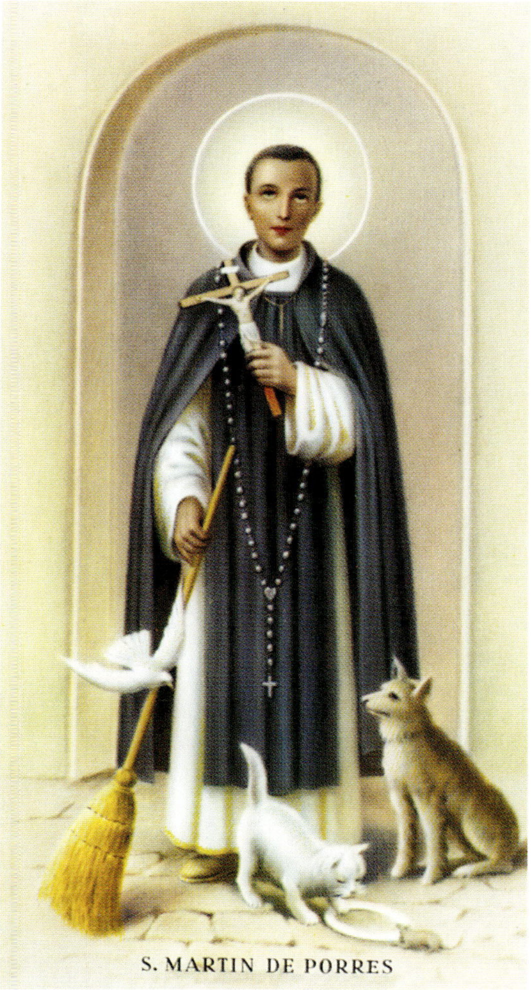

During a plague he tended, all by himself, to sixty sick people. He also took care of **animals**, which he could not bear to see mistreated. He stooped to the lowliest animals of the farmyard, including even the mice, because in them, too, he saw the mark of the Creator; he spoke to them, and they obeyed him. **Dogs, cats, and mice** appear in his iconography because they used to go to him to be fed, tended, and medicated. **Mice** had him as a protector and used to gather at the end of the farmyard to be fed, without doing harm to others; he is therefore invoked against infestations of mice.

This was a fortunate period for Lima, since it contained not only Martin but also St. Toribius, St. Francis Solana, a Franciscan, the Dominican Tertiary St. Rose of Lima, and Blessed John Massias.

A violent fever led to Martin's death on November 3, 1639. This Dominican, regarded as a wonderworker and called "the father of charity," was canonized by John XXIII in 1962.

▷▷ Martin is invoked as protector of people of color; he also protects jurists, television, and the schools of Peru. He is invoked against infestations of mice.

▷▷ He is depicted in a **Dominican habit, holding a broom**, and with **farmyard animals: a dog, a cat, and mice, around him**.

Rose of Lima, Virgin

1586–1617
Memorial: August 23; *dies natalis:* August 24
Lat.: Rosa Limensis, Peruana; It.: Rosa da Lima; Fr.: Rose de Lima; Sp.: Rosa del Perù; Ger.: Rosa von Lima.

The saint was born to Gaspar Florese and Maria de Oliva, Spaniards who had settled in Peru. She was baptized Isabella, but because of her exceptional beauty she was first called Rose by Mariana, an Indian servant. The name stuck to her and was ratified at her confirmation, which was administered by Bishop St. Toribius in 1597 at Quive, to which the family had moved. She received an especially learned education for a woman of her time. While still a child, she consecrated herself to God and soon began a life of mortifications, fasts, penances, disciplines, hair shirts, and lengthy vigils. She entered the Dominican Order at the age of twenty but remained a Tertiary because there was no monastery of women in Lima; she received the habit in 1606 and took the name Rosa de Santa Maria.

She experienced ecstasies from Thursday to Saturday of every week and suffered the torments of the Passion; she loved to wear a **crown of thorns on her forehead** and to lie on shards of glass. She foretold her death a year in advance and died, amid great suffering, on August 24, 1617.

It is said that **flowers** bent their heads toward her and that a nightingale sang under her window during Lent. Her few writings bear witness to a spirit both ascetical and mystical.

Clement X canonized her in 1617 as the first saint of the Americas.

▷▷ Rose is the principal patron of South America, Peru, Lima, Callao (the port of Lima), the Spanish Indies, and the Philippines, and of a diocese named after her in California and another in Argentina. She is patron also of the Guardia Civile of Peru.

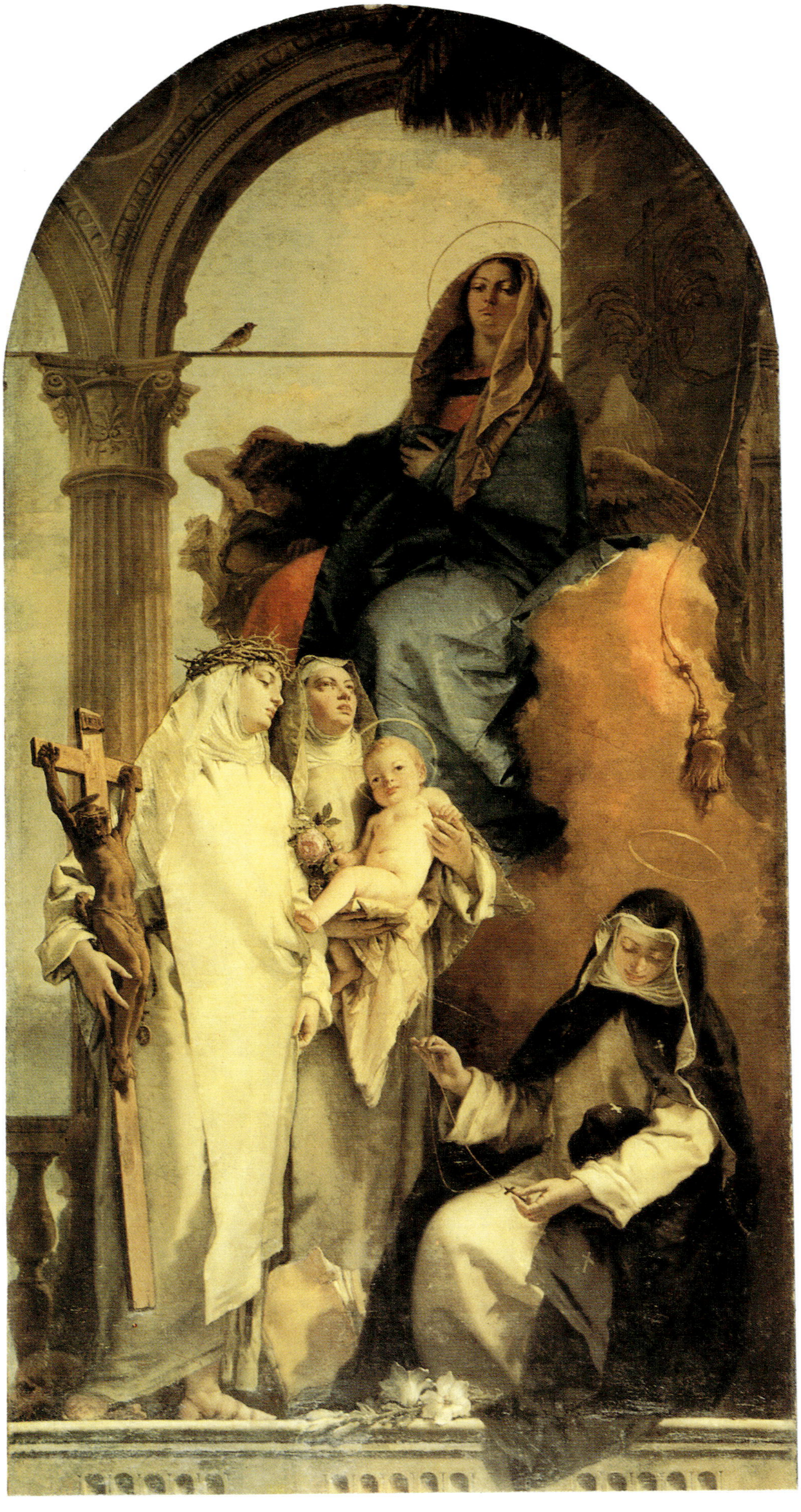

St. Agnes of Montepulciano, St. Rose of Lima, and St. Catherine of Siena at the Feet of the Virgin. By Giambattista Tiepolo (1696–1770) in the church of the Gesuati, Venice.
St. Rose is distinguishable by her roses and the Child Jesus. St. Rose is regarded as the St. Catherine of Siena of South America.

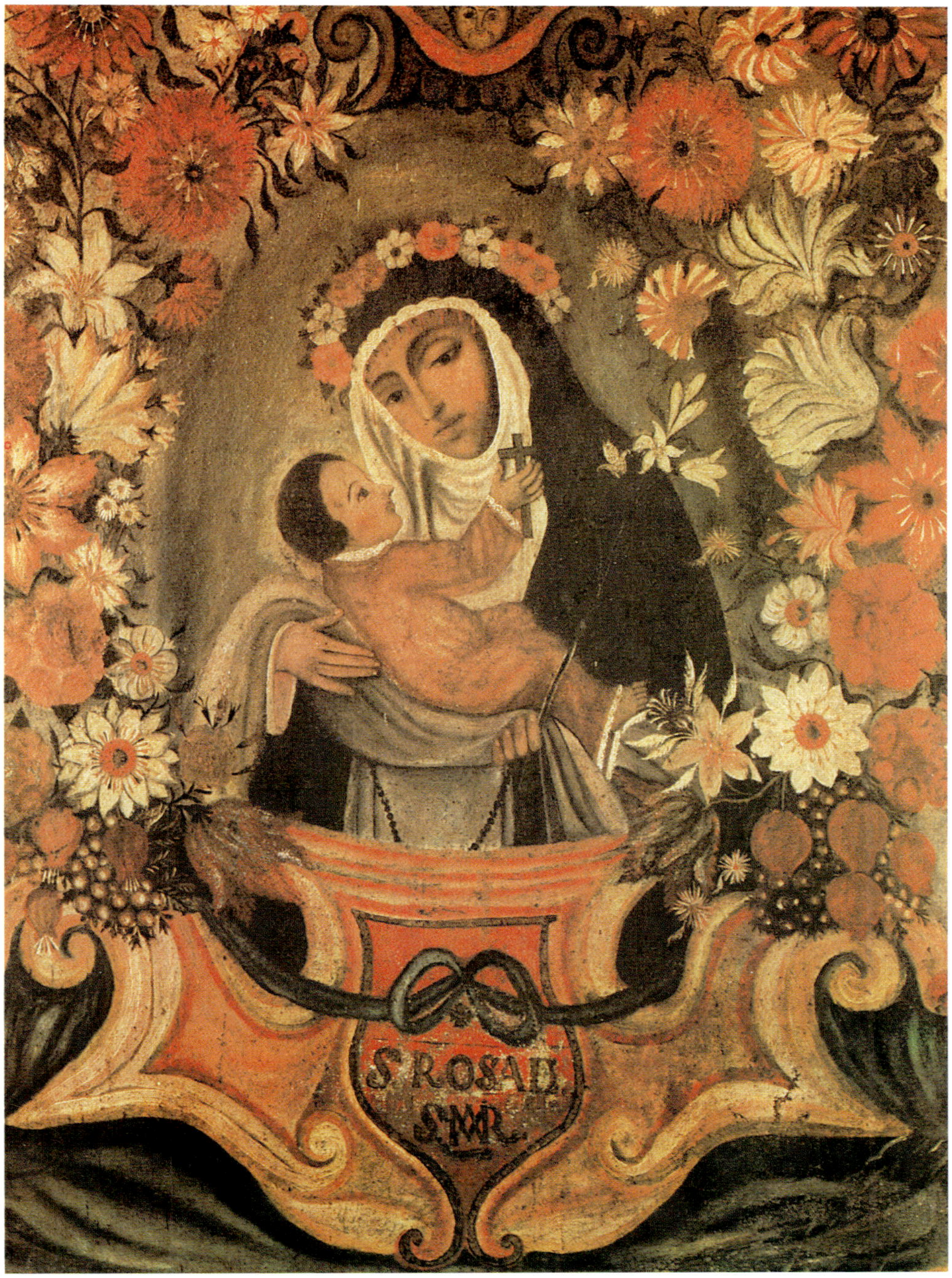

St. Rose of Lima.
18th cent., in the Museo del Banco Central, Quito, Ecuador.
Here is an example of colonial art in which the artist depicts the saints—and in this instance the first saint of the New World—in his own style and in the forms peculiar to a culture that was developing its autonomy.

Not only because of the miracle of the flowers but also because of her very name she is patron of gardeners and florists. Every home in Peru used to have an image of her, and the simple application of this image used to obtain miracles. In 1746 she protected Lima against an earthquake. She is also invoked against plagues.

▷▷ Rose is depicted as **young and beautiful, wearing a Dominican habit**. Roses in various forms are her principal attribute: she wears a **crown** or **rosary** of **roses and thorns**; she carries **roses** in her hand, or receives them from Jesus. In her ecstasies she contemplates the life of Jesus and was privileged to **hold the Child Jesus in her arms**. On the occasion of her canonization Clement X had her pictured holding a **bunch of roses on which the Child was resting**; this image became part of her iconography. The first image of her that was sent from Spain to Lima showed her in a Dominican habit, crowned with roses, and holding the Child Jesus in her right arm, while her left hand rested on a long **anchor**, a symbol of faith. She is also shown with the saints who were canonized along with her: Francis Borgia, Louis Bertrand, Gaetano of Thiene, and Philip Benizi.

Vincent de Paul, Priest and Founder of the Vincentians and the Daughters of Charity

1581–1660
Memorial: September 27
Lat.: Vincentius a Paulo; It.: Vincenzo de Paoli, di Paolo, de'Paoli; Fr.: Monsieur Vincent Depaul or De Paul; Sp.: Vicente de Pablo; Ger.: Vincenz von Paul.

This founder of the Vincentians and the Daughters of Charity was a man filled with the priestly spirit, a man who saw Christ in every sufferer and worked to form priests capable of helping the poor. The proper spelling of his name was Depaul, but this later changed to an Italian form: "De Paoli." He came from a poor family and was used to working in the fields, but he left his native place, Pouy, and went to the Franciscan convent in Dax in order to become a priest. He made unusual progress, entered the University of Toulouse, and was ordained in 1600 when he was only nineteen; he received his degree in theology in 1604.

He was captured by Turkish pirates during a sea voyage in 1605 and was sold to three different masters; together with the last one, a renegade Christian whom he converted, he crossed the Mediterranean in 1607 and landed in Provence. He then became a member of a group of priests who, under the guidance of Bérulle, were preparing for a reform of the clergy. He became a parish priest in Paris and then at Châtillons-les-Dombes; he became a tutor and chaplain to the powerful Gondi family, which supported his work. Meanwhile he had acquired a licentiate in canon law.

He started various foundations that met the needs of the poor and the rural population, who at that time were abandoned by everyone. He believed the sick and the poor needed help that was not merely occasional, and he therefore established a confraternity of devout persons who were committed to taking turns assisting all the needy sick. 1617 saw the birth of the first *Carità,* whose members described themselves as "Servants of the poor"; the name of one of the "Charities" in Paris was changed in 1629 to "The Ladies of Charity." (Soon men were called whose groups had a varied history but finally became in 1833 the "Conferences of St. Vincent de Paul.") The various "Charities" helped the saint in his charitable work, which covered a wide range of the needy: from foundlings to galley slaves, from the sick to slaves, and the starving.

Vincent then gathered around him a group of priests, and they began to preach missions in the countryside, with excellent results. The group soon became a "Congregation for the Missions": its members renounced ecclesiastical offices, preached only in the rural areas, taught catechism, and devoted themselves to convicts. These priests also became known as "Missionaries of St. Vincent," "Vincentians," or "Lazarists"; this last name was due to the fact that their first motherhouse was at the Parisian leprosarium of St. Lazarus.

Vincent's third foundation was the "Daughters of Charity": these were single country girls whom Vincent brought together to help the "Charities" in the cities. It was difficult for wealthy women to take a personal part in helping the needy, and therefore they provided the means for the works of mercy carried on by these country girls, who had no social obligations. In this work Vincent was aided by his spiritual daughter, St. Louise de Marillac.

St. Vincent, known as the "Father of the Poor," was one of the major authors of the seventeenth-century Catholic renaissance. He died in 1660 and was canonized in 1737.

He is depicted either with a **crucifix in his hand** or **carrying a child, with two others at his side**; these are his principal attributes.

▷▷ Vincent's traditional patronage of Madagascar was confirmed by Pius XII on November 9, 1949, and by John XXIII on October 25, 1961. He is patron of abandoned children and orphans, nurses, slaves, convicts, and prisoners. He is invoked by those who lose their parents. Leo XIII proclaimed him patron of Catholic caritative associations on May 12, 1885.

▷▷ He is depicted wearing a **black cassock**; his face is that of a man **on in years but not old**, smiling and serene, and with **children** in his arms and at his side.

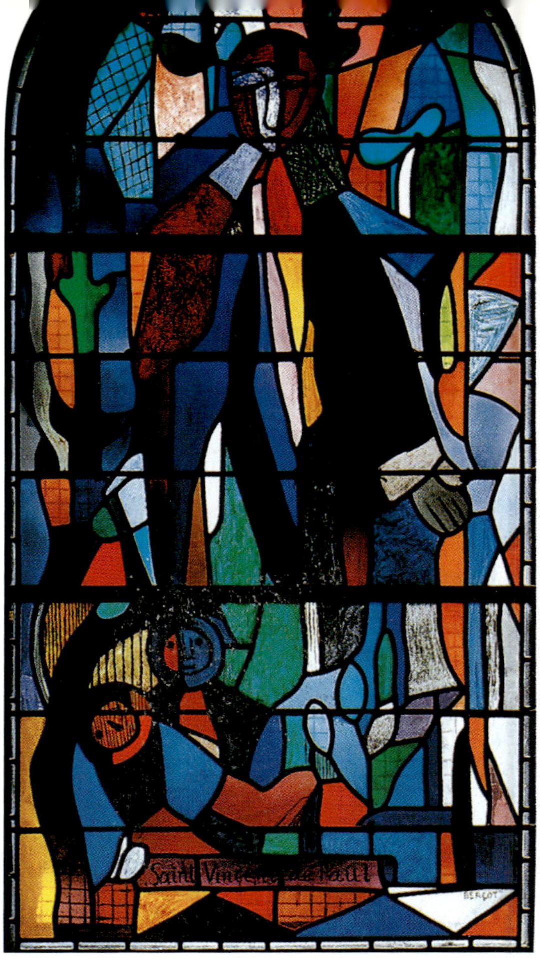

St. Vincent de Paul.
Stained-glass window, 1950, by P. Berçot, in the church of Notre Dame de Toute Grâce, Plateau d'Assy.

St. Vincent de Paul.
19th-cent. plaster devotional statue, Lizzano in Belvedere, Bologna.
St. Vincent is often shown with children, whose care he promoted.

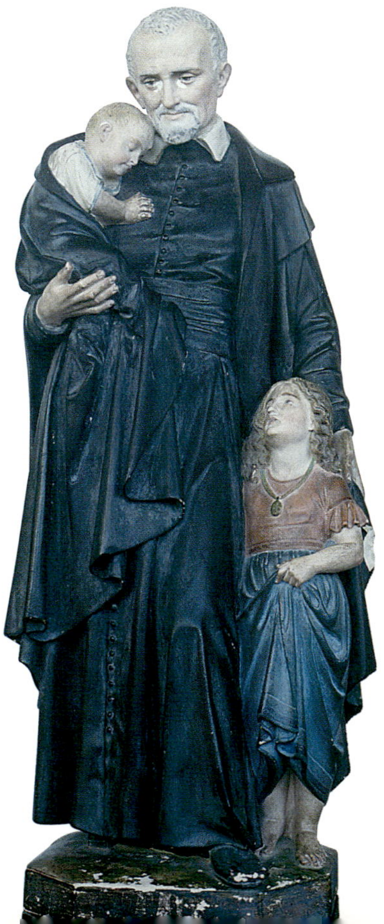

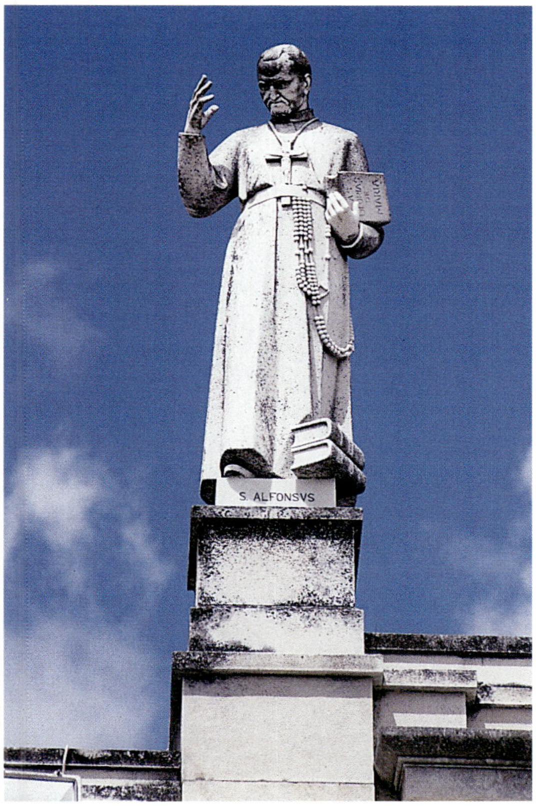

St. Alphonsus Maria Liguori.
Statue, from the beginning of the 20th cent., in the porch of the sanctuary in Fatima.

Alphonsus Liguori, Bishop, Founder of the Congregation of the Most Holy Redeemer, and Doctor of the Church

1696–1787
Memorial: August 1
It.: Alfono Maria de'Liguori; Fr.: Alphonse de Liguori; Sp.: Alfonso de Ligorio; Ger.: Alfons von Liguori.

Alphonsus preached and wrote many books aimed at helping people to live a Christian life. He was born in Naples and founded the Congregation of the Most Holy Redeemer, known as the Redemptorists, which was consecrated to the Redeemer and dedicated to giving popular missions in a complicated age that was marked by great faith but also by the growth of indifferentism and expediency. He became bishop of Sant'Agata dei Goti (Benevento) in 1762. He was present, in an ecstasy, at the death of Pope Clement XIV, and he himself died in 1787.

Alphonsus wrote the well-known Christmas carol *Tu scendi dalle stelle, o Re del cielo* ("Come down from the stars, O King of heaven"), which bears witness both to his love of the Child Jesus and to his pastoral talent, which evangelized in accurate and simple language.

▷▷ In the course of time Alphonsus became stooped, and his images differ greatly, showing him sometimes as a young and erect man, sometimes as old and stooped. He is often shown **in prayer before a crucifix**; the **crucifix** and the **rosary** are his principal attributes.

Jean Marie Baptiste Vianney, Curate of Ars

1786–1859
Memorial: August 4
Lat.: Ioannes Maria Vianney; It.: Giovanni Maria Battista Vianney; Fr.: Jean-Baptiste Vianney, le curé d'Ars; Ger.: Der Pfarrer von Ars, der heilige Tor.

This son of peasants was born in Dardilly near Lyons, and his childhood ran concurrent with the French Revolution. He made his First Communion in 1799 at a Mass celebrated by a recusant priest, that is, one who had not sworn fealty to the revolutionary government. This witness led Jean to think of the priesthood. He lacked talents and was unable to read and write until he was seventeen. Despite his not having the necessary education, he presented himself to Charles Balley, the parish priest of Écully, who was so struck by the young man's worth that he accepted him. After many difficulties he was ordained a priest in 1815 and remained three more years with his teacher. When Balley died, Jean was appointed assistant priest of Ars-sur-Formans, and became its pastor in 1821. Within ten years he had changed the life of the area by his example, by a preaching which, without being unusually learned, touched hearts, and, above all, by his constant presence in the confessional, where he remained for sixteen or seventeen hours a day. People came to him from all sides, drawn by his ability to understand souls and guide them.

Throughout his life he was tormented by the thought of his inadequacy and twice attempted to leave the parish. When he died on August 4, 1859, throngs attended his funeral. Pius XI canonized him in 1925 and, in 1928; proclaimed him patron of all parish priests. John XXIII devoted his encyclical *Nostri sacerdotii primitias* to Vianney.

Jean was tireless in his ministry; he allowed himself only a half-hour of sleep and ate only a few boiled potatoes. The devil did not spare Jean his visits and disturbed his nights by pulling on his feet.

▷▷ Vianney is patron of priests and, in particular, of pastors and curates.

▷▷ His image, deriving from some contemporary depictions, is that of a **thin** man, **emaciated** from fasting and dressed in the **garb of curates of that time**.

St. Jean Marie Baptiste Vianney.
This is the best-known portrait of the holy Curé of Ars.

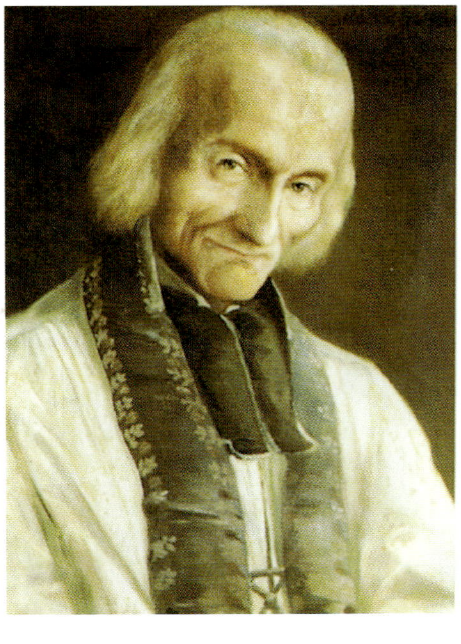

John Bosco, Priest and Founder of the Salesian Order and the Institute of the Daughters of Mary Help of Christians

1815–1888
Memorial: January 31
Lat.: Ioannes Bosco; It.: Giovanni Bosco; Fr.: Jean Bosco; Sp.: Juan Bosco; Ger.: Johannes Bosco.

This saint's work was devoted entirely to the young. He was born in Becchi, an outlying hamlet belonging to Castelnuovo d'Asti. At the age of nine he had a vision showing him that his destiny was to win to the faith those young people who, far from God, were like wild animals that had to be turned into lambs.

John began gathering boys around him, on Sunday evenings after Vespers, by calling them to a game of acrobatics he had learned at fairs; then, when they had played, he would repeat to them the sermon he had heard at Mass. After making his Communion, he went off to be a laborer on a dairy farm, with the result that until 1831 he was able to study only sporadically. He completed his elementary and junior high school studies in a few years' time and in 1835 was able to be invested as a cleric. He had already founded the "Society of Joy," the goal of which was the avoidance of everything unworthy of a Christian, the scrupulous fulfillment of duty, and joy.

In order to pay for his schooling he worked hard every evening, performing the most varied tasks: he was a tailor, a blacksmith, a carpenter, and other things as well. After the years in the seminary he was ordained a priest in 1841. He began his life's work and for five years his place of prayer had no fixed abode; his boys, drawn by his joy and the prospect of a meal, followed him everywhere. Finally, at Valdocco, a chapel was built with the name of St. Francis de Sales, which later gave Don Bosco's group its name—the Salesians; there he was able to gather the young in a more permanent way.

His activity was accompanied by visions which showed him the future and encouraged him; meanwhile he wrote his first works. In 1858 he want to Rome and told Pius IX of his plan to found a congregation dedicated to the education of the young. This marked the beginning of a huge undertaking. Without ever getting into the area of politics, Don Bosco succeeded in overcoming the difficulties he met as time passed; he often served as mediator between the Italian government and the Holy See. The Basilica of Mary Help of Christians which he wanted was completed in three years, in 1868. In 1872 he founded the Institute of the Daughters of Mary Help of Christians for the education of young girls.

The work of the Salesians expanded; thus trade schools were opened that removed the young from the streets and from forced idleness and vice. Bosco's life was filled with undertakings that were carried out with tireless zeal, courage, and broad vision. Religion, reason, and kindness were the three fixed points of his work, the motto of which was "Everything through love, nothing by violence." His life unfolded during difficult years in the history of Italy, a time when relations between state and Church were changing. Don Bosco was the same priest whether dealing with the poor or with the mighty.

▷▷ John is patron of apprentices, the young, publishers, educators, and pedagogues. On January 17, 1958, Pius XII proclaimed him patron of Italian apprentices and young workers.

▷▷ Don Bosco is always shown in a **cassock** and with **boys around him**.

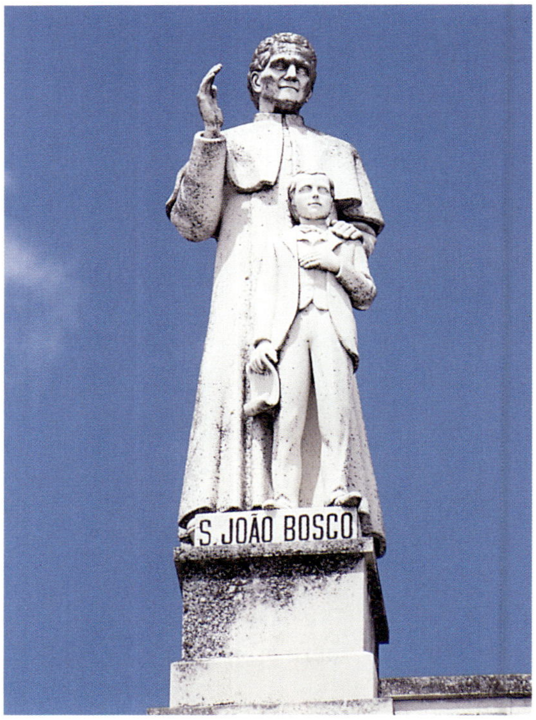

St. John Bosco.
Statue, from the beginning of the 20th cent., on the porch of the sanctuary in Fatima.

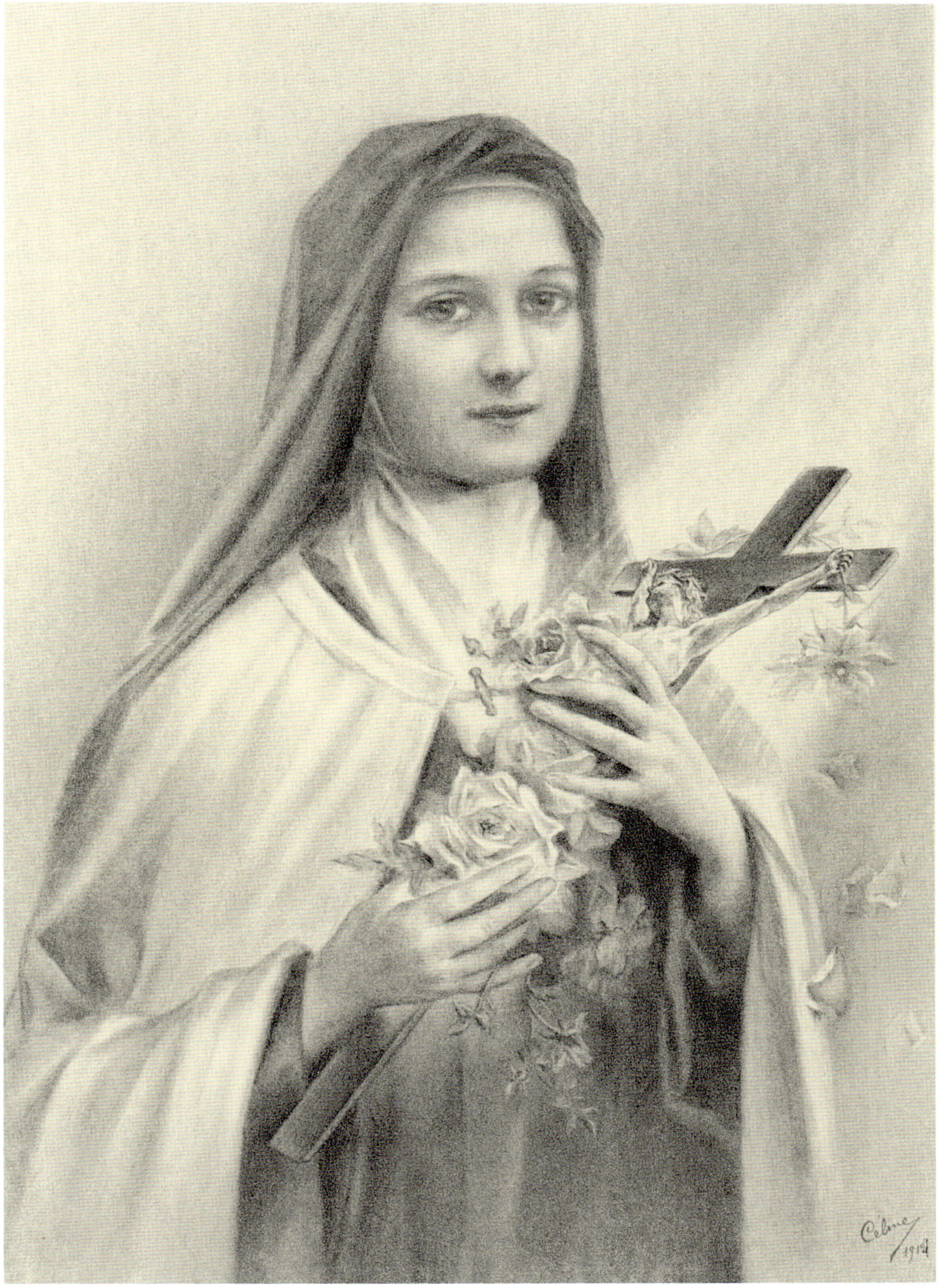

Theresa of the Child Jesus, Carmelite Religious and Doctor of the Church

St. Theresa with Roses.
This drawing, made in 1919 by Sister Genevieve of the Holy Face, Theresa's sister, is the basis for the most widespread representation of the saint.

1873–1897
Memorial: October 1; *dies natalis:* September 30
Lat.: Teresia a Jesu Infante; It.: Teresa di Gesù Bambino, Teresa del bambin Gesù, del Volto Sancto; Fr.: Thérèse de Lisieux ou de l'Enfant Jésus, la Semeuse de roses; Sp.: Teresa del Niño Jesús; Ger.: Theresia vom Kinde Jesu, von Lisieux.

Theresa, known also as Theresa of Lisieux, was the ninth and last daughter of Joseph Stanislaus Martin and Maria Zelia Guérin, and was baptized Maria Françoise Theresa. She experienced suffering at an early age, her mother dying when she was four; but she tells us that at the age of only two she decided to become a sister. She learned very quickly to pray and at the age of three desired "not to refuse God anything." At the age of six she became a semi-boarder of the Benedictine nuns of Lisieux, to which place her family had recently moved. She fell ill on March 25, 1883, and was cured on May 13 by the Virgin's smile. Her First Communion on May 8, 1884, with its complete union with Jesus, was the beginning of a life surrendered without reserve to merciful Love and so bent on the conversion of sinners and the salvation of souls that it made her patron of the missions.

In 1886 she obtained the permission of her father and then of the religious superiors to enter Carmel at the age of fifteen. She took the veil in 1888, together with the name Theresa of the Child Jesus and the Holy Face and pronounced her vows on September 8, 2890. Not infrequently she was tormented by the thought of not pleasing God, but in the Scriptures she discovered God's love for the little ones, and she trusted that the arms of Jesus would carry her to heaven. In 1895, by order of the superior, she began to write *The Story of a Soul,* in which she told of a spiritual journey marked by the awareness that only "a holocaust offering to merciful Love" can restore the order broken by sin and that a soul united to God draws after it all those it loves. It was, moreover, a journey not lacking in interior struggles and harsh times of dryness, which were always surmounted by abandonment to God. Tuberculosis caused Theresa's death on September 30, 1897.

She had said that from heaven she would let fall a **shower of roses**, that is, of graces, and that is what happened, confirming her sanctity. She was canonized in 1925.

▷▷ On December 14, 1927, Pius XI proclaimed her, together with Francis Xavier, patron of all missionaries and all missions. Pius XI also proclaimed her patron of Russia on October 28, 1932. She is patron of France as well.

▷▷ In the photographs we have of her, she is shown wearing a **Carmelite's habit**, often **contemplating the cross** and holding an **armful of roses**.

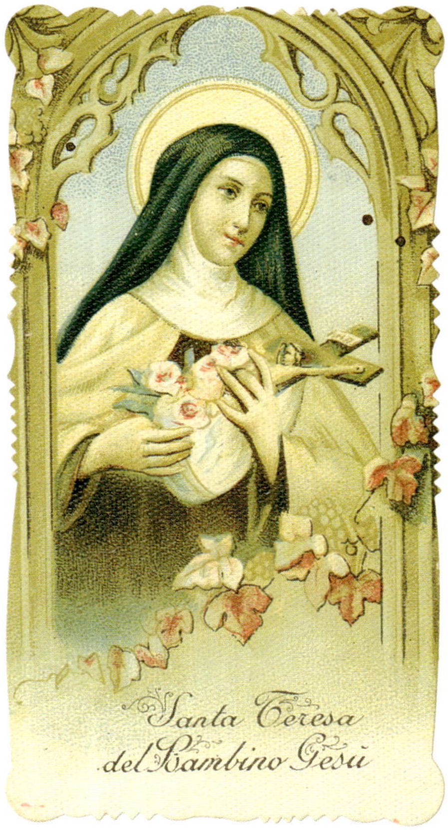

St. Theresa of the Child Jesus.
Small devotional image, 20th cent.

Leopold Mandic, Priest of the Friars Minor Capuchin and Confessor

1866–1942
Memorial: July 30
Lat.: Leopoldus (Bogdan) Mandic de Castronovo.

Leopold was a Capuchin priest on fire with zeal for Christian unity and the ministry of reconciliation. He was born in 1866 at Bocche di Cataro in Castelnuovo, entered the convent at the age of sixteen, and took his vows at Udine in 1888. He was ordained in Venice in 1890; after going to Padua in 1909, he remained there until his death on July 30, 1942. He was only about four-and-a-half feet tall, awkward, stooped, and always sickly; he spent his life in the confessional, remaining there fifteen hours a day. He was thus almost a saint without a history, and yet such were his ties to the people of Padua that, contrary to the norm that friars should go from convent to convent frequently, he was left in Padua; a brief removal from there in 1923 was immediately cancelled by superiors at the persuasion of the bishop of Padua. At the end of 1988 the volumes containing the appeals of pilgrims to St. Leopold already numbered 290.

Much of the convent was destroyed during the war, but Leopold's cell remains intact, as does the chapel of Our Lady, where he said Mass and spent long periods in prayer. These are the places, together with the tomb, to which the faithful come. They see the few poor things that are his relics: the chalice for Mass, the little whip for penance, the breviary, the footstool he used in reaching to things above his head, a folded shirt, and his last habit.

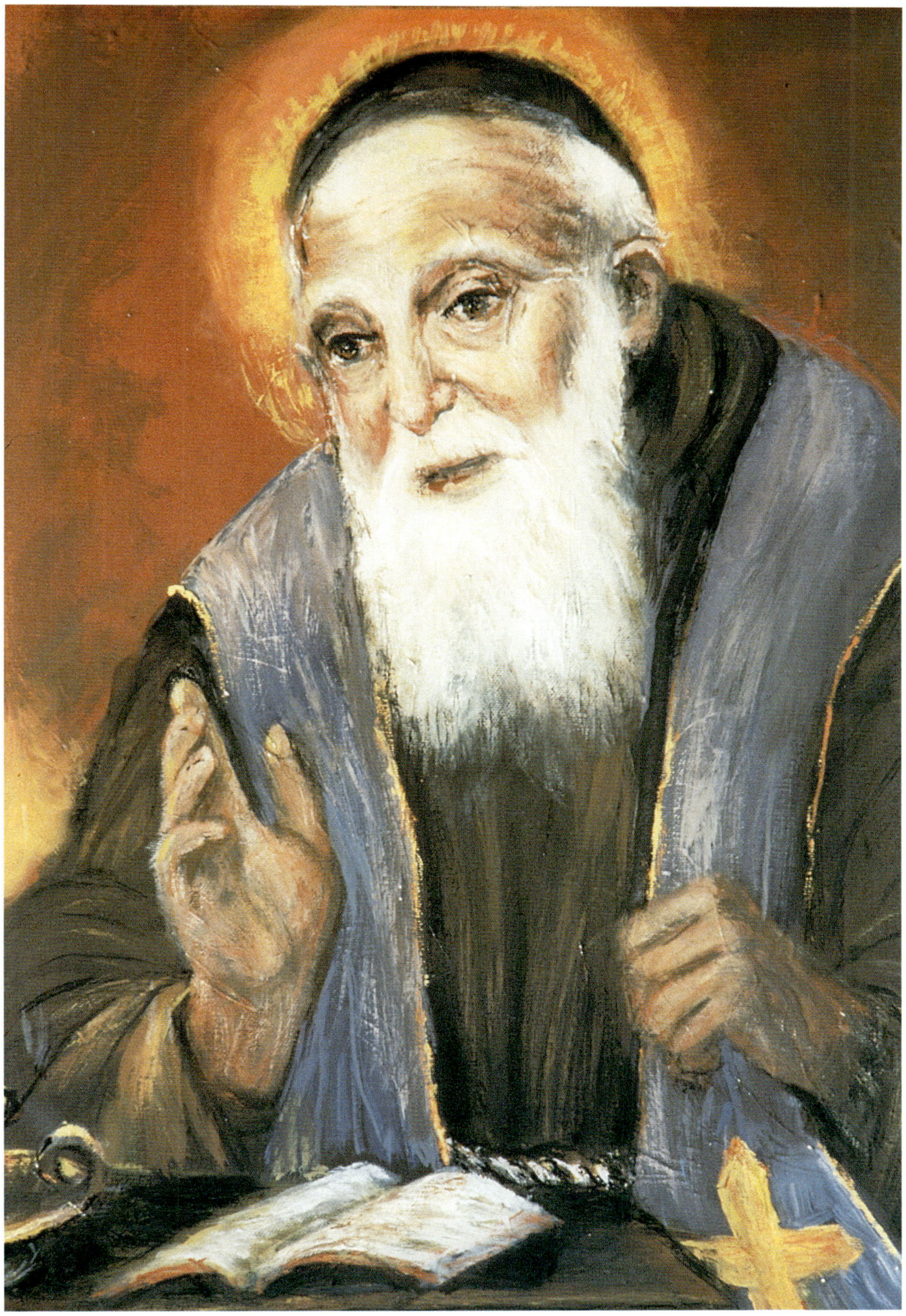

St. Leopold Mandic.
Portrait, 20th cent.

Leopold loved his habit and kissed it and wanted to die in it, because the habit expresses the state of the heart.

He is a saint without a history, but the churches of Italy have slowly been filled by his images; this is because, like Anthony, Leopold is a brother who does not disappoint. Pilgrimages, whether of individuals or of groups, arrive continually, and the crowds naturally increase during the week of his feast day, around May 12. John Paul II canonized him in 1983.

▷▷ Leopold is protector of confessors.

▷▷ He is depicted in his **Capuchin habit**, with a **long beard and white hair**, in the act of giving absolution. A **skullcap** and a **violet stole** are his attributes.

Frances Xavier Cabrini, Virgin and Foundress of the Missionaries of the Sacred Heart of Jesus

1850–1917
Memorial: December 22
Lat.: Francisca Xaverio Cabrini; It.: Francesca Saverio Cabrini.

This saint's entire concern was for immigrants. She was born at Sant'Angelo Lodigiano as a thirteenth child. She became a teacher and, when her parents died, she expressed a desire to become a religious, but the pastor to whom she told this sent her to teach in the orphanage of Lodi. She made her profession in a new institute, the Sisters of Providence, of which she soon became superior; she took the name Frances Xavier in honor of the great missionary to the Indies. The community was disbanded; the bishop, claiming not to know of any missionary institute such as she wanted, suggested that she found her own. This she did, and in 1880, together with seven companions, inaugurated her Institute of the Missionaries of the Sacred Heart of Jesus in the House of Providence. Her heart inclined her to the East, but Leo XIII wanted her in America, where the situation of the emigrants was very troubling; he told her, "Your China will be the United States." This "mother of the emigrants" became familiar with their problems on the voyage across the ocean. When she reached New York, she was tireless in quickly organizing initial help for the poorest, while also caring for the sick and the orphans. This was the period in which she built houses, schools, emergency clinics, and, finally, a large hospital. She returned several times to Europe and, because of the great flowering of vocations, opened thirty foundations in eight countries. Her works consisted of asylums, schools, boarding schools for boys, girls' boarding schools, orphanages, workshops, hospitals, clinics, chapels, catechisms, congregations for different classes of people, and visits to families, prisons, and mines. Her work advanced with great rapidity. Death took her unexpectedly in Chicago on December 22, 1917. It is estimated today that she left sixty-seven foundations and thirteen hundred missionaries.

Leo XIII regarded her as a very holy woman; Pius X called her "the apostle of the gospel"; and Benedict XV acknowledged her as "filled with the Spirit of God."

Her strength came from obedience, humility, and daily meditation; as superior, she emphasized prayer, silence, poverty, hard work, and complete and constant obedience. She asked nothing of others that she herself was not ready to do.

By a special dispensation from Pius XI, the process for her beatification began very quickly, and he beatified her on November 12, 1938. Pius XII canonized her in 1946.

▷▷ Frances was proclaimed patron of emigrants by Pius XII on September 8, 1950.

▷▷ A statue of the saint, the work of E. Tadolini, is in the Basilica of St. Peter in Rome, in one of the niches reserved for founders. Her iconography has been determined by a photograph taken of her in 1914. She is dressed in the **habit of her Institute** and holds a **cross** in her hand. Her principal attribute is a **heart on fire**.

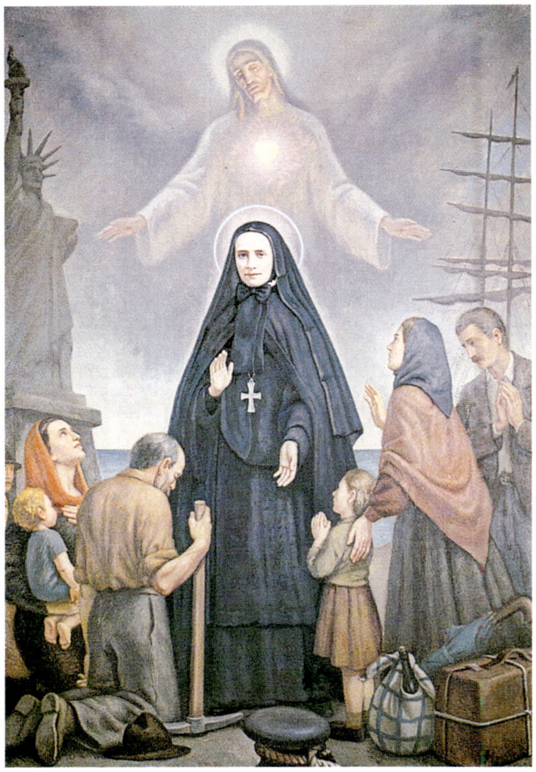

St. Frances Xavier Cabrini.
This picture was published in a pamphlet of the Missionaries of the Sacred Heart of Jesus. It shows the saint in the midst of immigrants who have arrived in America.

Theresa Benedicta of the Cross, Virgin, Carmelite, Martyr, and Patron of Europe

1891–1942
Memorial: August 9
Lat.: Teresia Benedicta a Cruce (Editha) Stein; It.: Teresa Benedetta della Croce.

Edith Stein was born in Breslau, Germany (now Wroclaw, Poland), German by nationality, Jewish by birth, and the last of eleven children. Her mother, who became a widow shortly after, raised her in the Jewish tradition, but later on, and for a long time, Edith declared herself an atheist. Beginning in 1916 she was assistant to phenomenological philosopher Edmund Husserl. After being deeply impressed by a widow's trust in God and by reading a biography of Theresa of Avila, she met philosopher Max Scheler and became acquainted with Christianity and Thomism. She was baptized in the cathedral of Cologne, taking the name Theresa Hedwig. She then taught German and history in the convent of

Arrival of Edith Stein, Sister Theresa of the Cross, in Auschwitz.
By M. Celeste, 20th cent., in the General Curia of the Discalced Carmelites, Rome.

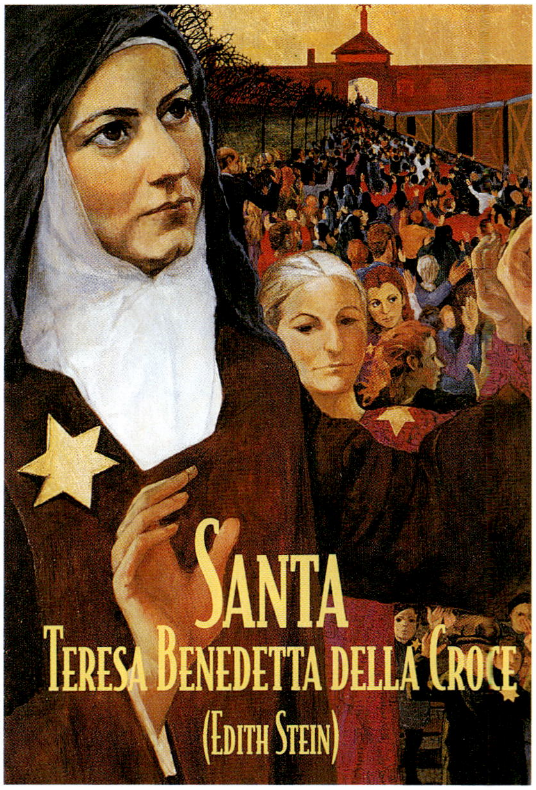

the Dominican nuns of St. Magdalene in Speyer (Palatinate). Her conversion led her to rethink Aristotelian-Thomistic philosophy in the light of phenomenological thought; she later became a teacher in the German Institute of Scientific Pedagogy in Münster. Finally, on April 15, 1934, she made a definitive choice and entered the convent of the Discalced Carmelites, taking the name Sister Benedicta of the Cross. In 1936 one of her blood sisters was also baptized and entered Carmel.

When the persecution and mass deportations of Jews began in 1938, superiors transferred Edith to the convent of Echt in Holland. The deportations reached even there, however, and on August 2, 1942, she and her sister were captured and then, on August 9, sent to Auschwitz-Birkenau, where they died that same day in the gas chamber known as the "White House." Edith was prisoner no. 44074. On the way she had said to her sister: "Come! Let us go for the sake of our people."

During the transfer from Holland she had consoled her companions with the words: "Even here, Jesus is in our midst." When the train stopped at Schifferstadt in the Palatinate, she managed to send a note to her Carmelite sisters in the monastery of Speyer. In Schifferstadt, a memorial stone still recalls the final piece of writing of the "martyr with the Jewish star."

Pope John Paul II canonized Edith on October 11, 1998.

▷▷ She has been proclaimed a patron of Europe.

▷▷ Her iconography shows her in **Carmelite dress** with the **Star of David** on her habit; in the background is **barbed wire** and a **concentration camp**. Her principal attribute is the **cross** which she holds in her hand.

on the following pages:

The Saints at the Gate of Paradise.
A detail from the general judgment on the western facade of the church of St. George at the monastery of Voronetz, Romania.
The saints are being led to the gate of paradise by St. Peter, who holds the key and leads Paul by the hand; the other saints follow. While there is obviously an effort to make at least some saints different and recognizable, the very sameness of the golden haloes gives the sense of viewing a closely unified multitude, a single body.

The Lamb and the Virgins.
Miniature from the commentary of Beatus Liébanus (11th cent.) on the book of Revelation.
The miniature faithfully represents the passage in St. John's text: "Then I looked, and there was the Lamb, standing on Mount Zion! And with him were one hundred forty-four thousand who had his name and his Father's name written on their foreheads. And I heard a voice from heaven like the sound of many waters and like the sound of loud thunder; the voice I heard was like the sound of harpists playing on their harps, and they sing a new song before the throne and before the four living creatures and before the elders. No one could learn that song except the one hundred forty-four thousand who have been redeemed from the earth. It is these who have not defiled themselves with women, for they are virgins; these follow the Lamb wherever he goes. They have been redeemed from humankind as first fruits for God and the Lamb, and in their mouth no lie was found; they are blameless" (Rev 14:1-5).
In the heaven that is marked by a circle of stars can be distinguished "the four living beings," who would become symbols of the evangelists (since they have the heads of a man, a lion, an ox, and an eagle) and the eight elders. On Mt. Zion, which blooms with palms, olive trees, and grain, stands the Lamb, who has been victorious through the cross, which he carries like a banner. He is surrounded by singing virgins, who belong solely to God and who accompany the singing on their harps. The saints are here represented as a single company and, while there has clearly been an effort to individualize each face, they are presented as, and felt to be, the one, inseparable family of the Lamb, a family begotten by the Spirit.

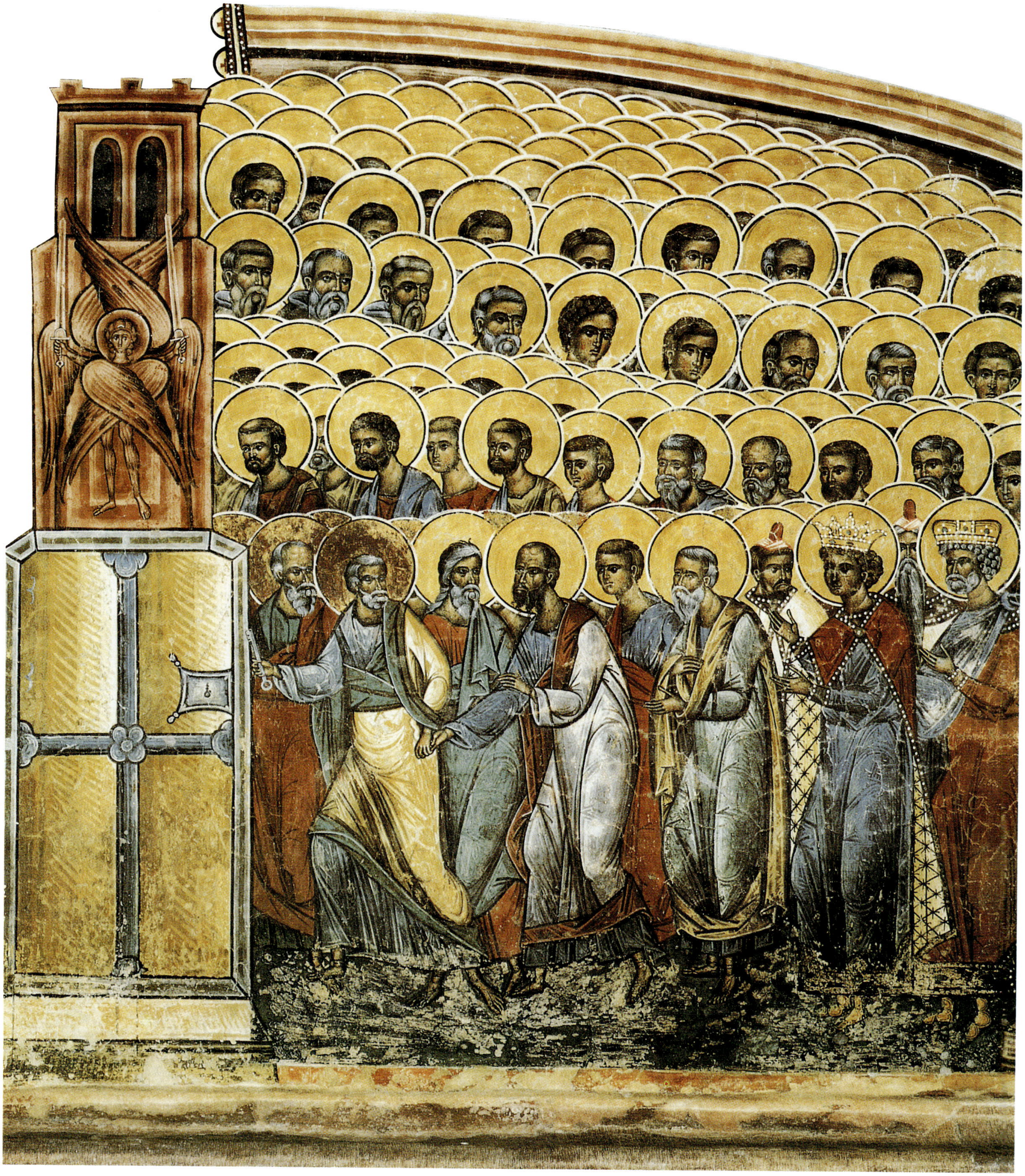

Dictionary of Saints
with Their Attributes

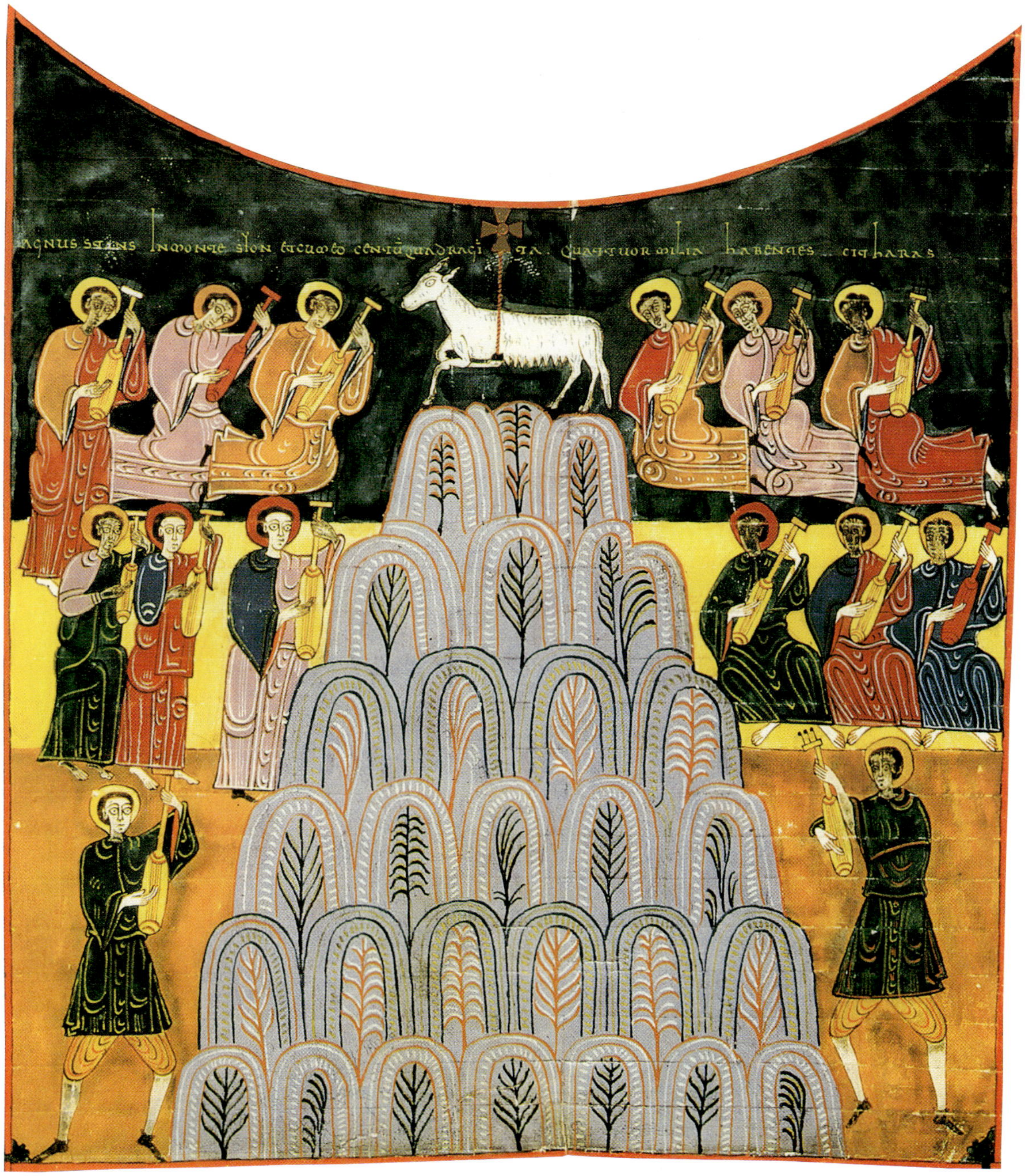

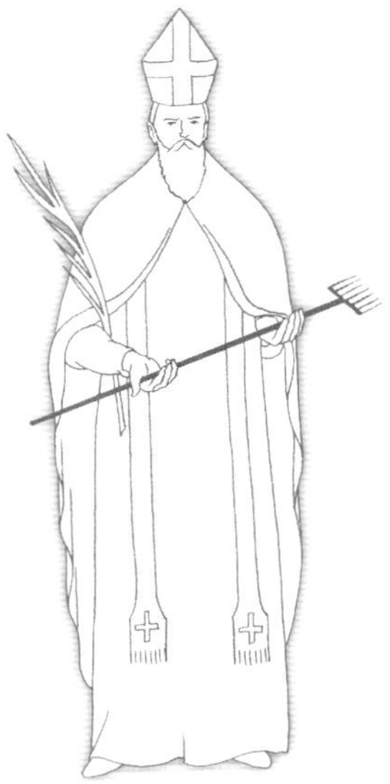

Adalbert of Prague (p. 137)
Principal attribute: seven-pronged skewer, episcopal garb.
Another: cruet of wine.

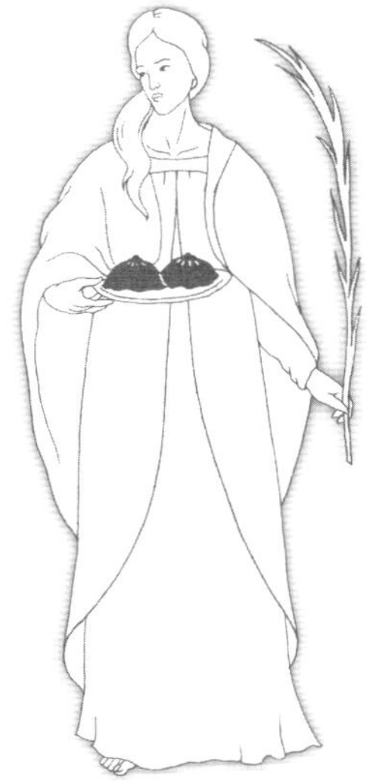

Agatha (p. 88)
Principal attribute: one or two severed breasts.
Others: pincers, knife, tongs, fire, palm, Etna erupting, veil, two mottoes: M.S.S.H.D.E.P.L. and "Do not give offence to Agatha's native land, because she avenges insults"; and an old man, i.e., St. Peter accompanied by a boy with a lamp.

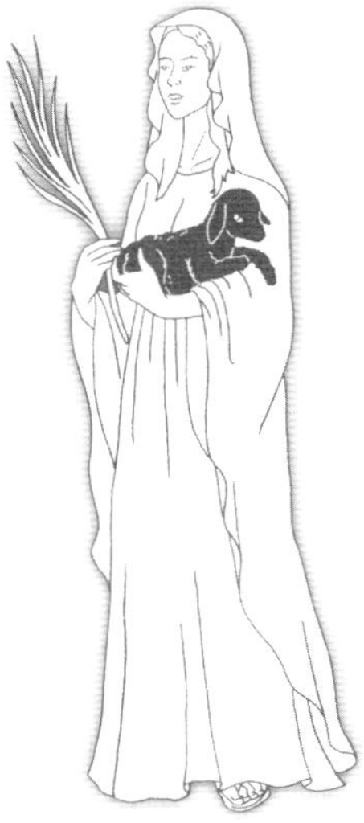

Agnes (p. 90)
Principal attribute: a lamb.
Others: a dagger, very long hair.

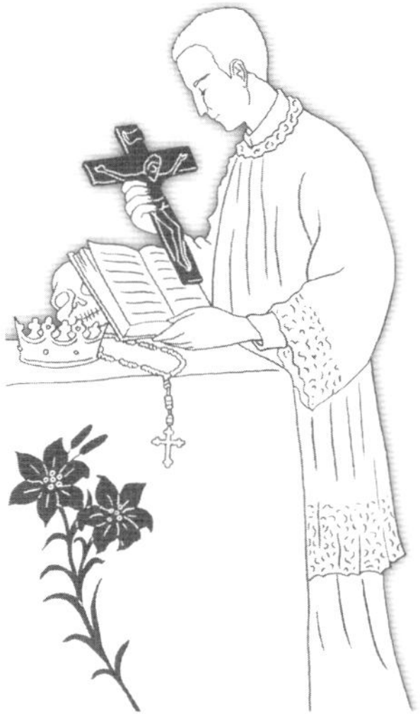

Aloysius Gonzaga (p. 201)
Principal attributes: Jesuit novice in white surplice, lily, crucifix.
Others: rosary, skull, discipline, ducal crown at his feet.

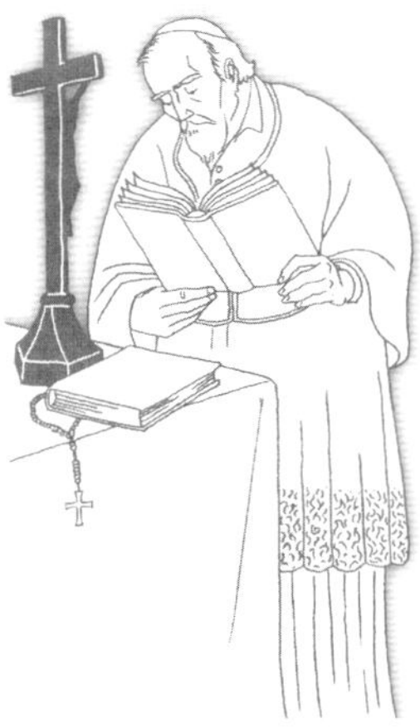

Alphonsus Maria Liguori (p. 207)
Principal attributes: crucifix and rosary.

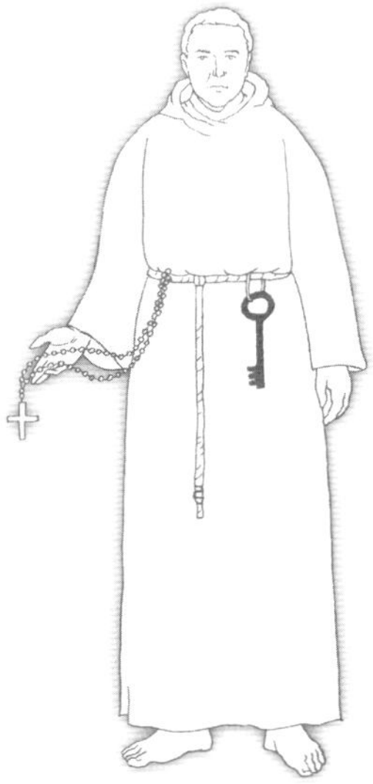

Alphonsus Rodriguez (p. 196)
Attributes: key on cincture, Jesuit habit.
Another: rosary on cincture.

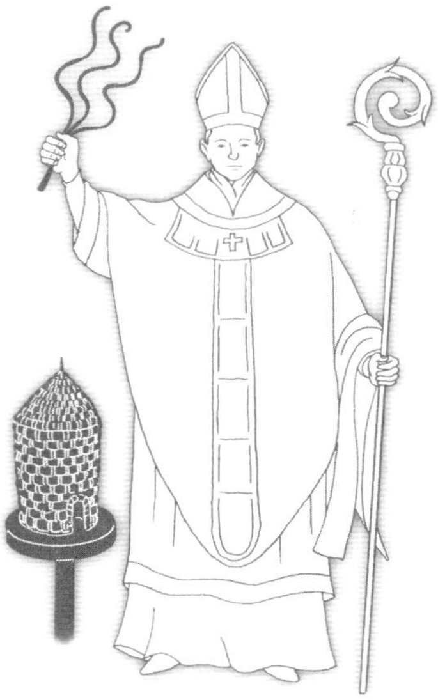

Ambrose of Milan (p. 106)
Principal attributes: beehive, three-corded whip, episcopal garb.
Others: bees, child in a crib, bones.

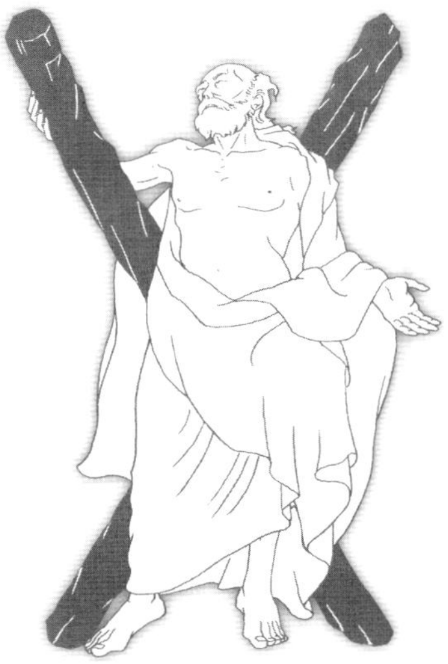

Andrew (p. 61)
Principal attribute: X-shaped cross.
Others: nets, rope.

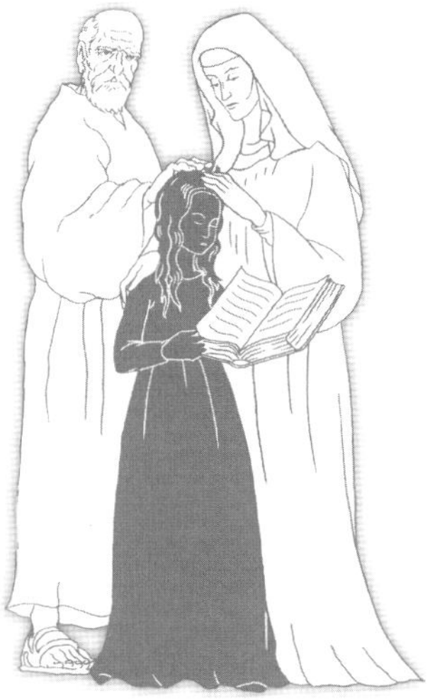

Anne and Joachim (p. 37)
Principal joint attribute: Mary as a child.
Another: a pair of doves.

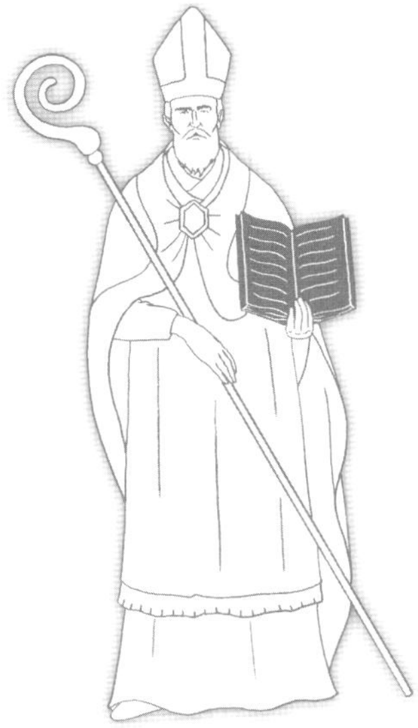

Anselm of Aosta or of Canterbury (p. 138)
Principal attribute: book.
Another: heretics supine at his feet.

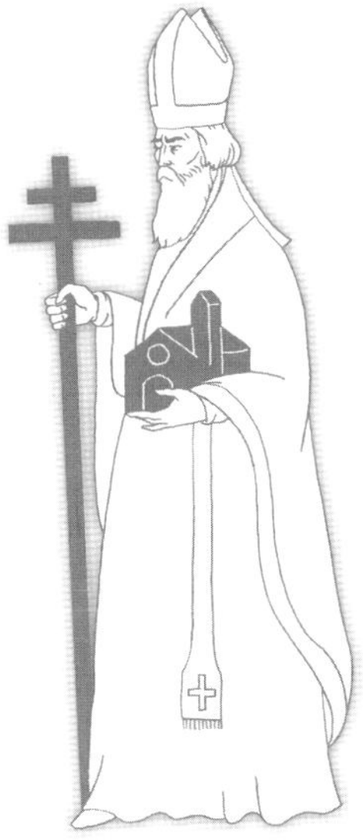

Anskar or Oskar of Corbie (p. 130)
Principal attributes: episcopal garb and episcopal cross.

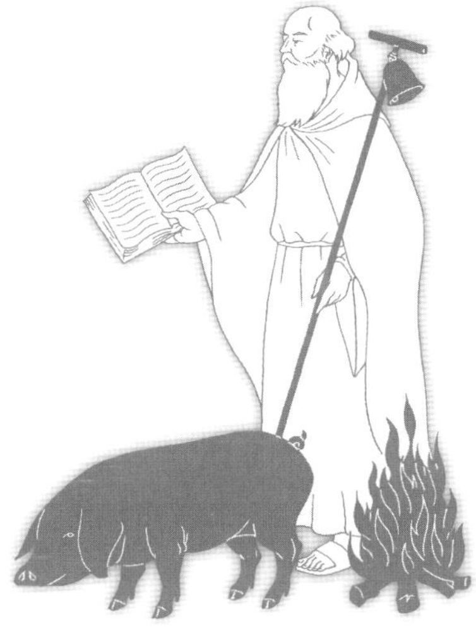

Anthony Abbot (p. 100)
Principal attributes: T-shaped staff, small pig, fire, monastic garb.
Others: little bell, farmyard animals, such as horses, dogs, pigs, all of them together.

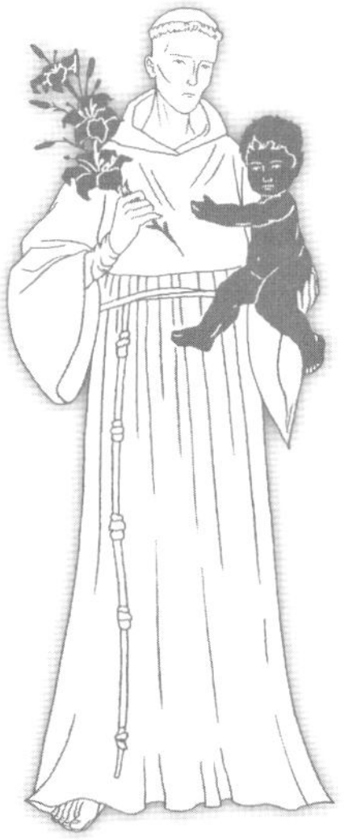

Anthony of Padua (p. 155)
Principal attributes: Child Jesus, lily, Franciscan habit.
Another: a book.

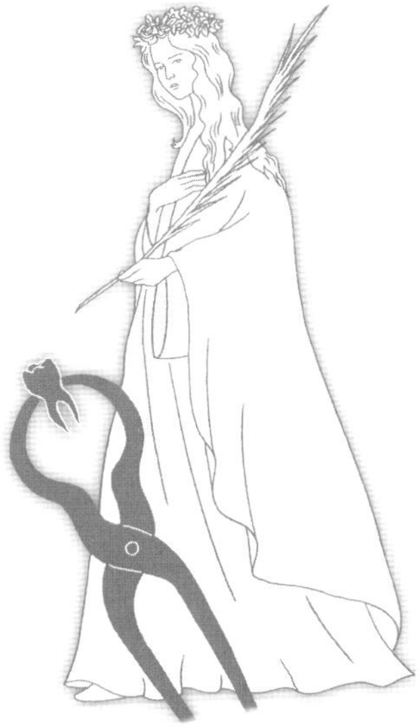

Apollonia (p. 80)
Principal attribute: tongs, sometimes gripping a tooth.

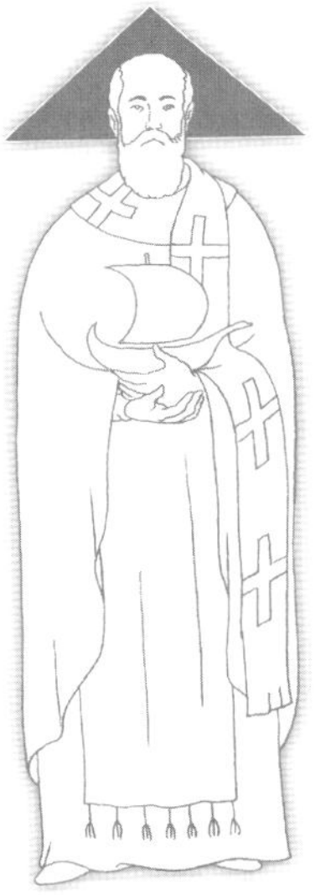

Athanasius the Great (p. 103)
Principal attributes: luminous triangle, episcopal garb.
Another: a boat.

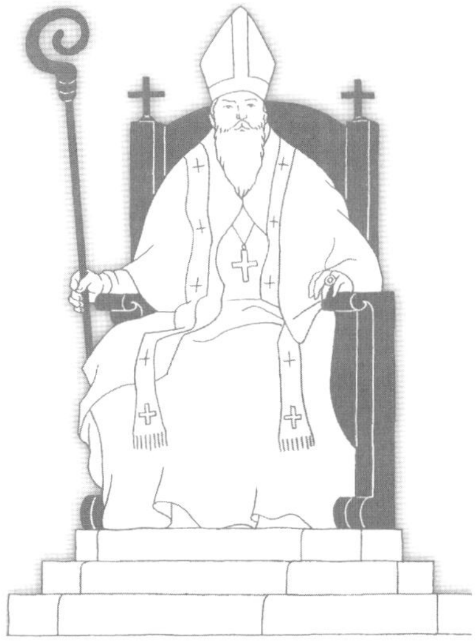

Augustine of Canterbury (p. 122)
Principal attributes: throne and episcopal garb.

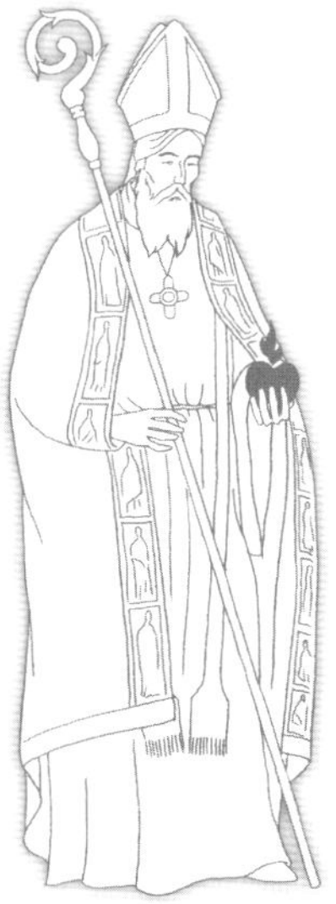

Augustine of Hippo (p. 108)
Principal attributes: a heart, sometimes pierced by three arrows, and episcopal garb.
Others: a book, his mother, a child pouring water into a hole with a shell.

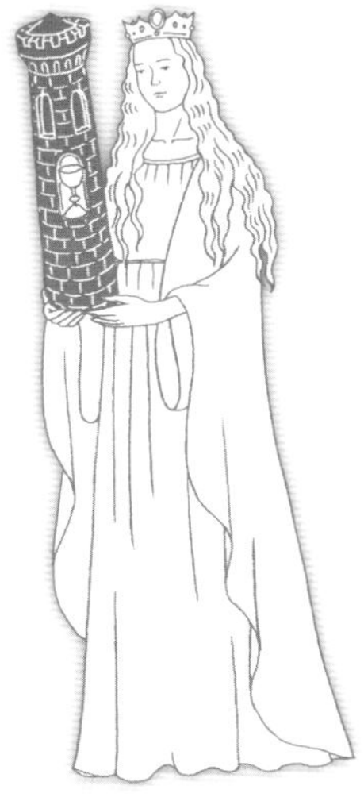

Barbara (p. 95)
Principal attribute: tower with three windows.
Others: peacock feather, cannon and cannon balls, chalice with Host, her father and torturers at her feet.

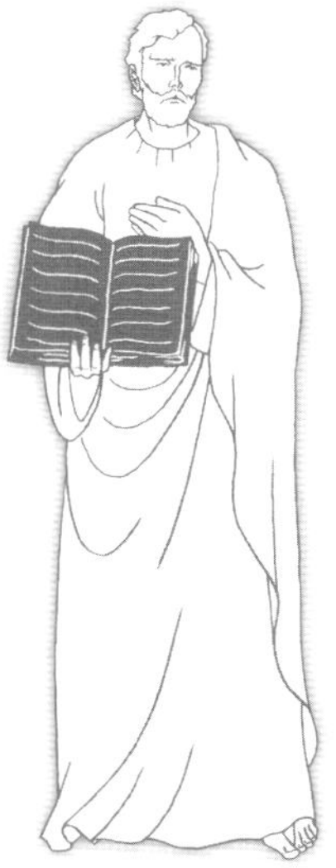

Barnabas (p. 74)
Principal attribute: Gospel of Matthew.
Another: stones.

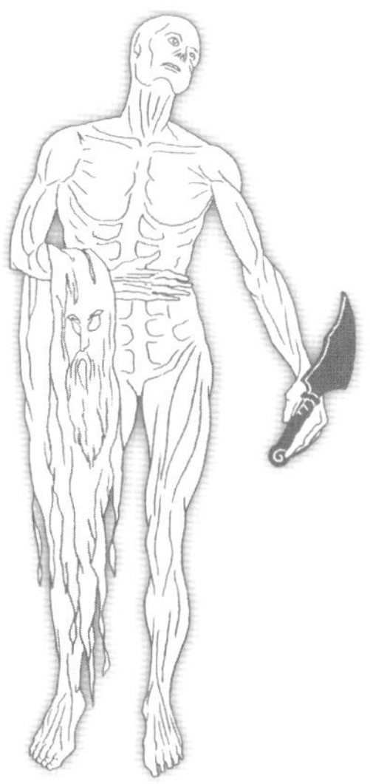

Bartholomew (p. 68)
Principal attribute: his skin.
Another: a knife.

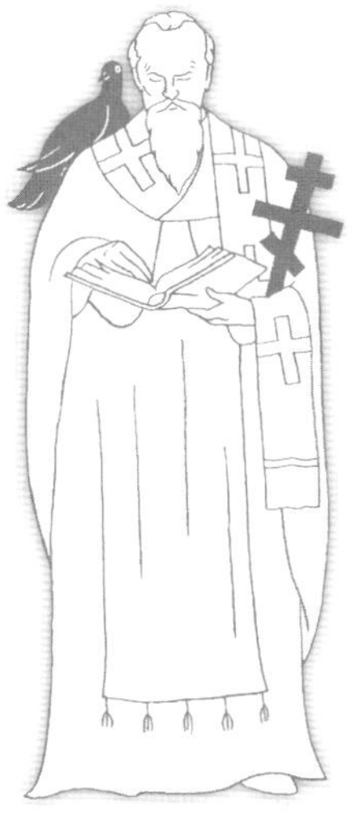

Basil the Great (p. 110)
Principal attributes: homophorion, dove of the Holy Spirit, episcopal garb.
Another: a red cross.

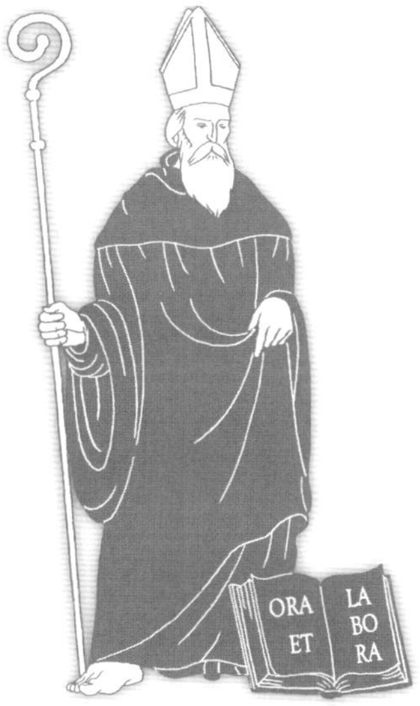

Benedict of Nursia (p. 118)
Principal attributes: black monastic garb, staff, book with inscription: "Pray and Work."
Others: a raven with bread in its beak, cup with two serpents, whips, broken sieve.

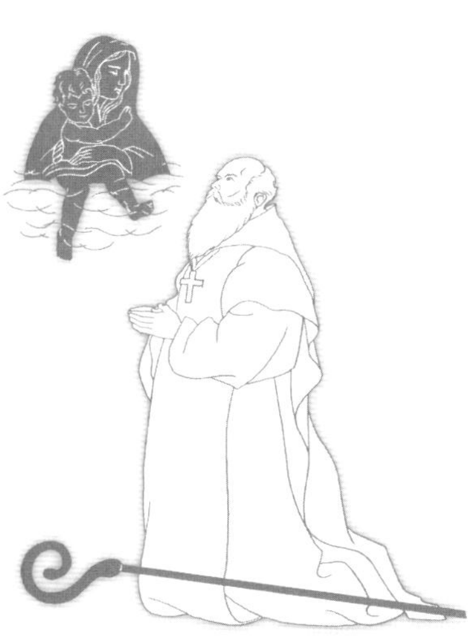

Bernard of Clairvaux (p. 145)
Principal attributes: white Cistercian habit, pastoral staff at his feet, the Virgin Mary.
Others: beehive, chained dragon, three miters at his feet, quill, book, white dog, wagon wheel, instruments of Christ's passion.

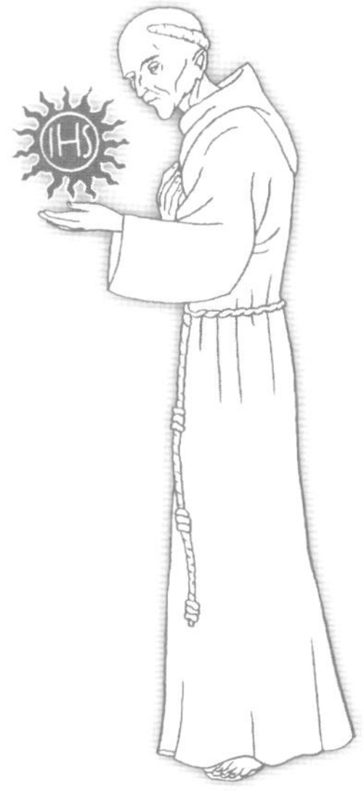

Bernardino of Siena (p. 177)
Principal attribute: the trigram *IHS*.
Others: three pastoral staffs or miters at his feet, dove of the Holy Spirit, city of Siena.

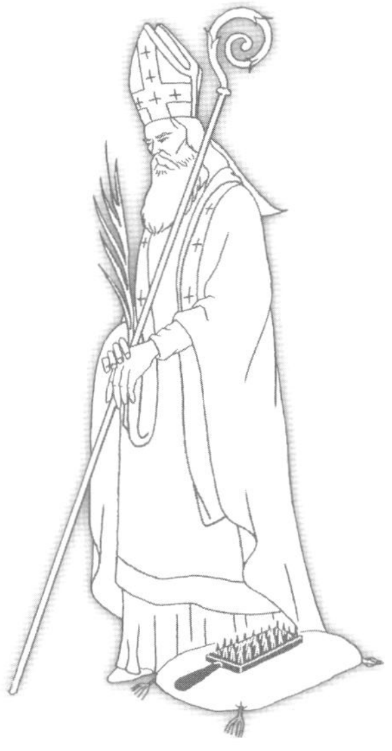

Blaise of Sebaste (p. 98)
Principal attributes: carder's combs, episcopal garb.
Another: candles.

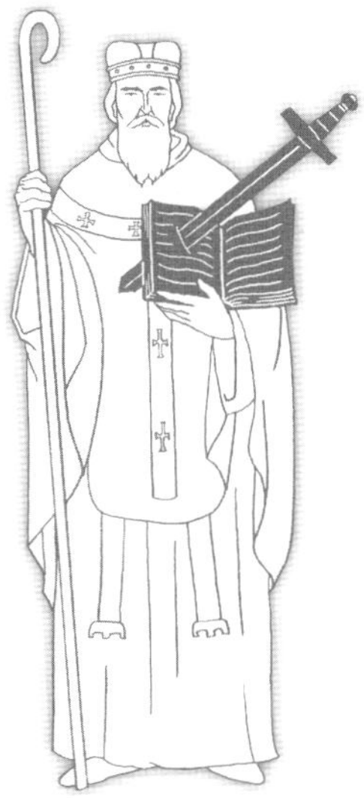

Boniface of Mainz (p. 126)
Principal attributes: miter, pastoral staff, Evangeliary pierced by a spear, episcopal garb.
Another: an axe.

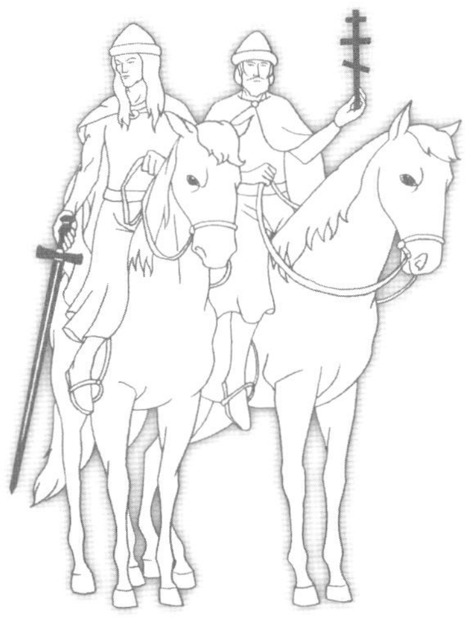

Boris and Gleb of Kiev (p. 134)
Attributes: beard (Boris), sword, conical cap of skin, Russian cross.

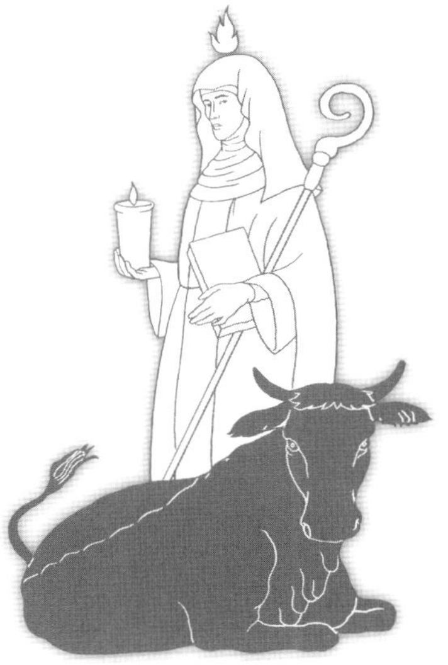

Bridget of Kildare (p. 111)
Attributes: a cow at her feet, the white Cistercian garb of an abbess.

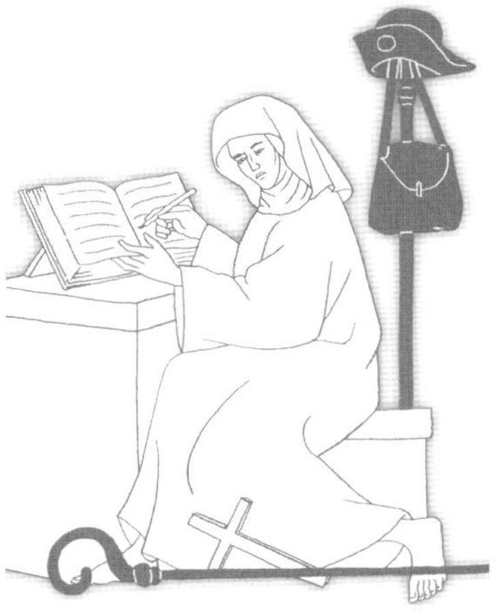

Bridget of Sweden (p. 171)
Principal attributes: as a pilgrim, staff, knapsack with the keys of Rome and the palms of Jerusalem, wide-brimmed hat; as an abbess, monastic dress, pastoral staff, headdress of the Brigettines.
Others: heart on fire, with a red Jerusalem cross, cross, crown, book and inkstand, widow's veil, escutcheon with the lion of Sweden.

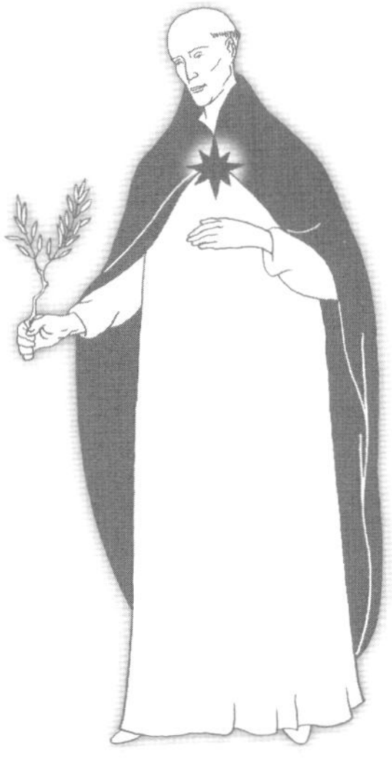

Bruno of Cologne (p. 141)
Principal attributes: white robe, black cloak, star on his breast.
Others: miter and pastoral staff at his feet, skull, a crucified Christ on a wooden cross, olive branch.

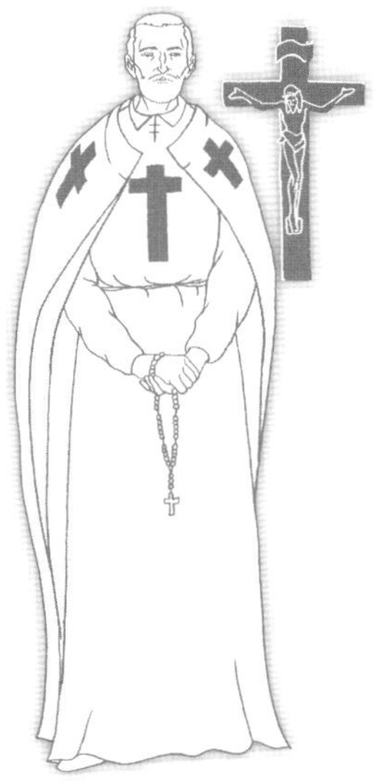

Camillus of Lellis (p. 199)
Principal attribute: red cross on a cassock.
Others: book, rosary, angel, skull.

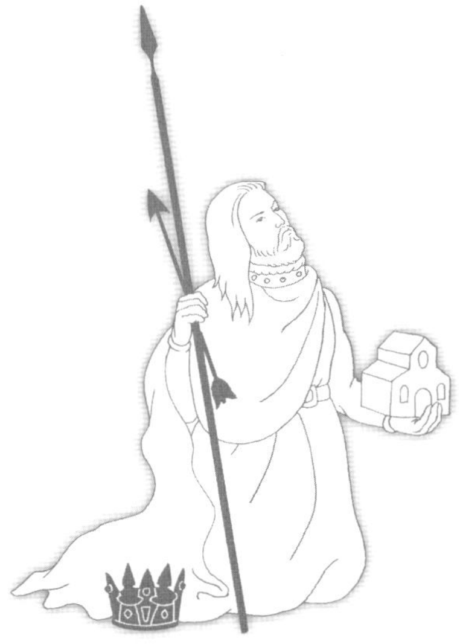

Canute IV (p. 139)
Principal attributes: royal garb, spear, arrow, royal crown at his feet.
Another: a model of the cathedral in Odense.

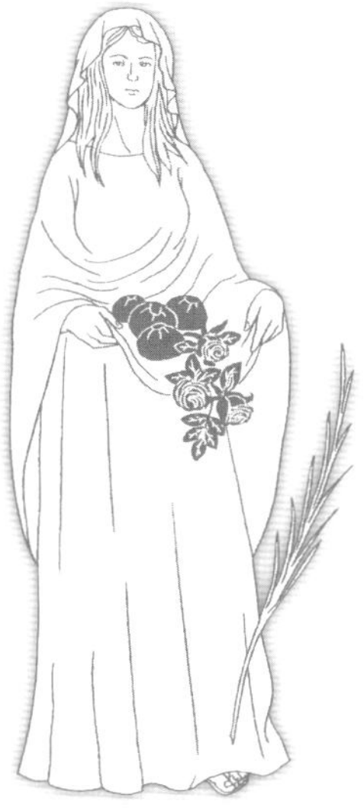

Casilda of Burgos or of Toledo (p. 140)
Attribute: roses in the folds of her habit.

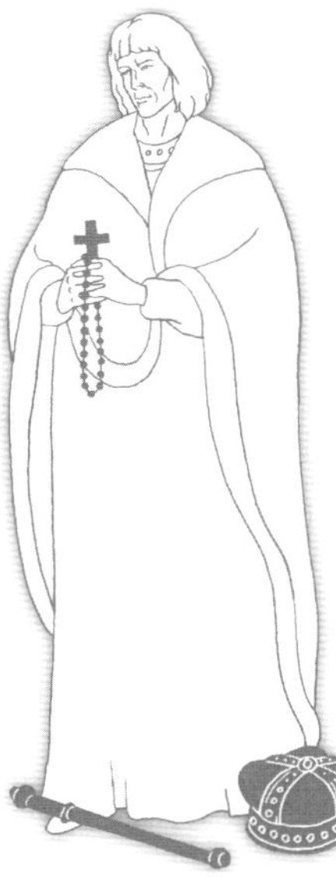

Casimir of Lithuania (p. 184)
Attributes: scepter, royal garb, ducal crown or hat (often at his feet), lily, rosary, cross.

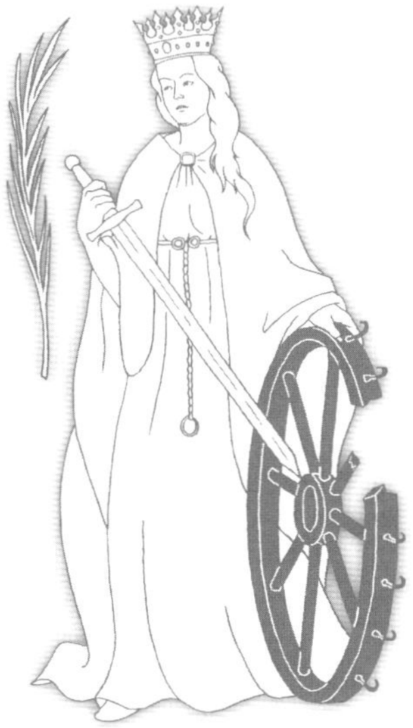

Catherine of Alexandria (p. 98)
Principal attribute: broken wheel with hooks.
Others: crown, princely garb, book, sword, ring.

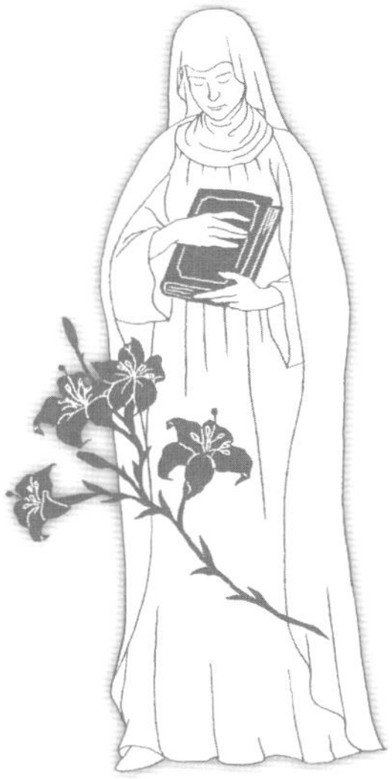

Catherine of Siena (p. 175)
Principal attributes: Dominican white habit and black cloak, lily, book.
Others: crucifix, heart, crown of thorns, stigmata, dove.

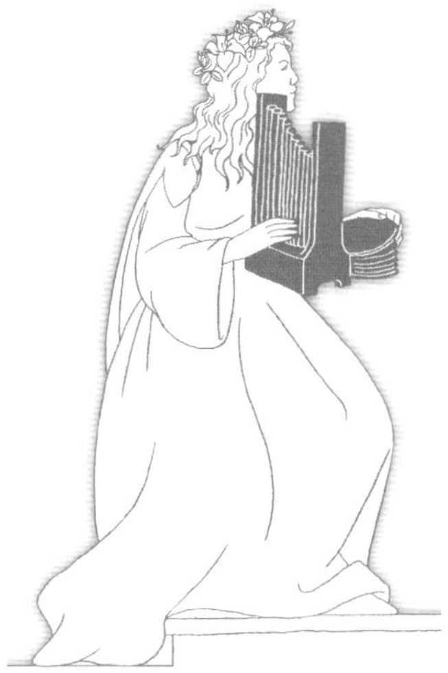

Cecilia (p. 78)
Principal attribute: musical instrument.
Others: crown of roses and lilies, wound in the neck.

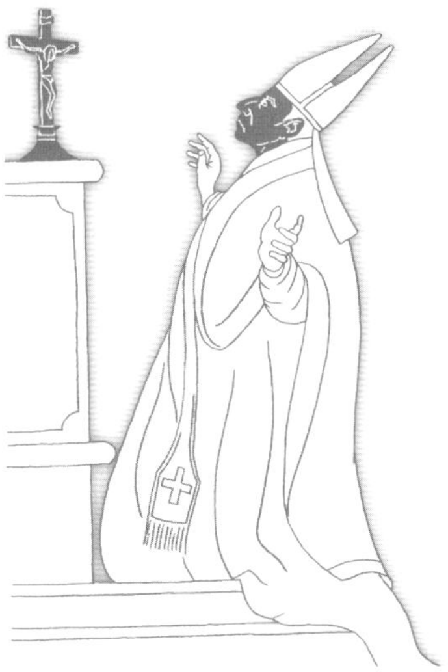

Charles Borromeo (p. 196)
Principal attributes: aquiline nose, crucifix, cardinal's cape.
Others: the plague-stricken, fiery weapon, Holy Nail.

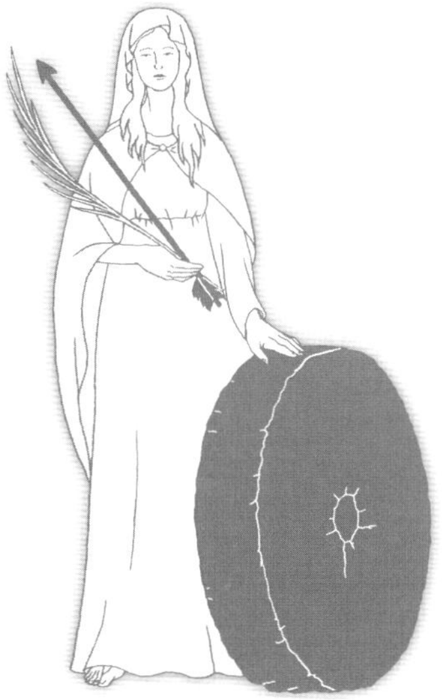

Christina of Bolsena (p. 82)
Principal attributes: arrow, millstone.
Others: tongs, serpents.

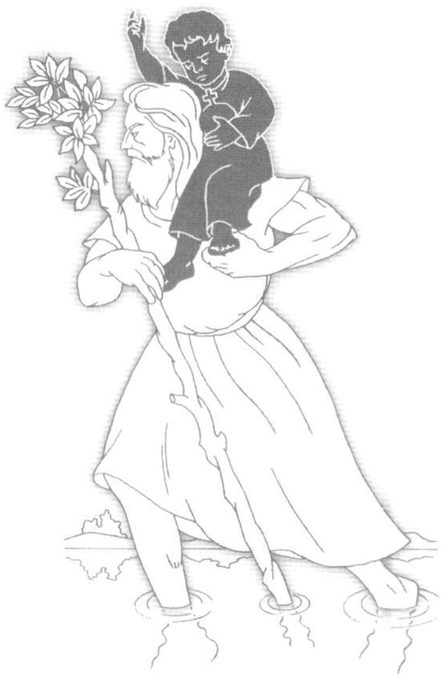

Christopher (p. 96)
Principal attributes: giant stature, Christ Child on his shoulders.
Others: leafy staff, river with fish, monk.

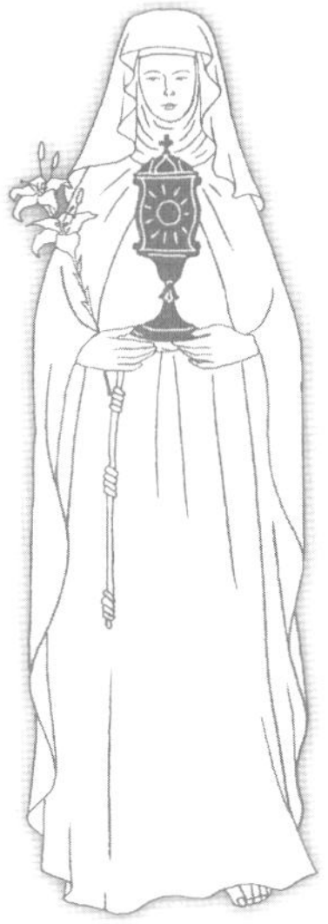

Clare of Assisi (p. 161)
Principal attributes: monstrance, Franciscan habit.
Others: rope cincture with three knots, cross, olive branch, lily, lamp.

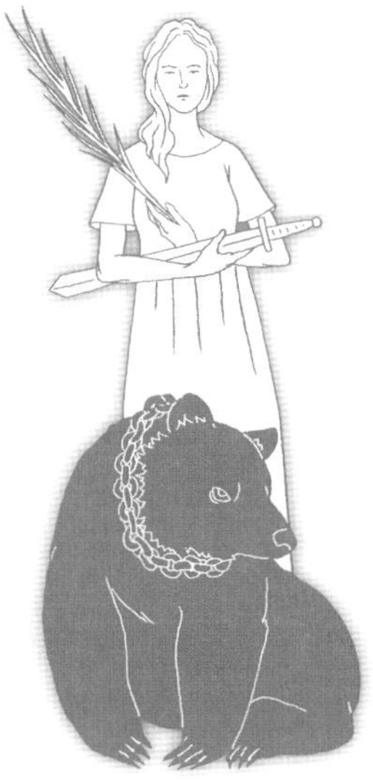

Columba of Sens (p. 80)
Principal attribute: female bear.
Another: peacock feather.

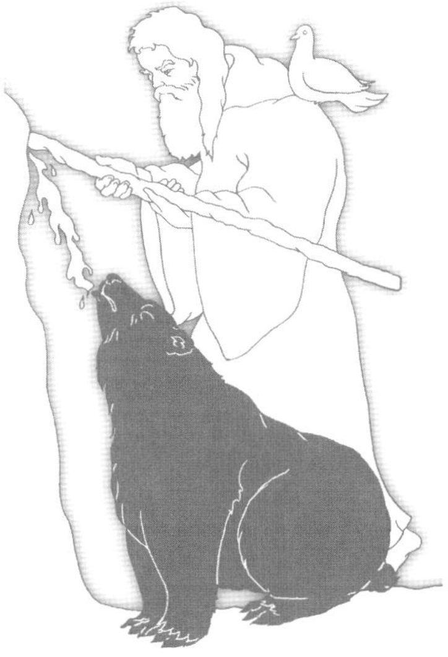

Columbanus of Bobbio or of Luxeuil (p. 123)
Principal attributes: white or black monastic garb, bear, motto: "We belong to Christ, not to ourselves."
Others: sun, dove, scourges, fountain.

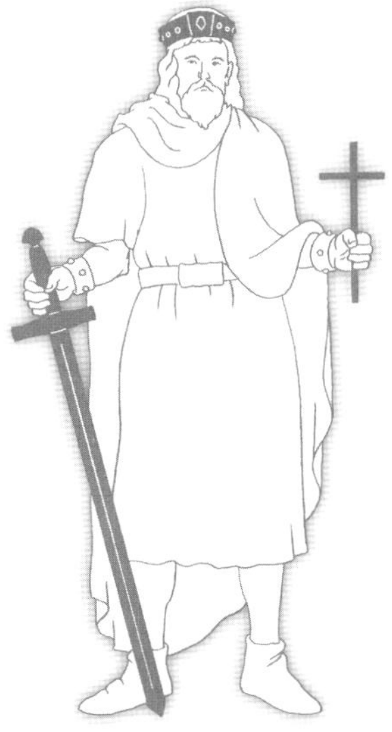

Constantine of Cornwall (p. 124)
Attributes: sword, cross, crown.

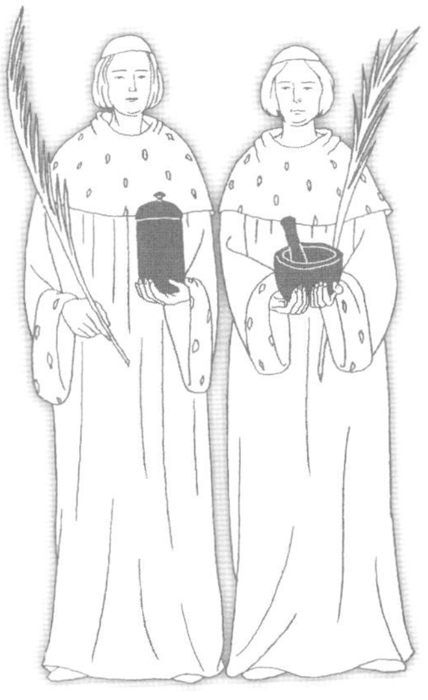

Cosmas and Damian (p. 84)
Principal attributes: vials, surgical instruments, pharmacist's mortar, box of ointments, scalpel, spatula.
Others: comb, shears, urinal.

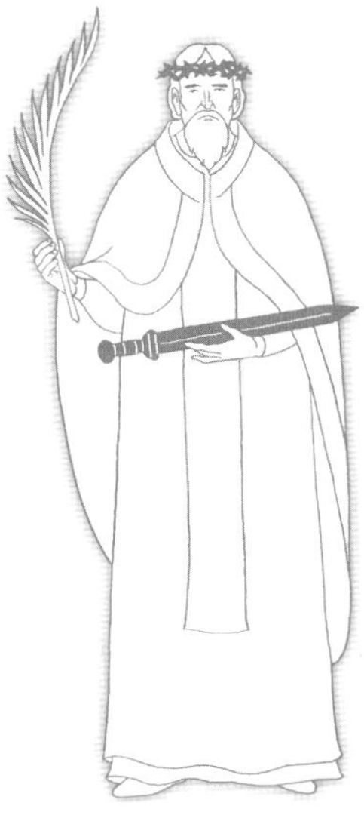

Cyprian of Carthage (p. 80)
Attributes: sword, crown, episcopal garb.

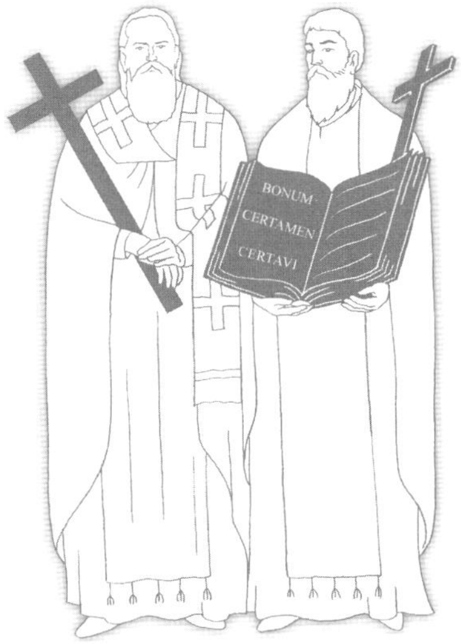

Cyril and Methodius (p. 131)
Attributes: the two always together; for Methodius: beard, episcopal garb; for Cyril: book with motto.

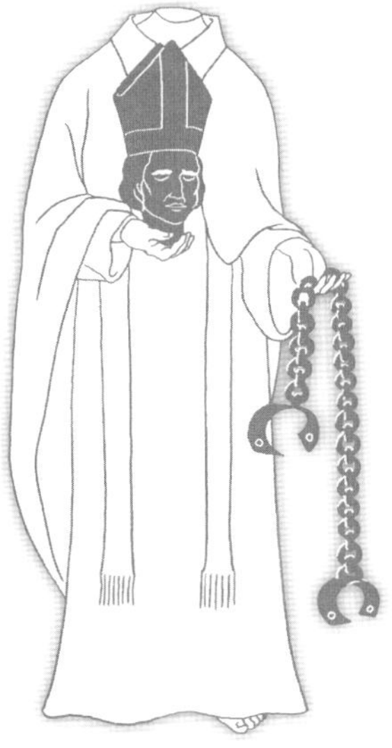

Dionysius of Paris (p. 81)
Principal attributes: episcopal garb, his mitered head in his hand.
Another: chains.

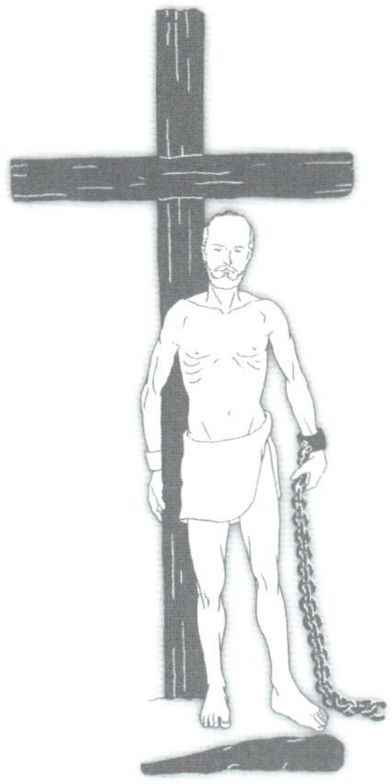

Dismas, the Good Thief (p. 52)
Attributes: chain, cudgel, cross.

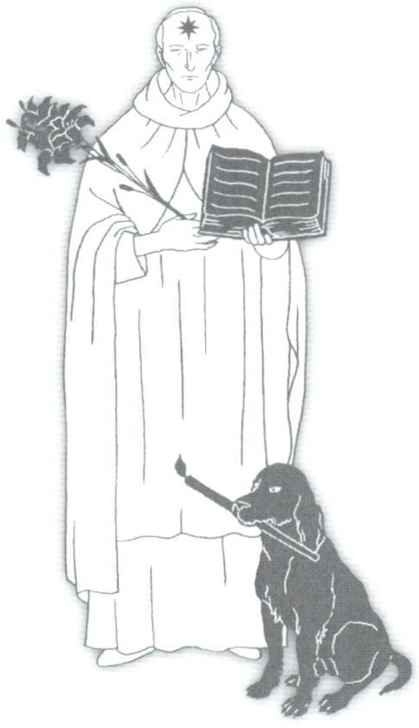

Dominic Guzmán (p. 157)
Principal attributes: Dominican habit, dog with torch or candle, star on forehead, lily, book.
Others: rosary, angel.

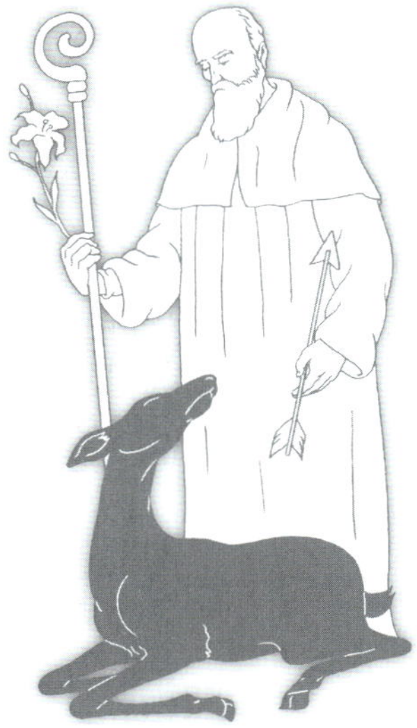

Egidius (Giles), Abbot (p. 125)
Principal attributes: black habit, pastoral staff, deer.
Others: arrow, lily.

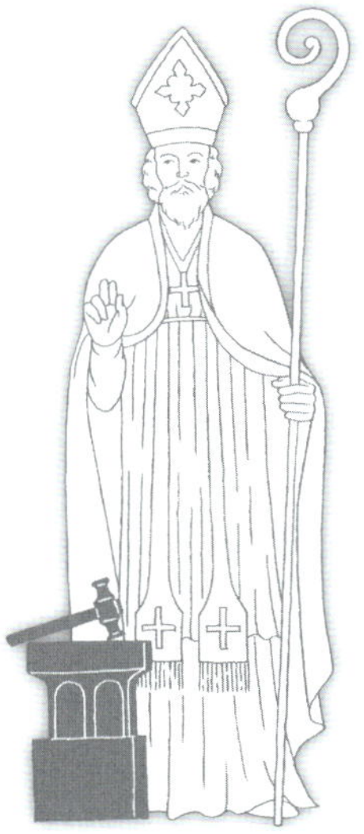

Eligius (p. 124)
Principal attributes: hammer, anvil, tongs, episcopal garb.
Others: scales, chalice, ring.

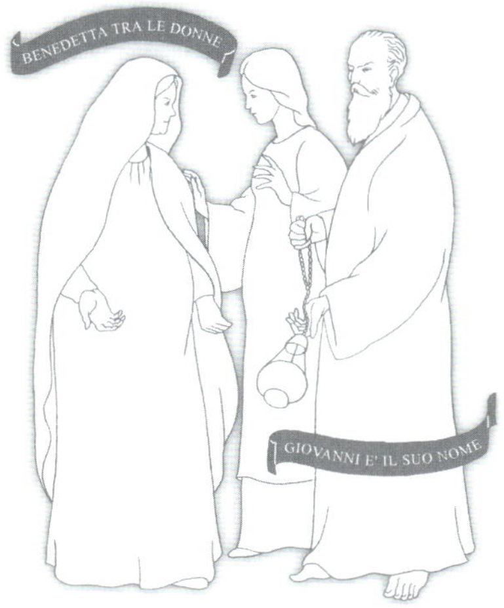

Elizabeth and Zechariah (p. 43)
Principal attributes: for Elizabeth: scene of the Visitation; for Zechariah: motto "John is his name," and thurible.

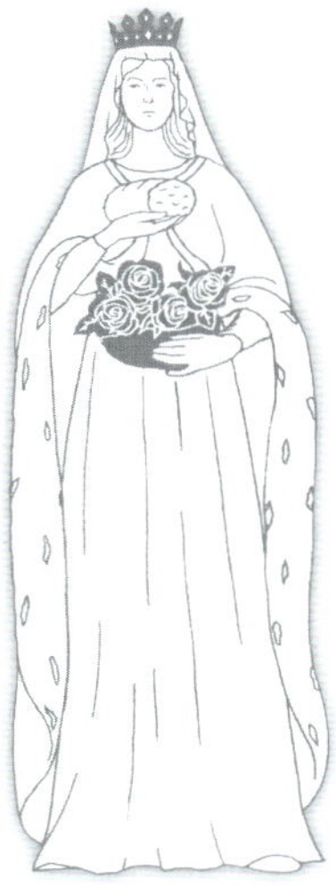

Elizabeth of Hungary (p. 159)
Principal attributes: roses in the folds of her cloak, royal garb, crown.
Others: three crowns, model of a church.

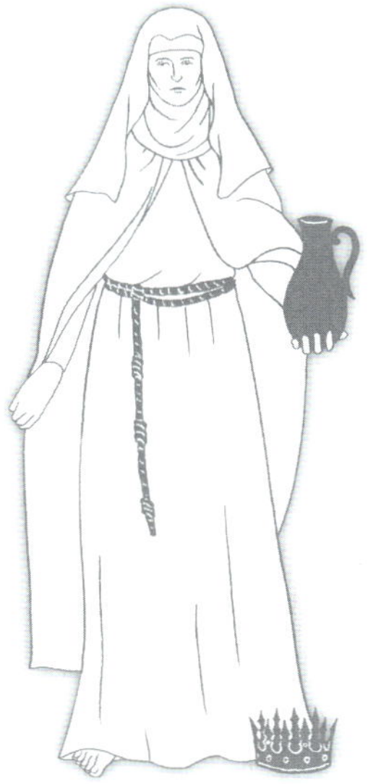

Elizabeth of Portugal (p. 168)
Principal attributes: royal crown, widow's garb, cincture with three knots, carafe.

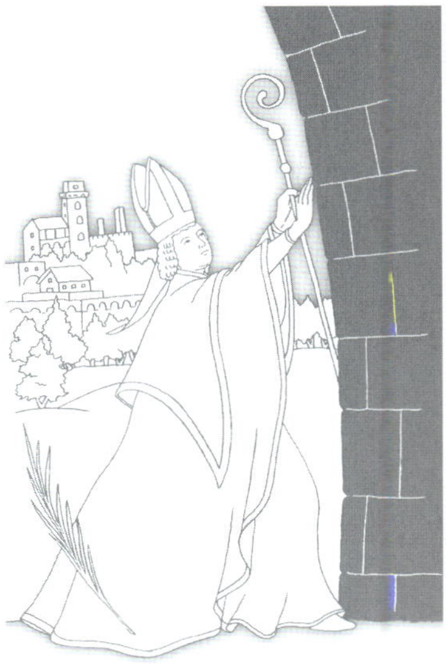

Emidius of Ascoli (p. 97)
Principal attributes: episcopal insignia, gesture of building an edifice.
Others: head in hands, model of a city.

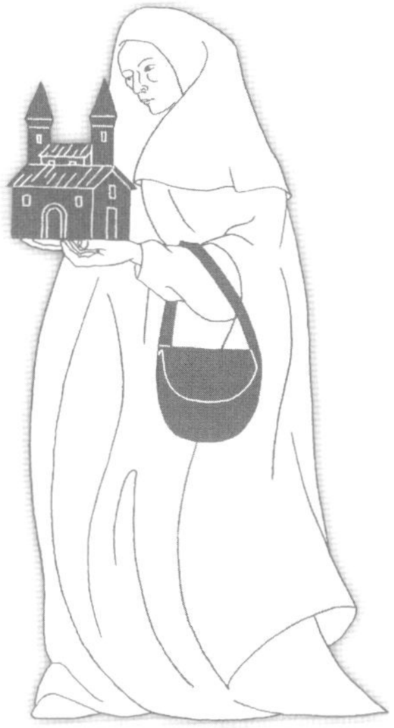

Emma of Gurk (p. 134)
Attributes: widow's veil, models of the monasteries she founded, bag of money.

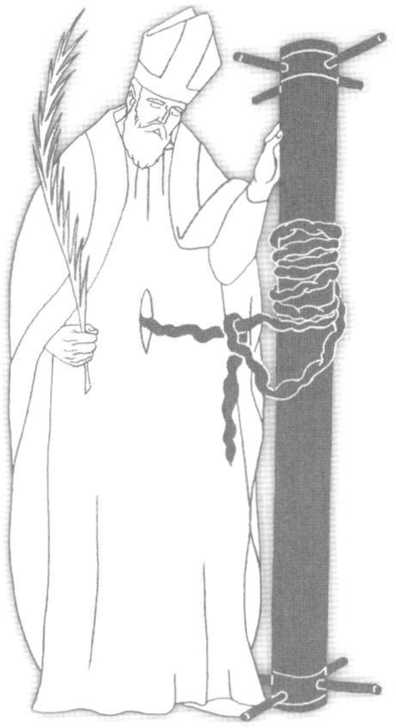

Erasmus of Gaeta (p. 85)
Principal attributes: episcopal insignia, windlass.
Another: nails.

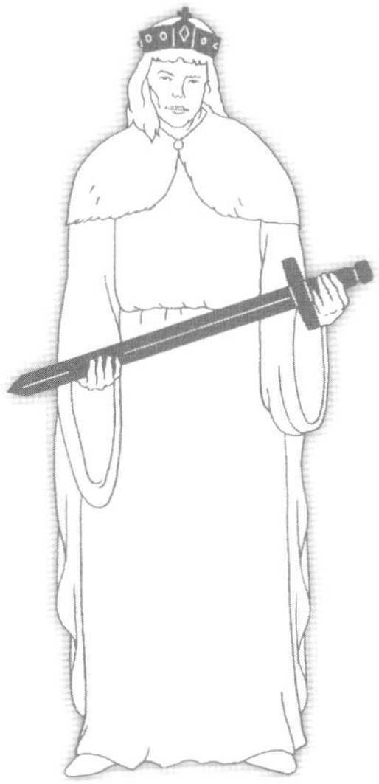

Eric of Sweden (p. 147)
Attributes: royal insignia, sword.

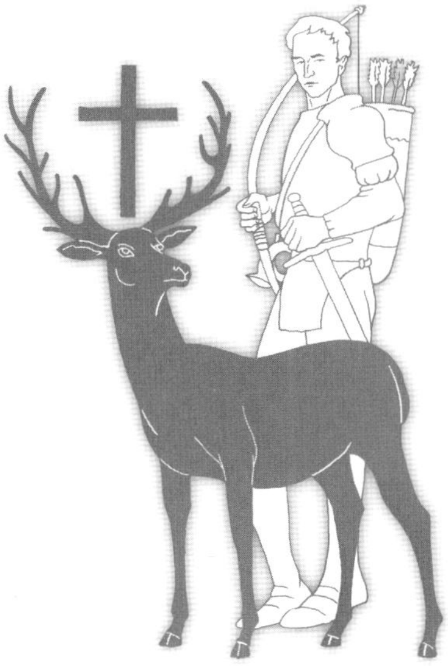

Eustachius (p. 75)
Principal attribute: deer with cross on its head.
Others: hunting implements, hunting horn.

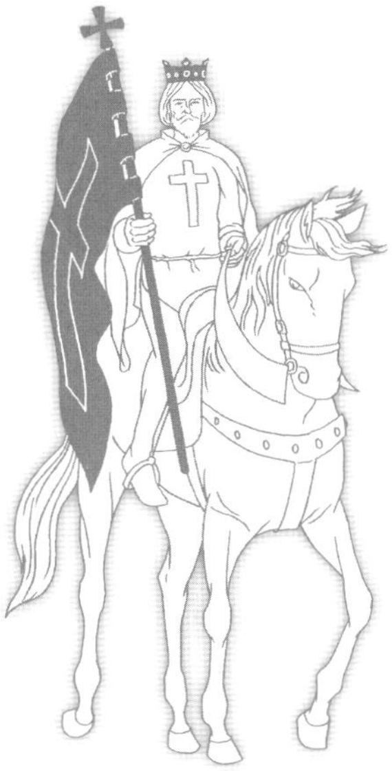

Ferdinand III of Castile (p. 162)
Principal attributes: crown and scepter, Crusader's banner.
Others: key, small statue of the Virgin.

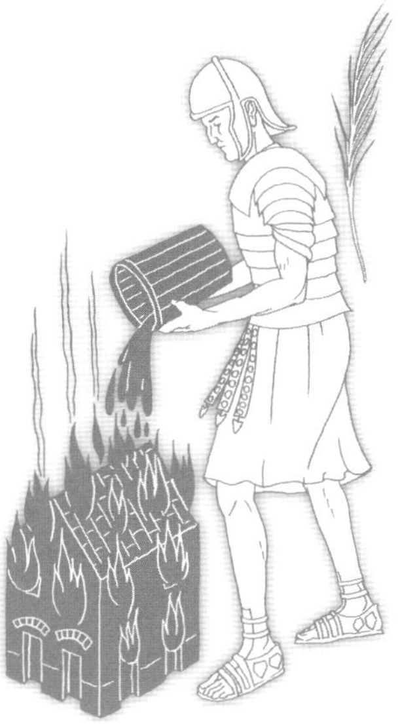

Florian of Lorch (p. 86)
Principal attributes: military dress, bucket with water pouring from it.
Others: millstone, stork's nest.

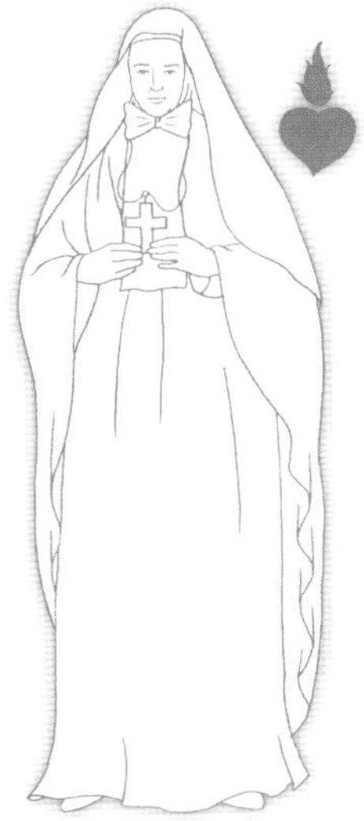

Frances Xavier Cabrini (p. 212)
Attributes: habit of her congregation, cross, heart of Jesus.

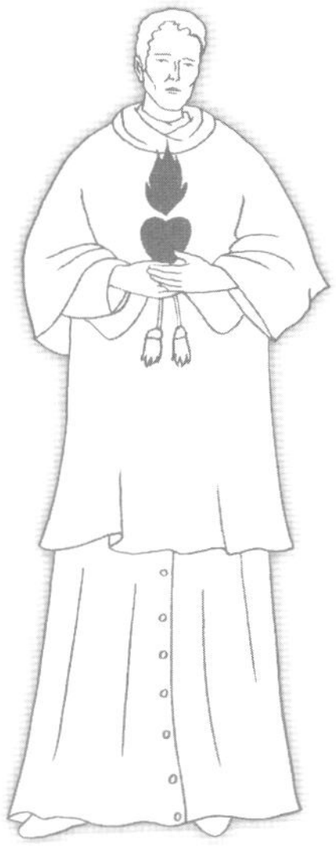

Francis Borgia (p. 191)
Principal attributes: heart on fire, Jesuit habit.
Others: crucifix, monstrance, ducal crown at his feet, crowned skull.

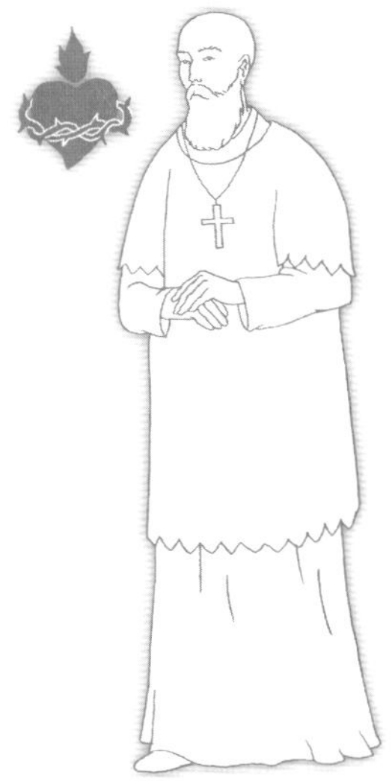

Francis de Sales (p. 200)
Attribute: heart of Jesus, crowned with thorns.

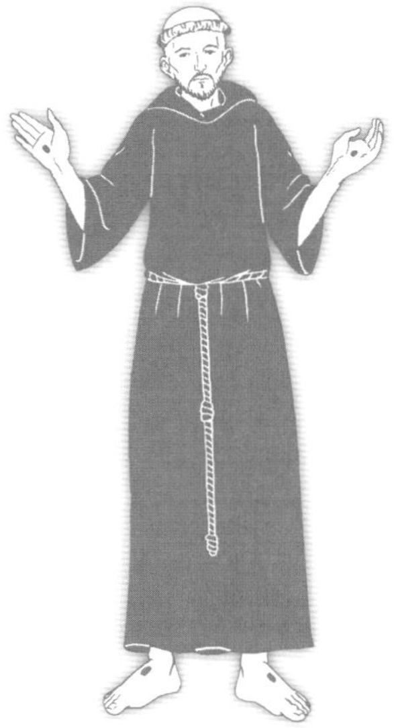

Francis of Assisi (p. 152)
Principal attributes: Franciscan habit, stigmata, cincture with three knots.
Others: crucifix, wolf, birds.

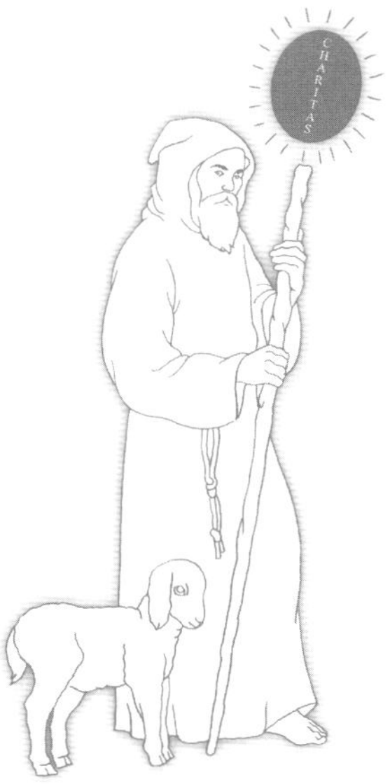

Francis of Paola (p. 182)
Principal attributes: staff in hand, motto "Charity," Franciscan habit.
Another: a little lamb.

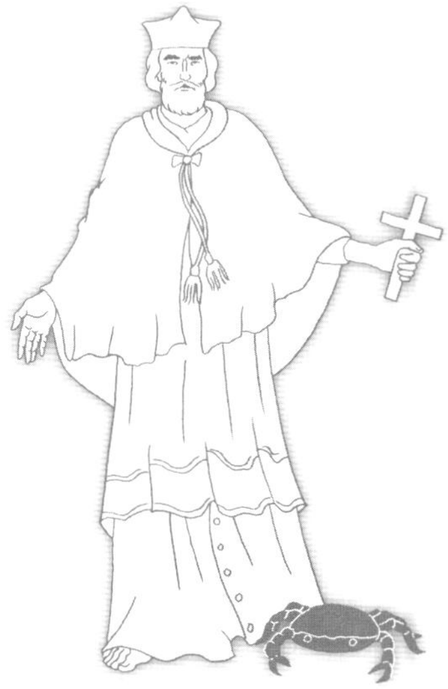

Francis Xavier (p. 189)
Principal attributes: crab at his feet, Jesuit habit.

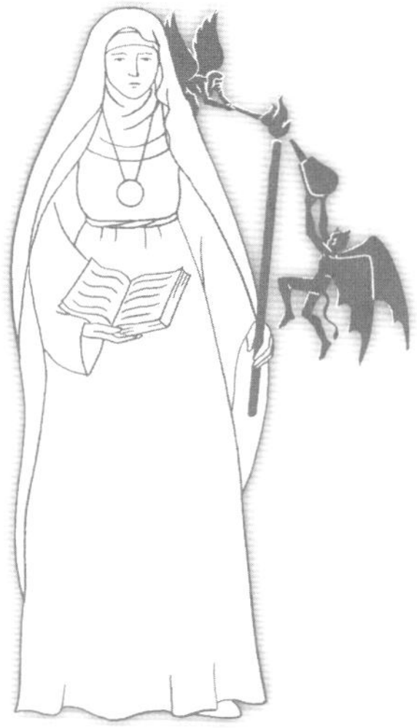

Genevieve of Paris (p. 107)
Principal attribute: candle, with the devil blowing it out and an angel relighting it.
Others: crook, spindle, medal with cross.

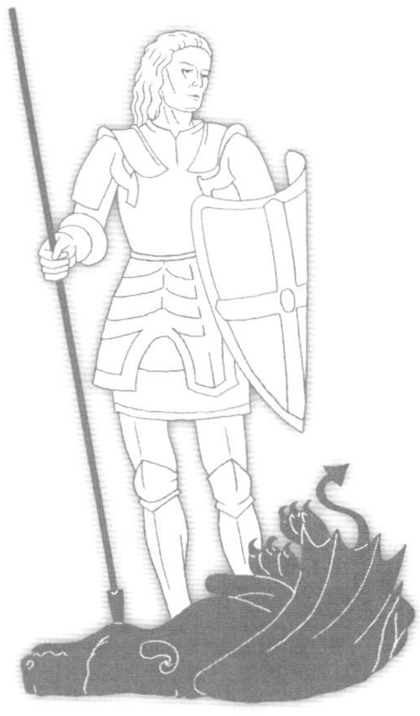

George of Lydda (p. 86)
Principal attribute: dragon pierced by spear.
Others: banner with cross on it, princess, white horse.

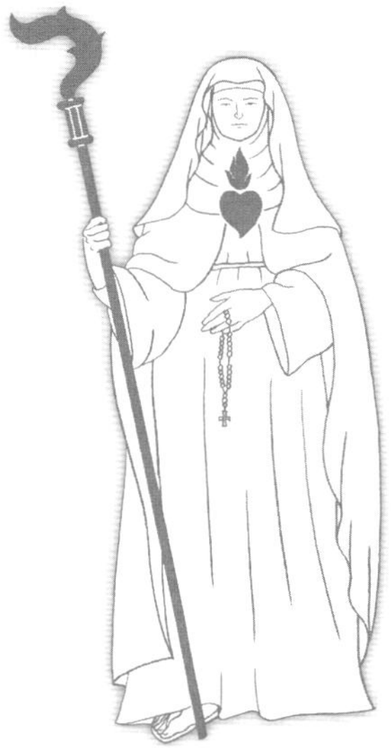

Gertrude of Helfta (p. 167)
Principal attributes: pastoral staff, flaming heart with image of adolescent Jesus, motto, white Cistercian habit.
Another: crown held up by angels.

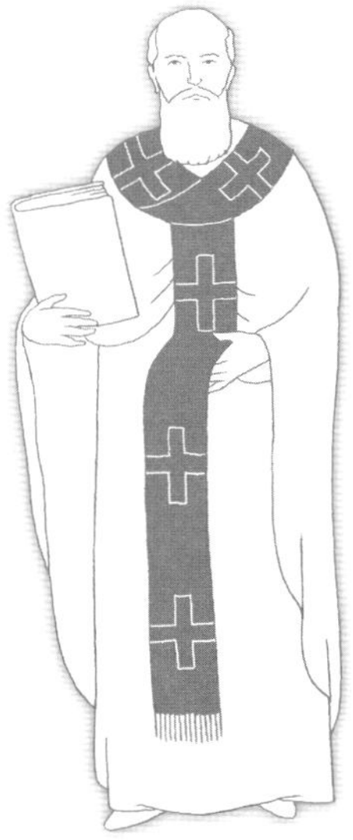

Gregory of Nazianzus (p. 115)
Attributes: episcopal garb, often shown with friend St. Basil.

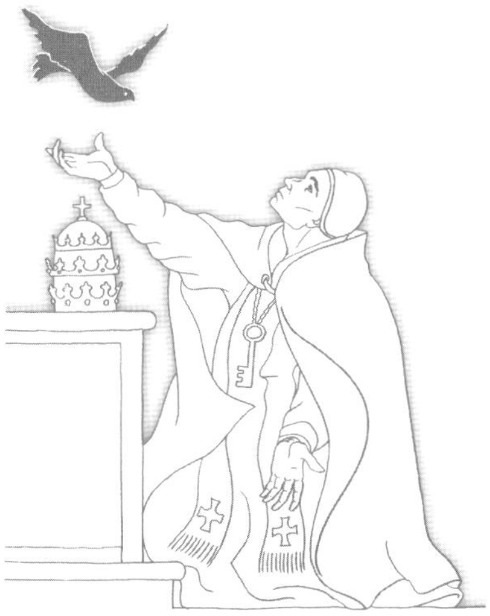

Gregory the Great (p. 120)
Principal attributes: tiara, dove of the Holy Spirit.
Others: papal cross, pontifical keys, celebration of Mass.

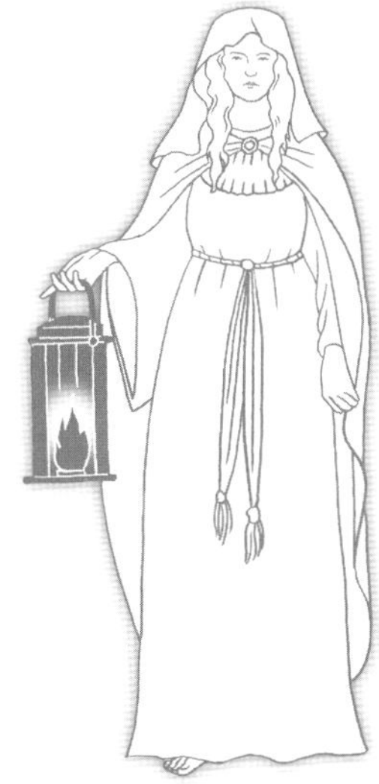

Gudula of Brussels (p. 127)
Principal attribute: lantern.
Another: devil extinguishing and angel relighting lantern.

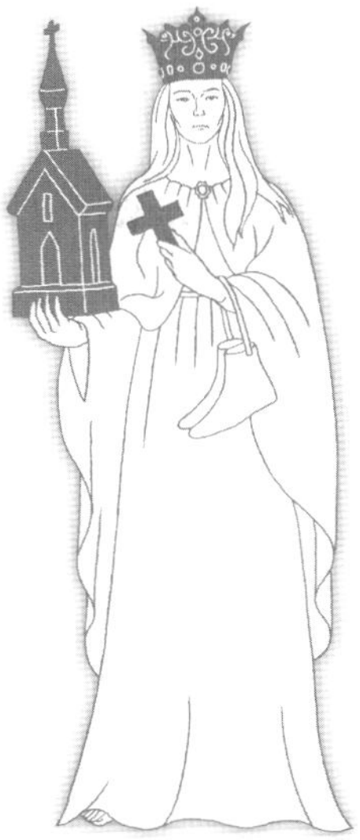

Hedwig, Queen (p. 160)
Principal attributes: royal crown and dress, bare feet, shoes in her hand, cross.
Others: image of the Virgin, model of a church.

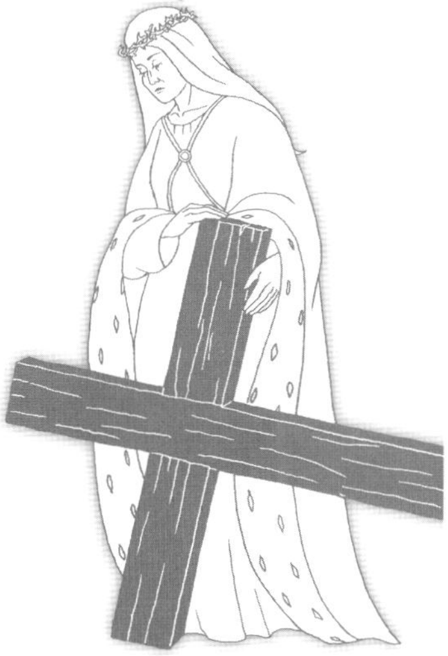

Helen, Mother of Constantine (p. 100)
Principal attribute: cross.
Others: nails, imperial crown and crown of thorns.

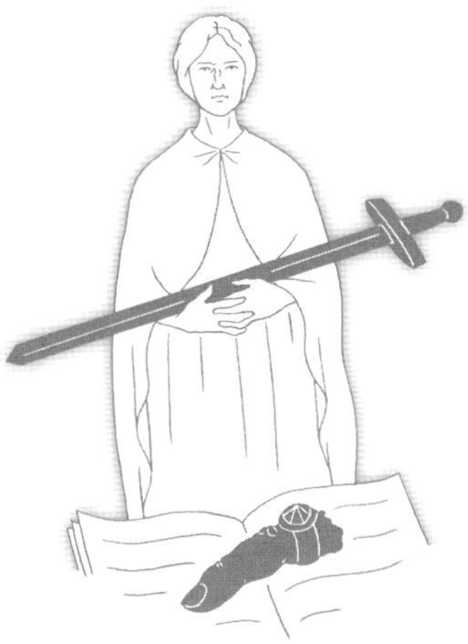

Helen of Skövde (p. 146)
Attributes: sword, severed finger lying on Evangeliary.

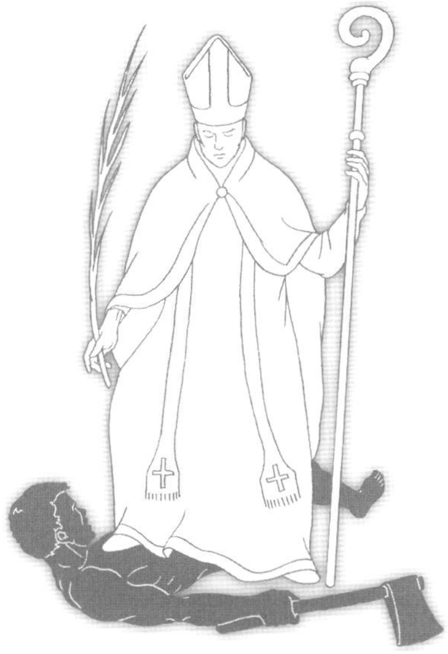

Henry of Uppsala (p. 147)
Attributes: episcopal garb, assassin armed with axe and being trampled.

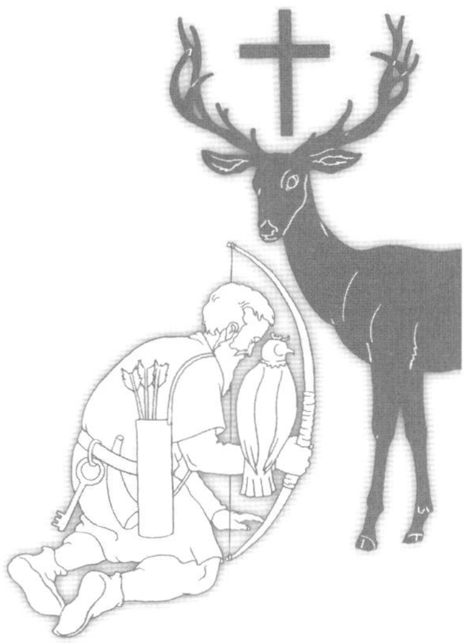

Hubert of Liège or of Maastricht (p. 129)
Principal attributes: deer with cross on its head, episcopal garb.
Others: stole, key, horse, dog, hunting horn, falcon on his wrist.

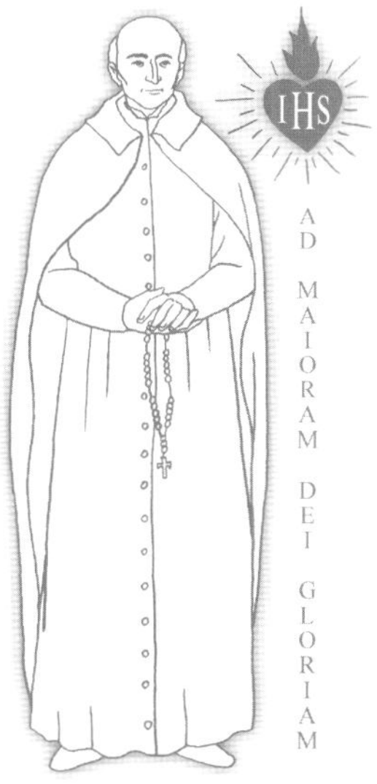

Ignatius of Loyola (p. 186)
Principal attributes: flaming heart of Jesus, *IHS, AMDG,* Jesuit habit.
Another: book of the *Rule*.

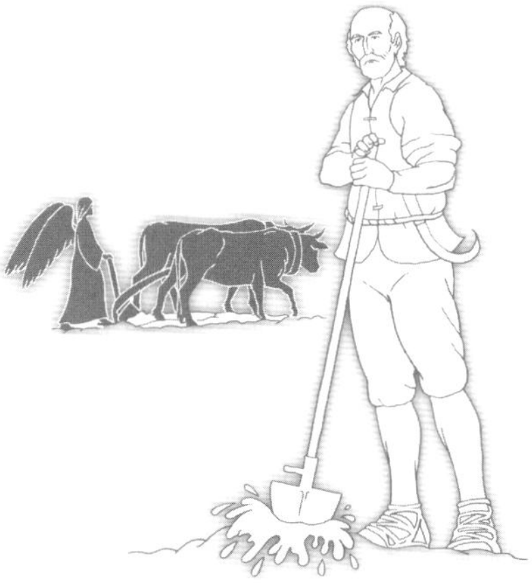

Isidore of Madrid, Farmer (p. 143)
Principal attributes: angels, ox-drawn cart, spade, spring.

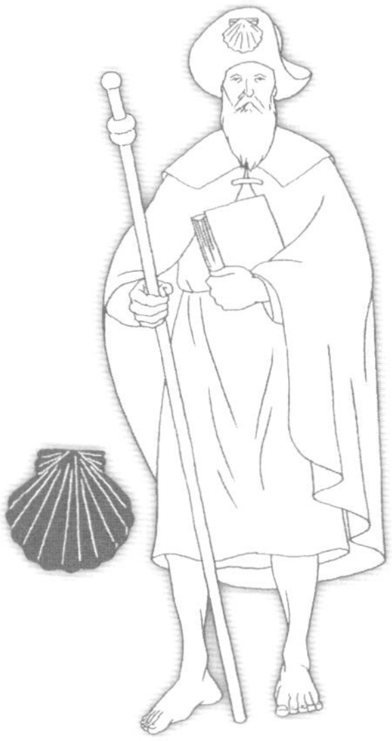

James the Greater (p. 62)
Principal attributes: shell, pilgrim's staff, canteen or gourd, broad-brimmed hat, cloak.
Others: white Crusader's banner, whirling sword and severed head of a Moor, horse.

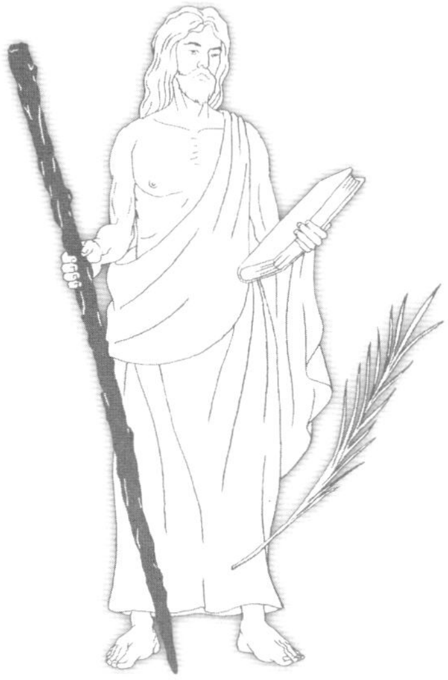

James the Lesser (p. 67)
Attribute: walking stick.

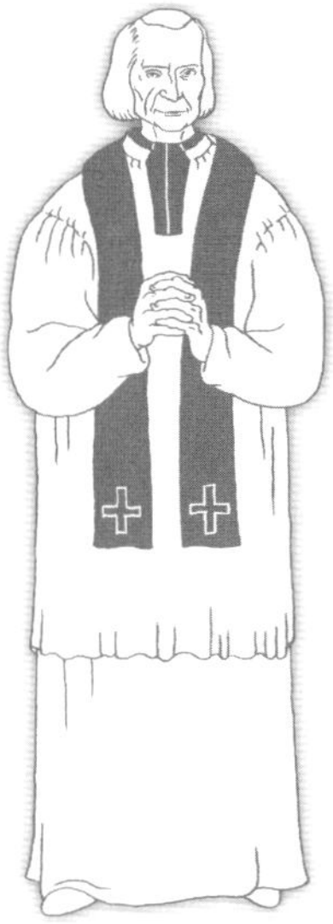

Jean Marie Baptiste Vianney (p. 207)
Attributes: emaciated but smiling face, cassock.

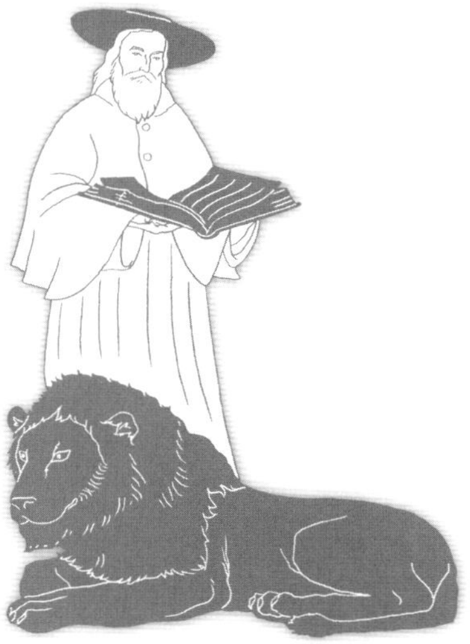

Jerome (p. 114)
Principal attribute: lion.
Others: crucifix, stone, skull, rosary, clay lamp, cardinal's cloak and hat, book, eyeglasses.

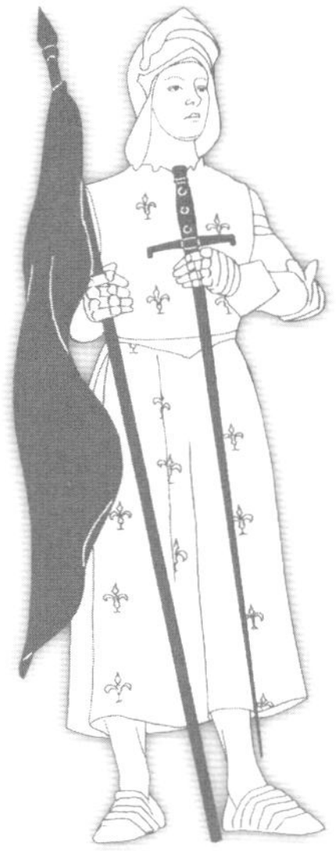

Joan of Arc (p. 181)
Principal attributes: armor, sword, standard.
Another: pyre.

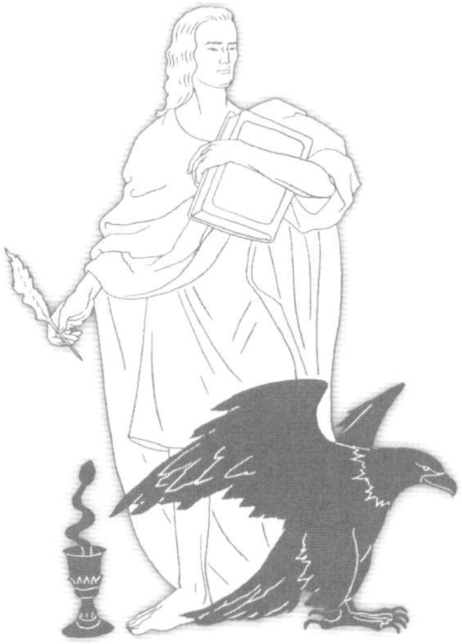

John, Apostle and Evangelist (p. 64)
Principal attribute: eagle.
Others: cup with serpent emerging from it, palm, four horsemen of the Apocalypse, cauldron.

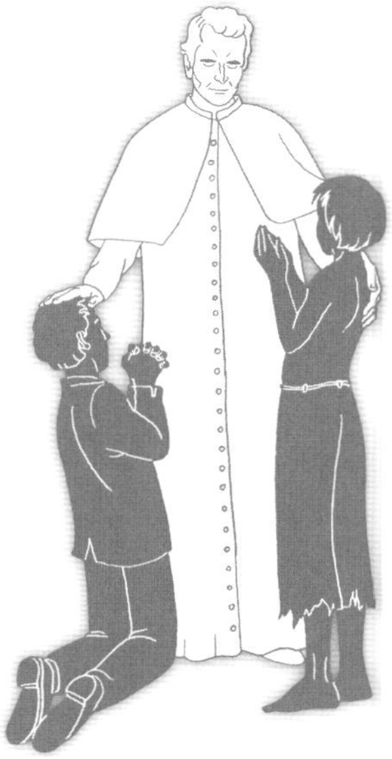

John Bosco (p. 208)
Attributes: cassock, boys around him.

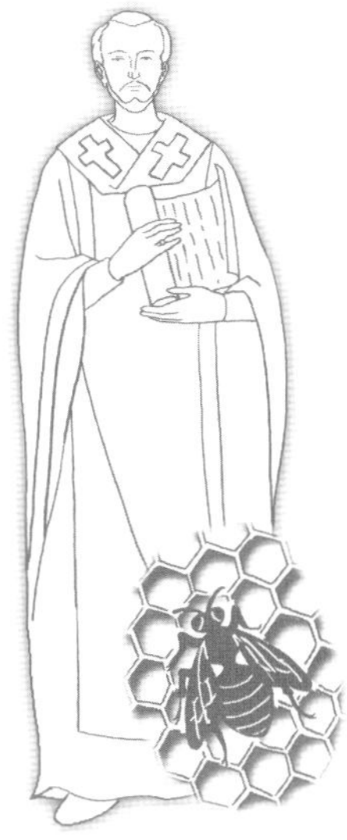

John Chrysostom (p. 103)
Principal attributes: beehive, episcopal garb.
Another: parchment scroll.

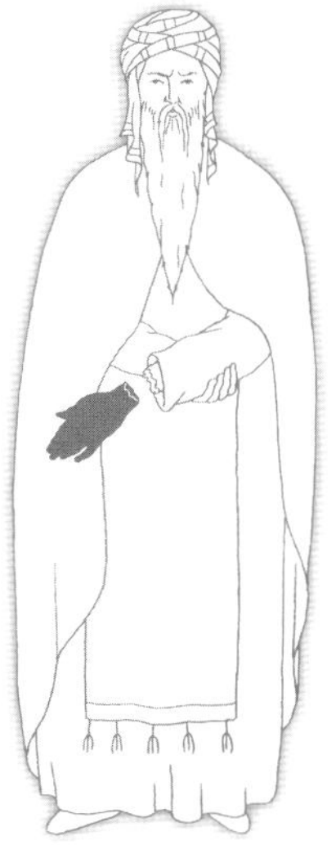

John Damascene (p. 128)
Attributes: severed hand, episcopal garb.

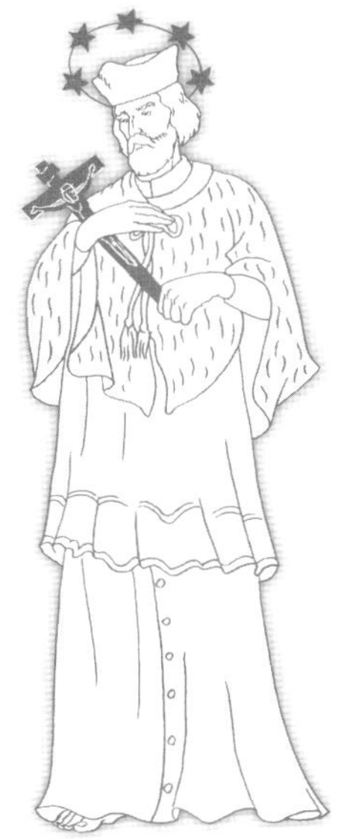

John Nepomuk (p. 174)
Principal attributes: halo of stars, crucifix, garb of a canon, biretta, mozetta.

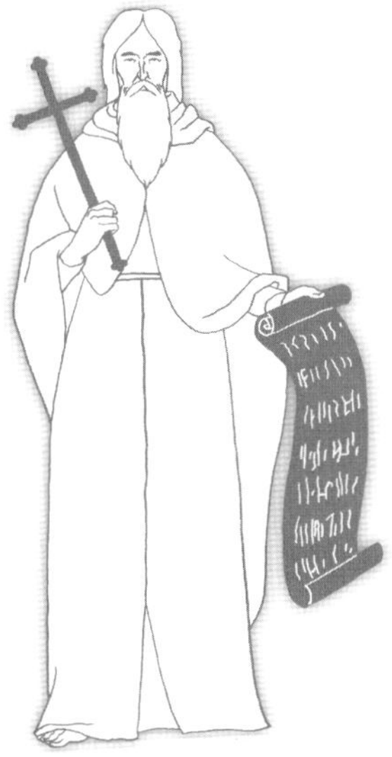

John of Rila (p. 133)
Attributes: cross, monastic garb.

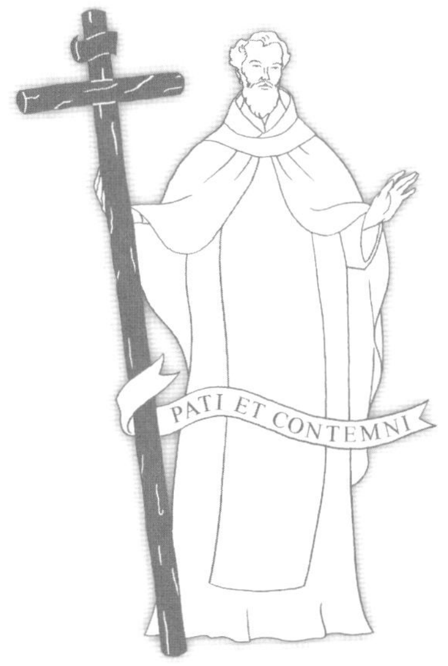

John of the Cross (p. 195)
Attributes: cross or crucifix, motto: "To suffer and be scorned," Carmelite habit.

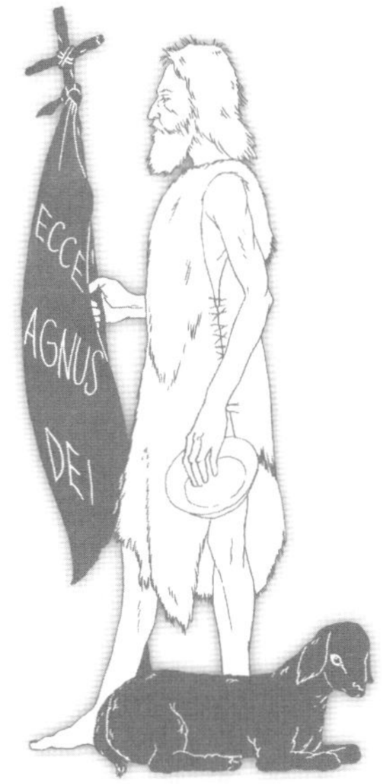

John the Baptist (p. 44)
Principal attributes: lamb, cross with motto: "Behold the Lamb of God."
Others: garment of skins, shell.

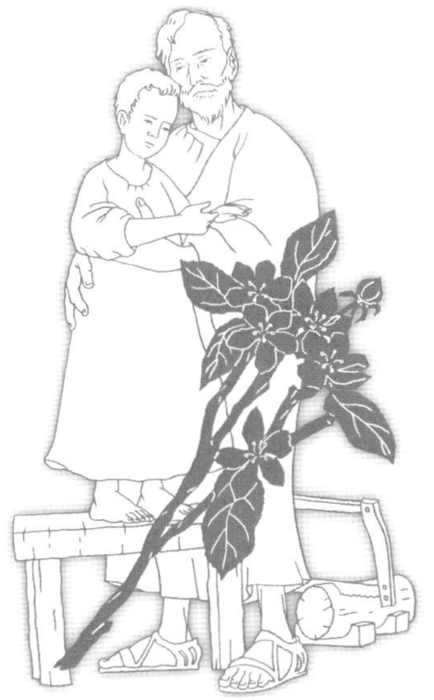

Joseph (p. 40)
Principal attributes: Child Jesus, flowering staff.
Others: lily, dove, pair of doves, saw, axe, plane, carpenter's square.

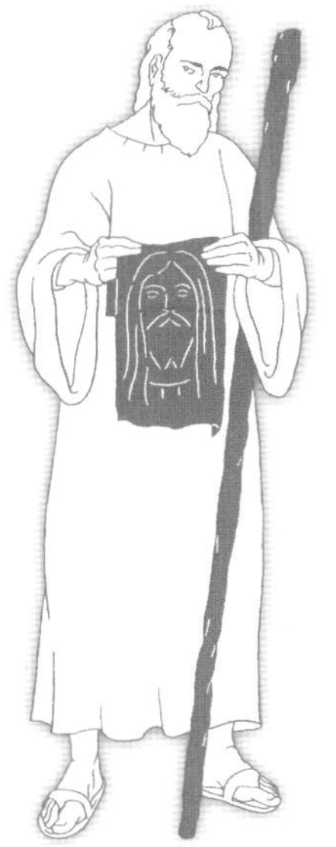

Jude Thaddeus, Apostle (p. 70)
Principal attributes: image of Jesus, staff with which he was struck.
Others: axe, halberd, square, cross with long shaft.

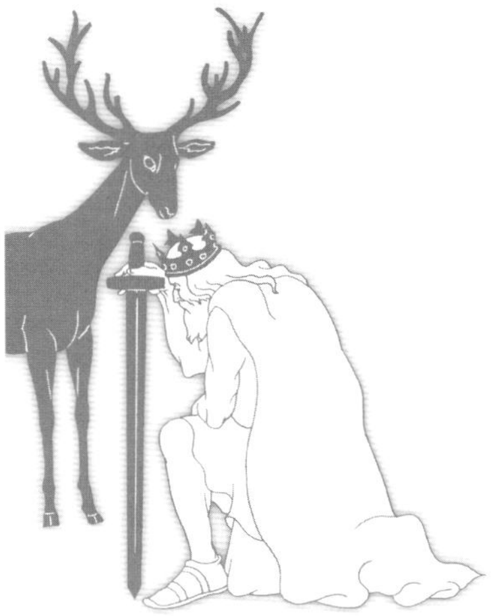

Ladislas, King of Hungary (p. 142)
Principal attributes: royal crown, sword, deer.
Others: two angels, standard, beard.

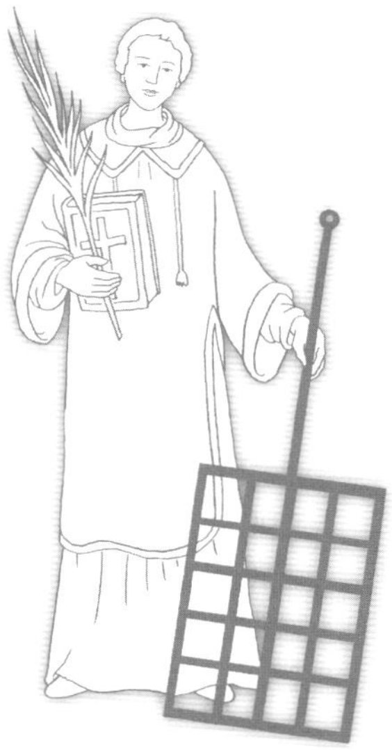

Lawrence (p. 77)
Principal attribute: grill.
Another: dalmatic.

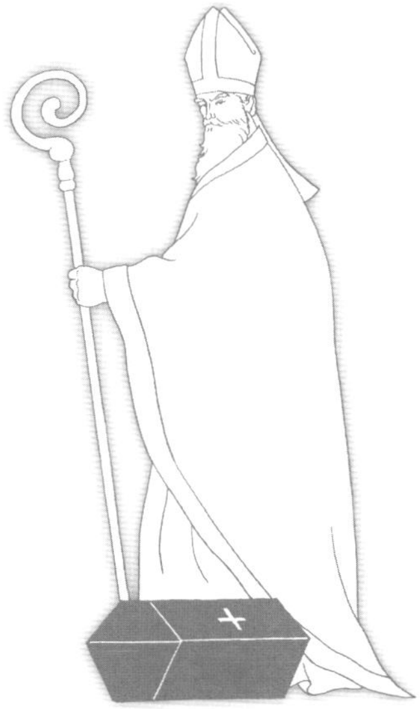

Lazarus of Bethany (p. 46)
Principal attribute: burial bandages.
Others: episcopal garb, coffin.

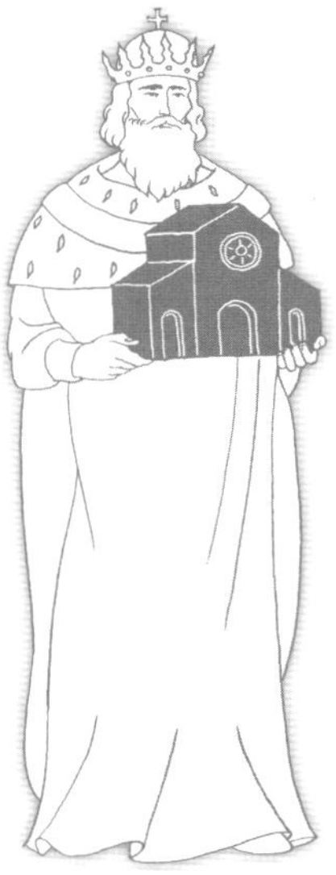

Leopold III of Austria (p. 144)
Principal attribute: model of an abbey.
Another: two baskets.

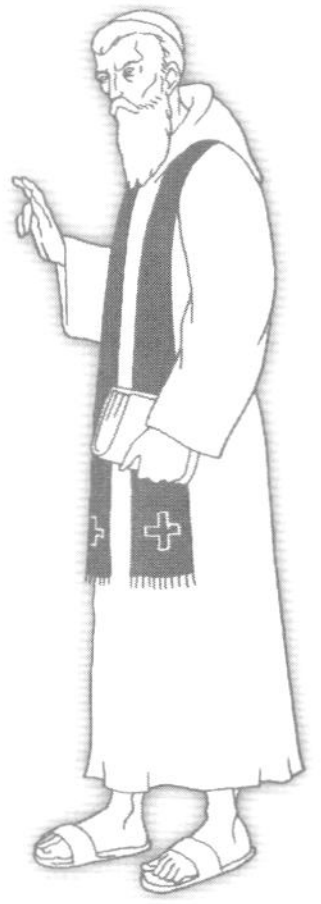

Leopold Mandic (p. 210)
Principal attributes: violet stole, skull cap, Franciscan habit.

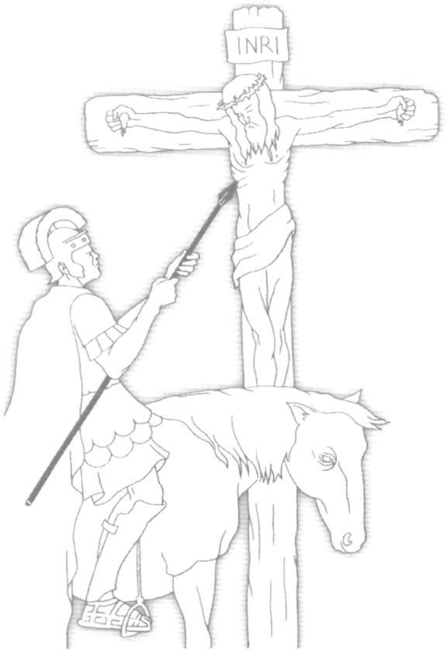

Longinus of Caesarea, Centurion (p. 51)
Attributes: spear, military dress.

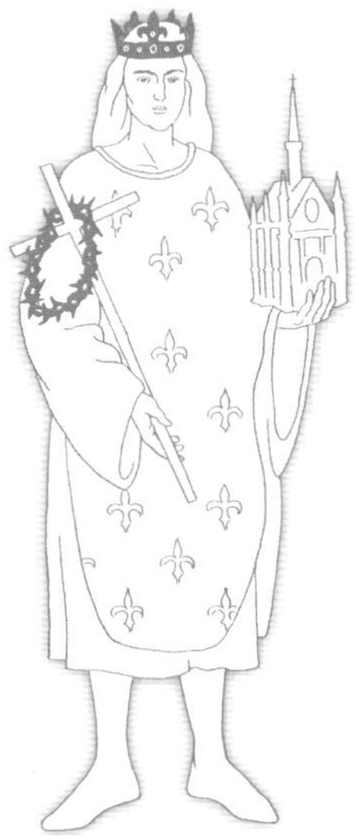

Louis IX, King of France (p. 163)
Principal attributes: royal dress, crown, ermine cape, lilies of France, cross.
Others: crown of thorns, nails of crucifixion, model of the Sainte-Chapelle.

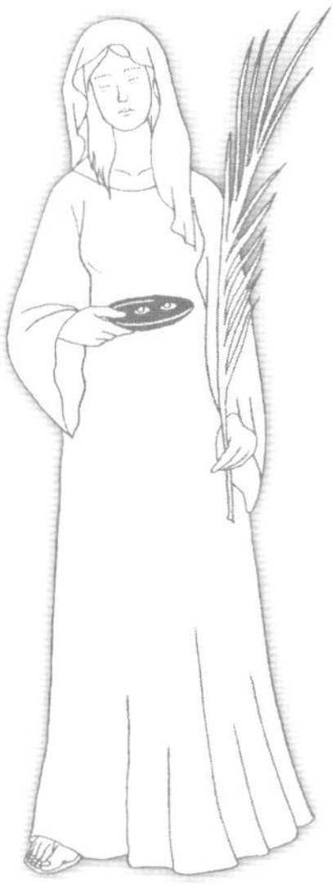

Lucy (p. 89)
Principal attribute: eyes.
Others: sword or dagger, oxen, flames, lighted lamp, candle, background of stars.

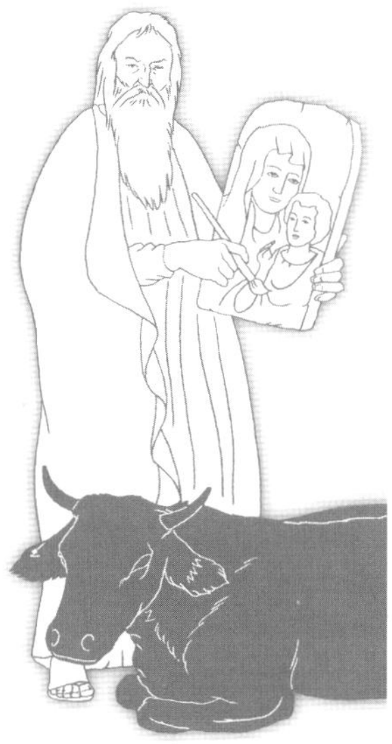

Luke, Evangelist (p. 72)
Principal attribute: ox.
Others: portrait of Mary and Child, physician's instruments.

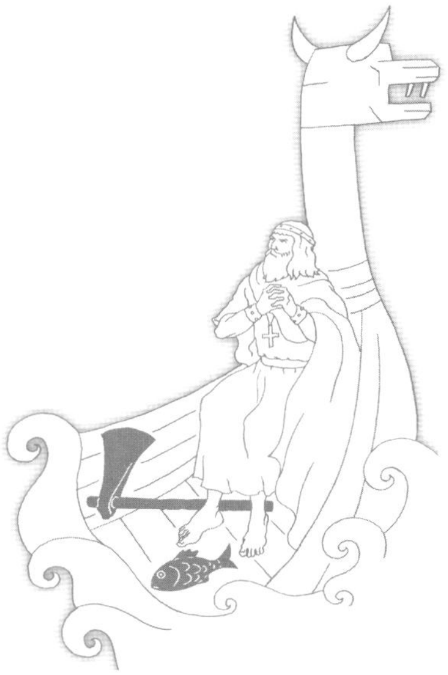

Magnus, Martyr (p. 144)
Attributes: axe, fish.

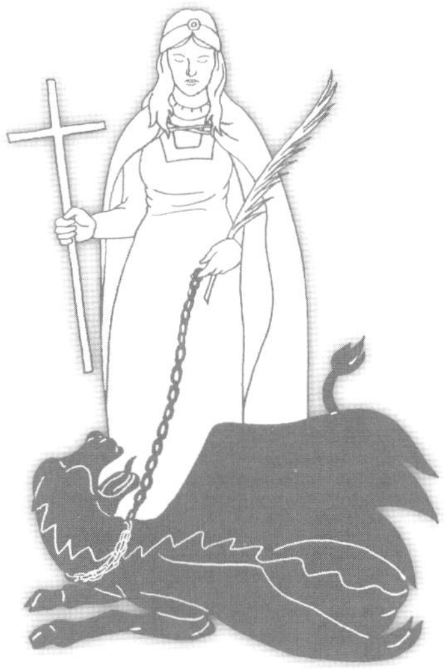

Margaret of Antioch (p. 92)
Principal attributes: crown, dragon, cross with long vertical shaft.
Others: torches, iron combs.

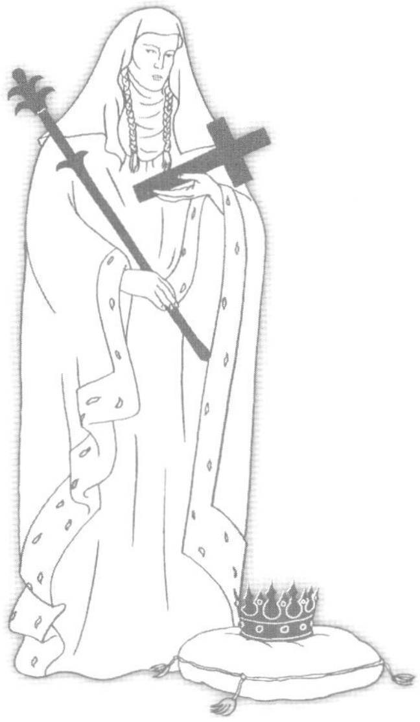

Margaret of Hungary (p. 142)
Attributes: crown at her feet, scepter, cross, royal dress.

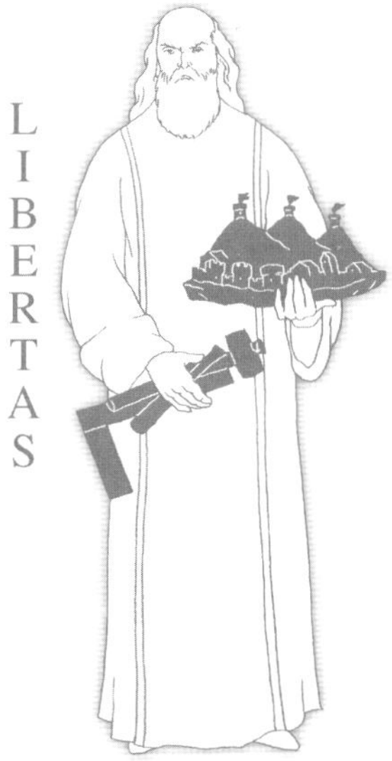

Marinus (p. 83)
Principal attributes: the three peaks of Mount Titan, the motto "Liberty."
Others: bear, tools of work, i.e., hammer, chisel, square.

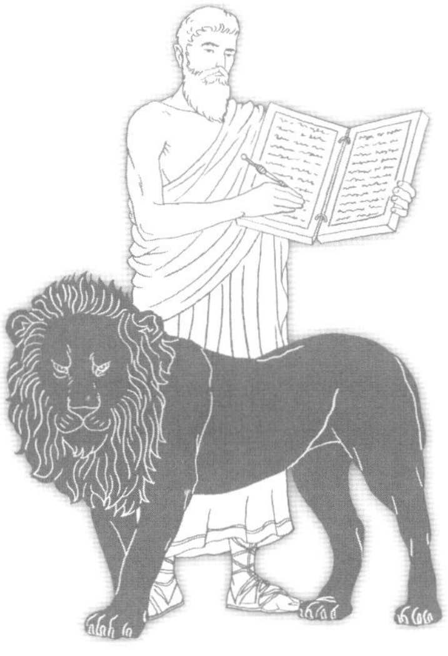

Mark, Evangelist (p. 71)
Attribute: lion.

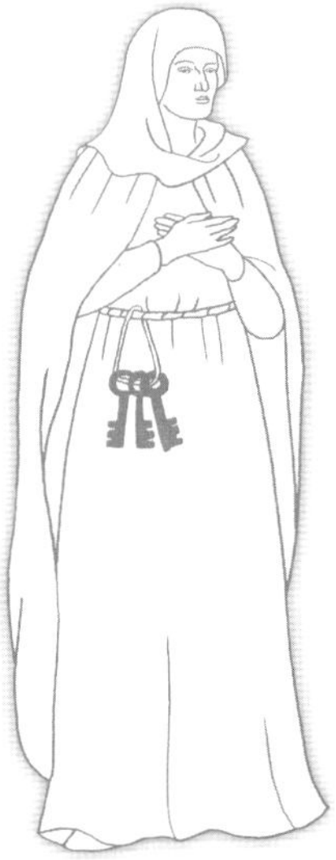

Martha of Bethany (p. 48)
Principal attribute: keys on her belt.
Others: spoon, broom, aspergillum, chained dragon.

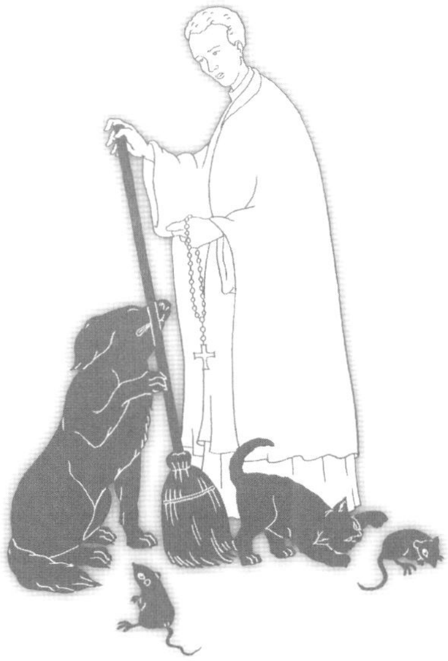

Martin de Porres (p. 202)
Attributes: broom, dog, cat, mice, Dominican habit.

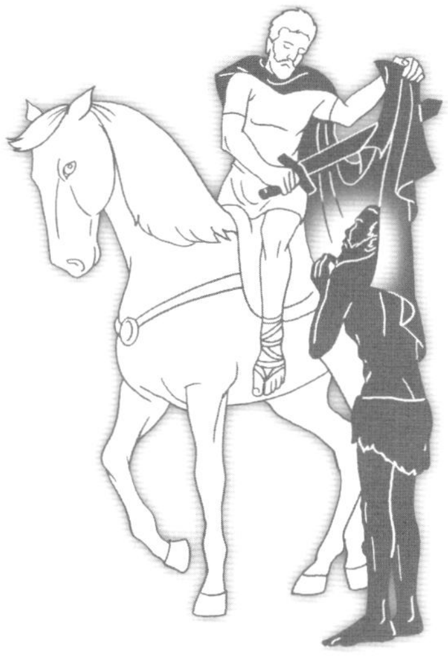

Martin of Tours (p. 104)
Principal attributes: cloak shared with beggar, goose, episcopal garb.

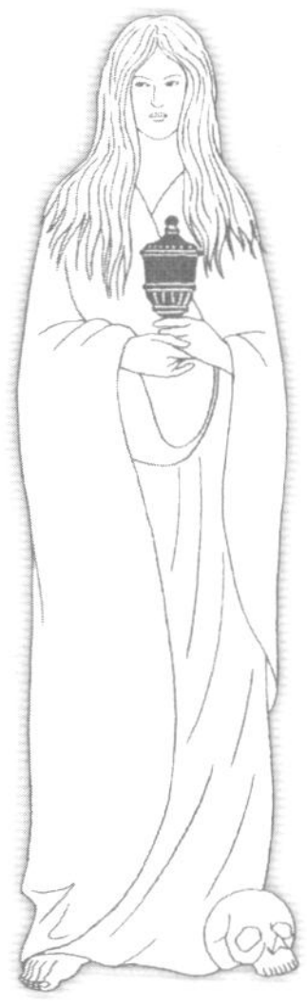

Mary Magdalene (p. 49)
Attributes: jar of ointment, unfastened hair.

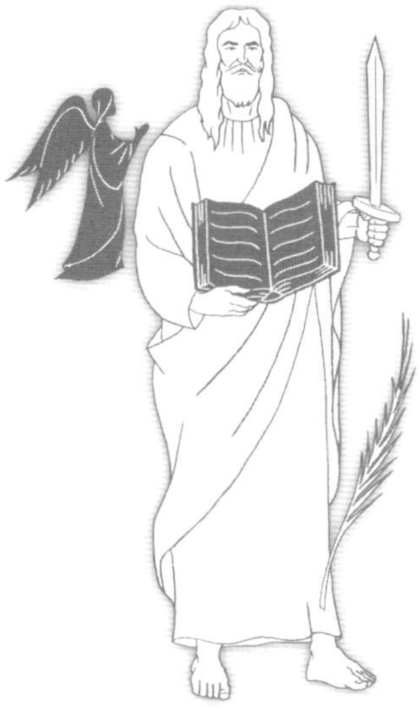

Matthew, Apostle and Evangelist (p. 69)
Principal attributes: angel or human face.
Others: bag of money, scales, sword.

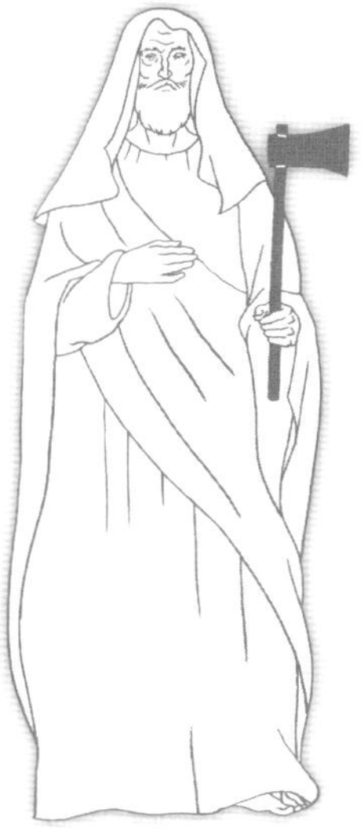

Matthias, Apostle (p. 71)
Attributes: axe or halberd or sword.

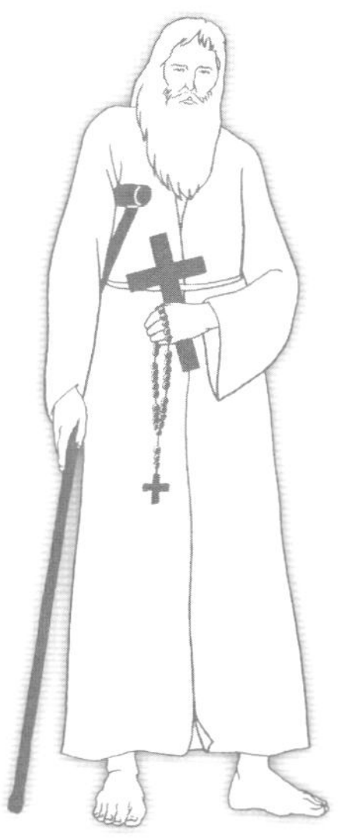

Nicholas of Flue (p. 184)
Attributes: bare feet, crutch, rosary, cross.

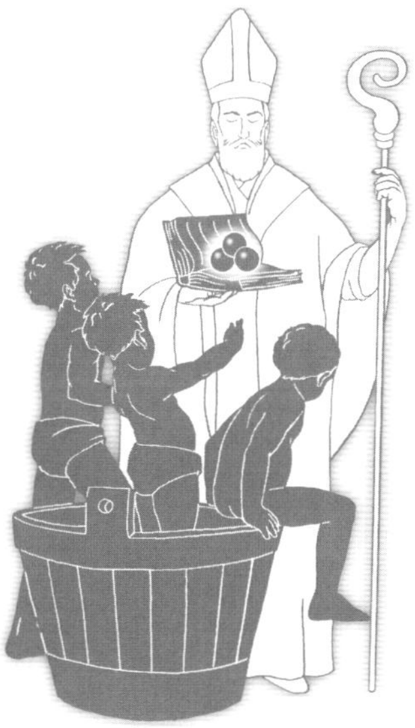

Nicholas of Myra and of Bari (p. 111)
Principal attributes: three spheres (bags of money), episcopal garb.
Others: three children, three young girls,

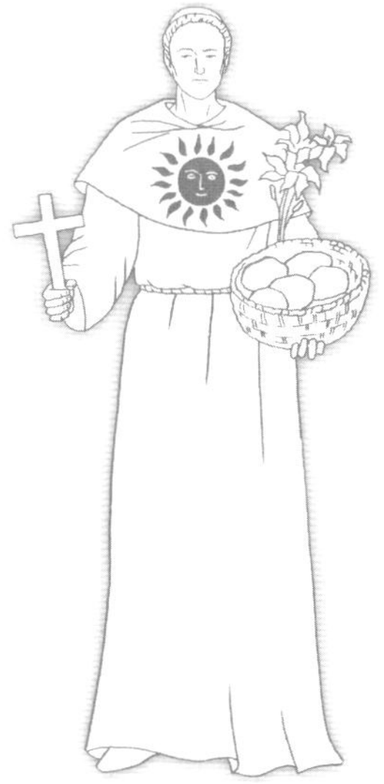

Nicholas of Tolentine (p. 166)
Principal attributes: on his breast a star with face within it, black Augustinian habit.
Others: skull, crucifix flowering with lilies, rolls, partridges.

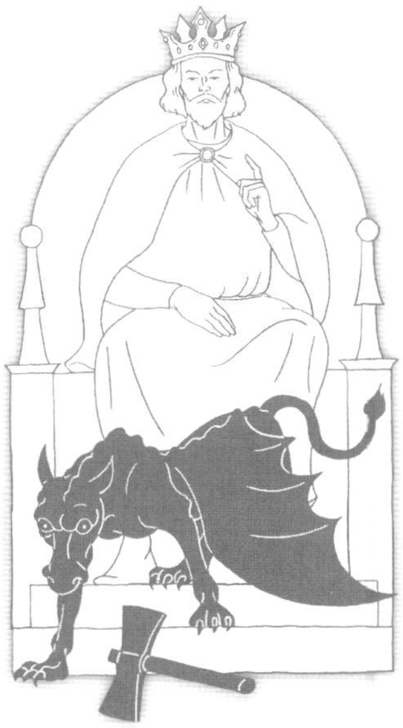

Olaf of Norway (p. 136)
Principal attributes: crown, two-edged axe, chained dragon.
Others: tankard, ship.

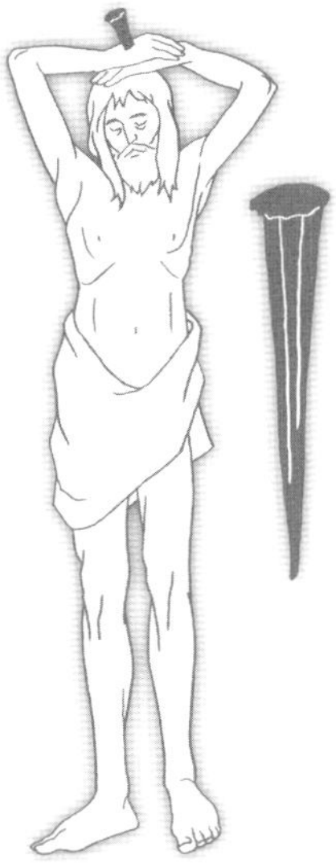

Pantaleon of Nicomedia (p. 94)
Principal attribute: nail.
Others: healed child, physician's implements: urinal, ampulla of ointment.

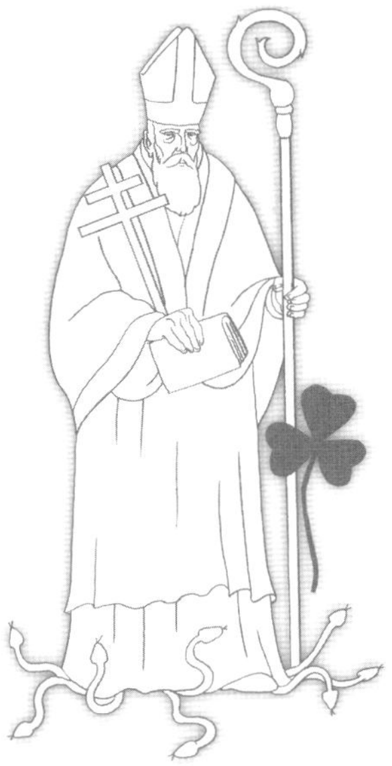

Patrick of Ireland (p. 117)
Principal attributes: shamrock, pastoral staff, episcopal garb.
Others: snakes, fires of purgatory.

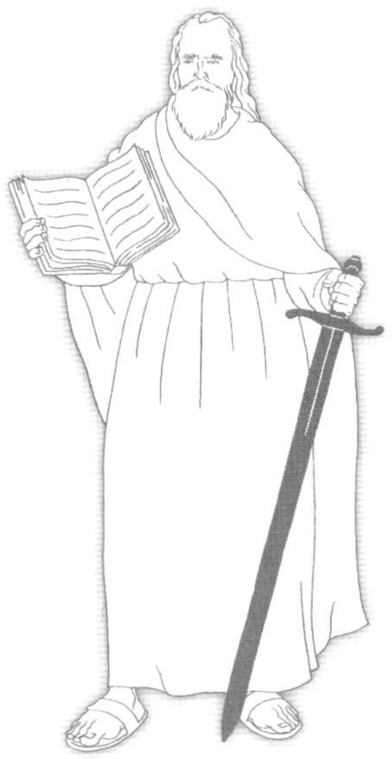

Paul of Tarsus (p. 60)
Principal attribute: sword.
Another: basket.

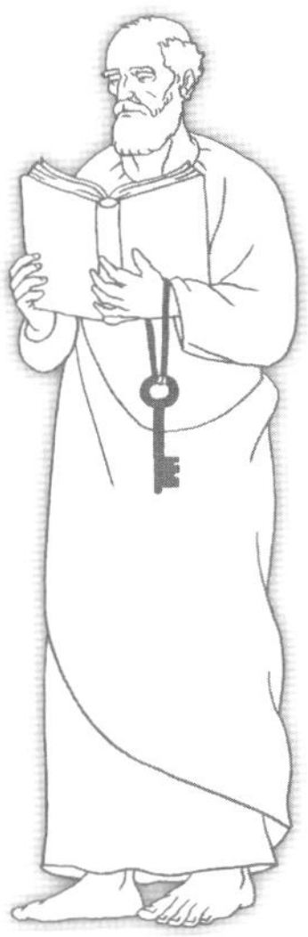

Peter, Apostle (p. 57)
Principal attribute: papal keys.
Others: fishing rods, nets, rooster, chains, ship, inverted cross, tiara, papal cross.

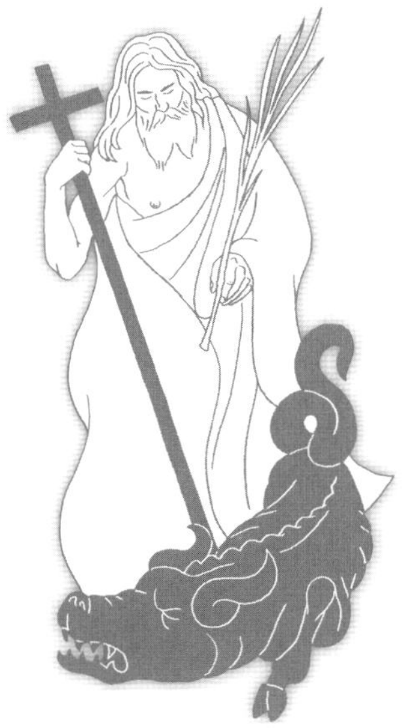

Philip, Apostle (p. 68)
Principal attribute: cross, sometimes inverted.
Others: dragon, stones.

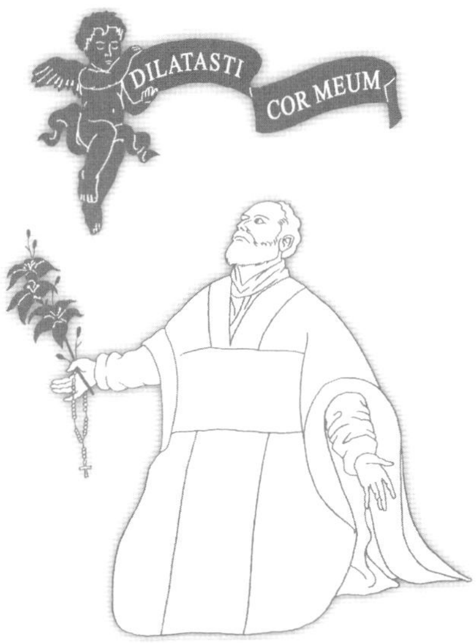

Philip Neri (p. 193)
Principal attributes: rosary, lily, angel with scroll and motto, cassock, biretta.
Another: garland of roses.

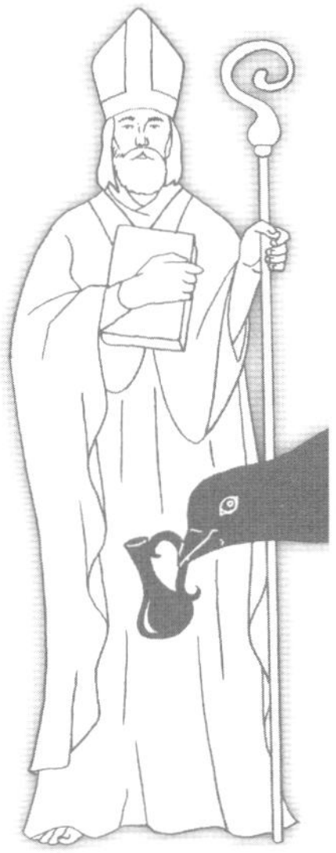

Remigius (p. 118)
Principal attributes: dove with cruet, episcopal garb.
Others: book, lamp.

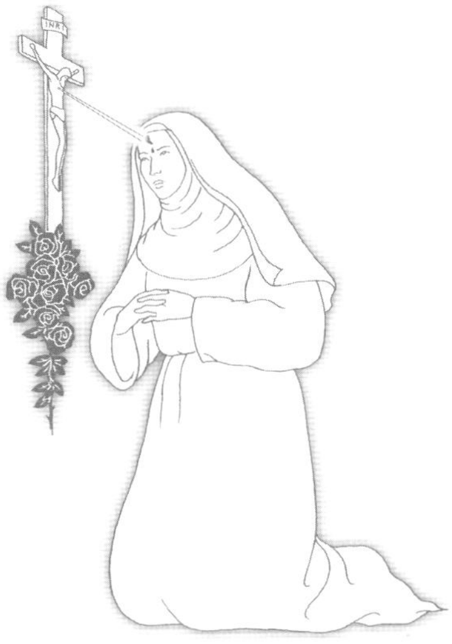

Rita of Cascia (p. 180)
Principal attributes: thorn in forehead, crucifix, black Augustinian habit.
Others: roses, bees.

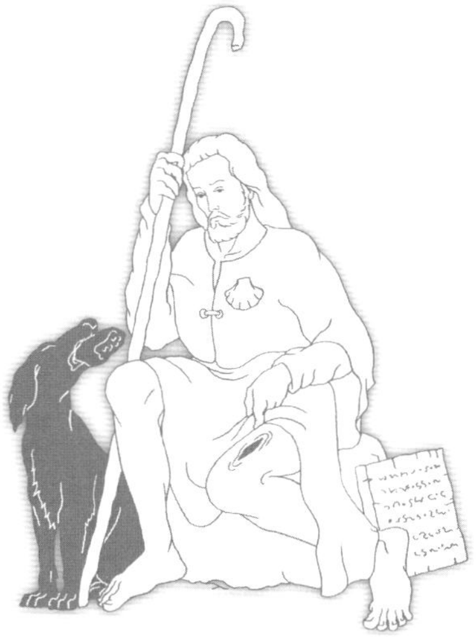

Roch (p. 169)
Principal attributes: wound on one thigh, dog offering a piece of bread.
Others: cape, pilgrim's staff, broad-brimmed hat, tablet with writing on it.

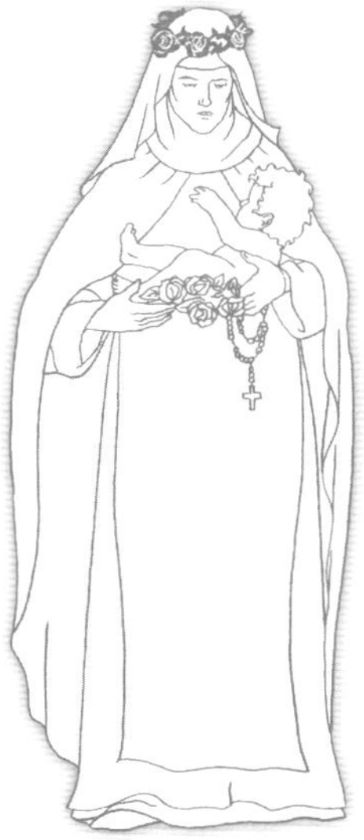

Rose of Lima (p. 203)
Principal attributes: rose or crown of roses, Dominican habit.
Others: Child Jesus, anchor.

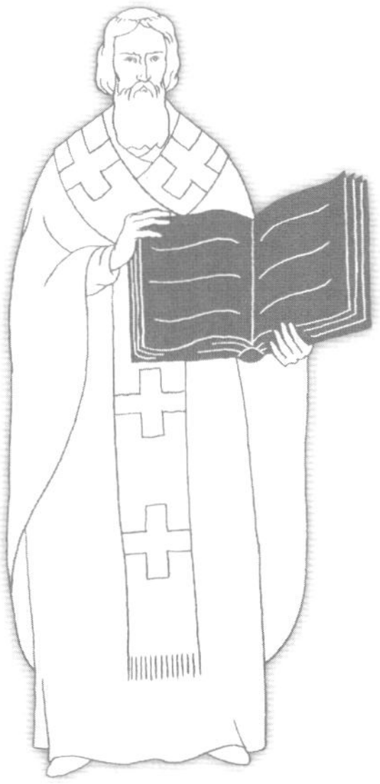

Sabas of Serbia (p. 148)
Attributes: book, his father St. Simeon, a monk, episcopal garb.

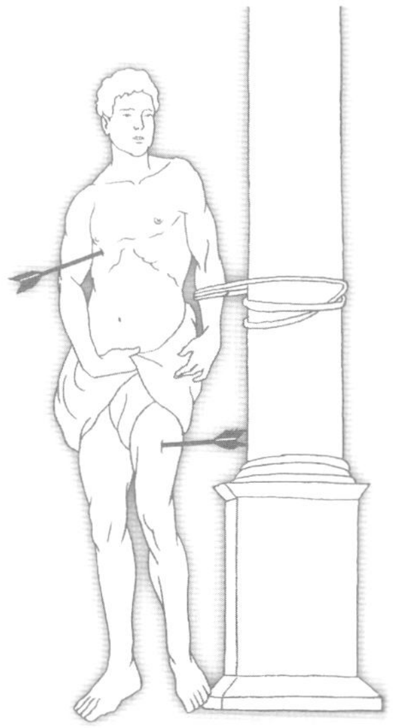

Sebastian (p. 82)
Attributes: arrows, seminaked body.

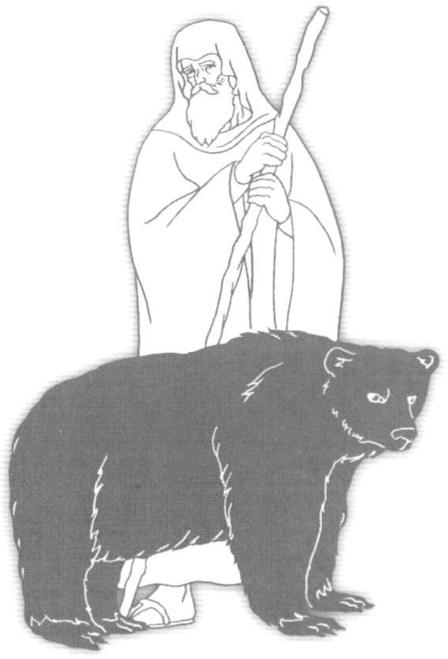

Sergius of Radonezh (p. 173)
Attributes: bear, monastery, monastic garb.

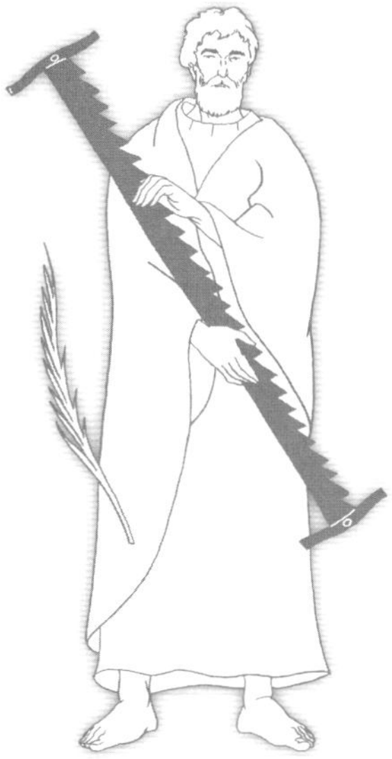

Simon, Apostle (p. 71)
Attribute: saw.

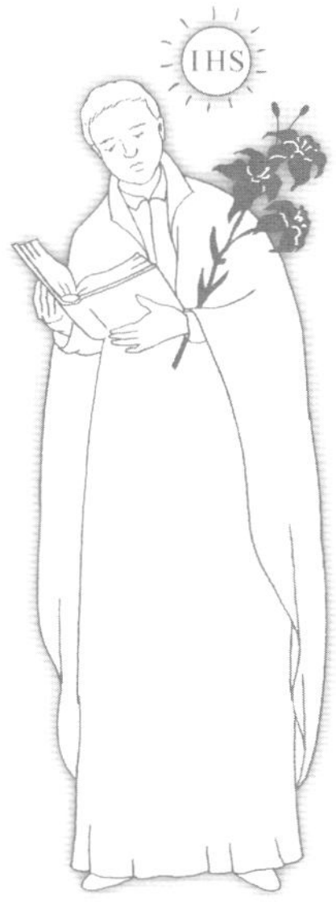

Stanislaus Kostka (p. 198)
Principal attributes: lily, Jesuit habit.
Others: Child Jesus, Most Blessed Sacrament.

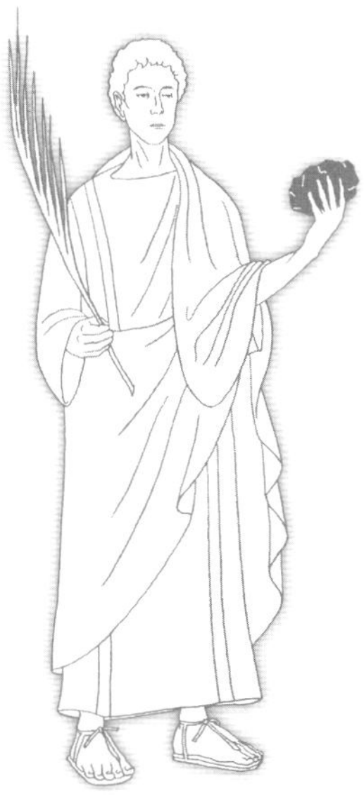

Stephen, Protomartyr (p. 74)
Principal attribute: stones.
Another: dalmatic.

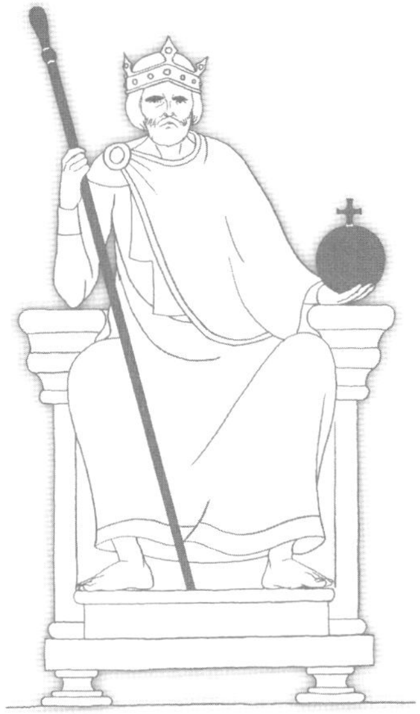

Stephen of Hungary (p. 137)
Attributes: crown, scepter, globe topped by a cross.

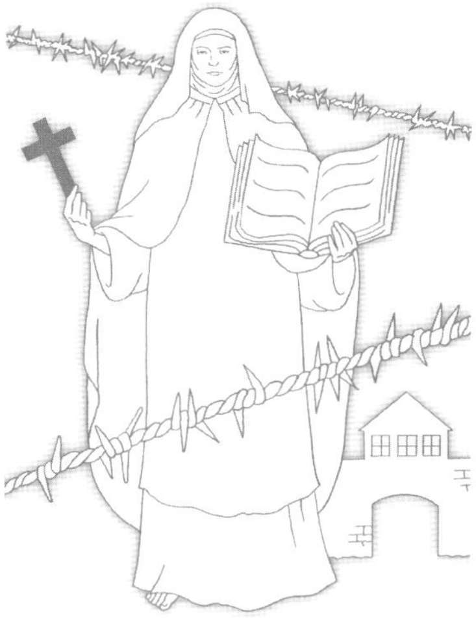

Theresa Benedicta of the Cross (p. 212)
Principal attributes: cross, Carmelite habit, book.
Others: Star of David, concentration camp.

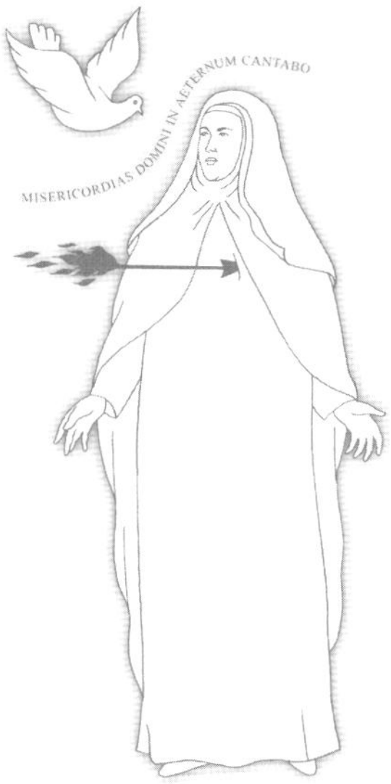

Theresa of Avila or of Jesus (p. 193)
Principal attributes: fiery arrow, Carmelite habit.
Another: dove.

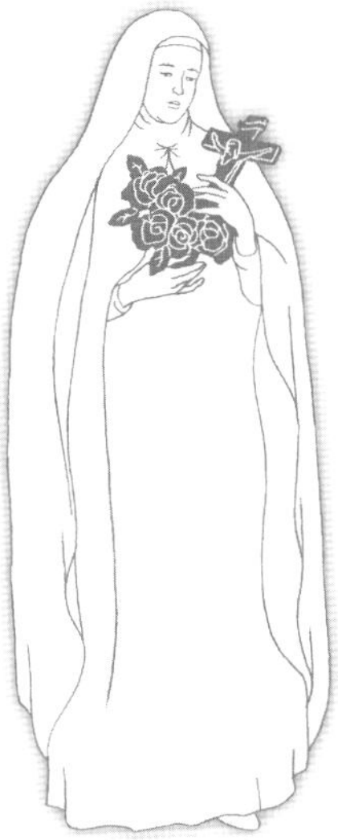

Theresa of the Child Jesus or of Lisieux (p. 209)
Attributes: Carmelite habit, crucifix, roses.

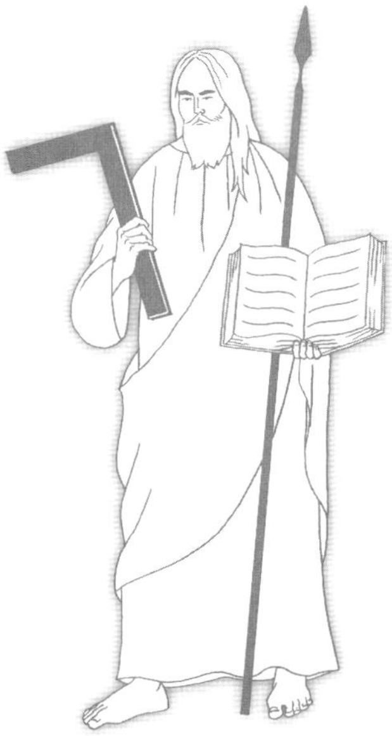

Thomas, Apostle (p. 66)
Principal attributes: square, spear.
Another: the Virgin's cincture.

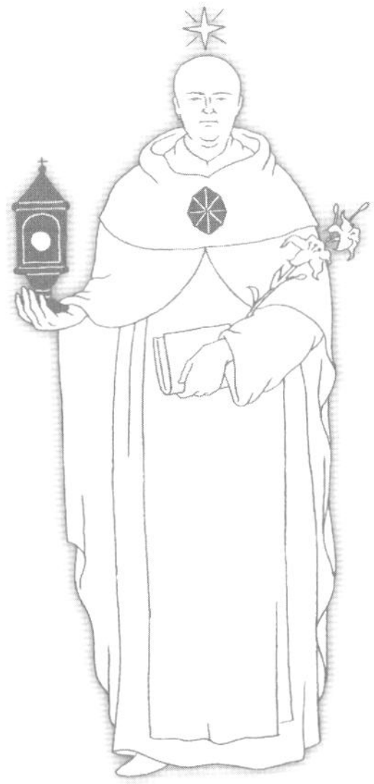

Thomas Aquinas (p. 165)
Principal attributes: ruby on breast, Blessed Sacrament, Dominican habit.
Others: dove of the Holy Spirit, cincture, star or small sun, lily, wings.

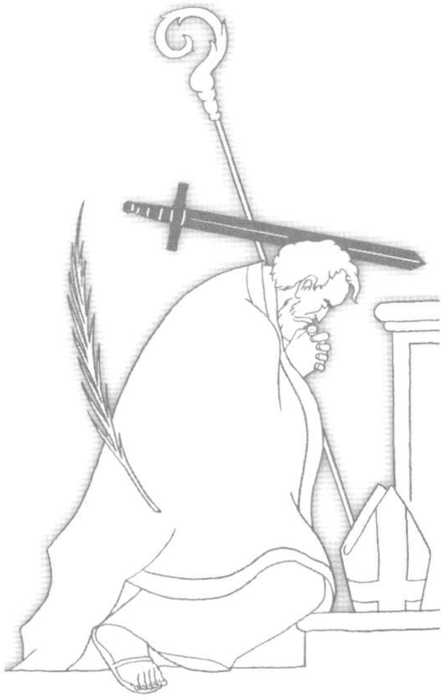

Thomas Becket (p. 150)
Attributes: chancellor's robes, honorary neck-chain.

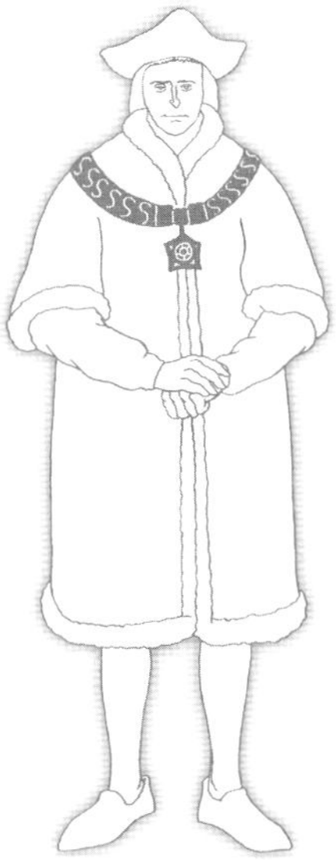

Thomas More (p. 185)
Attributes: robes of a chancellor, honorary neck-chain.

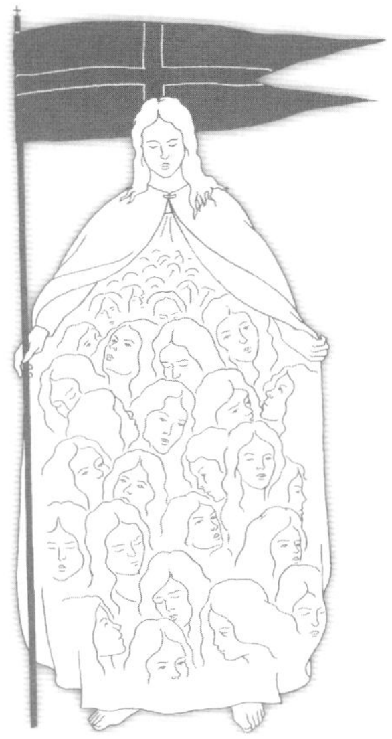

Ursula and the Eleven Thousand Virgins (p. 115)
Principal attributes: young companions, banner with cross, cloak.

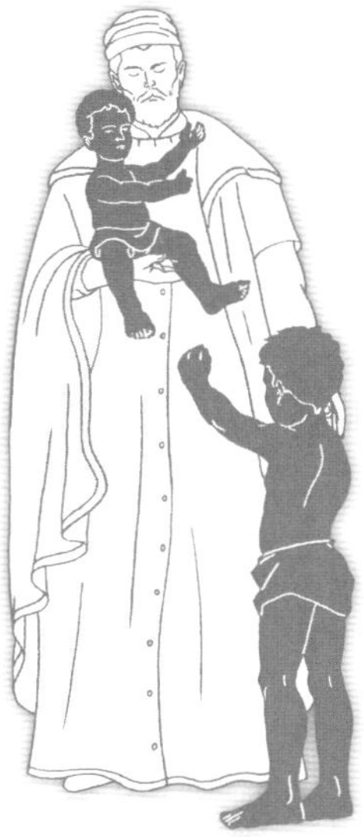

Vincent de Paul (p. 206)
Attributes: boys, crucifix, cassock.

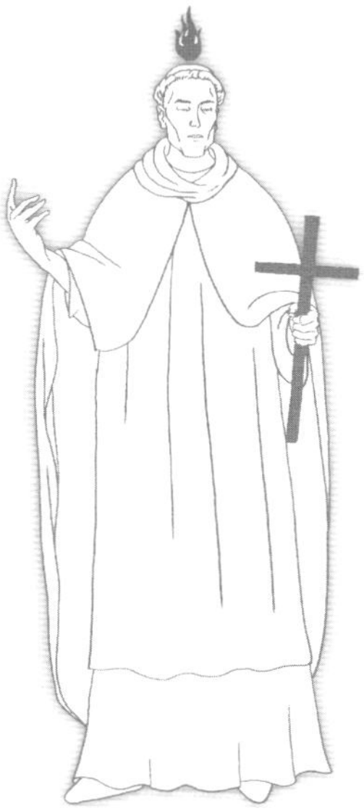

Vincent Ferrer (p. 177)
Principal attributes: flame on his head, crucifix, right hand raised, Dominican habit.
Others: lightning, trumpets, banner, baptismal font.

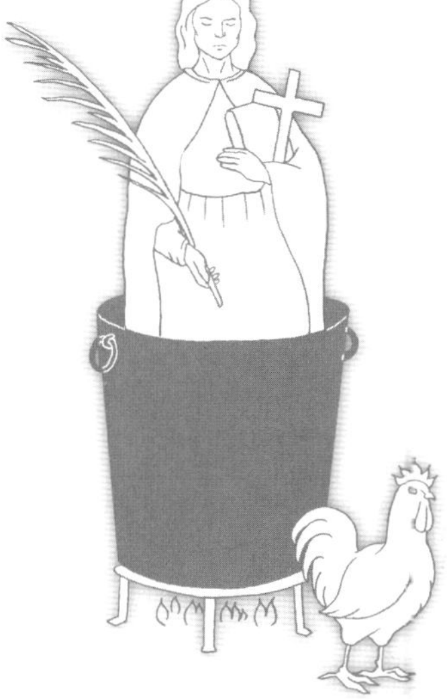

Vitus (p. 83)
Principal attribute: cauldron.
Others: lion, clay lamp, white rooster.

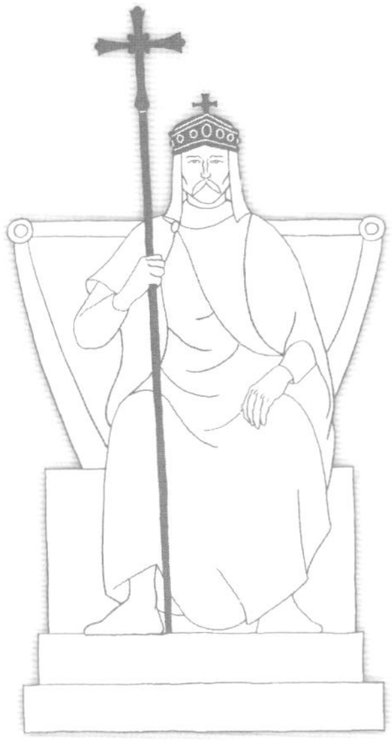

Vladimir of Kiev (p. 134)
Attributes: crown, cross, throne.

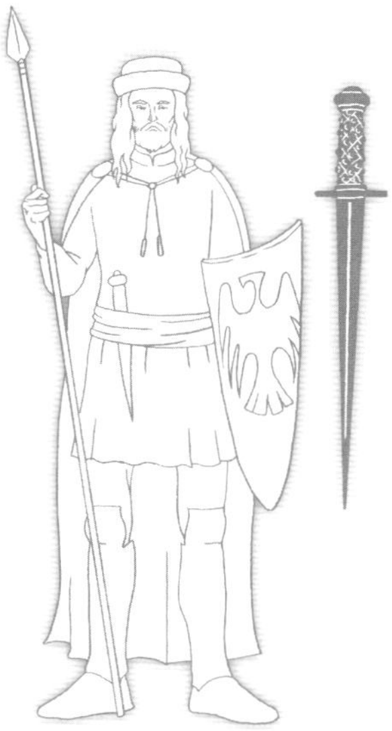

Wenceslas of Bohemia (p. 132)
Principal attributes: dagger, armor, spear, shield, ducal hat.
Others: cluster of grapes and a torch.

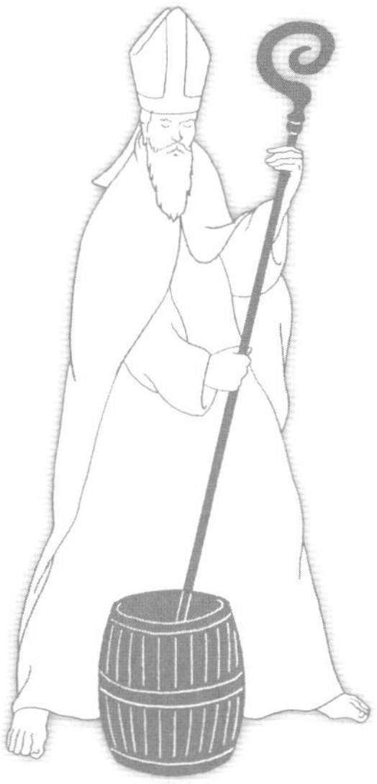

Willibrord (p. 130)
Attribute: pastoral staff which he dips into a cask.

Index of Attributes

Photograph Credits

The photographs are from the Jaca Book Archive, except for the following:

Apostolic Library, Vatican: 39, 75, 154

Archive of the CSCP: 22, 83, 92, 97, 136, 140, 158, 166, 170, 172, 180, 184, 207 (bottom), 209

Athenon Publishing, Athens: 130–131

BAMS Photo: 189, 198

Bavarian State Library: 48

Fernando Lanzi: 37, 40, 42, 43, 54, 59, 61, 62, 63, 66, 68, 70, 71, 74, 77, 78, 80, 84, 86, 88, 101, 102, 104, 121, 123, 129, 131, 132, 134, 142, 144, 145, 155, 156, 159, 160, 167, 169, 174, 193, 195, 200, 201, 203, 206, 207 (top), 208, 211

Isber Melhelm: 85 (top), 87, 101, 110, 115

Luigi Giannetti, Fontana Liri: 65

Maintenance Office of the Cathedral, Milan: 52

Museum of the St. Ferdinand Royal Academy of the Fine Arts, Madrid: 196

Nidwald Museum, Stans, Switzerland: 184

Parish of St. Willibrord, Echternach, Luxembourg: 130

Photographic Archive of the Supervisor of the Artistic and Historical Treasures of Rome: 51

Photothèque Zodiaque: 38, 107

Rheinland Photographic Archive: 111

St. Matthew National Museum, Pisa: 171

The authors thank Gianfranco Contri for the information on St. Olaf and his iconography.

Composition of the texts and selection of images:
News SpA, Milan

Printing and binding:
D'Auria Industrie Grafiche SpA,
S. Egidio alla Vibrata (TE)